Theories, Concepts and Discoveries in Historical Studies

Theories, Concepts and Discoveries in Historical Studies

Edited by **Trevor Bowen**

CLANRYE
INTERNATIONAL

New Jersey

Published by Clanrye International,
55 Van Reypen Street,
Jersey City, NJ 07306, USA
www.clanryeinternational.com

Theories, Concepts and Discoveries in Historical Studies
Edited by Trevor Bowen

International Standard Book Number: 978-1-63240-490-9 (Hardback)

Printed in the United States of America.

Contents

Preface

The term History is derived from the Greek word 'historia', meaning knowledge acquired by investigation and inquiry. It essentially is an academic discipline of the social sciences, which refers to the recording of events in the past, and studying how it relates to humans. Information is recorded and collected from numerous sources to create History.

History aims to narrativise and analyse the past in a sequence, in order to objectively determine the patterns of cause and effect. The origins of the subject can be traced to 5th-century BC, when a Greek historian Herodotus, along with his contemporary Thucydides, helped form the foundations for history, as we understand it today. In fact, in the Western tradition, Herodotus is considered the 'father of history'.

Today, the term covers cosmic, geologic, and organic history as well. The modern study of history as an academic discipline is wide-ranging. Practitioners in this field are encouraged to question historical discourses and approach and deconstruct them from every possible angle. With the subaltern narrative also being an important focus area, research in this field is also very exciting.

I'd like to thank all the contributors for sharing their findings with us to enrich this book. Their researches and efforts towards this book are sincerely appreciated.

Editor

Over and Undershot Waterwheels in the 18th Century.
Science-Technology Controversy

Danilo Capecchi

Dipartimento di Ingegneria Strutturale e Geotecnica, Università La Sapienza, Rome, Italy

The present paper concerns the development of theory and experiments on water wheels in the 18th century. At that time, as a result of a growing demand for energy, a better understanding of the functioning of watermills, even at the theoretical level, was required in order to improve their efficiency. A hint about the evolution of the theory of wheels in the 19th century is reported also. We have tried to clarify the role played by some protagonists as Antoine Parent, Jean-Charles de Borda and John Smeaton. Their role has not been fully recognised even in contemporary studies. Then some considerations are developed on the relationships between science and technology on this particular subject, concluding that it was a happy and well-balanced marriage.

Keywords: Waterwheels; Hydraulic Machine; Science-Technology; History of Hydraulics

Introduction

Hydraulic machines can be of different kinds; for a synthetic description see (Singer, 1957; Strock & Teague, 1952; Cardwell, 1965; Syson, 1980). In the present paper reference is made to waterwheels only, for their widespread diffusion and since their development allows for an understanding of the science-technology relationship. Mainly two types of waterwheels exist: the undershot waterwheels and the overshot waterwheels, whose difference is shown in **Figure 1**. There is also another interesting wheel, intermediate between the two, the breast wheel, in which water enters from the mid points—or breast—of the wheel.

In the undershot machines, water flows beneath the wheel and hits blades or paddles evenly diffused around the periphery of the wheel. They are moved by the impulsion of the particles of water. In the overshot machines water is led above the wheel. Instead of blades, there are often buckets which get filled with water and move the wheel by means of the water gravity itself.

The waterwheel steadily evolved since its introduction 2000 years ago, to pump water and mill grain. It is not clear where it had its origin; it is clear however that it rapidly spread out as described by Roman, Greek and Chinese sources. There is evidence that the familiar vertical waterwheel developed within the Roman Empire and rapidly spread out; the undershot waterwheel was more common (Denny, 2003). Overshot wheels required a large head (2 - 10 m), therefore they were usually confined to hilly areas, or required extensive and expensive auxiliary constructions. On the other hand, undershot wheels, could operate with a small head (0.5 - 2 m), hence they could be located on small streams in flat areas, near to population centres. It is widely considered that the most dramatic industrial consequences of waterwheels occurred in the Middle Ages, when the scale of milling considerably increased with the de-velopment of large towns. Their considerable economic and social impact may be judged by the increased application of waterwheels. From grinding wheat and pumping water in antiquity, water powered mills evolved to forge iron, full cloth, saw wood and stone, and for metalworking and leather tanning (Denny, 2003: p. 194).

In the 18th century the waterwheels received new attention because of the rising of the manufacturing industry and its increasing request of energy. As soon as all the places suitable to install wheels run out, the only way to increase energy was to increase the efficiency, which called for an intervention of scientists and technicians. The problem of efficiency of waterwheels and their history in the 18th century has been the object of rather recent studies (Reynold, 1979; Cardwell, 1965, 1967), which also make general considerations on the role of the hydraulic energy in society. However, it must be said that in some cases these studies present some errors when interpreting the precise contribution of scientists. For example Parent is accused of committing faults he is actually not guilty of while de Borda is given undeserved merits.

The purpose of the present paper is to clarify these misunderstandings and also to present some reflections on the interaction between science and technology in this particular field, in the 18th century. The first point has been developed by considering the contributions on theory and practice of waterwheels published in the scientific journals of the time, mainly the *Mémoires* de l'Académie des science de Paris and the *Philosophical transactions*. A great attention was paid to explain the writings of the 18th century authors without judging them on the basis of the modern standards of mechanics and hydraulics. For the sake of simplicity, some concepts of mechanics of the 18th century were given for granted hoping the presentation to be comprehensible enough for a contemporary reader. The

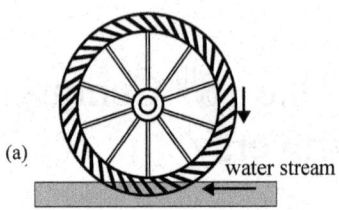

(a)

water stream

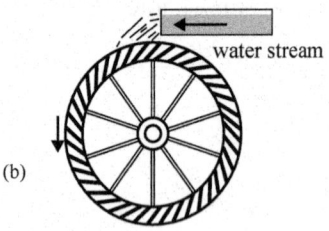

water stream

(b)

Figure 1.
Examples of undershot wheel (a) and
overshot wheel (b).

second point concerning the relationship between science and technology is also based on the content of the mentioned scientific journals. However, the conclusion drawn in such a case are not comprehensive and a more targeted study would be necessary. This notwithstanding some indications can be drawn.

Science and Technology

At the beginning of the 18th century an increasing need of energy was felt by the emerging factories, especially in England. Before the introduction of steam the only way to get energy from nature was by means of the motion of water and air. Waterwheels were suitable machines to collect energy form the rivers. However the available streams of water were limited and an increase of energy could come only by improving the efficiency of the hydraulic machines.

Both scientists and engineers devoted themselves to the task. Hydrodynamics at the beginning of the century was scarcely developed. Only the theoretical results reported by Newton in the second book of his masterpiece, *Philosophiae naturalis principia mathematica* (Newton, 1972) and by Torricelli in his *Opera geometrica* (Torricelli, 1644: p. 265) and the experimental analysis of Edme Mariotte in his *Traité des eaux et autres corps fluides* (Mariotte, 1686) were of some help. In this situation scientists could consider very simplified models only. On the other side engineers, or at least some of them, were no longer practical men; they knew hydraulic quite enough and, mainly, had a scientific attitude versus experiments which were carried out using models of reduced size and accurate measurements. There were thus elements for science and technique to cooperate.

Scientists were the first to be involved. But the results they found were useless from a practical point of view because they were far from the actual findings. For this reason the development of the hydraulic machines in the whole 18th century was greatly influenced by engineers that experimented different kinds of wheels, in particular overshot wheels and wheels with curved blades.

Difference between theory and practice was hardly accepted by the scientific community, thus the need to interpret the ex-

perimental results was pressing. But it took nearly a century from the first theoretical analysis, that of Parent in 1704 (see below), to reach a satisfactory interpretation of the hydraulic phenomena and to suggest a way to build more efficient machines thanks to the studies of French engineers, especially Poncelet (Poncelet, 1825, 1827).

Theoretical Studies

The first attempts to measure the efficiency of waterwheels were carried out by scientists and contributed to the development of hydrodynamics. For example, Edme Mariotte measured the force of water stream by means of a counterbalancing weight, drawing the conclusion that the force varies as the square of the velocity of impact (Mariotte, 1686: p. 205); a result which was already provided by Newton on theoretical basis (Newton, 1726: Part II, Theorem 27). A sophisticated analysis on the undershot wheels was soon given by Antoine Parent in 1704 (Parent 1745: pp. 116-123, 323-338).

Antoine Parent's Analysis of Undershot Wheels

In his memoir *Sur la plus grande perfection possible des machines* (Parent 1745) Parent considered the idealized system of wheels of **Figure 2**, deprived of any friction. A fluid (water) flows through a channel from left to right; it spins the large wheel CBD (**Figure 2**) as a consequence of the force exerted by the fluid in B. The rotatory motion of FGH is transmitted by means of teeth to the small wheel HMR, around whose axis a rope wraps and lifts a weight. The fluid flows through the channel EB with uniform velocity V; the larger wheel CBD rotates with constant angular velocity and the velocity at point B of the immersed blade is equal to x, so that the relative velocity of the water with respect to the blade is V-x. Parent wanted to calculate the weight p that the smaller wheel HMR is able to lift with velocity u.

He made the following assumptions: (a) the force exerted by the water flow on the blade in B is proportional to the square of the relative velocity between the blade and the water; (b) the Galilean principle of moments (the principle of virtual velocities) can be applied—as the friction is negligible—assuming that a steady state is reached in which the forces are balanced. There were also some assumptions not made explicit, although fundamental; (c) only one blade at a time is considered immersed in water; (d) the stream is considered to be perpendicular to the blade. Parent indicated with P the force exerted by the fluid in B with the blade at rest (then with a relative speed of the fluid equal to the absolute velocity V); and called *natural effect of the fluid* (effect naturelle) the product PV (Parent 1745: p. 326). The product pu of the weight p lifted by its velocity u is the (general) *effect of the fluid*. Assume with Parent: $B = AB$, $b = AH$; $C = LH$; $c = LI$, Q the weight p necessary to equilibrate P[1].

The relation between P and Q is given by the principle of virtual velocities as $Q = \alpha P$; where $\alpha = BC/bc$ measures the ratio of the virtual displacements of the blade B (horizontal) and the weight $p = Q$ (vertical). When the wheel CBD rotates,

[1]Note that in his calculations Parent used the same symbol P to indicate both the suspended weight which equilibrates the wheel and the force exerted on the blade. We prefer to differentiate the symbols, retaining the symbol P for the force exerted on the blade and indicating the suspended equilibrating weight as Q.

Over and Undershot Waterwheels in the 18th Century. Science-Technology Controversy

3

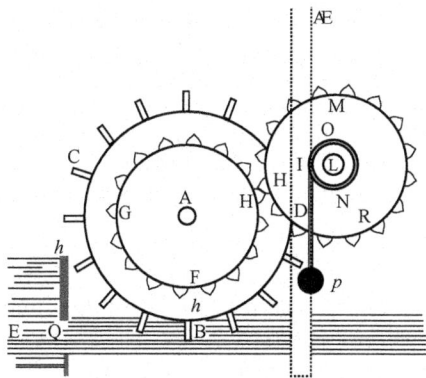

Figure 2.
Parent's undershot wheels

instead of P which is proportional to V^2, the force on the blade in B is P^*, lower than P and proportional to $(V-x)^2$, being $V-x$ the velocity of the water relative to the wheel. The weight p can be raised with uniform velocity, i.e. the weight to be equilibrated with P^* (because its motion is assumed to be uniform) is $p = \alpha P^*$; consequently:

$$Q : p = V^2 : (V - x)^2 \qquad (1)$$

which is an equation between x and p. Quite surprisingly for a modern, Parent chose to solve it with respect to x instead of p, which gives:

$$x = V \frac{\sqrt{Q} - \sqrt{p}}{\sqrt{Q}} \qquad (2)$$

With simple kinematical considerations, the velocity u of the weight p is obtained:

$$u = x \frac{bc}{BC} = V \frac{\sqrt{Q} - \sqrt{p}}{\sqrt{Q}} \frac{bc}{BC} \qquad (3)$$

and the effect of the fluid pu:

$$pu = V \frac{\sqrt{Q} - \sqrt{p}}{\sqrt{Q}} \frac{bc}{BC} p \qquad (4)$$

If the geometry of machine (bc and BC) and the absolute velocity V of the fluid are kept as constant, the effect of the machine only depends on p. Parent found the maximum value with the use of *Calculus*:

Art. V. If one now assumes B, C, b, c as constants and p is decreased, or decreased as far as possible, that is to say, we do it through all changes in size which is possible, the value that makes the machine to produce its greatest effect, there will be p variable in the general values of the effect of the preceding article, and taking the differential of the value, namely, $\overline{\sqrt{P} - \frac{2}{3}\sqrt{p}} \times V \frac{bc}{BC\sqrt{P}} dp$ with the purpose to equate it to zero (according to the method of the infinitesimals) it results the equality $\sqrt{P} = \frac{3}{2}\sqrt{p}$, i.e. $\frac{2}{3}\sqrt{P} = \sqrt{p}$, and finally $\left(\frac{4}{9}P = p\right)$ (Parent 1745: p. 331)[2].

From the value $p = 4/9\ Q$ which makes maximum the effect Parent obtained the maximum value of the effect itself simply

by substituting this value of p in the expression (4), also considering the equilibrium relation $Q = P\ BC/bc$:

$$pu = \frac{4}{27} PV \qquad (5)$$

i.e. the effect of the fluid is 4/27 of the natural effect. The optimal value of velocity can be obtained from Equation (2), resulting in $x = V/3$. Notice the all these values are independent of the machine geometry and of the fluid velocity.

If one wants to evaluate the efficiency of the machine, i.e. the ratio between dissipated *living force*[3] and work made in a second—as was done by many scientists and engineers of the 18th century, such as Smeaton, Daniel Bernoulli for instance—this can be made by reworking the Equation (5), assuming that the velocity V results from a downfall from the height H, such that $V^2 = 2gH$ (Torricelli's law). Being A the section of the vein of fluids (**Figure 3(a)**), γ the mass density of the fluid, $q = \gamma AV$ the flow (mass in a second), the force P and the product PV are respectively $P = \gamma AV^2 = 2g\gamma AH$[4] and $PV = 2g\gamma AVH = 2gqH$; thus Equation (5) gives:

$$pu = \frac{8}{27} qgH \qquad (6)$$

But qgH is exactly the living force dissipated per unit of time $(1/2qV^2)$ and pu the work made (per unit of time) by pu, thus the efficiency is 8/27. Parent however did not give this association probably because he could not write $P = \gamma AV^2$, as he only knew that P is proportional to AV^2. Indeed when considering the case of the fluid falling from the height H, he evaluated the effect assuming for P its static value $P = \gamma gH$, with γ the specific mass, g the acceleration of gravity and A the area of the fluid vein (see **Figure 3(b)**). The effect resulted then:

$$pu = \frac{4}{27} A\gamma gHV = \frac{4}{27} qgH \qquad (7)$$

i.e. one half of that obtained assuming for P its dynamic value $P = \gamma AV^2 = 2g\gamma AH$ (see **Figure 3(a)**). This is indeed an incongruence, because if Parent, as it seems from his reasoning, was considering a wheel immersed in a river then he should assume for P the dynamic value; if instead he was assuming that the wheel was placed in a channel having the same width of the blade, P is correctly evaluated by the static value, but the dynamic analysis leading to the Equation (5) is not tenable.

Apart from the last consideration that is not central, it can be said that Parent's approach is elegant and with no errors; its limitations are due to the idealization of the model. His results can be regained at ease using modern notations and concepts.

---

[2]Art. V. Si l'on suppose donc maintenant B, C, b, c constant & que l'on diminue, ou que l'on augment p autant qu'il est possible; c'est à dire, qu'on le fasse passer par tous les changements de grandeur dont il est susceptible, afin de trouver sa valeur qui fasse produire à la Machine son plus grand effet on aura p variable dans le valeur générale de l'effet de l'article précèdent, & prenant la différentielle de cette valeur, savoir, $\overline{\sqrt{P} - \frac{2}{3}\sqrt{p}} \times V \frac{bc}{BC\sqrt{P}} dp$ afin de l'égale à zéro (selon la méthode des Infiniment petits) il résulte l'égalité $\sqrt{P} = \frac{3}{2}\sqrt{p}$, d'où l'on tire $\sqrt{P} = \frac{3}{2}\sqrt{p}$, & enfin $\left(\frac{4}{9}P = p\right)$. In this quotation, to be coherent with my symbols, P should be replaced by Q.
[3]Living force is the term used in the 18th century to indicate twice the kinetic energy; so the living force of a body with mass m and speed v is given by mv^2.
[4]The relation $P = \gamma AV^2$ is a classical results of dynamics of fluids.

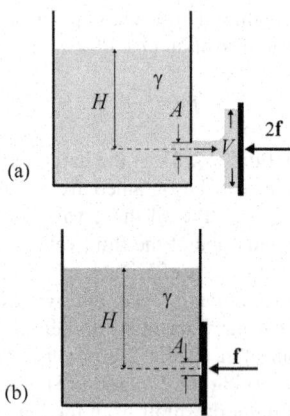

Figure 3.
Dynamic (a) and static (b) forces of a fluid.

To this purpose see (Denny, 2003) where also the analysis of the overshot wheel is reported. Although Parent's analysis was idealised, its results were adopted by many scientists of the 18th century such as John Theophilus Desaguliers (1683-1744), Colin Maclaurin (1698-1746) (Smeaton, 1776: pp. 452-455), Jean D'Alembert (1717-1783) and Leonhard Euler (1707-1783) included.

Jean-Charles de Borda's Analysis

Jean Charles de Borda (1733-1799), in the *Memoire sur les roues hydrauliques* of 1767 (de Borda, 1767), much later than Parent's one, when hydrodynamics had become a mature science, reconsidered the problem of the efficiency of the water wheels. He studied several situations. Besides the classical undershot wheel with plane blades he also studied a wheel with curved blades and an overshot wheel. Here the first case is referred to, while the latter is discussed in one of following sections. The case of the wheel with curved blades is not discussed because it was too difficult a problem for de Borda to solve and was satisfactory solved only in the 19th century (Poncelet, 1825, 1827; Coriolis, 1831, 1835).

De Borda derived the behaviour for the undershot wheel with plane blades starting from the analysis of the wheel having a vertical axis. Since a detailed presentation of de Borda results would be too long, his result will be summarized adapting them to Parent's problem and symbols, also considering that de Borda's text contains many misprints. Moreover as he used two different approaches, one based on the principle of living force[5] the other based on D'Alembert principle (D'Alembert, 1758: pp. 73-75), which however gives the same result, for the same reason of economy the latter only is referred.

At the beginning de Borda assumed, as Parent did, that the single blade was moving with velocity x (de Borda's symbol V), impacted orthogonally by a fluid stream with velocity V (de Borda's symbol B). But the hydrodynamic context is different; while Parent assumed the force on the blade resulting from the friction in a medium, de Borda assumed an impact of the water on the blade moving in a narrow channel as large as the blade. According to D'Alembert principle the impact force of the blade and water is proportional to the lost motion given by the relative velocity $(V\text{-}x)$. If q (de Borda's symbol E) is the flow of

---

[5]In modern term the principle of conservation of mechanical energy.

the fluid (mass for second) the quantity of motion lost in an interval of time Δt is given by $q(V\text{–}x)\,\Delta t$. The quantity of motion acquired by the weight p is given instead by $p\Delta t$. For the equilibrium, the use of the principle of virtual velocities leads to the relation: $pbc\Delta t = q(V - x)BC\Delta t$ and the effect pu, considering that $u = x\ bc/BC$, is given by $pu = qx(V - x)$, which has its maximum for $x = V/2$ with a value:

$$pu = \frac{1}{4}qV^2 \qquad (8)$$

Assuming that V *is* generated by a downfall of water H, it is $V^2 = 2gH$ and the previous relation becomes:

$$pu = \frac{1}{2}qgH \qquad (9)$$

Thus the efficiency of the undershot machine would be 1/2 (i.e. 50%), that is a much higher value (twice) than that found by Parent. Notice that Equation (9) is ours, obtained completing de Borda reasoning; however somewhere in his memoir (de Borda, 1767: p. 284) he explicitly said that the theoretical maximum efficiency of the undershot machine is 1/2. Adding that in practice this result is never reached, he stated that the lower value 3/8 should be assumed (de Borda, 1767: p. 285).

In a comment de Borda tried to justify his result which is different from Parent's one:

What my solution says is contrary to what has been said so far by the mathematicians who worked on the matter who all found that to produce the greatest impact on a paddle wheel, it should be left to the paddles one third of the velocity of the fluid that hits them, and here I show what this result is based on. It is considered but one paddle on this wheel AB, against which the force is sought of the shock of the fluid; it was found by calling B the velocity of the fluid and V that of the paddle, that the shock was proportional to $(B - V)^2$ and as the effect of the impeller is necessarily proportional to the speed of the blades multiplied by the shock of the fluid, the effect of the wheel was given by $V (B - V)^2$, from which it is obtained for the *maximum V* = 1/3 B; but it was observed that the movement in question, the action of the water is not exerted against an isolated blade, but against several blades at a time, and that these blades closing all the breading of the small canal and removing from the fluid the velocity that this has more than that, the amount lost by the fluid, and therefore the shock experienced by the paddle movement is no longer proportional to the square of the difference in fluid velocities and pallets, but only to the difference in the speed; from which it follows that the effect is represented by $V (B - V)$, and not by $V (B - V)^2$; now matching $V (B - V)$ to a *maximum*, we find V = 1/2 B (de Borda, 1767: pp. 273-274)[6].

A reader, not only a modern one, cannot but remain confused by this argumentation. It seems unrelated from the analysis summarised above, the correctness of which is not discussed here. There are neither theoretical nor experimental argumentations justifying the assertion that when there is more than a blade immersed in the water the force of impact should vary as $(V - x)$ instead as $(V - x)^2$. Why this comment when de Borda has theoretically already proved that for a single blade the force of impact varies as $(V - x)$? This is a mystery, that becomes still greater by noticing that de Borda had good reason not to carefully scrutinise and accept his theory, as it was in good agreement with experience, at least as far as efficiency and velocity of the wheel are concerned (see Smeaton's comments, hereafter).

In the secondary literature it is sometimes argued that Parent made calculation errors, and the true efficiency of the undershot wheel is 8/24 instead of 4/27 (Cardwell, 1967; Reynolds, 1979). De Borda would instead have found exact results if he had corrected the error due to the approximation in considering a wheel at the time and a factor two which Parent had neglected:

> In 1767, Borda published a short paper correcting the two main errors of Parent and harmonising theory with experiment (Cardwell, 1967: p. 212).

Parent's theory is actually correct if properly intended. The difference with de Borda's one depends on the different hydraulic context assumed by the two scientists.

Empirical Investigations

John Smeaton Investigations on Undershot Wheels

The first systematic experiments on waterwheels were probably those of the English engineer John Smeaton (1724-1792) who in 1759 published *An experimental enquiry concerning the natural powers of water and wind to turn mills, and other machines, depending on a circular motion*, before de Borda's memoir. He compared under and overshot wheels.

Smeaton's attention to water wheels was due to the demand of English industry for an improvement of the efficiency of existing water wheels. Being not convinced of Parent's results he performed numerous experiments on the model shown in **Figure 4**, where ABCD is a reservoir which collects water for recirculation after its action on the waterwheel. Water is pumped out of the waterwheel via a hand pump (MN is the handle of the pump, L the pump rod) to another reservoir DE. The water in DE was maintained at a constant level by observing the graduated rod FG, while the water released on the wheel was controlled by the rod HI. A rope connected to the axle of the wheel in O and led through the pulleys P and Q raised a pan of weights, R, used for measuring the wheel's output. The apparatus could be adapted to test overshot wheels as shown by the dotted line in the cross-sectional view.

Smeaton defined the *original power* of the water as the product between the quantity of water expounded in a given time and the height that water comes down from. The *effect* of the machine is the sum of the weight raised by the action of this water and the weight necessary to overcome the friction, multiplied by the height the weight will be raised to in a given time. The efficiency is the ratio between effect and power (Smeaton, 1759: p. 106-107). In one of his experiments where the power was 3970 pounds × inches in a minute (the product of the flow of 264.7 lb of water multiplied by the height of fall of 15 inches), by varying the raised weight, he found that the maximum effect corresponded to 1266 pounds × inches in a minute (the product of a weight of 9.375 lb raised to and height of 135 inches), for an efficiency of 1266/3970 = 32%, greater than that provided by Parent (25%) but lower than that provided by de Borda (50%). The ratio between the velocity of the blades of the wheel and the velocity of water was often greater than that foreseen by Parent, arriving in some cases close to 1/2 instead of 1/3. Also the weight raised was much greater, (3/4) instead of 4/9 of the equilibrating weight (Smeaton, 1759: p. 115). Smeaton justified the difference between theory and experiment as a consequence of different assumptions:

> It must be remembered, therefore, that, in the present case, the wheel was not placed in an open river, where the natural current, after it has communicated its impulse to the float, has room on all fides to escape, as the theory supposes; but in a conduit or rate, to which the float being adapted, the water cannot otherwise escape than by moving along with the wheel. It is observable, that a wheel working in this manner, as soon as the water meets the float, receiving a sudden check, it rises up against the float, like a wave against a fixed object; insomuch that when the sheet of water is not a quarter of an inch thick before it meets the float, yet this sheet will act upon the whole surface of a float, whose height is 3 inches; and consequently was the float no higher than the thickness of the sheet of water, as the theory also supposes, a great part of the force would have been 10 ft, by the water's dashing over the float (Smeaton, 1759: pp. 113-114).

[6]Ce que ma solution vient de me donner, est contraire à ce qu'ont dit jusqu'à présent les Géomètres qui ont travaillé fur cette matière en effet, tous ont trouvé, que pour faire produire à une roue à palettes le plus grand effet possible, il ne fallait laisser prendre aux palettes que le tiers de la vitesse du fluide qui les frappait, & voici sur quoi ce résultat était fondé. On ne considérait dans cette roue qu'une seule palette A B, contre laquelle on cherchait la force du choc du fluide; on trouvait, en appelant B la vitesse du fluide & V celle des palettes, que le choc était proportionnel à $(B - V)^2$ & comme l'effet de la roue est nécessairement proportionnel à la vitesse des palettes multipliée par le choc du fluide, on avait l'effet de la roue représenté par $V (B - V)^2$ d'où on tirait pour le *maximum* $V = 1/3\ B$; mais il fallait observer que dans le mouvement dont il s'agit, l'action de l'eau ne s'exerce pas contre une palette isolée, mais contre plusieurs palettes à la fois, & que ces palettes fermant tout le panage du petit canal & ôtant au fluide la vitesse qu'il a de plus qu'elles, la quantité du mouvement perdu par ce fluide, & par conséquent le choc qu'éprouvent les palettes, n'est plus proportionnel au carré de la différence des vitesses des fluides & des palettes, mais seulement à la différence de ces vitesses d'où il suit que l'effet est représenté par $V (B - V)$, & non pas par $V (B - V)^2$; or égalant $V (B - V)$ à un *maximum*, on trouve $V = \frac{1}{2}B$.

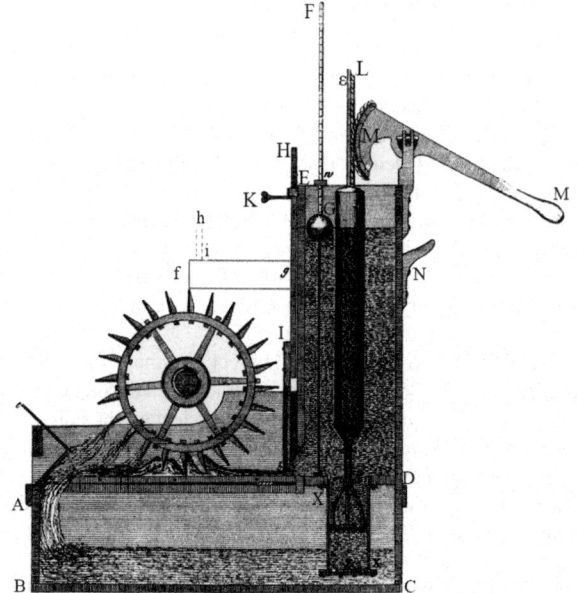

Figure 4.
Smeaton's experimental set (Smeaton, 1756: p. 102).

In a subsequent paper Smeaton reassumed his experimental results, rhetorically exaggerating the difference between experimental and theoretical findings, asserting also that for large wheel (as the wheels of actual mills), the efficiency is greater arriving up to 50%:

> I have found be the commonly received doctrine among theoretical mechanics [...] that, where the velocity of water is double, the adjutage or aperture of the sluice remaining the same the effect is eight time; that is not as the square but as the cube of the velocity [...].

> For if that conclusion were true, only 4/27 of the water expended could be raised back again to the height of the reservoir from which it had descended, exclusively of all kinds of friction, &c. which would make the actual quantity raised back again still less; that is, less than one-seventh of the whole; whereas it appears from Table I of the said volume (Smeaton, 1759), that in some of the experiments here related, even upon the small scale on which they were tried, the work done was equivalent to the raising back again about one quarter of the water expended; and in large works the effect is still greater, *approaching towards half, which seems to be the limit for the undershot mills, as the whole would be the limit for the overshot mills* [emphasis added][...].

> The velocity also of the wheel, which according to M. Parent's determination, adopted by Desaguliers and Maclaurin, ought to be no more than one-third of that of the water, varies at the *maximum* in the above mentioned experiments of table, between one third and one half but in all the cases there related, in which the most work is performed in proportion to the water expended and which approach the nearest to the circumstances of great works, when properly executed the *maximum* lies much nearer to one half than one third (Smeaton, 1776: pp. 456-457).

Antoine de Parcieux's and John Smeaton's Experiments on Overshot Wheels

The overshot waterwheel received no attention by the scientists probably because there was the spread opinion that they had the same efficiency as the undershot ones (Reynolds, 1979: p. 274). This was the opinion of Leonhard Euler also, who in his work of 1754 denied that the overshot wheel had any advantage over the undershot ones (Euler, 1754: p. 198). Bernard Forest de Belidor (Belidor, 1782: p. 286) referred that an undershot wheel is six times more efficient that an overshot one, while Desaguliers on the contrary affirmed that a "well-made overshot mill" may be ten times more efficient than an undershot wheel (Desaguliers, 1744: p. 532).

The first known study on the subject was that of Antoine de Parcieux (1703-1768) which is usually classified as an engineer though member of the Académie des sciences de Paris. The interest of de Parcieux derived by the desire of Madame de Pompadour to have current water from the small river the Blaise in Crésy, raising to a height of 50 meters. Because of the small flow of the river, an undershot wheel would not have been able to satisfy the request.

De Parcieux was brought to think that the efficiency of the overshot wheels should be higher than that of the current undershot wheels by assimilating the water, that descends and works as an engine for the water that should be raised, to two weights which are located on two opposite sides of a pulley and are connecters by a rope.

> I soon saw that I could get a much better use of water weight, considering it as weights which falling raise others: but how has one to take the wheel (de Parcieux, 1759: p. 607)[7].

He said to have made experiments with a pulley using as power a weight of 96 ounces which raised weights of 24, 32, 40, etc. ounces registering the amount these weights rise in one second, i.e. the velocity in the first part of motion. The velocity ranged from 85 inches per second for a weight of 24 ounces to 20 inches per second for a weight of 72 ounces (de Parcieux, 1754: p. 609).

On the basis of his results de Parcieux suggested a simple experiment by imagining two waterwheels equal to each other but with their buckets inclined in opposite directions. The wheel receiving the falling water was able to raise water in the other wheel under the condition that the raised water was less than that falling one. And, in the same way as in a pulley, the speed of the wheels will depend on the ratio between falling and raising weight. In the limit, if the wheels rotate very slowly, the amount of raised water will be equal to that fallen, and the efficiency of the overshot waterwheel will reach 100%.

The explanation, on the greater efficiency of wheels that rotate slowly actually has no weight. The experiment of the pulley is of course truthful, but here accelerated motions are concerned. In the case of the waterwheel there is instead a stationary motion. In this situation it can be shown that the velocity of the wheel, at least ideally, has no influence on the efficiency. The greater efficiency actually registered for the overshot wheels that rotate slowly depends on the construction methods and operation. In (Denny 2003) the reasons for the efficiency of the overshot wheels to decrease with the increasing of speed are illustrated.

With his apparatus, Smeaton was able to experiment an overshot wheel with water flowing from the tape indicated with *fg* in **Figure 4**. He found that using the same wheel with plane blades, the efficiency was double than that of the undershot wheels and confirmed the results obtained by de Parcieux, that the efficiency of the wheel increased by slowing its speed.

Smeaton was convinced that most of the difference between over and under wheels were due to the loss of living force of the water in the latter case associated to its change in shape during impact. He also proposed an (unsatisfactory) explanation for the increase of efficiency of the overshot wheel by slowing the speed of the wheel, assuming that at the higher speed the efficiency of the water pressure was lower.

> When the velocity is *greater* [water] does not press so much upon the bucket as when it is less, the power of the water to produce effects will be greater in the less velocity than in the greater: and hence we are led to this general rule, *that*, caeteris paribus, the less the velocity of the wheel, the greater will be the effect thereof (Smeaton, 1759: p. 133).

---

[7] Je vis bientôt que je pouvais tirer un bien meilleur parti du poids de l'eau, en la considérant comme des poids qui en descendant, en enlèveraient d'autres: mais quelle vitesse falloir il faire prendre à la roue.

In the subsequent years Smeaton performed many experiments on the impact of non-elastic bodies assuming that the loss of living force in the impact was due to a change of shape of the bodies. The following quotations resumes Smeaton's ideas about the energy (modern term) required to change the shape of a body.

To obviate this, those of the old opinion seriously set about proving, that the bodies might change their figure, without any loss of motion in either of the striking bodies.

[...]

On the other hand, if it can be shown that the figure of a body can be changed, without a *power*, then, by the same law, we might be able to make a *forge hammer* work upon a mass of soft iron, without any other power than that necessary to overcome the friction resistance, and original *vis inertiae*, of the parts of the machine to be put in motion: for, as no progressive motion is given the mass of iron by the hammer (it being supported by the anvil). no power call be expended that way; and if none is lost to the hammer from changing the figure of the iron, which is the only effect produced, then the whole power must reside in the hammer, and it would jump back again, to the place from which it fell, just in the same manner as if it fell upon a body perfectly elastic, upon which, if it did fall, the case would really happen: the power, therefore to work the hammer would be the same whether, it fell upon an elastic or non-elastic body; an idea so very contrary to all experience (Smeaton, 1782: pp. 342-343).

Thanks to Smeaton, at least in Great Britain, the overshot wheels became dominant, and contrasted the success of steam machines.

However much Mr. Smeaton's valuable observations may have been disregarded by authors, they have not been lost to practical men... [As a result of his experiments] he determined to apply the water, in all cases, so that it should act more by its weight, and less by its impulse; and the advantage gained by that improved construction was found to be fully equal to his expectation. It was afterwards so generally adopted and improved upon by himself and by other engineers in this country, that although undershot water-wheels were, about fifty years ago, the most prevalent, they are now rarely to be met with; and wherever economy of power is an object, no new ones are made (Reynold, 1979: p. 291).

In his *Hydrodinamica* of 1738 Daniel Bernoulli reinterpreted Parent's result calculating in 8/27 the theoretical efficiency related to the living force of the flowing water before the impact upon the blades of the wheel. Bernoulli concluded that the small efficiency of the undershot wheels had to be ascribed to the fact that part of the water living force is lost to keep still the high speed of the water flowing after that the impact against the paddles of the wheel has occurred (Bernoulli, 1738: p. 193). Johann Albrecht Euler—a son of Leonhard—in a memoir submitted in 1754 for a prize competition, which he actually won, analysed separately undershot, gravity and reaction wheels (Euler, 1754). For the undershot wheel he found out Parent's result, i.e. an efficiency equal to 8/27 (Euler, 1754: p. 12). For the gravity wheel (the overshot ones of **Figure 5**) Euler con-

cluded that if the buckets were large enough to collect all the water of the stream and if the diameter of the wheel was equal to the height of the fall, the efficiency of the gravity wheel would be 100%.

Smeaton did not know Daniel Bernoulli's work, neither probably Johann Albrecht Euler's. Equally, at least in 1759, Smeaton did not know de Borda's analysis of the overshot wheels which, though correct, needed to be interpreted.

De Borda, considering a very idealized wheel whose buckets did not leave water, drew the conclusion that an overshot wheel as in **Figure 6**, where the stream of water MN is tangent to the wheel, reaches its maximum effect when $BH = 0$ and the wheel rotates with zero velocity, confirming that the efficiency of this kind of wheel increases by lowering the speed of rotation. Actually de Borda was not precise. Indeed, after a substantially correct analysis, he concluded that the effect of the overshot wheel, using Parent's symbols is given by (de Borda, 1770: p. 281):

$$pu = q\left[\left(\sqrt{2gh} - x\right) + g\frac{H-h}{x}\right]x \qquad (10)$$

with $h = BH$ and $H = BE$, with reference to **Figure 6**. He correctly concluded that the maximum of the efficiency is reached for $h = 0$; but incorrectly that x should be zero. Indeed for $h = 0$ the previous relation should be rewritten as:

$$pu = q\left[g\frac{H}{x}\right]x = qgH \qquad (11)$$

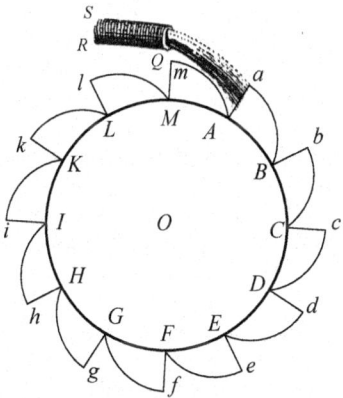

Figure 5.
Euler's gravity wheel (Euler, 1754: Tab. II)

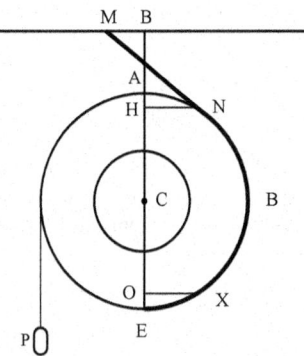

Figure 6.
de Borda's wheel (de Borda, 1767: p. 286).

which indicates an efficiency of 100% and the independence of the velocity x of the wheel. However, at the end of his paper (de Borda, 1770: p. 286), De Borda noticed that the efficiency is in fact substantially independent of x, as its change with x is rather small.

Further Development in the 19th Century

In the 19th century the development of the hydraulic machines was brought in the frame of applied mechanics, where theory and practice were carried out by the same people, the modern engineers, determining a great improvement in the efficiency of all kind of machines. A prominent role was played by the military engineers of the *École de applications de l'Artillerie et du Génie*, in particular Jean Victor Poncelet (1788-1867) and Arthur Jules Morin (1795-1880).

These engineers were so much involved in mathematics and physics as to consider themselves more scientists than practitioners; for instance they addressed their memories to the Académie des science instead to technological journals. They made extensive use of experiments, but not as much as they should to verify the effectiveness of the general mechanical theories behind their designs. The experiments instead had two main purposes. From the one hand they had to highlight some minor defects of the machines to be corrected after a theoretical review of the problem; on the other hand they should furnish numerical values of selected correction factors which allowed transition from theoretical to practical formulas. This was not due to errors in the theory but to simplified assumptions. For example very often the conservation of living forces—or the work—was assumed and then no friction was taken into account; its effect was evaluated by performing experiments under different operating conditions and arranging tables of correction factors.

After some preparatory work (Belhoste, 1994) Poncelet prepared the *Mémoire sur les roues verticales à palettes courbes mues par en dessous, suivi d'expériences sur les effets mécaniques de ces roues* concerning the undershot waterwheels. It was presented before the Académie des science in 1824 and published in the *Annales de Chimie et Physique* in 1825, with minor revisions (Poncelet, 1825); an improved version was published in 1827 (Poncelet, 1827). Poncelet's purpose was to satisfy Lazare Carnot (1753-1823) (and de Borda) requirements for an efficient machine: avoiding loss of living force by impact and by the release of water with significant speed. He reached his goal by assuming curved and inclined blades as shown in **Figure 7**; probably not a new idea, but a good idea that was not pursued with the due firmness:

> The idea to substitute curved blades to plane blades of the old systems seemed so naturel and simple that one can think that its arose to everyone; so I did not attribute a great merit to it. But because the simplest ideas are often those which found the most difficulties to be accepted, I did not want limit myself to theoretical speculations (Poncelet: pp. 144-145)[8].

---

[8] L'idée de substituer des palettes courbes aux palettes droites de l'ancien système parait si naturelle et simple, qu'il y a lieu de croire qu'elle sera venue à plus d'une personne; aussi n'ai-je pas la prétention de lui attribuer un grand mérite; mais, comme les idées les plus simples son fort souvent celles qui rencontrent le plus de difficultés à être admises, je n'ai pas voulu m'en tenir à des aperçus purement théoriques.

With these devices the undershot wheels could reach, at least theoretically, an efficiency of 100%. The water wheel as proposed by Poncelet is now known as *Poncelet wheel*. Later studies and experiments highlighted some weakness of Poncelet wheels (Belhoste, 1994), which however spread out and for a long time were competing with the water turbine introduced by Benoit Fourneyron (1802-1867) proposed to replace the waterwheel around 1830 (Fourneyron 1840). Contrary to the common belief, turbines did not replace the waterwheels and their design was only in the syllabus of engineering faculties at least until 1940. They disappeared only after the Second World War. Today new attention is paid to properly designed water-wheels, both undershot and overshot, as an economical solution to get energy from water streams with low head (Muller, 2004).

Conclusion

In the early 18th century, as a result of the growing demand for energy, a better understanding of the functioning of the waterwheels, even at the theoretical level, was required in order to improve their efficiency. At the time there was a widespread belief among scientists that it did not really matter which type of wheel to study because the effectiveness would have to be the same for all types of wheels, probably because at an intuitive level one could think that the living force (the kinetic energy) of water is communicated always in the same way.

Despite the theoretical knowledge of hydraulics was very limited, in 1704 Antoine Parent could write a very interesting work on the hydraulics of the undershot wheels that preserved its value for most of the century. Parent's result was not in a perfect agreement with practice and some differences persisted in comparison to experimental research. Smeaton work was for sure of much interest. He finally pointed out what should have been clear to everyone, that is that the overshot wheels could have much higher efficiency, up to twice, than undershot, at least as regards the wheels used in the 18th century.

Meanwhile hydrodynamics was developing thanks to the theoretical work of Leonhard and Johann Euler and D'Alembert, who had also made it possible theoretical investigation of the operation of water wheels. But their theoretical work written on the subject had a very limited impact on the technological development of the wheels, mainly because they were not read by engineers, in particular, they were not read by Smeaton and were soon forgotten. Thus the legacy the experiments and the theoretical speculations of the 18th century left to the 19th century consists mainly of the two points concerning the optimization of the efficiency of water wheels:

a) the impact of the water upon the paddles of the wheel should be avoided;

b) the wheel must move so that the water is unloaded with the minimum possible speed.

These conclusions were collected by Lazare Carnot (Carnot 1786) who based his theory of machines on the conservation of living force and impact for insensible degrees. The problem of the efficiency of waterwheels was dealt with in a different fashion in the 19th century by French engineers, such as Morin and Poncelet. They clarified that the efficiency does not depend on the kind of wheel (over or undershot) but on the way they are designed.

If one had to summarize in a few words the role of science in the technology of water-wheels, he would be attempted to say that it was modest, almost none at all as claimed by Reynolds

Mémoires des Experinces en grand, relatives à la nouvelle Rene

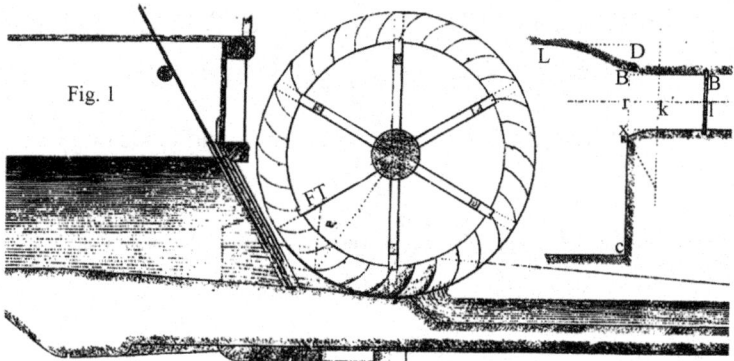

Fig. 1

Figure 7.
Poncelet wheel (Poncelet, 1827: Planche 1)

(1979) and Rupert Hall (1961). In our opinion there was instead a fruitful interaction between science and technology. In fact, the application of rational mechanics based on a high formalization had a limited impact, which instead will have a profound influence on the technology of the 19th century. On the contrary, less formalized theoretical considerations had a decisive role, despite their high degree of idealization, such as those of Parent and de Borda. The hydrodynamical studies aimed at assessing the pressure of fluids also had decisive importance. Moreover, considering De Parcieux's and Smeaton's peers as foreign to science, as was done by some historians asserting the low influence of science on technology, is certainly debatable and not shared by all. For example, Musson and Robinson (1969) considered Smeaton's contribution as an example of the direct application of science to technology.

REFERENCES

Belhoste, B. (1994). La formation polytechnicienne: 1794-1994. Paris: Dunod.

Belidor, B. F. (1782). *Architecture hydraulique, ou l'art de conduire, d'élever et de ménager les eaux pour les différens besoins de la vie (1737-1739)*. Paris: L. Cellot.

Bernoulli, D. (1738). *Hydrodynamica, sive de viribus et motibus fluidorum commentarii*. Strasbourgh: Dulsseker J. R.

Cardwel, D. S. L. (1965). Power technologies and the advance of science. *Technology and Culture, 6*, 188-207.

Cardwell, D. S. L. (1967). Some factors in the early development of the concepts of power, work and energy. *The British Journal for the History of Science, 3*, 209-224.

Carnot, L. (1786). *Essai sur les machines en général (1783)*. Dijon: Defay.

Coriolis, G. (1831). Mémoire sur le principe des forces vives dans le mouvements relatifs des machines. *Journal École polytechnique, 21*, 268-302.

Coriolis, G. (1835). Sur les équations du mouvement relatif des systèmes de corps. *Journal de l'École Polytechnique, 24*, 142-154.

D'Alembert, J. (1758). *Traité de dynamique*. Paris: David.

de Borda, J. C. (1770). *Sur les roues hydrauliques* (pp. 270-287). Mémoires de l'Académie des Sciences de Paris.

De Parcieux, A. (1759). *Mémoire dans lequel on démontre que l'eau d'une chute destinée à faire mouvoir quelque machine* (pp. 603-605). Histoire de l'Académie Royale des Sciences de Paris, année 1754. Paris: Imprimerie Royale.

Denny, M. (2003). The efficiency of overshot and undershot waterwheels. *European Journal of Physics, 25*, 193-202.

Desaguliers, J. T. (1744). *A course of experimental philosophy, vol. 2*. London: Innys W. et al.

Euler, J. A. (1754). *Enodatio quaestionis quomodo vis aquae aliusve fluidi cum maximo lucro ad molas circum agendas aliave opera perficienda impdendi possit?* Gottingen: Kubler D.F.

Euler, L. (1754). *Maximes pour arranger le plus avantageusement les machines destinées è élever de l'eau par le moyen des pompes* (pp. 185-232). Mémoires de l'Académie des Sciences de Berlin. Berlin: Auder et Spenner

Fourneyron, B. (1840). *Memoires sur les turbines hydrauliques*. Liege: Leroux.

Hall, A. R. (1961). Engineering and the scientific revolution. *Technology and Culture, 2*, 333-341.

Mariotte, E. (1686). *Traité des eaux et autres corps fluides*. Paris: Estienne Michallet.

Musson, A. E., & Robinson, E. (1969). *Science and technology in the industrial revolution*. Manchester: University Press of Manchester.

Newton, I. (1972). *Philosophiae naturalis principia mathematica* (3rd ed.). Cambridge: Cambridge University Press.

Parent, A. (1745). Sur la plus grande perfection possible des machines. Histoire de l'Académie Royale des Sciences de Paris, année 1704. Paris: Martin G., Coignard JB., Guerin HL., pp. 323-338.

Poncelet, J. V. (1825). Mémoire sur les roues verticales à palettes courbes mues par en dessous, suivi d'expériences sur les effets mécaniques de ces roues. *Annales de Chimie et de Physique, 30*, 136-188, 225-257.

Poncelet, J. V. (1827). *Mémoire sur les roues verticales à aubes courbes mues par en dessous, suivi d'expériences sur les effets mécaniques de ces roues*. Metz: Thiel.

Reynolds, T. S. (1979). Scientific influences on technology: The case of the overshot waterwheel, 1752-1754. *Technology and Culture, 20*, 270-295.

Singer et al. (1957). *A history of technology, Vol. 3*. Oxford: Clarendon Press.

Smeaton, J. (1759). An experimental enquiry concerning the natural powers of water and wind to turn mills, and other machines, depending on a circular motion. *Philosophical Transactions of the Royal Society of London, 51*, 100-174.

Smeaton, J. (1776). An experimental examination of the quantity and proportion of mechanic power necessary to be employed in giving different degrees of velocity to heavy bodies from a state of rest. *Philosophical Transactions of the Royal Society of London, 66*, 450-475.

Smeaton, J. (1782). New fundamental experiments upon the collision of bodies. *Philosophical of the Royal Society of London, 72*, 337-354.

Storck J., & Teague W. (1952). *Flour for man's bread: A history of milling*. Minneapolis: University of Minnesota Press.

Syson, L. (1980). *The watermills of Britain*. London: David and Charles.

Torricelli, E. (1644). *Opera geometrica*. Florentiae: Masse & de Landis.

2

Les Châteaux de Landiras et de Montferrand and Their Seigneurial Families

—Part One: Setting, Medieval History, and Genealogy

Donald A. Bailey
Department of History, University of Winnipeg Winnipeg, Manitoba Canada

Apart from Arnaud Communay's "Genealogical Essay", as he himself noted (1889: v), the Montferrands of the Bordeaux region have been neglected.[1] The present approach to their history initiated in research on the Château de Landiras, whose baronial family tended to heiresses until one of them married a Montferrand. So began a four-century association of the "first and second baronies of Guyenne"! This first part will describe the socio-geographical settings of the two branches, some of their medieval experiences, and then proceed to presenting the combined genealogies—a task not previously attempted. The second part will narrate their respective and blended subsequent histories.

Keywords: Montferrand de Guyenne; Landiras; Saint Jeanne de Lestonnac; Bordeaux; Hundred Years' War; French Revolution; Bertrand III; Pierre II; Lesparre; de Goth; de la Roque-Budos; Communay; Graves Wine

Geographical Setting

About thirty-five kilometres southeast of Bordeaux, one finds the name Landiras attached to a small stream, a village and *commune*, and a château. The town's medieval significance is indicated by its holding perhaps as many as four fairs each year (on 2 or 3 February, 11 November, the second feast of Easter, and the second feast of Pentecost), as well as a market every Sunday (Baurein. 1876: III, 206; Féret, 1874: II, 446). Yet in modern times, the city has only grown from 1535 in 1726 to 2061 residents in 2009 (Baurein, III, 205; Wikipedia; cf. Baurein: II, 205). The town's patron saint was St. Martin, whose feast day is the same 11 November as the town's fourth annual fair; the local 12th-century church bears his name (Féret, II, 446).[2]

Almost three kilometres to the west of the town, one finds an imposing château, beside the ruins of a 14th-century castle, the principal site of the renowned *seigneurie* of Landiras. The original grand edifice was a 12th-century square fortress, with towers at each corner and its main door protected by two other polygon towers, surrounded by a moat. Eventually demolished, only a few ruins, one tower or citadel, and part of the moat remain (Jouannet, 1837: I, 275; cited in Communay: lxxiv, n. 8). Today's château was built in the early 19th century beside the original site.

For their part, the Montferrand family possessed from early times a strategically important site, dominating the mouths of the Garonne and Dordogne Rivers and so the port city of Bordeaux.[3] The barony extended into the parishes of Ivrac, Bassens, Sainte-Eulalie, Saint-Pierre de Quinsac, Montferrand, Ambarès, and La Grave-d'Ambarès (Communay, xliv, n. 4; cf. Grasset, 50). Across from Bordeaux and a little downstream, the *château fort* ("castle") of Saint-Louis-de-Montferrand, in the parish of Saint-Pierre de Bassens, presided over its territory like a "veritable sentinel".[4] Indeed, the Kings of England often appointed a Montferrand (from one branch or the other) as *sénéchal* (*grand-bailli*)[5] of Bordeaux. Only in 1591 was the city able to purchase the specific property and have the château destroyed.

---

[1] Though presenting several Montferrand families throughout France, F-A de La Chenaye Des Bois ignored the one in Guyenne in his multivolume grand Dictionary of French nobility (1770-1778).

The name "Montferrand" refers both to towns and to various, quite different families. Speaking at least of the Bordelaise extended family, one source insists that "Monferrant" is the modern spelling, the "-d" ending being found occasionally "in the old titles" (Féret 1889: III, 469). Not all modern scholars respect this opinion.

[2] This is Saint Martin of Tours (ca. 315-8 November 397).

[3] There's an historical conundrum here, however, for it would be just as likely that the Montferrand castle had served, and been seen as serving, to protect Bordeaux as much as to threaten it. What's the story?

[4] Grasset, Jean, Pastureau, 1981 (hereafter: Grasset). I can't find these striking words in the text, but they are in the virtual poster advertisement for the book on the Internet. Grasset certainly reiterates the point in diverse words (49, 94 & 109).

[5] It's not clear why several of my sources redundantly state someone was a *balli/sénéchal*! Either term refers to an agent of the king or of a lord governing a jurisdiction termed a *baillage* or a *sénéchaussée*, respectively, the former usually found in northern France and the latter generally in the south ("*Grand*" was merely a way of distinguishing a royal agent from others). This delegated authority covered administrative, military and even judicial functions.

Earliest References

The name "Landiras" (formerly, also spelt "Landirans", or "Landirats" in Gascon) is found in the archives as early as the late 12th century. The "-as" termination of words in the Gascon language "suggests some sort of grandeur, as disagreeable as excessive" (Baurein: III, 204).[6] Rostand, *seigneur* de Landiras, sold a fourth part of the *dîme* of Barsac in 1173 to Guillaume Le Templier, archbishop of Bordeaux, who made a gift of the *dîme* to his cathedral (Baurein: III, 161 & 207; and Lopes, 1884: 216). A Rostand de Landiras again appears in a 1236 charter. More than a half century later, we find another Rostand de Landiras and his sister, Isabelle de Landiras (1230/35-ca. 1279),[7] wife of Gaillard de La Mothe (1230-1279), who probably had a sister, Clairemonde de La Mothe. These four appear to have left an orphan niece/daughter, Clairemonde (or Esclaremonde) de La Mothe-Landiras (ca. 1260-1301 or '28). The seneschal Jean de Graily, from Gex, near Geneva,[8] may have married "aunt" Clairemonde de La Mothe (Bailey, 2006: 30-32)[9] and arranged to have his nephew, Jean Roussel de Saint-Symphorien, also originally a Savoyard, marry her niece, the wealthy heiress of Landiras.[10] This Jean Roussel appeared in a document of the year 1290, issued by Edward I of England (1272-1307), which empowered him to look after his uncle's estate while the latter was in the Holy Land.[11]

Landiras's medieval reputation was as "the second barony in Guyenne", with the Montferrand barony reputed as "the first". But it was not always so: Landiras appears to have had no natural advantages for becoming a significant medieval barony. Earlier, Lesparre—one of the largest and oldest baronies in the Bordelaise (Baurein: I, 142)—was seen as the region's "second barony". Yet as Lesparre came into and then passed out of the possession of the barons of Landiras, their respective influence was exchanged. And so it was with the originally powerful barony of Blanquefort, whose brief association with the Montferrand family seems to have coincided with a transfer of

preëminence from the former to the latter. Apart from strategic marriages and capricious genetics, I am not sure how the barony of Landiras attained such prominence. The same factors no doubt aided the Barès family, who morphed into the Montferrand. But in their case, their principal *château fort*, Saint-Louis-de-Montferrand, dominated the Bordelaise and so gave natural advantages for its prominence. Even the powerful Dukes of Aquitaine were never able to bring the barons of Montferrand under their sway.

Both lordships included many and diverse *seignieuries*, *baronnies*, and even a *vicomté* or two, and we have tried to respect these distinctions throughout. Some transfers of title or *terre* were not truly natural, since the Kings of England sometimes arbitrarily transferred titles, suspiciously without reason (Baurein: II, 94; cf., *idem.* III, 273). In addition, as the Kings of France struggled to gain control over territories theoretically under their suzerainty, they made other transfers as rewards for fidelity or punishments for disloyalties. Thus, for example, the barony of Lesparre was taken from Pierre II de Montferrand-Landiras in 1541, but descendents pretended to the title for several generations (Baurein: I, 159/160).

Attaining Medieval Prominence

The barony of Landiras attained prominence when, as we have seen, Jean Roussel de Saint-Symphorien married its heiress, Clairemonde de La Mothe-Landiras, around 1290. For his uncle, Jean de Graily, had won such favour with King Edward I of England that he was made *sénéchal* of Bordeaux. Jean de Graily had even twice served as a crusader in the Holy Land. Just over sixty years later, John de Stratton (another non-Bordelaise) married a later heiress of Landiras, Isabeau de Saint-Symphorien, and soon brought further importance to the barony. Their daughter's marriage to Arnaud de Preissac brought Landiras into association with the barony of Lesparre, as well as several other important lordships, and made it the second barony in Guyenne—with the baron's right to hold the bridle of the Archbishop's horse in processions (Grasset: 50). Soon after her marriage, this Marguerite de Stratton inherited the seigniory of Uzeste from the last male of the de Goth family. Then, in 1410, a third heiress in three generations brought the Landiras and Montferrand dynasties together.

A few words more concerning John of Stratton, who arrived in Guyenne in 1355. In 1377, he was defeated in a battle against Charles V's Constable Bertrand du Guesclin on the Lacapere plateau, with the result that the château de Landiras temporarily passed under French suzerainty.[12] In 1379, the Stratton couple received (as compensation?) from King Richard II (1377-1399) the goods, situated in the Bazadais, seized from the rebel Gaillard de Goth, seigneur de Roaillac, a descendant of our Indie de Goth's uncle (Anselme, 1967: II, 173, 176 & 183)[13]—see next paragraph. Among other offices and remunerations, Richard II made Jean de Stratton *châtelain et connétable* (castellan and constable) of the château of Bordeaux on 26 August 1382 (Baurein: IV, 289). His widow was confirmed in these privi-

---

[6]Many details concerning Landiras and its region may be found in "Saint-Martin de Landiras," article XXXII, in Baurein *Variétés bordeloises*, vol. III, 204-08. (All translations from the French are by the author.)

[7]Dates presented like this "(1230/35-ca. 1279)" indicate the range of disagreement concerning a birth, a marriage, or a death.

[8]Jean III de Graily (1220/30-1303) descended from a noble Savoyard lineage, but he became a servant of the King of England on the other side of France, serving him both in the Bordeaux region, eventually as seneschal de Bordeaux, and twice in the Holy Land. His career and his marriages clearly established his (and his nephew's) family in Guyenne, and justified a changed nomenclature: "Jean I"!

[9]The marriage of the seneschal Jean de Graily is both important and obscure—important because he was an ancestor of Henri de Bourbon-Albret-Foix de Navarre, who became Henry IV of France, and obscure because many sources identify no known spouse. (See Casanovas, 1991: 140, n. 832). Many have him marry Clairemonde de La Mothe-Landiras (for details of these sources see Bailey, 2006: 30-32), but supposed descendents of this match soon peter out. Curiosity aroused, I thought the mystery could be solved by seizing on a one-source mention of a same-name aunt for Clairemonde; this resolution was problematical but it responded to diverse claims that uncle and nephew had married the same person (*loc. cit.*). "Ahnentafel" concurs with four of the standard sources (#7104).

[10]Jean Roussel (b. ca. 1250) was the son of Guillaume Roussel de Saint-Symphorien (b. ca. 1220) and Guillermine (or Guillemette) de Graily (b. ca 1225, daughter of Pierre de Graily and sister of the seneschal of Guyenne). An Internet source for this information gives his wife's name as Esclarmonde de La Mothe (1260-af. 1328); this source does not know the name of Clairemonde's mother, another knows the mother only as Isabelle, while a similar source knows the names of neither of her parents.

[11]For more details, see "Branches collatérales des Montferrands," 1. The next few paragraphs owe much to this source.

---

[12]This must have been a part of the Battle of Eymet, in which Bertrand II de Montferrand also fought.

[13]This would be Gaillard I de Goth. Ansleme (1987: II, 176) describes Gaillard I's ambiguous relations with the English and French kings and penalties incurred around 1345, but then has Gaillard die before November 1371, that is, before the confiscation mentioned above. In fact, though, Gaillard died after 1380 ("Family de Goth").

leges in 1408. It may have been Jean de Stratton who built the dominating château de Landiras in 1377.[14]

For their part, the 1303 marriage of Armaudin III de Barès's to Indie de Goth significantly aided the Montferrand ascendency by virtue of Indie's uncle. Bertrand de Goth, Archbishop of Bordeaux (from 1297), was soon to be elected Pope Clement V (1305-14). The *château fort* de Monferran [*sic*] was magnificently rebuilt (Communay: 1).[15] Their son Bertrand I married Régine de Durfort, the daughter of the *seigneur* de Blanquefort,[16] then the first baron of Guyenne, and of Marqueze/ Marquesse/Marquise de Goth (Bertrand's mother's niece). And *their* son Bertrand II felt justified in changing the family name from Barès to Montferrand. Grandson Bertrand III (1380-1435/46) was among the several in the family to be made *chevalier de l'ordre de la Jarretière* (knight of the [English] Order of the Garter). Already baron and lord of Montferrand and several other places, including Pondesac (which today gives its name to the *canton* in which the *commune* of Landiras is found),[17] he became *châtellain* of the strategic *château fort* de Blaye-et-Sainte-Luce and seneschal of Bordeaux (*sénéchal* or *grand bailli de Guyenne*). The "most illustrious of the Montferrands" (Grasset: 97), he was "the first baron in Guyenne" and a favourite of the English king.

In 1401, Bertrand III married Marguerite d'Astarac, who bore him one or two sons, Jean I de Montferrand (bf. 1404-1442) becoming the heir of his father's Montferrand lands. It was through Bertrand's second marriage, in 1410, to the rich heiress Na Isabeau de Preissac, that the titles and lands attached to Landiras entered the family. *Dame* de La Trau, de Landiras, etc., she was the only child of Bernard Arnaud de Preissac, who was also, like the Baron de Montferrand, a knight ("*chevalier*") and "one of the most valiant warriors of his century" ("Montferrand", 7). Landiras was by now the "second barony" of Guyenne, and the Baron of Preissac was himself seneschal of

Marennes and governor of Mortagne. This marriage therefore brought together the two most prominent families of Guyenne.

One might see such a "skillful matrimonial policy" being extended (reversed?), when, for example, the heiress Isabelle de Montferrand brought the viscounties of Uza & Aureilhan and other possessions into her 1572 marriage to Pierre II de Lur, so constituting "the original nucleus of [this] family's patrimony" (Figéac, 1996: I, 244).

Once attaining prominence, the Montferrands had created heraldic arms, a new device which entered general use in the early 13th century. An English lay description of their arms would be: "Alternating lines of gold and red, edged by a black border dotted with bezants".[18] The marriage of Bertrand III de Montferrand and Na Isabeau de Preissac-Landiras meant a reconfiguring of the coats of arms of both families. The joint arms may be found in a 17th-century rendering in the choir of the church of Saint-Michel-de-Rieufreyt, a town a little to the north of Landiras earlier given into Gaillard de Landiras's jurisdiction.[19] In the upper left and lower right corners are reproduced the vertical gold and red lines surrounded by a black border with bezants that we have just encountered as the Montferrand arms. In the upper right and lower left corners are those of Landiras: on a silver (code for "white") background is placed a red cross, on which sit five gold ("yellow") stars, one in the centre and one on each arm of the cross. Superimposed in the centre of the coat of arms, where the four crests meet, is the Preissac symbol: a tongued, clawed lion with paws in the air.[20]

The Hundred Years' War
(1337-1454)

At the time of the coming together of the Montferrand and Landiras families, France and England were more than halfway through the Hundred Years' War. Officially initiated in 1337 by Edward III's claim to the throne of France and by troublesome French aid to the Scots, then sustained also by commercial ambitions, the underlying reasons were also concerned with the English kings' desire for more independence in their position as French vassals. Not only had Normandy been lost to France less than a hundred and fifty years earlier (and it was to be the site of many battles and the temporary re-establishment of Eng-

[14]The 2009 labels on bottles of the château's wine state a château was erected in 1306, a date rather early for it to have been built by Jean de Stratton, as suggested by Marc-Henry Le May (1995: 765). When was the castle built whose ruins one sees today? (Le May's recent edition of *Bordeaux... et ses vins* has the fullest discussion of the history of the Château de Landiras of the entire series launched in 1850 by Charles Cocks. But the series's area of expertise lies elsewhere and perhaps cannot be relied upon for the accuracy of every detail. Still it's all we have on this rather central matter!)

[15]That is, the first page of the documentation ("pièces justificatives"). The introduction (pp. xii-xix), together with its Genealogical Table, is a principal source for information throughout this article.

[16]Edward II had given Blanquefort to Bertrand de Goth in 1308 and it soon passed into the Durfort family (Courcelles, 1824: IV, "de Blanchefort [*sic*]", 5, note [in Courcelles, pagination starts over with each family]). (What does "give" mean here, since the de Goth and Blanquefort families had intermarried the century before? Sometime before 1289, Régine de Goth la jeune [she had an elder sister with the same name] married Bernard de Durfort, sgr de Flamarens [d. bf. 1329]). Courcelles, 1826: VI "de Goth ou de Gout", 17. Indie de Goth was a sister born just before the second Régine. Alternatively, Régine was an elder sister, the younger being named "Reine", and it was the elder who married Bernard de Durfort ("Famille de Goth/Gotz/ Gout"). For more about Indie de Goth, see note 29 below.

In 1338, Edward III transferred the seigneurie de Blanquefort to Gaillard Roussel de Saint-Symphorien, sgr de Landiras, after Gaillard de Durfort's "treason". When Gaillard de Durfort et de Duras reattached himself to Edward III, however, the seigniory of Blanquefort was returned to him (Baurein: II, 169). Durfort was made governor of Calais; he died at Poitiers.

[17]He was also Baron de Langoiran, sieur de Rions and seigneur de Veyrines, Agassac, and Soussans, for example. "Baron is a title given by the king to his most faithful servants" ("Les Seigneurs de Landiras_2").

These possessions indicate an important Montferrand presence in the Landiras region before the intermarriage of the two.

[18]Described as "Palé d'or et de gueules, à la bordure de sable, chargée de besans d'argent," these arms are in another version stated to have precisely *eight* bezants. Decoding this description, we note the word for wooden stakes ("pal"), here used as a verb ("palé") to mean dividing what become lines into pairs; gules ("gueules"), from gule (gullet), a heraldic term for red educed from the term for an ermine-died collar; the sable, a dark-brown small carnivorous animal, which lent its name to the colour black; and bezants, originally Byzantine gold coins, minted in Europe also in silver, and represented in heraldry simply as small disks. (When not referring to something like coins, the word gold was often simply heraldic code for "yellow", so the lines above might better be described as alternating "yellow and red".)

[19]As early as 1307, Jean Roussel de Saint-Simphorin [*sic*] was described as "Seigneur Haut-Justicier de la Paroisse" (Lord High-Justice of the Parish) of Saint-Michel de Riufreyt [*sic*], but it appears that the actual exercise of this office had to be demanded and received by son Gaillard de Saint-Simphorin in 1340 (Baurein: III, 82/3).

[20]Professor Liliane Rodriguez, of the University of Winnipeg, was immensely helpful in interpreting the terms for the Preissac portion of this coat of arms.

A reproduction of these arms, on the left of a rectangle shared with those of Jeanne de Lestonnac, may be found at "Sainte-Jeanne de Lestonnac... JeanneEnfance". The quoted descriptions are from "Branches collatérales des Montferrands" under "SAINT-SYMPHORIEN," 1.

lish sway), but French pressure on English governance in Aquitaine was persistent and growing.[21] The Maisons de Montferrand and de Landiras were to be continually active throughout the War, and one lord or another often travelled to England to offer advice or raise troops.

Early in 1345, the year before the war's first great battle (at Crécy), our Bertrand I de Montferrand was among the many Aquitainian lords invited by Edward III to participate in a major joust at Windsor Castle. At this "gathering of the Knights of the Round Table", Edward learnt of a renewed threat to his French territories and so decided to send a large force, commanded by Henry, Earl of Derby, to engage the French in Guyenne. Following the ensuing battle at Bergerac, in August 1345, both Bertrand I de Montferrand and his brother Amanieu were knighted. Henceforth, male members of the family were entitled to call themselves "chevaliers". Son Bertrand II fought at both Poitiers (1356) and Eymet (1377).

Jean II Roussel de Saint-Symphorien-Landiras participated in that same meeting of the Knights of the Round Table in England as had Bertrand I de Montferrand. However, his own notable French campaigning was ten years later, with Edward the Black Prince (1330-1376), rather than in the expedition in which Montferrand was active. Indeed, Saint-Symphorien-Landiras fought beside the Prince of Wales in England's second great victory of the war, the battle of Poitiers (19 September 1356), in which the King of France, John II the Good (1350-1364), was taken prisoner. The baron of Landiras and Blanquefort accompanied the Black Prince and his royal captives to England. Jean Froissart (ca. 1337-after 1400), the famous French chronicler of the Hundred Years' War, eulogized the barons of Landiras in the following terms: "From this era and up to the conquest of Guyenne, we see the lords of Landiras marching at the head of the Bordelaise nobility and taking part in the most important affairs" (cited in "Branches... des Montferrand": 2).[22]

Throughout the first half of the Hundred Years' War, the papacy found itself mired in its own struggles, and here too, the Montferrands were twice peripherally involved. In wars of an earlier generation, the kings of both France and England had sought to tax the wealthy bishoprics and monasteries within their respective jurisdictions. In this effort they were vigorously opposed by the papacy. The culmination of the dispute was the rough handling of Boniface VIII by agents of King Philip IV and the Pope's premature death. The succeeding pope was the Frenchman Clement V, who moved the papacy and its bureaucracy to Avignon, in the French-dominated Rhone Valley. We have seen that it was Clement's niece, Indie de Goth, who had married Armaudin III de Barès, baron of Montferrand.

Now, in the second half of the Hundred Years' War, the difficulties following efforts to return the papacy to the city of Rome had led to schism in the Church, with the election of two rival popes after 1378 and then three competing popes after 1409. Towards the end of this crisis, the Roman pope was Gregory XII (1406-1415), favoured by the English, most German states and others, and the Avignonese pope was Benedict XIII (1394-1423), whose papal decisions tended to reflect French interests.

The putative and the actual Montferrand archbishops of Bordeaux (sons of Bertrand II de Montferrand), Jean de Montferrand (1409-1410) and David de Montferrand (1413-1430), made their allegiance to the Roman pope, Gregory XII, which reflected the influence of and their support for the English side in the war.[23] Archbishop David was present at the meeting on 4 May 1415, held in the Chapter of Saint-Seurin (the meeting room in an ancient basilica in Bordeaux), which attempted, before the decisive English victory at Agincourt in October, to negotiate an Anglo-French truce, scheduled to be signed by the end of the year (Baurein: IV, 290). After this victory, Henry V (1413-1422) married the French princess Catherine of Valois and also added Normandy and other parts of northwestern France to his domains on the Continent. As it happened, his brother's illegitimate daughter, Mary of Bedford,[24] was in 1435 to marry into the newly established Landiras branch of the Montferrand family. Her husband,[25] eventually executed in Poitiers, pursued perhaps the most dramatic career of all the late-medieval Montferrands.

The story now passes to the second article, while we pause to

---

[21]Historians won't need to be reminded of England's long and complex role in governing extensive parts of France: 1) Long after their 1066 conquest of England, the Dukes of Normandy continued to defend their rights in France, significantly augmented by Geoffrey of Anjou's marriage to Margaret of England—until John lost the last of these territories to Philippe Augustus in 1214. The victories at Crécy, Poitiers and Agincourt effectively re-established this suzerainty. 2) Two years after his marriage to Eleanor (or Aliénor) of Aquitaine (ca. 1122-1204), Henri d'Anjou had become Henry II of England (1154-1189). Essentially the southwest quadrant of France, Eleanor's Guyenne was to spend the next three centuries closely tied to and often dominated by its English overlords—a phenomenon ended only in 1453.

[22]The Internet source cited writes that this assessment was recounted by [Léo] Drouyn [1816-1896]. (The conquest mentioned here was the one by the English in 1373. The "final" reconquest, in 1450-1453, by the French, was of course after Froissart's death.)

[23]David de Montferrand became bishop of Dax in 1408 and archbishop of Bordeaux after 17 May 1413. Despite ill health, he was called to London to advise on French affairs, but died there on 31 May 1429 (Mas-Latrie, 1889, 1397; and Fisquet, 1864: 332-33). Alternatively: bishop of Dax in 1406 and died in 1430 (Communay: Genealogical table & xx); archbishop of Bordeaux in 1414 (Féret, 1889: III, 468).

Elder brother Jean de Montferrand cannot accurately be listed as archbishop of Bordeaux (despite Communay: loc. cit.). As part of the dis- putes among rival popes and bellicose kings, Jean was named archbishop by a bull of Gregory XII, dated 12 December 1409, but 1) was opposed by the incumbent, Cardinal François II Hugocinio (or Hugocio or Hugotion; Francesco Uguccione, abp. 1384-1412), who had assisted in the attempt to dethrone Gregory at the Council of Pisa in 1409, and 2) was also opposed by the cathedral chapter and "tous les ordres de la ville"; Jean died in the midst of this dispute and the Cardinal continued in office (Grasset: 51; Communay xx). Alternatively, François II became archbishop of Bordeaux only in 1389 (Fisquet: 229-32). Another story makes no mention of "David", but erroneously assigns all his offices to Jean de Montferrand (Grasset: 51).

[24]This "girl bastard of Lancaster", born of an unknown woman, is identified variously as Mary Plantagenet, Mary of Lancaster, ... of Bedford, ... of England. Remembered in history as the Duke of Bedford, her father, John of Lancaster (1389-1435), was appointed regent of France (1423-1433) for his nephew, Henry VI, and then regent of England (1433-1434). He was to become the first of the two royal-blood Dukes of Kendal in the 14th century; for the third duke, Jean de Foix, see note 7, in Part Two. For the fourth, we again encounter royal blood, in the early 20th century (Bailey, 2006: 34).

Baurein (I, 157) states that her dowry was 500 livres tournois in lands and guaranteed income. With the duke's death before all the dowry was transferred, Pierre de Montferrand became in part dependent upon the good graces of the English king Henry VI, the duke's universal heir.

[25]By incorrectly stating that Pierre II, this son of Bertrand III and Na Isabeau, died after August 1437, the Internet source "Montferrand" (7) creates confusion for where his story picks up (10). Being the eldest child of a 1410 marriage, Pierre II de Montferrand would not normally have a grandson old enough to marry before 1435. "Montferrand" has most probably confused his date of death with that of his mother. Pierre I de Montferrand, then, would not be the unnumbered "Pierre" on page 7, but rather the Pierre-Amauvin de Monferrand (d. before 1349) of page 1.

examine the genealogies of these allied families. Just who were the proprietors of the châteaux de Montferrand and de Landiras?

The Genealogies

These genealogies seek two objectives together, both important: one is to show the most accurate names, titles and dates the current author can unearth; the other is to indicate the discrepancies in the secondary sources. The hope is that readers will know, if not whom to trust, then at least where any given source differs from others. The best known, with its extensive family tree, is that by Arnaud Communay, and it will form our base for the Montferrands. Unless a source states "born in" or "died in", there is occasional uncertainty about whether shown dates are regnal or life. Taken at face value, some of Communay's dates suggest an heir's possession of title during a father's lifetime! Where alternate suggestions lack, I have simply reiterated what dates are offered, even though several simply cannot conform to other dates offered by the same source. (For example, a person cannot marry earlier than he or she is born!) Sometimes accepting Communay, sometimes not, scrupulous attention has been given to whether the precise title be *seigneur*, *baron* or *vicomte*.

Numerous duplications of names and numbers, both from cadet houses and from merely similar names held by scattered siblings, have seriously misled impatient genealogists. Furthermore, "Jean" is occasionally named "Jehan" or "Jehannot"; Bertrand, Bernard & Bérard same interchangeable, as do Amaubin, Amaudin, Arnaudin & Almalvin. Also marriage to cousins re-lated through females often goes unnoticed. For all these reasons, I have tried to recover younger siblings, including females, and to indicate clearly the connections. With some hesitation, I have offered the names of wives hitherto largely unknown, as well as including some rarely mentioned earlier or later wives who left no succession. Then, what about numbers? To get three "Jean"s before our Jean IV (Jehan de Landiras), we have to count two in the Cancon branch, the latter being Jehan's contemporary. But François IV de Landiras is older by a century than François II and III in the Cancon branch; and Pierre II de Landiras, the same with respect to Pierre I in the senior branch! Are the numbers just Communay's arbitrary way of working from left to right across his table? A further challenge is to trace titles, for a male is conventionally identified/listed as possessing titles and properties that only entered his supervision by marriage (that is, not inheritance from either parent).

Naturally, many disagreements among the sources were of some significance. Internet sources, especially Wikipedia and several enthusiastic genealogists, have been an immense (not always acknowledged) assistance in adding to or correcting printed sources, but they present so many uncertainties and contradictions that they, too, can only be used with great care. (Amateur genealogists can be fine and tenacious antiquarians, but they may also lack the historian's skill in judging what they've found.) Many of the abundant dates are only approximate, and some no doubt incorrect—and so a challenge for my successors to rectify. The large Roman Numerals denote generations (Communay); the occasional immediately following Arab Numerals denote where siblings succeed one another (Bailey).

The Senior Maison de Montferrand/Montferran/Montferrant

I. **Tiso de Barès (or Wareys)** (documented as a living adult in 1168)
　　"Varèze" or "Varesio" (Courcelles, 1826: VI, "de Goth ou de Gout", 17).
　　[one or two missing generations]

II.* **Amanieu de Barès**, *écuyer*, sgr de Montferrand (1242-1255); "GeneaNet" (not in Communay),
　　(d. 1242) Abbot (n.d.: 327)

II. **Amaubin/Amaudin I de Barès** (1242-1271), *sénéschal* de Lannes (Could Amanieu and Amaubin be the same person?)
　　= Gaillarde de Castillon
　　　Brother: Étienne de Barès (1278-1283) = Marguerite de Castillon　　m.s.p.[26]

III. **Amaubin II de Barès** (1265-1280), baron de Montferrand in 1265
　　= Marguerite de Preissac[27] (Pressac—Grasset: 51; Marquèze de Prechac—"GeneaNet")
　　　Brother: Tridon de Barès (fl. 1265) plus five other siblings without posterity
　　　　　　　= ??? d'Anglade
　　　　　　　>son Arnaud de Barès (fl. 1331) = ??? de la Roque
　　　　　　　　　>dgtr Renaud de Montferrand, sgr d'Aiguille (1363-1397)
　　　　　　　　　　　= ??? de Chabannes
　　　　　　　　　　　　　>son Guillaume de Montferrand (1391-1399)　　m.s.p.
　　　OR: Amauvin II le Jeune de Barès (ca. 1260-1285)
　　　　　　= Gaillarde (?) de Montferrand

IV.* **Pons de Montferrand** (1250-1312)
　　= Thalèse de ??? (b. 1267)　　(These dates from "Généalogie mes ancêtres")
　　Pierre Armauvin III is **their** son (which would make him "V")
　　(These three paragraphs from "Informations généalogiques" and "Arbre généalogique").

IV. **Pierre-Amaubin/Arnaudin III de Barès** (1280-1339/49), brn de Montferrand[28]
　　Or **Almalvin III de Barès** (Courcelles: VI, "de Goth ou de Gout", 17).

---

[26]"M.s.p." = "mort sans posterité" (died without issue). Below: "N. de ..." = name unknown.

[27]I am unable to place Marguerite de Preissac, let alone connect her with the line we meet later. Cf. Gastelier de la Tour (1770).

[28]Alternately, Pierre Amauvin (1290-1349), marriage in 1308, with Indie dying in 1328 ("Arbre généalogique de Jean Michel Ducosson"). Though also possessed of errors, this site presented the entire family tree and sometimes filled in gaps below, most notably life dates for Isabelle de Preissac.

= 1303 Indie/Inde de Goth/Got/Gout (d. 1324/35);[29] or 1285-1328 ("Mes arbres")
    brings in the *baronnie* de Veyrines/Vérines; mother of succession
= 1330/40 Mabille de Colomb (1333-1371)—neither mrg. date fits suggested life dates!
    (her full name, dates, and later mrg. date from "GeneaNet")
    Brother (?): Amalvin de Varèze (b. ca. 1314), sgr de Montferrand = 1328 Yolande de Pons

V. **Bertrand/Bérard/Bernard I de Barès** (1320/24-1351) or ca. 1310-1351 ("Mes arbres")[30]
    brn de Montferrand & *châtelain* de Blaye-et-Sainte-Luce; knighted in 1345
= ca. 1335 N. de Durfort (b. ca. 1315/20)   (Régine de Durfort, dgtr of sgr de Blanquefort*)
    Brother: Amanieu

VI. **Bertrand II de Montferrand** (1345/50; baron 1365-1409/10), *chevalier banneret*
    —the first to replace "Barès" by "Montferrand" as the **family** name*
= ca. 1365/70 Rose d'Albret (1355-1393), *dame* de Pondesac

VII. **Bertrand III[31] de Montferrand** (1380; baron 1409-1435/46), brn de Langoiran & de Veyrines,
    sgr d'Agassac, de Soussans de Podensac, & sr de Rions, *châtelain* de Blaye, *sénéchal* de Guyenne,
    chevalier de l'ordre Jarretière ("Order of the Garter"),
    gouverneur de Marmande (d. 1446*[32])
= before 1409 Isabeau de Pons ("Informations généalogiques")[33]
= April 1401 (Communay, xxi; & for April, Grasset, 51)[34] Marguerite d'Astarac (1385-1410);
    Or 1382-1404 ("GENI"); mother of elder, Montferrand succession
= 1410 (Communay & Grasset, 51); 1408 (Bourrousse de Laforre, 1883: IV, 241);
    1409 (?)   Isabeau/Isabelle de Preissac/Pressac (1390-1437); mother of junior, Landiras succession
    Bertrand III's brothers & sister (with *Maison d'Uza*):
      Jean (d. 1410), never properly archbishop of Bordeaux [see note 23, above]
      VII. *François I, sgr de Montferrand* (d. bf. 1456)—*Maison d'Uza (or Uzar)*
        = ca. 1415 Jeanne/Jouine/Jouyne Sans de Pommiers (ca. 1390-bf. 1457),
          vicomtesse de Fronsac et *d'Uza*, *dame* de Belin & Biscarosie
        Or no known wife ("Informations généalogiques")
      [VIII.] *Bertrand/Bérard de Montferrand & d'Uza* (ca. 1415-1471)[35]
        = ca. 1445/47 Marie de Lalande (af. 1488), (see note 38)
          (two later marriages for her)
        Brother: Jehannot de Montferrand (b. bf. 1425)
          = 1435* Johanette de Foix (b. bf. 1425*)
          >son Bertrand* (*="Informations généalogiques")[36]
      [IX.1] *Catherine de Montferrand, vicomtesse* d'Uza from 1469
        = 1466 Gilles d'Albret, sgr de Castelmoron   m.s.p.
      [IX.2] *Isabeau de Montferrand, vicomtesse* d'Uza (b. 1459)

---

[29]It may be worth pointing out that Indie's mother is sometimes identified as Miramonde de Mauléon (d. ca. 1348), who was, however, to be her father's second wife (mrd. May 1309) and who bore him no children. Arnaud-Garcie de Goth (1245/50-ca 1312) had married Blanche de Mauléon (1250-1286) in 1269, who bore him nine children. Initially, Anselme, vol. II, simply lists Miramonde as de Goth's wife, but in vol. IX of the 3rd ed. (1733), "Additions et Corrections", he cites/adds Blanche as the first wife and mother of the children (382). For Blanche's dates and family name (or is this another confusion with de Goth's second wife?—cf. next paragraph in this note), see "Généalogie Famille de Carné". She has been also named Blanche Lambert (1255-1309) ("Mes arbres"). "1386" was once mentioned as her date of marriage. Would Blanche and Miramonde have been sisters or aunt & niece? For more on Indie de Goth, see note 16 above.

    Does another source blend these women by naming de Goth's first wife "Blanche (Mirland) de Mauleon" (b. ca. 1248, mrd. 1269)? The husband in this case is called "Arnaud-Garsie de Lomagne, vicomte de Lomagne & d'Auvillars" (ca. 1250-1312), who sired among other children an illegitimate son "Arnaud-Garsie de Goth" (ca. 1285-after 1339)! "Our Royal... Ancestors". Let us note that the *vicomte* de Lomagne is elsewhere identified as "Arnaud-Garsie de Goth"; these needn't be different persons! Note: Garcie/Garsie.

    "Généalogie mes ancêtres" (a site I cannot find now!) also dates Bertrand's birth to 1310.

[30]Speaking of the husband of Marguerite d'Astarac, but perhaps subsuming his father & grandfather too, Communay (xxi) writes that "Bérard" and "Bernard" can sometimes be found for the more common "Bertrand".

[31]These three asterisks (in V., VI. and VII.) denote information from Grasset, 1988: 51.

[32]A Dutch Internet genealogy offers interesting, sometimes disparate details. First, it is virtually alone in denominating the family as barons of "Saint-Louis-de-Montferrand", which does link the family to the site of their château. (In fact, the commune officially dropped "Saint-Louis-de-" from its name only in the French Revolution, during the *Convention nationale*, 1792-1795.) Second, almost every person has slightly different dates from those suggested above: Pierre-Amaubin III (1285-1345), Bertrand I (1315-1350), Bertrand II (1345-1409; marriage in 1475), Bertrand III (1380-1445). "Genealogieonline".

[33]"Informations généalogiques" alone offers this earlier wife, Isabeau de Pons.

[34]Alternative mrg. dates for Marguerite d'Astarac: "before 22 March 1394, old style" (Baurein: III, 75), possible, but rather early; bf. 1409 ("Informations généalogiques"); 1446 (!), ("Ahnentafel, #774").

    Did Marguerite d'Astarac have two sons, Pierrre, sgr de Soussans, and Jean ("Cdelmars", "Informations généalogiques" & "RootsWeb")? These sources are aware that Isabeau de Priessac had a Pierre by Bertrand III as well. But nothing further is anywhere said of this earlier Pierre.

[35]Bertrand's becoming a prisoner of the English [*sic*, not "of the French"?], the marriage was not immediately consummated. Bertrand's sister, Isabeau de Montferrand, married Guischarnaud de Saint-Martin. Most of the information concerning Bertrand (Bérard) and his d'Uza descendents comes from Courcelles (1825: V, "d'Uza", 41-44, a note: "Fragment sur la Maison de Montferrand").

[36]A natural daughter of Gaston de Foix, Johanette de Foix brought the *seigneurie* de Fargues to the Montferrands (Baurein: III, 231-32). Communay's table says no issue. (Would the mother's illegitimacy have denied the inheritance to her off spring?) OR: is Jeannette the wife of Jehannot's cousin Jean I? In either case, her son is named Bertrand.

           = 1472 Pierre II de Lur, brn de Longa (1462-1515)[37] (Cf. Maison de Cancon)
       David, bishop of Dax, 1406 or '08; archbishop of Bordeaux (1413-1429/30)
       Jeanne = 1408 Jean II de Lalande (1375-1420)[38]
       Marguerite = sgr de Massidan

VIII. Jean I de Montferrand (b. 1404/10; baron 1435-1442) or b. 1402 (Chenaye des Bois: V, 418) or 1405 ("Cdelmars");
        or d. 1441 ("Cdelmars"; Abbot, 237); killed at siege of Langon[39]
   = ca. 1420 unknown woman (Communay, Table; "Informations généalogiques")
      Or   = 1435 Jeanne/Johannette de Foix ("Cdelmars")

IX.   Bertrand IV de Montferrand (1435; baron 1442-1474), brn de Langoiran (till ca. 1454)
        sgr de Margaux (from 26 May 1447[40]), *conseiller et chambellan du duc* de Guyenne
      = ca. 1450/54 Jeanne de Luxe
        <u>Sister:</u> Catherine de Montferrand (b. ca. 1420/22) = 1440   David de Faubournet
          ("Arbres Généalogiques / Ducusson"—the earlier birth date and date of marriage)
          >son Jean de Faubournet, sgr de Montferrand & Puybeton (ca. 1445-ca. 1572)
          = 1481 Bernadine de Lavedan (ca. 1450-after 1517)
            ("Généalogie Famille de Carné; Chenaye Des Bois, V, 418)
            >dgtr Marguerite de Faubournet-Montferrand
            = 1499 Pons de Gontaut, brn de Biron, as his second wife
              >son Jean I de Gontaut, sgr de Montferrand[41]

X. Gaston I de Montferrand (1454/71-1498/1504), *conseiller et chambellan du roi* de France,
        gouverneur de Bourg, *sénéchal* de Bazadais
   = 1473 Catherine de Lescon (b. 1463?!)
   = 14 mars 1483 Jeanne/Jehanne de Maingot de Surgères; mother of next generation
        Gaston's brother & his descendents—*Maison de Cancon*:
       X.   *Jehan/Jean II de Montferrand*, (b. af. 1454), *vicomte de Foncaude*,[42]
           sgr de Castelmoron et Gironde (Grasset: 113)
        = 1494 Louise de Juge (ca. 1480-af. 1520), *comtesse de Castres*[43]
      XI. *Charles III de Montferrand-Cancon-Foncaude* (af. 1494-ca. 1557)
        = 1526 Marie de Verdun de Hautesvignes, *dame de Cancon*
        > dgtr Marguerite de Montferrand mrd Charles II de Montferrand of the senior branch,
        her distant cousin
        > dgtr Marie de Montferrand-Cancon married Louis de Lur, *vicomte* d'Uza (1535-1573),
        grandson of Pierre de Lur and Isabeau de Montferrand, *vicomtesse* d'Uza[44] (Cf. d'Uza)
        <u>Other Siblings:</u> of three brothers, David de Montferrand (af. 1494–af. 1562), *comte* de Castres
          = 1529/30 Marie Dubedat/de Bedat
        >son Raymond (Robert) de Montferrand (d. 1621) ("Informations généalogiques")
        = Marthe de Cours; and then Marie de Lamouroux
          >dgtr Jeanne ("Arbre généalogique")[45]
     XII.1. *Jean III de Montferrand-Cancon-Foncaude* (af. 1526-1595)
        = 1556 Barbe de Pons (1520-1595)   m.s.p.
     XII.2. *François II de Montferrand-Cancon-Foncaude* (ca. 1536-1625),
        succeeded senior Montferrand branch in 1591
        = 1577 Claire de Pellegrue (b. bf. 1562)
      XIII. *François III de Montferrand-Cancon-Foncaude* (af. 1577-Oct. 1660),[46]

---

[37]Isabeau being only thirteen years old, the marriage was not consummated till 20 January 1474. Pierre was born of Marie de Fayolle (b. 1415), Bertrand II de Lur's second wife (Courcelles: V, "de Lur", 40-41).

    Earlier, the same source mentions the grandson of Bertrand's first wife, Jean de Lur (son of Bertrand III & Catherine de Gontaut-Biron) as married to an Isabeau de Montferrand (*Ibid.*, 27 & 32), a woman we cannot identify. Is it possible that this apparent uncle Pierre/nephew Jean should be seen as the same person?

[38]Their granddaughter, Marie de Lalande (daughter of Jean III and Jeanne de Foix), married her father's cousin, Betrand/Bérard de Montferrand-d'Uza.

[39]I can date specific sieges of Langon (& Blaye) to 1339 & 1345 [*sic*], but to resolve the disagreement of sources about Jean de Montferrand's death, the best I can say is that Charles launched a major offensive in Guyenne in 1442! In his Introduction, Communay (xxv) dates Jean's death to 1471 (typo for change to 1441?).

[40]Baurein: II, 93. The *terre* de Margaux was a dependency of the *châtellenie* de Banquefort (*ibid.*, 94).

[41]John I de Gontaut was the last in this line to bear the Montferrand title. (Courcelles, 1822: II, "de Gontaut-Biron", 22; Chesnaye Des Bois, II, 285; Anselme, II 22; Moréri: I, 896—for this point & others in the text above).

    Concerning Bernadine de Lavedan (Jean de Faubournet's wife) see François IV de Montferrand-Landiras (note 67).

[42]Whence and when the *vicomté* de Foncaude? Communay has an entire chapter III, "Vicomtes de Foncaude" (li-lxiv), in which he just ascribes the title to Charles III & Jean III (lvi-lvii) without anywhere explaining its origins. He has Charles cede Foncaude to his brother David (82-84).

[43]This marriage was arranged by Louise's mother, Marie d'Albret, but opposed by her father, Boffile de Juge, *comte* de Castres (Communay: 47, where he erroneously names the groom "Charles", rather than the correct "Jean" (*ibid.*, 39).

[44]Courcelles writes, without correction (!), that it is believed Marie was the last of the Montferrand-Cancon line (1825: V, "d'Uza", 47, n. 1). Marguerite and Marie had another sister, also named Marguerite (who married Jacques deigneur [*sic*] Angevyn), and two brothers. ("Informations généalogiques").

[45]"Arbre généalogique" presents David as if he were his father's uncle.

[46]"After 1572", offers "Informations généalogiques", for François III's birth, yet the same source and all others have his parents marry only in 1577.

premier baron de Guyenne, *conseiller du roi*
= 1625 Jacquette de Beauxoncles (bf. 1616-1635)   m.s.p.[47]
Or mrd. 27 Oct. 1526 ("Arbre généalogique/André Decloitre")

XI. **Pierre I de Montferrand** (1513-1547) —Pierre is missing from Abbot (327)
= ca. 1508 Marie/Madelaine de Carmain et de Foix

XII. **Charles I de Montferrand** (1513; baron 1547-1548)
= 15 or 19 March 1534 Françoise d'Aydie de Ribérac (a widow)
demoiselle de la chambre de la reine (Communay, xxxiv; Grasset, 113)

XIII.1. **Charles II de Montferrand** (d. 1574/5),[48] *premier baron* de Guyenne,
maire et gouverneur de Bordeaux (1569-??)
= 1574 Marguerite de Montferrand (Charles's cousin)[49]   m.s.p.
Siblings: two brothers died young; Catherine = Jean de Laminsans, brn d'Auros
>dgtr Catherine = Jean d'Achard des Augiers, sgr de Mauconseil & de Villeneuve
>son, Charles Achard, tried to claim the château & *terre* de Montferrand in 1591 (Communay, xliii, note 1)

XIII.2. **Guy/Gui de Montferrand** (ca. 1540; baron 1575-1591),[50] *chevalier de l' ordre du roi*
= Jeanne d'Eschelles (d. 1594); "Dechelle" (Grasset, 113 & 115)
(Son Gédéon died a month before his father[51])

THUS, the titles and remaining properties passed to *François II de Montferrand-Cancon-Foncaude* (d. 1625), (see above), a distant cousin. François II's son, *François III*, died in October 1660 without heirs, and all passed to the Maison de Landiras.

The pre-Montferrand Maison de Landiras/Landirans/Landirats

I. **Rostand/Rostang/Rustand de Landiras** (documented as living in 1173)
[one or two missing generations?]

II. **Rostand ?? de Landiras** (documented as living in 1236)
[one or two missing generations?]

III. **Rostand ?? de Landiras**; brother of …

IV. **Isabelle de Landiras** (1230/35-ca. 1279) = Gaillard de La Mothe (1230-1279)[52]

V. **Clairemonde/Esclaremonde de La Mothe-Landiras** (ca. 1260-1301 or af. 1328)
= 27 September 1280 (?) **Jean Roussel de Saint-Symphorien**[53] (b. bf. 1269);
after 1307/8 exercised the rights of high and low justice in the parishes of Illats,
Lassats, Guillos, Brachs, & Saint-Michel-de-Ruifreyt

VI. **Gaillard Roussel de Saint-Symphorien**, sgr de Landiras (1279/80-1340),
in 1340 received the same rights of high and low justice in the parishes mentioned as had his father,
again in 1342 (Baurein: III, 83);
in 1338, the *seigneurie* de Blanquefort was transferred to him by the king of England after Gaillard de Durfort's "treason"
= Jeanne de Vaux (Buathier, 1995: 71)[54]   or
= 1309 Jeanne de Soler (b. 1299)[55] [most sources say "an unknown woman"]

VII. **Jean II Roussel de Saint-Symphorien**, sgr de Landiras (ca. 1310/20-????)
= January or July 1343 Na-Aupeys de La Mothe et de Roquetaillade (b. bf. 1333)[56]
Or Na-Alpais ("Ahnentafel" #6206)
Brother or Half-Brother: Pierre de Saint-Simphorin [*sic*] (d. 1382)

---

[47]François III de Monferrand-Cancon-Foncaude had a younger brother of the same name (ca 1597-1620), who had become a knight of Saint-Jean de Malte/St. John of Malta.

[48]Let us note here that while Féret (III, 468-69) seems to have an accurate grasp of essential events, he skips generations and assigns Charles II's exploits to "Gaston II". Or is this last just a typo or a jumping over to the Landiras branch?

[49]She was the granddaughter of Jehan II de Montferrand, baron de Cancon & *vicomte* de Foncaude, the brother of her husband's great-grandfather, Gaston I de Montferrand (and so from another cadet branch of this senior house).
Thus, we can see that the dynastic strategies of aristocratic marriages sometimes stretched Church law against marrying even moderately distant relatives. (Only one source mentions papal dispensation for marrying a cousin.)

[50]When Charles II succeeded to Montferrand, etc., Guy succeeded to the barony of Langoiran (Féret: III, 468).

[51]Yet on 8 March of the year of father's and son's deaths, Gédéon sold four *chevaux de guerre* (Communay, Doc. XLIV, 125-26).

[52]"Les Seigneurs de Landiras_1" states that Gaillard de la Mote [*sic*] became sgr de Landiras in 1284; with seneschal Jean I de Grailly marrying Clairemonde de la Mote the following year; and Jean Rossel [*sic*] receives the *seigneurie* from Edward III [*sic*] in 1315. If we allow Gaillard (and Isabelle) to live so long, he could be so recognized, whether as husband or as widower in place of his daughter; and recognition by Edward II would not be unwelcome. But otherwise, this is all erroneous.
One source has Gaillard de La Motte related to the de Goth family, which we've met above.

[53]Many sources have Jean Roussel married by 1290, yet born ca. 1320! Of these, only one offers for him another (earlier than Clairemonde?) wife, namely Alpais de La Mothe ("Ahnentafel", 13th generation, # 6206).

[54]Buathier gives Gaillard & Jeanne three children: Jean, Pierre and Agnès. If sought independently, however, the only "Jeanne de Vaux" to be found on the web married a Louis de Montalembert in 1450—over a century later!

[55]Most sources marry Gaillard in 1309 to Jeanne de Soler and give them only a son, Pierre (d. 1382).
Another source gives Pierre to Gaillard & Jeanne de Soler, while ascribing a half-brother Jean to Gaillard & no named mother. Buathier does include a second marriage, in 1309, to Jeanne de Soler. "Informations généalogiques" gives only the latter marriage for Gaillard Roussel. In short, the identity of Jean's mother is uncertain.

[56]Birthdate for Na-Aupaïs de la Mothe & precision of marriage to 16 July 1343 (Buathier, 71).

"otherwise called de Landiras, *chevalier*" = Marie de Colomb (1325-1393)
part owner of the Isle-Saint-George by a title of 1374 (Baurein: III, 37).
>dgtr Marie Roussel = Jean I de Lalande (1340-1407)
>son Jean II de Lalande (1375-1420) = 1408 Jeanne de Montferrand[57]
>son Jean III de Lalande (1409-1491) ("GeneaNet")

VIII. **Isabelle/Isabeau/Ysabé de Saint-Symphorien**, *dame* de Landiras (ca. 1345/50-1391 or 1408 or 1424)[58]
= 1358/66 **John of/Jean de Stratton** (ca. 1340-1395) or **Estratonne** (Baurein: III, 80).
(In Baurein, IV, one also finds "Destratone" and "Destratonne".)
or d. bf. February 1400 ("Branches ... des Montferrand" [2])
châtelain et connétable du château de Bordeaux (Baurein: IV, 289)
[perhaps the builder of the imposing château de Landiras (Lemay, 1995: 765)]

IX. **Marguerite de Stratton-Landiras** (ca.1370-1424/27), *dame* de Saint-Symphorien-Bazadais
= **Bernard- (or Bermond-)Arnaud) de Preissac**[59]   (b. ca. 1350), ("Préchac" in the Gascon Rolls),
soudan/soudic de La Trau,[60] sgr de Didonne, de Portets, d'Arbanats, & de Lesparre, etc.,
grand-bailli de Marennes, *gouverneur* de Montagne, *chevalier de la Jarretière*

X. **Isabeau de Preissac-Landiras** (1390-perhaps 1437), *dame* de La Trau, de Portets, de Lesparre,
d'Uzeste & de Saint-Symphorien-Bazadais; "Isabeau de La Trau"(Baurein: I, 157); (mother of Pierre II)
= 1410[61] **Bertrand III de Montferrand** (earlier marriage to Marguerite d'Astarac, mother of Jean I)

The Cadet Maison de Montferrand, Seigneurs de Landiras

XI. [if numbering as from the Landiras lineage, but in order to align with the Montferrand generations ...]
VIII. **Pierre II de Montferrand-Landiras** (af. 1410-1454) [younger half-brother of Jean I de Montferrand],
soudan de La Trau, *dit* brn de Lesparre,[62] de Langoiran & de Landiras, sgr de Portets,
d'Arbanats, de Uzeste, de Daurange (d'Audenge?), de Daureigne (d'Origine?),
de Guillac, de Saint-Michel de Rivière-Froid, & *du péage* de Guillos,
sieur de La Tour de Bessan,[63] *gouverneur* de Blaye
=   bf. 1435 Marie Plantagenet de/Mary Plantagenet of Lancaster/of Bedford/of England (1420-1459/63)
Siblings: Pierre **or** Pey de Montferrand le jeune (Communay) **OR** Bertrand,
baron de Montferrand, de Frespech, de Langoiran, etc.
(Bourrousse de Laforre: IV, 241), (d. 1437)   m.s.p.;
Jeanne (Gaillarde);   Marcotte;
Isabeau de Montferrand (1415-1464) = 1435 François de Gramont (ca. 1410-1462);
and Marguerite de Montferrand = (?) Jacques Angevin, sgr de Rauzun, Civrac, Pujols, Bladignac, etc.?
(Courcelles: VI, "de Durfort", 143, n. 1)
>dgtr Jeanne Angevin = Jean de Durfort, *chevalier*, sgr de Duras & Blancquefort,
mayor of Bordeaux, who became governor of Cremona during the Italian invasion

---

[57]Daughter of Bertrand II de Montferrand and so sister of Bertand III & sister-in-law of Isabeau de Preissac, *dame* de Landiras (see below).

[58]At least two sources identify Isabelle's father as Gaillard rather than Jean II, thereby confusing father and grandfather. Baurein identifies Na-Aupuys as daughter of the *dame en partie* (so, heiress in part) de Roquetaillade, sister of Pierre de la Mothe, sgr. de Langon. (Are this sister and brother in any way related to Clairemonde de La Mothe-Landiras, the grandmother of the husband of their daughter/niece?) Baurein spells the mother's name "Na-Aupays" & the daughter's "Ysabé de Saint-Simphorin" (III, 207). Baurein references a document of 7 April 1424 that refers to *both* mother (Isabeau) and daughter (Marguerite) as "Dames de Landiras" (III, 208), which need only to establish a point, not an indication that the mother was still living. Without equivocation, Baurein dates the Saint-Symphorien-Stratton marriage to "as early as 1358", and for their longevity, gives us the date 1391, actually for both spouses (III, 207/8).
Alternatively: "Isabeau, *dame* de Landiras, Bessan de St-Symphorien" (ca. 1250 [*sic*]-ca. 1424); John Stratton, "constable de Bordeaux, sr de Landiras" (ca. 1350-ca. 1400); married in 1366 ("Ahnentafel", 12th generation, # 3102 & 3103).

[59]"Bernard Arnaud de Preissac, knight (*chevalier*), captain of a company of *hommes d'armes*, ..., was one of the most valiant warriors of his century, contributed immeasurably to the victory of the battle of Cocherel, where he fought at the head of the Gascons on King Charles V's side, was there badly wounded and received from the king the most striking marks of his gratitude and was a guarantor (*conservateur*) of various treaties between France and England" [my translation] (Chenaye des Bois: ?, 508, quoted in "Montferrand"). Cocherel was fought 16 May 1364, between the kings of France and Navarre (with some English on the Navarese side).

[60]The château de La Trau had been built by Pope Clement V and turned over to Arnaud Bernard de Preissac (d. 1310), his brother-in-law, as governor, but under the recently-new-to-Europe title of "soudan" (from "sultan"—sometimes "soudich"). Bacque translates the title as "défenseur" (1908: 19). Bernard-Arnaud de Preissac was his great-grandson (Beltz, 1841: 265, note 1, & 268). By 1384/5 Richard II of England had given permission to hold a market and fairs in Arbanats/Darbenatz, a parish in the jurisdiction of the baronnie of Portets (Betz: 268; Baurein: III, 75). Bourrousse de Laforre reiterates the titles of Bermond-Arnaud de Preyssac, but with the spelling sgr. "d'Arnanats" (1883: IV, 241).

[61]For the various suggestions for dating the Montferrand-Preissac marriage, see note 34, above.

[62]Bertrand III had claimed Lesparre in right of his wife, Isabeau de Preissac, but was awarded Madaillon as indemnity. Pierre raised the claims again, and was given Langoiran instead in 1446. Henry VI gave Lesparre to John Holland, Earl of Huntingdon; Charles VII awarded it in 1450/51 to Amanieu d'Albret, sr. d'Orval (d. ca. 1463). Communay (????); Baurein (I, 159-60); Abbot (325), who alone mentions Huntingdon; Ribadieu gives Huntingdon as an example of how the English king sowed disputes among his vassals (1990: 192). Lost in Pierre's demise of 1454, Langoiran was retrieved by his nephew Bertrand IV and later sold by Guy de Montferrand in 1590 to meet debts (Abbot, 323). Alternately, Bertrand IV possessed Langoiran and was responsible for the (temporary) loss; it was sold by Gaston I on 28 June 1578 (Communay: Doc. XLIII, 121-25).

[63]This extensive list is owed to Communay (1). But after Landiras, he introduces his list merely by "ensemble des terres...", so not each item that follows need be considered a *seigneurie*, most notably not the "*péage*" (toll gate). Of course, we have his and many others' authority that most are. (Elsewhere, giving all the sometime possessions over the centuries, he lists *seigneuries* and *maisons nobles* together [vii]).

IX. **François IV de Montferrand-Landiras** (ca. 1440-1501), sgr de Budos[64] & de Cernés (Saint-Léger-de-Balson)[65]
   = ca. 1470 Yolande Carrion (b. ca. 1450)[66] OR Bernadine de Lavedan (ca. 1450-af. 1517)[67]
      Siblings: Thomas, sgr d'Aigille (d. ca. 1470), Bertrand, sgr de Montbadon (d. ca. 1470),
         Mathilde (yet Communay says all "died young")
   X. **Thomas de Montferrand-Landiras**[68] (1470; baron 1514-1523/40), d'Uzeste and Portets:
      = ca. 1500 Unknown woman   OR Yoland Carrion (b. ca. 1450)
      Siblings: Perre [*sic*] (b. 1469), Catherine & Jeanne
XI.1. **Pierre III de Montferrand-Landiras** (d. 30 May 1540)   m.s.p.
XI.2. **Gaston I de Montferrand-Landiras** (d. 1540)[69]   m.s.p.
XI.3. **Jehannot de Montferrand-Landiras,** *baron de Portets* (1501-1561) (or b. 1510),[70]
      ("Cdelmars"; "GeneaNet"; & "Arbre généalogique")
      = 1535 Marguerite de Grignols/Talleyrand-Grignols (ca. 1520-bf. 1561),
         (Communay, "Cdelmars"; "GeneaNet" & "Arbre généalogique")[71]
         mother of Portets succession (viz. Gaston *et seq.*)
      =   Françoise de Pompadour (d. 1580)
         XII. *Gaston de Montferrand-Portets = ???*
         XIII. *Mathurin de Montferrand-Portets*   m.s.p.
XI.4. **Jehan/Jean IV de Montferrand-Landiras** (1505; baron 1559-1573/80)[72]
      admitted to the *ordre de Saint-Michel* in 1570[73]
   = 1545 Jacquette de Rayet
XII.   **Gaston II de Montferrand-Landiras** (d. early 1597)
   = 1573 (Saint) Jeanne de Lestonnac (1556-1640)
      Siblings: Barbe;   Marie = Bernard de Faverolles, sgr de La Planche;
         Catherine = Antoine de Chanteloube, sgr de Branda;
         Marguerite = François de Sentout
XIII. **François V de Montferrand-Landiras** (1580-1619/20), sgr de St-Morillon, *bourgeois* de Bordeaux,
      gentilhomme ordinaire de la chambre du roi in 1603, *capitaine d'une compagnie des chevaux légers*[74]
   = 3 July 1600 Marguerite de Cazalis (1583-1620)

---

[64]Given that the Montferrand-Landiras patrimony would fall to the La Roque-Budos family in the middle of the 18th century (cf. note 30, in Part Two), this earlier, brief ownership of Budos should be noted: André de Budos's loyalty to the King of France cost him his lands from 1421 until his son's repossession in 1460. In 1440, the English crown had assigned the *seigneurie* to François IV de Montferrand, who, in the 1443 Capitulation of Dax, however, promised to render Budos, Castelnau and Cernés to Charles VII. Instead, François preferred to offer his son Bérard as hostage than to execute the terms of the treaty. Nonetheless, in 1446 the château de Budos was assigned (temporarily) to Jean, comte de Foix. Bacque (1908: 19) (I offer these details in faith even though the same source has Jeanne de Lestonnac born in the château de Landiras and founding her Order in Toulouse! Furthermore, Bérard de Montferrand appears to be the hostage of the English king, when the post-Dax circumstances would suggest the French?!)

[65]"Les Seigneurs de Landiras_1", indeed, lists Saint-Léger-de-Balson in parenthesis after Cernés.

[66]Yolande Carrion married François IV according to Communay (table). Their children and some dates were confirmed by "RootsWeb's WordConnect Project".

[67]"Arbre généalogique" and "Informations généalogiques" give Yolande Carrion to Thomas de Montferrand and assign Bernadine de Lavedan to his father. Both women would be a little too old for marriage to Thomas. However, these respective assignments of Yolande and Bernadine do happen often enough for one to be cautious in denying either's accuracy.

For another Bernadine de Lavedan, see Bertrand IV de Montferrand, in the senior house. A third Bernadine married Jean/Jeannot de Montault (Anselme: ?, 605; Chenaye Des Bois: ?, 262). "Bernadine" appears to be one of the fifteen most frequently given names within the Lavedan family ("Généalogie.com"), and we have found both 1450 and 1460 given to one or another Berdadine de Lavedan who died in 1517. "Our Royal ... Ancestors".

[68]"Les Seigneurs de Landiras_1" inserts a Gaston, *sénéchal* de Guyenne in 1465 between François and Thomas.

[69]One source ("Informations généalogiques") offers no wife or date of marriage for Gaston I de Montferrand-Landiras, but gives him two children (Gaston II and Pierre), who are more likely those of his youngest brother, Jean IV.

[70]If Jehannot really was born in 1510 (and "Jean IV" in 1505), we have a better explanation for why it would be Jehannot who established a cadet house. That is, Jehan (Jean IV) would follow the two elder, deceased brothers into the succession, while the younger, fourth brother, Jehannot, would have to be content with an appanage or two, as per the 1559 agreement mentioned by Communay (lxx). Then, should Jehannot figure in the Landiras succession at all, let alone before Jehan/Jean IV? They could have been co-proprietors. Anything is possible, of course, so an elder brother might have, for one reason or another, decided to establish a cadet line. Cf. note 14, in Part Two.

[71]The date of marriage is from Courcelles: III, "de Grignols", 260.

"Talleyrand" is included only by Communay (lxx), but not without probability; the comté de Grignols had been in the Talleyrand house since "time immemorial" (Courcelles: III, "de Grignols", 258).

"GeneaNet" offers a marriage date of 1513 (which brings it into striking clash with the only known suggestions of her birth date, *viz.* 1520, let alone her husband's), and then as much as offers her brother-in-law (Jean [IV], "co-seigneur de Landiras") as her first child. Then, three more children: Gaston de Montferrand (father of Mathurin [which matches other information], Isabeau and Marie de Montferrand), Jacquette de Montferrand (to be wife of François de La Cropte sr de Meinardie, and then mother of Jeanne de La Cropte), and Isabeau de Montferrand (to marry Raymond de Fortebride).

[72]A largely reliable source nonetheless has Jean IV die in 1563 ("Informations Généalogiques"), when most have him present at his son's wedding ten years later.

"Montferrand" does not help us keep the family's succession straight during these generations. Among other things, it merely indicates that Jean de Montferrand-Landiras had posterity and then inconsistently suggests that his second-oldest brother, Gaston I, was the father of Gaston II (11-12).

[73]"Jean de Montferrand" is listed for 1571, with the title "sgr de Portelz [*sic*]" (Colleville & Saint-Christo, n.d., 109), which would suggest his brother Jehannot, but **he** had died in 1561. Cf. note 14, in Part Two.

[74]Identified as "Bourgeois de Landiras de Montferrand" by "GeneaNet/François", a site which furnishes several additional dates for the next few generations. Also by "Les Auschtzky de Bordeaux".

   Sisters: Marthe (b. 1586) & Madeleine (b. 1588) became nuns;[75]
      Cittérée Jeanne (1587-1635) = François de Chartres, sgr d'Arpaillant/Arpailhan (d. 1644)
         >dgtr Marie de Chartres, O.D.N. (1640)
XIV. **Bernard de Montferrand-Landiras** (b. 1600), *marquis* de Landiras (Sept. 1651)
      Succeeded to remaining properties & titles of the senior branch in 1660
      = 19 Jan. 1647 **or** 21 Oct. 1646 ("Les Auschtzky de Bordeaux") Marie-Delphine (or Delphinette) de Pontac (1627-af. 1675)
XV.1. **Joseph-François de Montferrand, mrqs de Landiras & brn de Montferrand** (d. 1698),
      Grand sénéchal de Guyenne et de Libourne (Communay has Jean-Joseph)
      = unknown woman   m.s.p.—or not?![76]
XV.2. **Léon de Montferrand, mrqs de Landiras & brn de Montferrand** (ca. 1659-6 May 1717)
      premier baron de Guyenne, *grand-sénéchal* de Guyenne (declared hereditary on 21 April 1705)[77]
      = Elizabeth de Rizaucourt (a daughter died young)
      = 13 September 1700 Catherine de Meslon (1683-1724); mother of succession
         Sisters: Marie-Catherine de Montferrand (1654-1731), O.D.N. (1720);
            Louise de Montferrand (?)
XVI. **François-Armand V de Montferrand, mrqs de Landiras & brn de Montferrand**
            (1704-18 August 1761), *grand-sénéchal* de Guyenne
      = 1721 Thérèse-Jeanne du Hamel (d. 29 August 1761)
      son: Charles-Hyacinthe (March 1730-2 October 1751); and
      dgtr: Suzanne de Montferrand, O.D.N. (1745)
      François-Armand's sisters: Henriette Catherine Olive de Montferrand, O.D.N. (1728);
         Marie Catherine Lucie de Montferrand (b. 1707), O.D.N. (1731), ("GeneaNet");
         Delphine de Montferrand (b. ca. 1702), *baronne* de Beychevelle[78]
            mother of the succession
            = 1720 Étienne-François de Brassier (ca. 1685-1744), sgr de La Marque
XV.1. **François Armand de Brassier, mrqs de Landiras & brn de Montferrand** (1723-1768)
      = Mathive Jeanne Françoise Thérèse de Pommiers   m.s.p.
XV.2. **Étienne de Brassier, mrqs de Landiras & brn de Montferrand** (1725-1787)[79]
      (*célibataire*)   m.s.p.
XV.3. **Delphine de Brassier, marquise de Landiras & baronne de Montferrand** (1722/25-1795)
      = 23 June 1745 Michel-Joseph de La Roque, baron de Budos (ca. 1715-1770)
XVI. **François-Armand de La Roque-Budos, mrqs de Landiras & brn de Montferrand**
            (ca. 1750-1825), *capitaine de dragons* et *chevalier de l'ordre de Saint-Louis*; *émigré*
      = 14 April 1787 Catherine de Ménoire de Barbe (1765/66-1792)
         Siblings: Charles François Armand de La Roque-Budos (b. 1762)[80] and
            Marguerite de La Roque-Budos (d. 1820)[81] = 1775 Jean-Baptiste-Calixte de
            Montmorin (1727-1781), marquis de Saint-Hérem, *maréchal des*
            camps et armées du roi
XVII. **Catherine Delphine de La Roque-Budos, mrqse de Landiras & brnne de**
            Montferrand (1789-1860)
      = 1814 Léon, baron de Brivazac (1774-1860) or b. 1776 (Bacque & O'Gilvy, 1856: I, 392);[82]
         émigré (1798-1802), (O'Gilvy (1856: I, 392)

---

[75]Marthe and Madeleine de Montferrand professed as *Religieuses Annunciades* in 1604 and then transferred to their mother's *Order/Company of [the Daughters of] Mary Our Lady*, in 1622 ("GeneaNet").

[76]One source gives them a son, François Joseph Lombard de Montferrand (1700-1770), *marchand* de Bordeaux, who in 1725 married Marie Labory, daughter of Pierre François Labory, *bourgeois* de Landiras. "Les Auschtzky de Bordeaux" (Génération 3; 1.2). If father Joseph-François really was the elder brother, why did the inheritance pass to his nephew? The same source has Joseph-François as the son of Bernard on his own *fiche* and as the son of Joseph François on the latter's *fiche*. These *fiches* also imply that Léon (dates, no titles) was the elder brother, yet Joseph François (no dates!) apparently bore all the Landiras titles at some point.
   Communay also appears to acknowledge a son, Pierre François de Montferrand, *vicomte* de Foncaude (150, but not in his table).
   Abbot, after creating doubts with his Pierre and two Gastons as sons of Jean IV (above), now has a "François IV" die after 1698 and then, after brother Léon, he offers François Armand (d. 1761) with a sister "Marie Brassier" (327).

[77]From here into the French Revolution every marquis de Landiras, baron de Montferrand is the *premier baron* de Guyenne and *grand-sénéchal* de Guyenne.

[78]A site so helpful concerning her parents and siblings aids yet further in calling this daughter Delphine de Montferrand, in contrast to the name of the nun Marie-Catherine suggested by others (Communay; "GeneaNet").

[79]Baurein writes (in 1784-86) that M. de Brassier "est le seigneur actuel", a statement that the "Nouvelle Edition" (1876) made no effort to update (III, 208).

[80]This Charles François Armand de La Roque and his widowed mother, Delphine de Brassier, sold much of the estate in 1793, during François Armand's absence. Some sources have "Charles" precede his elder brother's names, so it is difficult to distinguish them.

[81]Marguerite was Saint-Hérem's second wife. Anselme, IX (2), 956. The barony of Beychevelle passed to this daughter, after two generations associated with Landiras. Both mentions of her younger brother's duel only identify him as her brother (see the text at note 36 in Part Two).

[82]Féret (III, 100) confirms 1814 for the marriage. Bacque dates the marriage to 1801 (rather early, for the bride would have been twelve and the husband not yet back from England) and either offers no date of death or suggests 1821. But the 1821 date is offered by Bacque as if it were the death of the elder of two sons named "Léon". (A death before ten was not uncommon, followed by giving the same name to another.) The corrections and some additional information (here & below) is from Garrric (n.d.).

XVIII. **Léon II Armand de Brivazac** (1823-1889)
= 1860 Alice Louise Caroline de Lur-Saluces (1836-1901)[83]

Conclusion

Bare as these Genealogies have attempted to be, the discerning reader has already seen quite a variety of historical perspectives and experiences. The narratives earlier in this article and in the next flesh out the experienced histories of the Montferrand and Landiras dynasties. Whether genealogical "fact" or historical "interpretation", much remains in dispute or completely unknown, but our presentation of the diversity of opinion will contribute, we hope, to the resolution of some of the uncertainties.

Acknowledgements

The author wishes to thank the Discretionary Grant Program, Research and Innovation Committee, of the University of Winnipeg (Winnipeg, Manitoba, Canada), for generously agreeing to fund the publication of these articles. He is also most grateful to Marshall Bailey and Kathleen Sweeney for their making possible the research trip to Bordeaux.

REFERENCES[84]

Abbot, P. D. (n.d.) *Provinces, pays and seigneuries of France*. Canberra.

Ahnentafel of Jean Vincent brn [sic] St. Castin d'Abbedie. Accessed 10 January 2013 and since.

Anselme, P. [Pierre Guibours] (1967). *Histoire généalogique et chronologique de la maison royale de France, des pairs, grands officiers de la Couronne et de la maison du roi et des anciens barons du royaume*. Paris: Libraires Associés; New York: Johnson Reprint, 1726-1733.

Arbre Généalogique/André Decloitre. Accessed 21 February 2013 before and since.

Arbre Généalogique/Jean Michel Ducusson. Accessed 21 January 2013, before and since. To be highlighted, however, is his site's offering one of the amplest genealogies of the family to be found anywhere, though not always internally consistent nor easy to interpret. http://gw2.geneanet.org/jmducosson?lang=fr&m=N&v=de%20MONTFERRAND

Les Auschtzky de Bordeaux. http://bertrand.auschitzky.free.fr/AuschitzkyHTML/fiches/fiche6333.htm

Bailey, D. A. (2006). Les mystères de la maison des Grailly-Foix-Candale. *Revue de Pau et du Béarn, 33*, 29-41.

Baudrillart, Alfred, Van Cauwenbergh, Étienne, & Aubert, Roger (Eds.) (1937). *Dictionnaire d'histoire et de géographie ecclésiastiques*.

Baurein, A. J. (1876). *Variétés bordeloises; ou Essai historique et critique sur la Topographie ancienne et moderne du Diocese de Bordeaux (1784-86)*. Bordeaux: Féret et Fils.

Beltz, G. F. (1841). *Memorials of the order of the garter, from its foundation to the present, with biographical notices of the knights in the reigns of Edward III and Richard II*. London: William Pickering.

Boidron, B., & Lemay, M.-H. (2001). *Bordeaux: Ses environs et ses vins classés par ordre de mérite* (16e éd.). Bordeaux: Féret et Fils.

Bourrousse de Lafforre [Pierre] J[ules] (1860-1883). *Nobiliaire de Guyenne et de Gascogne; Revue des familles d'ancienne chevalerie ou anoblies de ces provinces, antérieures à 1789, avec leur généalogies et arme*. Paris: Dumoulin; Bordeaux: Féret et Fils; Paris: H. Champion.

Branches Collatérales des Montferrands. http://perso.internet.fr/driout/SAINT-SYMPHORIEN, htm (accessed 27 December 2002).

Buathier, H. (1995). *Jean Ier de Grailly; un chevalier européen du XIIIe siècle*. MEX (Valais).

Casanovas, F. M. (1991). *Les Ancêtres d'Henri IV*. Paris: Éditions Christian.

Chenaye des Bois, François Aubert de La (1980). *Dictionnaire de la Noblesse...*. Paris: Berger-Levrault.

Communay, A. (1889). *Essai généalogique sur les Montferrand de Guyenne, suivi de pièces justificatives*. Bordeaux: Vve Moquet.

Courcelles, Jean Baptiste Pierre Julien, chevalier de (1822-1833). *Histoire généalogique et héraldique des pairs de France, des grands dignitaires de la Couronee, des principales familles nobles du Royaume...*. Paris: Arthus Bertrand.

Delmars, C. Mes ancêtres nobles. Accessed 21 January, 2 March 2013, and between.

Dynastie de Grailly. Accessed 28 August 2004. http://web.genealogie.free.fr/Les_dynasties/Les_dynasties_celebres/France/Dynastie_de_Grailly.htm

Family de Goth. Accessed 24 February 2013 and since. http://racineshistoire.free.fr/LGN/PDF/Goth.pdf

Féret, É. (1874). *Statistique générale... du département de la Gironde*, vol. II. Paris: G. Masson; Bordeaux: Féret et Fils.

Féret, É. (1889). *Statistique générale... du département de la Gironde*, vol. III. *Première partie, Biographie*. Paris: G. Masson; Bordeaux: Féret et Fils.

Fisquet, M. H. (1864 et seq.). *La France pontificale (Gallia christiana): Histoire chronologique et biographique des archevêques et évêques de tous les diocèses de France depuis l'établissement du christianisme jusqu'à nos jours, divisée en 18 provinces ecclésiastiques* [the volume "*Métropole de Bordeaux*"]. Paris: E. Repos.

Foras, le comte E.-Amédée de (1992). *Armorial et nobiliaire de l'ancien Duché de Savoie*. Geneva: Slatkine.

Garric, A. (n.d.). Léon Armand de Brivazac. *Essai de Généalogie*.

Gastelier de la Tour, D.-F. (1770). *Généalogie de la maison de Preissac, tirée du Nobiliaire historique de la province de Languedoc*. Paris.

Généalogie mes Ancêtres.

Généalogie.com. http://www.genealogie.com/nom-de-famille/LAVEDAN.html

Généalogie Famille de Carné. Accessed 23 February 2013, 2 March 2013 and between.

Genealogieonline. Accessed 23 February 2013.

GeneaNet/pierfit. Diverse Montferrand, Lestonnac and Grignols searches. Accessed 21 & 28 February, 2 March 2013, and other occasions.

GENI. Accessed 6 April 2013. http://www.geni.com/people/Marguerite-d-Astarac/6000000000460332132

Grasset, J. P., Jean, Ph., & Pastureau, J. L. (n.d.; 1981). *Le Pays de Montferrand des origines à la Révolution; ou Essai d'histoire locale*. Bordeaux: G.G.E.L.E.P.

Grasset, J. P., Jean, Ph., & Pastureau, J. L. (n.d.; 1981). Les seigneurs de Montferrand-Ville. Virtually a poster promotion on the Internet for the book!

Informations Généalogiques. Genealogie de Jean-Michel Ducosson, Created March 2006. Accessed 2 & 22 January, 21 & 23 February, and 2 March 2013.

---

[83]Note the presence of a "de Lur" again. Cf. the *Maisons* d'Uza and de Cancon.

[84]How can this list be kept useful and grateful, without being cluttered or pretentious? The research attack, in addition to consulting solid reference books, was to Google most of the individuals mentioned here and then click on several of the offered links, for comparisons and comprehensiveness, then pursuing most relatives and even properties individually. Below, I shall list, to the fullest extent my recollection allows, the generic names of the sites to which I am indebted, but not always their internet coördinates. The latter are many and long, and often the only word changed is the name of the person concerned. So, my conclusion, dear readers, is to advise you to Google directly whoever interests you by his or her name, but to remain open, creative and persistent in your search.

http://www.genealogie33.org/pduc/dat716.htm

Jouannet, François Vatar de (1837). *Statistique du département de la Gironde*, T. I. Paris: P. Dupont.

Lemay (1995). *Bordeaux...et ses vins*. See Boidron.

Lopes, J. [Hierosme] (1882-1884). *Histoire de l'Église métropolitaine et primatiale Saint André-de Bordeaux (1688)*. Rééd., annotée et complétée par l'abbé Callen. Bordeaux: Féret & Fils.

Mas-Latrie, Comte Louis de (1889). *Trésor de chronologie d'histoire et géographie pour l'étude et l'emploi des documents du Moyen Age*. Paris: Victor Palmé.

Montferrand. Accessed 3 December 2002 and in January 2013. http://perso.club-internet.fr/driout/MONTFERRAND.htm

Moréri, L. (1759). *Le grand dictionnaire historique, ou le mélange curieux de l'histoire sacrée et profane*. Paris: Les Libraires Associés.

Our Royal… Ancestors. Accessed 23 February 2013 and earlier. http://our-royal-titled-noble-and-commoner-ancestors.com/p3886.htm#i116712.

Roots Web. Accessed 6 April 2013. http://archiver.rootsweb.ancestry.com/th/read/GEN-MEDIEVAL/2003-10/1065637694

RootsWeb's Word Connect Project: BEVAN BATES ATKINSON and KIDD Ancestries.

Les Seigneurs de Landiras_1. Comité historique de Landiras. Accessed 2 January 2013.

Les Seigneurs de Landiras_2, Comité historique de Landiras. Accessed 5 January 2013.

3

Reflections on the Scientific Conceptual Streams in Leonardo da Vinci and His Relationship with Luca Pacioli

Raffaele Pisano

Centre Sciences, Sociétés, Cultures dans leurs Evolutions, University of Lille 1, Lille, France

Leonardo da Vinci (1452-1519) is perhaps overrated for his contributions to physical science, since his technical approach. Nevertheless important components concerning practical problems of mechanics with great technical ability were abounded. He brought alive again the Nemorarius' (fl. 12th - 13th century) tradition and his speculations on mechanics, if immature made known how difficult and elusive were the conceptual streams of the foundations of science for practitioners-artisans. Leonardo also had an interesting and intense relationship with mathematics but merely unhappy insights in his time. The meeting with Luca Bartolomeo de Pacioli (1445-1517) was very important for da Vinci since proposing stimulating speculations were implemented, but they were not definitive theoretical results. In this paper historical reflections notes on mechanics and mathematics in da Vinci and his relationships with Pacioli are presented.

Keywords: *Scientia de Ponderibus*; Mathematical Renaissance; da Vinci; Pacioli; Mechanics

An Outline

The emergence of the figure of the engineer seen as a technician in some way educated in sciences, is a characteristic feature of the XV century and the first half of the XVI. Indeed this is perhaps the main feature of science, where the reduced creativity (real or apparent) of *pure* scientists, was counterbalanced by the great creativity of *applied* scientists. A short list is sufficient to give an idea of the dimension of the phenomenon: Mariano di Jacopo called Taccola (1381-1458), Leon Battista Alberti (1404-1472), Francesco di Giorgio Martini (1439-1501), Leonardo da Vinci, Vannuccio Biringuccio (1480-1539), Francesco de' Marchi (1504-1576), Giovanni Battista Bellucci (1506-1554), Daniele Barbaro (1513-1570). Although there were no public funding to encourage scientists to devote their efforts to the study of technical applications and to the improvement of their knowledge, a common ground arose, particularly in Central and Northern Italy. The link between engineers and scientists emerged, at least in part, through the creation of some technical centres in the courts of the principalities which had been set up. This was the case of Medici's court in Florence, but also, and perhaps more importantly, the court of Milan under Francesco Sforza with its very rich library. Particularly in Urbino, Francesco di Giorgio Martini (1480-1490) wrote a translation of Vitruvius (see book X on machines) into Italian, questionable from a philological standpoint and Piero della Francesca (1415-1492) one of the greatest mathematicians and painters of the time, should be reported (Pisano, 2007, 2009; Pisano & Capecchi, 2008, 2009, 2010a, 2010b, 2012).

Leonardo introduced the concept of *pratica* (Gille; Sarton) as the basis of any of his studies, defining it either as observation, a study of buildings, of human anatomy and natural phenomena, or as an experiment aimed at checking up the calculations derived from his observation. On the other hand, he defines himself *discepolo della sperienza*. To him, from *experience* we can derive, beyond good building practices, also rules that are not only the expression of aesthetic research but principally requirements for the proper performance of the *building organism*, considered at the same time as a living organism or a *macchina-ingegno*. He is an artist but also a technician and a scholar and it would be a mistake, assuming a position systematically too antithetic to the official thesis, to assimilate his notes to a definitive work of art. Then, we must say that an indirect continuity in a bend toward science shown by Leonardo emerges when considering that the themes he dealt with had already been studied in early 1400 by Taccola who was interested in the scripts of mechanics and military technology of Pneumatica by Philon of Byzantium (280-220 B.C.). As the majority of engineers by that time, Leonardo also studied the engineering works by Heron from Alexandria (fl. I-II? B.C.) though considered useless toys (Heron, 1575, 1893, 1900, 1999). On the other hand, they got enthusiastic before the futuristic technical designs by Leonardo in that when not copying it, they were strongly influenced by them, such as Hero's engine, windwheel, vending machine, force pump, Heron's fountain et al. Gille ends up his book with a hope:

All our engineers were men of war. [...]. But the enquiry remains open: it might bring to light other works still languishing in the dust of libraries, it might also provide a more precise analysis of the notebooks which have never been published and which are full of information[1].

In spite of because no Greek and Latin knowledge he learnt, it is reasonable to think that he had no direct access to classical ancient works; on that he wrote interesting annotations in the *Codex Atlantico* and *Codex Leicester* (ex *Codex Hammer*). On his classical language education he wrote:

I know very well that because I am unlettered some presumptuous people will think they have the right to criticize me, saying that I am an uncultured man. What unintelligent fools[2]!

Introduction

The privileged geographical position of Italy in the Mediterranean caused interesting commercial exchanges with Africa and the Middle East that favoured the free circulation and the widespread of Greek works throughout Italy and Northern Europe. On the other hand, when the Turks captured Constantinople (1453) many Greek scholars moved to Europe (several of them to Italy as well), taking with them important manuscripts and making the knowledge of the classical culture more accessible, compared with the past 12th and 13th centuries. The translation into Latin straight from the Greek language made their contents more reliable. Reliability increased thanks to the invention of movable type printing (ca. 1450) by Johann Gutenberg (1400?-1467?). Approximately, since 1474 they started to print works of mathematics, astronomy and astrology in Italy. The edition[3] (*Elementa geometriae*) by Giovanni Campano di Novara (1220-1296) might have been one of the first translations of the *Elements* by Euclid (fl 300 BC) in its Latin version (Knorr, 1978-1979, 1985; Busard, 2005). It included speeches from *Arithmetica* by Jordanus de Nemore, commentary on Euclid by Anaritius (865-922) and several additions by Campano, too. In such a climate and until Renaissance the image of the new scientist, seen also as a student of natural phenomena, emerged. He was seen as a new type of scientist, re-born and re-qualified, not just an interested and clever astrologer and medieval theologian. Above all he looked now independent from a hypothetical and *general pre-established design*. However, the reconcilement between the divine plan and the new mathematical truths could converge into an outlined project, still divine under many aspects, considering God as the engineer who had planned a cosmological design in mathematical and geometrical terms. God as an engineer allowed a certain *chance* of studying the divine product that is nature interpreted in mathematical terms, since in this way the object of study was still confined to a religious matter. In fact, this would explain why, among other things, the majority of the Renaissance scientists were theologians as well (of course not usually theologians in the sense of their principal employment) who preferred to inquire into nature instead of the Holy Scriptures. Therefore each discovery or mathematical invention was seen as the product of God's engineering work[4]. Though this new way of conceiving it science was limited to the learned and the rich only, since they had a knowledge of Latin and Greek. The spread of the new culture by print was hampered by two factors. First, a lot of technicians, such as architects and engineers, would have probably welcomed the application of geometry and mathematics as *theoretical science* to arts, navigation and architecture but the precarious diffusion of school education did not give the pioneers of *scientia activa* access to the necessary scientific heritage. Thus, according to some thought currents of history of mathematics, the expectation about the spread of the classical culture, instead of encouraging the highest erudition among mathematicians and, in general, of scientific topics, paradoxically seemed to exclude just the new-born class of scientists-mechanics who, far more numerous than theoretical scientists, felt a strong interest in the introduction of mechanical devices or of calculating ones within their treatises. Secondly, theoretical knowledge was the only one to be considered full and definitive, therefore experience was meant to be of secondary use, so the discoveries of technicians were ignored, eventually causing a strange regression toward the medieval culture typical of the Scholastics of 12th century. In particular, due to the lack of mathematical devices, technicians would feed their knowledge through the development of so-called procedures *by comparison*. Modelling by similitude were typical, after daily practice and based upon *make mistakes and correct*, almost to represent a sort of a practical, e.g., handbook of architecture. The scientific applications will flow into the new technology and will require more and more the integration of local activities and the managing skill of the artisans. This integration and the new reference to the Euclidean geometry will bring together with other physical-mathematical factors— that will be the case study of the present thesis—to the realization of the first projects, after *the aestimatio* modelling, that is approximated and designed on the spot.

Mostly, at the end of the Middle Age mathematics was taught essentially at universities and at abacus schools. In the university, mathematics was taught in the *quadrivium* (arithmetic, geometry, astronomy and music) of the faculties of arts, that while maintaining their autonomy, were instrumental to the training of future physicians and theologians (Duhem, 1988: X; Grant, 2001; De Ridder-Symoens, 2003; Grendler, 2002). The medical faculties of the early Renaissance were usually those in which mathematics had more space. Medicine was, in fact, connected to the study of astrology, which required the students to have rudiments of Ptolemaic astronomy and then knowledge of elements of geometry and arithmetic. Professors of these subjects were the masters of liberal arts of the *quadrivium*, whose teaching and research many of the mathematical works of the XV century are connected. However the place occupied by mathematics was still marginal and also the level of mathematical knowledge, which except for some teachers was limited to what was indispensable for the exercise of astrology. In fact it did not cover the study of so many Greek classics that at the time were already available in Latin translations from Arabic of the XII century.

During the 16th - 17th centuries mechanics was a theoretical science and it was mathematical, although its object had a physical nature and had social utility. Texts in the Latin and Arabic Middle Ages diverted from the Greek. In particular al-Farabi (ca. 870-950) differentiates between mechanics in the

---

[1] Gille, p 240; see also: Hall, 1997.

[2] da Vinci, *Codex Atlanticus*, f. 119v.

[3] Maybe made by Abelard of Bath (12th century) and annotated and edited by Campano. The edition in fifteen books, *Preclarissimus liber elementorum Euclidis perspicacissimi* [...] will published by Erhard Ratdolt in Venezia (1482). It is based on an Arabic translation from original Greek manuscript.

[4] Of course one should also take into account *Liber naturae* (for ex: Numbers, 2006; Harrison, 1955; Vanderputten, 2005; Ophuijsen, 2005; Kusukawa, 2012; Jesseph, 2004; Pedersen, 1992; Biagioli, 2003; Marcacci, 2009).

science of weights and that in the science of devices. On the other hand, the science of weights refers to the movement and equilibrium of weights suspended from a balance and aims to formulate principles. The science of devices refers to applications of mathematics to practical use and to machine construction. In the Latin world a process similar to that registered in the Arabic world occurred. Even here a science of movement of weights was constituted, namely *Scientia de ponderibus*. Besides this there was a branch of learning called mechanics, sometimes considered an activity of craftsmen, other times of engineers (*Scientia de ingeniis*).

On the *Scientia de Ponderibus*

The *scientia de ponderibus* saw the birth in the Arabic land (Capecchi, 2012, 2011). The status of a distinct *Scientia* to the science of weights first appeared in al-Farabi's (ca. 870-950) *Iḥṣā' al-'ulūm* (*Enumeration of the sciences*). In particular he definitely distinguished between science of weights and sciences of devices or machines. Al-Farabi (Schneider 2011) took six distinct sciences: language, logic, mathematics, nature, metaphysics and politics. The mathematics was divided into seven topics: arithmetic, geometry, perspective, music, science of weights and sciences of machines (Capecchi & Pisano 2013) or devices:

> As for the science of weights [emphasis added], it deals with the matters of weights from two standpoints: either by examining weights as much as they are measured or are of use to measure, and this is the investigation of the matters of the doctrine of balances (umūr al-qawl fi l-mawāzīn), or by examining weights as much as they move or are of use to move, and this is the investigation of the principles of instruments (uṣūl al-ālāt) by which heavy things are lifted and carried from one place to another.
> As for the science of devices [emphasis added], it is the knowledge of the procedures by which one applies to natural bodies all that was proven to exist in the mathematical sciences... in statements and proofs into the natural bodies, and [the act at] locating [all that], and establishing it in actuality. The sciences of devices are therefore those that supply the knowledge of the methods and the procedures by which one can contrive to find this applicability and to demonstrate it in actuality in the natural bodies that are perceptible to the senses[5].

The *Scientia de ponderibus* was different from Greek mechanics (Clagett and Moody [1952] 1960); Brown 1967-1968) both for the scope-Greek mechanics placed transportation of weights, instead of their equilibrium, at the centre—and for the methodology—the *Scientia de ponderibus* charged only of the theoretical foundations of equilibrium and not applicative aspects (Capecchi & Pisano, 2013; Pisano, 2013). The *Scientia de ponderibus* was also different from the mechanics of the early XVI, the *centrobaric*, a discipline developed in the wake of the rediscovery of Archimedes (fl. 287-212 B.C.) which was concerned mainly with the mathematical problems of determining

the geometric centres of gravity of plane figures and solids (*Ivi*).

The new science of weights was characterized by a strong deductive system, in which components of qualitative and ideas in physics (Locqueneux) were formulated *more geometrico*. The most common historical point of view is that the science of weights originated from interplay of Aristotelian physics and the physical-mathematical theories of Archimedes and probably Euclid (Renn), on the equilibrium of bodies (Archimedes, 2002; Clagett, 1964-1984; Tartaglia, 1565a; Dijksterhuis, 1957).

From a methodological point of view the majority of treatises in the science of weights followed what is often called dynamical or more properly kinematical approach, in which the equilibrium is seen as a balance of opposing forces and the movement, virtual or real, has an important role. In these treatments the Aristotelian dichotomy, but not only, between the natural and forced, upward and downward, motions, disappears for they are considered on the balance, in which the weight is also the natural cause of lifting other weights. The geometrical approach, like the one carried out by Archimedes, is certainly uncommon, so that some historians does not even consider it as part of the science of weights.

In the Latin Middle Ages various treatises on the *scientia de ponderibus* circulated (Clagett 1959), as already mentioned in the introduction of this work. Among them, the most important are the treatises attributed to *Elementa Jordani super demonstratione ponderum* (version E), *Liber Jordani de ponderibus* (cum commento) (version (P)), *Liber Jordani de Nemore de ratione ponderis* (version R) (Capecchi & Pisano, 2013). They were the object of comments up to the 16 century. It is not well known the distribution of the original manuscript; what is sure is that *Liber Jordani de Nemore de ratione ponderis* (version R) finished in Tartaglia's hands and was published posthumous in 1565 by Curtio Troiano as *Iordani opvsculum de ponderositate* (Tartaglia, 1565b; see also Tartaglia, 1554).

Generally, when the so-called *scientia pratica* of the Renaissance is referred to, we are reminded of engineers and, consequently, of Leonardo da Vinci, the great scholar who sums up a multiplicity of competences that nowadays would be considered as different crafts: from the engineer, architect, scientist to the artist (Pisano, 2007, 2009). Although some studies, such as from Pierre Duhem (1861-1916), Roberto Marcolongo (1862-1943), Clifford Truesdell (1919-2000) and Bertrand Gille (1920-1980) suggest a review of Leonardo da Vinci's role as a genius, in favour of a more human figure of a *learned man*, endowed with a quick intelligence, e.g. not all his designs about machines sprang out straight of his vision (Marcolongo, 1932; Truesdell; Gille).

The XV century records a check on the growth in the development of science and the publication of scientific papers. The check existed of course for the science of weights, too. In this case it also depended on the fact that the discipline, formulated axiomatically had reached its complete internal maturity and only the proposition of new problems would have lead to an evolution. Although until the early years of the XVI century no new major scientific treatise was written[6], except the *Summa de arithmetica, geometria, proportioni et proportionalità*[7] (hereafter *Summa*, Pacioli, 1494) and *De divina proportione* (Pacioli, 1509) by Luca Pacioli, it must be said that in this period the

---

[5]Othman, 1949: pp. 88-89. Interesting correlated comments are in Abattouy 2006, p. 12. See also Schneider, 2011; Abattouy, Renn, & Weinig, 2001. In the secondary literature one can also see the science of weights proposed as science of balances and science of weight lifting: Ibn Sina (980-1037), al-Isfizārī (1048-1116), al-Khāzinī (1115-1130).

[6]One can also see *Questiones super tractatum de ponderibus* (Pellicani) by Biagio Pellicani of Parma (d. 1416).
[7]The *Summa* was a teaching textbook mainly concerning general algebra.

foundations of a major renovation were laid down, with the breaking of the spirit of the scholasticism system and the repudiation of the principle of authority, particularly that of Aristotle (384-322 B.C.), the rediscovery of Plato (427-347 B.C.) and Pythagoras (570-495 B.C.) and the valorization of mathematics which was the premise for the new philosophy of nature of the second half of the XVI century (Pisano, 2011).

On Leonardo's Approach to Mechanical Science

In ancient Greece the term Μηχανική was used when referring to machines and devices in general. To be more exact, it was intended to mean the study of simple machines (winch, lever, pulley, wedge, screw and inclined plane) with reference to motive powers and displacements of bodies (Capecchi & Pisano, 2008, 2010a, 2010b). Historically works considering these arguments were referred to as *Mechanics*, from Aristotle, Heron, Pappus Alexandrinus (290-350 A.C.) to Galileo (1564-1642). None of the treatises entitled *Mechanics* avoided theoretical considerations on its object, particularly on the lever law. Moreover, there were treatises which exhausted their role in proving this law; important among them are *The Euclid book on the balance* by Euclid and *On the Equilibrium of Planes* by Archimedes (Archimedes, 2002). The Greek conception of mechanics is revived in the Renaissance, with a synthesis of Archimedean and Aristotelian routes. This is best represented by *Mechanicorum liber* by Guidobaldo dal Monte (1545-1607) who reconsiders *Mechanics* by Pappus (Pappus, 1588, 1970) maintaining that the original purpose was to reduce simple machines to the lever (dal Monte, 1581, 1588).

With the Renaissance in the XV century the medieval mathematics is joined by the new mathematics, or rather the rediscovered ancient Greek mathematics to which the humanist movement gave a great contribution. The essential role of Italian humanism in the renaissance of mathematics during the XV and XVI centuries was well documented in (Rose, 1975). Many humanists returned from their travels to Byzantium with codes of Apollonius (262-190 A.C.), Ptolemy (90-168 A.C.) Pappus, Heron written in Greek. In the early XVI century, within a few decades, many revisions and translations of classics were delivered, i.e., including the *De expetendis et fugiendis rebus* (1501) by Giorgio Valla, sort of rich encyclopaedic anthology of Greek scientific texts[8] where

> [...] the starting point for this renaissance of mathematics was the correction of Greek mathematical texts, to be undertaken by those who were expert in both the Greek language and astronomy. To make the refurbished traditions of Greek mathematics available to mathematicians generally, Regiomontanus from at least 1461 was engaged on a series of Latin translations. But by 1471, this means of communication was revolutionised by Regiomontanus' discovery of the new invention of printing. Through printing, an astonishingly rapid and accurate dissemination of texts and translations become possible that had been inconceivable in an age where manuscripts represented the sole means of circulating the written word. In its fusion of mathematics, Greek and printing Regiomontanus' publishing Programme of 1474 marks the formal beginning of

the renaissance of mathematics[9].

It should however be said that the reacquisition of mathematical techniques was rather slow. The humanist thought carried on meta-mathematical character concerned a new role that mathematics acquired within the philosophy of the Platonic and Pythagorean instances. On that the role played by Pacioli, which was in the same time teacher of abacus and *magister theologiae*, was crucial. This job allowed him to mediate the culture of technicians and learned men. Nevertheless the biblical metaphysical idea inspiring *frà* Luca Pacioli in his dedicatory letter "[...] Fratris Luca de Burgo Sancti Sepulcri, ordinis minorum, sacre theologiae Magistri [...]" (Pacioli, *Summa*, f. 3r) to Guidobaldo da Montefeltro (1472-1508) as "Ad Illustrissimum principem sui Ubaldum Duces Montis Feretri, Mathematice discipline cultorem serventissimum [...]" (*Ibidem*) was that the book of nature (later on resumed by Galileo[10], too) is written in mathematical characters:

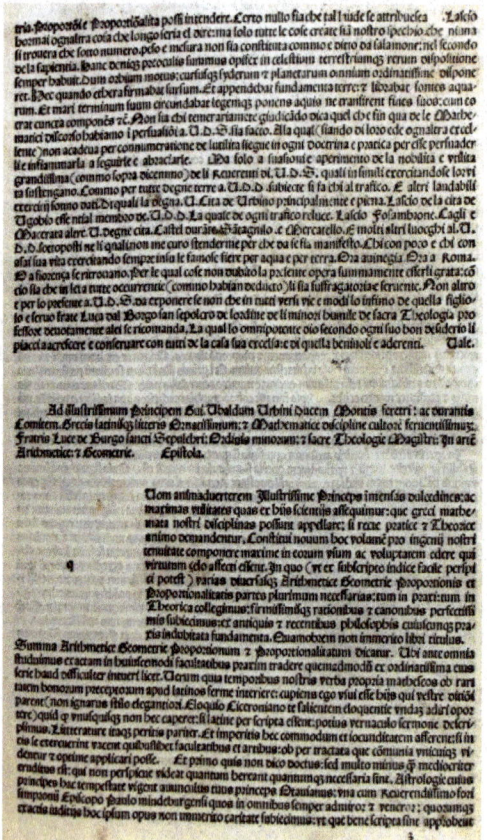

Let all create beings be our mirror, as no one will found to be constituted but as number, weight and measure, as said by Salomon in the second book of the Sapientia[11].

Figure 1.
Plate from the initial part of the dedicatory letter by Pacioli (Pacioli, *Summa*, f. 3r)[12].

---

[8]*De rebus expetendis et fugiendis* consisted of 49 books, 30 on sciences. Valla's book also contains interesting notes on Archimedes' works.

[9]Rose, 1975, p. 110.
[10]Galileo, 1890-1909. See also: Galluzzi & Torrini, 1975-1984; Pisano, 2009d; Pisano & Bussotti, 2012; Marcacci, 2009.
[11]Pacioli, 1494, *Summa*, f. 4r. Evidently, he alludes to the biblical text around I century BC.
[12]Source: Max Planck Institute for the History of science–Echo/Archimedes Project [via http://echo.mpiwg-berlin.mpg.de/content/historymechanics/archimdesecho/archimedes-intro].

It is evident from the large production of the secondary literature with respect since his was more the mentality of the engineer. Leonardo's notebooks are not organized and minor eloquent[13] of the others authors at his time. He was a brilliant scholar, very intelligent and a great worker. His questionable assumptions on mechanics make known how complex, hard and mysterious were the conceptual streams science for its early practitioners. Taking into account that modern historiography (Pisano, 2009 and refs) reached the conviction that Leonardo got his results in part from other sources or that he would have written them previously together with other authors, we can reasonably make the hypothesis that the abundance of materials about his scripts and the lack of it in other cases could also be due to greater care when searching the documents of the brilliant scholar. Therefore it is difficult to make a hypotheses about an artist's inspiration. In fact, without a proper method of historical inquiry it is not so easy to deduce from his manuscripts what one author takes from another and what really represents scientific continuity or discontinuity (Pisano, 2009a, 2009b).

Leonardo's mechanics speeches are effetely scattered notes, often repeated with slight variations, sometimes with inconsistencies. Although attempts were made to reach a chronologically consistent order, the different scholars have not yet obtained results sufficiently shared, also because Leonardo had the habit of putting his hands to the manuscripts and edit them with continuous additions and deletions (Capecchi & Pisano, 2013). The only valid criterion is the search for the logical consistency and the persistence of certain statements over others. For example:

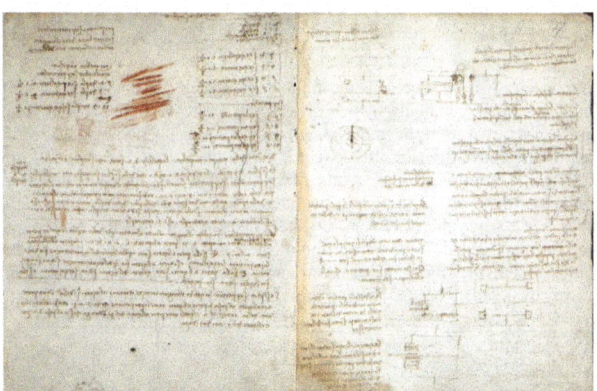

Gravity is an accidental power, which is created by motion and infused into bodies out of their natural site[14].
[...]
Gravity, force and accidental motion (material motion), together with percussion are the four accidental powers, by which all the evident work of mortal beings have their origin and their death[15].

Figure 2.
Studies on gravity and force[16] (da Vinci, *Codex Arundel* f. 37r).

Here Leonardo refers to the four powers (with a modern language, forces). Regarding the gravity it can be said that Leonardo married the Aristotelian thesis considering it as the tendency of bodies to reach their natural place[17]. For Leonardo gravity is caused by motion:

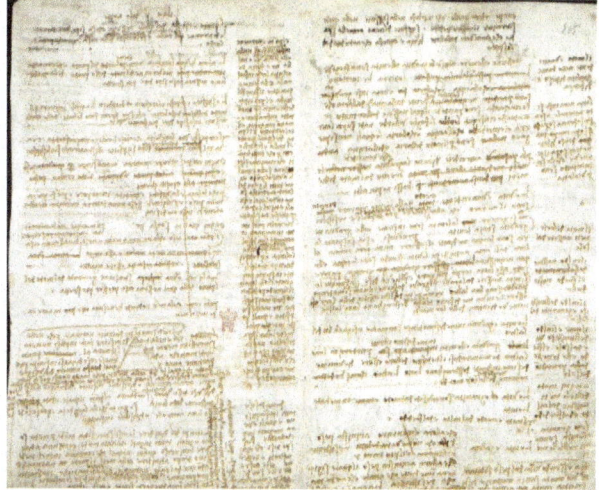

No element has in itself gravity or levity if it does not move. The earth is in contact with the air and water and has in itself neither gravity nor levity; it has not stimulus neither from the water nor from the surrounding air, unless by accident, which originates by motion. And this teaches us the leaves of herbs, born above the earth, which is in contact with the water and the air, which do not bend if not for the motion of air or water[18].
[...]
Gravity be an accident created by the motion of the lower elements into the upper[19].

Figure 3.
Studies on gravity (da Vinci, *Codex Arundel* f. 205r).

In brief, a body shows its gravity if, following an upheaval of the underlying parts, an imbalance of the upper parts is determined (Capecchi & Pisano, 2013). More problematic is the interpretation of the term force. On the purpose, quite clarifying was the following famous quotation, which is interesting from a literary point of view also, as a very effective example of scientific prose, in which studies have suggested the influence of the neo-Platonic philosophy of universal animation (*Ivi*).

It seems the impetus of scholastic conception (i.e., Oresme, Buridanus) which is generated in the bodies by the motion transmitted to it by another body, for example by the hand that launches a stone. Leonardo distinguishes between natural gravity and accidental gravity (Capecchi & Pisano 2013). The former is the ordinary one and is invariant, the latter is not clearly defined or at least is not defined in a unique way. According to Duhem (Duhem, 1905-1906: I, pp. 114-115; Duhem, 1906-1913), this term was used by the schoolmen as a synonym of impetus and Leonardo, following the ideas of Albert of Saxony (ca. 1316-1390) who assumed the natural gravity concentrated in the centre of gravity, would consider also the accidental concentrated in a point, named the centre of accidental gravity:

---

[13]See, e.g., Martini's works on machines with several notes Leonardo da Vinci's hand were re-discovered.
[14]da Vinci, *Codex Arundel* f. 37r. See also: da Vinci, 1940: p 31.
[15]da Vinci, *Codex Forster II*, f. 116v. See also: da Vinci, 1940: p 32.
[16]The *Codex Arundel* is a collection (London, British Library) of papers written in his characteristic left-handed mirror-writing (reading from right to left), including diagrams, drawings and brief texts, covering a broad range of topics in science and art, as well as personal notes. It consist of 283 folia concerning physics-mechanics—and mathematics-optics and Euclidean geometry—(Euclid, 1945) architectural and territorial studies (Pedretti, 1998). Source: London British Library [via http://www.bl.uk/manuscripts].

[17]On that some arguments, sometime *forced* are in: Duhem, 1905-1906: I, pp. 16-17.
[18]da Vinci, *Codex Arundel*, f. 205r. See also: da Vinci, 1940: p 30.
[19]*Ibidem*.

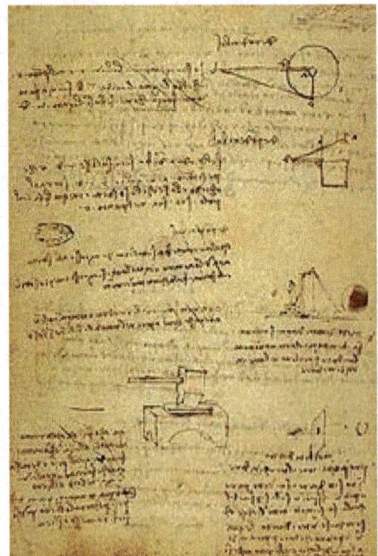

Force I say to be a strong spiritual virtue, an invisible power, which is caused by accidental external violence of motion and placed and infused into bodies, which are moved from their natural habit [the rest] and bent by giving them active life of wonderful power: constrains all created things to change form and site, runs with fury to her desired death and comes diversifying through the causes. Slowness makes her great and quickness weak, she comes into being from violence and dies for freedom and the greater the sooner is she consumed. Drives away in a rage what is opposed to her decay; she wants winning, to kill by her causes any constraints and winning, she kills herself. She becomes stronger where she finds a stronger contrast. Nothing will move without her. The body from which she originates does not change form or weight[20].

Figure 4.
Studies of the equilibrium of weights and of impact ("percossa")[21] (da Vinci, *Ms. A* f. 1v).

Each body has three centres of figure, one of which is a natural centre of gravity, the other of the accidental gravity and the third one of the magnitude[22].

On Leonardo's Approach to Statics Science

Leonardo's contribution to statics (Pisano, 2009a; Capecchi & Pisano, 2007) concerns the rule of composition-decomposition of a force along two given directions. The problem to be solved was to find the tensions of two inclined ropes supporting a weight. The forces of the ropes also were associated with weights[23].

Leonardo besides to formulate the rule also correctly proved it[24]. The analysis of texts has however led us to believe that in this case Marcolongo's analysis is correct and actually Leo-

nardo recognized the rule of weight distribution in two ropes supporting a weight. There are of course, as typical in Leonardo (Pisano, 2009a), situations in which the rule is loosely worded, and sometimes wrongly (Capecchi & Pisano, 2013). However, although there are no certain dating criteria, the analysis of the manuscripts shows a long series of examples with a lot of correct arguments that can leave no doubt that Leonardo reached a conscious knowledge of the rule of composition of forces. The following quotations start from the intuitive finding that the weight distribution depends on the obliquity of the ropes.

> On weight. If two ropes converge to support a heavy body, one of which is vertical the other oblique, the oblique one does not sustain any part of the weight.
> But if two oblique ropes would support a weight, the proportion of weight to weight would be as the obliquity to obliquity.
> For ropes that descend with different obliquity from the same height, to support a weight, the proportion of the accidental weight of the ropes is the same as that of the length of these ropes[25].

Here by using the word *obliquity*, Leonardo rather than to the slope refers to the length of the ropes—see the final part of the previous quotation—while the accidental weight could be understood as the tension of the ropes. The statement is patently incorrect, but one could think that Leonardo had confused and meant to speak of the inverse ratio of obliquity, which is still wrong but at least the tendency is correct. In the following passage Leonardo's is not a typo, because he clearly states that the weight is divided into proportion of the angles formed by the ropes with the vertical, which is clearly false (Capecchi and Pisano 2013):

Let consider two lines concurring in the angle which sustains the weight, if you draw the perpendicular which divides this angle, then the weights [tensions] of the two ropes have the same ratio as that of the two angles generated by the above division. If between the two lines *ac* and *ec*, which form the angle *c*, from which the weight *f* is suspended, the perpendicular *dc* is drawn that divides this angle into two angles *acd* and *dfe*, we say that these ropes will receive the weight in proportion equal to that of the two angles they form and equal to the proportion of the two triangles. And the perpendicular that divides the angle of this triangle will split the gravity suspended in two equal parts, because passing through the centre of such gravity[26].

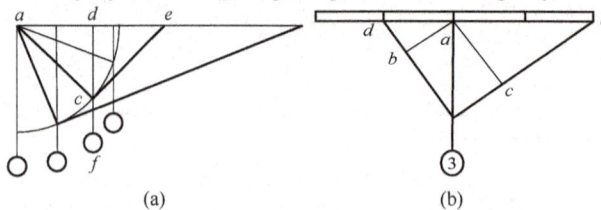

(a)   (b)

Figure 5.
(a) A wrong instance of decomposition of forces[27]; (b) A correct instance of decomposition of forces[28].

It is reasonable to suppose (Capecchi, 2012; Capecchi & Pisano, 2013) that Leonardo might have thought to a weight hanging from the middle of a rope in which the greater the obliquity—i.e. the angle they form with the vertical—the larger the tensions in the rope (*Ivi*).

---

[20]da Vinci, *Ms. A*, f. 34v. See also: da Vinci, 1940: pp. 253-254.
[21]Source: Istituto e Museo di Storia della Scienza, Firenze, Italy [via http://brunelleschi.imss.fi.it].
[22]da Vinci, *Codex Atlanticus* f. 188v (b). See also: da Vinci, 1940: p. 45.
[23]Of course the modern difference between force-weight (vectorial quantity) and mass (scalar quantity) is taken into account.
[24]This is normally not recognized by historians and even Duhem (who did not study the *Codex Arundel*) suggested only as a possibility that Leonardo understood the rule. Marcolongo only asserted with no doubt his priority.

[25]da Vinci Ms. E f. 70 r. See also: da Vinci, 1940: p. 142.
[26]da Vinci, Ms. E f. 71r. See also: da Vinci, 1940: p. 143.
[27]Capecchi & Pisano, 2013.
[28]*Ibidem.*

Marcolongo (Marcolongo, 1932) argues, however, that these wrong results date back to the years before 1508, when Leonardo had not yet reached his final idea which is well expressed in the passage:

> For the sixth and ninth [propositions], the weight 3 does not split into the two real arms of the balance in the same proportion of these arms, but in the proportion of the potential arms[29].

Here Leonardo asserts, without proving it, that the suspended weight is supported by tensions b (left) and c (right) having inverse ratio to the potential arms ab and ac, i.e.: $b:c = a:ab$. The relation, correctly, allows to find the ratio of tensions in the two ropes (Capecchi & Pisano, 2013).

In other *Codex*, Leonardo proves the asserted relation and also indicates the way to evaluate the absolute value of the tension in each rope. He introduces the terms: *potential lever* and *potential counter lever* (*Ivi*). The potential lever corresponds someway to the potential arm, the potential counter lever is the horizontal segment connecting one support of a rope to the vertical from the suspended weight. The reading of the following quotation is useful to illustrate the use of these terms. The potential lever associated to the arm *fm* is *fe*, the potential counter lever is *fa*.

Here the weight is sustained by two powers, i.e. *mf* and *mb*. Now we have to find the potential lever and counter lever of the two powers. The lever *fe* and the counter lever *fa* will correspond to the power *mb*. The appendix *eb* is added to the lever *fe*, which is connected with the engine *b*; and the appendix *ab* is added to the counter lever *fa*, which sustains the weight *n*. By having endowed the balance with the power and the resistance of engine and weight, the proportion between the lever *fe* and the counter lever *ab* should be known. Let *fe* be 21/22 of the counter lever *fa*. Then *b* supports 22 when the weight *n* is 21[30].

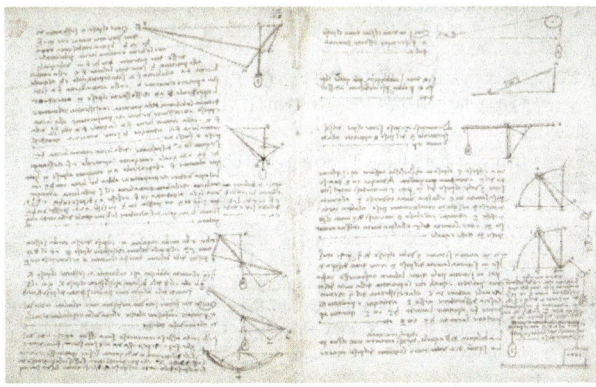

(a)

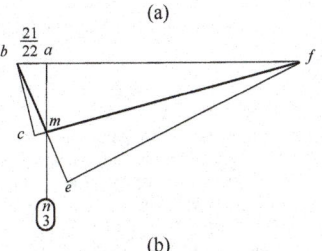

(b)

Figure 6.
(a) Studies on levers[31] (da Vinci, *Codex Arundel* f. 7v); (b) Potential lever and potential counter leve[32].

Attention is centred on the rope *bm* with the aim to find its tension. A similar argumentation can be repeated for the rope *fm*. Basically Leonardo imagines the rope *fm* as *solidified*, i.e. as a rigid beam hinged at *f*. According to his embryonic concept of moment of a force, Leonardo asserts the validity of the following relation: $b:n = fa:fe$, where b is the tension of the rope *bm* and n is the suspended weight. He gives as an example $fa:fe$ $= 21:22$; for $n = 21$ it results $b = 22$. Previous quotation deserves some comments. First: the idea to solidify the rope anticipates what is commonly named solidification principle, according to which if a body is in equilibrium its state is not perturbed by adding additional constraints[33].

In others folia Leonardo da Vinci's observations on beams concern either the axial and flexional behaviour. For this last issue he focused more attention on its buckling. These considerations are interesting though not always formal and precise experimentally.

Finally, Leonardo is more concerned with deformability than strength (Capecchi & Pisano, 2013). The reason could be that he refers mainly to the timber used in building-war-machines and ships.

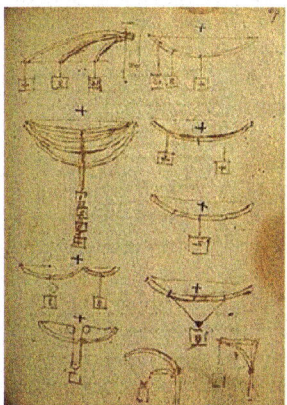 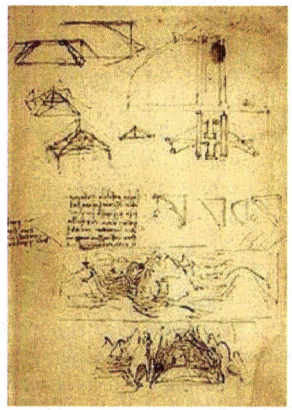

Figure 7.
Studies on beam[34] (da Vinci, *Codex Forster II*, f. 89v).

Figure 8.
Studies of the resistance of arches[35] (da Vinci, *Codex Arundel*, f. 224r).

These beams are very thick and resistant to failure, so they are essentially dimensioned for deformation.

> [A] One beam of 6 braccia is stiffer the double in its middle, than four equal sized beams of 12 braccia joined together[36].

Based on recent researches (Pisano, 2009; Capecchi & Pisano, 2010, 2013), the previous observation of Leonardo is in accordance with modern theory of elasticity of beams: a supported beam of constant section, highlighted l by means of a concentred force f applied to *mezzeria*.

The arrow v is mathematically interpreted by the following formula:

$$v = \frac{1}{48}\frac{fl^3}{EI} \tag{1}$$

[29]da Vinci, *Codex Arundel*, f. 1v. See also: da Vinci, 1940: p. 171.
[30]da Vinci, *Codex Arundel*, f. 7v. See also: da Vinci, 1940: p. 179.
[31]Source: British Library [via http://www.bl.uk/manuscripts].
[32]Capecchi & Pisano, 2013.

[33]This principle has been used to study deformable bodies by many scientists, including Stevin, (Dijksterhuis, 1955), Lagrange, Cauchy, Poinsot, Duhem (Capecchi, 2012; Pisano & Capecchi, 2013).
[34]Source: Istituto e Museo di Storia della Scienza, Firenze, Italy [via http://brunelleschi.imss.fi.it].
[35]*Ibidem*
[36]da Vinci L, *Codex Atlanticus*, f. 211rb, [p. 562r].

where *E* is the longitudinal modulus and *I* the moment of inertia of the section. From the previous track and considering (1), from 6 to 12 arms, that is, doubling the light, the same section and force *f* by formula above the arrow increased 8 times or *rigidezza* (rigidity) decreases 8 times. But 4 of 12 auctions arms absorb each 1/4 of the force *f* to which the arrow of four auctions together is equal to that of an individual charged with 1/4 *f*. The fall of each beam of 12 arms worth 1/4 to 8 times so it is only 2 times that of an arm of 6. It is thus the result of Leonardo in [A].

On Leonardo's Approach to Mathematical Science

Nowadays Leonardo da Vinci's cultural matrix seems clear. Historians agree in considering the Aristotelian physics as the main source of his mechanics. According to such studies from the analysis of *Codex* by Leonardo, it was possible to deduce some of the titles of the manuscripts[37], not entirely scientific, used by Leonardo for the researches: Abū Yūsuf Yaʿqūb ibn Isḥāq al-Kindī (801-873 A.C.) *Libellum sex quantitatum*, Gaius Plinius Secundus called Pliny the Elder (23-79 A.C.), *Naturalis Historia*, Aristotle[38], *De phisica* and *De metheoris*, Euclid, *De ponderibus*, *De levi et ponderoso fragmentum*, John Peckham (1225 ca-1292) *Perspective ciommunis*, Piero de' Crescenzi (1233-1320?) *De Agricultura*, Mondino de' Liuzzi (1270-1326) *Anathomia*, Paolo dell'Abaco (1282-1374) *Recholuzze del maestro Pagolo astrolacho*, Leon Battista Alberti (1404-1472) *De pictura*, Cristoforo Landino (1424-1498) *Formulario di epistole volgari*, Francesco di Giorgio Martini (1439-1501) *Trattato di architettura militare e civile*, Giovanni di Mandinilla, *Tractato delle più maravigliose cosse e più notabili*, Luca Pacioli, *De divina proportione*, and Giorgio Valla (1447-1500) *De expetendis et fugiendis rebus*, etc. Thus, even if Leonardo da Vinci's research works concern almost exclusively the fields he practiced as a technician, a need of a mathematical-geometrical[39] abstraction and of rationalization seems to emerge; apparently neglected until then by technicians, there was an exigency to define technique through observation and the mathematical explanation of phenomena. Nonetheless it is worth remarking that a consequence of this early form of *discontinuity* is the fact that Leonardo da Vinci's method surely did not spring out of nowhere. It is rooted in the scientific tradition of the Aristotelian school, further than in the Archimedean one. More specifically, many are the traces of Aristotle' thought to be found in Leonardo, starting with the concept that the knowledge of *universal things* (*the furthest from our senses, in contrast with the singular things which are the closest to our sensible perception*) is acquired by means of reasoning based on primitive truths that cannot be proved; the latter can be known by induction, that is by means of data of the sensible perception stored in our memory.

At the same time, Leonardo draws on Archimedes' *scientia*,

in particular he shares the methodology based on the mathematical and geometrical study of the equilibrium that is he follows the rational criteria that the mathematician from Syracuse had set to determine the centres of gravity. Thus the relationship between Leonardo and the mathematics were influenced by many factors, especially his close friendship with Luca Pacioli. Nevertheless his results were enough immature with respect to the deep mathematical ideas born by Luca. In the following attempts by Leonardo to work with fractions before his meeting with Luca Pacioli is reported:

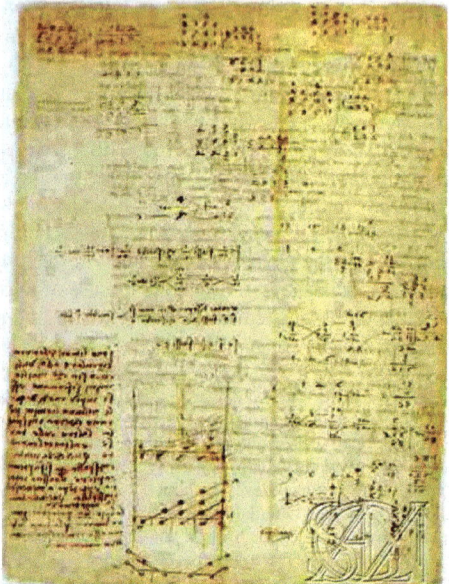

[Leonardo wrote]

"sarà $\frac{12}{12}$ cioè $\frac{1}{0}$ [...]" "[...] $1\frac{1}{12}$,$1\frac{1}{2}$ [...]"

[Then, he correctly transforms in "[...] $\frac{13}{12}$,$\frac{7}{6}$,$\frac{3}{2}$ [...]"

[Now he sums these 3 fractions and obtains:] $\frac{216}{78}$

[Of course the result is wrong. The right one is

$\frac{45}{12}$ that is $\frac{15}{4}$

[He confused "12" as denominator. *Idem* ambiguous calculus are possible to read in the *Codex L*, f. 10v, f. 21v[40] and in the *Codex Atlantico*, f. 665r (Bagni & D'amore, 2007)].

Figure 9.
Rules to calculate fractions (da Vinci, *Codex Atlanticus*[41] f. 191v).

---

[37]Leonardo did not finish his speeches on *On the sky* (*Sul cielo*) and *On the world* (*Sul mondo*) would have to combine the researches of astronomy to those of geology. The few notes that there are often appear contradictory: on the one hand they show that Leonardo believed the Earth at the center of the system, on the other hand sometimes express concern about the motion of the Sun. In some passages only the comments around celestial bodies was then reduced to issues of lighting, within art and science speculations.

[38]See also: Aristotle, 1853, 1949, 1955a, 1955b, 1963, 1984, 1996, 1999; Cartelon.

[39]An interesting work on geometry during Islam period is Maitte, 2003.

[40]The *Codex L* is part of a set of manuscripts: *A, B, C, D, E, F, G, H, I, K, L, M*. They are archived at the Institute of France, Paris (France). They consist of twelve manuscripts, some bound in parchment, leather or cardboard. They have different sizes, the smaller one is the number M (10 × 7 cm), the larger one is C (31.5 × 22 cm). By convention each of them are named by a letter of the alphabet, from A to M (omitting J), for a total of 964 folia. The topics covers from military art, optics, geometry, hydraulic and flight of birds. A probably date might be fl. 1492-1516. Source: Istituto e Museo di Storia della Scienza, Firenze, Italy [via http://brunelleschi.imss.fi.it].

[41]The codex is the largest collection of Leonardo's sheets (end of the sixteenth century by the sculptor Pompeo Leoni (1531-1608) who dismembered many original notebooks. ca. 1478-1518 and consists of 1119 sheets. It is archived in *Biblioteca Ambrosiana* Milano, Italy and contains studies on science and technology, architectural projects, town planning, biographical records and personal notes. Source: Biblioteca Ambrosiana [via http://www.ambrosiana.eu].

On the Scientific Relationship between Leonardo and Luca

By considering the complexity and the huge literature on Pacioli's mathematics, before focusing on Pacioli-da Vinci scientific relationship, just few notes on Pacioli's arithmetical approach are reported.

The theory of proportions[42] plays a central role in the project of mathematization of knowledge proposed by Pacioli. It is interesting to remark the fifth[43] book of Euclid's *Elements*. It derived and commented by second part of the *VI Distinction* in the *Summa de arithmetica, geometria, proportioni et proporzionalità* (1494) where Pacioli claims his definitions of proportionality[44].

> If you well study, in all arts, you will found the proportion as the mother and queen of all of them, and without it you cannot exertion[45].

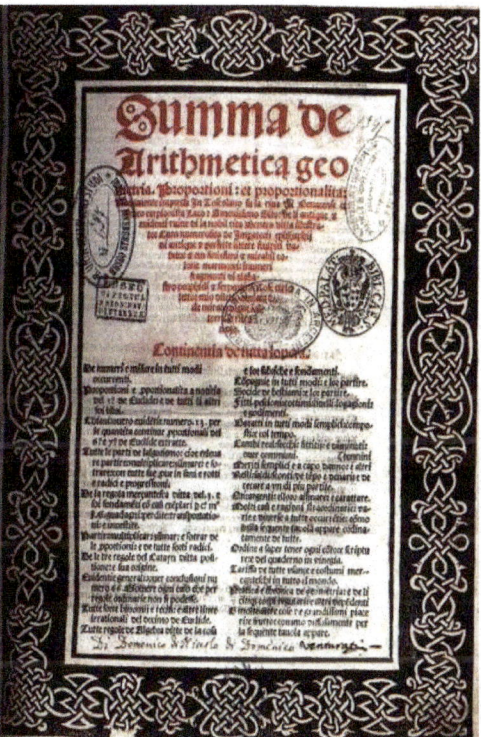

Figure 10.
Plate from *Summa* by Pacioli (Pacioli, *Summa*, f. 1r)[46].

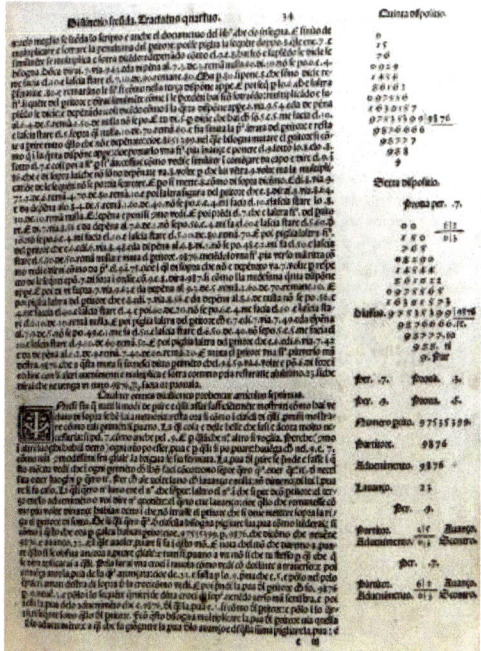

Figure 11.
Mathematical arguing in Pacioli's *Summa* (Pacioli, *Summa*, f. 34r)[47].

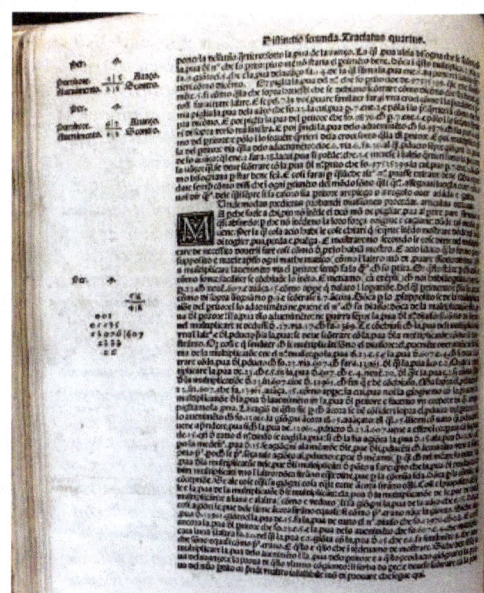

In a modern formalism. Given four proportional quantities
$$x{:}y = z{:}w$$
being m equimultiple of the first and third, and being n equimultiple for the second and fourth, one obtain:
$$ma = ny \text{ and } mz < nw$$
$$ma > ny \text{ and } mz = nw$$
$$ma > ny \text{ and } mz < nw$$
$$ma > ny \text{ and } mz > nw \text{ with } mx/ny > mz/nw$$
$$ma < ny \text{ and } mz < nw \text{ with } mx/ny < mz/nw$$

Figure 12.
Mathematical arguing in Pacioli's *Summa* (Pacioli, *Summa*, f. 34v)[48].

---

[42]Since the literature on Pacioli is very large, some examples and maybe more adequate arguments are reported only.
[43]In *vulgare* text by Federico Commandino (1509-1575) the definitions are: "[V, Def. 5] Magnitudes are said to be *in the same ratio*, the first to the second and the third to the fourth, when, if any equimultiples whatever are taken of the first and third, and any equimultiples whatever of the second and fourth, the former equimultiples alike exceed, are alike equal to, or alike fall short of, the latter equimultiples respectively taken in corresponding order [...]. [V, Def. 6] Let magnitudes which have the same ratio be called *proportional.*" (Commandino, 1575, Defs. 5-6; see also Commandino, 1565).
[44]"Dico con Euclide in quinto proportionalità in communi ene solo similitudine de più proportioni e al manco de doi" (Pacioli, *Summa*, 72v).
[45]Pacioli, *Summa*, 78v.
[46]Source: Max Planck Institute for the History of science– Echo/Archimedes Project [via
http://echo.mpiwg-berlin.mpg.de/content/historymechanics/archimdesecho/archimedes-intro].

[47]Source: *Ibidem.*
[48]*Ibidem.*

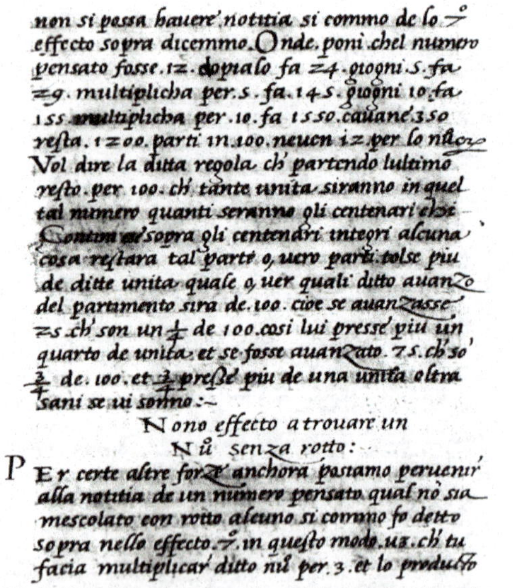

non si possa hauere notitia si commo de lo effecto sopra dicemmo. Onde poni chel numero pensato fosse 12. doptralo fa 24. qtogni s. fa 9. multiplicha per s. fa 145. qtogni 10 fa 155 multiplicha per 10. fa 1550. cauane 350 resta 1200. parti in 100. neuen 12 per lo nůeu Vol dire la ditta reqola ch' partendo lultimo resto per 100. ch' tante unita siranno in quel tal numero quanti seranno qli centenari ebi Contien sopra qli centendri integri alcuna cosa restara tal parti o uero parti tolse piu de ditte unita quale o uer quali ditto auanzo del partamento sira de 100. cioe se auanzasse s ch' son un ¼ de 100. cosi lui presse piu un quarto de unita et se fosse auanzato 75. ch' so ¾ de 100. et ½ presse piu de una unita oltra sani se ui sonno.

Nono effecto a trouare un Nů senza rotto:

PEr certe altre forze anchora possamo peruenir alla notitia de un numero pensato qual no sia mescolato con rotto alcuno si conuno fo detto sopra nello effecto. in questo modo ua ch' tu facia multiplicar ditto nů per 3. et lo productoò

Ninth effect for seeking a number without fraction [*rotto*]: [In modern language, given *x*, by using Fibonacci, we can calculate:] [...]

$$\frac{3\dfrac{3x}{2}}{9} = \frac{x}{4}$$

Figure 13.
On the fractions (Pacioli, *Viribus*, 20v, 21r)[49].

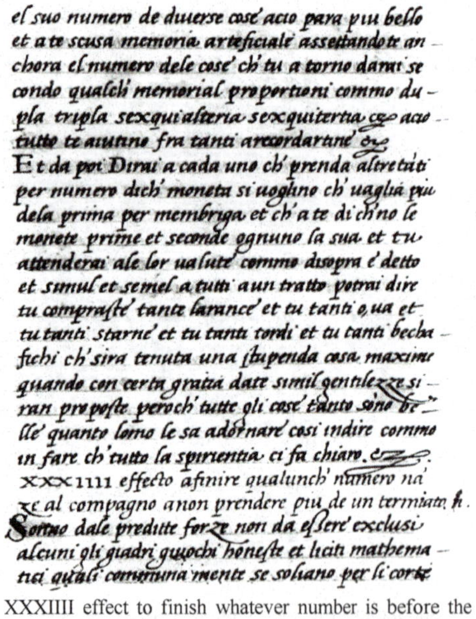

el suo numero de diuerse cose acio para piu bello et a te scusa memoria arteficiale assettandote anchora el numero dele cose ch' tu a torno darni secondo qualch memorial proportioni commo dupla tripla sexquialtera sexquitertia ce acio tutte te aiutino fra tanti arecordartene ce Et da poi Dirai a cada uno ch' prenda altretati per numero dich' moneta si uoglino ch' uaglia piu dela prima per membriga et ch' a te di ch' no le monete prime et seconde ognuno la sua et tu attenderai ale lor ualute commo disopra è detto et simul et semel a tutti a un tratto potrai dire tu comprasti tante larance et tu tanti o ua et tu tanti starne et tu tanti tordi et tu tanti becha fichi ch' sira tenuta una stupenda cosa maxime quando con certa graiza date simil gentilezze si ran proposte peroch' tutte qli cose tante sono belle quanto lomo le sa adornare cosi indire commo in fare ch' tutto la spirientia ci fa chiaro ce ce xxx 1111 effecto afinire qualunch' numero na ce al compagno a non prendere piu de un terminato h. Sonno dale predicte forze non da essere exclusi alcuni qli quadri qiuochi honeste et liciti mathematici aquali comunamente se soliano per li corte

XXXIIII effect to finish whatever number is before the company, not taking more than a limiting number. [...] [For example two persons must reach 30 by summing alternatively numbers between 1 and 6. The one who reaches 30 wins. The artifice consists in making choice of the numbers 2, 9, 16, 23. Indeed, if I reach 23, as my opponent can only add a number between 1 and 6, he will reach at most 29 and I just have to add 1 to win. We find the other safe numbers with backward reasoning].

Figure 14.
On the recreational maths games (Pacioli, *Viribus*, 73v-74r)[50].

[49]Source: Biblioteca Universitaria di Bologna [via http://www.uriland.it/matematica/DeViribus].
[50]*Ibidem.*

With concern Leonardo, he wrote down earlier meeting with Pacioli, transcripts of his handful of whole passages of the Summa. On 10th November 1494, in Venice, finally released in print in Latin, Luca Pacioli's *Summa arithmetic, geometry, proportions et proportionality*. Luca inspired Leonardo, and he was counselor, teacher and translator. Leonardo bought *Summa* (119 *soldi*) as he claimed (da Vinci, *Codex Atlanticus*, f. 288r f. 104r, f. 331 r) and notes: "Learn multiplication of the roots by master Luca" (da Vinci, *Codice Atlanticus*, f. 331r [120r]). Thus, from 1496 to 1504 Leonardo studied Luca Pacioli's works and summarizes his theory of proportions (da Vinci, *Codex Madrid*, 8936). Based on that, he expressed his interest in geometry expressing both in the drawings for *De divina proportione* ([1496-98] 1509), that for his readings on Euclid (clearly only for first 6 books and part of the tenth. Leonardo faced the problem of irrational numbers, the ratio between incommensurable segments, side and diagonal of the square, the radius and the circumference and the problem of the so-called deaf roots (*radici sorde*).

Thus, after his meeting (1496) with Luca, Leonardo was busy in geometry and mechanics adopting new mathematical and geometrical assumptions forwarded by *Maestro* Luca. In the following examples on geometrical and mechanical problems are reported:

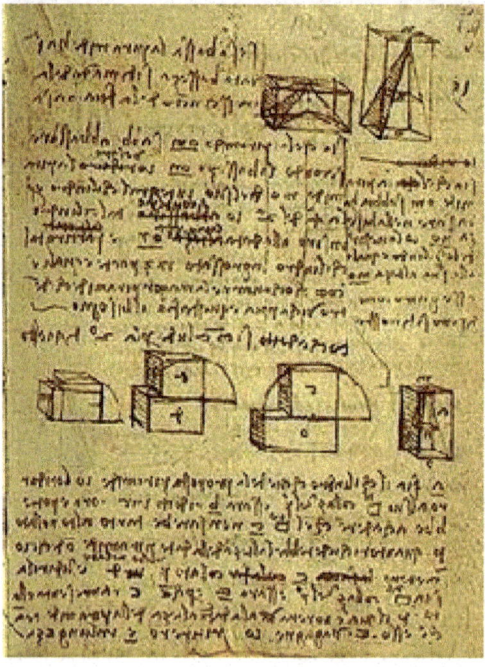

Figure 15.
Stereometric studies after Leonardo and Luca meeting[51] (da Vinci, *Codex Forster I*, f. 19r).

Particularly geometrical figures were presented for the first time in the *Codex Forster*[52] and finally included *De divina proportione* (1498) are evident examples.

[51]Source: Istituto e Museo di Storia della Scienza, Firenze, Italy [via http://brunelleschi.imss.fi.it].
[52]This *Codex Forster* is composed of two manuscripts totalling 159 leaves. The Ms. I (1497) presents studies of mechanics, ornamental knots and plaits and of architecture. The Ms II (1495) records Leonardo's research in physics and mechanics (force, gravity, weight and movement). Particularly the *Codex Forster I* from f. 14r to f. 22r includes speeches on *Summa*'s theory.

Generally speaking, Leonardo tried to develop a process of theoretical and experimental research (Rogers) that starts from tasks and requirements of a practical nature and then develops theoretical considerations, compared with the classical and medieval primary sources of scientific knowledge, to be verified experimentally, in order to build up general mathematical rules applicable to specific cases. Particularly he used pragmatic and realistic approach to the mathematical problems. Leonardo does not seek absolute rigour in the results of his research, but an approximation recognized as useful, clearly an attempt to rationalize all human activities, including his own (Pisano, 2009; Pisano & Rougetet, 2013).

With Leonardo, it very often recurs, perhaps for the first time, the idea of an absolutely efficient *building-machine* (Pedretti, 1978, 1999). Within it daily activities are made rational and mechanic: e.g. a fireplace automatically operated, a laundry, the model of a stable. The building is conceived as a *living organism* but, at the same time, in a sense, taking Vitruvio' concepts to the extreme, he suggests also the way round. In other words, living organisms too—men and animals—are turned into *machines*. In this sense, he detects in any organism, living or not, a unity of process and function based on movement and considers animals as a human body and buildings as a whole of mechanical devices, that he calls *elementi macchinali* (*machineries*) *Bird is a device performing after a mathematical law and nature cannot make animals move without mechanical devices* Leonardo da Vinci's considerations around such *mechanical elements* and his studies of anatomy are really interesting, proving study and performance methods very similar. This *uniformity of treatment* emerges in his drawings as well, either anatomic, where bones and muscles are handled as geometrical schemes of *ingegni*[53], or of machines and tools, in which relevant specific elements insist, such as the cannons-columns[54] that seem to claim the universality of the planning project. Thus, it is evident that the studies by Leonardo represent an important and partly correct attempt to formulate a general theoretical organization involving greater formalization—than his predecessors—which can clear up and preview, e.g. the deformability of bodies in mechanics and architecture. One of his aims was to avoid further planning mistakes to ensure the proper functioning of the *building-human organism* and of the *building-machine*[55].

Unlike Leonardo, Luca implemented an *artimetization* of the theory of proportions (Pacioli's Summa, 77-78rv) which is based on the *Book V*, and above based on the *Book VII* (the first of the three arithmetic books of the *Elements*) that provided to use the proportions in practical scope of the calculation, and using the concept of *denominator*. The subject of the proportions is the core of the scientific program of *mathematization* pursued by Luca. The latter adopted a practice to use ratio by the denominators, since he frequently adopted Euclidean definitions of in the seventh book of the *Elements*, equivalently of practice use adopted at that time by non mathematicians, that is by philosophers. At that stage he uses which the selected list of names as presented in the *Arbor proportionis*.

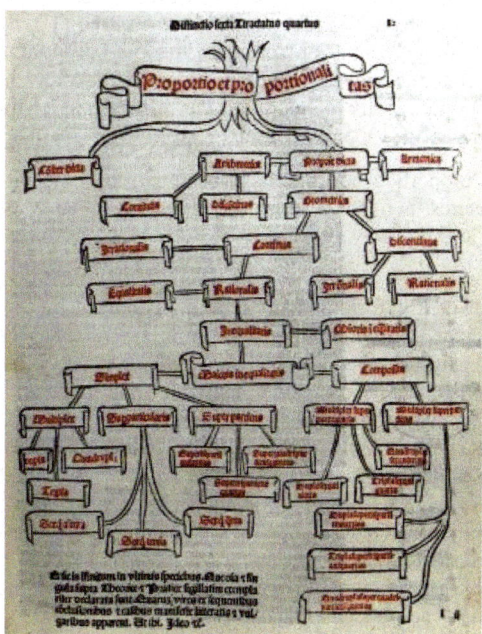

Figure 16.
The *Arbor proportionis et proportionalitatis* by Pacioli (Pacioli, *Summa*, f. 82r).

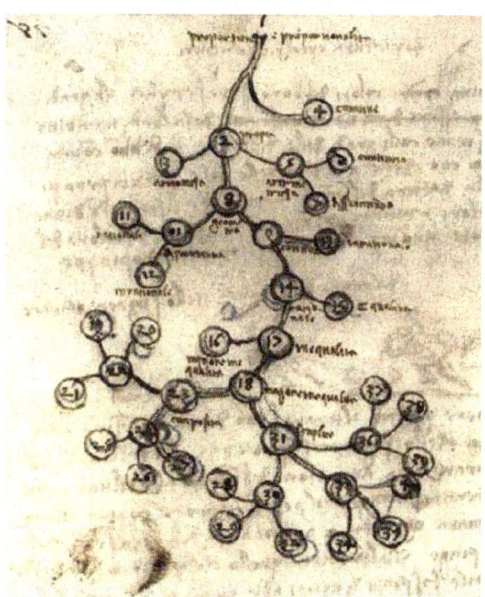

Figure 17.
The *Arbor proportionis et proportionalitatis* by Leonardo (adapted by Pacioli's *Arbor*) (da Vinci, *Codex Madrid*, Ms. II, f. 78r)[56].

___

[53]da Vinci, *Codex Windsor*, RL 12656; see also f. 17r.

[54]da Vinci, *Codex Atlanticus*, f. 28v.

[55]In this way he is remote from his contemporaries. Later, toward the end of the Renaissance this new way to decide the theory that assumed a particular cultural value mainly proceeding towards an *analytical* perspective of conceiving mechanics that seemed to be coming to a crossroads: *physical or mathematical science*? That way another historiographic problem emerges (Pisano, 2009; Pisano & Gaudiello, 2009): a crucial continuity-discontinuity problem appears when a theory is included in another theory, e.g. mathematics in mechanics (*rational mechanics*), astronomy in mechanics (*celestial mechanics*) mathematics in thermodynamics (analytical theory of heat), mechanics in engineering (*structural mechanics*).

[56]The *Codex Madrid* is a recent Codex rediscovered in 1966 consists of 157 folia concerning Leonardo's activity in Firenze on plans for military architecture carried out (Piombino), maps of the Tuscan region, notes on painting and studies of optics. A final booklet, arbitrarily attached to the manuscript, contains Leonardo's studies (1491-1493) for the casting of the equestrian monument to Francesco Sforza.

Leonardo is interested in Pacioli's works and reported it his three codes (da Vinci, *Madrid II, Forster II* (1°); *Id., Ms. K*. The *Codex Madrid II* (da Vinci, *Codex Madrid II*, Ms. 8936), contains from folio 46v to folio 50r, a summary of the *Sixth distinction* of the Pacioli's *Summa*, dedicated to the proportions and proportionality. In fact, the *Codex Forster II* (1°), by folio 14r to folio 22r contains notes on the theory of proportions that lead back to the *Summa*. Finally in the *Ms. K* (da Vinci, *Ms. K*), dotted by numerous references to the propositions of Euclid's Elements (*Book V*), one can read:

> The proportion is not only to be found in numbers and measures, but also in sounds, weights, intervals of time, and in every active force in existence[57].

The sentences belongs to *Summa* by Pacioli (Pacioli, *Summa*, f. 69r) which in turn, he belongs to the comment by Campano adapted for his Euclidean work (Pacioli, *Euclidis*, f. 32rv-33r). With regard to the geometry, Leonardo was interested in construction of regular polygons with ruler and compass, rather that problems of constructing a square sum of two data. On can see, e.g., the problem by dividing the circumference in 3, 4, 5, 6, 7, 8 equal parts up to the maximum of 48 sides (da Vinci *Codex Atlanticus*, f. 11v). The speech are randomly distributed in the manuscripts where few precise explanations are proposed by Leonardo only adding by *ragione* (*reasoning*, a sort of proof). In effect they are not really proofs, rather they are fast explanations (da Vinci, *Codex Forster III*, fs. 68v-69r).

Final Remarks

Finally, Leonardo met Luca in Milan (1496). The friendship and mutual respect between the two are very strong as Pacioli wrote in the first pages of *De divina proportione* around a scientific challenge (*duello scientifico*) that took place at the court of Ludovico il Moro on the February 9, 1498, (clergy, theologians, doctors, engineers and inventors of new things and Leonardo shared it). Leonardo learnt concepts, methods, proofs and *avversaria* for the statement to refute (*inimica*). The geometry of Leonardo is therefore more cultured, and obtained by Pacioli (and indirectly by Euclid). In particular, golden section presented to him by Luca, who calls it *Divine proportione*.

Very known are the drawings of Leonardo in the divine proportion by Luca so I avoided to be reported.

Acknowledgements

I would like to thank the two reviewers for their valuable comments and suggestions to improve the quality of my paper.

REFERENCES

Abattouy, M. (2006). The Arabic transformation of mechanics: The birth of science of weights. *Foundation for Science Technology and Civilisation, 615,* 1-25

Abattouy, M., Jurgen, R., & Weinig, P. (2001) Transmission as transformation: The translation movements in the Medieval East and West in a comparative perspective. *Science in Context, 14,* 1-12.

Archimedes (1558). *Archimedis opera non nulla a Federico Commandino Urbinate nuper in latinum conversa et commentariis illustrata.* Apud Paulum Manutium, Aldi F. Venetiis

Archimedes (2002). On the equilibrium of planes. In T. L. Heath (Ed.), *The works of Archimedes* (pp 189-220). New York: Dover.

Aristotle (1853). On the definition and division of principles. In: O. F. P. Owen (Ed.), *The organon, Or logical treatises, of Aristotle* (pp. 263-266). London: Bohn H G.

Aristotle (1949). *Aristotle's prior and posterior analytics. A revised text with introduction and commentary.* Oxford: The Oxford University Press.

Aristotle (1955a). *De caelo.* The Tech Classics Archive of M.I.T

Aristotle (1955b). *Mechanical problems.* In: W. S. Hett (Ed.), *Aristotle. Minor works.* Cambridge: William Heinemann.

Aristotle (1963). *Minor works.* Heinemann, Cambridge, London: The Harvard University Press.

Aristotle (1984). *The complete works of Aristotle.* Princeton: The Princeton University Press.

Aristotle (1996). The principles of nature-physics. Oxford: The Oxford University Press.

Aristotle (1999). *Physics.* Oxford: The Oxford University Press.

Bagni, G. T., & D'Amore, B. (2007). Leonardo e la matematica. In: I. Marazzani (Ed.), *La matematica e la sua didattica* (pp. 3-7). Bologna: Pitagora.

Bellucci, G. B. (1598). *Nuoua Inventione di fabricar Fortezze, di varie Forme in qualunque sito di piano, di monte, in acqua, con diuersi disegni, et un trattato del modo, che si ha da osseruare in esse, con le sue misure, et ordine di levar lepiante, tanto in fortezze reali, quanto non reali.* Venezia: Roberto Meietti.

Biagioli, M. (2003). Galileo e Derrida: Il libro della natura e la logica del supplemento. In *Rinascimento ser* (pp. 205-232). Firenze: Olschki.

Brown, E. J. (1967-1968). *The scientia de ponderibus in the later Middle Ages.* Ph.D. Dissertation, Madison: University of Winscosin .

Busard, H. L. L. (2005). *Introduction to the text. Campanus of Novara and Euclid's elements I.* Stuttgart: Franz Steiner Verlag.

Capecchi, D. (2011). Weight as active or passive principle in the Latin and Arabic scientia de ponderibus. *Organon, 43,* 29-58

Capecchi, D. (2012). *The history of virtual work laws.* Basel: Springer.

Capecchi, D, & Pisano, R. (2007). Torricelli e la teoria dei baricentri come fondamento della statica. *Physis, XLIV,* 1-29

Capecchi, D., & Pisano, R. (2008). La meccanica in Italia nei primi anni del Cinquecento. Il contributo di Niccolò Tartaglia. In *Proceedings of XXV SISFA Congress* (pp. C17.1-C17.6). Milano: University of Milano.

Capecchi, D., & Pisano, R. (2010a). *Scienza e tecnica nell'architettura del Rinascimento.* Roma: CISU.

Capecchi, D., & Pisano, R. (2010b). Reflections on Torricelli's principle in mechanics. *Organon, 42,* 81-98.

Capecchi, D., & Pisano, R. (2013). *Tartaglia's science of weights. The Mechanics in XVI century.* Dordrecht: Springer

Cartelon, H. (1975). Does Aristotle have a mechanics? In Barnes et al. (Eds.), *Articles on Aristotle. Vol. I: Science.* London: Duckworth.

Clagett, M. (1959). *The science of mechanics in the Middle Ages.* Madison: The University of Wisconsin Press.

Clagett, M. (1964-1984). *Archimedes in the Middle Ages, Madison-Philadelphia, memoirs of the American Philosophical Society.* Oxford: The Clarendon University Press.

Clagett, M., & Moody, E. (1960). *The medieval science of weights. Scentia de ponderibus.* Madison: The University of Wisconsin Press.

Comandino, F. (1565). *Federici commandini vrbinatis liber de centro gravitatis solidorum.* Bononiae: Ex Officina Alexandri Benacii.

Comandino, F. (1575). De gli elementi di Euclide libri quindici. Con gli scholii antichi. Tradotti prima in lingua latina da m. Federico Commandino da Vrbino, & con commentarij illustrati, et hora di ordine delli istesso trasportati nella nostra vulgare, et da lui riueduti in Vrbino: appresso Domenico Frisolino In Vrbino: in casa di Federico Commandino.

da Vinci, L. (1940). *I libri di meccanica nella ricostruzione ordinata di Arturo Uccelli preceduti da una introduzione critica e da un esame delle fonti.* Milano: Hoepli.

dal Monte, G. (1581). *Le Meccaniche dell'Illustrissimo Sig. Guido Ubaldo dè Marchesi del Monte, tradotto in volgare dal Sig. Filippo*

---

[57]da Vinci, *Ms K*, f. 49r; see also *Codex Forster I*, folia. 1-40.

Pigafetta. Venezia: Evangelista Deuchino.

dal Monte, G. (1588). *In duos Archimedis aequeponderantium libros paraphrasis.* Pisauri: Hieronymum Concordiam.

de Ridder-Symoens, H. (1992). *A history of the university in Europe. Vol. I. Universities in the Middle Ages.* Cambridge: The Cambridge University Press.

Dijksterhuis, E. J. (1957). *Archimedes.* New York: The Humanities Press.

Dijksterhuis, E. J. (1955). *The principal works of Simon Stevin, vol. I.* Amsterdam: C. V. Swets & Seitlinger.

Drachmann, A. G. (1967-1968). Archimedes and the science of physics. *Centaurus, 12,* 1-11.

Duhem, P. M. (1905-1906). *Les origines de la statique* 2 vol. Paris: Hermann.

Duhem, P. M. (1906-1913). *Etudes sur Léonard de Vinci.* Paris: Hermann.

Euclid (1945) The optics of euclid. Trans. by Burton, H. E. *Journal of the optical society, 35,* 357-372.

Galileo, G. (1890-1909). *Le opere di Galileo Galileo: Edizione nazionale sotto gli auspici di sua maestà il re d'Italia.* Firenze: Barbera.

Galluzzi, P. (1988). *Leonardo da Vinci: Engineer and Architect.* Montreal: Montreal Museum of Fine Arts.

Galluzzi, P., & Torrini, M. (1975-1984). *The works of Galileo Galilei's disciples 2 Vols. Correspondence.* Firenze: Gunti-Barbera (In Italian).

Gille, B. (1966). *Engineers of the renaissance.* Cambridge, MA: MIT Press.

Grendler, P. F. (2002). *The universities of the Italian renaissance.* Baltimora: The Johns Hopkins University Press.

Hall, B. S. (1997). *Weapons & warfare in renaissance Europe.* Baltimore: The John's Hopkins University Press.

Harrison, P. (2006). The book of nature and early modern science. In: K. van Berkel, & A. Vanderjagt (Eds.), *Book of nature in early modern and modern history* (pp. 1-26). Leuven: Peeters.

Heath, T. L. (2002). *The works of Archimedes.* New York: Dover Publications Inc.

Hero, A. (1575). *Heronis alexandrini spiritalium liber. A federico commandino urbinate, ex graeco, nuper in latinum conversus.* Urbini: Frisolino Domenico.

Hero, A. (1893). Les mécaniques ou l'élévateur de Héron d'Alexandrie Arabic text and French translation by Carrà de Vaux. *Journal Asiatique, 9,* 386-472.

Heron, A. (1900). Herons von Alexandria Mechanik und Katoptrik. In L. Nix, & W. Schmidt (Eds.), *Heronis Alexandrini opera quae supersunt omnia.* Leipzig: Teubner.

Heron, A. (1999). *Heron alexandrinus mechanica.* English translation by Jutta Miller.
http://archimedes.mpiwg-berlin.mpg.de/cgi-bin/toc/toc.cgi

Jesseph, D. M. (2004). Galileo, Hobbes and the book of nature. *Perspectives on science, 12,* 191-211.

Knorr, W. R. (1978-1979). Archimedes and the "elements": Proposal for a revised chronological ordering of the Archimedean corpus. *Archive for History of Exact Science, 19,* 211-290.

Knorr, W. R. (1985). Archimedes and the pseudo-Euclidean 'catoptrics': Early stages in the ancient geometric theory of mirrors. *International Archive on the History Science, 35,* 114-115; [1986] 28-105.

Kusukawa, S. (2012). *Picturing the book of nature: Image, text and argument in sixteenth-century human anatomy and medical botany.* Chicago, IL: The Chicago University Press.

Locqueneux, R. (2009). *Une histoire des idées en physique. Vol. 57. Cahiers d'histoire et de philosophie des sciences.* Paris: Vuibert.

Maitte, B. (2003). *La géométrie dans les arts décoratifs islamiques.* Le Caire: CFCC.

Marcacci, F. (2009). *Galileo Galilei, sidereus nuncius. Traduzione e commento di giustini PA.* Roma: The Lateran University Press.

Marcolongo, R. (1932). *La meccanica di Leonardo da Vinci.* Napoli: Stabilimento Industrie Editoriali Mendionali. [Id. 1937 (1937). *Studi vinciani. Memorie sulla geometria e la meccanica di Leonardo da Vinci.* Napoli: Stabilimento Industrie Editoriali Meridionali.

Numbers, R. L. (2006). Reading the book of nature through American lenses. In K. van Berkel, & A. A. Vanderjagt (Eds.), *Book of nature in early modern and modern history* (pp. 261-274). Leuven: Peeters.

Van Ophuijsen, J. M. (2005). The two fold action of mind in Aristotle's proto-book of nature. In K, van Berkel, & A. Vanderjagt (Eds.), *Book of nature in antiquity and the Middle Ages* (pp. 1-12). Leuven: Peeters.

Othman, A. (1949.) *Farabi: La statistique des sciences.* (2 ed.). Cairo: Dar al-fikr al-'arabi.

Pacioli, L. (1494). *Summa de arithmetica, geometria, proportioni et proporzionalità.* Venezia: Paganino de' Paganini.

Pacioli, L. (1496-1508). *De viribus quantitatis.* Bibliotheca: University of Bologna.

Pacioli, L. (1509). *De divina proportione opera a tutti gli'ingegni perspicaci e curiosi necessaria* [...]. Venezia: Paganino de' Paganini.

Pacioli, L. (1509). *Euclidis megarensis, philosophi acutissimi mathematicorumque omnium sine controversia principis, opera a Campano interprete fidissimo tra[s]lata..* [...]. Venezia: Paganino de' Paganini.

Pappus, A. (1588). *Mathematica collectiones a Federico Commandino urbinate in latinum conversae.* Pisauri: Hieronimum concordiam.

Pappus, A. (1970). *The Arabic version of the mathematical collection of Pappus Alexandrinus Book VIII.* Ph.D. Dissertation. Cambridge: The University of Cambridge Press.

Pedersen, O. (1992). *The book of nature.* Città del Vaticano: The Vatican Observatory Publications.

Pedretti, C. (1978). *Leonardo architetto.* Milano: Electa. [Id., 1999 Leonardo. Le macchine, Giunti Editore, Firenze 1999; et refs. on Codex]

Pedretti, C. (1998). *Leonardo da Vinci, Il codice arundel 263 nella British library. 2 vols.* Firenze: Giunti.

Pisano, R. (2013b). Historical and epistemological reflections on the principle of virtual laws. Submitted to *Archive Internationales d'Histoire des Science.*

Pisano, R., & Capecchi, D. (2013b-forthcoming). *Conceptual and mathematical structures of mechanical science between 18th and 19th centuries.* Almagest, in Press.

Pisano, R. (2007). Brief history of centre of gravity theory. Epistemological notes. In M. Kokowski (Ed.), *Proceedings of the 2nd ESHS Congress* (pp. 934-941). Krakow.

Pisano, R. (2009a). Continuity and discontinuity. On method in Leonardo da Vinci' mechanics. *Organon, 41,* 165-182.

Pisano, R. (2009b). Il ruolo della scienza archimedea nei lavori di meccanica di Galilei e di Torricelli. In E. Giannetto, G. Giannini, D. Capecchi, & R. Pisano (Eds.), *Proceedings of XXVI SISFA Congress* (pp. 65-74). Rimini: Guaraldi Editore.

Pisano, R. (2009c). On method in Galileo Galilei' mechanics. In H. Hunger (Ed.), *Proceedings of ESHS 3rd Conférence* (pp. 147-186). Vienna: Austrian Academy of Science.

Pisano, R. (2009d). Galileo Galileo. Riflessioni epistemologiche sulla resistenza dei corpi. In E. Giannetto, G. Giannini, & M. Toscano (Eds.), *Relatività, Quanti Chaos e altre Rivoluzioni della Fisica* (61-72). Rimini: Guaraldi Editore.

Pisano, R. (2011). Physics-mathematics relationship. Historical and epistemological notes. In E. Barbin, M. Kronfellner, & C. Tzanakis (Eds.), *European Summer University history and epistemology in mathematics* (pp. 457-472). Vienna: Verlag Holzhausen GmbH-Holzhausen Publishing Ltd.

Pisano, R., & Bussotti, P. (2012). Galileo and Kepler. On theoremata circa centrum gravitates solidorum and mysterium cosmographicum. *History Research, 2,* 110-145.

Pisano, R., & Capecchi, D. (2009). *Il ruolo della meccanica ne le fortificationi di Buonaiuto Lorini* (pp 797-808). Napoli: Cuzzolin Editore.

Pisano, R., & Capecchi, D. (2010a) Galileo Galilei: Notes su trattato di fortificazione. In A. Altamore, & G. Antonini (Eds.), *Galileo and the Renaissance Scientific Discourse* (pp. 28-41). Roma: Edizioni Nuova Cultura.

Pisano, R., & Capecchi, D. (2010b) On Archimedean roots in Torricelli's mechanics. In S. A. Paipetis, & M. Ceccarelli (Eds.), *The genius of Archimedes. Proceeding of an internal conference* (pp.

17-28). Syracuse.

Pisano,R., & Capecchi, D. (2008). La meccanica in Italia nei primi anni del Cinquecento. Il contributo di Niccolò Tartaglia. In P. Tucci (Ed.), *Proceedings of XXV SISFA Congress* (pp. C171-C176). Milano. http://www.brera.unimi.it/sisfa/atti/index.html

Pisano, R., & Capecchi, D. (2009). Il ruolo della meccanica ne Le fortificationi di Buonaiuto Lorini In Cuzzolin (Ed.), *3 Convegno di Storia dell'ingegneria*, vol. II (pp. 797-808). Napoli.

Pisano, R., & Gaudiello, I. (2009). Continuity and discontinuity. An epistemological inquiry based on the use of categories in history of science. *Organon, 41*, 245-265.

Pisano, R., & Rougetet, L. (2013-forthcoming). *Quelles mathématiques trouve-t-on chez Leonardo da Vinci et chez Luca Pacioli?* In press.

Renn, J., Damerow, P. & McLaughlin, P. (2003). *Aristotle, Archimedes, Euclid, and the origin of mechanics: The perspective of historical epistemology*. Berlin: The Max Planck Institute for the history of science of Berlin.

Rogers, K. (2005). *On the metaphysics of experimental physics*. New York: Palgrave Macmillan.

Rose, P. L. (1975). *The Italian renaissance of mathematics*. Geneve: Droz.

Sarton, G. (1953). *Leonardo de Vinci, ingenieur et savant*. Paris: Colloques Internationaux.

Schneider, J. H. J. (2011). Philosophy and theology in the Islamic culture: Al-Farabi's de scientiis. *Philosophy Study, 1,* 41-51.

Tartaglia, N. (1554). La nuova edizione dell'opera Quesiti et inventioni diverse de Nicolo Tartaglia brisciano Riproduzione in facsimile dell'edizione del 1554. In A. Masotti (Ed.), *Commentari dell'Ateneo di Brescia*. Brescia: Tipografia La Nuova cartografica.

Tartaglia, N. (1565a). *Archimedes De insidentibus aqueae, Lib. I et II, in Iordani Opvscvlvm de Ponderositate*. Venetia: Apud Curtium Troianum Navò.

Tartaglia, N. (1565b). *Iordani opvscvlvm de ponderositate, nicolai tartaleae stvdio correctvm novisqve figvrisavctvm*. Cvm Privilegio Traiano Cvrtio, Venetiis, Apvd Curtivm Troianvm.

Truesdell, C. (1968). *Essay in the history of mechanics*. New York: Spinger.

Vanderputten, S. (2005). Exploring the book of nature? Human history and natural history in monastic historiography from the Middle Ages. In K. van Berkel, & A. Vanderjagt (Eds.), *Book of Nature in Antiquity and the Middle Ages* (pp. 151-166). Leuven: Peeters.

4

Temple as the Site of Struggle: Social Reform, Religious Symbols and the Politics of Nationalism in Kerala

M. R. Manmathan

Department of History, Farook College, Calicut University, Kerala, India

The temple entry movement of the 1920s and '30s in Kerala, South India, has become a landmark in the history of social reform and nationalist movements for its uniqueness and sweeping success. Popular history has presented the episode as an integral part of the Nationalist Movement and the Gandhian Constructive Programme mainly because the temple-entry issue was endorsed by the Kerala State Congress Committee and the agitation was concluded under its auspices. But this popular and idealist impression of the movement has been challenged from various quarters. It is pointed out that there have been very little attempts at linking the event with the advancing civic rights movement led by the lower caste people for freedom of worship and social equality which was gaining a radical turn by the 20s and 30s; the pressure exerted by the untouchables to achieve civic freedom even at the cost of renouncing Hinduism had created an alarming situation which no caste-Hindu could ignore. Even more surprising is the absence of academic attempts to link the agitation with the Malabar Rebellion of 1921; in fact the Rebellion had challenged the very survival of the Congress organization in Kerala; this factor forced them to retreat from the earlier secular plane to a religious idiom of politics for which the question of temple-entry served their purpose. The Temple entry movement, therefore, has to be studied in the light of the antipathy shown by the Congress towards popular and radical agitations and in the context of its growing tendency to incline towards Hindu symbols in politics as a means to escape addressing vital and burning social issues.

Keywords: Temple-Entry; Constructive Program; Vaikam Satyagraha; 1921 Rebellion; Religious Conversion; Indian National Congress

Introduction

Social reform movements of early twentieth century Kerala differed from their north Indian counterparts in certain basic features. Firstly, they overlooked individualistic and usually female-oriented reform programs and confronted inequalities among Hindu castes, which were more glaring in Kerala than anywhere else in India. At the early stages of the all-India reform movements the "evils" of society, mostly inflicted upon women-sati, the prohibition on remarriage of young widows, purdah, the custom of early marriage, and lack of educational opportunities for them-engaged the reformers' attention, and crusades for laws to protect (mostly high-caste) women and the founding of institutions to support and educate them defined the practical reform programs (Heimsath, 1978: pp. 24-26). In Kerala, women's causes never caught on[1]; Kerala's social evil was caste. Secondly, they were all caste/community movements;

preoccupation with community-subjects marked their social presence. The process of the "construction of Hinduism" (Muraleedharan, 1996; Viswanathan, 2003), which was one of the focal points of the early social reform movements of North India, both as a desperate resistance against colonialism ("Resistant Hinduism" against "Renascent Hinduism", Young, 1981) and as a prospective nationalist program, was only a succeeding agenda for the reformers of Kerala[2]. In other words, what was at stake was primarily the status relationship between communities; the formation of a unified Hindu religious community, by forging a symbolic unity of castes through the portal of the temple[3], was not taken up seriously till the early 1920s. Thirdly,

---

[1] Mainly for the reason that society had been impregnated with mother-right cultural norms and thus women—except in Nambutiri Brahmin and some Muslim households—were already liberated. Customs like Sati, female infanticide, and the disfigurement of widows which so enraged Indian social reformers, failed to emerge from the mother-right culture of Kerala. Widow remarriage, a highly charged issue throughout India, caused no ripples either, because most low caste and Nair widows freely remarried. Among the Nambutiris mature marriage was the norm, not child marriage, and so widowhood could not claim major attention among their reformers. Infant marriages among all communities were rare.

[2] The Renaissance intellectuals focused mainly on relieving Indian religion of the features most attacked by Christian missionaries and to remodel Hindu religion in accordance with the Judeo-Christian conceptions o monotheism and anti-idolatry. This process of shaping Hindu religion acf cording to a totally alien concept is termed as "Construction of Hinduism".

[3] "Hinduism... does not meet the fundamental requirements of a historical religion of being a coherent system; but its distinct religious entities do. They are indeed religions; while Hinduism is not" (Stietencron, 1989: p. 20) The lower caste Hindus had their own shrines (*kavu*), the belief system and ritual practices of which were basically different from that of the Brahmanical temples. The Izhava social reform movement was a campaign to "sanskritze" their social customs, rituals and ceremonies: Aryan gods to replace primitive deities ("to obtain high gods for lower castes", Lemercinier, 1984: p. 248), learning of Sanskrit and founding of school for Vedanta and the congregation of monks.

these movements played a very insignificant part in the anti-British nationalist opposition (Houtart & Lemercinier, 1978: p. 5). The outstanding enemies here were internal, and the British colonist appeared to the depressed communities as an element favorable to their emancipation, since it was he who had been responsible for the abolition of slavery and for so many liberal reforms. For the upper castes too the British offered opportunities for emancipation, since educational progress and changes in marriage rules were largely dependent on their consent. In general, thus, the attitude of the caste associations towards the emerging nationalist movement was one of distrust and caution.

Against this background, my attempt here is to discuss how the temple-entry movement of the 1920s and '30s signified the above mentioned features and determined the nature and general course of nationalist politics in Kerala. It rejects the nationalist proposition of the temple-entry movement as a great humanitarian and philanthropic endeavor mediated by the Gandhian programme of social upliftment (Pilla, 1986: pp. 357-368; 409-415; Chandra, 1989: pp. 224-234; Menon, 2001: pp. 141-163; 316-331; Menon, 1997: pp. 74, 82) towards creating a "community of equals" and places it against deep social pressures from below. In fact the episode of temple entry agitation represented a conclusive act of the movement for civil rights led by the untouchable castes from the early nineteenth century (Jeffrey, 1978a: pp. 136-169). But the Congress involvement in the struggle in the 1920s, and even later, should be examined from two political standpoints—a shrewd drive to pacify lower caste radicalism (Aloysius, 2010: p. 181) (which was aggravated by religious conversions) and to find a quick deliverance from the moral setback inflicted by the Rebellion of 1921 (which in fact threatened to destroy the very foundations of the Congress in Kerala). The highly complicated socio-political environment brought about by the rebellion problematized both the future course of nationalist political action and the status quo of existing community and class relationships upon which nationalist politics had laid its roots.

This paper, apart from examining the role of lower caste radicalism in engendering the temple-entry movement, examines the hitherto unexplored story of the impact of the 1921 Rebellion in putting pressure on the Congress to deviate from its earlier secular stance to an apparent Hindu idiom of politics. Historians have noted this point earlier (Jeffrey, 1978a; Menon, 1994) but a serious effort to develop it into a polemic has not been undertaken. My attempt here is to create a counter-narrative, not by depending on any new sets of empirical data, but through a re-reading of the existing texts, which are, however, mostly of elite origin. Sources having subaltern inclination are rare, but those that are available from the part of both the Izhavas and the Mappilas are certainly made use of; the missionary and colonial records are treated with care as they represent another set of elite sources. The paper would first trace out the social situation of nineteenth century Kerala, the long history of the movement for civil liberties and the politics of rising nationalism, and then proceed on to discuss how the temple entry agitation reflected the concerns of the caste Hindus about the growing lower caste radicalism and attempted at addressing it through social reform measures.

Historiography

Though there are plenty of literature on the civil liberties movement, the nationalist struggle and the 1921 Rebellion, and a few attempts at connecting the temple entry movement with the conversion issue, there are practically no attempts at linking it with the 1921 rebellion. The Census Reports of Travancore and Cochin from 1871 to 1941 as well as the manuals of Travancore (Aiya, 1906; Pilla, 1940) and Cochin (Menon, 1911) contain rich data on the condition of the untouchable castes. The two manuals of Malabar (Logan, 1887; Innes, 1908) discussed the role of the colonial state as instrumental in emancipating the downtrodden. Some of the anthropological studies taken up during this period (Thurston, 1909; Iyer, 1909, 1939) discussed the social condition and inter-caste relationships to analyze how customs and traditions stood to counter the engagement with modernity. We have three important pieces of missionary literature (Day, 1863; Mateer, 1871, 1883) which looked down at the "primitive" and "superstitious" customs and systems of the people of the land and placed Christianity as a great redeeming force. Two recent studies also have tried to locate missionary intervention and the presence of a powerful Christian community as decisive factors in the modernization of Kerala society (Kawashima, 1988; Onwerkerk, 1994).

Academic studies on the social and religious reform movements of Kerala in general and the Izhava reform movement in particular placed them against the existing "context" (of caste, social evils, deprivation) and the impending forces of modernity (new education, missionary activity, colonial agency and the rising middle class consciousness) and analyzed the varied factors which helped or obstructed the potential of different social groups to appropriate reformism as a means to overcome their state of deprivation. (Rao, 1979; Isaac & Tharakan, 1988; Jeffrey, 1994). There were also attempts at examining the factors for the radicalization of the Izhava caste movement and its later inclination towards left-wing ideology (Jeffrey, 1978b). Some scholars considered missionary presence as instrumental in the gradual radicalization of the Izhava movement and the slow expansion of its emancipation agenda (Pulapilly, 1976). There were also attempts at analyzing the ideological foundations of the reform movements and to identify the unique features of the "Kerala Renaissance" (Houtart & Lemercinier, 1978; Heimsath, 1978, 1982).

On the Malabar Rebellion we have an unending series of literature belonging to diverse ideological streams ranging from colonial to nationalist and Marxist to subaltern. Discussion on the Rebellion has generally been focused on whether they were communal or agrarian uprisings, or whether they were motivated by economic or religious imperatives. Despite "fanatical outbreak" being the predominantly shared official version of the uprisings, agrarian grievances as a possible factor did not remain totally unnoticed. Two early exponents of the religious interpretation (Conolly, Strange), while recognizing the poverty and destitution of the Mappila "fanatics", rejected them as a reason for the "outbreaks". In contrast, Logan identified agrarian discontent as the main causative factor, but underlined the turbulence and fanatical character of the Mappilas (Logan, 1887). The government held that Mappila religiosity exacerbated by nationalist politics was the prime moving force behind the rebellion of 1921 (Tottenham, 1922; Nair, 1923; Hitchcock, 1925). More recent studies have attempted to interpret the militancy of the Mappilas as a means of defending the frontier of Mappila society-internal frontier was with the Hindu society dominated by landholding Brahmins and the external frontier with the Europeans, from Portuguese to the British. The nineteenth century uprisings were jihads to defend the internal Islamic frontier.

The rebellion of 1921 was different in that it was directed towards an identifiable political goal, i.e., establishment of an Islamic kingdom (Dale, 1980). The nationalist version is represented mainly by the autobiographical sketches of the Congress leaders which, while justifying the decision of the Congress to uphold the Khilafat issue, found fault with the government policy of repression and the irrationality and intense religiosity of the Mappilas (Nambutiripad, 1965; Nair, 1971; Menon, 1986). A dominant section of left wing historians followed an essentially economic interpretation, treating agrarian discontent as the prime factor with religion as a means of mobilization (Nambutiripad, 1952; Hardgrave, 1977; Dhanagare, 1977; Wood, 1987; Gangadharan, 1989; Panikkar, 1989). Among them Panikkar's study stood different in that it treated the context (anti-British feeling and the urge to free from the exploitation of the propertied classes) and ideology (religion translated discontent into action and provided the vision of an alternate society) equally decisive. A recent study examined the uprisings from a subaltern perspective and placed the Mappila insurgency along subalternity and religiosity, which are specific to premodern consciousness, in order to exonerate it from the alleged blemish of "communalism" and "jihadism" (Ansari, 2005).

For a survey of the nationalist movement in Kerala we have several studies, both panegyric and critical. Studies which followed the official Congress view (Pilla, 1986; Menon, 1997; Menon, 2001) perceived the shifting strands of nationalist position with reference to its primary (anti-colonial) preferences and its (umbrella-type) all-class and secular character. The disposition of the Congress in taking up the internal issues affecting class/caste relations on a secondary footing has been justified on this premise but it is further argued that the constructive program was actually devised to serve this purpose—to supplement political action through social and humanitarian work (including efforts to eradicate untouchability)—which aimed at cleansing the nation of blots which stood against true and ideal nationhood. The nationalist reading of the temple-entry movement followed such a glossy picture: uplift of the depressed sections of Hindu community through constructive program was an integral part of the work of the Indian National Congress in Kerala (Menon, 2001: pp. 141-163; 316-331). That the dual task taken up by the Congress, to build the nation and to construct a solid Hindu community, was not a mistaken strategy; in the context of the predominantly Hindu majority nation-state, the appropriation of Hindu religious symbolism was not incongruous (Chandra, 1989: pp. 230-234). A critical stream against the nationalist position came from various quarters, especially the left and the subaltern-dalit groups. The left perceived the nationalist movement as having had an implicit class agenda which got reflected in its ideology and method of political action and argued that the constructive programme was devised to establish Congress hegemony over low castes and untouchables and to pacify the mounting "pressures from below" which threatened to offset the interests of the dominant social groups who were steering the movement (Nambutiripad, 1952: pp. 131-132; Sarkar, 1990: p. 230). An article on Guruvayur satyagraha, while treating it as a part of the nationalist movement, analyzed the role of factionalism within the Congress as a possible reason for diverting the Civil Disobedience Movement (CDM) into a social struggle and attributed the failure of the struggle to the basic limitations of the Congress attitude towards untouchability (Gopalankutty, 1981). The Dalit perspective blamed Gandhi for perceiving untouchability simply as a religious issue, not as a question of civil right, and hence in practice, it appeared to counter their own idea and struggles for emancipation (Aloysius, 2010: p. 181; Ravindran, 1988).

Two studies have tried to link the temple-entry agitation with the struggle for civil rights and the inner politics of the nationalist movement (Jeffrey, 1978a; Menon, 1994). While the former identified the "modernizing" impact of colonialism and the "civilizing" impact of missionary work as decisive in the creation of a powerful middle class and a congenial ideological environment leading to radicalization of the reform process, the latter discussed the difference in the degree of power and deprivation among hierarchically arranged social groups in the traditional social order and presented the nature of their response to colonialism/nationalism on the basis of the degree to which the changes which took place under the colonial system favored their emancipation/retention of privileged position.

The Social Spectrum of Kerala

The caste structure of colonial Kerala stood different from the pan-Indian scenario. The existing varna and jati system varied from the ideal four-fold model with the total absence of the Vaishyas and a very marginal Kshatriya presence; the traditional trading and commercial functions were by and large the preserve of the non-Hindu communities like the Jews, Muslims and Syrian Christians and the ruling lineages of medieval Kerala were substantially drawn from Sudra-Nair caste who however were gradually elevated to Kshatriya-Samanta status. Brahmins (including the Kerala Brahmins called Nambutiris and the immigrant Tamil and Kannada groups) constituted a mere 1% of the population of the land but they occupied the upper echelons of ritual hierarchy and owned substantial landed properties. The populous, martial and matrilineal caste of the Nairs, who were the ruling class and constituted a substantial portion of the military force in the pre-British era, were accorded higher status for being "clean sudras" which led the Brahmins to enter into alliance with them by arranging liaisons with their women[4] and by entrusting them with the management of their landed estates and temples. All of the above groups along with the several tiny castes of temple-servants called Ambalavasis constituted the elite Hindus (savarna). All the castes below the Nairs were avarnas (untouchables) and included, in terms of hierarchy, the Izhavas, Pulayas, Cherumas, Parayas and Nayadis. In addition there were the fishing and tribal communities. Pulayas, Parayas and Cherumas served as agrestic laborers and occupied very low social position and economic power tantamount to serfs. Defilement practices consisting of untouchability, unapproachability and even un-seeability determined inter-caste relations and was apparently influenced by the notion of hierarchy. The savarna-avarna divide mediated by socioeconomic and political inequalities hardened and dehumanized relationships between social groups.

An examination of the position of the Izhavas in the traditional social structure reveals the range and magnitude of diverse kinds of relative deprivation. They are an ethnic category, found all over South India (Izhavas and Shannars in South Tra-

---

[4]Such conjugal alliances were called *sambandham* in which the male partners were just "visiting husbands" and the wives along with their children lived in matrilineal extended households maintained by impartible joint property. This practice was popular among matrilineal castes like the Nairs, Kshatriyas and Ambalavasis who had liaisons with the Brahmins.

vancore, Chovans in North and Central Travancore and Cochin, Tiya in Malabar, Billava in Tulunad, Nadar in Tamil Nadu and Idiga in Mysore) and the various cognate castes in Kerala constitute a large ethnic bloc. The most popular theory is that the Izhavas were migrants from Ceylon (Aiya, 1906: pp. 398-402; Thurston, 1909: pp. 292-418; Innes, 1908: pp. 124-125; Logan, 1887: p. 80) and were Buddhists by faith (Kunhuraman, 1925; Aiyappan, 1965: p. 119). The occupation of the Izhavas in the traditional caste order was coconut plucking and toddy-tapping, though they were engaged as tenant cultivators, agricultural laborers, weavers and coir workers. They also practiced ayurveda and astrology and had a tradition of military service (Iyer, 1909: p. 298). The Izhavas ranked lower than the Nairs and above the Cherumas/Pulayas in the caste hierarchy. Though the Izhavas were at the top of the category of castes who caused distance pollution, they had to keep a distance of 36 feet from the Nambutiri Brahmins and were not allowed to enter temples managed by the upper castes. They also did not have the right to use public roads and wells of the upper castes (Aiyappan, 1944: p. 39) and were denied admission in caste Hindu schools and government jobs. Their women were not allowed to wear upper garments or any ornaments. The Nairs often demanded unpaid labour (uzhiyam) from them (Mateer, 1871: p. 43; Day, 1863: p. 322). Under the existing three-tier agrarian social structure, most Izhavas occupied the position of sub-tenants or agricultural laborers. Most of the janmis were Nambutiris, Kshatriyas or aristocratic Nairs. Kanam tenants who held the lease for a period of twelve years (but sub-leased them) were mainly Nairs. Verumpattam was the lease for a three year tenure and Izhavas and Mappilas were the prominent sub-tenants. Agricultural laborers formed an important category, and this consisted of the Izhavas, Pulayas and Cherumas.

The political attitude of the Mappila community of Malabar represented a more complex pattern. Mappilas (or Moplahs), the Muslims of Malabar, traditionally trace their origins to the ninth century, when Arab traders brought Islam to the west coast of India (Miller, 1992: pp. 40-45). By 1921, they constituted the largest—and the fastest growing—community of Malabar. With a population of one million, 32 percent of that of Malabar as a whole, the Mappilas were concentrated in south Malabar, i.e., in the Ernad, Valluvanad and Ponnani taluks of the erstwhile British Malabar described in colonial records as "fanatical zone" (Innes, 1908: p. 89). In Ernad taluk, the center of the rebellion, they formed nearly 60 percent of the population and in Walluvanad, 35 percent. The community has been characterized as consisting of pure Arab settlers, of the descendants of the Arab traders and women of the country, and of converts to Islam from the lower Hindu castes (Innes, 1908: p. 26). The Mappilas were a mercantile community concentrated along the coast in urban centers. Segregated from the Hindu population in separate settlements, they had considerable autonomy, and under the Zamorin of Calicut, they enjoyed prestige as well as economic power (Zaynu'd-Din, 1942). From the sixteenth century, with the rise of Portuguese power in challenge to Mappila commercial interests, the greater portion of the community moved into the interior of Malabar and increasingly came to be agricultural tenants, low in status and desperately poor (Dale, 1980: pp. 54-82). In sharp contrast to the general prosperity enjoyed by the Mappilas of the North (where early converts included propertied classes of the high castes), the Mappilas of South Malabar were principally converted from the

lower Tiyya, Cheruman and Mukkuva castes, for whom "the honor of Islam" brought freedom from the disabilities of ritual pollution. It was in these inland areas of the south and among the poorest sections of the population that the Mappila community expanded most rapidly (Hitchcock, 1925: p. 9).

During the successive invasion of Hyder Ali and Tipu Sultan, in the late eighteenth century, Malabar was thrown into social turmoil. The Mappilas tried to reap political and economic gains from it by declaring their proprietorship rights over their tenurial lands and by remitting land tax directly to the government defying caste-Hindu landowners (Dale, 1976; Miller, 1992: p. 81; Menon, 1999). The caste Hindus responded to this hopeless situation by fleeing from Malabar and seeking refuge in the self-proclaimed Hindu state of Travancore after either disposing of their property or deserting them to the Mappilas (Narayanan & Kesavan, 1983: p. 275). The situation was also significant in that large number of lower caste Hindus utilized the opportunity to enhance their social prestige by embracing the religion of the new rulers (Kunju, 1989: p. 79). The defeat of Tipu and the subsequent British land settlement policies in Malabar, leading to the restoration of the social and economic position of the dominant castes, severely affected the position of the Mappilas in South Malabar—by imposing enormous amount of rent and by fixing heavy renewal fees on tenurial contracts (melcharth) (Panikkar, 1989: pp. 1-48), they were oppressed in particular. Reduced to insecure tenancy, vulnerable to rack renting and eviction at the hands of Hindu janmis sustained by British courts, the Mappilas responded in a series of outbreaks[5]. During the course of these nineteenth century outbreaks, the number of conversions to Islam heightened dramatically. In converting to Islam, those of lower castes were not only freed from the traditional social disabilities of the outcaste, but they joined a community of resistance wherein their protest against janmi tyranny was supported by their fellow Muslims (Hardgrave, 1977: p. 62)[6]. The recurrent Mappila riots of the 19th century were, to a large extent, in spite of their predominant religious character (Dale, 1975), defensive responses to, or retaliatory acts against, such tyrannical acts and in that sense were essentially economic phenomena (Gough, 1968-1969). The sweeping militancy of the Mappilas and the exceptional enthusiasm they expressed in violating traditional caste dharma combined with the rise in their demographic strength intensified the

---

[5]The term "outrage" was used by the British to refer to those outbreaks of Mappilla violence in which the attack usually against a nambutiri or Nair landlord; sometimes against a European official or a convert who had slipped back into the Hindu fold and thus threatened community solidarity was followed climactically by the religious suicide of all involved, in the secure knowledge that by their martyrdom they would attain the houri bliss of Paradise. The incidents in which the mappillas "sought actively their own death", 29 in number between 1836 and 1919, were normally suppressed in a few days and involved in each case a relatively small number of people. Only in eight of the outbreaks did more than ten Mappillas become martyrs (or shahids) (Hardgrave, 1977: p. 62).

[6]The Census of India, Madras (1871: p. 7) noted that the Cherumas "have to a large extent embraced Mohammedanism, and in so doing have raised themselves and their successors in the social scale. The tyranny of caste no longer affects the Mussalman converts and under these circumstances it is no cause for surprise that the Mussalman population on the Western Coast should be fast increasing". Subsequent Census Reports recorded the continued Mappila increases and actual declines in the number of Cherumas reported. Between 1871 and 1881, the Mappila population of Malabar increased by 12.3 per cent, compared to only 3.4 per cent of non-Mappilas (Census of India, Madras, 1881: pp. 39-40). Between 1881 and 1891, Mappilas increased by 18 per cent, in comparison to a 10 per cent increase for Hindus (Census of India, Madras, 1891: p. 67).

social distance between the Mappilas and the high caste Hindus (Miller, 1992: p. 98). The setback inflicted on the material interests of the dominant groups had started to articulate slowly in the form of religious polarization and in widening the communal divide.

In 1852, a special commission, headed by T. L. Strange, was appointed to investigate the causes of the outbreaks. Strange rejected the view that the disturbances had their origin in agrarian discontent or poverty and attributed it to religious fanaticism stirred by the teachings of ambitious priests. He recommended a repressive policy, enacted into law in the Moplah outrages Act, XXIII and XXIV of 1854. A special force of police was raised in Ernad to enforce these measures (Logan, 1887: pp. 570-571). The failure to quell the outbreaks despite strong police measures persuaded the government to appoint William Logan, the District Collector, as Special Commissionaire, in 1881, to enquire into land tenures and tenant rights in Malabar. Logan believed the problem to be rooted fundamentally in the early British misunderstanding of the traditional relationship of the *janmi* to the land. Rather than seeing the *janmi* as one of several agricultural classes with rights to the land and its produce, British officials viewed him as rather like an English landlord to be protected with the force of Law (Logan, 1887: p. 584). However, the government refused to implement his recommendations which is evident from the statement of District Collector Innes who writing at the turn of the century attributed the outbreaks to "three main causes, poverty, agrarian discontent and fanaticism, of which the last is probably the chief" (Innes, 1908: p. 89).

The establishment of British rule marked the beginning of a social transformation. A notable feature was the consolidation of diverse political units into larger administrative ones. By 1793 the whole of Malabar came into the hands of the British and became a district of the Madras presidency. Travancore and Cochin continued under princely rule but as subordinate allies of the British and guided by a British officer called Resident in administration. The consolidation of power in the British hands led to the introduction of a uniformity in basic legislation. Slavery was abolished in Malabar in 1843 by the British and through Royal Proclamations in Travancore and Cochin in 1853 and 1854 respectively (Basu, 2008: pp. 57, 62-63). But in the realm of land tenure and educational progress law and custom stood opposite to each other. In 1793 the British recognized the *janmi* as the owner of the land and *kanakkar* as the lease, holding a mortgage. Thus the *verumpattakar* tenants were dependent on their lords and if they revolted against the landlord, they were evicted. From the beginning of the nineteenth century, large number of schools was started by the Christian missionaries to impart education to the converted people. Taking queue from them, the governments of Travancore, Cochin and Malabar opened schools, but it benefitted the Nairs and the Syrian Christians. As untouchables, the Izhavas could not profit from them but the mission schools provided them openings for education. The strong anti-British attitude of the Mappilas kept them away from English education for a long time. The Tiyyas of Malabar and the Muslims of Travancore fared well and did not face much deprivation; under direct British rule, the Tiyyas could prosper educationally and socially and as traders and landowners, the Muslims of the princely states could make use of the possibilities opened up by modernity (Logan, 1887: p. 144; Iyer, 1909: p. 283).

The Civil Rights Movement

Kerala began to experience the impact of colonial modernity from the early decades of the nineteenth century, the ramifications of which were felt in the public sphere in different times and in different degrees. One of the most important impact was felt in the social realm, in the form of efforts at reforming customs and democratizing social relationships. It was the (Protestant) Christian missionaries (such as the London Mission Society (L.M.S) in Southern Kerala, Church Mission Society (C.M.S) in Central Kerala and Basel Evangelical Mission Society (B.E.M.S) in Northern Kerala) who took the pioneering steps in promoting social reforms; they actively engaged in spreading the message of reform by imparting modern education to the untouchables and encouraging the new converts to openly question symbols of caste oppression and rules of ritual pollution (Aiya, 1906, I: p. 525; Manavalan, 1990: p. 120). The revolt of the Christian converted Shannar/Nadar women of Southern Travancore to get their right to wear upper garments really shook southern Travancore in the first half of the nineteenth century (Hardgrave, 1968)[7]. Similarly, the activities of the missionaries and the pressure exerted by them played a decisive role in coercing the governments to abolish slavery in both Travancore and Malabar in the middle of the nineteenth century (Basu, 2008: p. 74). The missionaries were also the first to introduce print-culture in Kerala. They utilized the print media to oppose customs and practices which had contradicted with modern outlook and human reason (Anderson, 1983: pp. 41-49)[8]. The efforts of the missionaries had had its desired effect, especially among the lower castes, and large mass of such people became converts to Christianity. But missionary appeal failed to much impress the upper or middle level caste groups; even the untouchable caste of the Izhavas took advantage of the new opportunity and the newly acquired knowledge to attain upward social mobility within the existing Hindu social order through radical social reform (Sahodaran, 1920: pp. 290-294; Jeffrey, 1974: p. 48)[9].

Early attempts at social reform were followed by organized struggle for social change which also had its genesis in the princely state of Travancore. Though being conservative and very vigilant in protecting the old social order, the government had started "modernizing" the state by founding schools, roads, law courts, and efficient bureaucracy. Meanwhile, a powerful middle class, which had been developing among the untouchable caste of the Izhavas, grew more and more frustrated over the state policy of keeping them away from government schools and service. In 1896 the Izhavas of Travancore submitted a huge memorandum (signed by 13176 men known as *Izhava Memorial*) calling upon the government to open public schools and services to them (Rao, 1979: p. 34). The failure of such

---

[7]The struggle is examined from various viewpoints. While some people from within the caste see it as part of an epic struggle to free the lower classes from feudal domination (Yesudas, 1975), the missionary perception take it as the triumph of decency and Christian values (Mateer, 1883: Ch.XXXIV). Hardgrave regards it as part of a wider movement within the caste order of south India for the Nadars to raise their status in the social hierarchy (Hardgrave, 1969).

[8]Anderson attributes the success of European Reformation to print-capitalism and stresses the coalition between Protestantism and print-capitalism.

[9]*Sahodaran*, the magazine published by the radical Tiyya lawyer C. Krishnan from Calicut, urged the Izhavas to concentrate on reforming Hinduism from within as no other religion was so liberal and tolerant. Jeffrey added that as large number of Izhavas prospered, they were able cautiously to imitate the manners of Nairs.

early steps persuaded them to turn towards more radical measures under a strong organization, that is, the S.N.D.P. Yogam under the powerful leadership of Sri Narayana Guru. The Yogam took up a two-pronged struggle—the fight for social equality and freedom of worship and the internal reform of the Izhava caste to make it a model community (Pulappilly, 1976: pp. 35-39). The radical demands raised by the S.N.D.P. in Travancore, such as the freedom to use public roads and temple-entry and representation in government jobs and legislatures, and the strategy of mass struggle they adopted to achieve their demands, clearly reflected their resolve to transform—not merely to reform—the existing social structure (Heimsath, 1982: p. 33). In British Malabar, the state did not adhere to caste rules and hence the lower castes could get recruited into even higher government posts (Menon, 1901: p. 182; Kesavan, 1968: pp. 263-270). Thus the Tiyyas in Malabar were not as deprived as their Izhava counterparts in Cochin or Travancore and hence militant lower caste social reform movements failed to take roots in Malabar.

By the 1920s the movement for civil liberties was taking new proportions. As already noted, the lower caste untouchables had expressed their resolve to better their social position through mass conversion (to Christianity in southern and central Kerala and to Islam in northern Kerala) and to distance themselves with the politics of nationalism since the Indian National Congress was identified to represent upper caste interests and to perceive the colonial master as a potential ally in the path to social emancipation. But the middle level caste of the Izhavas who till then refused to experiment the possibilities of the politics of religious conversion and worked to occupy a "respected place in Hindu society" than to satisfy with a "doubtful Christian role between contemptuous Syrians and polluting Pulaya converts" (Jeffrey, 1974: p. 48), now began to seriously think of renouncing Hinduism for getting a more honorable status in the civil society. The Congress decision to uphold the cause of temple-entry stemmed from this predicament, because religious conversion was slowly growing into a vital social issue capable of subverting the existing social equilibrium solidly rooted in birth rights and hereditary social privileges.

The Nationalist Politics

The nature of political awakening in Kerala differed in the three political regions in accordance with the prevailing political climate—while in Malabar where direct colonial rule existed, nationalist movement had made deep inroads by the beginning of the Gandhian era but in the princely states of Travancore and Cochin they were at low ebb. In Travancore and Cochin, political condition of the princely state weakened the possibilities of the spread of a strong nationalist movement and hence the rising middle class of both the upper and lower castes concentrated on promoting community interests (Kesavan, 1968: pp. 356-357). This was the background of the Izhava memorial, and the Abstention Movement of the 1930s, in which various deprived groups formed a coalition forum called Joint Political Congress to press forward their middle class demands for reserved representation in government jobs and legislatures in accordance with population strength against the huge monopoly of the Nairs and Brahmins. The non-cooperation or civil disobedience movements of the 1920s and 30s did not make any political effects here; politics of the princely states evolved around social issues, skillfully masterminded by caste/community organizations.

The nationalist movement came relatively late to "sleeping Malabar". While a District Congress Committee had been formed in 1908, it was not until 1916, with the beginning of the Home Rule Movement that Malabar began to awaken politically. The fifth Malabar District Conference was held at Manjeri in 1920 with Annie Basent in chair in which the extremist group could pass a resolution in favour of tenancy reforms against the moderate stand who under Basent boycotted the proceedings. The demands for tenancy reform came principally from the class of *kanakkar*, substantial tenants who were largely intermediaries between *janmis* and the vulnerable *verumpattakkar*, tenants-at-will. The *janmis* were mostly Nambutiri Brahmins, the *kanakkar* were disproportionately Nairs and the *verumpattakkar* were overwhelmingly drawn from the Mappila community and from Tiyyas, Cheruman and other depressed Hindu castes. The Nair *Kanakkar*, prosperous and articulate in defense of their interests, had long been active before government commissions and in the Madras legislative assembly in efforts to secure more favorable tenancy rights for themselves. But it was not until 1920, in linking the tenancy issue with the Congress-Khilafat struggle for Swaraj, that the tenancy movement gained momentum. The Congress was still a predominantly Hindu organization, dominated largely by Nair lawyers from the *kanakkar* class. The rise of the Khilafat issue[10] and Gandhi's decision to link it with the noncooperation movement fundamentally transformed the character of the Congress (Nambutiripad, 2005: p. 42)[11].

Non-cooperation was formally launched on August 1, 1920, and on the 18th of that month Gandhi and Shaukath Ali visited Calicut to bring its message. Khilafat committees began to sprout in Malabar and official reports revealed that Mappilas of Ernad were more interested in the tenant cause and only on upholding that issue the agitators could make any advance (Tottenham, 1922: p. 4). Agrarian tension increased in the light of the rumor of an impending tenancy reforms in Malabar and while landlords increasingly evicted tenants, Nair leaders of the Congress sought to mobilize the active support of the Mappila cultivators—both for tenancy reforms and in the name of Khilafat. Intense campaigning for Khilafat scared the official circles, in the light of "fanatic outbreaks" of the past, and ignorance and backwardness of the Mappilas, which led them to ban public meetings (Madras Mail, 1921, Feb. 8: 9; Ap. 27: 8); expansion of the tenancy movement under Congress auspices spread alarm among landlords and officials alike. In the context of all these the All Kerala Provincial Congress was held at Ottappalam on 26 April 1921, in which large number of Khilafat volunteers in uniform attended (Panikkar, 1989: p. 132) and an *ulema* conference exhorted all Muslims to support the Khilafat as a religious duty and to join the Congress to fight for the Khilaft through the struggle for swaraj. A tenants' conference convened at Ottappalam strongly supported resistance to land-

---

[10]The Khilafat movement sought to preserve the integrity of the Ottoman Empire and the Turkish Sultan as the Caliph. The movement beginning in 1919, protested against British support for the dismemberment of the Ottoman Empire and the abolition of the Caliphate. The Indian movement was led by the Ali Brothers (Shoukath and Muhammad) but Congress soon supported the issue as Gandhi saw in it a golden opportunity to weld Hindu-Muslim unity and combine anti-British issue of Khilafat with the movement for Swaraj through non-violent noncooperation.

[11]E.M.S. wrote that a striking solidarity had developed between the Mappilas and the class of lawyers, journalists and politicians (i.e., Congressmen) who brought them into nationalist politics; both were lured by tenant interests, and looked forward to get a tenancy legislation passed.

lords and Government in the form of noncooperation (Hardgrave, 1977: p. 70). Congress leaders like K. P. Kesava Menon and K. Kelappan addressed several Khiafat conferences (Menon, 1986: pp. 82-83). The "wonderful" organization of the Khilafat movement (Madras Mail, Aug. 8, 1921: p. 6) and the traditional system of communication among the Mappilas (Hitchcock, 1925: p. 3), along with the official anxiety over the Mappilas utilizing the newly forged solidarity to redress their immediate grievances (Tottenham, 1922: p. 26) forced the government to take strong punitive measures against them which, within a few days, led to the eruption of a violent uprising.

The rebellion actually started with the Tirurangadi incident in which nine Mappilas were killed in police firing while a group of 2000 people marched to the police station demanding the release of their fellowmen taken into custody during a police action at the Mambram mosque in search of some Khilafat volunteers (Hitchcock, 1925: pp. 31-34). Thereafter violence erupted which was marked by widespread attack on symbols of government authority, such as police stations, courts and record offices and cutting of railway and telegraph lines. Landlords-Nambutiris and Nairs—were the principal victims of the attacks, several of whom fled from the area to the nearby towns of Calicut or Trichur. At the earliest stages, Hindus were clearly involved, but with time and growing violence (and with the proclamation of the Khilafat kingdom in south Malabar), their numbers rapidly diminished (Hardgrave, 1977: p. 83), which imparted a communal color to the rebellion. For almost six months the "Mappila zone" was under the control of the rebel leaders. The government soon resorted to reinforcements which led the rebels to retire into safe areas and to fight a guerilla war. There were frequent reports of rebel atrocities, sporadic incidence of violence against Hindus and cases of forced conversions to Islam (Nair, 1923: pp. 76-79)[12]. This has been attributed primarily to two factors: the impression among many rebels of the movement leading to the establishment of an Islamic state and to the widespread suspicion of Hindus acting as informants for the government (Panikkar, 1989: pp. 179, 198). By the beginning of 1922 the rebellion was crushed causing heavy casualties on the rebel side and all the leaders were soon arrested or shot dead[13]. Panikkar identified at least three patterns of rebel activity in the whole course of the rebellion. The initial political mobilization was effected by the Khilafat and Congress activists who were soon rendered ineffective and the actual course of the revolt thereafter developed outside the political movement in which it had initially developed. In this second, but short-lived, stage the locally influential leaders took over the direction of the rebel proceedings but ceased to be effective when the army operations began. In the third and crucial stage, the insurrection was now conducted by the rural poor themselves, either under grass-root level leadership or without any recognizable leadership at all. The pattern of rebel proceedings underlined a consciousness primarily rooted in an opposition to

the landlord and the colonial state. Against the selective and limited nature of rebel violence (against the janmis and their servants) of the nineteenth century, in 1921 a distinction was made between the lenient and exacting landlords (although attitude towards Europeans was uniformly hostile); several of the latter category were executed and murders and physical assaults on others were largely punitive actions against collaborators and informers of the British army (Panikkar, 1989: pp. 198-199).

In the context of the eruption of violence and the evolution of the revolt into a communal outbreak the Congress withdraw its support to their earlier ally, the Mappilas. The Congress leaders were in fact taken by surprise at the unexpected developments. But their activity was confined to the two trips they made to the rebel area in the early stage of the rebellion; afterwards they remained passive spectators-partly because they could not approve of the rebel action and partly because of their lack of confidence in being able to influence the rebels (Panikkar, 1989: pp. 149-151). The attitude of the Congressmen drove the Mappilas to identify the Congress with the Hindus (Panikkar, 1989: p. 189). The relief and reconstruction measures undertaken after the rebellion also underlined the communal divide—the Congress was active only among the Hindu refugees. The years that followed the suppression of the Rebellion and the withdrawal of the non-cooperation movement made it extremely difficult for the Congress organization to function in Malabar. K. P. Kesava Menon, the Congress leader, described the situation thus: "For a long time after the rebellion no public activity was possible in Malabar. Enmity towards the Congress was evident everywhere. The authorities stated that the Congress had brought down calamity on the country through participation in the Khilafat agitation. They even wanted all the Congressmen in Malabar to be imprisoned. The Muslims complained that those who had induced them to join abandoned them when police oppression and firing by the troops started" (Menon, 1986: p. 128). The caste-Hindus who were opposed to the Congress, on the other hand, denounced them for supporting the "foolish" and "fanatic" Mappilas and for inciting them to plunge into a violent action (Yogakshemam, 1921, 11: 47, 2). The Congress leadership sadly realized that the first political struggle it undertook in Kerala ended in tragedy and the alliance with the Mappilas proved self-annihilating as they not only not refused to adhere to Gandhian ahimsa but advanced it into a class and community struggle. More disturbing was the sense of unity evinced by the Mappilas and their resolve to sacrifice for a cause which was alien to the Hindu tradition and hence incompatible to "national" interests.

The Congress could not recover from the fatal blow inflicted on its morale by the rebellion for long; it could not think of political campaigning—even to summon a Congress meeting. It tried to overcome this political lethargy by focusing on the social front and by drifting towards political journalism. This was the background of the birth of the nationalist newspaper Mathrubhumi and the launching of the Vaikam satyagraha (Menon, 1986: pp. 139-149; Gangadharan, 2008: p. 248; Nambutiripad, 2005: pp. 65-68)[14]. The temple entry movement in fact

---

[12]The pro-British Madras Mail was in the forefront in this venture. The anti-Mappila reaction was presented by the Mail in its daily reporting and in a (later) series on "The Moplah Rebellion". It referred to the "innate characteristics" of the Mappila as "his mad fanatical fury, his murderous spirit and his reckless disregard for life" (Madras Mail, 1921, Nov. 14: 5; Nov. 15: 7). Gopalan Nair's Malabar Rebellion devotes 21 pages to atrocities allegedly committed by the Mappilas against the Hindus (Nair, 1923: pp. 52-72).

[13]Official figures recorded 2339 rebels killed, 1652 wounded and 5955 captured. K.P. Kesava Menon estimated that as many as 10,000 may have lost their life in the rebellion (Menon, 1986: p. 116).

---

[14]Mathrubhumi Daily was started in 1923 from Calicut with K. P. Kesava Menon as its founder editor. Congress leaders and people sympathetic to the nationalist movement helped to raise the necessary funds. It consciously tried to propagate nationalist and patriotic sentiments as well as a spirit of Hindu unity.

provided the Malabar Congressmen with a programme, and a lease of life, as it opened before them a safe field of activism; it shifted the centre of activity to further south where Mappilas were absent and furnished with a fine opportunity to compensate for the earlier "disastrous" alliance with the Mappilas by fighting for a Hindu cause (Jeffrey, 1978a: pp. 153-154)[15]. The Congress was turning more Hindu and more rightist; communities of foreign religious affiliation were increasingly identified as external to the national self and as threatening "national" interests.

The Temple-Entry Movement

The political and social atmosphere of Kerala in the 1920s and 30s grew tense with the Indian National Congress upholding the cause of temple entry. In 1924 the Congress organized the vigorous 20 month long satyagraha at the Vaikam temple with the simple aim of securing the right to use the approach roads of the temple for the untouchables. While the upper castes and non-Hindus including Christians and Muslims freely used the temple roads, the untouchables like the Izhavas and Pulayas were forbidden to pass through them. The Izhavas were on the verge of a revolt over the question of caste pollution and viewed it as an obvious act of social injustice and open violation of human rights. The S.N.D.P. Yogam was seriously discussing the means to overcome this social stigma. Since the Izhavas had their own temples in which they themselves acted as officiating priests, their eagerness to get access to *savarna* temples was more a matter of civil rights than a question of freedom of worship. T. K. Madhavan, the prominent leader of the S.N.D.P. Yogam and the true spirit behind the satyagraha, managed to get a resolution passed at the Congress session in 1923 at Kakinada on the question of the removal of untouchability. The Kerala Pradesh Congress Committee (KPCC) decided to launch a satyagraha at Vaikam on this basis (Menon, 1986: pp. 160-164). Gandhi blessed the satyagraha but cautioned against non-Hindu participation and non-savarna leadership in it as it was strictly a Hindu cause and a golden opportunity for caste-Hindus to atone for a heinous sin (Young India, 1925: p. 135; Proceedings, 1925). The satyagraha attracted countrywide attention and people from all over India reached Vaikam to support the struggle. The *savarna-jatha* (upper caste march) organized under the leadership of Mannath Padmanabhan to the capital Trivandrum, to impress upon the king of the urgency of the demand, truly reflected this spirit. The prolonged campaign and the direct involvement of Gandhi forced the authorities to come to a settlement according to which all the approach roads, except the eastern one, of the temple were thrown open to all people irrespective of caste and community. The modalities of the agreement was a subject of intense debate and the Congress was blamed for deserting the struggle halfway and for effecting the agreement only to the Vaikam temple (Ravindran, 1988: pp. 144-149). Due to this reason, several similar struggles had to be waged for the same purpose subsequently. As a result, in 1928, approach roads to all temples in Travancore were thrown open to all people (Menon, 1984: p. 327).

The second satyagraha struggle under the K.P.C.C. against caste based pollution, but now to get the temple open to all

Hindus, was organized in 1931-32, in the course of the C.D.M, at the Guruvayur temple in Malabar. While the struggle at Vaikam was a social reform measure divorced from any political movements, at Guruvayur it was integral to a political program (Gopalankutty, 1981). Nevertheless, in Kerala, the zeal for social reform overshadowed the rising countrywide political enthusiasm; for the K.P.C.C. the temple-entry issue was more important than the C.D.M. and leaders like Kelappan concentrated heavily on the question of untouchability (Mathrubhumi, 1931, Ap. 6, June. 21, July. 29, July. 31 & Sep. 10; 1932, March. 5, March. 27 & Aug. 4). Gandhi also asked the satyagrahis to detach the struggle from all its political affiliations and from the organizational links of the Congress in order to rescue it from government repression and to ensure its success. Though the temple-entry agitation was perceived as tantamount to the "struggle against imperialism" by some of its leaders (Gopalan, 1973: p. 28) as it kept vigil against disunity and factionalism, what really prompted the Congress to confine the struggle to temple-entry was the bitter experiences of 1921[16]. The Zamorin, who was the trustee of the temple, however, refused to step down to negotiate a settlement which led Kelappan to start a fast unto death which, however, was withdrawn under the advice of Gandhiji (Mathrubhumi, 22 Sep. & 4 Oct. 1932). The satyagraha as a whole was finally terminated before achieving any of its declared objectives. A period of three months was given to the Zamorin to effect temple-entry, failing which Gandhi would himself offer satyagraha; but it was postponed and did not take place at all. A referendum was held among the caste Hindus of Ponnani taluk, where the temple was situated, which revealed that 70% of them supported the cause of temple entry (Mathrubhumi Weekly Temple Entry Special Issue, 16 Nov. 1937). N.P. Damodaran, one of the leaders of the satyagraha, later recollected that though the agitation failed to meet its immediate objective, it created a climate in favour of temple entry (Damodaran, 1981). The movement for temple entry registered its crowning victory when the Travancore government made the temple entry proclamation in 1936 by which all temples in Travancore were thrown open to all Hindus (Menon, 1984: pp. 327-328). Nevertheless, the temples of Cochin and Malabar remained closed before the *avarnas* till 1947.

Politics of the Temple-Entry Movement

The temple-entry movement was important for several reasons. Firstly, it was a conscious effort on the part of the Congress to integrate the various castes and communities under the Hindu fold through social and religious reform, which represented a powerful domain of the nationalist movement. Temple could rally diverse sections together without dislodging the existing power relations and a symbolic unity could pacify lower caste radicalism. The Congress decision to take up the issue in Kerala was certainly in the context of the inclusion of the removal of untouchability as part of the Gandhian constructive program and its decision to fight out social evils in accordance with the nation-building project, but the constructive

---

[15]In an interview K. P. Kesava Menon revealed that for the Congressmen from Malabar district, the temple-entry campaign gave an opportunity to revive interest—at a safe distance—in a Congress that had suffered a severe setback with the Mappila rebellion of 1921 (cited in Jeffrey, 1978a: pp. 153-154).

[16]The fear of the Mappilas loomed large even in the 30's and during the salt march it is reported that salt law had been broken all over Malabar except in the erstwhile "rebel" areas. Moreover, the procession on foot from Payyannur, heading for the Guruvayur satyagraha stopped short of the "rebel" area. The marchers took a train from Feroke to Tirur "because of a rumor that the Mappilas would prevent them from moving into Ernad" (Menon, 1994: pp. 103-104).

programme itself betrayed its elitist character (Kooiman, 1995: p. 45; Onwerkerk, 1994: p. 56). Writings of Gandhi in the early twenties, and even later, revealed how the Congress leadership was getting seriously troubled by lower caste radicalism and the increasing volume of religious conversions (Young India, 27.10. 1920: 135; 04.06.1925: 135; 19.01.1921: 6; 04.05.1921: 3; 27. 04.1921: 5; 22.09.1921: 11; 29.09.1921: 12; 13.10.1921: 13; Harijan, 11.02.1933; 31.10.1936)[17]. Of equal importance was the basic limitation of the anti-untouchability program: it searched for a moral solution to repair inequalities to recast the nation but without dislodging the basic social structure[18]. The Congress leadership in Kerala also refused to address the economic content or power relationships rooted in it but rather took it as a question of equality within religion and an unfortunate aberration from scriptural injunctions.

Secondly, the heated debates unleashed by the Izhava middle class on religious conversion was acquiring political and economic dimensions. C.V. Kunhuraman, the firebrand leader of the S.N.D.P. and the editor of *Kerala Kaumudi* had made the alarm signal by urging the Izhavas to renounce Hinduism if the upper castes did not support their cause of temple entry (Kunhuraman, 1936). A section of the Izhavas enthusiastically welcomed the suggestion. Though there were differences of opinion as to which religion they should opt—whether Christianity, Islam or Buddhism—the challenge fell like a bombshell on the *savarna* groups. Although conversions had been taking place among the untouchables from very early times and its pace had considerably increased by the nineteenth and early twentieth centuries, the '20s and '30s were special because now the challenge came from the Izhavas who though "are *avarnas* are rich and educated" (Kelappan, 1925). The loss of the middle class was exceptionally harmful as they could threaten—as in the case of the Christian middle class of central Travancore (Jeffrey, 1978a: pp. 153-154)—the material pursuits of the upper caste Hindus. A powerful section within the S.N.D.P—including Kumaran Asan, T. K. Madhavan and A. Ayyappan, and of course Sri Narayana Guru too—stood for a reformed Hinduism (Kesavan, 1968: pp. 274-276). But radicals held fast to the idea of conversion; preferably to Buddhism against the Sri Lankan background of the Izhavas (Kunhuraman, 1925); this had lent

space to speculations, that the conversion issue was a pressure tactic to enforce a reform of customs. However, it had its desired effect: caste Hindus increasingly began to realize the need of ritual reform which is evident in the rhetoric against conversions with a stress on the innate quality of Hinduism (Thampan, 1932; Nambutiripad, 1932). The Nair aristocracy fanned Nair communal passions against the Christian capitalists who were buying up their land and prestige (Isaac & Tharakan, 1988: p. 166). Leaders like "Mannam, who was not a Gandhian and was in general opposed to the Congress", participated in the Vaikam Satyagraha for his concern over the loss to Hinduism of converts to Christianity (Onwerkerk, 1994: p. 59). The temple entry movement under the leadership of the Congress thus represented an attempt at forging a consolidated Hindu identity and to discourage conversions which was engendered by disabilities enforced by the caste system. Religious conversion could cause trouble to the caste Hindus because "it reduced their rhetorical constituency" (Jeffrey, 1978a: p. 143). The writings of Kelappan clearly demonstrated how the temple-entry movement was directly linked to the threat posed by religious conversions (Kelappan, 1925; 1932a; 1932b)[19].

Thirdly, the Congress interest in the temple-entry struggle was an attempt to offset the damage caused to its prestige and honor by the incidents of 1921. Congress leadership tried to escape from the initial shock by expressing its "firm conviction" that the non-cooperation and Khilafat movements were in no way responsible for the outbreak. The Congress view was recorded in the resolution of the Working Committee in September 1921, expressing a "sense of deep regret over the deeds of violence done by the Mappilas in certain areas of Malabar" and resolved that the rebellion was not caused by the Khilafat or Non-cooperation movements, and that the causes of the rebellion had nothing to do with these movements (Sitaramayya, 1946: p. 216). Prominent Congress leaders in Kerala shared this view as is understood from Kesava Menon's comment that "it was wrong to have connected the Khilafat problem with the Nationalist Movement" (Menon, 1977: p. 48). Congressmen in Kerala were under siege for upholding the Khilafat issue and forging an alliance with the "fanatic" Mappilas which brought about "great hardships to the Hindus and dishonor to the land". The committees appointed by the Congress failed to make a comprehensive and objective enquiry into the cause of the rebellion, which led to develop controversies with strong political and communal overtones. K. Moidu Maulavi, Khilafat leader and staunch nationalist, reiterated his firm conviction that the rebellion was a struggle for freedom, it started as an anti-imperialist rising, although "in the end the British authorities had succeeded to an extent in degrading it into a communal conflict" (Maulavi, 1981: pp. 136-141; 152-154). But Kesava Menon stated (later) that it would not be correct to consider the "Mappila Rebellion" as part of the Nationalist movement because the rebels "were motivated more by religious zeal and

---

[17] In a series of articles entitled "The Removal of Untouchability" wrote in *Young India* and *Harijan*, Gandhi viewed conversion rather more inspired by the desire for material benefits than for spiritual needs. The lower caste people were getting converted because of untouchability which has to be eliminated not only to cleanse Hinduism of its evils but to attain swaraj also. Foreign rule in India is a divine punishment for following this curse which "is a crime against god and humanity". In fact untouchability was not a part of original Hinduism and hence those who threaten to abandon Hinduism are deceiving their religion. He consoled the untouchables that their low social stature is not due to their fault and urged the *savarna* people to take up the removal of untouchability as an act of atonement before they were too late to do so.

[18] "Untouchability was both a moral and political problem: the former because its eradication involved undermining its moral legitimacy and changing, or at least softening, Hindu attitudes; the latter because it was deeply rooted in the highly unequal structure of power relationship between the upper castes and the harijans and could not be removed without restructuring it. It had therefore to be fought at both levels. Gandhi's campaign was conducted only at the moral and religious level. Hence he concentrated on caste Hindus…, appealed to their sense of duty and honor, mobilized their feelings of shame and guilt, and succeeded in achieving his initial objective of discrediting untouchability and raising the level of the Hindu… consciousness. Since he did not organize and politicize the harijans, stress their rights and fight for a radical reconstruction of the established social and economic order, Gandhi's campaign was unable to go further" (Parekh, 1989: pp. 245-246).

[19] K. Kelappan, the great Gandhian Congressman and the foremost champion of the temple-entry movement in Kerala, in his article on the Vaikam Satyagraha (1925: pp. 42-45), justified the struggle in the context of the increasing tendency of the lower castes, especially Izhavas, to renounce Hinduism. In another article written around the time of the Guruvayur Satyagraha, he expressed great concern over the harms caused by conversions. This article is specially noted for his attitude of the Muslim "other"; they are perceived as a threat to the nation and national unity; mainly because of their solidarity and stress on international brotherhood (1932a: pp. 7-8). He also suggested a "secular" programme the government should follow to curb the growth of (Muslim) communalism (1932b: pp. 4-5, 10).

interest in the Khilafat than by true national consciousness" (Menon, 1977: p. 48). In their highly illuminating accounts of the event, two other prominent Congress leaders—K. Madhavan Nair and Mozhikunnath Brahmadathan Nambutiripad—traced the origin of the rebellion back to the high-handed British policy of repression (Nair, 2002; Nambutiripad, 1965). By attributing the violence of 1921 to the official atrocities, they justified the decision of the Congress to ally with the Mappilas but regretted for associating with a group still unfit for a modern and secular political struggle—and thus justified the official Congress position rejecting the struggle as a part of the national movement. They also shared the colonial perception of the uprising as nothing but a "riot" and treated the Mappilas as "wild" and "fanatic" people who could not be trusted or easily tamed.

Neither did the rebellion confine its impact to Malabar politics alone. The widespread propaganda recounting awesome details of the "Hindu suffering" at the hands of the Mappila rebels gave birth to an aggressive Hindu campaign, at first against the "cruel Mappilas" and later against Muslims in general. On the other hand, the sufferings of the Mappilas deeply moved Muslims all over India. Frantic appeals for helping them received generous response from the North. All these affected the relationship between the Hindus and Muslims all over India. "The exaggerated tales (about the rebellion)... inflamed feelings. The cry of Hinduism in danger was raised and movements of *Shuddhi* (reconversion) and *Sanghathan* (organization) planned. A vicious cycle of accusation and counter-accusation was set up which created the heat in which the tender plant of Hindu-Muslim unity began to wither" (Chand, 1972: p. 497). The "communal antagonisms generated by the Malabar Rebellion" (Brown, 1972: p. 329) and the steadily advancing nationalist discourse centered on religious and cultural nationalism greatly strengthened the concept of the Muslim "other" to the extent that even the great Izhava reformer and poet Kumaran Asan wrote a tale of the Rebellion villainizing the Mappilas in which he told the tale of a Nambutiri girl thrown desolate by the "cruel Muhammedans" during the revolt of 1921 (Asan, 1969). Similarly, in his "statement" attached to the 1970 edition of K. Madhavan Nair's *Malabar Rebellion*, K. Kelappan shared the concern of the Congress leadership towards the "minority Hindus of Ernad" against the "illiterate", "ignorant" and hence "rude" Mappilas (Nair, 2002: ix-xii)[20].

The fear of the Mappilas for their "lack of civility", the widespread concern over the hardships of the (upper caste) Hindus who had escaped from the affected areas to take shelter in the nearby town of Calicut or in the princely states of Travancore and Cochin, the cooperation extended by Congress to the relief measures undertaken by the Arya Samaj, which was also very active in reconverting the Hindus who were converted to Islam, (Ansari, 2005: p. 64) the total breakdown of the organizational structure of the Congress and its inability to carry on even normal political activity in the face of official retribution and

popular distrust in its programs, all forced the Congress to retreat to a Hindu idiom of politics (Menon, 1994: p. 78). Gandhi's statement—"The Moplahs are Muslims"—reveals the stereotypical character-construct of the Muslim (Ansari, 2005: p. 73). The leadership of the Congress in Kerala could not get out of the shock inflicted by the events of the rebellion, especially the attack of the Mappila rebels on caste Hindus. This was not surprising because in Malabar caste system conformed to a kind of class order: the caste Hindus were the landlords or the prominent leaseholders of the area while the Mappilas were the sub-tenants under them (Panikkar, 1984). Among the higher castes in particular, it is observed, the attitude towards Islam was coloured by the way in which Islam impinged upon their interests (Misra, 2004: p. 20). That the lower caste tenants refused to rebel against their upper caste lords in Malabar clearly revealed the manner by which caste hierarchy and the mode of class response got enmeshed. The higher castes could realize that the threat posed by conversion to their interests could only be countered by bringing various caste groups together on some common issue and by reforming social practices which segmented them; efforts to forge a symbolic unity among Hindu communities around the question of temple-entry appeared a useful weapon to discourage the untouchable castes to get attracted to religions which promised to emancipate them. For the dominant groups, religion offers the necessary ideological justification for existing social divisions, makes these divisions appear non-antagonistic and holds together a potentially divided society into a single whole (Chatterjee, 1989: p. 172).

Thus, the championing of the temple-entry cause (mainly at Vaikam) provided the Congress with a big lease of life: it gave a platform for action with a strictly non-political program; it saved them from official surveillance as the centre of activity was shifted to the safe environs of the princely state of Travancore; it eschewed the fear of communal tension because the Mappila factor was absent in Travancore (Menon, 1994: pp. 103-104) and above all, it provided the Congress with an opportunity to expiate for the "sin" of allying with the "dangerous" Mappilas by upholding a "Hindu" cause. Congressmen played the role of an arbiter between various Hindu castes, which in fact signaled a retreat from secular political activity, but it opened before them a program of action after the "Mappila" rebellion (Menon, 1994: p. 80).

Conclusion

The temple-entry movement decided the future course of politics in Kerala at least in three respects. Firstly, it provided a conclusive end to the civil rights movement undertaken by the untouchable castes leading to the attainment of the right of universal temple-entry. The questions of religious disability and freedom of worship slowly subsided to become less and less powerful to command the discourse of civic life and political culture. The debates centered on religious conversion as a means of social emancipation also faded out altogether (Isaac & Tharakan, 1988: p. 168; Narayanan, 2011). The (upper caste) leadership of the Congress was able to coerce the caste-Hindus to compromise on the question of temple-entry as the only viable means to ward off religious conversion which challenged the very survival of the Hindu community. Secondly, with the success of the temple-entry agitation the conversion movement certainly began to wane in Kerala, but it greatly undermined the secular image of the Congress for its propagandist role in dis-

---

[20]Chatterjee (1995: p. 126) writes that the fact that Indian nationalism is synonymous with "Hindu nationalism" is an entirely modern, rationalist and historicist idea. The notion of "Hinduness" is not defined by any religious criteria at all. There are no specific beliefs or practices which characterize this "Hindu" and the many doctrinal or sectarian differences among Hindus are indifferent to this concept. Even anti-Vedic and anti-brahmanical religions as Buddhism and Jainism count here as "Hindu". Clearly excluded from this *jati* are religions like Christianity and Islam. The criterion for inclusion and exclusion is determined by their historical origin. Buddhism and Jainism are 'Hindu' because they originated in India while Islam and Christianity originated outside and are, therefore, foreign.

seminating the so-called "Essentials of Hinduism" and in seeking to forge a (Hindu) "community of equals" (Menon, 1994: p. 80) through a common bond of religiosity and uniformity of religious worship around temples. In that sense the temple-entry movement marked a definite stage in the process of the disjunction of folk religion and other currents of religion. Religion is no longer divided into lower religion and higher religion, but into religion and superstition (Sontheimer, 1995: p. 396). Hence it was a *shuddhi* movement—to cleanse religion of blots identified incompatible with modernity and the essentials of nationhood. The temple-entry satyagraha attains significance against the dual task taken up by the Indian National Congress —to construct a modern nation-state and to mould a national (Hindu) religion. But it had its disastrous consequences—in driving religious minorities away from the organizational fold and ideological appeal of the Congress. The bitter experiences of 1921 followed by the conscious involvement of the Congress in the affairs of religious nationalism forced the Mappilas to keep away from nationalist politics and slowly drift towards a marked sectarian identity. The slow but steady drift of the Mappilas into communal politics became inevitable (Panikkar, 1989: p. 190). Thirdly, the struggle for temple-entry helped in delivering the Congress from the moral setback it faced after the Malabar rebellion, but in the unique social context of Kerala where reform movements had succeeded in shaping an ideological environment in favor of social equality, its withdrawal from direct politics to engage with socio-religious issues, disregarding more important questions of material deprivation and class disparities, transcending caste/religious affiliations, reduced its political constituency and created a fertile ground for the proliferation of left political ideology in subsequent times. Moreover, in the 1930s, the strong communal and caste consciousness let loose by the agitation against caste disabilities could lead the poor towards class consciousness (as caste roughly coincided with class in Kerala). With the Temple entry Proclamation in Travancore in 1936—"the final act in the embourgeoisment of society" as Nambutiripad saw it (Jeffrey, 1978: p. 82)—the middle class members were accorded the right to use temples and abruptly lost interest in the poor of their own caste. But the political excitement awakened among the poor and low caste could not be made to go away; it lay ready to be developed into class consciousness.

REFERENCES

Newspapers/Periodicals
Harijan
Madras Mail
Mathrubhumi Daily
Mathrubhumi Weekly
Mitavadi
Sahodaran
Yogakshemam
Young India

Government Publications
Aiya, V. N. (1906). *The Travancore State manual, I&II*. Trivandrum: Travancore Government Press.
Cornish, W. R. (1874). *The census of India 1871, Madras Vol. I, Report*. Madras: Government Press.
Hitchcock, R. H. (1925). *A history of the Malabar rebellion, 1921*. Madras: Government Press.
Innes, C. A. (1908). *Madras District gazetteers, Malabar I*. Madras: Government Press.
Logan, M. (1882). *Report of the Malabar special commission 1881-2, I.*

Madras: Government Press.
Logan, W. (1887). *Malabar manual, I*. Madras: Government Press.
McIvery, L. (1883). *Census of India, 1881, Madras, Vol. I, Report*. Madras: Government Press.
Menon, C. A. (1911). *Cochin State manual*. Ernakulam: Government Press.
Menon, M. Sankara. (1901). *Census of India, Vol. 20 (Cochin) Part I (Report)*. Ernakulam: Government Press.
Pillai, T. K. V. (1940). *Travancore State manual, Vol. I*. Trivandrum: Travancore Government Press.
Proceedings of the Conference held at Mr. Idamturuttil Devan Neelakantan Nambutiripad's House, Vaikam on 10 March 1925. *Correspondence on the Vaikam Satyagraha, Vol IX*, English Records, Secretariat, Trivandrum.
Stuert, H. A. (1893). *Census of India, 1891, Madras, Part. I Report*. Madras: Government Press.
Tottenham, G. R. F. (1922). *The Mappila rebellion, 1921-22*. Madras: Government Press.

Autobiographies
Kesavan, C. (1968). *Jeevitasamaram*. Kottayam: National Book Stall.
Maulavi, M. (1981). *Atmakatha*. Kottayam: SPCS/National Book Stall.
Menon, K. P. K. (1986). *Kazhinja Kaalam*. Calicut: Mathrubhumi Books.
Nambutiripad, E. M. S. (2005). *Atmakatha* (6th ed.). Thiruvananthapuram: Chintha Publishers.

Books
Aiyappan, A. (1944). *Iravas and culture change*. Madras Government Museum Bulletin, 1.
Aloysius, G. (2010). *Nationalism without a nation in India*. New Delhi: Oxford University Press.
Anderson, B. (1983). *Imagined communities: Reflections on the origin and spread of nationalism*. London: Verso Editions and NLB.
Ansari, M. T. (2005). Refiguring the fanatic: Malabar, 1836-1922. In S. Mayaram, M. S. S. Pandyan, & A. Skaria (Eds.), *Subaltern studies, XII* (pp. 36-77). Delhi: Permanent Black and Ravi Dayal.
Asan, K. (1969). *Duravastha (Distress)*. Trivandrum: Sarada Book Depot (Rpt).
Brown, J. M. (1972). *Gandhi's rise to power: Indian politics, 1915-1922*. Cambridge: Cambridge University Press.
Chand, T. (1972). *History of the freedom movement in India, III*. New Delhi: New Delhi Publications Division, Government of India.
Chandra, B. (1989). *India's struggle for independence 1857-1947*. New Delhi: Penguin Books.
Chatterjee, P. (1989). Caste and subaltern consciousness. In R. Guha (Ed.), *Subaltern studies: Writings on South Asian history and society, No. 6* (pp. 169-209). Delhi: Oxford University Press.
Chatterjee, P. (1995). History and the nationalization of Hinduism. In V. Dalmia, & H. Von Steitencron (Eds.), *Representing Hinduism: The contraction of religious tradition and national identity* (pp. 103-128). New Delhi: Sage Publications.
Cooiman, D. (1995). *Communities and electorates: A comparative discussion of communalism in colonial India*. Amsterdam: V.U. University Press.
Dale, S. F. (1980). *Islamic society on the South Asian frontier: The Mappilas of Malabar, 1498-1922*. Oxford: Clarendon Press.
Day, F. (1863). *The land of Perumals or Cochin and its past and its present*. Madras: Oantz Brothers at the Adelphi Press.
Gangadharan, M. (2008). *The Malabar rebellion*. Kottayam: D.C. Books.
Hardgrave Jr., R. L. (1969). *The Nadars of Tamilnad: The political culture of a community in change*. Berkeley: University of California Press.
Isaac, T. M. T. & Tharakan, P. K. M. (1988). Sree Narayana movement in Travancore. In S. K. Sreevastava & L. Sreevastava (Eds), *Social movements for development* (pp. 155-177). Allahabad: Chugh Publications.
Iyer, L. A. K. (1909). *The Cochin Tribes and castes*. Madras: Higginbotham's.
Iyer, L. A. K. (1939). *The Travancore Tribes and castes*. Trivandrum: Government Press.
Jeffrey, R. (1978a). Travancore: Status, class and the growth of radical

politics, 1869-1940—The temple entry movement. In R. Jeffrey, (Ed.), *People, princes and paramount power: Society and politics in the Indian princely states* (pp. 136-169). Delhi: Oxford University Press.

Jeffrey, R. (1994). *Decline of Nair dominance: Society and politics in Travancore, 1847-1908.* New Delhi: Manohar.

Kawashima, K. (1988). *Missionaries and a Hindu state: Travancore 1858-1936.* New Delhi: Oxford University Press.

Kunhuraman, C. V. (1936). *Izhavarude mathaparivarthana samrambham (Religious conversion enterprise of the Izhavas).* Kottayam: Kaumudi Press.

Kunju, A. P. I. (1989). *Mappila Muslims of Kerala.* Trivandrum: Sandhya Publishers.

Lemercinier, G. (1984). *Religion and ideology in Kerala.* Delhi: D. K. Agencies.

Manavalan, P. (1990). *Kerala samskaravum Kraistava missionarimarum (Kerala culture and Christian missionaries).* Kottayam: DC Books.

Mateer, S. (1871). *The land of charity: A descriptive account of Travancore and its people.* London: John Snow & Co.

Mateer, S. (1883). *Native life in Travancore.* London: W. H. Allen & Co.

Mathew, G. (1989). *Communal road to a secular Kerala.* New Delhi: Concept Publishing Company.

Menon, A. S. (1984). *A survey of Kerala history.* Madras: S. Viswanathan Pvt Ltd.

Menon, A. S. (1997). *Kerala and the freedom struggle.* Kottayam: D.C. Books.

Menon, D. M. (1994). *Caste, nationalism and communism in South India: Malabar, 1900-1948.* New Delhi: Cambridge University Press.

Menon, K. P. K. (1977). Some aspects of the nationalist movement in Malabar. In K. P. S. Menon (Ed.), *Kesava Menon* (pp. 43-48). Calicut: K. P. Kesava Menon 90th Birthday Celebration Committee.

Menon, P. K. K. (2001). *History of the freedom movement in Kerala, Vol. II.* Thiruvananthapuram: Department of Cultural Publications.

Menon, M. G. (1989). *Malabar rebellion, 1921-1922.* Allahabad: Vohra Publishers.

Miller, R. E. (1992). *Mappila Muslims of Kerala: A study in Islamic trends.* Madras: Orient Longman.

Misra, A. (2004). *Identity and religion: Foundations of anti-Islamism in India.* New Delhi: Sage Publishers.

Nair, G. G. (1923). *The Moplah rebellion, 1921.* Calicut: Norman Printing Bureau.

Nair, K. M. (2002). *Malabar kalapam (Malabar rebellion).* Calicut: Mathrubhumi Books.

Nambutiripad, E. M. S (1952). *The national question in Kerala.* Bombay: People's Publishing House.

Nambutiripad, M. B. (1965). *Khilafat smaranakal (Khilafat reminiscences).* Kozhikkode: Navakerala Co-operative Publishing House.

Narayanan, M. G. S., & Kesavan, V. (1983). A history of the Nambutiri community in Kerala. In F. Stall (Ed.), *Agni: The Vedic ritual of the fire altar* (pp. 256-278). Delhi: Motilal Banarsidas.

Onwerkerk, L. (1994). *No elephants for the Maharaja: Social and political change in Travancore 1921-47.* New Delhi: Manohar Publishers.

Panikkar, K. N. (1984). Peasant exploitation in Malabar in the nineteenth century. *Journal of Kerala Studies, 11,* 155-185.

Panikkar, K. N. (1989). *Against lord and state: Religion and peasant uprising in Malabar, 1836-1921.* Delhi: Oxford University Press.

Parekh, B. (1989). *Colonialism, tradition and reform: An analysis of Gandhi's political discourse.* New Delhi: Sage Publications.

Pilla, A. K. (1986). *Congressum Keralavum (Congress and Kerala).* Trivandrum: Prabhath Book House.

Rao, M. S. A. (1979). *Social movements and social transformation: A study of two backward classes movement in India.* Delhi: MacMillan.

Ravindran, T. K. (1988). *Vaikam satyagraha and Gandhi.* Trivandrum: Sri Narayana Institute of Social and Cultural Development.

Sarkar, S. (1990). *Modern India, 1885-1947.* Madras: Macmillan.

Sitaramayya, P. (1946). *The history of the Indian national congress 1885-1936.* Bombay: Padma Publications Ltd.

Sontheimer, G. D. (1995). The erosion of folk religion in modern India: Some points for deliberation. In V. Dalmia, & H. Von Steitencron, (Eds.), *Representing Hinduism: The contraction of religious tradition and national identity* (pp. 389-398). New Delhi: Sage Publications.

Thurston, E. (1909). *Castes and tribes of southern India, II.* Madras: Government Press.

Viswanathan, G. (2003). Colonialism and the construction of Hinduism. In G. Flood (Ed.), *The Blackwell companion to Hinduism* (pp. 23-44). Oxford: Blackwell.

Von Stietencron, H. (1989). Hinduism: On the proper use of a deceptive term. In G. D. Sontheimer, & H. Kulke (Eds.), *Hinduism reconsidered.* Delhi: Manohar.

Wood, C. (1987). *The Moplah rebellion and its genesis.* New Delhi: People's Publishing House.

Yesudas, R. N. (1975). *A people's revolt in Travancore: A backward class movement for social freedom.* Ernakulam: Kerala Historical Society.

Young, R. F. (1981). *Resistant Hinduism: Sanskrit sources on anti-Christian apologetics in early nineteenth century India.* Vienna: De Nobili Research Library.

Zaynu'd-Din, S. (1942). *Tuhfat-al-Mujahidin.* Translated by S. M. H. Nainar. Madras: University of Madras.

Articles

Basu, R. S. (2008). Pulayas in Kerala: The nineteenth century emancipation question re-explored. *The ICFAI University Journal of History and Culture, 2,* 47-76.

Dale, S. F. (1975). The Mappila outbreaks: Ideology and social conflict in nineteenth century Kerala. *Journal of Asian Studies, XXXV,* 85-97.

Dale, S. F. (1976). The Mappilas during Mysorean rule: Agrarian conflict in eighteenth-century Malabar. *South Asia, 6,* 1-13.

Damodaran, N. P. (1981). Oru sathyagrahathinte katha (The story of a satyagraha). *Mathrubhumi Weekly,* 22-25.

Dhanagare, D. N. (1977). Agrarian conflict, religion and politics: The Moplah rebellion in the nineteenth and early twentieth centuries. *Past and Present, 74,* 112-141.

Gopalankutty, K. (1981). The Guruvayur satyagraha, 1931-32. *Journal of Kerala Studies, 8,* 43-55

Gough, K. (1968-1969). Peasant resistance and revolt in South India. *Pacific Affairs, XVI,* 526-554.

Hardgrave Jr., R. L. (1968). Breast cloth controversy: Caste consciousness and social change in southern Travancore. *Indian Economic and Social History Review, 5,* 171-187.

Hardgrave Jr., R. L. (1977). The Mappilla rebellion, 1921: Peasant revolt in Malabar. *Modern Asian Studies, 11,* 57-99.

Heimsath, C. H. (1978). The functions of Hindu reformers—With special reference to Kerala. *The Indian Economic and Social History Review, XV,* 21-39.

Heimsath, C. H. (1982). From social reform to social struggle. *Man and Development, IV,* 29-34.

Houtart, F., & Lemercinier, G. (1978). Socio-religious reform movements in Kerala: A reaction to the capitalist mode of production. *Social Scientist, 6,* 25-43.

Jeffrey, R. (1974). The social origins of a caste association, 1875-1905: The founding of the S.N.D.P. Yogam. *South Asia, 4,* 39-59.

Jeffrey, R. (1978b). Matriliny, marxism and the birth of the communist party in Kerala, 1930-1940. *Journal of Asian Studies, XXXVIII,* 77-98.

Kelappan, K. (1925). Vaikam satyagraham. *Matrubhumi Onam Special,* 42-45.

Kelappan, K. (1932a). Mathavum samudayavum: Mathaparivarthana sramam kondulla dosham (Religion and community: The harms caused by religious conversion). *Matrubhumi Weekly, 10,* 7-8.

Kelappan, K. (1932b). Mathavum samudayavum: Oru swathantra government cheyyendathenthellam (Religion and community: What should an independent government do). *Mathrubhumi Weekly, 10,* 4-5.

Kunhuraman, C. V. (1925). Tiyyarku nallathu buddhamatham thanne (Buddhism is better for the tiyyas). *Mitavadi Special, II,* 6-24.

Menon, D. M. (1999). Houses by the sea: State formation experiments in Malabar, 1760-1800. *Economic and Political Weekly, 34,* 1995-

2003.

Muralidharan, M. (1996). Hindu community formation in Kerala: Processes and structures under colonial modernity. *South Indian Studies, 2,* 234-259.

Nambutiripad, E. M. S. (1937). *Congress socialist.* 7-9.

Nambutiripad, K. S. (1932). Matha parishkaram (Religious reform). *Mathrubhumi Weekly, 10,* 7-8.

Narayanan, M. G. S. (2011). Malayala manorama. *Sunday Supplement, IX.*

Pulapilly, C. K. (1976).The izhavas of Kerala and their historic struggle for acceptance in the Hindu society. *Journal of Asian and African Studies, XI,* 24-46.

Thampan, M. R. V. (1932). Kshetra pravesanam (Temple-entry). *Mathrubhumi Weekly, 9,* 5-6.

5

Technology as a Mode and Manifestation of Being: An Assessment of Its Applications

Theodore John Rivers
Independent, Forest Hills, USA

The objective of this paper is to demonstrate how technology's being is revealed through its applications, which is expressive by means of the mode and manifestation of its being. The designation of technology as a mode of being refers to its nature, and the designation of technology as a manifestation of being refers to its activity as proof of technology's being. Both mode and manifestation indicate how the being of technology is applied. Although distinguishable as two aspects of technology, both mode and manifestation are essential to revealing the essence of technology and its interplay with the world. Since human culture has a technological underpinning, the applications of technology not only reveal its metaphysics, but also indicate its importance to human culture. In addition to technology's underlying method, these applications also pertain to the artifacts (or objects) of invention, mathematics, the consciousness of time, writing, alphabetization, science, and society.

Keywords: Technology

Introduction

Technology is expressive of the choices humanity makes. Unless we encounter extraterrestrials that might be similar to us technologically, we can say that technology is primarily associated with humans. This statement is true while knowing that some animals possess a rudimentary technology, such as the building of nests by birds, the constructing of dams by beavers, and the use of simple tools by chimpanzees. Essentially, technology helps to form the basis of human culture, and it is culture, among other factors, that lies at the foundation of human reality. Although the manner by which humans live in the world determines the use of technology, it should be apparent that modern technology is culturally more inclusive than premodern technologies. Collectively, technology is more than occasionally present; it is omnipresent. Technology comes into being because humanity's being becomes, that is, it is by means of becoming that the being of technology is revealed. This revelation indicates that technology is a dependency because it is based on creative ingenuity, but it is also true that humans have willingly made themselves excessively dependent on its being. Although it is not our concern to discuss the moral implications of technology, it should be kept in mind that technology always has moral consequences because it is the result of human choices.

The essence of technology, if it possesses one, is its presence, which is expressive of its involvement in the world. Technology is the embodiment of human creativity that is the result of the upsurge of our ontological freedom. It is embedded in human choices, occupied by the decisions humanity makes, and committed to the means intended for its projected ends. Embeddedness, occupation, and commitment reveal technology's presence that is a description of a process that is all-consuming. Technology signifies a plan or inducement toward a course of action. It would be a simple step to go from this thought to the realization of the nearly endless applications of technology throughout time. Although the past is always a victim of interpretation, any hermeneutical attempt of it should be guided by the pursuit of truth unaffected by emotion or deception. Humanity's alignment with technology should be sufficient to continue its presence and its impact.

When expressed within this context, technology's importance is self-evident. It is revealed in many ways, beginning with the nature of conceptualization and its relationship to truth. Because human reality is involved with the act of the becoming of being, the latter is the way in which technology makes its appearance in the world, that is, the act of becoming is the conduit for the appearance of the being of technology (Olsen, 2009: pp. 40-61). Although the fundamental characteristics of technology have been discussed many times before, suffice it to say that its applications demonstrate its importance at the present time and anticipate its continuation in the future.

Technology is also supported by the formation of concepts and their necessity for human action. Nevertheless, there is no immediate contact with the world unless it is affected by concepts that help with comprehension. As a requirement for everything we do from spatial orientation to numerical calculation, concepts allow us to understand the world because they are part of the essential framework on which comprehension is based. Conceptualization is associated with the mental process that allows humans to function in the world, and the world may be equated with the summation of social relationships (society), or the physical environment (nature). In addition to these two distinctions, there is also the single human being, that is, the self, from which individuality and self-consciousness are derived (Fodor, 1998: pp. 23-29).

As essential as concepts are to humans, they are not extant in the world because they exist only in our heads. A concept is a mental representation from which identity is derived when individual human beings interact with the world or with other individuals. Concepts are played out in the world because the latter is the platform from which action takes place. Therefore, without the world, there would be neither individuals nor concepts. The truth of this relationship should be self-evident, and it supports the idea that concepts and the cognitive development that is associated with them are culturally, not biologically, derived (Donald, 1991: pp. 119-122).

If concepts are related to culture, it should be asked how they are created. And by culture, reference is made not to distinct ethnicities or nationalities, but to human culture in general from which humanity's experiences are based, the experiences that are grounded in the challenges of living in a changeable world, conditioned by the longing to satisfy basic needs, and hounded by life's uncertainties. Human culture by means of evolution has led to the development of concepts, that is, to the development of mental representations that humanity needs for survival. If human understanding reveals a greater complexity, this complexity is imposed on the world. Therefore, mental representation signifies the means by which human culture laid a basis for cognitive development that distinguished humans from other primates.

Because a concept is a mental representation that is derived from perceptions, the latter is not only recognition of mental and physical stimuli, but also an interpretation of them. The integrations of perceptions concern everything. When defined in this way, perceptions become part of a systematic approach to reality because a system concerns the integration of components into a unified whole. Technology plays a key role in helping to satisfy fundamental needs, beginning with methods and organizations and expanding to all manner of applications. Although wants are often confused with needs, both are dependent on technology, which is true even for physiological needs that originate biologically, but are affected technologically.

We should ask how technology becomes the result of conceptualization. Although emanating from the use of ontological freedom that results from a perception of the world, technology is characterized eventually by its applications. Once conceived, technology may be devised, and when devised, it may then be used. Since applications make technology useful, it is creativity that characterizes technology. The manner by which this is done indicates the means by which technology is rendered real in the world.

Technology as a Mode and Manifestation of Being

The metaphysics of technology is derived from the becoming of being because technology is demonstrative of a process. Although becoming denotes a procedure from which being springs forth, it also denotes the modification of being that already exists. Since becoming, as an expression of being, supplements the being that is, it lies at the threshold of the enlargement of being from which creativity originates. But this process must not be confused with the notion of development or evolution because the latter represents a specific type of be-

ing. To develop or evolve usually means to bring something forth from latency, as a way of improving or elaborating something. To come into being means to appear where previously there was no appearance or presence, as a way of springing forth or coming into existence. For example, the materials used in a book already exist in trees for paper or resin for ink, but they do not constitute the being of a book until a book comes into being. Likewise, when a book is destroyed, it will cease to be. The being of a book concerns its presence, and it is through its presence or the projection of its presence that it comes into being.

This process is demonstrated in two ways, that when combined, reveal the nature of technology. First, and more essentially, technology is a mode of being that refers to the nature or the underlying basis to its being. It concerns the means of doing something as a way of positing its existence. Since mode is the medium through which existence appears, it is the way in which technology shows the underlying mechanism of its presence. A mode of being is indicative of the presence of being in general, just as technology's mode of being reveals its presence, that is, its bearing on the world. The second part of this process concerns technology as a manifestation of being. Since manifestation is indicative of the presence of something as proof of it's being, it indicates that the doing of anything, even the doing of technology, is the result of its presence. The mode and manifestation of technology reveal it's being, which is the being that we give it.

Of these two attempts to understand the being of technology, we may conclude that although mode and manifestation are related, one of them may be more fundamental than the other. Since a presence presupposes an essence, we might conclude that a mode of being is antecedent to its manifestation, but it is difficult to separate them. Logically, we might say that if manifestation is an effect of being, then mode is its cause; but metaphysically, they are inseparable. Therefore, for all practical purposes, we should regard the mode and manifestation of the being of technology to be conterminous.

These thoughts are merely preparatory to a discussion of technology's applications. Although other applications could have been selected, the ones that are discussed below are fundamental to human culture.

Method

An analysis of technology should begin with the concept of method. Although not necessarily progressive, technology's method is developmental. It is no understatement to say that its method expresses more than what is supposedly evident by the nature of any means to its corresponding end. Although means and ends are reciprocal to each other by the very nature of their being, technology's method is much more fundamental because it lies at the core of their relationships. Just as it is inconceivable to think of technology without making reference to process, it is also inconceivable to think of technology without considering its method. Since the latter intensifies the idea of involvement, it is a feature that is fundamental to technology. But it is not redundant to describe method as methodic when the latter signifies a procedural turn of events. If technology's method is not procedural, it cannot be methodic.

Technology's method is not to be confused with methodology. A method is the description of how to do something, but it is not a description of the underlying principles on which it is based. Nevertheless, how method is perpetuated indicates a great deal about it. It may be perpetuated by all types of means, by those expressed directly from the context to which they are derived, but technology may also be expressed indirectly by a motley of seemingly lesser means, such as custom, environmental considerations, or economics. Overall, method is most meaningful not with any means, but with a means that is useful, purposeful, and manipulative. We might say that method is a form of perception, but it is not the equivalent of invention. Nevertheless, method is the result or product of invention (Buchler, 1961: pp. 12-13).

Because method is an artifice that presupposes the completion of its tasks, it may be perceived as an agent that allows its tasks to be actualized. Since technology is the effect of its characteristics (notably, rationality, materiality, accumulation, and process), it is also distinguished by a process that accompanies these characteristics and projects them onto the world. Technology's method is twofold: it is a characteristic of technology, and the medium or conveyance of technology itself. If this condition were not true, then technology would not be linked to processes, procedures, and all manner of organization.

An understanding of method in general and its relationship to technology in particular must not be confused with the idea that technology is little more than a matrix or framework, which is proposed by Heidegger as the principle feature of technology (Heidegger, 1977: pp. 11-16, 25-33)[1]. We should emphasize that technology is multilayered, made up of several interdependent characteristics, none of which is more important than another. Nevertheless, technology's method is variable because the circumstances that help to define it are not static, but subject to change. Although circumstances may appear that could lead to new methods, essentially method concerns the improvement of those procedures that already exist. It is repeatable, but not necessarily predictable.

Because technology's method is associated with its essential characteristics, one type may serve as a paradigm for others, but technology does not innately possess any method. If a paradigm is a pattern in the sense of a composite of features or a representative sample that is based on concepts or practices that depicts a way or manner of doing something, even if this is a

---

[1]According to Heidegger, technology is a mode or manner of revealing truth in which something unknown, such as an object or technique, is brought forth into the world, or to use Heidegger's terminology of this revelation: a "challenging, setting-upon revealing". Because technology is associated with truth, it is hidden (to use an ancient Greek concept) and must be revealed through human ingenuity. Therefore, technology is situated somewhere, waiting to be discovered by humans. But Heidegger's interpretation ignores non-being, the description for those things that do not exist. Does technology reside somewhere waiting to be revealed by human ingenuity, or does it not exist at all until invented by humans? An answer to this question is fundamental to an understanding of technology. Heidegger's interpretation makes humans important, but in a subordinate role. More importantly, Heidegger ignores the becoming of being in relationship to technology. Since becoming concerns a process for the realization of being, as discussed in Aristotle, Metaphysics, Bk. II, 2 (994a34-994b2), this process is never complete. Even when inhibited or isolated, technology should continue indefinitely into the future.

Heidegger also contends that we are provoked by technology, and implies that as a result, we are determined by it. Behind this understanding, Heidegger identifies a framework (Gestell in German) that compels humans to respond to technology. It is this framework that makes technology compelling, but this interpretation leaves little room for human responsibility. Heidegger's interpretation of Gestell should not be equated with method because although technology acquires a method, the latter is only one feature of technology's application.

way of perceiving reality, then a paradigm is a method. It is a structure around which reality revolves at a particular time and place and from which rules may be derived (Kuhn, 1996: pp. 42-44).

Similarly, method is not a model because a model serves merely as a representation of something, as a plastic miniature can represent a model of an airplane. Although method may be explained as a conceptual model, this relationship is true only in so far that there is an underlying reality to method. Otherwise, a conceptual model would exist theoretically, but not actually. Therefore, we should conclude that method presupposes some type of practical application, since it constitutes more than a mental construction. When method becomes standardized, it is standardization that allows us to speak of the completion of tasks. It is similar to the function of society, in which its individual parts, when applied, are integrated into a whole because society in general manifests a particular conception of reality. In its affiliation with technology, method reveals the effectiveness of its being. It is for this reason that the indefinite article "a" is not used with the noun "method" to fix its identity. Thus, we may speak of method, but not a method because the identity of technology's method is not known.

And it is through effectiveness by which method is most meaningful. Wherever we look, we are likely to discover a heartfelt means by which technology is put into effect. Indeed, what would be the effect of tools, devices, machines, and products, without some manner in which they have an influence on the world? And the same may be said of techniques, which are subordinate parts of method, that is, specialized approaches to completing something. Although these technological effects could be used in ways different from their original intent, nevertheless, they were invented for specific goals, as a chisel was invented to chip and form rock, or the sport of golf was developed based on the mastery of techniques with different clubs.

Artifacts as Tools, Devices, Machines, and Products

An analysis of technology's applications must also emphasize its material artifacts, which began with the first tools. Given that the first tools were most likely unaltered stones utilized by hominids, all other technologies, except for a few that are genuinely original, are directly related to their predecessors. Anything that humans have produced also incorporates some type of technique, such as the technique of cultivating plants, or making clay pots, or extracting metal from ores. And when anything is made, techniques are created, beginning with a simple procedure and evolving into more elaborate ones. Technology is based on the accumulation of its results, evolving from the simplest to the more complex (Arthur, 2009). Because technology is made up of several interrelated characteristics that are used, elaborated, extended, modified, or reinvented, it is the result of many factors, only one of which is accumulation. And since accumulation is related to technological efficiency, the latter indicates that the best possible means should be selected when completing a task. If no means exist, then one can be invented.

A distinction should also be noted about the artifacts of technology, particularly, the definition of a tool as a device, and a device as a tool. We should not be confused about the reciprocal relationship because tools and devices since both are universal descriptions of the artifacts of technology. A device is an invention designed for a specific purpose, but this definition is applicable as well to tools that are devices that work manually or mechanically. Therefore, tools and devices may have equivalent descriptions, but the definition of a machine is also relevant in so far that it is a more elaborate device. To say that a machine deals with fixed and movable parts would designate even a shaduf as a machine because it has a fixed weight at one end that is moved to counterweight a basket at the other end to scoop up water for irrigation. If a shaduf is a simple machine, then many other devices associated with antiquity are also, such as the lever, pulley, inclined plane, or wedge (McNeil, 1990: pp. 17-18).

As already noted, technology in large part concerns artifacts of invention, which evolved from the simplest techniques of scavenging for meat from dead animals by hominids and early humans to hunting them with weapons of wood and stone. Eventually, humans become nomads who hunted animals and gathered fruits, nuts, and roots. A comparison of the rudimentary technology, for example, of Paleolithic humans during the Ice Age and our own technology leaves much to be desired, in fact, almost everything. Having no domestic implements except for the needle used to sew animal skins together to make clothes and boots, even lacking the bow and arrow, Paleolithic humans survived because they had fire, and could use it to cook food and stay warm. As primitive as the technology was for Paleolithic humans, the fact that they had technology that aided their existence is proof of their innovative ability as an essential characteristic of their being.

Eventually, the hunter-gatherer became a herder of animals, and later, a cultivator of plants. In addition to food, animals were also used for other purposes: clothing (derived from their skins), transportation, physical power, and protection. Because a settled way of life became the predominant life style for many people and led to civilization, permanent agricultural settlements gave rise to dietary changes whose techniques were included in the so-called Neolithic revolution that began in the fourth millennium BCE. These techniques involved the development of procedures, beginning with the identification of potentially useful plants that could be cultivated, and ending with the preservation of seeds for the next growing season. By trial and error, agriculture entailed the invention of special tools for working the land, and techniques for maximizing the likelihood of successful cultivation.

Similarly, other technologies were also affected, such as the making of clothing (the loom), pottery (the potter's wheel), and metal utensils and weapons (metallurgy). Apart from the use of various minerals found lying on the ground, metallurgy became a specialty because it entails the substitution of one component of metallic ores with another (usually sulfur) through the application of high temperatures, a procedure that took several centuries to perfect.

The tools and machines that were developed in prehistory and antiquity, and that served as an introduction to the sophisticated counterparts of later generations include all major categories of technological innovation. From the hoe to the plow, the water mill to the windmill, the abacus to the computer, the water clock (clepsydra) to the mechanical clock, the telegraph to the telephone, the cannon to the automobile, the motor to the generator, the technologies of the past have influenced the technologies of later generations. It is impossible to think of technology without making reference to its artifacts, as enumerated above, and its artifacts are expressive of the being of technology, a revelation of humanity's continuous application

of the need to assist human existence by modifying nature. And the effects of this need are everywhere and in every aspect of our lives. Because inventive ability is emphasized through tools and machines that indicate how society acts and reacts, invention is indicative of the being of technology as a force in history. When applied, invention is transformed into innovation. And the accumulation of innovations represents a process of ingenuity, exerting an influence on humanity much greater than its original purpose.

Mathematics

Formal schooling usually includes an introduction to mathematics. Even when this introduction is limited to arithmetic, it is accompanied by the idea that numbers and mathematical functions are natural, that is, they are not fabricated. Since the study of mathematics concerns the idea that numbers in particular and mathematical entities in general exist independently of human beings, this idea has little significance for anyone who is not concerned about the origin of mathematics, but much significance for anyone who thinks that numbers are a valid topic for reflection. Hence, it is to philosophy of mathematics where the notion of mathematical concepts is pertinent. It is within this context that mathematics is perceived either to exist apart from human reality or remains dependent on it, that is, mathematics is either innate within itself or created.

Of course, numbers would have no bearing if they could not be understood. Some animals, such as pigeons and chimpanzees, may be assumed to possess a rudimentary numerical ability (Honig, 1993: p. 62; Thompson, 1995: pp. 199-200), but the latter must be differentiated from the symbolization associated with numbers. We may conclude, to which science gives support, that numbers reflect a mental identification that is the result of the perception of physical objects. They are not descriptions of what are naturally in the world, but enumerations of how objects are perceived (Russell, 1956: p. 529). A number is an idea with its corresponding meaning of enumeration that we impose on the world. Indeed, we may find many things in the world, but nowhere will we find numbers. Although constituting an important part of human reality, numbers are real as concepts, but not real as things (Carnap, 1983: p. 42). To write a number on a piece of paper does not confer reality. A number is a concept represented by a numeral, as the Arabic numeral 4 (or the Roman numeral IV) stands for the number that immediately follows the numeral 3 (or III) in a progression of symbols. Despite being used in association with objects, numbers lack factual content and are not verifiable empirically, since they are merely mental representations of things.

Arithmetic, as the simplest area of mathematics, is an extension of object identification. Like many other things we do, arithmetic is a reflection of everydayness, but it is also a reflection of the need to modify its conditions. Therefore, every person should have a fundamental understanding of mathematics because of the human capability of counting and identifying objects. It is from object identification that humans are able to add and subtract, multiply and divide (Lakoff & Núñez, 2000: pp. 77-78). All other areas of mathematics from algebra and geometry to trigonometry and calculus are artificialities. They are expressions of human consciousness imposed on the being of the world.

Why would we need higher forms of mathematics? Although algebra originated in antiquity, it later concerned the substitution of letters for numbers in arithmetical equations, a substitution that was expanded in the sixteenth century by the French mathematician François Viète (Hazewinkel, 1988: p. 73). We should ask why there would be a need for a branch of mathematics that seems to make the latter deliberately complex. Although algebra was invented as a tool to discover unknown quantities in mathematical equations, the use of letters for numbers attempted to uncover universal formulas when applicable to similar examples.

As is widely known, geometry concerns uncovering the mathematical relationships between points, lines, angles, and solids. We can refer to the first known historical reference to geometry in The Histories, written by Herodotus in the fifth century BCE that describes the desire to measure land in Egypt after the annual flooding of the Nile (Herodotus, 1998: pp. 135-136). The practicality of geometry is evident as a means of reassessing land measurements that in turn is applied to many other occasions when referring to space and distance. Geometry became a simple tool for the practical application of mathematics.

Similarly, trigonometry concerns the mathematical relationships of the sides and angles of triangles. It was developed, most likely, as an extension of geometry, particularly, for the use of surveying land in the determination of boundaries, and the construction of roads and buildings. It was developed as an applied science, and fulfilled a rudimentary step in the study of mathematical functions when no quantitative value is known, which mathematically is described as a variable.

The branch of mathematics that expands trigonometry and that deals with the differentiation and integration of functions of one or more variables is known as calculus. It concerns analyzing one set of numbers in relationship to another. Differential calculus concerns finding the rate of change between these two sets. The opposite operation to differentiation is integral calculus in which change as a factor is already known, but the result of change is not. As introduced independently by Isaac Newton and Gottfried Wilhelm von Leibniz in the seventeenth century, differential and integral calculus are essential to understanding the movement of objects in space. Apart from the calculation of gravity, the invention of calculus had a technical application because ballistics (the study of missiles and trajectories) was directly related to astronomy. Once the science of ballistics was developed, aeronautics was rendered possible as well.

We must conclude that if arithmetic is innately conceptual, then all other branches of mathematics must be extensions of elementary mathematics. Because of the way these extensions are utilized, they may be described as technological modifications of basic mathematics, since they are organizational approaches to reality. They are used, for example, to construct buildings, to measure canals for irrigation, to erect aqueducts or roads, to calculate the trajectory of satellites into the atmosphere, to create all types of devices, to formulate images in pixels—all of which, whether ancient or modern, are the result of applied mathematics, an application that would be unnecessary or undesirable in a society in which the being of technology has lesser importance. As we said above, mathematics is the technological effect of a numbering system derived from the identification of objects. Although mathematics evolved into the systematic study of the symbolic relationship between quantities, it remains at heart the result of a self-expression that has been technologized into a highly skilled scientific discipline.

It is a revelation of how the world, itself the result of human activity, can be explained as an extension of humanity's mental positing of the world. Because mathematics is an example of the workings of human ingenuity, it is one way in which humanity gives meaning to the world.

Writing and Alphabetization

Whether humans can speak or are mute, and they are not paralyzed, they all communicate in some way, but the most useful form of communication is writing. In non-literate cultures in which traditions are past down orally to succeeding generations, the inability to commit traditions to writing, or to record new discoveries, relegate their cultures to an inferior position. Nevertheless, speech offers only a partial conception of language, which is supplemented by the practicality of writing.

But writing is dependent on texts. Is a text defined solely by the fact that it is written down, or does it transcend its medium? Materially, a text is commonly defined by a clay tablet, stone stele, papyrus, vellum, paper, or electronic transmission that it depends on, but a physically related medium portrays a text (even when electronically devised) from only one perspective. In a sense, texts are transcendent, although they are tied to their medium, as they are tied historically to the age in which they are produced[2]. Therein lies a major difference between literate and non-literate cultures.

Naturally, a textual transcendence is dependent on future generations. Although countless original texts have been lost in the past, they may continue to exert an influence because copies had been produced, such as those texts laboriously copied by monks in European monasteries during the Middle Ages, or reprinted for modern use by the printing press. Since texts presuppose the existence of writing, conversely we can say that writing presupposes the existence of texts, or at least the assumption that somehow they must exist. If writing and texts are associated with literacy, then their absence is associated with illiteracy (Stock, 1983: pp. 3-4, 8).One can be taught to read and write without a dependency on texts, but it may be presupposed that reading and writing are somehow related to them. We should also ask if texts exert an influence on our collective memory, but it is not our task to assess whether or not this influence is long lasting. It is possible that a tradition, idea, or remembrance may be lost because conditions, either deliberate or accidental, may have been set in place that have allowed for forgetfulness.

These thoughts, however, are merely preparatory to an understanding of writing. Although language is phonetic because it depends on sounds as a means of communication, writing also intensifies it. This relationship is evident when we reflect that language is based on distinct sounds, each represented by a sign, which when written may be preserved indefinitely. Language, of course, is more than just sounds because it is derived from conceptualizations that are the result of human interaction with the world. Despite being adversely criticized for attributing signs as the only requirement for language, Ferdinand de Saussure in the early twentieth century concluded that language begins with representation of signs through concepts (Saussure,

---

[2]Texts bring to mind their importance to religions, from the Vedas to the Quran, from the Old Testament to the New Testament of the Bible. Even for Martin Luther, faith in the Bible guaranteed salvation, but this conclusion presupposed the technology of writing.

1983: pp. 28-29, 98, 146).

Because a written language presupposes the existence of signs, either logographic, pictographic, or alphabetic, signs would be non-existent without a written language. Although it may be concluded that writing began in Mesopotamia in the late fourth millennium BCE, no alphabet existed at that time. The development of writing represents a slow, laborious process, and reflects the increasingly complex nature of human culture, especially, as a result of urbanization. The earliest writing emphasized consonants only, although the sound of vowels was included in the pronunciation of words. Because writing originally addressed practical matters that served as descriptions of commodities used in trade or donations made to local temples, it heightened the preservation of data without relying on memory. In Mesopotamia, cuneiform fulfilled this function, and in Egypt, hieroglyphics. Writing also acquired importance because it became the means that distinguished history from prehistory. And by writing we are not referring to casual markings or signs on objects for a specific purpose, but a system of preservation of cultural significance for a general purpose. Essentially, writing denotes a system of communication, not a conglomerate of isolated signs.

The simplification of writing was accompanied by the invention of the alphabet. Although the Phoenicians may be attributed with modifying the alphabet, they were not its innovators. The alphabet in a most rudimentary form is attributed to the Canaanites when they lived and worked in the Sinai Peninsula, although assigning their writing to a precise date is difficult. This earliest alphabet evolved as a simplification of hieroglyphics, which itself is a highly sophisticated and stylized system of pictographs that originally represent an object or a sound (Gardiner, 1957: p. 8). The alphabet is based on letters, not pictures, and above all, it is not based on objects. In this sense, writing is not natural, but artificial. The alphabet gave rise to letters as representations of sounds. It is an example not only of a technological application that transcends the natural world, but it is also an indication of technological civilization itself.

The alphabet associated with the Sinai Peninsula and later with Palestine, respectively known as Proto-Sinaitic and Proto-Canaanite, must be distinguished from a cuneiform alphabet that developed at Ugarit in western Syria in the fourteenth or thirteenth century BCE (Puech, 1986: pp. 197-198). The Proto-Sinaitic alphabet is considered to have been developed between the seventeenth or sixteenth centuries BCE (Naveh, 1987: pp. 26-27). It later influenced the alphabets associated with the Phoenicians, Greeks, and Romans. Although the introduction of letters for vowels is accredited to the Greeks, the Phoenician alphabet, emphasizing consonants only, had an influence on the Aramaic alphabet from which Hebrew and Arabic developed.

Writing is a way of recording information so that it may be preserved. It is a way in which other people, who may or may not be directly involved in writing themselves, may benefit from it. Because writing appeals to a much larger audience than the audience immediately intended by authors of particular works, it has an influence far greater than many other human endeavors, which is now augmented by the internet. Even when attempting to understand an ancient people, the preservation and decipherment of their writing give insights into their culture. Although these thoughts may explain why writing is important, they do not explain why alphabetization was invented. Actually, we should not ask why any one alphabet was invented.

Instead, we should ask why alphabets in general, some earlier and some later, were invented.

Nevertheless, there have been several explanations for the origin of the alphabet, such as an attempt to preserve a people's literature, or an effort to leave a mark of one's presence, or an intensification of writing that serves as a substitution for speech, or a proposal to develop a national script, but none of these explanations seem to address the fundamental reason why an alphabet was invented. Although these explanations hold some practicality, they do not seem to reveal its underlying necessity. Of course, after its invention, the alphabet was adopted by many cultures for different purposes over vast expanses of time. The fact that there were the proto-Sinaitic and cuneiform alphabets should lead to the conclusion that alphabets facilitate and simplify the technology of writing, and illustrate their importance to human culture (Coe & Van Stone, 2001: p. 20)[3]. More important than any one alphabetic script is the idea of alphabetization itself as the means for the increased importance of the technology of writing that communicates with a present generation and preserves information for future generations.

Writing is a learned experience that promotes factual information for practical purposes, which then may be applied to other endeavors, such as literature. Although many literary works, such as the Epic of Gilgamesh, the Iliad and the Odyssey, or Beowulf were originally oral, they were subsequently committed to writing, which increased their importance to their respective cultures. The same phenomenon is also applicable to the legal customs or laws of a primitive people. Writing is the means by which the influence of the past may be extended into the future. Therefore, the past acquired new meanings when preserved in writing because writing allowed memory to be projected indefinitely into the future. Like mathematics, the invention of writing has lent itself to humanity's innovative accumulation and indicates that the metaphysics of technology is demonstrative of a process of becoming.

Science

The definition of science has changed over the ages, but for the present age, science is far more specialized in its analysis of reality when compared with the more general applications of science in the past. Although many topics that qualified as science in antiquity would be categorized in the modern age as pseudoscience, it is not our intention to pass judgment on what legitimately was science in a former age. Nevertheless, regardless of the age in which it appears, we should ask how science is related to technology. Although there may be some confusion about the influence of science on technology, there should be no confusion about the influence of technology on science. Science and technology evolved with distinct objectives. Science concerns an understanding of the manner in which knowledge about reality is acquired, no matter how far reaching that may be, but technology concerns the practical applications of that knowledge. As a result, a distinction evolved between theory and practice. But as technology invaded the exclusive areas of science, the latter lost its purely theoretical basis and was rendered technical instead. We should speak of science's technologization more than technology's scientification. Since technology dominates everything we do, it could just as easily

---

[3]The Landa or Mayan alphabet is not an authentic alphabet, but an artificiality created by Diego da Landa, a sixteenth century Catholic bishop, who wanted to convert the Maya to Christianity.

function without regard for usefulness. This is to say that method takes precedence over practicality (Habermas, 1974: pp. 253-256). In this sense, practicality loses its importance because the bulk of our emphasis revolves around technology's performance to the exclusion of everything else which is manifested through technology's prolific ubiquity.

In some way, science has always been associated with technology, at least in so far as technical applications are concerned. But in the modern age, technological apparatus, instruments, devices, and procedures commandeer science. No longer independent and no longer superior, science has been rendered subordinate to technology, since the triumphs of science are rendered possible only because of benefits made available by technology. For example, chemistry has advanced considerably because of the refinement of laboratory equipment, and without it, chemistry would have progressed little since the time of Lavoisier. If science has become more technical, its technicality is attributable to its technologization, which would seem to be true in both western and non-Western cultures (McGinn, 1990: pp. 22-27).

The displacement of science by technology, or at least the accelerated influence of technology on science, occurred with greater intensity in the nineteenth century when the industrial revolution took place (Pollard, 1981: pp. 85-87, 142-148). At that time, the techniques of technology were greatly aligned with the methods of science. No longer could science proceed without the benefit of technology, although technology does benefit from the discoveries of science that, for example, allow for the invention of better tools and machines. The alignment of science with technology occurred by a gradual process that resulted in the manifested presence of technology in all aspects and in all places of the world. Consequently, we may describe the technologization of society more as a process of degree rather than kind.

The advancement of modern technology, and therefore its relationship with science, is essentially twofold. First, technology has benefited from the past because of its historic evolution, to which initially it made a minor contribution, but from which eventually it was the principal beneficiary. And this past is attributed to the European Middle Ages, which gave to technology its dynamic forward directedness that was acquired from Christianity and a Christian culture (Benz, 1966: pp. 121-142). Second, the method of science had changed at the end of the Middle Ages that initiated not only a new way of looking at reality, that is, a new science, but also a new way of applying this knowledge that facilitated a new technology. This new method formed the basis of the scientific revolution, in which technology was "implied as a possibility in the metaphysics" of the new science (Jonas, 1974: pp. 47-48).

But more than its implication and its Christian underpinning, technology came to represent metaphysics itself. It surpassed the science that resulted from the scientific revolution and replaced the metaphysics of the Middle Ages, that is, technology superseded Christianity as the foundation of the metaphysics of Western civilization. Ultimately, technology became expressive of the metaphysics of the world at large. More than being in the world, technology is expressive of the being of the world. It owes a debt, in part, to the past for the impetus in accomplishing this goal. To express these thoughts in other words, we might say that humanity's being is reflected unto technology. It demonstrates that technology's mode of being is revealed as a manifestation of ourselves.

Time-Consciousness

Because of sundials, water clocks, and mechanical clocks (and by extension, quartz digital clocks and watches), time reckoning has evolved as a consequence of time's computation. But more than time reckoning, it is time-consciousness that concerns us. In fact, time-consciousness—itself an effect of technology—is rendered possible primarily because of the reckoning of time. Of these three different inventions described above, it was the mechanical clock, conceived and developed in the late Middle Ages, that led to time's mechanization, in which time is not only compartmentalized into smaller and smaller units, but also rendered into a commodity that could be regulated, manipulated, and projected. Above all, time-consciousness exerts an influence on daily life as to transform completely an undefined understanding of time into a motif that penetrates everything. If time was not an important feature of the human psyche before the invention of the mechanical clock, it certainly has become one since its invention, whose ticking manifests a presence of time's fragmentation. Everything from birth to death is now adjusted or tempered by time-consciousness. The vehicle for making money or pursuing pleasure, for devotion to one's family or the pursuit of idleness occurs by means of the consciousness of time, which inevitably is followed at some point by the fear of wasting it. Consciousness of the passing of time dominates all aspects of life. Because the telling of time in many languages relates to a description of time derived from the clock, the latter has acquired a meaning far beyond its original intent (Rivers, 2000: pp. 225-226).

The augmentation of time by means of technology is not to be confused with natural cycles or so-called economic cycles representative of the effects of prosperity (or its lack) because they do not obliterate technology's progressive momentum. The fact that there is a cycle of anything does not preclude the linearity of time, which is the result of the Christian conception of time (and its biblical background) that helped with technological progress. Likewise, the difference between time internally experienced, which is ontological (a natural metaphysical phenomenon), and time externally given, which is artificial (an unnatural metaphysical phenomenon), is exaggerated by technology. This exaggeration plays a part in the distortion between the future and its absorption by the present, so that the possibility of the future seems to be consumed by an ever-present present, a characteristic that is attributable to the clock. Consequently, the perception of time is variable, ranging from mandatory obligations to free time, from an emphasis of time as a quality to its emphasis as a quantity. In fact, time acquires a power hereto non-existent because its quantity enables it to become the means of accomplishing anything (Blumenberg, 1986: p. 223).

Nevertheless, how would society be made aware of time reckoning if there was no way to be informed of it, if there was no clock in the town square, or if there were no watches? If time were not tied to specific hours of the day, what use is time-consciousness? Since the invention of the mechanical clock, which itself had a slow and localized influence in medieval monasteries before it had an influence on society in general, time-consciousness took much time to be perfected. Likewise, other changes in the past have also taken considerable time, even centuries, to have an impact, such as the use of the wheel, domestication of plants and animals, or writing. Even as late as the eighteenth century, time-consciousness had no influence on people who had little need for it (Landes, 1983: pp. 227-228).

Time-consciousness is not inherent in the being of being human, but it is a mode or manner of an awareness of temporality as a characteristic of being. Time-consciousness is a technological artificiality, but temporality is an ontological reality. There is no being without time, and no time without being. Since temporality is a characteristic of being, it may be supplemented by time-consciousness that is artificially induced by technology. Whether or not human reality has benefited by this relationship is not the issue. Calculating the time of day by noticing the rising and setting of the sun, or by reading the stars after the sun has set gave the first glimpses of the passing of time that goes back to time immemorial; but these simple happenings lacked the precision of time-consciousness with its positive or negative connotations. Like so many other happenings, once a threshold has been crossed, it is impossible and anachronistic to go back. As in other endeavors, technology is the result of an accumulative process. It is based on the choices of the past that help to set the conditions of the future.

How much has time-consciousness changed human culture? How much has it altered forever the way the world is perceived? If time-consciousness can be ignored and the world can continue without time's overbearingness, then time-consciousness is irrelevant, but the world has changed because it has been compartmentalized. Even when time awareness is rejected and people move to a remote island somewhere, this desire is chosen most likely because they are conscious of time. This rejection of time-consciousness is the immediate result of the cognizance of time's ubiquitous presence (Griffiths, 1999: pp. 11-15).

Society

Human society is a social structure definable by networks of interaction among its members who generally demonstrate a willingness to work cooperatively, and who often show a sense of fairness, or at least mutuality. Although society may also refer to chimpanzees, baboons, bees, and ants, for our purposes we will limit the use of this term to humans only. Because the societal relationships manifested by these other animals are the result of evolution, the benefits of cooperation among members of one's own species, human or non-human, should outweigh any advantages supportive of individuality. As far as humans are concerned, the social structure associated with cooperation originates between two or more people, and most commonly within a family, even if the latter consists of a husband and wife cohabiting without children.

Related to the idea of association is the notion that society denotes a type of organization, and it is organization that is particularly important. How an individual reacts to another lays the basis for society, whether expressive of identity that is based on ethnicity, culture, social solidarity, or patterns of authority. Like the system introduced into Chinese society by Confucius whose goal was the maintenance of stability in an uncertain time, society in general deals with relationships between and among individuals, families, communities, countries, cultures, and by extension, civilizations.

One should ask if social mechanisms associated with society are derived from interactions between people that require more than one person, or derived from the human brain that is individually based and not initially tied to other people. Regardless of its derivation, it is the interaction between people that is the basis for society because if humanity were reduced to only one individual, there would be no need for (and no benefit derived from) other people. Society does not exist when humanity is reduced to a sole survivor.

Indeed, what need would there be for society unless it achieved something that individuals could not achieve alone. In some sense, when compared to politics, we may say that society is similar to a confederal system in which a central government has the power to do something that individual state governments cannot do efficiently for themselves and from which central governments derive their power. Similarly, if the purpose of society is the attainment of social goals, these goals are variable. They would differ among societies, but they would also differ within them, as if each enclave within a community or country denotes a distinct society with noticeable differences, such as the associations of a crime family, a religious community, an ethnic neighborhood, personal affiliations within a profession, or any subdivision of a culture. Societies regulate some type of social order, but they become more complex when they reveal elaborate patterns of control. Nevertheless, we are not concerned with the alleged stages of social evolution that impact the development of society, but with the importance of society in general.

Society comes into existence from the interaction of at least two people, and therefore, it is as old as humanity itself. The question for us to ask, therefore, is self-evident: If society is natural, to what extent is it influenced by technology? Or we may rephrase the question: How have different technologies given rise to different societies? Since culture determines what makes us human, we are defined by willful human choices. It is a common conclusion within anthropology that humanity is defined culturally, not biologically. It is this distinction that separates humans from other life forms. If society could be defined solely by biology, then it would hardly be subject to technology.

Anthropologically, culture may be defined as a configuration of the natural order. Because the relationship of the natural order with an alleged "human nature" is determined by biology, we must conclude that human nature is a distortion because it supposedly is a description of qualities that all humans share. An accurate definition of human nature should include physiological traits because humans are mammals. Non-physiological traits that would more accurately define the nature of humans are traditionally excluded because these traits are variable. It is variability that indicates that culture, not biology, is what defines us. Therefore, the designation of human nature from any other perspective as a definition of culture is a misnomer.

It should be apparent that society helped cognitive development, and it is fundamental to the promotion of social behavior. Given that human society is often compared with simian societies, it is more complex than the latter and entails greater organization. Any elaborate organization implies some type of technology. When referring to society, its structure reveals that its individual components are combined in particular ways that form integrated wholes. Society concerns the means by which individuals are incorporated into a framework. The process in which this integration takes place is technological. But societies are not passive because they develop through conflict, that is, through deliberate actions that shape cooperation and form complex institutions. One type of conflict concerns warfare, and another type concerns trade. Therefore, conflict may have negative and/or positive consequences, both of which are affected by technology.

It may be impossible to uncover the conditions that led to the first human societies, but the transition from pre-human (or hominid) to human society most likely included the development of spoken language because the latter is paramount for cooperation, without which well-developed social relationships would be impossible. Regardless how long it may have taken to develop language with all its complexities, changes in kinship and even the development of myth may have been important for its evolution (Barnard, 2011: pp. 92-93, 109). The social cooperation that was needed for hunting and gathering helped in the development of society, both of which evolved with an increase in brain size, and all of which facilitated the development of language. Experiences evolved into traditions that could be perfected, and traditions evolved into societies that could be expanded. As a result, cultural evolution was the beneficiary of these events.

Since spoken language entails the designation of sounds for distinct entities, early humans must have developed words as a way of understanding the world. Nevertheless, we should be mindful that to look for the origins of anything is really to seek the causes that answer all our questions. Such a quest is both beyond our reach and highly suspect (Bloch, 1953: pp. 29-30). The earliest tools, which were unmodified stones, were used by hominids, but the skills required for the flaking and chipping of them came much later and probably were associated with the development of speech. Thus, technology, language, and cooperation (or altruism) are associated with human society and played a part is its development (Hurford, 2007: pp. 268-271).

It should go without saying that technology is a human phenomenon. Although one person can invent a technology, any social application it may acquire must be distinguished from its invention. This idea concerns the truth that technology is more than a human phenomenon; it is also a social one. For example, was the wheel invented for the benefit of one person who had wares to transport, or did several people contribute to its invention for their mutual benefit, such as its use for ceremonial reasons? It is possible that the wheel could have been invented for either purpose, but it was only after it was applied among many people that it acquired social significance, that is, acquired an importance to society. And we should also consider the environmental conditions that may or may not have allowed the wheel to be useful (Basalla, 1988: pp. 9-10). Although individuals precede society, society is followed by humanity. And by humanity we mean the qualities of being human, which takes place when individuals cooperate and become integrated parts of a group and promote its well-being. It is at this point where technology achieves its greatest impact, that is, when inventions appear, when they are modified, even when they are abandoned.

These thoughts lead to another. If society is a type of social organization, then it is a type of method. But we do not have to ask where this organization originates. It is apparent that we create it because societies are variable based on the cultural conditions from which they evolve. Although societies must address the human condition to which all people are subject in the satisfaction of basic needs, how societies deal with these conditions vary widely. An introduction to cultural anthropology reveals the infinite variety of human societies. It indicates that society, for example, is characterized by the way in which

it uses technology in maintaining life, in protection from harm, in food production, in education, in planning for the future. These examples are expressions of social mechanisms that bind people together and promote solidarity of the entirety of human life. They indicate that technology's presence is expressive of a fundamental truth about the nature of society, a truth that indicates that the social structure of society is supported and promoted by means of technology, in fact in everything we do in our lives. Without it, society would be represented by a disjointed assemblage of human beings struggling to maintain daily existence. Metaphysically, we may say that society, as the embodiment of human reality, reveals its own being, that is, the being of the world, by means of technology.

Conclusion

Technology is the result of human ingenuity, originating from ontological freedom, influenced by conceptualization, and given actuality through the manipulation of the world. Together, these factors help to describe the essence of technology. As we said above, technology's involvement reveals its essence. Its interaction with the world is embedded in our choices, occupied by our decisions, and committed to the means that are projected to their ends. Since the essence of technology is founded upon its presence, the latter is fundamental to its being. Technology is made real initially through praxis, since praxis is how technology's engagement is played out. For example, writing is a mode of technology. It maintains a presence through its exercise of symbolization, but writing in itself is not essential to technology. Writing may be important for communication, society, and human progress, but it is not fundamental to technology's essence. The technological importance of writing does not concern what is written, but rather the process or manner of writing. It concerns the symbolization of signs and letters, that is, the substitution of written words for things. Whether these words are written in Arabic, Urdu, or Greek is incidental. It is the idea of writing, rather than its form, that makes writing important. And technology's being is applicable to all the categories we have discussed above. Therefore, the being of technology, regardless of the form it takes, concerns its overriding reality, as if it possesses an aura of some distinct quality or breadth of vision. Although any being, that is, any entity, possesses potentiality because being denotes existence, nevertheless, potentiality may not be actualized. It should be assumed, however, that technology's being would have an impact on the world by its mere presence, which is expressed through its applications.

As we said above, the being of technology is expressed through its applications, which begins with the nature of conceptualization and its relationship to truth. Once technology is conceptualized, it may be devised and used. Applications are the means by which technology is made evident, from the first tool to the last, from a simple procedure to the most complex, from a particularized technique to a generalized method. Because it participates in human activity, technology is one link between thought and action, that is, between thinking about the world and creating it. It manifests the completion of tasks when its designated means attain their ends. Like art or literature, technology is a phenomenon that transforms humans and changes the world. It is the means by which humans express their being, that is, technology is the way in which humans reveal their being to the world. And what is the world if not our inheritance of the cultural conditions of the past that result from innovative accumulation (Ogburn, 1964: pp. 24-27).

REFERENCES

Arthur, W. B. (2009). *The nature of technology: What it is and how it evolves.* New York: Free Press.

Barnard, A. (2011). *Social anthropology and human origins.* Cambridge: Cambridge University Press.

Basalla, G. (1988). *The evolution of technology.* Cambridge: Cambridge University Press.

Benz, E. (1966). *Evolution and Christian hope: Man's concept of the future from the early fathers to Teilhard de Chardin.* Frank, H. G. (Trans.). Garden City: Doubleday.

Bloch, M. (1953). *The historian's craft.* Putnam, P. (Trans.). New York: Knopf.

Blumenberg, H. (1986). *Lebenszeit und weltzeit.* Frankfurt: Suhrkamp.

Buchler, J. (1961). *The concept of method.* New York: Columbia University Press.

Carnap, R. (1983). The logicist foundations of mathematics. In P. Benacerraf, & H. Putnam (Eds.), *Philosophy of mathematics: Selected readings* (2nd ed., pp. 41-52). Cambridge: Cambridge University Press.

Coe, M. D., & Van Stone, M. (2001). *Reading the Maya glyphs.* New York: Thames & Hudson.

de Saussure, F. (1983). *Course in general linguistics.* Bally, C., & Sechehaye, A. (Eds.) with collaboration of Riedlinger, A., Harris, R. (Trans.). London: Duckworth.

Donald, M. (1991). *Origins of the modern mind: Three stages in the evolution of culture and cognition.* Cambridge, MA: Harvard University Press.

Fodor, J. A. (1998). *Concepts: Where cognitive science went wrong.* Oxford: Clarendon Press.

Gardiner, A. (1957). *Egyptian grammar: Being an introduction to the study of hieroglyphs* (3rd ed.). Oxford: Oxford University Press.

Griffiths, J. (1999). *Pip pip: A sideways look at time.* London: Flamingo.

Habermas, J. (1974). *Theory and practice* (abridged 4th ed.). Viertel, J. (Trans.). Boston: Beacon Press.

Hazewinkel, M. (1988-1994). *Encyclopaedia of mathematics.* Dordrecht: Reidel.

Heidegger, M. (1977). *The question concerning technology and other essays.* Lovitt, W. (Trans.). New York: Harper & Row.

Herodotus. (1998). *The histories.* Waterfield, R. (Trans.) with an introduction and notes by Dewald, C. Oxford: Oxford University Press.

Honig, W. K. (1993). Numerosity as a dimension of stimulus control. In S. T. Boysen, & E. J. Capaldi (Eds.), *The development of numerical competence: Animal and human models* (pp. 61-86). Hillsdale: Erlbaum.

Hurford, J. R. (2007). *The origins of meaning: Language in the light of evolution.* Oxford: Oxford University Press.

Jonas, H. (1974). Seventeenth century and after: The meaning of scientific and technological revolution. In L. E. Long (Ed.), *Philosophical essays: From ancient creed to technological man* (pp. 46-82). Englewood Cliffs: Prentice Hall.

Kuhn, T. S. (1996). *The structure of scientific revolutions* (3rd ed.). Chicago: University of Chicago Press.

Lakoff, G., & Núñez, R. E. (2000). *Where mathematics comes from: How the embodied mind brings mathematics into being.* New York: Basic Books.

Landes, D. S. (1983). *Revolution in time: Clocks and the making of the modern world.* Cambridge, MA: Belknap Press.

McGinn, R. E. (1990). *Science, technology, and society.* Englewood Cliffs: Prentice Hall.

McNeil, I. (1990). *An encyclopaedia of the history of technology.* London: Routledge.

Naveh, J. (1987). *Early history of the alphabet: An introduction to West Semitic epigraphy and palaeography* (2nd ed.). Jerusalem: Magnes Press.

Ogburn, W. F. (1964). *On culture and social change: Selected papers.* Duncan, O. D. (Ed.). Chicago: University of Chicago Press.

Olsen, J. K. B. (2009). Becoming through technology. In J. K. B. Olsen, E. Selinger, & S. Riis (Eds.), *New waves in philosophy of technology.* Basingstoke: Palgrave Macmillan.

Pollard, S. (1981). *Peaceful conquest: The industrialization of Europe, 1760-1970.* Oxford: Oxford University Press.

Puech, É. (1986). Origins de l'alphabet. *Revue biblique, 93,* 161-213.

Rivers, T. J. (2000). The conception of time and its relationship to technology. *Research in Philosophy and Technology, 19,* 215-231.

Russell, B. (1956). Definition of number. In J. R. Newman (Ed.), *The world of mathematics: A small library of the literature of mathematics from A'h-mose the scribe to Albert Einstein.* New York: Simon & Schuster.

Stock, B. (1983). *The implications of literacy: Written language and models of interpretation in the eleventh and twelfth centuries.* Princeton: Princeton University Press.

Thompson, R. K. R. (1995). Natural and relational concepts in animals. In H. L. Roitblat, & J.-A. Meyer (Eds.), *Comparative approaches to cognitive science* (pp. 175-224). Cambridge, MA: MIT Press.

6

Reclaiming Realism for the Left: Gar Alperovitz and the Decision to Use the Atomic Bomb

Peter N. Kirstein

History Department, St. Xavier University, Chicago, USA

Sixty-seven years after the decision to use the atomic bomb in World War II, controversy remains whether the United States was justified in using fission bombs in combat. Gar Alperovitz, the great revisionist historian, in his *Atomic Diplomacy* and *The Decision to Use the Atomic Bomb* transformed our knowledge of the geopolitical motives behind the atomic attack against Japan at the end of World War II. These uranium and plutonium-core bombs were political, not primarily military in purpose and motive behind their deployment. His analysis will be compared to realists such as Hans Morgenthau, Kenneth Waltz, Henry Kissinger and George Kennan who for the most part questioned unrestrained violence and offered nuanced views on the wisdom of using such indiscriminate, savage weapons of war. The paper will explore Alperovitz's classic argument that out of the ashes of Hiroshima and Nagasaki, the A-bomb drove the incipient Cold War conflict. American national-security elites construed the bomb as a political-diplomatic lever to contain Soviet power as much as a military weapon to subdue Japan. The views of various political and military leaders, President Truman, Henry Stimson, James Byrnes, General George C. Marshall, Admiral William Leahy and General Dwight Eisenhower are assessed.

Keywords: A-Bomb; Alperovitz; Realism; Hiroshima; Truman

Realism and War

At 8:15 in the morning on August 6, 1945 the world changed forever when the United States launched the nuclear age with an air-burst atomic bomb that exploded in the skies over Hiroshima, Japan. The city-busting carnage was repeated on August 9 with the destruction of Nagasaki in the final days of World War II. The cataclysmic potential for mass destruction of humankind had not occurred on such a scale since the Columbian invasions and subsequent extermination of the Native American settlements beginning in the late fifteenth century (Crosby, 1987). The decision to use the atomic bomb raises questions ranging from its impact on international peace and security to whether the atomic bomb advanced the national interest.

Realism does not worship the use of force in all circumstances. Examples of realism shall be examined that explore with nuance in theory and direct examination the use of the A-bomb against a conventionally armed Japan. Realism emphasizes the use of power in pursuit of the national interest in a world of anarchy. Alperovitz's writings investigate many dimensions that are relevant to the realist critique that begin to emerge in Thucydides's epic history of the Peloponnesian War in the fifth century B.C.E.

Athens informed the Lacedæmonians in speeches before their assembly that they must submit to Athens' greater power and avoid rhetorical efforts to prevent domination. They are told that "the secret being that where force can be used, law is not needed." Thucydides, anticipating the anarchy of realism that requires a muscular approach in defending the national interest, quotes the Athenians, "that the weaker must give way to the stronger" (Thucydides, 1951). The militarily dominant Athenians, in their war against Sparta, subdue the neutral islanders of Melos who had complained they were "debar(red) from talking about justice and invite us to obey your interest" (Thucydides, 1951). Neither conditional surrender nor negotiation were permitted: surrender or die was the Athenian option.

The pursuit of the national interest by war and rejecting non-violent conflict resolution is morally repugnant. Pope Paul VI in his "World Day of Peace Message in 1976", described the atomic bombings of Hiroshima and Nagasaki as a "butchery of untold magnitude" (National Conference of Catholic Bishops, 1983). Atomic bombs are indiscriminate. They kill babies, fathers, mothers, brothers, sisters, children, hospital patients, doctors, trees and gardens. Classmates, books, animals in zoos, life savings, sidewalks, engagements, marriages, and highways are destroyed (Sebald, 2003).

It is instructive to apply America's launching of nuclear war to realism and its variants that developed between the wars and subsequently during the Cold War between the United States and the Soviet Union. Realism is not a monolithic ideology and one may glean a broad spectrum of analysis that can be applied as a counter argument against the decision to use the atomic bomb at the end of World War II.

E. H. Carr was an anti-imperial, Marxist historian whose works on modern Russian history may endure as long as those in the realm of international-relations theory (Ghosh, 2007). He was one of the early forerunners of classical realism and skeptical of a universality of moral principles that should govern humankind. His between the wars critique of Wilsonianism, a favorite target of realists determined to challenge lofty headed idealism, was less than absolute. While various critics described Carr's "scathing critique" of idealism, the "harmony of interests," and the search for a comprehensive moral code of justice, his writings are almost lyrical in their denunciation of the indiscriminate use of force unrelated to military necessity (Snow, 2000).

While Carr remains faithful to the tradition of classical realism that the pursuit of power and not international moral principles is essential for nation-state survival, he rejects the use of military force if arbitrarily and indiscriminately destructive. Carr's distinct manifestation of idealism emerges from the realist:

> All agree that there is an international moral code binding on states. One of the most important and most clearly recognised items in this code is the obligation not to inflict *unnecessary* death or suffering on other human beings... This is the foundation of most of the rules of war, the earliest and most developed chapter of international law (Carr, 1961).

Carr and Irving Critique

In a footnote, Carr observes with some conditionality that following World War I, modern warfare has blurred the distinction between combatant and non-combatant immunity. While attacking the latter might be "essential to... military purpose," Carr does not sanction a reckless or murderous disregard of avoiding non-combatant carnage in war (Carr, 1961). During World War II there was mass scale horrific destruction of non-combatant populations. Strategic bombing killed one and a half million civilians in urban areas across the globe including Dresden, Cologne, Hamburg, Tokyo, Osaka, Yokohama, and London (Simic, 2003). As the violence mounted in a war without mercy, nations waged total war upon defenseless, non-combatant populations that were targeted along with military bases, armies in the field, and key naval staging areas. One's status had no bearing on whether a person would be targeted; only one's distance from a conventional or nuclear explosion would determine life or death (Rhodes, 2007). Even Secretary of War Henry Stimson's removal of Kyoto from the nuclear-target list was intended to preserve the ancient capital's historic treasures but not its population (Carr, 1961).

If nation states reject any obligation to accept international regimes, according to Carr, than international morality is impossible (Carr, 1961). Yet nations that attempt to universalize their values are equally repugnant. Carr compares nations that claim a universality of their principles to Hitler's assertion that Germany and the fittest are "the bearers of a higher ethic". Clearly referring to Wilsonian hubris, he eloquently denounces the bombast "that American principles are the principles of humanity" (Carr, 1961). Carr advocated some adherence to international norms but not if it rested on nationalistic fervor emanating from hegemonic ethnocentrism (Carr, 1961).

David Irving wrote in the opening sentence of *Hitler's War*: "To Historians is granted a talent even the gods are denied—to alter what has already happened!" (Irving, 1990). In addition to

historians, nation-states and other ruling elites have unwarranted influence in selecting and defining the components of public memory. Race, class, and gender are powerful factors in determining whose history gets written, whose history is memorialized in museum display, and whose history is deemed important or relegated as nonhistory. While everything in the past is history, the historical record includes what influential elites—the press, the fawning professor-academic class, various ethnic groups, the government and the media—believe can advance their interests. Dominant groups control history by controlling the present and thus memory of a civilization.

Revisionism and the A-Bomb

Gar Alperovitz in his major revisionist works, *Atomic Diplomacy: Hiroshima and Potsdam, the Use of the Atomic Bomb and the American Confrontation with Soviet Power* and *The Decision to Use the Atomic Bomb* avoids directly the moral question of whether the atomic bomb was justified as a weapon of war (Alperovitz, 1985, 1995). Yet his stunning analysis of transformative revisionist history argues convincingly that the Truman administration's decision to use the atomic bomb at the end of World War II was not militarily needed to defeat Japan and that the standard defense of the bomb's use is egregiously flawed.

Alperovitz has created a new past in challenging the architects of the atomic era and those who dominated its historical significance. His magisterial writings that appear in books and essays contain five major revelations: 1) In the months before the A-bombs were unleashed in August, 1945, the United States had several viable options to end the war without resorting to weapons of mass destruction; 2) These options were not created in postwar-revisionist New Left history but were known at the time at the highest levels of government. In particular, Japan was looking for a way to end the war and retain its emperor through intense diplomacy with Russia; 3) The atomic bomb was essentially a diplomatic weapon to contain and even roll back Soviet influence in Central and Eastern Europe in the early days of the Cold War (Alperovitz, 1985); 4) The weapons' principal military purpose was not to defeat an already defeated Japan, but to preempt greater Soviet influence in Asia that might result from a protracted, sustained role after it entered the Pacific War; 5) The atomic bomb was not necessary to defeat Japan or prevent a high-casualty invasion of its home islands (Alperovitz, 1985).

Manhattan Project and Targeting

The Joint Chiefs of Staff initially ordered that Hiroshima, Kyoto, Kokura, and Niigata escape conventional bombing to preserve pristine targets to measure and admire the destruction of atomic bombs. (Correspondence ("Top Secret") of the Manhattan Engineer District, 1945) Hiroshima and ultimately Nagasaki became urban-atomic experiments because conventional bombing had not reduced them to ashes. Major General Leslie R. Groves, the director of the Manhattan Project, ordered a post-attack assessment report. The report confirmed Hiroshima was chosen since it was "relatively untouched by previous bombing, in order that the effect of a single atomic-bomb could be determined" (Manhattan Engineer District, No Date). This was a strong indication that Hiroshima was not considered a high-value strategic military target.

While the Manhattan Project report stated atomic targets should have "high military strategic value," it was ignored with the indiscriminate atomic bombings of urban populations. The report emphasized that the A-bomb should have a "morale effect upon the enemy" (Manhattan Engineer District, No Date). It affirmed an advantage of fission weapons is the "sheer terror it struck into the people of the bombed cities," and "terror resulted in immediate hysterical activity" including "flight from the cities" (Manhattan Engineer District, No Date). Fission is a term borrowed from biological cell division and refers to the neutron splitting of a uranium or plutonium nucleus into two smaller and similar sized nuclei.

Clearly, the decision to use the atomic bomb was not to reduce Japan's capacity to wage war as two cities were marked for destruction because of revenge, racism, and a desire to field test these new weapons of mass destruction (Dover, 1986; Takaki, 1985). President Harry S. Truman's diary during the Potsdam Conference contained this entry: "The Japs are savages, ruthless, merciless and fanatic" (Bernstein, 1991). Many more targets were planned. One-hundred thousand persons had already been incinerated in fire-bomb raids of Tokyo during a single night in March, 1945 (Freedman, 2007). Because Tokyo was of "great psychological value," Thomas Farrell, deputy commanding general and chief of field operations of the Manhattan Project, urged its nuclear annihilation when more fission bombs became available (Farrell, 1945). On one level it was an inevitable escalation of conventional-strategic bombing.

The Target Committee meeting on April 27, 1945 had declared that the 20th Air Force conventional bombing of urban areas had "the prime purpose in mind of not leaving one stone lying on another" (Correspondence ("Top Secret") of the Manhattan Engineer District, 1945). Philip Morrison was one of several Manhattan Project nuclear physicists and engineers on Tinian who loaded the "Fat Man" Nagasaki implosion-triggered plutonium A-bomb onto *Bockscar*. This was the B-29 Stratofortress that carried the weapon to the skies over Nagasaki with the eponymous reference to Captain Frederick C. Bock. Ironically he switched aircraft just prior to takeoff and Major Charles Sweeney was at the controls of *Bockscar* (Rhodes, 1986). Morrison after the war reflected: "But I wondered: Is this the right thing to do... We knew a terrible thing had been unleashed... We obviously killed a hundred thousand people and that was nothing to have a party about... This would reduce a city of three hundred to four hundred thousand people to nothing but a sink for disaster relief, bandages and hospitals" (Terkel, 1984).

Realism's Approach to War

Realism's concern that worldwide anarchy requires a unilateralist pursuit of its national interest is not absolute. Realism is seen as rejecting economic, social, and human-rights violations in third countries as germane in developing a nation's strategic approach to foreign policy. Pragmatists tell us that realism is disciplined with a focus on limiting American foreign policy to pursuing the national interest through the use of power (Haas, 1997). While clearly less committed than internationalists or pacifists to defining how power might be used or enforcing the laws of war, its founding intellectuals questioned the ethics of atomic war at the beginning of the nuclear age.

Reinhold Niebuhr, the influential, realist theologian, drifted from Marxism to realism during his great career as a public intellectual. Such ideological musings are evident in his *Moral Man and Immoral Society*. Niebuhr alternated between opposition and support of various nuclear policies during the Cold War. He opposed publicly the dropping of the atomic bombs on Hiroshima and Nagasaki and was a signatory of a Federal Council of Churches statement that opposed the atomic detonations over Japan. James B. Conant was president at Harvard on leave during the war when he served as chair of the National Defense Research Committee. He was a major architect of the Manhattan Project and served on the pivotal Interim Policy Committee on Atomic Energy (Interim Committee). He complained to Niebuhr about his support of the anti-nuclear bomb petition and received an ambivalent apology that stated the atomic weapons were "evil... in order to do good" (Lears, 2012; Kirstein, 2009).

Hans Morgenthau attacked the hypocrisy of the Roosevelt administration's condemnation of indiscriminate warfare resulting from Japan's attack on Canton and Russia's assault on Finland in the 1930s when the United States and others perpetrated far more ruthless strategic bombing during World War II. He places the atomic attacks as the culmination of the progression toward total war:

> Hiroshima and Nagasaki are stepping stones... in the modern morality of warfare... The national interest in the destruction of enemy productivity... and the opportunity the modern technology presents of satisfying that interest, have had a deteriorating effect upon international morality (Morgenthau, 1985).

Contrast this analysis with Herman Kahn's graduated deterrence and the escalation-dominance catechism that would drive nuclear war-gaming scenarios during the Cold War. Morgenthau ruefully predicted that the incorporation of nuclear weapons as "normal instruments of warfare would mean the destruction of... viable societies." To construe their utility as a super weapon that can decisively determine the outcome of war "would not be a rational means to the rational ends of foreign policy but instruments of desperation denoting suicide and genocide" (Morgenthau, 1985).

A-Bomb and Diplomacy

Avoiding a final invasion of Japan and the myth of saving a million American casualties have been the most enduring defense of the decision to use the atomic bomb. The preliminary invasion, Operation Olympic, was not scheduled to begin until November 1, 1945 on the southern island of Kyushu. The full-scale Operation Coronet invasion across the Tokyo Plain would not commence until March 1, 1946, almost seven months after the Hiroshima bombing (Alperovitz, 1985). Other military or diplomatic options could have been pursued during the intervening period. Alperovitz believes the United States hastily used the bombs just before and after the Soviet Union decided to end its neutrality in the Pacific War.

The US deployed the atomic bombs not as a winning weapon but as a preemptive nuclear war to deter Soviet influence in Manchuria and Japan (Alperovitz, 1985). Months before the Olympic and Coronet ground invasions would occur, the United States dropped uranium and plutonium-core nuclear weapons over Japan. It was a geopolitical decision to effectuate a strategic advantage over the Soviet Union in America's expanding Northeast Asian empire, dominate the peace in occupied Japan, and strengthen its yet to be named "containment" policy in Eastern Europe.

At the Moscow Foreign Ministers Conference in October 1943, almost two years before the Manhattan Project would produce combat-ready nuclear weapons, the Roosevelt administration pressured the Soviets, then engulfed in epic conflict with the Wehrmacht and sustaining the majority of the war's casualties, to enter the Pacific War (Alperovitz, 1985; Baker, 1976). Joseph Stalin was more preoccupied with national survival after the Nazi "Barbarossa" invasion of June 22, 1941, but agreed with Hitler's defeat in sight at the Yalta Crimea Conference in February, 1945 to terminate its state of non-belligerency with Japan. Russia would end its state of neutrality with Japan within two to three months after its defeat of German forces. It surrendered on May 8 and, ninety-two days later on August 8, Russia invaded Japanese-occupied Manchuria from its bases in Siberia. The Truman administration chose not to allow the impact of the devastating loss of Russian non-belligerency to register fully with Japan. It was fighting alone without an ally in what was suddenly a conflict against the two greatest powers on Earth. Truman also chose not to allow Japan ample time to comprehend its atomic vulnerabilities following the "Little Boy" Hiroshima attack (Horowitz, 1971). The day after the Soviet Union initiated its Yalta pledge to enter the war and three days after the first atomic bombing, "Fat Man" destroyed Nagasaki.

Truman postponed the Potsdam Conference that was held in a suburb outside bomb-ravaged Berlin during the summer of 1945 hoping that a nuclear test might allow a unilateralist approach in dominating post-war Japan (Alperovitz, 1985). The conference began July 17 the day after the successful atomic-bomb "Gadget" explosion at the Trinity site in New Mexico. Truman wanted confirmation that the A-bomb worked before suddenly reversing long-term American policy that ending the Pacific War required a Soviet-American coalition (Alperovitz, 1970). The "Little Boy" gun assembly, uranium Hiroshima bomb was then shipped to Tinian in the Marianas as Truman anticipated a nuclear ending to World War II would preempt a sustained Russian entry into the war. The 1945 Russo-Japanese conflict was a six-day war from August 8 to August 14 when Emperor Hirohito announced a surrender.

Russia and the Bomb

James Byrnes, Truman's personal representative on the Interim Committee, dominated policy formulation on how and not whether the atomic bomb would be used. Byrnes becomes secretary of state in July while still serving on the Interim Committee. Army Chief of Staff General George C. Marshall, in the spirit of allied transparency, suggested at a May 31, 1945 Interim Committee meeting that two Russian scientists attend the New Mexico A-bomb test and observe its unprecedented power. Byrnes rejected any sharing of information with the Soviets on S-1, the codename for the Manhattan Project (Correspondence ("Top Secret") of the Manhattan Engineer District, 1945).

After Trinity, British Prime Minister Winston Churchill endorsed the American abandonment that urged Russian entry into the Pacific War: "we should not need the Russians" and "European problems" would be more manageable with a "far happier prospect in Europe" (Churchill, 1953). Cold War power-maximizing thinking took precedence over preserving the solidarity of the wartime alliance. Nuclear weapons were the great equalizer that would preempt Russian influence in post-war Japan and manage its domination of Red Army liberated Central and Eastern Europe. P. M. S. Blackett's classic observation stated, "the dropping of the atomic bomb was not so much the last military act of the Second World War, as the first major operation of the cold diplomatic war with Russia" (Steiner, 1977).

At Potsdam there was a brief exchange when Truman obliquely informed Stalin that the United States had developed a new weapon against Japan. The words "atomic" and "nuclear" were not used (Alperovitz, 1985). Henry Kissinger a realist scholar-statesperson stunningly states that Truman revealed to Stalin "the existence of the atomic bomb" (Kissinger, 1994). Kissinger without documentation claims that "undoubtedly" Stalin's "paranoia" induced the Soviet leader to construe this atomic revelation as "intimidation" (Kissinger, 1994). Kissinger's depiction of the exchange contrasts sharply with that of Churchill who observed intently the Truman-Stalin conversation from a distance of five yards. Churchill described Stalin as "delighted" but "had no idea of the significance" of Truman's vague reference to a more destructive weapon (Churchill, 1953).

The prime minister and Truman agreed they no longer "needed" Soviet intervention in the Pacific War. Two days after the July 16 plutonium A-bomb test in a New Mexico desert, Churchill composed a note for his War Cabinet that Truman told Stalin only "the simple fact" of a new weapon but "at all costs refused to divulge any particulars" (Churchill, 1981). Truman told Churchill after the July 24 conversation with Stalin that he asked no questions and Churchill believed had "no special knowledge of the" atomic bomb (Churchill, 1981). Unlike the expansive Churchill, the laconic Truman devotes a mere three sentences in his memoirs on his encounter with Stalin. Yet he confirms a "casually" delivered account of a "new weapon of unusual destructive force" and corroborates Churchill's observation that the Soviet leader appeared pleased (Truman, 1951).

Kissinger makes another speculative but interesting assertion that Stalin knew about the existence of S-1 before Truman did (Kissinger, 1994). Stalin probably was aware of the Manhattan Project based on Soviet intelligence prior to Secretary of War Henry Stimson's comprehensive April 25 S-1 briefing of the new president after the death of Franklin Roosevelt (Harrison-Bundy Files, 1942-1946). F. D. R. was aware of likely Soviet intelligence assets during the developmental stage of the atomic bomb. Stimson had alerted Roosevelt as early as September, 1943 of its wartime ally's penetration of the Manhattan Engineer District (Sherwin, 1973). Yet Stalin had little conception of the atomic bombs' magnitude of scale before the attacks on Hiroshima and Nagasaki (Patterson, 2000). Kissinger's air of authority that Stalin was fully informed about the atomic bomb through a combination of espionage and Truman's alleged atomic revelation at Potsdam is highly speculative. He ignores the Anglo-American determination to retain indefinitely an atomic monopoly as the Grand Alliance was beginning to unravel with Cold War division and competing imperial overstretch. The ethnocentric belief that the Russians were not capable of developing an atomic bomb for several decades fed the arrogance of atomic monopoly amidst a world of inferior technological actors (Sherwin, 1975).

Kissinger avoids any citation of Alperovitz's work and relies instead upon counter-revisionist scholars such as John Lewis Gaddis. While presenting himself as a Metternichian acolyte committed to realism and pragmatism in external affairs, Kissinger actually confirms Alperovitz's revelation that the A-bomb's use was intended in large measure to intimidate the Russians into accepting containment and America's technological mastery in the postwar period. Kissinger supported Byrnes's objective to use American atomic might to pressure the Soviet Union to embrace free elections in Poland and throughout Eastern Europe (Maier, 1978; Alperovitz & Messer, 1991-1992; Bernstein, 1991). The "awesome power of the atom bomb... would have strengthened the American bargaining position" (Kissinger, 1994). Kissinger laments the failure of Byrnes's atomic diplomacy to control Soviet behavior yet strikingly avoids any lamentation much less referencing of the atomic bomb's impact on the citizens of Hiroshima and Nagasaki.

Military Leaders and A-Bomb

Classical realism emphasizes "the central role of power, the primacy of national interest, and the pervasiveness of conflict" (Spanier & Hook, 1998). Military leaders orchestrate the use of power in war. They are intimately involved in decision making as it pertains to strategy and tactics. They literally defend the putative national interest and participate in defining it. In World War II, senior military officials were widely respected and admired. General Dwight Eisenhower would follow Truman as the thirty-fourth president and General George C. Marshall would serve as secretary of state and defense.

Opposition to a unilateral nuclear war was not limited to liberal-internationalist scientists working at the Metallurgical Laboratory (Metlab) of the University of Chicago (Kirstein, 2001). Alperovitz demonstrates that many senior military leaders opposed abandoning conventional warfare in the final days of World War II. Eisenhower told Stimson before the nuclear assaults that "he had a feeling of depression... that dropping the bomb was completely unnecessary... as a measure to save American lives" (Alperovitz, 1970). Eisenhower later proclaimed, "It wasn't necessary to hit them with that awful thing" (Alperovitz, 2011). In March 1945, General Curtis LeMay directed B-29 indiscriminate, low-altitude, nighttime burnings of some sixty-three Japanese cities prior to Hiroshima. He declared after Japan's surrender: "The war would have been over in two weeks... The atomic bomb had nothing to do with the end of the war at all" (Alperovitz, 2011). Admiral William D. Leahy was the nation's senior military officer serving as chair of the Joint Chiefs of Staff and chief of staff to Truman. He "believed war is not to be waged on women and children." Leahy stated "they went ahead and killed as many women and children as they could which was just what they wanted all the time." Elsewhere in his memoirs he refers to the atomic attacks as "barbarous" (Alperovitz, 1985, 1995).

Arguments over Bomb Use

Truman's declared revenge was a motive in his announcement of the bombing of Hiroshima: "the war from the air at Pearl Harbor... has been repaid many fold." Yet the "Little Boy" bomb was a nuclear Pearl Harbor with a sneak attack on an unsuspecting nation (Harrison-Bundy Files, 1945). While Pearl Harbor was horrific and tragic, it was tactical and directed against battleships and airplanes. Supporters of the decision to use the A-bomb dismiss the necessity of announcing the existence of the weapon prior to attack; Japan deserved no sparing of suffering that American technological prowess might deliver. Advocates of an atomic warning believed it was a moral imperative prior to atomic ruin. No atomic warning was contained within the Potsdam Declaration that Truman, Churchill, and nationalist China Generalissimo Chiang Kai-shek signed on July 26, 1945. The exclusion of Russia from signing the declaration was a clear signal to Stalin that the United States was attempting now to bypass previous entreaties to enter the war. The use of the atomic bombs without warning to Japan or Russia indicate the desire on the part of the United States to contain Soviet power in Asia (Hasegawa, 109).

Morrison also witnessed the plutonium-gadget test at Trinity in the appropriately named desert, Jornada del Muerto (Journey of Death). In a postwar interview he said: "I was of the opinion that a warning to the Japanese might work. I was disappointed when the military said you don't warn... Now, of course, I don't think the bombing was justified" (Terkel, 1984).

Probomb advocates also opposed a non-lethal demonstration, as Marshall advocated, for fear it might be a dud or if conducted in Japan, American POW might be brought into a pre-announced ground-zero site (Steiner, 1977). The Truman administration rejected a demonstration of the atomic bomb off Tokyo bay, in the United States, or in some sparsely populated area to stun Japan into surrender. Several scientists from Metlab issued the Franck Report on June 11, 1945, which recommended a demonstration on a "desert or a barren island" to forestall widespread "horror and revulsion" (Kirstein, 2001). Physicist Edward Teller, a strong supporter of nuclear weapons and a major figure in the development of the hydrogen bomb, noted in his memoirs that a demonstration over Tokyo Bay might have convinced Japan that ending the war was necessary for its survival (Teller, 2001).

Japan was defenseless. American naval assets surrounded and effectuated a "strangling blockade" of Japan (Stimson, 1947). The war of burning cities had reduced the nation to rubble. Its navy was virtually destroyed and air force and air defense incapable of retarding attack. Truman and Byrnes, however, opposed any modification of unconditional surrender terms that would allow Japan to retain its emperor in exchange for surrender. Japan's emperor was considered a deity and the incarnation of perfection. The evidence, while not conclusive, strongly suggests a Japanese surrender prior to Hiroshima if guaranteed the preservation of its monarchy (Alperovitz, 1995). Alperovitz demonstrates American intelligence in breaking the Japanese code was privy to its frantic démarche with Russia to conclude a mediated settlement of the war with the preservation of the chrysanthemum throne. Only Byrnes among senior civilian officials rejected outright any modification of unconditional surrender that Roosevelt had declared in an almost impromptu manner at a press conference during the first allied-war conference at Casablanca in January 1943 (Alperovitz, 1995).

Truman's rejection of conditional surrender through diplomacy prevented a possible shortening of the war without the introduction of nuclear weapons (Sherwin, 1975). If a belligerent believes that surrendering could have the most egregious consequences for state survival, there are no inducements to end the fighting other than abject surrender to a more technologically advanced and remorseless enemy. After Japan's surrender the United States preserved the emperor within the framework of a constitutional monarchy (Alperovitz, 1995).

The use of the A-bomb and the Soviet decision to intervene occurred at virtually the same time. August 6 and 9 were the fateful days of Hiroshima and Nagasaki and the Soviet Union attacked Manchuria on August 8. Yet Alperovitz believes it was the Soviet entrance into the war that was the decisive event leading to Japan's surrender. The Russian declaration of war was a crushing failure for Japanese diplomacy and that alone might have ended the war. Emperor Hirohito informed senior Army officers and soldiers on August 14, the day he declared surrender, that "The military situation has changed suddenly. The Soviet Union entered the war against us... Now that the Soviet Union has entered the war, to continue under the present condition... would only result in further useless damage... Therefore ... I am going to make peace" (Alperovitz, 2011).

Defenders of the decision to use the atomic bomb claim it hastened the end of the conflict and was responsible for sparing over a million American and Japanese lives. Numerous documents and Alperovitz's revisionist history suggest strongly the decision to use the atomic bomb did not shorten the war. The United States Strategic Bombing Survey stunningly concluded in July 1946, "that certainly prior to December 31, 1945, and in all probability prior to November 1, 1945, Japan would have surrendered even if the atomic bombs had not been dropped, even if Russia had not entered the war, and even if no invasion had been planned or contemplated" (Feis, 1970). It concluded the "atomic bombs did not defeat Japan" (Bernstein, 1976).

Supporters of the decision to use the atomic bomb assert that the horrific atomic ending of World War II served notice that nuclear war was too dangerous and has deterred subsequent use of these weapons. Opponents of the bombing of Hiroshima and Nagasaki claim it launched a nuclear arms race. America's nuclear ending of World War II created even greater international instability with vertical and horizontal nuclear proliferation. Atomic bombs were replaced in many arsenals with thermonuclear weapons in the 1950s and eventually were deployed on a lethal triad of bombers, ICBMs, and SSBN submarines. The United States during the Cold War manufactured 70,000 nuclear weapons that stole $5 trillion that might have been used for vital domestic programs (Connelly et al., 2012). It's been estimated that the destructive yield of the world's nuclear arsenals approached an equivalence of 1.5 million Hiroshima bombs (Stone & Kuznick, 2012). Nine nations now possess either atomic or hydrogen-nuclear weapons. Eight are declared nuclear weapons states: the United States, Russia, China, United Kingdom, France, India, Pakistan and the Democratic People's Republic of Korea. Only Israel has refused to acknowledge officially its nuclear weapons' status. There are still thousands of strategic nuclear weapons in the world's arsenals on hair-trigger alert status, despite some reductions in the START I (1991), START II (1993) and New Start (2010) treaties. The latter will "limit" Russia and America to 1550 deployed strategic warheads and 700 launchers within seven years (Baker, 2010).

Neo-Realism and Nuclear Weapons

Kenneth N. Waltz's neo-realism describes the international-state system as adrift in anarchy and "interdependence among them is low" (Waltz, 2010). Imposing on the state system a strongly suggestive Marxian materialist conception of history, Waltz argues the structure of the world order governs external state behavior regardless of national preference. Marx's dialec-

tical materialism also minimizes human consciousness and volition in determining inevitable progressive cataclysmic change. Forces of revolutionary and societal tumult unfold independently from human will as substructural productive forces and productive relations undergo seismic inevitable transformation (Feuer, 1959). Robert Keohane also identifies elements of Marxian theory in realism's deterministic analysis of hegemonic domination and state behavior (Keohane, 1989).

Waltz believes nation-states, independently of their will, create balances of power to prevent hegemonic subjugation. The United States according to Waltz rearmed after World War II despite "a strong wish not to" (Waltz, 2010). He argues that Hiroshima and the development of nuclear weapons did not create a "new world" since "the perennial forces of politics are more important than the new military technology" (Waltz, 2010).

The global order, however, is structurally dynamic and America "has played a leading role in transforming the international system over the past sixty-five years" (Department of Defense, 2012). The nuclear era was revolutionary and created a new world out of "a world destroyed" (Sherwin, 1975). Our capacity to attain global annihilation reached a new level of terror and magnitude. Whether or not a structural realist determinism conditions interstate behavior, human-made institutions consist of sentient beings. They can adopt new strategies of self-preservation to cope with the present danger of a nuclear Armageddon. This is the challenge that lies ahead. Hiroshima led to nuclear proliferation as states attempted to either balance their power or pursue a mindless strategy of nuclear dominance. Yet the old tactics of power and the pursuit of the national self-interest in a world of thermonuclear warheads are hopelessly inadequate and must challenge the determinism of realism and neorealism.

Waltz, a structural theorist desires the spread of nuclear weapons. He welcomes the expansion of the nuclear club in the post-Hiroshima world as a stabilizing deterrent that mitigates anarchy and reduces armed conflict. Waltz described the fission bombs that destroyed Hiroshima and Nagasaki as "Model-T bombs" and noted inaccurately they were small because they could fit into a B-29 (Sagan & Waltz, 2003). "Fat Man", the larger of the two fission bombs, was eleven feet in length, weighed 4.5 tons, and had a yield of about twenty-one kilotons (Kirstein, 2003). They could barely fit into the bomb bay of the *Enola Gay* and *Bockscar* B-29 strategic bombers (Rhodes, 1986). They were large and B-29s had to be modified to fit them into the bomb bay. The modifications included the removal of all four bomb bay doors and the outer fuselage section between the two bomb bays (*Washington Times*, 2011).

Waltz believed, however, the nuclear climax of World War II demonstrated that nuclear weapons were small, hard to preempt, and useful in restraining additional war. He argued nuclear-weapon states through deterrence will always refrain from initiating a first-strike nuclear attack due to the uncertainty they could avoid a second-strike retaliatory nuclear response (Waltz, 2003). Nations will keep their nuclear-powder dry for fear they cannot escape retaliation. In Waltz's world nuclear proliferation contributes to strategic stability as "the gradual spread of nuclear weapons is better than either no spread or rapid spread" (Waltz, 2003). Horizontal proliferation according to Waltz' neo-realism preserves the peace as more nations grow increasingly wary of initiating a nuclear exchange (Waltz, 2003). Mutual Assured Destruction (MAD) preserves the peace and averts nuclear destruction.

Strategic Bombing

In the pre-Hiroshima era, nations were eager to introduce more deadly and destructive weaponry onto the battlefield. World War II's nuclear ending reflected this conventional mindset when the United States used its fission bombs as the latest version of strategic bombing. Waltz claims poison gas and chemical weapons were not introduced in the war due to an informal deterrence in the absence of a monopoly of these systems. When both sides to a conflict possess weapons of mass destruction, conflict is avoided and peace through mutual assured destruction is maintained (Waltz, 2003). Even a few nuclear weapons can go a long way in preserving a state of non-war according to Waltz. Whether a nuclear-tipped world can permanently avert the use of these weapons places undue faith in theory and a belief that the structural dynamics of the interstate system are indefinitely predictable.

George Kennan, the architect of containment, represented a softer side of realism in asserting that World War II in particular and the use of violence in general retards the advancement of civilization and inhibits the spread of democratic values:

> But, basically, the democratic purpose does not prosper when a man dies or a building collapses or an enemy force retreats... And this is why the destructive process of war must always be accompanied by, or made subsidiary to, a different sort of undertaking aimed at widening the horizons and changing the motives of men and should never be thought of in itself as a proper vehicle for hopes and enthusiasms and dreams of world improvement (Kennan, 1951).

The unrestrained, intimidating rhetoric of the Potsdam Declaration is palpable: "We call upon... Japan to proclaim... the unconditional surrender of its armed forces, and to provide proper and adequate assurances of their good faith in such action. The alternative for Japan is prompt and utter destruction." Thucydides described a similar statement from the Athenians prior to attacking the island of Melos. In their colloquy with the Melians, the Athenians reject their plea for justice and conflict resolution: "Then you do not adopt the view that expediency goes with security, while justice and honor cannot be followed without danger" (Thucydides, 1951). The Melians are told they have a choice between "war and security," the latter meaning survival by surrendering to Athens (Thucydides, 1951).

Potsdam Declaration and Truman Threat

As Truman returned across the Atlantic from Potsdam on the USS *Augusta*, the White House released a written statement announcing the bombing of Hiroshima and the existence of the nuclear age (Truman, 1955). As seen with Athens and the Potsdam Declaration, the strong order the weak to surrender or die:

> We are now prepared to obliterate more rapidly and completely every productive enterprise the Japanese have above ground in any city. We shall destroy their docks, their factories, and their communications... If they do not now accept our terms they may expect a rain of ruin from the air, the like of which has never been seen on this earth (Harrison-Bundy Files, 1945).

Newly elected British Labour Prime Minister Clement Attlee also announced the Hiroshima bombing and released a statement Churchill had prepared prior to his General Election defeat and abrupt departure from Potsdam (Harrison-Bundy Files, 1945). It also threatened continued nuclear annihilation of Japan: "It is now for Japan to realize in the glare of the first atomic bomb which has smitten her what the consequence will be of an indefinite continuance" of the conflict (*New York Times*, 1945). Indeed three days after Hiroshima "Fat Man" produced 75,000 casualties in Nagasaki.

The Potsdam Declaration in thirteen paragraphs of threats and frenzied rhetoric proclaimed that "stern justice shall be meted out to all war criminals, including those who have visited cruelties upon our prisoners" (National Diet Library, 2011). Yet on August 6 and August 9, American prisoners of war were knowingly sacrificed in the atomic attacks. American POW were known to be held in Kokura but it made no difference where their camps were in Japan because the Target Committee did not want Japan to have a prisoners' veto over US target selection (Farrell, 1945).

American POW were also nuclear casualties in Nagasaki. General Farrell tersely described the killing of American prisoners of war in Nagasaki: "There was a prisoner of war camp in Nagasaki and that some few prisoners were made casualties by our bombing" (Farrell, 1945). LeMay admitted after the war, "I suppose if I had lost the war, I would have been tried as a war criminal" (Rhodes, 1995).

Alperovitz was determined to reexamine the past and develop a new history of understanding acts of violence with such great import. The realist perspective in no small measure contributes to the revisionist assault on the standard history of the bomb. It supports the use of force to advance the national interest and some realists supported the atomic attacks. Yet realism as seen above frequently requires reasonable moral restraint and yes, overarching ethical standards before resorting to the use of force that invariably destroys so many lives.

REFERENCES

Alperovitz, G. (1985). *Atomic diplomacy: Hiroshima and potsdam, the use of the atomic bomb and the American confrontation with Soviet power*. New York.

Alperovitz, G. (1970). *Cold war essays*. New York: Anchor Books.

Alperovitz, G., Messer, R. L., & Bernstein, B. (1991-1992). Correspondence: Marshall, Truman, and the decision to drop the bomb. *International Security, 16*, 204-221.

Alperovitz, G. (2011). On the sixty-sixth anniversary of the bombing of Hiroshima. Fire Dog Lake. http://my.firedoglake.com/garalperovitz/2011/08/05/on-the-sixty-sixt h-anniversary-of-the-bombing-of-hiroshima/

Alperovitz, G. (1995). *The decision to use the atomic bomb and the architecture of the American myth*. New York: Vintage.

Bernstein, B. (1991). Eclipsed by Hiroshima and Nagasaki: Early thinking about tactical nuclear weapons. *International Security, 15*, 149-173.

British Statements Reviewing the Allies' Cooperation in Development of Historic Missile (1945) *New York Times, 8.*

Carr, E. H. (1961). *The twenty years' crisis, 1919-1939: An introduction to the study of international relations*. London: Macmillan.

Churchill, W. (1953). *The Second World War: Triumph and tragedy* (Vol. 6). Cambridge: Houghton Mifflin.

Churchill, W. (1981). *The Second World War: Triumph and tragedy*. New York: Houghton Mifflin.

Connelly, M., Fay M., Ferrini, G., Kaufman, M., Leonard, W., Monsky, H., Musto, R., Paine, T., Standish, N., & Walker, L. (2012). "General,

I have fought just as many nuclear wars as you have": Forecasts, future scenarios, and the politics of Armageddon. *American Historical Review, 117,* 1431-1460.

Correspondence ("Top Secret") of the Manhattan Engineer District (1945). Notes of the Interim Committee meeting. Roll 5, National Archives-Great Lakes Region.

Correspondence ("Top Secret") of the Manhattan Engineer District (1945). Notes on the initial meeting of the Target Committee. Roll 1: National Archives-Great Lakes Region.

Correspondence ("Top Secret") of the Manhattan Engineer District (1945). Recommended action by the JCS. Roll 1: National Archives-Great Lakes Region.

Crosby, A. W. (1987). *The Columbian voyages, the Columbian exchange, and their historians.* Washington DC: American Historical Association.

Dower, J. (2007) Lessons from Iwo Jima. *Perspectives, 45,* 55-57.

Dower, J. (1986). *War without mercy.* New York: Pantheon Books.

Farrell, T. F. (1945). "Report on overseas operations—Atomic bomb," 3. Roll 13, Manhattan Engineer District History, Records of the Defense Nuclear Agency.

Feis, H. (1970). *The atomic bomb and the end of World War II.* Princeton: Princeton University Press.

Freedman, L. (Ed.) (1994). *War.* Oxford: Oxford University Press.

Haas, R. N. (1997). *The reluctant sheriff: The United States after the cold war.* New York: A Council on Foreign Relations Book.

Harrison-Bundy Files Relating to the Development of the Atomic Bomb, 1942-1946 (1945). Text of Mr. Churchill's statement. Roll 6: National Archives: Great Lakes Region.

Harrison-Bundy Files Relating to the Development of the Atomic Bomb (1945). Statement of the president of the United States. Roll 6: National Archives: Great Lakes Region.

Harrison-Bundy Files Relating to the Development of the Atomic Bomb, 1942-1946 (1945). Memo: Discussed with the president. Roll 4: National Archives—Great Lakes Region.

Hasegawa, T. (2009). Were the atomic bombings justified? In Y. Tanaka, & M. Young (Eds.), *Bombing civilians: A twentieth-century history* (pp. 97-134). New York: The New Press.

Horowitz, D. (1971). *Free world colossus: A critique of American foreign policy in the cold war.* New York: Hill and Wang.

Horowitz, D. (1976). Hiroshima and the cold war. In P. R. Baker (Ed.), *The atomic bomb: The great decision* (2nd ed.) (pp. 66-70). New York: Dryden Press.

Irving, D. (1990). *Hitler's war.* New York: Avon.

Kennan, G. F. (1951). *American diplomacy: 1900-1950.* Chicago: University of Chicago Press.

Keohane, R. O. (1989). *International institutions and state power: Essays in international relations Theory.* Boulder: Westview Press.

Kirstein, P. N. (2001, March). *False dissenters: Manhattan Project scientists and the use of the atomic bomb.* American Diplomacy, University of North Carolina. http://www.unc.edu/depts/diplomat/archives_roll/2001_03-06/kirstein_manhattan/kirstein_manhattan.html

Kirstein, P. N. (2009). Hiroshima and spinning the atom: America, Britain, and Canada proclaim the nuclear age, August 6, 1945. *The Historian, 71,* 806-827.

Kirstein, P. N. (2003, July-August). Terrorism from the sky: The destruction of Nagasaki. *New Ground,* 12-15.

Kissinger, H. (1994). *Diplomacy.* New York: Touchstone Book.

Lears, T. J. J. (2012). Pragmatic realism versus the new American century. In A. J. Bacevich (Ed.), *The short American century* (pp. 82-120). Cambridge: Harvard University Press.

Maier, C. S. (1978). Revisionism and the interpretation of cold war origins. In C. S. Maier (Ed.), *The origins of the cold war and contemporary Europe.* New York: New Viewpoints.

Manhattan Engineer District (ND). The atomic bombings of Hiroshima and Nagasaki. Roll 14: National Archives-Great Lakes Region.

Marx, K. (1959). A contribution to the critique of political economy. In L. S. Feuer (Ed.), *Marx and Engels: Basic writings on politics & philosophy* (pp. 42-46). Garden City, NY: Anchor Books.

Morgenthau, H. (1985). *Politics among nations: The struggle for peace and power* (6th ed.). New York: Knopf.

National Conference of Catholic Bishops (1983). *The challenge of peace: God's promise and our response.* Washington DC: United States Catholic Conference.

National Diet Library, Japan (2004). *Birth of the constitution of Japan.* http://www.ndl.go.jp/constitution/e/etc/c06.html

Patterson, T. G., & Clifford, J. (Eds.) (2000). *American foreign relations* (Vol. 2). Boston, MA: Houghton Mifflin.

Rhodes, R. (2007). *Arsenals of folly: The making of the nuclear arms race.* New York: Alfred A Knopf.

Rhodes, R. (1995). *Dark sun: The making of the hydrogen bomb.* New York: Simon & Schuster.

Rhodes, R. (1986). *The making of the atomic bomb.* New York: Touchstone.

Sebald, W. G. (2003). *On the natural history of destruction.* New York: Random House.

Sherwin, M. J. (1975). *A world destroyed: The atomic bomb and the grand alliance.* New York: Alfred A. Knopf.

Sherwin, M. J. (1973). The atomic bomb and the origins of the cold war: U.S. atomic-energy policy and diplomacy, 1941-45. *American Historical Review, 78,* 945-968. http://www.jstor.org.ezp.sxu.edu/stable/1858347?seq=12

Simic, C. (2003). Conspiracy of silence. *The New York Review of Books,* 8-10.

Snow, D. W. (2000). *When America fights: The uses of U.S. military force.* Washington DC: CQ Press.

Spanier, J., & Hook, S. W. (1998). *American foreign policy since World War II.* (14th ed.). Washington DC: CQ Press.

Steiner, A. (1977). Scientists and politicians: The use of the atomic bomb reconsidered. *Minerva,* 249-264.

Stimson, H. (1947). The decision to use the atomic bomb. *Harpers Magazine, 194,* 97-107.

Stone, O., & Kuznick, P. (2012). *The untold history of the United States.* New York: Gallery.

Takaki, R. (1995). *Hiroshima: Why America dropped the atomic bomb.* Boston: Little, Brown.

Teller, E. (2001). *Memoirs: A twentieth-century journey in science and politics.* Cambridge: Perseus.

Terkel, S. (1984). *The good war: An oral history of World War II.* New York: Norton.

Truman, H. S. (1955). *Memoirs by Harry S. Truman: Year of decision* (Vol. 1). Garden City, NY: Doubleday.

U.S. Department of Defense. (2012). *Sustaining U.S. global leadership: Priorities for 21st century defense.* Washington DC: Department of Defense.

U.S. Strategic Bombing Survey (1976). In B. Bernstein (Ed.), *The atomic bomb: The critical issues* (pp. 52-56). Boston: Little, Brown.

Waltz, K. N. (2003). More may be better. In S. D. Sagan, & K. N. Waltz. *The spread of nuclear weapons: A debate renewed* (pp. 3-45). New York: Norton.

Waltz, K. N. (2010). *Theory of international politics.* Long Grove, IL: Waveland Press.

Thucydides (1951). *The complete writings of Thucydides: The Peloponnesian War.* New York: Random House.

Washington Times (2007). *Newsletter, No. 12.* http://www.cooksontributeb29.com/uploads/5/8/6/5/5865941/howlett_interiors1.40.pdf

7

Forest History Snapshot: Forest Industry Woodlands Operations Locations Prior to Mergers and Acquistions

Thomas J. Straka

School of Agricultural, Forest, and Environmental Sciences,
Clemson University, Clemson, USA

Forestry industry was a major owner of timberland in the United States over most of the twentieth century. This timberland was seen as a cost-effective means to supply their lumber and pulp mills. They were an important owner, with some of the most productive and intensively-managed timberlands in the country. Beginning in the 1980s, other investors realized the value of timberland assets and actively pursued acquisition of the forest products companies and their timberland assets. Mergers and acquisitions were common within the industry as a means to discourage takeovers. These timberlands were traditionally managed by woodlands operations located near the mills. These operations defined classic timber towns, with names like Crossett, Georgetown, Bogalusa, and Millinocket becoming synonymous with the mill and the woodlands. Woodlands operations are nearly extinct as few mills still own timberlands; what might remain is a small wood procurement organization at the same location. These woodlands operations were an important part of forest history and their locations provide much insight into the historical patterns of industrial forest management. Major forest industry woodlands operations are identified by geography and size as a means to record a fading historical artifact of forest history.

Keywords: Forest Industry; Woodlands Operations; Woodlands Departments; Locations

Introduction

The vertically-integrated forest products industry was a major owner of private timberland in the United States over most of the twentieth century (Zinkhan, Sizemore, Mason, & Ebner, 1992). At the peak of its timberland ownership in the late 1980s and early 1990s, the vertically integrated forest products industry owned nearly 28.5 million ha of timberland in the United States (Block & Sample, 2001; Sampson, DeCoster, & Remuzzi, 2000). Today, the industry owns approximately 9 million ha. The forest products industry has divested itself of most of its timberland over the last twenty five years (Gunnoe & Gellert, 2011). Some of the timberland was spun off as separate entities; real estate investment trusts (REITs) that just held the timberland asset. The four major timberland REITs today (Plum Creek, Weyerhaeuser, Rayonier, and Potlatch) own close to 7 million ha in the United States (Fiacco, 2010; Hickman, 2007). General investors own about 1 million ha of the former forest industry lands (Harris, 2007) and institutional investors, timberland investment management trusts (TIMOs) own approximately 11.5 million ha (Fiacco, 2010; Hickman, 2007; Straka, 2009).

These ownership changes are broad estimates. Transactions are still taking place, some of them very large, and areas owned are constantly changing. It is safe to say that the timberland owned by the vertically-integrated forest products industry has decreased by at least two-thirds and that the trend for divestiture of timberland by forest industry is continuing (Stein, 2011). What remains of forest industry are the smaller firms, many of them family-owned. Virtually all of the very large integrated firms are simply gone (Clutter, Mendell, Newman, Wear, & Greis, 2005; Harris, Baldwin, & Siry, 2011).

Several trends converged in the 1980s that caused the vertically-integrated forest products companies to divest of their timberlands (Clark & Howell, 2007). The traditional rationale for holding industrial timberland was future raw material supply (timber supply security), timberland investment return, tax advantages, and some control over the timber costs (Yin, Caulfield, Aronow, & Harris, 1998). This changed. First, the forest industry firms realized that the security of owning timberland to ensure a constant supply of raw material was an illusion. Ample raw material was available on the open market, including overseas, and often this supply was cheaper than the locally-produced one. Second, TIMOs and REITs were subject to lower tax rates than traditional forest products companies. Much of this timberland was prime for development and these new ownership vehicles provided more profitable ways to develop properties.

The main reasons forest industry sold timberland were 1) the need to increase shareholder returns; 2) the need to reduce debt, especially those firms that acquired other firms with debt financing; 3) firm restructuring to increase tax efficiency using REITs and subchapter S corporations; 4) tax strategies that allowed for reduced capital gains taxes; and 5) recognition that timber supply security was not as important as assumed in the past (the market would supply plenty of timber and land could be sold with timber supply agreements for the mills) (Clutter et al., 2005).

Investors in these timberlands saw an asset that 1) produced strong long-term financial returns; 2) had a low correlation with other asset classes (stocks and bonds) and thus reduced overall investment risk; 3) provided a good hedge against inflation; and 4) provided tax advantages (Fasano & Straka, 2009).

The catalyst was when timberland was identified as an undervalued asset that could be split off from the larger company for a profit (Binkley, 2007). Sir James Goldsmith started the process with the acquisitions of Diamond International and Crown Zellerbach (Clark & Howell, 2007). By the early 1980s a climate of hostile takeovers emerged and forest industry companies developed defensive strategies like limited partnerships holding the timberland assets (Binkley et al., 1996).

The rise of TIMOs also started in the 1970s with several pension funds diversifying into timberland investments (Binkley, 2007). The TIMO provided the acquisition and management services for portfolios of timberland for large institutional investors (like pension funds and insurance companies). At the same time some forest product companies divested of their timberland, putting it into subsidiaries that traded separately. Tax advantages also favored those that had timberland in separate real estate investment trusts (REITs). Both trends combined to separate timberland from the forest products companies (Irland, 2005). By the 1980s the transition to TIMO ownership from forest industry land or conversion of forest industry land to REITS was in full swing.

Changes in tax laws fueled industry divesting of timberland. The Employee Retirement Income Security Act of 1974 (ERISA) encouraged pension funds to invest in timberland (Binkley, 2007) and the 1986 Tax Reform Act removed a capital gains tax advantage for industrial ownership (Yin et al., 1998). Irland and Howard (1989) saw the increased activity in timberland ownership exchange resulting from issues like fiber supply control, timberland as collateral, timberland for investment, and timberland as a source of capital. As this transition played out, several major mergers and acquisitions took place in the industry (Diamond et al., 1999). Timberland emerged as an attractive nontraditional asset class.

By 1982 the first institutional investment in forest industry timberland began (Fu, 2012). Today, none of the larger traditional woodlands operations exist. A few of the smaller ones still exist (for now). The geographical locations of these operations correspond to the general location of forest industry timberlands. Woodlands operations are described in terms of size (timberland area owned) and location. This presents an historical perspective of where forest industry operated and where the "timber towns" used to be located. Forest industry had a huge impact on American development and these locations continue to have significant historical ties to the former dominant forest products industry.

Woodlands Operations

What was the traditional woodlands operation? It was the operational management unit for a large block or area of timberland. It represented the forest management structure for administering that large area of timberland. The structure tended to be decentralized with managerial authority radiating out to area offices and down to district offices. A woodlands operation could be small (perhaps 20,000 ha) to very large (perhaps 400,000 ha). Obviously, decentralization had to increase with overall size. Each operation had a headquarters office, for logistical reasons often located centrally to the timberland, that would report to a corporate or division headquarters.

American forestry has Central European roots and a strong administrative structure has always been a starting point in forest management. The earliest texts centered on a German framework of central control (Recknagel, 1913). An entire section of an early forest management textbook was devoted to forest organization (Chapman, 1931), with chapters devoted to subjects like principles of forest organization, evolution of forest organization, organization of a large forest enterprise, acquisition and consolidation of forests, boundaries, the coordination of land uses, the subdivisions of the forest area, and plans for development of the forest. Woodland operations tended to be very similar in appearance and structure; this was not a coincidence. Foresters were taught organizational structure from the same textbooks and differences were few. Modern forest management textbooks do not devote the same amount of space to the subject of forest organization, but it is still covered and the administrative framework has not changed from the early forestry development periods (Bettinger, Boston, Siry, & Grebner, 2009).

Industrial owners of timberland tend to be profit-motivated and usually develop extensive forest resource management plans for their resources (Davis, Johnson, Bettinger, & Howard, 2001: pp. 22-24; Leuschner, 1984: p. 256). Meyer, Recknagel, Stevenson, & Bartoo (1961: pp. 180-200) describe the forest as a business enterprise and illustrate the various function of a typical woodlands operation. The earlier textbooks were very detailed on setting up administrative structure, as it was a task that was a very current need. Chapman (1931: pp. 196-212) presented details on the subdivisions of the forest area, including administrative subdivisions, blocks, logging units, compartments, and subcompartments. These components comprise a woodlands operation. Chapman (1931: p. 198) explains there is an optimal size for a woodlands operation: "The administrative problem which such subdivisions seek to solve is the dual one of coordinating all the field work of a large organization while decentralizing it as much as possible. This result is accomplished by giving subordinate executives all the responsibility they can bear and depending on inspection to see the work is properly conducted. The size of the administrative unit has a direct bearing on the whole problem, as it must be adjusted to the volume and character of the business to be transacted within the area".

Davis (1966: pp. 247-261) described forest organization and subdivision. While he does not call his organization a woodlands operation, that is what he is describing. Davis (1966: pp. 248-249) discusses the factors influencing forest organization and subdivision: 1) establishment and maintenance of land ownership, 2) future acquisition plans, 3) scope and character of work to be done, 4) work load and supervision, 5) marketing area, 6) topography, 7) transportation facilities, 8) character of the forest, and 9) inventory and recordkeeping needs.

Davis (1966: pp. 252-253) presents organization charts for two typical large forest products organizations, one in the southeastern Unites States and one in the Lake States of the US

Both are headed by a Woodlands Manager, with an assistant manager and administrative assistants. The southeastern operation has a land department (with a nursery supervisor, equipment supervisor, and survey engineer) and a wood procurement department (with superintendents and field representatives). Plus, the southeastern woodlands operation has a technical department (forest inventories, research, and cruising and acquisition control) and conservation (public relations) department. The Lake States woodlands operation has a chief forester (forest management, silviculture, acquisition, inventory, wood quality and scaling, forest engineering, nursery, and forest pest problems). In addition, the Lake States operation has a production superintendent (with district foresters responsible for both land management and wood procurement), a forest products (marketing) manger, and a plant and equipment superintendent. Careful analysis of the various job functions will show both organizations accomplish exactly the same tasks.

Davis (1966: p. 254) summarizes what goes into the selection of a woodlands operation organization, size, and location: "a number of factors influence the size and character of field units. Work load and the kind of total organization are two of them. Also important are such things as an areas that be efficiently administered from a field headquarters without excessive time spent in travel, the need for the forest manager to become closely familiar with the forest, the location of schools and other urban services, and living and housing considerations for personnel". He summarizes the selection as: "The primary consideration is to get the job done efficiently".

These were the considerations that went into development and location of woodlands operations. Note that many had wood procurement departments attached or integrated into the woodlands department. The mills may have sold the timberland and gotten rid of the woodlands operations, but many retained the wood procurement operations. Thus, many of these locations still have timber-related operations. Many don't. That is just part of the interesting history of this large forest products industry transition.

Geography of the American Forest

Geography plays a large role in determining the locations of woodlands operations. Many operational factors were just discussed that impact location. But there is one large factor that breaks the operations into large geographical regions. The American forest based on tree species and forest composition is broken into a northern, southern, and western forest. Latitude divides the northern and southern forest, with the Appalachian Mountains allowing some northern tree species to expand their range into the South. The Great Plains separate the eastern and western forests. Then commercial factors like transportation costs, markets, geographical barriers (the Great Lakes, for example), natural transportation routes (the Mississippi River and the Great Lakes again), and native tree species further define the geographical regions of these operations. Generally, one can break the forest/woodlands regions into the Northeast or North, Lake States (Upper Michigan, Wisconsin, and Minnesota), the South (including east Texas and Oklahoma), and the West (with most the timber being in the Pacific Northwest).

Figure 1 illustrates the natural pattern just described. The northern and southern forest shows up quite well, with the darker Appalachian Mountain hardwood forests extending into the South. The Lake State forests stand out well and the western

forests show the large timber volumes in the Pacific Northwest. Woodlands operations will be characterized as northern, southern, Lake States, or western.

Figure 2 illustrates the pattern of industrial timberland holdings in the contiguous United States. The northern, southern, Lake States, and western forests are even more obvious on this map. The Lake States timberlands are quite distinct. Western timberlands are also distinct, even the concentration of timberland in the Pacific Northwest stands out. The eastern timberland is distinct, but the division between north and south is not obvious. It is generally based on "northern" and "southern" tree species. The historical Mason-Dixon line is a logical place to divide the two. The southern border of Pennsylvania is part of that line. Detailed maps and data analysis is available from the United States Department of Agriculture (USDA) Forest Service, Forest Inventory and Analysis. Much of it is produced to support the Forest and Rangeland Renewable Resources Planning Act (RPA) of 1974 that requires periodic analysis and reports on the nation's forest resources (Smith, Miles, Perry, & Pugh, 2009).

The most recent RPA data does not break out the industrial timberland. It uses a category of private corporate that includes all timberland administered by entities that are legally incorporated. Of course, that includes forest industry lands. REITs are also incorporated. TIMOs and many other types of forest holdings are also incorporated. Much of the old forest industry land is still in this category, as it moved from incorporated forest industry land to incorporated other timberland. The breakdown of private corporate land provides insight into timberland ownership. **Table 1** shows timberland area breakdown by region, giving an indication of where woodlands operations would be expected.

Based on **Table 1** most of the woodland operations ought to be in the South with just over half the timberland area. That will be shown not to be the case. Many firms decided to locate a woodlands operation in each forest region, even if some operations did not administer large areas. Many factors came into play in determining location, not just the timber resource. If one was to plot the locations of woodlands operations, the map would look similar to **Figure 2**. The location decision involved a tradeoff. Mill location and timber location drove the decision, but part of the function was wood procurement. So there was an advantage in not being located too close to competitors (so there would be less competition for outside wood). These location decisions were complex and often the optimal location was not the choice that seemed to make sense at first.

Figure 1.
Woody biomass, contiguous United States, 2012 (NASA Earth Observatory).

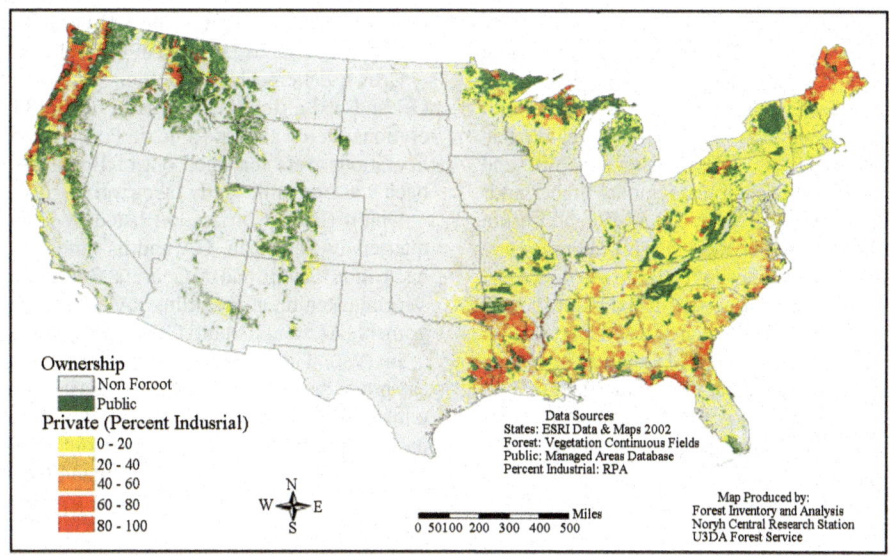

Figure 2.
Industrial timberland in United States, 2002 (USDA Forest Service, Forest Inventory and Analysis).

Table 1.
Private corporate timberland in United States by region, 2007 (Smith, Miles, Perry, & Pugh, 2009: pp. 192-194).

Region	Timberland ha (area)	Percent of timberland
North	9,283,000	5
South	23,067,000	21
Lake States	2,112,000	54
West	8,487,000	20

Woodlands Operations Locations

Timber Harvesting Magazine published a Wood & Woodlands Directory/Loggers' Buying Guide. The directory included most of the major woodlands divisions that operated in the United States. The directory was "a listing of personnel employed by the wood supply and forest management organizations of the nation's major industrial timber companies" (Timber Harvesting, various dates). The list of locations developed below came from this directory. The fifteen years from 1980 to 1994 were chosen as representative of the peak of the forest products industry and those fifteen directories were used to develop the listing.

There are multiple ways to organize the data. Size makes much sense and the listings will be by size, with the larges operations first. Within size grouping, the largest operations will be presented first. The directory did not include timberland areas owned. O'Laughlin & Ellefson (1982: p. 785) was the basis of all timberland area statistics.

Operations Managing 1,000,000 ha or More

These are the large multi-national corporations with huge timberland holdings backing major lumber, plywood, and pulp and paper mills. They tend to have a major corporate headquarters, often in New York City or nearby; Atlanta, Georgia and Portland, Oregon are also major headquarter cites. Timber-

lands and wood products tend to be a major division of the corporation and usually very large regional timberland divisions are established. Divisions tend to be organized geographically (Northeast, Midwest, Southeast, South Central, Rocky Mountain, and Pacific Northwest), by wood product (lumber, plywood, pulp and paper), or by historical ownership patterns (a division might be a purchased lumber company).

International Paper listed its corporate headquarters as New York in 1980 and its timberland area was 2,877,315 ha. It had Woodlands and Wood Products Operation headquartered at Mobile, AL, Dallas TX, and Memphis, TN. Woodlands operations were located at: Georgetown, SC; Natchez, MS; Camden, AR; Shreveport, LA; Augusta, ME; and Portland, OR. Over the fifteen years Erie, PA; Jackson, MS; and Gardiner, OR were added.

Weyerhaeuser Company listed its corporate headquarters as Tacoma Way, WA and its timberland area was 2,142,001 ha. They listed three land and timber regions centered at Columbus, MS; Mountain Pine, AR; and New Bern, NC; Wright City, OK; and Hot Spring, AR; and Tacoma, WA. *Timber Harvesting Magazine* was a southern magazine and some very western companies like Weyerhaeuser did not supply much data for their western operations.

Georgia-Pacific Corporation first listed its corporate headquarters as Portland, OR, but by the 1983 directory it was listed as Atlanta, GA. Its timberland area was 1,671,352 ha. In 1980 in the South they had two major divisions, one at Crossett, AR and one at Augusta, GA. The Crossett Division was broken into smaller timber operations in Arkansas and Mississippi. The Southern Division was broken into a Northern Timber Group at Alcolu, SC and a Southern Timber Group at Pine Mountain, GA. Other woodlands operations were at Bellingham, WA; Coos Bay, OR; Eugene, OR; Lyons Falls, NY; Fort Bragg, CA; Zachary, LA; Woodland, ME; and Toledo, OR. They also owned Hudson Pulp & Paper Corporation at Palatka, FL. Fifteen years later, after acquisitions and reorganizations, Georgia-Pacific's woodlands operations were at Woodland, ME; Wendell, NC; Watkinsville, GA; Cedar Springs, GA; Brunswick, GA; Palatka, FL; Jackson, MS; and Crossett, AR.

St. Regis Paper Company listed its headquarters as New York and its timberland area was 1,286,496 ha. St. Regis had a Northern Timberlands Division at Bangor, ME and a Southern Timberlands Division at Jacksonville, FL, plus a Lumber and Plywood Division at Tacoma, WA. The northern region had regional timberlands at Deferiet, NY; Rhinelander, WI; and Bucksport, ME. The southern division had regional timberlands at Jacksonville, FL; Pensacola, FL; Monticello, MS; and Lufkin, TX. They later added a Minnesota Region with operations at Bemidji, MN. By 1986 St. Regis was no longer in the directory.

Champion International Corporation was listed as headquartered at Stamford, CT and its timberland area was 1,216,889 ha. Champion International had a Gulf States Operation at Huntsville, TX; a Southeastern Operations at Greenville, SC; a West Coast Operations at Eugene, OR; a Rocky Mountain Operations at Missoula, MT; and a Lake States Operation at Norway, MI. By 1994 there was a Northern Timberlands at Bangor, ME; a Southern Timberlands at Greenville, SC; a Western Timberlands at Huntsville, TX; with a Technical Center in Jacksonville, FL.

Great Northern Nekoosa Corporation was listed in 1980 as owning 1,097,507 ha of timberland. It was operated as two divisions and a subsidiary (McCann 1994). Paper company mergers began well before the 1980s. In 1965 Great Southern Paper Company was merged into Great Northern Paper (Lehman Brother Special Collection, 2013) and in 1970 Great Northern Nekoosa was formed by the merger of Nekoosa Edwards Paper Company and Great Northern Paper Company (Steeves, 2009). The directory always listed Great Northern Nekoosa as two separate woodlands: Great Northern Paper Company at Millinocket, ME and Great Sothern Paper Company at Cedar Springs, GA. Nekoosa Papers Inc. was listed with a northern woodlands at Port Edwards, WI and a Southern Woodlands at Ashdown, AR.

Boise Cascade Corporation was headquartered in Boise, ID and owned 1,068,370 ha of timberland. Its Timber and Wood Products Group had a Southern Idaho Region at Emmett, ID; a Northeast Oregon Region at La Grande, OR; a Northwest Oregon Region at Monmouth, OR; a Southern Oregon Region at Medford, OR; a Northeast Washington Region at Kettle Falls, WA; a Central Washington Region at Yakima, WA; a South Atlantic Region at Moncure, NC; a Southeast Timberlands at Florence, SC; and a Midwest Woodlands at International Falls, MN. Boise Cascade also had an operation at DeRidder, LA called Boise Southern Company. By 1994 the Southeast Timberlands was listed at Charlotte, NC and there was a Rumford Mill Wood Department listed at Rumford, ME.

Operations Managing 1,000,000 to 500,000 ha

These were still large timberland operations and were often organized similar to the very largest firms. However, most had perhaps two divisions, often geographically based (northern and southern, southern and western, or northern and western). They are big enough to have product divisions. Often the corporate headquarters was at the larger or older of the two divisions. Some were located in a single geographical area. These firms tend to be fairly similar to the larger companies in terms of organization.

Scott Paper Company listed its headquarters as Philadelphia, PA and its timberland area was 743,812 ha. Scott had a North-east Operations at Winslow, ME and a Southern Operations at Mobile, AL. S.D. Warren was listed as a division of Scott Paper with a Timberlands Division at Fairfield, ME.

Crown Zellerbach Corporation was headquartered at Portland, OR and had a timberland area of 703,748 ha. It Northwest operations were managed out of Portland, OR and its Southern operations were managed out of Bogalusa, LA. Crown Zellerbach was one of the early take-over targets.

Union Camp Corporation listed Woodlands Division headquarters as Savannah, GA and its timberland area was 696,869 ha. Union Camp had a Georgia Region at Savannah, GA: A Virginia Region at Franklin, VA; an Alabama Region at Montgomery, AL; and a South Carolina Region at Eastover, SC.

In 1980, Time Inc., the magazine publisher, owned two forest products companies: Temple-Eastex Inc. and Inland Container Corporation, with a combined timberland area of 619,169 ha. Temple-Eastex was managed out of Diboll, TX, with an Eastex Division in Silsbee, TX. Inland Container was managed out of New Johnsonville, TN. Time spun off the companies and they became Temple-Inland Inc.

Burlington Northern Inc. had a Timber and Land Department at Seattle, WA and listed its timberland area as 603,791 ha. The department managed timberland in OR, WA, ID, and MT and sold logs and stumpage on the open market.

The Continental Group (Continental Forest Industries) had a Woodlands Division in Savannah, GA and listed its timberland area as 595,697 ha. Continental had a Savannah District at Savannah, GA; an Augusta Division at Augusta, GA; a Hodge Division at Hodge, LA; and a Hopewell Division at Hopewell, VA.

Diamond International Corporation listed its timberland area as 588,008 ha. It had a New England Land and Timber Division managed out of Old Town, ME, with a Maine Woodlands at Old Town; A New Hampshire Woodlands at Groveton, NH; a Minnesota Woodlands at Cloquet, MN; and a New York Woodlands at Plattsburg, NY. It also had a California Timber and Lands Division at Red Bluff, CA. Diamond International was one of the early takeover targets.

The Mead Corporation had its headquarters in Dayton, OH and listed its timberland area as 547,135 ha. Mead had Woodland Divisions at Chillicothe, OH; Stevenson, AL; Kingsport, TN; Escanaba, MI; and South Range, MI.

Potlatch Corporation is headquartered in Spokane, WA and listed its timberland area as 530,543 ha. It had a Northwest Division at Cloquet, MN; a Southern Division at Warren, AR; and a Western Division at Lewiston, ID.

Operations Managing 500,000 to 200,000 ha

These are the medium-sized firms. Most occupy a single region, rarely more than two regions. There tends to be a single timberlands division. Sometimes small geographical divisions are established within one geographical region. These companies were still major forestry/timberlands operations within their region; they just tended not to have a national focus. Much innovation came from these mid-sized firms.

Westvaco Corporation was headquartered at New York, NY and listed its timberland area as 494,121 ha. The Timberlands Division was headquartered at Summerville, SC. The Southern Woodlands was at Summerville, SC; the Virginia Woodlands was at Appomattox, VA; the West Virginia Woodlands was at Rupert, WV; and the Central Woodlands was at Wickliffe, KY.

ITT Rayonier Incorporated had a Southeast Timber Division headquartered at Fernandina Beach, FL and listed its timberland area as 433,823 ha. It had a Florida Operation Office at Fernandina Beach, FL and a Georgia Operations Office at Jesup, GA. They also had a Baxley Lumber Division at Baxley, GA.

Owens-Illinois, Inc. has a Forest Products Division managed out of Toledo, OH and listed a timberland area of 405,090 ha. They had a Northern Woodlands at Tomahawk, WI; a Southern Woodlands at Valdosta, GA; an Eastern Woodlands at Big Island, VA; and a Western Woodlands at Orange, TX.

Louisiana-Pacific Corporation was headquartered at Portland, OR and listed a timberland area of 356,123 ha. It had division offices in Beaverton, OR; Antioch, CA, Coeur D'Alene, ID; Samoa, CA; Escanaba, MI; Red Bluff, CA; Standard, CA; New Waverly, TX; and Ukiah, CA. They also owned Ketchikan Pulp Company at Ketchikan, AK. Later it had just a Western Division office at Samoa, CA and a Northern Division office in Hayden Lake, ID.

Container Corporation of America, owned by Mobil Corporation, listed its timberland area as 310,394 ha. It had two Timber Departments, one at Brewton, AL and one at Fernandina Beach, FL.

Kirby Forest Industries, Inc., owned by Santa Fe Southern Pacific Corporation, listed its timberland area as 264,664 ha. Its Woodlands Division was in Houston, TX and later at Silsbee, TX. Manville Forest Products Corporation (subsidiary of Johns Manville; Olinkraft) was headquartered at West Monroe, LA and listed its timberland area as 236,336 ha. The woodlands were managed out of West Monroe. Kimberly-Clark Corporation had a Division Headquarters at Coosa Pines, AL and listed a timberland area of 227,029 ha. Its woodlands were managed out of Coosa Pines and Waynesboro, GA.

Willamette Industries, Inc. was headquartered at Portland, OR and listed its timberland area as 221,768 ha. It had woodlands operations at Albany, OR: Ruston, LA; Campti, LA; Hawesville, KY; Centerville, TN; Bennettsville, SC; and Johnsonburg, PA. American Can Company listed its timberland area as 202,343 ha. It had a Lake States Woodlands at Green Bay, WI and a Southern Woodlands and Sawmills at Butler, AL. Masonite Corporation had a Fiberboard Division headquartered at Spring Hope, NC and listed a timberlands area of 201,129 ha. There was a Woodlands Division at Spring Hope plus a Southern Woodlands at Laurel, MS and a Western Lumber Division at Calpella, CA.

Operations Managing Less than 200,000 ha

While these were the smallest of the forest products companies, concentrated timberland area in small regions could create some relatively large single landholdings. But, in general, these were smaller timberlands, most always associated with a region or sub-region. All of these were large enough to be generally well-known in the forestry community.

Southwest Forest Industries had a Rocky Mountain Resources Division managed out of Flagstaff, AZ and listed its timberland area as 185,346 ha. Sierra Pacific Industries listed a timberlands area of 182,189 ha and was managed out of Arcata, CA. Packaging Corporation of America (owned by Tenneco) listed its timberland area as 169,563 ha and it had divisions in Filer City, MI and Counce, TN. Longview Fibre Company was headquartered out of Longview, WA and listed its timberland area as 165,112 ha. The woodlands were managed out of Long-

view.

Hammermill Paper Company had a Timberlands and Forest Products Divison at Erie, PA and listed its timberland area as 162,279 ha. It managed American Hardwood Industries, Inc. at Union City, PA; Amos-Hill Veneer & Lumber Company at Edinburg, IN; Frank Purcell Lumber Company at Kansas City, KS; Hammermill Hardwoods at Augusta, GA; a Northern Timber Division at Erie, PA; a Southern Timberlands Division at Selma, AL; and a Southern Forest Products Division at Selma, AL.

Federal Paper Board Company had a Riegelwood Operations at Bolton, NC and listed a timberland area of 100,768 ha. The woodlands were managed out of Bolton. Bendix Forest Products Corporation was headquartered at San Francisco, CA and listed its timberland area as 69,201 ha. The woodlands were managed out of San Francisco. The Pacific Lumber Company was headquartered at Scotia, CA and its timberland area is listed as 66,773 ha and its woodlands are managed out of Scotia.

Pope & Talbot, Inc. was headquartered in Portland, OR and has a listed timberland area of 52,609 ha. Medford Corporation had its headquarters in Medford, OR and listed its timberland areas as 35,612 ha. Arcata Redwood Company had a woodlands division in Humboldt County, CA and listed its timberland area as 30,756 ha. Bohemia Lumber Company was headquartered at Eugene, OR and had woodlands in Oregon and Northern California. Its timberland area was 28,328 ha.

Other woodlands operations were too small in timberland area to be listed in the O'Laughlin & Ellefson (1982 summary. They were still large enough to be listed in the woodlands directory. They were Abitibi Corporation at Alpena, MI and Roaring River, NC; Alabama River Woodlands, Inc. at Monroeville, AL; Allied Paper Incorporated at Jackson, AL; Alton Box Board Company at Jacksonville, FL; Appleton Papers Inc. at Combined Locks, WI; Arkansas Kraft Corporation at Morrilton, AR; Armstrong Cork Company at Macon, GA; Badger Paper Mills, Inc. at Peshtigo, WI; Bear Island Paper Company at Ashland, VA; Blandin Paper Company at Grand Rapids, MI; Bowater Incorporated with woodlands in Catawba, SC and Calhoun, TN; Brooks-Scanlon, Inc. at Bend, OR (with 93,482 ha); Brown Company at Berlin, NH; Brunswick Pulp Land Company at Brunswick, GA; The Buckeye Cellulose Corporation at Perry, FL; The Chesapeake Corporation of Virginia at West Point, VA; Chessie Resources, Inc. at Huntington, WV; The Cleveland-Cliffs Iron Company at Iron Mountain, MI; Coastal Lumber Company at Weldon, NC; Consolidated Papers, Inc. at Wisconsin Rapids, WI; Coos Head Timber Company at Coos Bay, OR and Dead River Company at Bangor, ME.

Other smaller woodlands were Finch, Pruyn & Company, Inc. at Glens Falls, NY; Flambeau Paper Corporation at Park Falls, WI; Georgia Kraft Company at Coosa, GA; Georgia Timberlands Inc. at Atlanta, GA; Gilman Paper Company at St. Marys, GA; The Glatfelter Pulp Wood Company at Spring Grove, PA; Green Bay Packaging Inc. at Green Bay, WI; Gulf States Paper Corporation at Tuscaloosa, AL; Hemphill-O'Neill Lumber Company, Inc. at Chehalis, WA; Interstate Paper Corporation at Riceboro, GA; Kaibab Industries at Phoenix, AZ; The Langdale Company at Valdosta, GA; Leaf river Forest Products, Inc. at New Augusta, MS; MacMillan Bloedel Inc. at Pine Hill, AL; Menasha Corporation at Otsego, MI; and Mosinee Paper Corporation at Mosinee, WI.

Other smaller woodlands were Pineville Kraft Corporation at

Pineville, LA; Pope & Talbot, Inc. at Portland, OR; Prentiss & Carlisle Company at Bangor, ME; The Proctor and Gamble Paper Products Company at Green Bay, WI; Publishers Paper Company at Oregon City, OR; St. Joe Paper Company at Port St. Joe, FL; Saunders Brothers at Westbrook, ME; Simpson Timber Company at Seattle, WA; Stilley Plywood Company at Conway, SC; Sonoco Forest Products at Hartsville, SC; South Carolina Industries, Inc. at Florence, SC; Stone Container Corporation at Columbia, SC; Texasgulf Inc. at Johnsonburg, PA; Thilmany Pulp and Paper Company at Kaukauna, WI; Vancouver Plywood Company at Florien, LA; Virginia Fibre Corporation at Amherst, VA; Wausau Paper Mills Company at Brokaw, WI: and W-I Forest Products, Inc. at Dinuba, CA with a timberland area of 72,843 ha.

Conclusion

Woodlands Divisions locations followed a very distinctive pattern. Divison locations listed were plotted on a map of the United States, producing a map that was not very usable. Division locations tended to be in clusters that produced a muddled, difficult-to-read map. **Figure 2** with does a better job of giving a general geographical perspective on location.

Several general observations are apparent. As one would expect Woodlands Divisions were located near the mills. Since the timberlands tends to be close to the mills, and the divisions close to the timberlands, that relationship follows common sense. The headquarters of the Woodlands Division, at least, would be close to the mills. Of course, some timberlands were spread out over fairly vast areas. Woodlands then would have some sort of regional pattern based on minimizing transportation and travel costs. Woodland Divisions (not the headquarters, but the operational first-level subdivisional level) would manage a timberland area of 20,000 to 100,000 ha. The lower end would be for smaller woodlands with limited area. The upper end would be very large woodlands with very large subdivisions.

National firms with timberland managed across the country usually had regional woodlands based on the North and South in the eastern United States, with the Midwest or Lake States usually managed separately. Eastern and Western Divisions were almost always the case, due to the large differences in timber types, logging conditions, and customs. Companies with large ownerships in the South usually managed them as a Southeastern Division and a Mid-South Division.

There is one strong influence on location that is not apparent from just studying the map and mill locations. Historical development of the industry has much influence on division location. For example, the pulp and paper industry developed in certain parts of the Northeast and Midwest. Those locations tended to have Woodlands Divisions. Many of the very early lumber companies with reasonably large timberlands were bought up by the larger firms. Crossett, AR; Georgetown, SC; Brunswick, GA; and Brewton, AL were early lumber mill towns. So history has aided in aligning these division locations.

Most of these Woodland Divisions no longer exist. However, the same factors that influenced how the locations were first selected and historical development have tended to encourage the TIMOs and REITs that acquired the timberlands to maintain operations offices at these same locations. While Woodlands Divisions were operational offices that directed large organizations that managed the trees on the ground, these new divisions are more managerial offices, with the field work usually contracted out to consulting forestry organizations. Locations have only changed moderately, but function is very much different.

The history of these locations is an important part of forest history and reveals much about management of the nation's private forest resource over the twentieth century. It tells a story of how forest management was organized and where forest industry was strongest. Timber was a vital natural resource that was crucial to the nation's development. Its history helps tell the history of the nation.

REFERENCES

Bettinger, P., Boston, K., Siry, J. P., & Grebner, D. L. (2009). *Forest management and planning*. Burlington, MA: Academic Press.

Binkley, C. S. (2007). The rise and fall of the timberland investment management organizations: Ownership changes in US forestland. In *2007 Pinchot Distinguished Lecture*. Washington, DC: Pinchot Institute for Conservation.

Binkley, C. S., Raper, C. F., & Washburn, C. L. (1996). Institutional ownership of US timberland: History, rationale, and implication for forest management. *Journal of Forestry, 94*, 21-28.

Block, N. E., & Sample, V. A. (2001). *Industrial timberland divestitures and investment: Opportunities and challenges in forest conservation*. Washington, DC: Pinchot Institute for Conservation.

Chapman, H. H. (1931). *Forest management*. Albany, NY: J. B. Lyon Company, Publishers.

Clark, S. A., & Howell, P. (2007). From Diamond International to Plum Creek: The era of large landscape conservation in the Northern Forest. *Maine Policy Review, 16.2*, 56-65.

Clutter, M., Mendell, B., Newman, D., Wear, D., & Greis, J. (2005). *Strategic factors driving timberland ownership changes in the U.S. South*. Athens, GA: Center for Forest Business, University of Georgia; USDA Forest Service; Southern Group of State Foresters.

Diamond, J., Chappelle, D. E., & Edwards, J. D. (1999). Mergers and acquisitions in the forest products industry. *Forest Products Journal, 49*, 24-36.

Davis, K. P. (1966). *Forest management: Regulation and valuation* (2nd ed.). New York, NY: McGraw-Hill Book Company.

Davis, L. S., Johnson, K. N., Bettinger, P., & Howard, T. E. (2001). Forest management: To sustain ecological, economic, and social value (4th ed.). Long Grove, IL: Waveland Press, Inc.

Fiacco, J. B. (2010). *A brief TIMO backgrounder*. Summerville, SC: Timberland Strategies, LLC.

Fu, C. (2012). *Timberland investments: A primer*. Brookline, MA: Timberland Investment Resources.

Gunnoe, A., & Gellert, P. K. (2011). Financialization, shareholder value, and the transformation of timberland ownership in the US. *Critical Sociology, 7*, 265-284.

Harris, T. (2007). Industry, TIMOs, REITs, the changing face of forestry: The new private forest landowners. *Forest Landowner, 66*, 3-5.

Harris, T., Baldwin, S., & Siry, J. (2011). *United States timberland markets: Transactions, values and market research*. Athens, GA: Timber Mart-South.

Hickman, C. (2007). *TIMOs and REITs*. Washington, DC: USDA Forest Service, Research and Development.

Irland, L. C. (2005). U.S. forest ownership: historical and global perspective. *Maine Policy Review, 14.1*, 16-22.

Irland, L. C., & Howard, T. E. (1989). Innovative forms of timberland ownership: What are the driving forces? *The Consultant, 34*, 32-37.

Lehman Brothers Collection (2013). Great Northern Nekoosa Corporation. Boston, MA: Harvard University, Harvard Baker Library Special Collections.

Leuschner, W. A. (1984). *Introduction to forest resource management*. New York, NY: John Wiley & Sons, Inc.

McCann, P. K. (1994). *Timber! The fall of Maine's paper giant... A chronicle of Great Northern paper Company in the 1980s and 1990s*. Ellsworth, ME: The Ellsworth American.

Meyer, H. A., Recknagel, A. B., Stevenson, D. D., & Bartoo, R. A.

(1961). *Forest management* (2nd ed.). New York, NY: The Ronald Press Company.

O'Laughlin, J., & Ellefson, P. V. (1982). Strategies for corporate timberland ownership and management. *Journal of Forestry, 80,* 784-791.

Recknagel, A. B. (1913). *The theory and practice of working plans (forest organization).* New York, NY: John Wiley & Sons.

Sampson, N., DeCoster, L., & Remuzzi, J. (2000). *Changes in forest industry timberland ownership: 1979-2000.* Alexandria, VA: The Sampson Group, Inc.

Smith, W. B., Miles, P. D., Perry, C. H., & Pugh, S. A. (2009). *Forest resources of the United States, 2007* (General Technical Report WO-78). Washington, DC: United States Department of Agriculture, Forest Service.

Steeves, B. H. (2009). Special Collections: Guide to the Great Northern Paper Company records, history. Orono, ME: University of Maine, Raymond H. Fogler Library.

Stein, P. R. (2011). Trends in forestland: Ownership and conservation. *Forest History Today, Spring/Fall, 2011,* 83-86.

Straka, T. J. (2009). Does your client own timberland? *Financial Advisor, 10,* 95-96.

Timber Harvesting (1980-1994). *Wood and woodland directory.* Montgomery, AL: Hatton-Brown Publishers, Inc.

Yin, R., Caulfield, J. P., Aronow, M. E., & Harris T. G., Jr. (1998). Industrial timberland: Current situation, holding rationale, and future development. *Forest Products Journal, 48,* 43-48.

Zinkhan, F. C., Sizemore, W. R., Mason, G. H., & Ebner, T. J. (1992). *Timberland investments: A portfolio perspective.* Portland, OR: Timber Press.

8

Communities Inferred from the Books of Samuel in the Old Testament of the Bible

Wei Hu

Department of Computer Science, Houghton College, New York, USA

The books of First and Second Samuel are part of historical books in the Old Testament of the Bible, which appear as a single book in Jewish scriptures. These two books record the critical transition of governing system in Israel from judges to kings and from 12 tribes to a centralized state. The three major characters in these books are Samuel priest, prophet and the last judge, Saul the first king of Israel, and David the second king, a man after God's own heart. These books contain many fascinating stories that present the life of Samuel, the rise and fall of Saul, the long journal for David to become king, and the establishment of his kingdom. In this study, we constructed a sequence of social networks from these two books based on the interactions of many characters and their locations. Our aim was to apply a computational approach to identifying the communities in these networks, which summarized the interactions between the key figures and others, along with their locations. As a result, the rich information of this part of Israel history was encoded and visualized concisely through this sequence of networks of communities in time.

Keywords: Samuel; Bible; Community

Introduction

The books of First and Second belong to the historical books of the Bible that record the history of the Israel, covering the time of this nation from conquering Canaan the promise land to the loss of this land through the Babylonian exile because of their disobedience to God (Payne, 1982; Magennis, 2011). These two books trace the social transition period of Israel from loosely organized 12 tribes to a centralized monarchy in the promise land, along with the political leadership change from tribal judges to kings. They provide a natural continuation of the book of Judges reflecting from the content overlapping between the start of the First Samuel and the end of the book of Judges. The time of the judges was a chaotic era in the history Israel since there was a repeated pattern of rebellion, oppression, and deliverance. In those days there was no king in Israel, but every man did that which was right in his own eyes (Judges, 17: 6). When Samuel, their prophet, priest, and the last judge, was quite old, the Israelites demanded a king, similar to the kings of the surrounding nations. However, the whole purpose of God creating the nation of Israel is to make this nation to be unlike all other nations (Exodus, 19: 5-6), as God Himself was the ruler, king, and God of Israel. Moses predicted Israel's desire for a human king in (Deuteronomy, 17: 14-20), but the human kings must serve as representatives of God's kingship over Israel.

The unity of contents of the First and Second Samuel suggests these two books are one book in reality as seen from the original Hebrew text (Gordon, 1999). Further, such division appears in the other books of the Bible such as First and Second Kings and First and Second Chronicles. These books were named after Samuel, because his life formed the foundation of First Samuel and he was a partial author of the book. Samuel was not merely an editor and a character of this book, but the author of the history of this critical period of Israel, who played a pivotal role in rise of kingship of Israel (Tsumura, 2007). These books are not a narrative of historical events solely, but rather to elucidate the significance of the divine guidance of the nation Israel, revealing God is the real maker of human history.

These two books primarily chronicle the life of Samuel (1 Samuel, 1: 12), the reign of Saul (1 Samuel, 13: 31), and the reign of David (2 Samuel), since they were essential in the establishment of the monarchy. In particular, these books give a comprehensive account of the life of David, a man of faith even while a man of weakness, as illustrated from his victories and struggles and his trust and reliance upon God. As the youngest of the eight sons of Jesse, David was born in Bethlehem and served as a shepherd during his childhood. Besides being a great king, David was also well known as a great psalmist as well as a great warrior. The description of David in the Bible, as a man after God's own heart (1 Samuel, 13: 14), is more detailed than any other Bible character except Jesus Christ. Furthermore, the name David is the third most often used name in the whole Bible, with Moses and Abraham being first and second respectively. In the New Testament, Jesus is described as a "descendant of David according to the flesh" (Romans, 1: 3) according to God's Davidic covenant recorded in (2 Samuel, 7).

The birth of Samuel was God's answer to his mother's faithful prayer. From the tribe of Levi, Samuel was the maker of

Israel kings and played a key role as God's messenger and leader, who found and anointed both Saul from the smallest tribe of Hebrews, Benjamin, and David from the tribe of Judah. He guided Israel's transition to kingship and bridged the periods of the judges and the monarchy. In addition to these three main figures, there were three more important characters in First Samuel, who were Eli that raised Samuel and the high priest prior to Samuel, Hannah mother of Samuel, and Jonathan son of Saul. Other key figures in Second Samuel were Joab the general of David's army, Bathsheba wife of Uriah and afterward of David, Nathan the prophet, and Absalom son of David. Nonetheless, the books of Samuel were cogently organized into stories of Samuel, Saul, and David, covering approximately the time period from 1050 to 970 BC (Gordon, 1999).

The books of Samuel capture so many attractive storied occurred in the history of Israel that are among the most famous from the entire ancient world (Tsumura, 2007). To discover the patterns of interactions among so many characters in these stories, we applied a community detection algorithm to a sequence of social networks made from these books. Our aim was to gain new insight into these interesting books, as God's word is a lamp to our feet and a light for our path.

Materials and Methods

Materials

The text of the Bible used in this study is from the King James version (1611 authorized version), downloaded from http://printkjv.ifbweb.com. Because First and Second Samuel are used as data in our study, this section provides some background information about three major characters in these two books, Samuel, Saul, and David.

Family of Samuel

Hannah and Elkanah were Samuel's mother and father who lived at Ramah. Elkanah was a Levite. He had another wife Peninnah who had children but Hannah had no children at the beginning of the book of First Samuel. Samuel had two sons Joel and Abijah.

Family of Saul

Saul was son of Kish from Gibeah, in the tribe of Benjamin. His wife was Ahinoam daughter of Ahimaaz. They had four sons and two daughters. The sons were Jonathan, Abinadab, Malchishua and Ish-bosheth, and the daughters were Merab and Michal. He had additional two sons, Armoni and Mephibosheth, born from his concubine Rizpah daughter of Aiah.

Family of David

David was born in Bethlehem, in the tribe of Judah. His father was Jesse. He had eight wives: Michal, daughter of Saul, Ahinoam the Jezreelite, Abigail the Carmelite, former wife of Nabal, Maachah, daughter of Talmai, king of Geshur, Haggith, Abita, Eglah, and Bathsheba, former wife of Uriah the Hittite. David also had at least one daughter, Tamar by Maachah. He had six sons born in Hebron: Amnon by Ahinoam, Daniel by Abigail, Absalom by Maachah, Adonijah by Haggith, Shephatiah by Abital, and Ithream by Eglah. By Bathsheba, his sons were: Shammua, Shobab, Nathan, and Solomon. He had others

sons born in Jerusalem by other wives.

Methods

Compared to random networks, real social networks exhibit several characteristic features such as small world, power law degree distribution, and community structures (Newman, 2010). A community in a network is a group of vertices that are densely connected inside the group but sparsely outside. In this study, we made use of Walktrap, a community detection algorithm, which relies on random walks on graphs to calculate a distance that could then be used to define the structural similarity between vertices. The advantage of the method is that this distance cab be computed efficiently. Finally, a hierarchical clustering algorithm is used to merge the vertices iteratively into communities. The intuition of this approach is that: random walks on a graph tend to get trapped into densely connected parts corresponding to communities (Pons & Latapy, 2006).

Division of First and Second Samuel into Segments

In order to make a sequence of social networks from the books of Samuel, we divided First Samuel into three logical segments, chapters 1-8 presenting the birth and life of Samuel and serving as an important preface for this book, chapters 9-15 describing the rise and fall of the first king Saul, and chapter 16-31 depicting God's choice of David to be Saul's successor, and David's long journey for accession to the throne. Similarly, Second Samuel was partitioned into four segments, chapters 1-4 showing David's victory over the house of Saul to become king of Judah, chapters 5-10 presenting the success of David's rule as king of all Israel, chapters 11-21 telling David's sins and their punishments, and chapters 22-24 covering David's faith, thanksgiving, and sin.

Social Network of First and Second Samuel

To gain a global perspective of First and Second Samuel, we present the Meta data of the social network made from the two books, including the appearances of Samuel, Saul, and David in each chapter, the social network from these two books, top 30 vertices of highest degrees in the network, and the histogram of degree distribution of all vertices in the network (**Figures 1-3**). The social network of First and Second Samuel displayed three characteristic traits of a real social network: small world with average geodesic distance of vertex pair = 1.847, power law degree distribution (histogram in **Figure 3**), and communities structures (**Figure 2**). The histogram in **Figure 3** suggested that vertices with small degrees are most frequent in this network.

Results

We present the communities found in a sequence of social networks from the segments of the books of Samuel as described in Section 2. With different colors these communities visualized the interactions of different characters and their locations, thereby rendering this part of Israel history with a sequence of networks of communities in time with a sense that a picture is worth a thousand words (**Figures 4-12**). Additionally, to give a quick summery of the chapters in each segment, the word clouds of top 50 most frequently occurred words in these chapters are displayed next to the network of the same chapters (**Figures 4-12**).

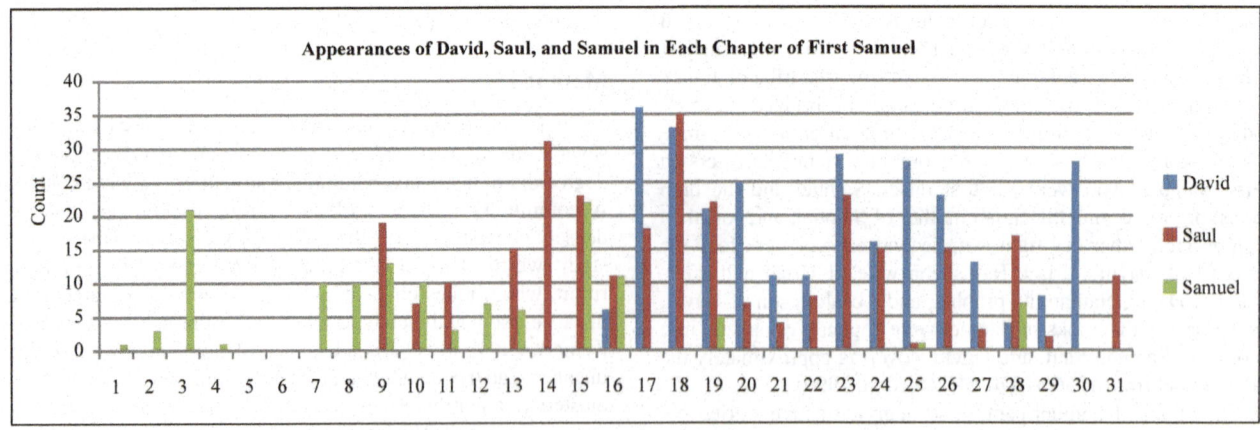

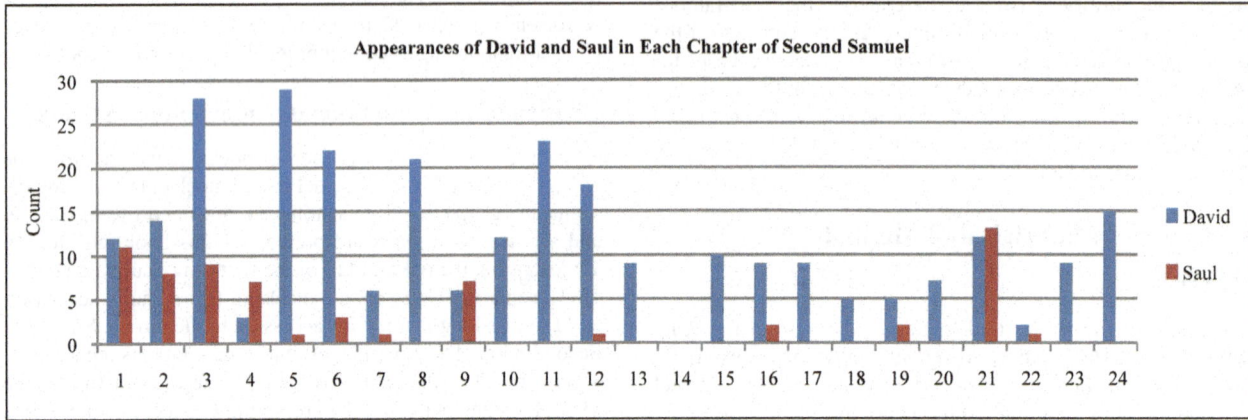

Figure 1.
Appearances of Samuel, Saul, and David in each chapter of First and Second Samuel.

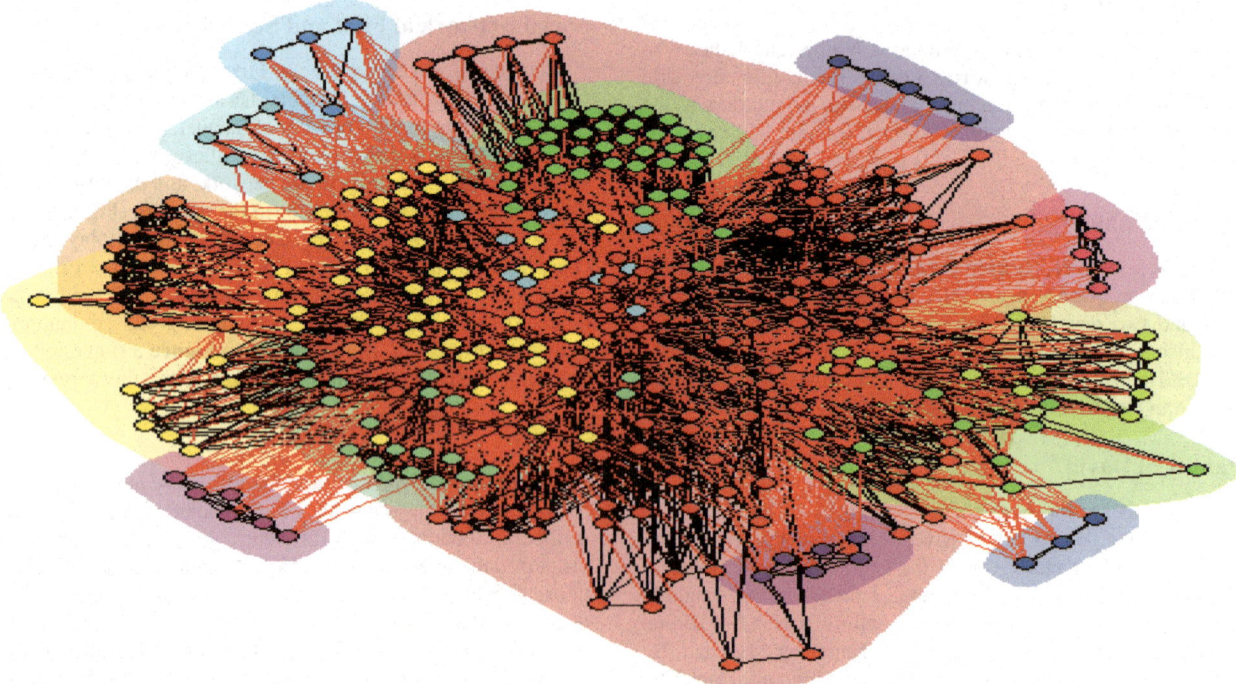

Figure 2.
Social network made from First and Second Samuel with 300 vertices, 8692 edges, and average shortest distance of vertex pairs = 1.847.

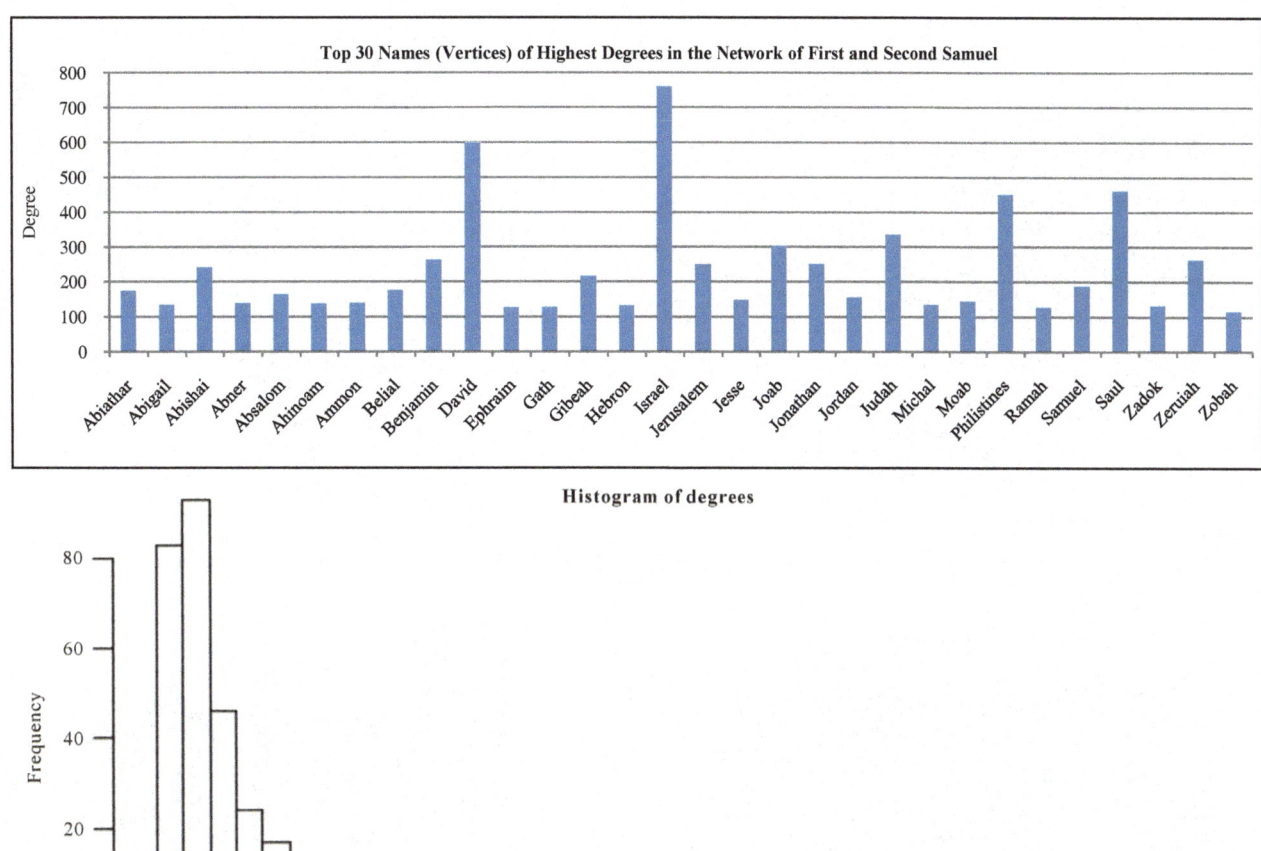

Figure 3.
Top 30 vertices of highest degrees and histogram of degree distribution with bin size = 20 in the network of First and Second Samuel.

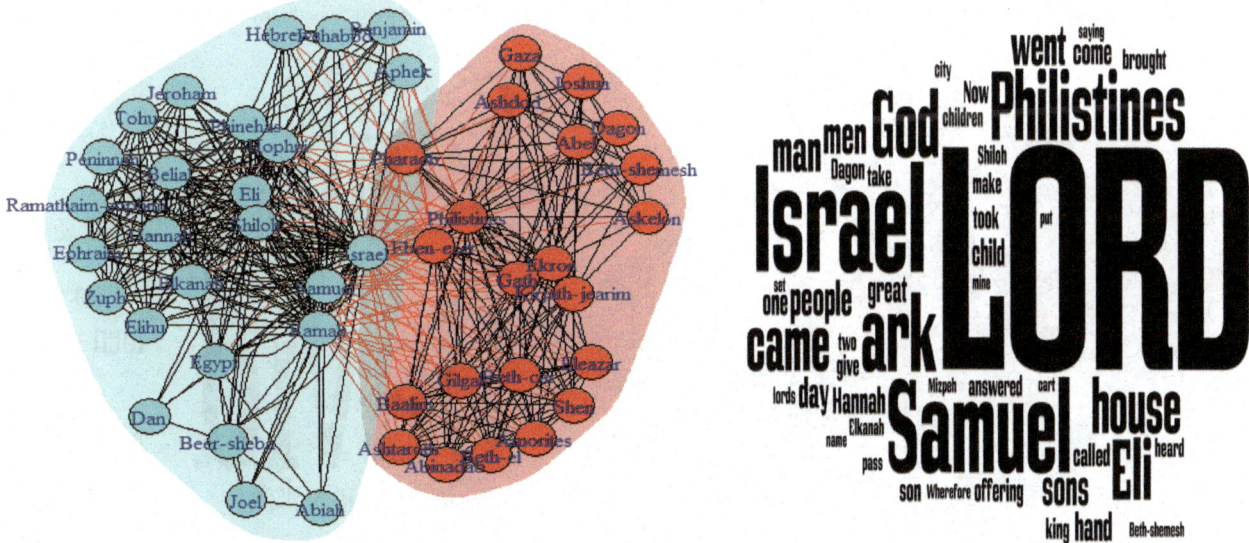

Figure 4.
Communities in the network of chapters 1-8 (left) and word clouds of top 50 most frequently occurred words in these chapters (right).

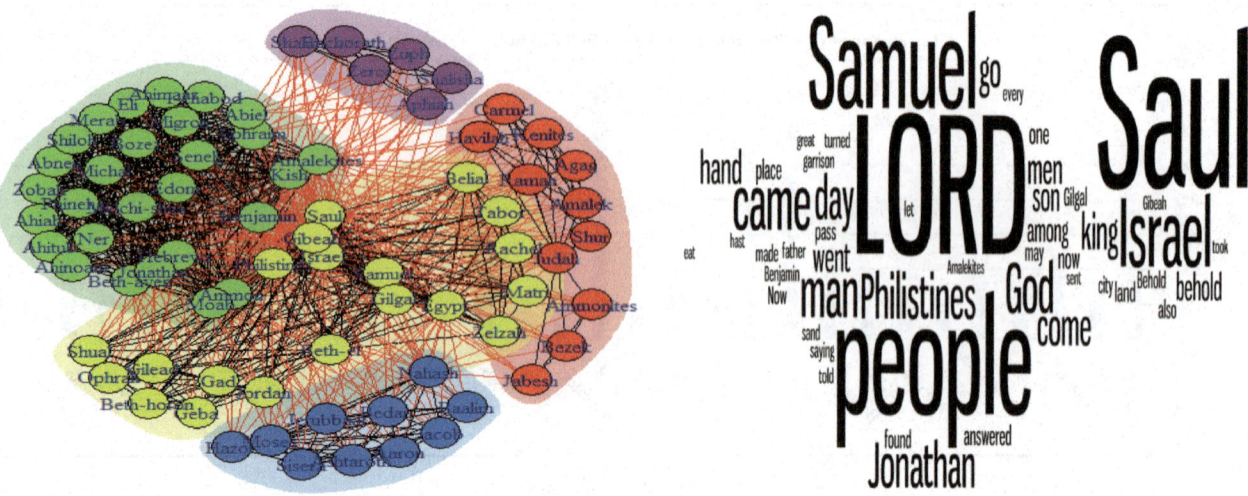

Figure 5.
Communities in the network of chapters 9-15 (left) and word clouds of top 50 most frequently occurred words in these chapters (right).

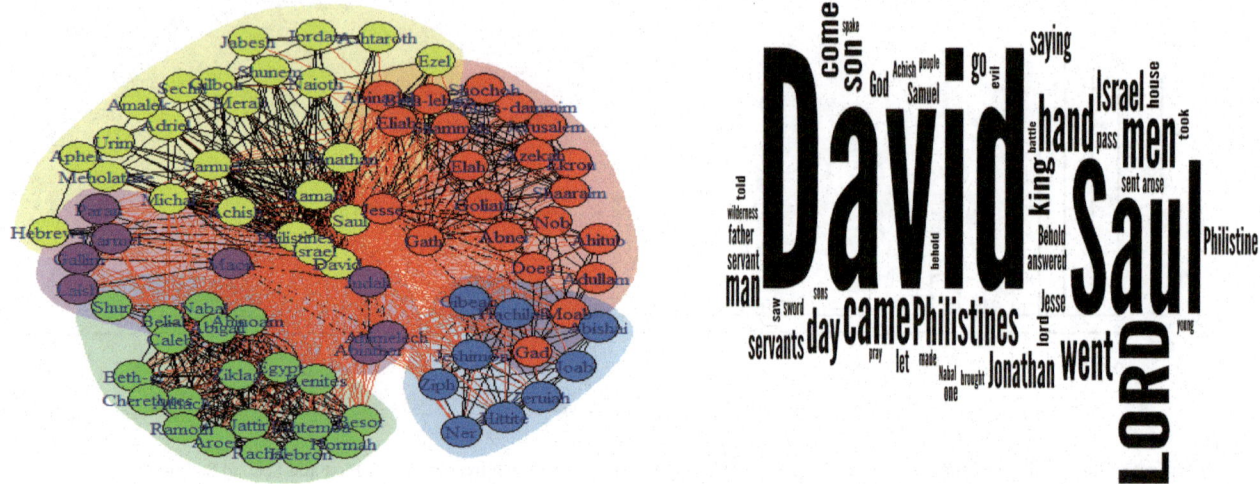

Figure 6.
Communities in the network of chapters 16-31 (left) and word clouds of top 50 most frequently occurred words in these chapters (right).

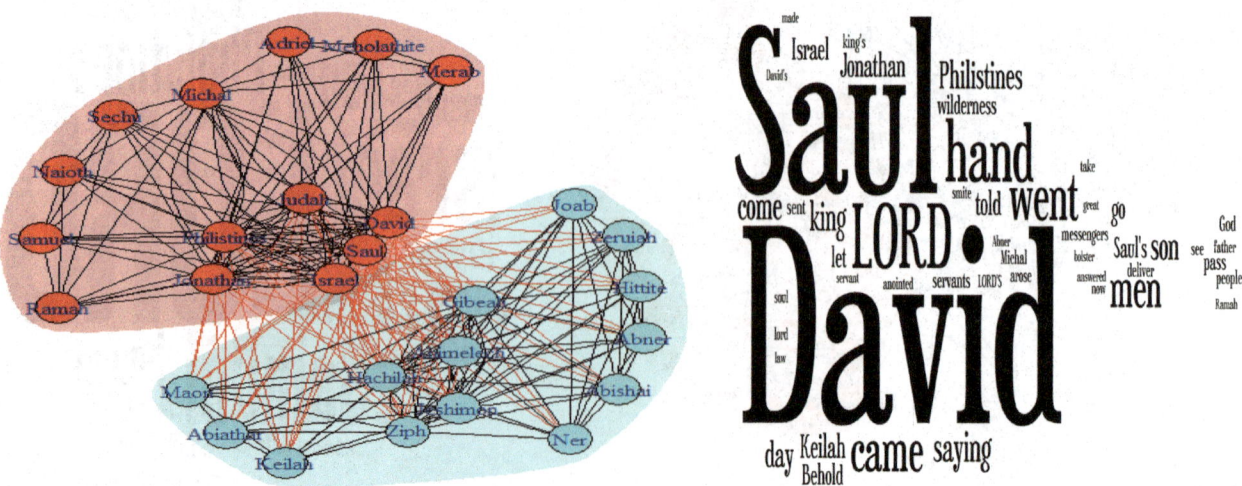

Figure 7.
Communities in the network of five chapters on Saul's Pursuit of David (left) and word clouds of top 50 most frequently occurred words in these chapters (right).

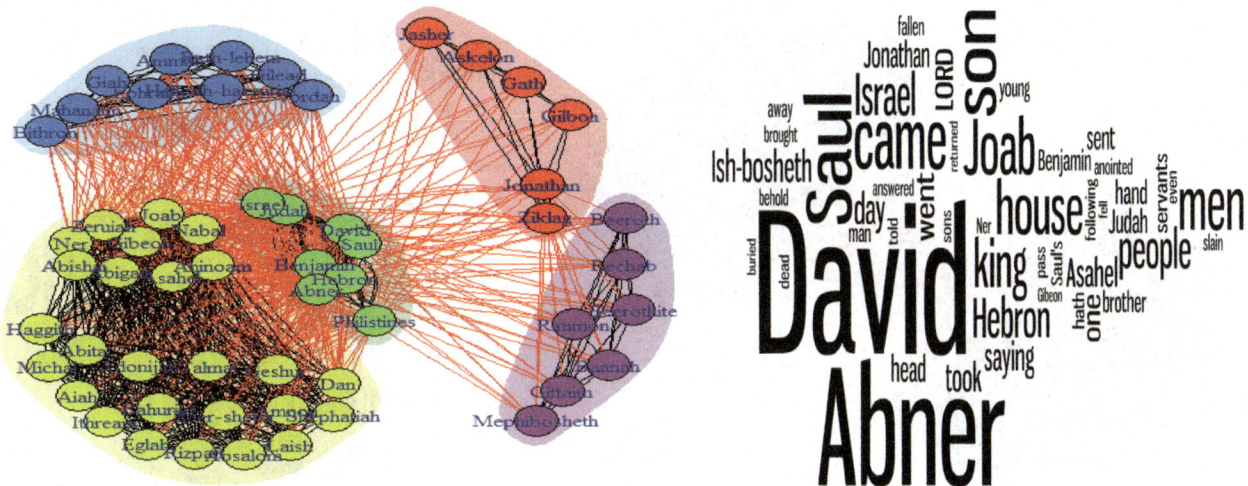

Figure 8.
Communities in the network of chapters 1-4 (left) and word clouds of top 50 most frequently occurred words in these chapters (right).

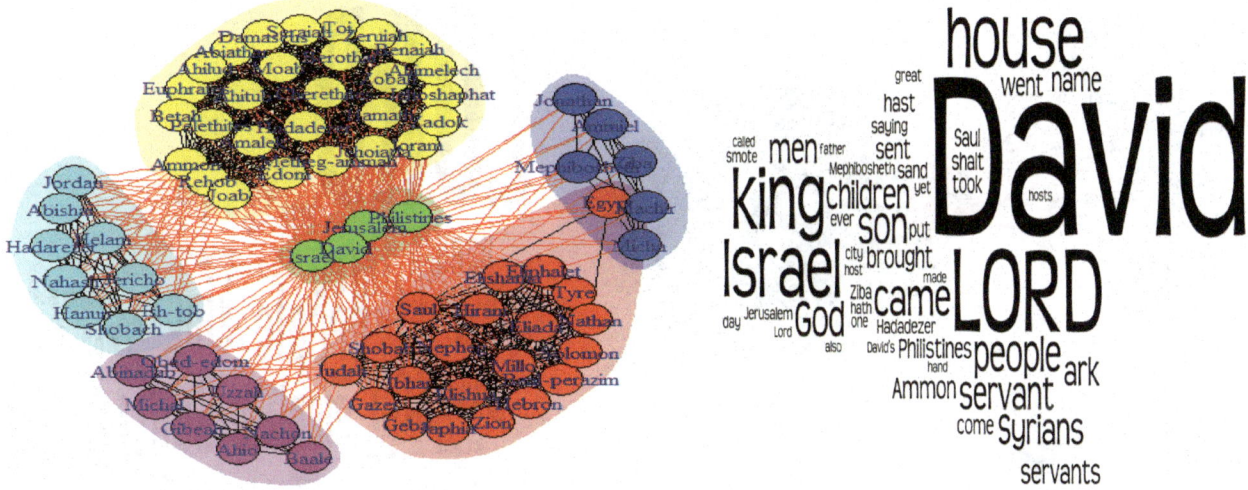

Figure 9.
Communities in the network of chapters 5-10 (left) and word clouds of top 50 most frequently occurred words in these chapters (right).

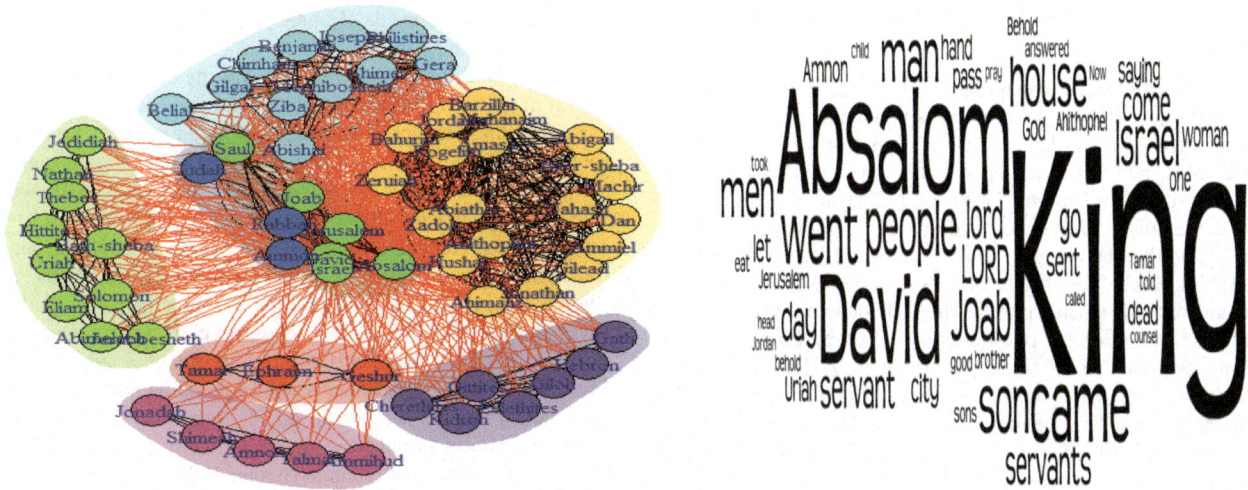

Figure 10.
Communities in the network of chapters 11-19 (left) and word clouds of top 50 most frequently occurred words in these chapters (right).

Figure 11.
Communities in the network of chapters 20-21 (left) and word clouds of top 50 most frequently occurred words in these chapters (right).

Figure 12.
Communities in the network of chapters 22-24 (left) and word clouds of top 50 most frequently occurred words in these chapters (right).

Communities in the Social Networks from First Samuel

Communities in the Social Network from Chapters 1-8

The main actor in these chapters is Samuel along with other key players such as Hannah, Eli and his two sons, Hophni and Phinehas, plus his grandson I-chabod, and Samuel's two sons Joel and Abijah. Born to Hannah and Elkanah, Samuel grew up in the temple at Shiloh, defeated Philistines at Mizpah, anointed Saul and then David, died and was buried at Ramah. The name Samuel meant "God has heard", as the child Samuel was given in answer to Hannah's prayer. These chapters present the life of Samuel, decay of the priesthood as shown by Eli and his two sons, and the Ark of the Covenant taken by Philistines when they won the battle against Israelites. But the Ark caused a disaster in the land of the Philistines and out of fear they returned the Ark back to Israel. Finally Israel asked for a human king.

Hannah was one of the two wives of Elkanah, and the other was Peninnah, who bore children to Elkanah, but Hannah re-

mained childless. One day Hannah and Elkhana went from their hometown Ramah to the temple at Shiloh, where Hannah prayed to God for a child while Eli was there. Eli was the high priest in Shiloh. God gave three sons and two daughters to Hannah including Samuel (1 Samuel, 2: 21). Samuel grew up in the presence of the Lord and established a school to train young prophets in Ramah. He also died and was buried there. He was the last of the judges, after whom Saul became king of Israel.

Eli's sons, Hophni and Phinehas, were wicked and the sons of Belial (meaning worthless) although served as priests, as they had no regard for the Lord. Eli was high priest and judge over Israel, but he did not take actions to correct them. One day a man of God came to Eli to inform him of God's judgment on his household: his descendents would die at an early age, Hophni and Phinehas would die on the same day, and another family of Aaron would be given the office of high priest. Hophni and Phinehas were slain in chapter 4. Phinehas's wife gave birth to a son I-chabod. As a judge, Samuele visited the area between Bethel, Gilgal, Mizpeh, and Ramah regularly. But his sons Joel and Abiah who also served as judges at Beer-sheba, judged unfairly.

Encoded with so much information about the stories happened during this period, this network showed two prominent communities with different colors, with Samuel, Ramah, and Israel being at the center of the whole network (**Figure 4**). The vertices Eli and Philistines were at the center of their own community. Samuel was close to Ramah and Eli close to Shilon. Eli's two sons Hophni and Phinehas were close to their father and also to Belial (meaning worthless), and Samuel's two sons Joel and Abiah were close to Beer-sheba where they served as priests. Vertex Philistines was connected to their three major cities, Ashdod, Askelon, and Gaza, where the temple of Dagon was located. Philistines captured the Ark after defeating the Israelites in a battle at a location between Eben-ezer where the Israelites encamped and Aphek where the Philistines encamped. In **Figure 4**, Israel and Eben-ezer were in one community colored light blue, and Philistines and Aphek were in the other community colored red.

Communities in the Social Network from Chapters 9-15

The main figures in these chapters are Samuel and Saul with a focus on the rise of King Saul. Saul was anointed king by Samuel and presented to Israel, rescued Jabesh-Gilead and was acclaimed king by Israel. These chapters describe Saul's victory over the Ammonites, Samuel's farewell speech to Israel, Saul's first failure to offer burnt offering by himself instead of by Samuel as priest, Jonathan's victory and Saul's second failure to follow the Lord's command to totally destroy Amalekites and their properties, and God's final rejection of Saul due to his disobedience. The events in Chapter 15 marked a turning point in Saul's life, since God instructed Samuel to anoint David as the next king of Israel in chapter 16. Samuel did not see Saul again until he died and he told Saul that "to obey is better than sacrifice" (1 Samuel, 22), a verse still having great value in our life today.

Saul's father Kish was close to him in the network (**Figure 5**). Kish was son of Abiel, the son of Zeror, the son of Becorath, the son of Aphiah. The commander of Saul's army was Abner son of Ner, Saul's uncle. Saul reigned from Gibeah, his hometown. The vertex Gibeah was next to Saul in the network, showing its close relationship to Saul. His family members were in the same community colored light green. In his farewell speech, Samuel reminded Israel of God's protection to them using Moses and Aaron as their heroes. Moses and Aaron were in one small community colored blue. Saul did not obey God's instructions from Samuel by making a burnt offering by himself at Gilgal and not destroying Amalekites and their properties. Samuel, Saul, and Gilgal were in the same group, but Amalekites was close the Saul but in another group.

Eli and Shiloh were at the boundary of the community colored light green and Ramah of Samuel was at the boundary of the community colored red, reflecting their reduced importance at this time.

Communities in the Social Network from Chapters 16-31

These chapters document the decline of Saul and the rise of David through the interplay between Saul and David, one as the current king and one as the successor to Saul and the next king. The stories presented in these chapters picture a clear contrast between Saul as a king after the people's own heart and David

as a king after God's own heart. They record David as an anointed king to replace Saul by God's selection, David's famous victory over Goliath, Saul's growing jealousy and quest to destroy David. Other topics included David fled from Saul, friendship of David and Jonathan, the defense of David by Jonathan and Michal, David fled to the priest at Nob, to the king of Gath, and to the cave at Adullam, Saul's revenge on the priests of Nob for having helped David, David's exile at Kehilah and in the wilderness of Ziph, David spared Saul's life in the Wilderness of Engedi, Nabal and Abigail, David spared Saul for second time, David fled to Achish, king of the Philistines, Saul went to the witch at Endor, Achish sent David back to Ziklag, David destroyed Amalekites, the death of Saul and his three sons including Jonathan.

The song of the Israelite women, "Saul has slain his thousands, and David his ten thousands" (1 Samuel, 18: 7), made Saul very jealous of David, revealing Saul's focus on earthly reputation. Instead, David placed a higher value on unseen over the seen. The flight of David against Goliath revealed their difference in character, since Saul was tall and David was just a boy at that time. David refused the physical protection of the king Saul's armor in favor of prayer and demonstrated his courage, wisdom, and faith, proving that he was the ideal man for the throne of Israel. Many of the older sons of Jesse were very impressive in their physical appearance, but God instructed Samuel to anoint the youngest son David, a shepherd boy, to be the next king after Saul.

It was a long journal for David from his anointing as a future king of Israel to eventually becoming king. During this whole period, David refused to take up the throne by forceful means but left it in the hands of God and waited for His timing. Saul pursued David into the desert where David spared his life twice, one in a cave and the other in Saul's tent while he was asleep. Still, Saul continued his pursuit. During this period, Jonathan developed a brother-like friendship with David. These chapters also record the weakness of David as he showed panics under the pressure of being pursued and lied to Ahimelech, the priest at Nob (1 Samuel, 21: 1-9), and to Achish the king of Gath (1 Samuel, 21: 10-15). These stories of Saul and David reinforced the supremacy of divine justice as articulated in Hannah's song: The proud will be humbled and the humble exalted.

Saul and his three sons, Jonathan, Abinadab, and Malchishua died on Mount Gilboa. Now Judah of David was at the center of the network, while Gibeah of Saul moved a little bit farther away from the center (**Figure 6**). Goliath, the champion of the Philistines, was in the red community and not very close to the vertex Philistines since this vertex is also strongly connected to other vertices. The couple, Nabal and Abigail, was in the same community colored light green and Zeruiah, David's sister, with her two sons, Joab and Abishai, were in the same community colored light blue. Samuel was in the center of the networks in **Figures 4** and **5**, but in this **Figure 6**, he was in a community colored yellow, not at the center anymore. David definitely entered the picture as a major character, along with another key player Jonathan, which was located in the center of this network. David and Jonathan were close to each other in the same group because of their friendship, and both of them were in the center. David was close to his father Jesse although they belonged to two different groups, and Jesse was connected to his other three sons, Abinadab, Eliab, and Shammah, and his hometown Bethlehem.

Saul's Pursuit of David

This story was the most interesting one in First Samuel, which displayed the opposite traits of Saul and David. Saul was trying to kill David, but David spared Saul's life not only once but twice. Each time after learning David had spared his life, Saul cried and promised David not to kill him anymore, but Saul continued his pursuit afterwards. We singled out the chapters that described the direct contact between Saul and David during this period and summarized each chapter below.

Chapter 18: All Israel and Judah loved David, so Saul became jealous of David. One day Saul hurled a spear towards David while he was playing the harp for Saul. But David eluded him twice. Saul promised to give his daughter Merab to David as his wife but Saul instead gave her to Adriel of Meholathite as wife. Saul's son Jonathan was very fond of David and protected David. David and his men went out and killed two hundred Philistines. Then Saul gave David his second daughter Michal as his wife.

Chapter 19: Saul tried to pin David to the wall with his spear as David was playing the harp, but David eluded him again. Saul then sent men to watch and kill David, and Michal helped David to flee. David went to Samuel at Ramah and then Saul went from a great well in Sechu to Naioth at Ramah to find David.

Chapter 23: The Ziphites went up to Saul at Gibeah and said, "Is not David hiding among us in the strongholds at Horesh, on the hill of Hachilah, south of Jeshimon?" So Saul pursued David from Keilah to the desert of Ziph and then to the wilderness of Maon. When a messenger came to Saul, saying the Philistines are raiding the land. Then Saul broke off his pursuit of David and went to fight the Philistines. Abiathar the priest was with David during this time.

Chapter 24: David spared Saul's life in a cave at En Gedi.

Chapter 26: Abishai and Ahimelech went with David to the camp of Saul at night. Abner son of Ner was with Saul as his commander of the army. Saul made his camp beside the road on the hill of Hakilah facing Jeshimon. David asked Ahimelech the Hittite and Abishai son of Zeruiah, Joab's brother, to go to Saul's camp by night. When David and others went into Saul's camp, he was asleep. So David spared Saul's life again.

Because of the direct interactions between the people of Saul and those of David, there was no clear separation between the followers of Saul from the followers of David as illustrated by the two communities identified in this network (**Figure 7**). However, these two communities did show Saul and David as being the center of both of them.

Communities in the Social Networks from Second Samuel

Chapters 1-10 of Second Samuel detail the rise of David's kingdom. Because of the resolution limit of the community graphs, we divided these chapters into two parts, chapters 1-4 and 5-10.

Communities in the Social Network from Chapters 1-4

The last part of First Samuel marks the end of Saul's life and Second Samuel opens with more details to the death of Saul. We have to remember that Saul had hunted David for many years prior to Saul's death. Chapters 1-4 record David's lament over Saul and Jonathan who died on the battlefield of Mount Gilboa, David was anointed in Hebron as king over Judah his

own tribe, Saul still had one surviving son Ish-bosheth who was crowned king over Israel, the war between the houses of David and Saul, David had six sons born in Hebron: Amnon, Kileab, Absalom, Adonijah, Shephatiah, Ithream, David asked Abner and Ish-bosheth to return his wife Michal, Joab had two brothers, Abishai and Asahel, Asahel was killed by Abner who was cousin to Saul and the commander-in-chief of Saul's army and went over to David, Joab murdered Abner for revenge, and finally Ish-bosheth was killed and the northern tribes asked David to rule the entire nation of Israel.

David, Israel, and Saul remained at the center of the network, and Saul was next to Benjamin, his tribe. Zeruiah, sister of King David, had three sons, Joab, Abishai and Asahel. David had six sons born in Hebron. All these family members of David were in the same group colored yellow. Jonathan was next to Gilboa where he and his father died. Abner was a prominent figure in these chapters as his name appeared 46 times and many David's activities occurred in Hebron while he was king over Judah, which explained the centrality of these vertices in the network (**Figure 8**).

Communities in the Social Network from Chapters 5-10

Chapters 5-10 include David united the kingdom and became king over Israel, David brought the Ark to Jerusalem, God's promise to David, David's victories over the enemies including Moab, Philistia, Zobah, and Syria, David's kindness to Mephibosheth son of Jonathan since David made a covenant with Jonathan, and David defeated the Ammonites and Syrians. David took Israel into several battles to win some of the promised land that had never been fully claimed.

The Davidic covenant recorded in chapter 7 is the theological centerpiece of this book. God made the house of David to prosper and in light of this the desire to build a permanent dwelling place for God arose in David. So he wanted to build a temple for worshiping God. Through the prophet Nathan, God informed David that He would not allow David to do so but his son Solomon would. Further God promised David that He would establish a house for David and the house and kingdom of David would endure forever before God and his throne would be established forever. God promised David that the Messiah, Jesus Christ, would come from the lineage of David and the tribe of Judah and would establish an everlasting kingdom. This promise to David was in fact the further unfolding of a previous promise God gave to Abraham in (Genesis, 15: 18). It also fulfills Jacob's promise that the scepter will never depart from Judah, David's tribe (Genesis, 49: 10).

One noticed that Saul moved from the center to a community colored red and Jerusalem became the center of this network, signaling the beginning of David's kingdom. In Hebron David reigned over Judah for seven years and six months and in Jerusalem he reigned thirty and three years over all Israel, as a result Jerusalem was at the center of this network. Judah and Hebron were in the same group colored red. Mephibosheth was next to his father Jonathan, and David showed graciousness to him due to the covenant between David and Jonathan (**Figure 9**).

Communities in the Social Network from Chapters 11-19

Chapters 11-21 cover David's sins and their consequences. For the sake of clear visual presentation, we divided these chapters into two groups, chapters 11-19 and 20-12. Chapter

11-19 describe David's adultery and murder, God's punishment on David, birth of Solomon, defeat of Ammon, rape of Tamar by Amnon, death of Amnon, and rebellion as well as death of Absalom.

David committed adultery with a married woman, Bathsheba, and got her pregnant. He then attempted a cover-up. When that failed, he conspired having her husband Uirah killed. Although David repented when the prophet Nathan confronted him regarding his sins and God forgave him, He promised David the judgment: "Now the sword shall never depart from your house" (2 Samuel, 12: 10).

The consequences of David's sins affected not only himself but also his family and his nation. Up to this point, three of David's son had died, Amnon, Absalom, and the first child born to David and Bathsheba. After the death of his elder brothers Amnon and Absalom, Adonijah, the fourth son of David, considered himself to be the rightful heir to the throne and proclaimed to be king when his father was dying. He was put to death after Solomon became king of Israel as successor of David (1 Kings, 2: 13-25). Amnon Absalom, and Adonijah died not only as punishments to David, but also because of their own sins. Absalom was prominently featured in these chapters. Completely different from Solomon, Absalom committed many heinous crimes such as sleeping with his father's concubines, plotting a conspiracy to kill his father.

Absalom was a new key player in this time, since he killed Amnon who rapped Tamar, rebelled against his father, and was killed by David's general Joab in the forest of Ephraim. After Absalom had killed Amnon, he fled to Talmai, the son of Ammihud, king of Geshur, since Absalom's mother was princess of Geshur. Ahithophel was a wise counselor of David, but during Absalom's rebellion against David, he betrayed David and became an adviser to Absalom. These names were next to each other in the network. The chief figures in David's adultery, Bathsheba daughter of Eliam, Uriah of Hittite, and Nathan, were in one community along with Solomon who had another name Jedidiah given by God through Nathan.

Communities in the Social Network from Chapters 20-21

Chapters 20-21 present the rebellion of Sheba son of Bicri, a Benjamite, three years of famine because Saul and his house put the Gibeonites to death, the revenge of Gibeonites, and the defeat of Philistines. In Canaan the Philistines were strong, having battles against Israel throughout the period of the judges. However, the leadership of Samuel, Saul and then David eventually made the Philistine threat declined.

Israel, Abishai, Daivd, and Judah were mentioned in both chapters, which explained why they were at the center of this network. Saul is at the boundary of the community colored blue (**Figure 11**).

Communities in the Social Network from Chapters 22-24

Chapters 22-24 conclude this book with final reflections on the life of David, showing the closing phase of David's reign, his faith through his psalm of praise to God, his thanksgiving in his last words, the names of his mighty men including Uriah of Hittite, and his sin of numbering people and the resultant plague as God's punishment, his construction of an altar.

Araunah, appeared in the blue community (**Figure 12**), was a Jebusite whose threshing-floor in Jerusalem was pointed out to David by the prophet Gad as an ideal site for building an altar of burnt offering to God. The destroying angel, sent to punish David for his sin in taking a census of his people, was withheld from his destruction near that threshing-floor. Araunah offered it to David as a free gift, but David insisted on purchasing it at its full price (2 Samuel, 24: 24), for he could not offer to God what cost him nothing. On the same location Solomon afterwards built the temple. Joab, a central figure in this network, was killed by Solomon according to David's command (I Kings, 2: 5-6). The end of this book seemed sad for Saul as he became a single outlier in this network, but David remained in the center of the network (**Figure 12**).

Discussion and Conclusion

Israel started as a nation of loosely organized tribes led by priests and heroes. The books of Samuel document Israel's transition from a group of 12 tribes ruled by judges, represented by the last two judges Eli and Samuel, to a united state ruled by kings, represented by the first two kings Saul and David. Through three central figures, Samuel, Saul, and David, two obeyed and one disobeyed, they demonstrate that God reigns by adapting to human situations to accomplish His plans and purposes, regardless of their response to Him. The history of Israel proves that trusting in God would lead to victory over their enemies whereas relying on their own strength would result in failure and defeat. It is interesting to notice that Saul, David, and Solomon all served as king of Israel for 40 years.

The service of Samuel brought to an end of judges and gave hope in a humanly desirable king. Saul, a man according to human flesh, was more concerned with earthly objectives than with spiritual matters of God. On the other hand, the kingship of David, a man according to the heart of God, demonstrated the characteristics of an ideal ruler relying on God in every situation, and brought hope in the coming Messiah. The books of Samuel document many positive achievements of David as well as his transgressions and punishments, which show that God remained loyal to His promise although David at times failed the covenant. God gave David and Bathsheba the child Solomon, whom later became king of Israel. He was merciful by safeguarding David during the rebellions of Absalom and Sheba. On the other hand, David confessed his sins before God, unlike Saul who always tried to excuse his sins, which made all the difference in their life, revealing that God hates and punishes sins but loves sinners. Hannah described God in (1 Samuel, 2: 3-10) as: He brings low the boastful, arrogant, mighty, full, rich, and wicked, and in contrast He exalts the feeble, hungry, barren, poor, low, needy and godly.

Through the communities found in a sequence of social networks from the books of Samuel, we could learn the roles played by key figures such as Eli, Samuel, Saul, David and their interactions with others during each important period. The community structures discovered from this sequence of networks visualized the interesting stories occurred during this critical transition of Israel from rule by judges to rule by kings.

Acknowledgements

We thank Houghton College for its financial support.

REFERENCES

Gordon, R. P. (1999). *1 & 2 Samuel: A commentary*. Grand Rapids:

Zondervan.

Magennis, F. T. (2011). *First and second Samuel (New Collegeville bible commentary: Old Testament)*. Collegeville: Liturgical Press.

Newman, M. (2010). *Networks: An introduction*. New York: Oxford University Press.

Payne, D. F. (1982). *I and II Samuel (OT daily study Bible series)*. Westminster: John Knox Press.

Pons, P., & Latapy, M. (2006). Computing communities in large networks using random walks. *Journal of Graph Algorithms and Applications, 10,* 191-218.

Tsumura, D. T. (2007). *The first book of Samuel (New international commentary on the Old Testament)*. Grand Rapids: Wm. B. Eerdmans Publishing Company.

9

Review Ph.D. Thesis: Psyco-Education Factors of Applying Visualisation in Science Education. Šiauliai University, Lithuania[*]

Raffaele Pisano[1,2]

[1]Sciences, Sociétés, Cultures dans leurs Evolutions, University of Lille 1, Lille, France
[2]Research Center for Theory and History of Science, University of West Bohemia, Plzen, Czech Republic

This paper presents a review of a Ph.D. Thesis by Renata Bilbokaitė, Natural Science Education Research Centre, Šiauliai University, Lithuania.

Keywords: History of Science and Science Education; Science and Society; Economy; I.T.

On the Author

Renata Bilbokaitė, already busy with research as junior worker at the *Natural Science Education Research Centre* at Šiauliai University, defends her Ph.D. Thesis at the same University in November 2012: *Psycho-Educational Factors of Applying Visualisation in Science Education. Language*: Lithuanian/English. Research supervisor: Prof. Dr. Vincentas Lamanauskas (Šiauliai University, Lithuania). The location of the defense is the *Academic Council of Education Studies* of Šiauliai University. The committee is composed of a distinguished and international members and opponents. Her doctoral studies involved 2009-2012 period. She prepared and published over 100 scientific articles in scientific journals, and presented over 80 works in international as well as national scientific and practical conferences, giving lectures for teachers, in the sphere of science education particularly focusing on applying visualisation in science education, management & quality in the higher education, image of pedagogues.

On the General Description and Topicality

The thesis is organized by an Introduction and three main chapters. 1) *Visualisation in science education: psycho-educational context concerning a state of art on the main objects and interactions of cognitive and socio-educational aspects*; 2) *Empiric psycho-educational factors of applying visualisation in science education on Epistemic-Exploratory-Diagnostic-Verification methodologies and related results*; 3) *Psycho-educational model of applying visualisation within science education*, the nucleus of the thesis on this new modelling approach in science education studies. Passionate and interesting *Discussion* and *Conclusions* included Recommendations for different kind of readers and an international and updated list of *References* close the volume of this notable doctoral research under an excellent and proficient supervision. A CD-Rom is annexed, too. The results of the dissertation research are illustrated by 72 figures and 31 tables.

The author has performed good orientation and wide educational and scientific knowledge of different parts of theory of science education considered in the thesis: epistemic analyses, analytical approach, and experimental approach included analysis of data.

The topic of thesis is contemporary and relevant in the context of up-to-date research in the sphere of science education, science and society. Particularly, a useful relevance of the Ph.D. thesis is

[...] is supposed by the complex assimilation of knowledge in Biology, Chemistry, Physics, Geography and Mathematics in comprehensive schools, which is affected by many factors, linked with conditions of the information representation within educational reality (p. 9).

The *Introduction* focus on the role played by the contemporary society, its transformations and technological progress related to science education and ITC.

The chapter one is mainly focused on *Application of aids in lessons of past*, present and future and aspects of learning-genders (9 paragraphs).

The chapter two ascribes on *Attention and memory within structures of mental models' formation and related motivations within the educational contexts* (7 paragraphs).

The chapter three is dedicated to study the methodology and results applied to epistemic and exploratory procedures of visualization in science education. It is composed of *Discussion, Conclusions* and *Recommendations*.

On the Aims, Methods and Benefits

The aims and methods are performed in the *Introduction* as well as the hypothesis and methods of the research. Thanks to the using of different fonts and structure of the text is proper and helps the reader to better orientation in the text.

One of the greatest problems within the reality of the science education is the inappropriate understanding of conceptions, phenomenon, topics and other elements of the content. Learners

---

[*]Short review.
In the running text of this paper some quotations are cited. The pages refers her Ph.D. thesis.

understand conceptions individually, constructing the own epistemic (p. 10).

Based on the well-declared *Researches Hypotheses* the main objective is psycho-educational factors of applying visualisation in science education. Particularly it "[…] is to analyse psycho-educational factors of applying visualisation during lessons of Biology, Chemistry, Physics, Geography and Mathematics in 9 - 10 forms, reasons for their heterogeneity, and the model of named factors." (p. 13). The author deeply precise the role played by theoretical and empirical sub-objectives concerning "[…] characteristics of visualisation within ontology of the image […]" (p. 14), and "[…] verify results of researches with empirical substantiation of attitude of Subjects of science education—teachers and students—towards reasons, affecting the higher need for externalised visual representations and their effect on heterogeneous groups of learners under aspects of gender and form." (*Ivi*). On that account an original *schema of research* methodology (p. 17) is originally proposed by the author.

The Ph.D. thesis ascribes two main methods: *theoretical and empirical-practical*. A data collection for exploring opinion of populations, e.g., "[...] Philosophical and social ontological aspect of the discourse of visualisation is revealed by analysing the meaning of externalised visual representations on aspects of postmodernism, globalisation, synergetics and innovations by supplementing with ontological importance for knowledge and information societies" is proposed (p. 18). The empirical-practical method mainly concerns "[...] benefits of applying visualisation in science education on psycho-educational aspect were gained during the empirically based theoretical discourse analysis" (p. 19).

From a methodological and pedagogical-scientific point of view I am also mostly appreciative of the clarity and precision of the exposition constantly paid attention both contents and understanding both for specialists and scientific and management readers, both Lithuanian and Western European scholars.

On the Results and Author's Recommendations

The results and modelling presented by the author are crucial and the overall technical intensity of the thesis is significant and typically for a very much qualified Ph.D. thesis: *Identifications of factors*, *Exploratory research*, *Diagnostic research*, *Verification of results* (Chapter 2, Section 2.2). "The Ph.D. thesis research results and the constructed model application of concrete aids of visualisation should be verified during lessons by forming questions if the similar positive factors exist in different classes, groups of students with different skills as well as on heterogonous aspects of gender, learning needs, educational environments and activities." (p. 32). Thus the results are very

original and certainly considerable such as important classes of science education, history and science education items within an international panorama. In fact some modelling and outlines are already published in highly reputable conferences and journals in science education and management & quality.

Particularly, the Ph.D. thesis ascribes two main results: conclusion within theoretical context and conclusions within *empirical-practical context*.

When it come the former, according to the author visualisation is indivisible from the image ontogenesis "[...] within the context of the psychological discourse, application of visualisation could affect the management (stimulations) of cognitive processes of the Subject-together with the artefact of external multimodal and multidimensional externalised representations" (pp. 33-34).

When it come the *empirical-practical context*: "[...] students in 9 - 10 forms experience learning difficulties in subjects of science education due to limitedness of activity of cognitive processes (perception, attention, memory and imagination)" [... and ...] attitude of teachers experts, it is identified that in disciplines of science education, classical visualisation methods and ways, presenting educational information, dominate, the usage of which during the last five years had a tendency to decrease and as it is planned—it is about to decrease in future" (p. 35).

The author close her results with a list of recommendations for different kind of readers: *authors of manuals*, *software*, *managers of publishing houses*, scientists and teachers (pp. 38-39 and correlated pages).

Conclusion

The structure of thesis conforms to principles and requests to the structure of a scientific Ph.D. thesis. The author studied and used appropriate number of international references sources used and cited in the thesis. It is the largely evidence of the deep theoretical knowledge and extremely good orientation in the problem discussed in science education. The word processing of the thesis appears also adequate. The using of different fonts and structure of the text is proper and helps the reader to better orientation in the text. Thus the Ph.D. thesis is well written and swell organized, with a suitable *Introduction* to interesting contents-chapters and through international references to cited works.

In my opinion, the author produced an urgent-emergency and a significant research and contribution of support for both science education readings, scientist-pedagogists and historians of science and natural science specialists.

The thesis by Renata Bilbokaitė performed all the conditions for gaining the PhD. degree in Science Education. The volume composition makes for absorbing reading.

10

Lagrange as a Historian of Mechanics

Agamenon R. E. Oliveira

Polytechnic School of Rio de Janeiro, Federal University of Rio de Janeiro, Rio de Janeiro, Brazil

In the first and second parts of his masterpiece, Analytical Mechanics, dedicated to static and dynamics respectively, Lagrange (1736-1813) describes in detail the development of both branches of mechanics from a historical point of view. In this paper this important contribution of Lagrange (Lagrange, 1989) to the history of mechanics is presented and discussed in tribute to the bicentennial year of his death.

Keywords: History of Mechanics; Epistemology of Physics; Analytical Mechanics

Introduction

Lagrange was one of the founders of variational calculus, in which the Euler-Lagrange equations were derived by him. He also developed the method of Lagrange multipliers which is a manner of finding local maxima and minima of a function subjected to constraints. He developed the method for solving differential equations known as the parameter variation method. In addition, he applied differential calculus to the theory of probabilities and did notable work in obtaining the solution of algebraic equations. Furthermore, in calculus Lagrange introduced a new approach for the interpolation of the Taylor (1685-1731) series. His famous treatise known as the Theory of Analytical Functions contains the path that leads to the foundation of group theory, anticipating the work of Evariste Galois (1811-1832).

In mechanics Lagrange studied specific problems, such as the three-body problem related to motion of the earth, sun and moon. By means of his Analytical Mechanics, he transformed Newtonian mechanics (Newton, 1952) into a branch of analysis, Lagrangian mechanics, which was a result of the application of the variational calculus to mechanical principles. Through this work, rational mechanics was able to fulfill the long desired Cartesian aim of becoming a branch of pure mathematics.

In relation to problems later called applied mechanics, Lagrange, in the works known as the Mélanges de Turin, studied the propagation of sound, making an important contribution to the theory of vibrating strings. He used a discrete mass model to represent string motion consisting of n masses joined by weightless strings. Then he solved the system of n + 1 differential equations, when n tends to infinity to obtain the same functional solution proposed by Euler (1707-1783). Lagrange also studied the integration of differential equations and made various applications to topics such as fluid mechanics, where he introduced the Lagrangian function

Lagrange's Analytical Mechanics was published in 1788, crowning a series of works and other important contributions previously developed by d'Alembert (1717-1783) and Euler (Euler, 1952). This book presents a model of formalized theory

in the same meaning that is now understood by modern physicists. The logical unity of this theory is based on the least action principle. However, the two dimensions of formalization and unification are the main characteristics of Lagrange's method.

Lagrange: A Biographical Note

Joseph-Louis Lagrange was born in Turin on January 25, 1736, under the name of Giuseppe Lodovico Lagrangia (**Figure 1**). His father was Giuseppe Francesco Lodovico Lagrangia and was Treasurer of the Office of Public Works and Fortifications in Turin. His mother was Teresa Grosso, the only daughter of a medical doctor from Cambiano near Turin. Lagrange was the eldest of their 11 children, but one of only two to live to adulthood.

Turin became the capital of the kingdom of Sardinia in 1720, sixteen years before Lagrange's birth. His family had French connections on his father's side. His grandfather was a French

Figure 1.
Joseph-Louis Lagrange (1736-1813).

cavalry captain who had left France to work for the Duke of Savoy. For this reason, Lagrange always leant towards his French ancestry. When he was young he signed his name Lodovico LaGrange or Luigi Lagrange, using the French form of his family name.

Lagrange's interest in mathematics began when he read a copy of Halley's 1693 work on the use of algebra in optics. He was also attracted to physics by the excellent teaching of Francesco Ludovico Beccaria (1716-1781) at the College of Turin, leading him to decide to follow a career in mathematics.

Returning to Mécanique Analytique, it was written by Lagrange during his period in Berlin and was approved for publication by a committee from the Academy of Sciences consisting of Laplace (1749-1827), Cousin, Legendre (1752-1833) and Condorcet (1743-1794). This book summarized all the work done in the field of mechanics since the time of Newton (1642-1727), being notable for its use of the theory of differential equations. In 1810, he commenced a thorough revision of his masterpiece, but he was able to complete only about two-thirds of this before his death in Paris, on April 10, 1813. He was buried in the same year in Panthéon in Paris. The French inscription on his tomb reads:

> Joseph-Louis Lagrange. Senator. Count of the Empire. Grand Officer of the Legion of Honour. Grand Cross of the Imperial Order of the Reunion. Member of the Institute and the Bureau of Longitude. Born in Turin on 25 January. Died in Paris on 10 April 1813.

Science and the French Revolution

The French revolution has a great importance as a fundamental transformation of European society from the social, political and scientific viewpoints. Besides the intellectual and cultural changes before the takeover of power by the bourgeoisie in France with direct consequences to the scientific production over a long period of his history, we should also mention other factors and aspects of this context.

The first important thing to note is the need of the new regime for new institutions in order to criticize and fight against the ideas of the *ancien regime*. These new institutions also appeared within the educational system as the best way to change mentalities and to prepare new technical and political elite to give continuity to the project of a new society announced by the Revolution.

The transformations in the educational system of France implied significant modifications in technical and professional education, because new creeds, new knowledges and new technologies had progressed, making it necessary to teach them. The development of engineering and its teaching is important in this context. A reformation of engineering instruction was necessary also because war with other European countries had stimulated the construction of fortifications, roads and bridges, and the development of artillery. This new context propelled France to apply scientific principles to industry, with the result that the new engineering had to provide universal scientific knowledge as well as tools and methods applicable in a diverse range of practical situations (Belhoste, 2003). As we know, Lagrange played an important role in the context of these transformations. He was the first professor of analysis, appointed for the opening of the *École Polytechnique* in 1794. In 1795 the *École Normale* was founded with the aim of training school teachers. Lagrange taught courses on elementary mathematics there.

Historical Considerations in *Analytical Mechanics*

First Part: Statics

Lagrange began his history of statics by defining this discipline associated with the concept of force. He states:

> Statics is the science of forces in equilibrium. We think, in general, of force or power as a cause, anything that impresses or tend to impress motion on the body under consideration; it is also by the quantity of impressed motion, or by its tendency, that a force or power must be estimated.

According to him, the objective of statics is to provide the laws that govern equilibrium. In this sense equilibrium appears as the destruction of several forces that oppose and annihilate them. These laws are based on three general principles, namely: a) the equilibrium of the lever; b) the composition of motions; c) virtual velocities. It is, thus, in the context of the historical development of these three principles that Lagrange rebuilds the history of statics.

Lagrange considers Archimedes (287 - 212 b. C.) as the only scholar from ancient times who had produced a theory of Mechanics, which is contained the latter's two books named *Aequiponderantibus*. Archimedes was also the author of the principle of the lever (Dijksterhuis, 1987). In modern times the contributions of Stevin (1548-1620), in his *Statics*, and Galileo (1564-1642), in his *Dialogues* (*Discorsi*) about motion, had transformed Archimedes' demonstration into a much more simple and useful concept (Galileo, 1988). However, it seemed to Lagrange that ancient mathematicians did not know of a method to generalize the principle of the lever to other simple machines, notably the inclined plane. This problem is also posed to the first modern mathematicians. Stevin presented the first exact solution to this problem independent of the lever theory. These considerations led him to the impossibility of perpetual motion. (See *Elements of Statics* and *Hypomnemata Mathematica*)

The second fundamental principle of equilibrium is the composition of motions. It is assumed that when two forces are acting in different directions on a body, these two forces are equivalent to one following the diagonal of the parallelogram. In all cases when there are several forces, the composition of two forces leads to a single force representing the whole system. For the equilibrium condition this force must be zero if there is no fixed point. This conclusion is found in any book of Statics, particularly in Varignon's new mechanics (Blay, 1992). In addition he derived a theory of machines using this principle alone.

The origin of this principle is attributed by Lagrange to Galileo, specifically in the second Proposition of the Fourth Journey in his *Dialogues* (*Discorsi*). Lagrange remarks that Galileo does not consider the entire importance of the Principle in his theory of equilibrium.

The theory of composed motions can also be found in the writings of Descartes (1596-1650), Roberval (1602-1675), Mersenne (1588-1648), and Wallis (1616-1703). As mentioned above, Varignon (1654-1722) used this principle for machines in equilibrium. His project of a new mechanics, presented in

1687, had this objective.

Let us look at the third principle, virtual velocities. This is understood as the velocity acquired by a body whose equilibrium is not maintained. The principle states that for the equilibrium the powers are in inverse ratio to the virtual velocities, estimated in the direction of the powers. Lagrange attributes the discovering of this principle to Galileo in his *Dialogues (Discorsi)*. (See the Scholium of the second proposition of the third *Dialogue*) In this context, Galileo also defines the *moment* of some weight or of some power applied to a given machine as an action, energy, or *impetus* to move the machine in a way that equilibrium is maintained between two powers with the condition that the moments are equals and in contrary sense. The moment is always proportional to a power (force) multiplied by its virtual velocity.

This notion of moment that came from Galileo was adopted by Wallis in his *Mechanics*, published in 1669. He emphasizes the principle of equality of moments as the main foundation for Statics, and thus applies this theory to machines. In parallel, Descartes summarizes Statics in a unique principle, which in fact is the same as proposed by Galileo, though presented in a new and general form. This principle is based on the force necessary to elevate a weight to a height. Afterwards it was used extensively to evaluate the capacity of a given machine or to compare machines with different capacities. The birth of applied mechanics, mainly with Lazare Carnot (1753-1823), uses this mechanical model extensively (Oliveira, 2012).

Another important principle described by Lagrange is Torricelli's principle. He was a famous disciple of Galileo and his principle is directly related to Galileo's concepts, or even are a consequence of Galileo's analysis. The principle states that when a system of bodies is in equilibrium its center of gravity is in the lowest position. In the condition of equilibrium the center gravity cannot go up or down due to infinitely small variations of position.

Lagrange enunciated the principle of virtual velocities in a general form as follows:

If in any system of bodies or material points, any one of them is submitted to forces, but the system is in the position of equilibrium and therefore we apply any small motion, as a consequence each point describes an infinitely small space which will express its virtual velocity; the addition of all forces multiplied by the displacement of its points of application following the direction of the force will be always zero, since we adopt as positive the displacements in the direction of the forces and as negative the displacements in opposite sense to the forces.

Lagrange also remarks that was Jean Bernoulli (1667-1748) the first to realize the great generality of the principle of virtual velocities, as well as its usefulness to solve statics problems. He mentions the letter addressed by Jean Bernoulli to Varignon in 1717 about this principle and other important developments, such as that of Maupertuis (1698-1759), who in 1740 proposed to Paris Academy of Sciences the name of the *Law of Rest*, and Euler who developed in his Memorials to the Berlin Academy in 1754.

Second Part: Dynamics

As in the previous section, Lagrange begins this topic defining dynamics by the effect that forces can cause on bodies, by accelerating or decelerating them. In addition, this science was entirely developed by modern mathematicians and physicists. Again, the name of Galileo arises as the one who presented the first fundamental concepts of dynamics. In addition, Galileo developed the kinematics of the free fall of heavy bodies, in which the law of inertia is also constantly present in the free fall, but also the motion of projectiles. Before Galileo forces were only discussed in the context of equilibrium conditions. In spite of the simplicity involving the falling of heavy bodies and the motion of projectiles, the determination of the laws governing these phenomena were unknown until Galileo. He took the first step and opened the way to advancing mechanics. Lagrange then refers to Galileo's master piece, calling it the *Dialogues About the New Science*, published in Leiden in 1637. Obviously, he means the *Discorsi*.

Following the development of mechanics, Lagrange studied Huygens' contributions, especially the latter's findings on pendulum motion and the mathematization of centrifugal force, which were fundamental steps towards the discovery of universal gravitation. Huygens' construction of a bridge between Galileo and Newton was of great importance (Taton, 1982).

Mechanics became a new science due to Newton's book known as *Mathematical Principles*, which appeared for the first time in 1687. With the invention of infinitesimal calculus it was possible to transform the laws of motion into analytical equations.

The theory of motion produced by driven forces is based on general laws of any motion impressed on a given body. These laws are derived from known principles which are inertia force and composed motion. As in Statics, Lagrange looks for general principles governing dynamics phenomena using the category of force as a unifying concept. Thus, he identifies these two already mentioned principles as the most general and fundamental. It is in the context of these two principles where Lagrange develops his historical considerations.

Galileo realized that the first principle enunciated and derived from the laws governing the motion of projectiles through the composition of horizontal motion with constant velocity with the vertical up and down motion modified by gravity acceleration. The case of falling bodies with the velocity acquired being proportional to the elapsed time, or the vertical displacement proportional to the time squared, was an important achievement made by Galileo using geometrical considerations in addition to experimental measurements with inclined planes.

After Galileo, Huygens (1629-1695) discovered the laws of centrifugal forces of bodies in circular motion with constant velocity, and used this knowledge to compare forces. As a result weight on the surface of the earth could be calculated as a centrifugal force. This was done in his *Horologium Oscilatorum*, published in 1673 (Huygens, 1673).

Newton generalized this theory to any kind of curve, thereby developing the science for varied motions with accelerated forces. He used a geometrical method and occasionally analytical calculation, though instead of differential methods he applied the series method. After Newton the majority of mathematicians that developed the theory of motion only generalized Newton's theorems, introducing differential expressions to solve many kinds of problems.

Lagrange then explains how to solve a dynamical problem by using three different perpendicular directions and decomposing forces and accelerations in these directions. The forces in any direction can be calculated by equating on one side forces and on the other the second the differential of space divided by the first differential of time squared. For curved trajectories, the decomposition had to be done in normal and tangential directions. Lagrange does not mention that it was Euler who applied this for the first time in 1752 in a manner different to Newton's second law (Truesdell, 1983).

Lagrange describes how the problem of shocks between hard bodies was studied, explaining the result of these interactions by means of the analysis of quantities of motion. He mentions that it was Descartes who first realized the principle behind this phenomenon. However, as confirmed by Lagrange, Descartes made a mistake in the application of the principle because he considered that the absolute quantity of motion was always conserved. After Descartes, Wallis was the first to have a clear idea of the principle and used it to discover the laws for the communication of motion in the context of shocks between hard and elastic bodies, as presented in his *Philosophical Transactions*, published in 1669, as well as in the third part of his treatise *De Motu*, which appeared in 1671.

One of the most important passages of Lagrange's text is dedicated to the d'Alembert principle. The *Treatise of Dynamics* written by d'Alembert and published in 1743 presented a general and direct method to solve, or at least to obtain the equations for, practically any dynamic problem (d'Alembert, 1743). The method proposed transformed the laws of bodies in motion to its equilibrium, thereby relating dynamics to statics. The principle enunciated by d'Alembert generalizes the work of some previous mathematicians, such as Jacques Bernoulli (1654-1705), with great simplicity.

We can enunciate the principle by studying the motion of various bodies which tend to move with velocities and in a direction so that changes in both are caused by their interactions. It is possible to visualize these motions as composed by what was really acquired and others that are destroyed in the interactions. If we consider only the final motions the bodies animated with them are in equilibrium.

It is important to emphasize that d'Alembert made useful applications to mechanical problems. However, this principle does not provide the necessary equations to solve different dynamical problems but rather provides the means to derive the equations from the conditions of equilibrium. Thus, by combining the principle with known principles of equilibrium, such as the lever principle or that of the composition of forces, we can find the equations for each problem with the help of some more or less complicated constructions. The difficulty is to evaluate the forces destroyed.

As discussed previously, the principle of virtual velocities leads us to a very simple analytical method to solve static problems. This same principle combined with the d'Alembert principle also provides a similar method to solve dynamical problems. Explaining this approach in more detail, the application of the principle of virtual velocities consists of the following methodology. For a given system containing several bodies that can be reduced to points being acted upon by any kind of force, if we apply to the system a small motion, each body displaces an infinitesimal space. If we multiply each force by the displacement of its point of application and add them for the whole system, the result is zero.

If we suppose the system is in motion, and considering that the velocities of each body can be decomposed in three fixed and perpendicular directions, the decreasing of these velocities will represent the motions lost along the same directions and their increasing will be the motions lost in the opposite directions. Thus, these lost motions will be expressed in general by the mass multiplied by the element of velocity and divided by the time element, and they will have contrary directions to the velocities. Using this approach it is possible to obtain a general formula to represent the motions of bodies which will provide a solution for any dynamic problem.

One of the advantages of the above mentioned formula is that it immediately offers the general equations which encompass the principles and known theorems about the *conservation of living forces*, the *conservation of the motion of the center of gravity*, the *conservation of the moments of rotation motion*, or the *principle of areas* and the *principle of least action*. These principles can be considered the general achievements of the dynamic laws and are the primary principles of this science. With this statement Lagrange proposed to explain its origins and developments.

The first mentioned principle, the conservation of living forces, was first presented by Huygens, but in a different form to how it is now known. In its origins, the principle represented the equality between the descending and raising of the center of gravity of several heavy bodies, in which descending in a group but raising separately, using the known properties of the gravity center, the space displaced by this center in any direction is expressed by adding the products of the mass of each body by the space displaced in the same direction divided the total mass. On the other hand, using Galileo's theorems, the vertical displacement of a heavy body is proportional to the square of the velocity acquired in free descent, as well as what can be reached by raising it to the same height. Based on these considerations, Huygen's principle can consider the motion of heavy bodies in which the sum of the products of the masses by the square of the velocities at each time is the same, since that the bodies motion be conjunctly in any way, or that they displaces freely to the same vertical heights. Huygens made these remarks in a short paper on the methods used by Jacques Bernoulli and the Marquis l'Hopital (1661-1704). Obviously, the principle postulated by Huygens is a particular application of the more general principle of conservation of energy, a concept which would appear only in the middle of the nineteenth century.

After these achievements, Daniel Bernoulli (1700-1782) derived from this principle the laws of fluid motion in vessels, which had not been previously dealt with. He reached this general principle in the Berlin memorials, published in 1748 (Bernoulli, 1968).

The great advantage of this principle is that it easily provides an equation between the velocities of the bodies and the variables which calculate their position in space in such a manner that, due to the characteristics of the problem, all these variables are reduced to one, with this equation being sufficient to solve completely the problem.

The second principle is due to Newton who, at the beginning of his *Principia*, demonstrated that the state of rest or motion of the center of gravity of several bodies does not change through their reciprocal action. This implies that the center of gravity of the system is at rest or in uniform linear motion unless it meets some exterior obstacle. Obviously this principle is useful to determine the center of gravity motion independently of individual bodies' motions, as it can provide three equations between the bodies' coordinates and time.

The third principle, more recent than the other two, seems to have been discovered simultaneously in different ways by Euler, Daniel Bernoulli, and Le Chevalier d'Arcy (1723-1779). According to Euler and Daniel Bernoulli, this principle involves considering the motion of several bodies around a fixed center. Hence, the sum of the products of the mass of each body by the circular velocity around the center is always independent of the mutual action among the bodies and is conserved unless some exterior obstacle is found.

The principle enunciated by d'Arcy, which appeared in the Memorial he presented to the Paris Academy of Sciences in 1746, is that the sum of the products of the mass of each body by the area described by its vector radius around the fixed center is always proportional to time. This principle generalizes Newton's theorem about areas due to any centripetal forces.

Finally, the fourth principle called the least action, in an analogy with Maupertuis' principle with the same name which had become famous. It involved considering the motion of several bodies acting among them and then taking the sum of the products of the masses by the velocities and the spaces described is a minimum. Maupertuis had derived this from the laws of the reflection of light and refraction, as well as of mechanical shocks. These studies appear in two Memorials, one presented to the Academy of Sciences of Paris in 1744 and the other to the Berlin Academy (Maupertuis, 1744).

Before being completely established as a principle, Euler made the first approach to it in his treatise on isoperimetric curves, printed in Lausanne in 1744, postulating that in the trajectories described by central forces, the integral of the velocity multiplied by the curve element is always a maximum or a minimum. This property which Euler did not recognize except for isolated bodies, as he mentioned, was extended to any motion of bodies acting among themselves, leading to this new general principle in which the sum of the products of the masses by the integrals of the velocities multiplied by the space elements is constant and a maximum or a minimum. It is a simple consequence of mechanical laws. This principle combined with the principle of the conservation of living forces following the rules of variational calculus directly provides all the necessary equations to solve each problem giving rise to a method to solve problems of motion.

Final Remarks and Conclusion

One of the aims most sought by physicists along the years has been the finding of a principle, the simplest possible, or some basic fundamental principles, which could fit all natural phenomena. Some tried to do this, as Lagrange's analysis demonstrates. D'Alembert did the same. In his *Preliminary Discourse* in the *Treatise on Dynamics*, one reads: *If the principle of the inertia of force, of composed motion, and of equilibrium, are essentially different from each other, as we cannot prohibit happening; and if, on the other hand, these three principles are sufficient for mechanics, one can reduce this science to the least number of principles possible, and assume that on these three principles there can be established all the laws of motion for any body in any circumstances, as I have accomplished in this work.*

In his famous *Fundamental Principles of Equilibrium and Motion*, published in 1803, Lazare Carnot states: *There are two ways to see mechanics and its principles. The first one is by considering it as a theory of forces, the causes that impress motion. The second is by considering it as a theory of motions themselves.* Here an important remark has to be made. Lagrangian mechanics is the development of mechanics using the second approach, the analysis of motions by themselves as defined by Carnot. However, with respect to history of mechanics, Lagrange adopts the concept of force to both statics and dynamics to explain its internal development, obviously because of the late development of the other concepts associated with motion that we know nowadays as the methods of energy.

Another important contribution in the historical considerations of mechanics made by Lagrange is that it highlights some developments which are not completely clear in the current literature. One example is his correct interpretation of d'Alembert's principle. As we know, from reading most mechanics or physics textbooks, this principle is always presented as a method to reduce a dynamical problem into a statics one. Lagrange, as in the original version of the d'Alembert principle, only considers the possibility of equilibrium where motions are destroyed. In other words, equilibrium means the conservation of the quantity of motion.

Lastly, the importance attributed by Lagrange to include in his masterpiece historical considerations about the development of mechanics, only confirms that the internal development of science is not independent of its historical development.

REFERENCES

Belhoste, B. (2003). *La formation d'une technocratie*. Paris: Belin, rue Féron.

Bernoulli, D. (1968). *Hydrodynamics*. New York: Dover Publication, Inc.

Blay, M. (1992). *La science du mouvement: De galilée à lagrange*. Paris: Belin, rue Féron.

D'Alembert, J. L. (1921). *Traité de dynamique*. Paris: Gauthiers-Villars et Cie Éditions.

Dijksterhuis, E. J. (1987). *Archimedes*. Princeton, NJ: Princeton University Press.

Euler, L. (1952). Methodus inveniendi lineas curvas maximi minimive proprietates gaudentes. In leonhardi euleri opera omnia, s. I, vol. XXIV, Lausanne.

Galileu, G. (1988). Discurso sobre as duas novas ciências, museu de astronomia e ciências afins, Rio de Janeiro.

Huygens, C. (1673). *Horologium oscilatorum*. Paris: Albert Blanchard Library.

Lagrange, J. L. (1989). *Mécanique analytique*. Paris: Éditins Jacques Gabay.

Maupertuis, P. L. M. (1744). *Accord des différents lois de la nature qui avaient jusqu'ici paru incompatibles*. Memoires de l'Academie des Sciences de Paris.

Newton, I. (1952). *Mathematical principles of natural philosophy*. London: Great Books of the Western World.

Oliveira, A. R. E. (2012). The role of the concept of work in the development of applied mechanics. Rome: SISFA.

Taton, R. (1982). *Huygens et la France*. Paris: Librairie Philosophique J. Vrin.

Truesdell, C. (1983). Essays in the history of mechanics. Berlim: Springer-Verlag.

Les Châteaux de Landiras et de Montferrand and Their Seigneurial Families

—Part Two: Two Families—One Destiny

Donald A. Bailey

Department of History, University of Winnipeg Winnipeg, Manitoba, Canada

Emerging from the Hundred Years' War, the Montferrand families acquired Renaissance associations, experienced internal divisions during the Reformation, generated Bordeaux's only saint, and came up to the Revolution with the usual noble financial challenges. Deeply opposed to the Revolution, they suffered confiscation and parcellization and barely held onto any property at all. The core estate of the Château de Landiras finds its modern renown in its fine *grave* wines.

Keywords: Montferrand de Guyenne; Landiras; Saint Jeanne de Lestonnac; Bordeaux; Hundred Years' War; French Revolution; Bertrand III; Pierre II; Lesparre; de Goth; de la Roque-Budos; Communay; Graves Wine

The Hundred Years' War Continued

Mary of Bedford, illegitimate daughter of John of Lancaster, was the last person mentioned in Part One.[1] Her husband was Pierre II de Montferrand, baron of Landiras, *soudan* of La Trau, etc., and lord of La Tour de Bessan.[2] Pierre's Anglo-French machinations (being both a vassal of the Duke of Guyenne, the King of England, and a sub-vassal of the King of France) twice took him from Guyenne to England and back again and were part of the events that eventually brought the War to an end. Montferrand-Landiras was also governor of Blaye-et-Sainte-Luce (today, Blaye), a town on the right bank of the Garonne crucial to the defence of Bordeaux, when French forces besieged it. The French were led by the now middle-aged Jean Dunois (ca. 1403-1468), count of Longueville, the famous "Bastard of Orléans", companion of Joan of Arc. A large assault forced Pierre II to abandon the town and take refuge in its château, which itself fell on 24 May 1451, only three days later. The city of Bordeaux was to capitulate on 23 June. Dunois gave generous terms and even let our Pierre II de Montferrand, in a private treaty, ransom his freedom for either 10,000 *écus* or the turning over of his son and nephew as hostages. He had to give up all his possessions, three of which would be returned provided that he swore an oath of fidelity to Charles VII of France (1422-1461) within six weeks.

Montferrand-Landiras then disappeared for about fourteen months,[3] but his English allegiance was revived in August 1452 by renewed French assaults on Guyenne. It had been Charles VII's moderation towards the Midi in general that had helped undermine the region's loyalty to the English crown, but now, in uncontested control, Charles imposed taxes and other obligations that provoked renewed disloyalties (Cocks, 1984: 24-25).[4] In reaction, Pierre de Montferrand sailed for England with

---

[1] Very few dates will be attached to individuals of either Montferrand branch in this article, since they may all be easily found in the earlier article's Genealogy. Chronological context should emerge from other dates mentioned.

[2] Pierre was often referred to by one of his mother's other titles, sire de Lesparre. Through Isabelle de Preissac, he was one of three heirs to the château de Lesparre after the death of Amanieu de Madaillan. An inquest in 1446 found that he was "the closest descendent, by his mother" (Barein, 1876: I, 159). He "took possession" in 1452 (Féret, 1889: III, 468).

Since Pierre received compensations for the non-payment of his wife's dowry only in 1450, Henry Ribadieu doubts (1990: 194, n. 2) the marriage was actually before 1435; yet John of Lancaster-Bedford had died in September 1435, so it's unlikely that Pierre would have sought the marriage afterwards. Among the compensations were the barony of Marennes and the *péage* (toll gate) of Hastingues (a *bastide*—walled town—in Landes, Aquitaine, founded in 1289 by John Hastings, then seneschal of Gascony).

Despite his apparently low credit at the English court, Pierre was charged to guard both Dax and Blaye, which were too far apart to defend simultaneously. Thus, his defence of Blaye (Ribadieu: 194). Bertrand IV de Montferrand meanwhile defended Bourg, but only half-heartedly after the fall of Blaye (*Ibid.*: 212). Ribadieu always refers to Pierre and Bertrand as "brothers", but Bertrand was the son of Jean, Pierre's half-brother. By the way, Ribadieu spells the family name "Montferrant", as Féret recommends (III, 469).

[3] Ribadieu suspects Pierre II de Montferrand-LaTrau-Lesparre-Landiras was ashamed of having signed with Dunois provisions that so benefitted him personally at the expense of Guyenne ("*qui liait sa fortune à la chute de sa patrie*", "which joined his fortune to the collapse of his country", 269).

[4] As heading the conspiracy, Cocks (1984) mentions "le sire de Lesparre et Pierre de Montferrand" as if they were distinct persons and says that the latter carried the title of "Souldich de l'Estrade" (25), which looks suspiciously close to "soudan de La Trau".

(Cocks was the first author of a work that, through at least the next seven editions, from 1868 to 1908, he co-authored with Édouard Féret and that by 2001 had seen sixteen editions.)

one of his distant relations, Jean de Foix.[5] As it happened, the Duke of Somerset (Edmund Beaufort, 1405-1455) was then preëminent at court, and he was looking for a way to re-establish his reputation and reinforce his influence after his disastrous loss of Normandy (D.N.B.: IV, 39). Montferrand's proposal gave him this opportunity, and so the council of Henry VI (1422-1461) was persuaded to offer a sizeable force, commanded by the now eighty-year-old John Talbot, first count of Shrewsbury (ca. 1373-1453), who had been unable to save Orléans from Jeanne d'Arc and Dunois in 1429.

After a few successful engagements, the English and their Guyennese supporters lost the decisive battle of Castillon, near Bordeaux, on 17 July 1453, and so, this time definitively, all their lands in France except Calais. Talbot and his son had lost their lives in the battle,[6] but Pierre de Montferrand-Landiras escaped to Bordeaux, which he and others attempted to secure. The château of Lesparre was taken and in part destroyed (Ribadieu: 319). On 9 October, at Montferrand, the treaty rendering Bordeaux to the French was signed, most of the generous provisions of 1451 retracted, and our baron and his uncle François de Montferrand-d'Uza-Belin were among a score of lords exempted from the amnesty and banished from France in perpetuity (Communay, 1889: 1; Cocks, 1984: 26).[7] After returning to London, however, a motley collection of émigrés organized a new enterprise against the French, with Pierre II de Montferrand-Landiras at their head. Landing at Médoc, he was arrested during a night-time attempt to enter what was officially no longer "his" château of Lesparre, taken to Poitiers for trial, and in July 1454 condemned and executed—in fact, decapitated and quartered, with pieces of his body nailed to the city gates (Féret: III, 468; Ribadieu: 381). The Hundred Years' War was finally over; Guyenne had been under English suzerainty for just short of three centuries.

The resulting confiscations require some attention, because, once again, the sources are not transparent. Between 1451 and 1454, this unfortunate baron of Montferrand lost two of his properties, both previously more important than Landiras itself: In April 1451, the seigniory of Lesparre had been transferred to Amanieu d'Albret (1425-1463/73), elder son of Charles II d'Albret, but without posterity himself. So Lesparre passed to a

brother's cadet grandson, Gabriel d'Albret ("La Maison d'Albret").[8] Already confiscated (when?), the château de La Trau was razed to the ground, with the *terre* being given to an unknown person.[9] The senior branch of the family was threatened by Charles VII's order to destroy the château of Montferrand, but nothing happened at this time.[10] Langoiran had been given to Pierre in 1446 in partial compensation for being denied Lesparre, then taken away in 1454 because of his treason, and transferred to the legitimatized bastard Jean d'Armagnac. Soon, Charles VII relented and as early as 1454 (?) restored ownership of their *biens* to the senior branch (Grasset, 1981: 97-98 & 113; Abbot, n.d.: 323 & 325)—OR was it Louis XI who in 1472 restored the properties to Bertrand IV's son, Gaston I (Féret: III, 468)? Charles VII's younger son, as Charles Duke of Guyenne, restored most of the properties of the Landiras branch, but the courts refused to transfer Lesparre back from the d'Albrets.

Restoration of Reputation after the War

François IV de Montferrand-Landiras, the son of Pierre II de Montferrand-Lesparre-Landiras and Mary Bedford, had been one of the hostages of the 1451 Blaye-et-Sainte-Luce treaty. He was reared at the court of Prince Charles of France, the duke of Berry, brother of soon-to-be King Louis XI (1461-1483). When Prince Charles was named Duke of Guyenne in 1469, Montferrand-Landiras was appointed his *premier panetier* (the person charged with supplying the prince's bread), while cousin and fellow hostage, Bertrand IV, became the prince's *conseiller et chambellain*.[11] Prince Charles, until his death in May 1472, was at the centre of most of the conspiracies against his brother the king, so any lingering resentment towards the French conquest of Guyenne would have made the young Montferrands at home in the prince's rebellions. But when the prince/duke died, François IV de Montferrand-Landiras entered the service of Pierre de Beaujeu, a member of the Bourbon family. In 1474 Beaujeu married Anne de France, Louis XI's daughter, who was to be regent for her young brother, King Charles VIII (1483-1498). Thus, his new service would have brought Montferrand-Landiras over to behaviour more supportive of the French crown. In fact, he had already participated loyally during Louis XI's last wars and later marched with King Charles into the Italian Wars. More than one baron of Landiras was to fight in these wars, as did their Montferrand cousins.

Bertrand IV de Montferrand, son of Jean I, the elder half-brother of the ill-fated Pierre II de Montferrand-Landiras and so heir to the senior line, also suffered from conflicting loyalties and so endured the confiscations and restorations just described. Through his 1473 marriage to Catherine de Lescun, Bertrand's son Gaston became associated with what had been one of the most famous factions at the French royal court on the eve of

---

[5]Baurein writes that Gaston de Foix gave his daughter to Jehannot de Montferrand, son of François de Montferrand, sgr. d'Uza (III, 231; Baurein spells it Uzar). Gaston de Foix was the father of our Jean de Foix, who was later to add Candale to his titles. The elder brother of François was Bertrand III de Montferrand, the father of Pierre de Montferrand-Landiras by his (second) marriage to Isabeau de Preissac-Landiras, and so Jehannot and Pierre were cousins germane, which made Jean de Foix and Pierre de Montferrand first cousins through marriage.

[6]But Talbot did leave his name on various sites in the Médoc part of the Gironde, as well as on a château and a fine wine there produced.

[7]Cocks (1984) makes the obvious point that, after 19 October 1453, the history of the province and that of the country were combined. (This time, it is Lesparre and de l'Estrade whom he cites as distinct persons. Cf. note 4.) Ribadieu says five were banished to England (365), rather than "a score"; it's he who names François.

By the way, Jean I de Foix-Candale was also taken prisoner at the fateful battle of Castillon and spent seven years in captivity. Back in England by 1460, he was able to make peace with the king of France in 1461-62, gave up all his possessions in England except the title Comte de Candale [= Earl of Kendal], and resumed lordship of his French estates, to the title of which he had added "Candale" (Bailey, 41, note 39). Cf. note 24, in Part One. The granddaughter of Jean de Foix-Candale and Margaret Kerdeston (aka "Marguerite de La Pole-Suffolk") was to marry Ladislaus (Vladislaus) II of Hungary and Bohemia in 1502, so making them ultimately the ancestors of the modern Hapsburgs, the Bourbon dynasty of France after Henry IV, and the Stuarts after Charles I.

[8]The court condemning Pierre II to death in 1454 stated that he "had never been seigneur de Lesparre except in name", but see note 2, above. The recipient, Amanieu d'Albret, was comte d'Orval, in Normandy. A seigneurie de Lesparre also turns up twice in the Grailly-Foix family.

[9]"Gérard d'Albret is named by Grasset (98), but I am unable to find this name anywhere—or any alternative recipient!

[10]Destroyed (Féret: III, 468); "lost only a few stones" (Grasset: 98); order carried out in 1591 (yet "demolished for the second time"?!), after the city of Bordeaux purchased the property (Grasset: 115).

[11]The French *conseiller* can mean either English "councillor" or "counselor/adviser", often easy to distinguish, but not here. A "chamberlain" manages the household of a noble or prince.

Joan of Arc's arrival there.[12] And Gaston was amongst the nobility of the Bordelaise obligated to the *ban et arrière-ban* ("mustering of the king's vassals for war") called up by Gaston de Foix in 1481 (Baurein: I, 434-36).[13] It was from Gaston de Montferrand's *second* marriage, in 1483, to Jeanne (or Jehanne) de Maingot de Surgères, that our senior line continued.

In these decades, the elder Montferrand branch sprouted two other, cadet dynasties. One, founded by Betrtrand III's brother François I (d. bf. 1456), sgr de Montferrand and (by marriage) viscount d'Uza, survived only three generations. But a later branch, titled "Cancon & Foncaude" and founded after 1474 by Gaston I's brother, Jean II de Montferrand, survived for six generations and, in fact, succeeded the senior branch before itself relinquishing titles and lands to the barons of Landiras. The Landiras branch indulged a similar experience, in the short-lived Portets branch of the family. A son of Thomas de Montferrand-Landiras, Jehannot de Montferrand, seems to have recognized his brother's claim to the main inheritance in 1559 and founded a parallel branch on a *seigneurie* brought into the family much earlier by Arnaud de Preissac.[14] The establishment of cadet lines attenuated sibling rivalry, but it also had the pragmatic goal of facilitating governance in an age without modern communication. Naturally, these dynastic enterprises mean numerous duplications of names and numbers, which, together with merely some similar names held by scattered siblings, have seriously misled impatient genealogists.

From the Italian Wars (1494-1559) to the Wars of Religion (1562-1598)

Towards the end of the 15th century, both branches of the Montferrand dynasty were again active, this time in the French invasion of Italy. These wars, too, involved dynastic claims, territorial ambition, and commercial advantages. But this time it was the French who won many of the famous battles, especially in the first decades, and then lost the war. The Austrian-Spanish Hapsburgs came to dominate most of Italy, while France's only gains (the bishoprics of Metz, Toul and Verdun) were in the Rhineland, far from the Italian peninsula. Francis I's (1515-1547) great victory at Marignano in 1515, however, did lead to the Concordat of Bologna, in which the king of France was recognized as supreme in all but name over the affairs, finances and appointments of the French (Gallican) church. Our François IV de Montferrand-Landiras participated in the campaign that opened the Italian Wars and culminated in a temporary triumph in Naples. His grandson, Jean IV, also fought as a

young man in Italy and later, as a royalist Catholic, in France. Pierre I de Montferrand, of the senior house, fought at the French disaster at Pavia in 1525, in which King Francis I was captured (Communay: xxxiii). His son, Charles I, also fought in Italy (Communay: xxxiv). Charles's two sons (Charles II and Guy) were to defend opposite sides in the French Wars of Religion.

The 16th century had seen a profound division within the Latin Church, which soon provoked religious civil wars in several countries. The reformed religion of John Calvin had a tremendous impact on his native land. Although it was never safe for Calvin himself to return to France, scores of other Genevan-trained pastors risked (and some lost) their lives to preach the new faith there. By the late 1560s, perhaps as many as one third of the French nobility had converted, thereby entailing most of their peasants, as well as significant numbers of merchants, lawyers, teachers and royal officials. The sudden death of King Henry II (1547-1559) during a joust to celebrate the end of the Italian Wars precipitated the French Wars of Religion. He left four sons under fifteen years of age and the fortunes of France in the untested, but competent, hands of his Italian widow, Catherine de Médicis (1519-1589). The wars ended only after the vigorous Protestant successor to the throne, Henry of Navarre (1589-1610), defeated or bought off his Catholic adversaries while negotiating his own (re)conversion to Catholicism in 1593, and after he then offered religious security to his former co-religionists in the Edict of Nantes (1598).

Jean IV de Montferrand-Landiras participated in this civil war on the royalist, Catholic side "with ardour", and in 1570 Charles IX (1560-1574) admitted him to the Order of Saint Michael (Grasset: 110).[15] Jean's son, Gaston II, remained loyal to the Catholic Valois kings; of this husband of (Saint) Jeanne de Lestonnac, more later. Their son, François V de Montferrand-Landiras, also *seigneur* de St Morillon and other places, became a *gentilhomme ordinaire de la chambre*[16] of Henry IV in 1603 and the captain of a company of light horse, posts which illustrate the family's modest status on the national stage.[17]

As for the senior branch, Charles II de Montferrand, first baron of the Bordelaise (Guyenne), became mayor and governor of Bordeaux in 1569. He boastfully carried out royal orders to extend the St. Bartholomew Day's massacre of Protestants to Bordeaux (250 killed). After several military engagements

---

[12]Catherine de Lescun was the daughter of Jean, bastard of Armagnac, called "de Lescun", count of Comminges and baron of Gourdon. An Armagnac from his *mother's* side, Jean d'Armagnac, a marshal (*maréchal*) of France, was also, among other charges, lieutenant-general of Guyenne; he was legitimized in 1463 (Anselme, 1967: VIII, 94-95).

[13]Remember that the Montferrands had made various marital alliances to the houses of Foix and Albret in earlier centuries, where the *seigneuries* of Lescun and Comminges, like that of Lesparre, were to be found. Furthermore, there had also been connections to the Armagnacs, since it was members of this family who were counts d'Astarac.

[14]See note 70, in Part One. The *seigneurie* of Portets had been under the authority of the *soudans* of La Trau since at least the 1380s. In 1587, Jean de Montferrand* sold Portets to Guillaume de Gasq, *trésorier de France* (Barein: III: 71 & 75). (*Trésoriers de France* were regional royal servants, not a unique & central officer.)

*Barein says "Jean", but Jehannot de Montferrand-Portets died in 1561 and Jean IV (Jehan) in 1580 at the latest, so a 1587 sale would have to have been made by the former's son (Gaston de Montferrand-Portets; no known dates) or, less likely, by the latter's son (Gaston II).

---

[15]Grasset simply has "Jean" admitted by Charles IX in 1570. Alternately, Jean de Montferrand-Landiras was admitted to the Order of Saint Michael in 1571, with the title Baron of Poltelz [*sic*], which had been his brother's title but which may have returned to a house that his heir's death reunited.

Montferrand is found in what is a second list under 1571, the first occasion when part of the list is termed "Qualifiés" (neither defined nor explained). Colleville & Saint-Christo (2001: 109). Let us note here that, by right of having been mayor of Bordeaux, Michel de Montaigne, who enters our story below, was also promoted to the *Ordre de Saint-Michel* (*Ibid.*: x).

[16]Of the regular noble or royal servants of noble background who ran errands or handled small tasks for his master, *un gentilhomme ordinaire* held such a position for at least a year, rather than, say, quarterly.

[17]There were, in fact, quite a few connections between this *gentilhomme ordinaire* and his master. King of France only from 1589, Henry IV had ruled the Kingdom of Navarre in the southwest of France since 1572. He was, furthermore, a friend of Michel de Montaigne, François V's great uncle. And as a member of the house of Bourbon, the king was a collateral descendant of Pierre de Beaujeu, whom François IV de Montferrand-Landiras had served towards the end of his career. Finally, since Henry IV's mother was Jeanne d'Albret (a house that ruled Foix as well as Navarre), there was also a distant family relationship between Montferrand-Landiras and his king.

against the Huguenots, he was killed by arquebus fire during the siege of Gensac in 1574 (Féret: III, 469) or in July 1475 (Communay: xxxiv). His marriage to his cousin Marguerite de Montferrand-Cancon being sterile, his younger brother, Guy de Montferrand, inherited the fiefs of Montferrand.

Guy de Montferrand-Loigoiran, however, was a Huguenot, the name given to French adherents of Jean Calvin, and so his military engagements were in opposition to those of his elder brother. On the eve of the bloody massacre of Huguenots in 1572 that broke out in Paris on St. Bartholemew's Day (24 August), he was somehow warned and took refuge in Saint-Germain-en-Laye (Communay: xl). Among his several military exploits during the rest of the decade, the most striking (and most tainted) was the capture of Périgueux (Dordogne) on 6 August 1575. The following three days saw an outbreak of murder and looting, in which even priests were not spared. Because of this event, which even exceeded the norm, the memoirs of the Huguenot Duke de Bouillon (Henri de La Tour d'Auvergne, viscount of Turenne: 1555-1623) describe Montferrand-Loigoiran as "one of the most cruel and irreligious men of his time" ("Montferrand": 14). Thiviers suffered similar pillaging later in the month, and also the rich abbey of Chancelade on 2 September. Realizing that Monferrand-Loigoiran's actions were not advancing the Huguenot cause, King Henry of Navarre dismissed him in 1577. The irritated baron therefore made his peace with Catholicism and lived out the remaining fourteen years of his life enjoying his two noble châteaux. He and his son Gédéon died in the same year, one month apart.

Once more, we meet divergent emphases: One asserts that, to meet her debts to the city of Bordeaux, Guy's widow, Jeanne d'Eschelles (who had died in 1594), sold the fief of Montferrand in 1595 (!) to her late husband's distant cousin (his sister-in-law's brother), François II de Montferrand-Cancon, scion of the younger branch of this senior line (source lost). Another asserts that Jeanne d'Eschelles sought to sell the fief and that the *jurats* (municipal officials) of Bordeaux, wanting to expand the city across the river and still finding the castle threatening to the city's interests, purchased the barony on 15 August 1591.[18] Thus, François II was obliged to begin a protracted process to recover it (Communay: xlii; Grasset: 109, 113 & 116). Regardless, the family had experienced financial difficulties throughout the century and had been selling off parcels since 1519 (Grasset: 113-15). The barony of Veyrines, for example, was sold (to the mayor and *jurats* of Bordeaux) in 1526 (Barein, II: 243), the barony of Langoiran in 1578 (Communay: Doc. XLIII, 121-25; Abbot dates the sale to 1590 [323]), and three-quarters of the barony of Portets, Castres and Arbanats in 1587 (Barein III: 71 & 75). Indeed, nobles all over Western Europe faced financial exigencies in this extremely inflationary century that forced frequent sales from their estates.[19] In interesting contrast to these sales, Thomas de Montferrand had "shared" some of his patrimony ("*biens*") with residents ("*habitants*") of Landiras in 1536 ("Les Seigneurs de Landiras_1"). Earlier, in 1518, he had given some land to the Syndics of the "Fabrique et Oeuvre"[20] of the church Saint-Hypolite d'Arbanats and to the syndics and parishioners of the parish for them to cultivate, in exchange for three religious services a year (at Christmas, Easter and Pentecost) for himself and his late parents (Barein: III, 76-77).

By a 1577 marriage to Claire de Pellegue, Guy de Montferrand's heir, François II, had sired seven children. Yet, despite his marriage in 1625 to Jacquette de Beauxoncles, their son François III died without heirs in October 1660. All four of his younger brothers having pre-deceased him, titles and properties passed to the Montferrand-Landiras branch.

Before abandoning the senior branch, however, let us suggest that its name and existence may be responsible for the relative historical obscurity of the Montferrands of Landiras. Once the details of the Landiras line's activities are discerned, one is surprised to find so little mention of it in the general histories of France. Since the name "Montferrand" identified both branches of the family and the elder line's château, records of achievements of the Montferrands of Landiras must often have been ascribed to their cousins. For instance, in one renowned history of France, the actions of Pierre II de Montferrand are, indeed, mentioned, but without any reference to his *seigneurie* of Landiras (Petit-Dutaillis, 1902: 111).[21]

Renaissance and Reformation; Saint Jeanne ("Joan") de Lestonnac (1556-1640)

While discussing the Wars of Religion, we alluded to Gaston II de Montferrand-Landiras. He may have trained as a lawyer and become a member of the Parlement of Bordeaux, and so a colleague of his future father-in-law, Richard Lestonnac.[22] He may otherwise have performed little of note himself during his less than twenty-year possession of the lands and titles adhering to this cadet branch of the house of Montferrand. But in 1573, he married Jeanne de Lestonnac, who was to become the family's most renowned member—the only saint born and bred in Bordeaux. Although only seventeen years old at the time of her marriage, Jeanne's life had already been filled with the drama of late 16th-century France.

The Massacre of St. Bartholomew's Day had occurred the year before this marriage. Jeanne's mother, Jeanne Eyquem de

---

[18]Jacques de Montignon, *maréchal* de France, came to take possession but found the castle occupied by Charles Achard, Charles and Guy's second cousin, grandson of Catherine de Montferrand-Laminsans; this claimant was persuaded to leave (28 August), and Bordeaux turned ownership over to the marshal (31 October 1591, how willingly is not clear—cf. Abbot: 327); François II de Montferrand-Cancon was able to buy the barony back between 1594 and 1607, but with the château demolished (Communay: Doc. XLV, 126-132).

It is hard to reconcile this genealogy with that offerered by GeneaNet (André Decloitre): Charles I's sister Catherine married Louis Jean de Laminsans, brn d'Auros, in 1514. But they had a son, Pierre Charles de Laminsans, who had posterity, so whence would come the claims of his sister's descendents? Sister Catherine de Laminsans married Jean Achard des Augiers (this agrees with Communay), but their sons were Jean and Robert, not Charles (Communay's attempted usurper of the Montferrand succession).

[19]Another example of property exchanges: in 1514, the owner of la Maison noble de Cagés did homage to Thomas de Montferrand; in 1574, Cagés was sold to "Messieurs Jean and Gaston de Montferrand"; and in 1580, it was sold by Gaston de Montferrand; in 1597, the new owner did homage for the property to Jeanne de Lestonnac, *dame* de Landiras (Barein: III, 126-127).

[20]The "fabrique" of a church was the group of clerics (and, after the Council of Trent, also laymen) charged with the administration of the communal goods of the parish (=vestry), while the "œuvre" was the church group specializing in charitable actions.

[21]We speak of the relevant volume in Ernest Lavisse's renowned series *Histoire de France*. Ribadieu does balance the two branches in his study of France's ultimate conquest of Guyenne.

[22]Or so claims "Les Seigneurs de Landiras_2". Communay (lxxii) makes no mention of this judicial position. Dast Le Vacher de Boisville, while confirming Richard de Lestonnac as becoming a *conseiller* (*clerc*), enrolled in the Parlement de Bordeaux on 1 June 1554 (41), has no mention of any Montferrand anywhere in the "Liste".

Montaigne, had joined the new faith and made every effort to bring up her daughter in it. Jeanne Eyquem's brother was Michel Eyquem de Montaigne (1533-1592), whose fame as essayist lay ahead of him. Both of the Eyquem parents were Roman Catholics, but the mother happened to be of Spanish-Jewish descent, and an attitude of religious forbearance appears to have pervaded the household. Although always a loyal Catholic despite his various philosophical doubts, Michel de Montaigne made many friends among the Protestants, including with the king of Navarre. Thus, the second basis of Montaigne's historical reputation was his devotion to the practice of toleration and reconciliation, at a time when the majority of Europeans and their monarchs were fanatical adherents of their respective faiths and willing to kill or die for them.

Let us, therefore, examine Jeanne de Lestonnac's background in more detail. Her maternal grandfather was determined that Jeanne Eyquem's brother would excel in erudition and so ordered that no one was to speak in his presence anything but Latin until Michel Eyquem was six years old. It should not surprise us, then, that young Jeanne, our saint's mother, also profitted from the family's erudition. Contemporaries later extolled her command of both Greek and Latin. Michel eventually studied law, travelled extensively, and returned to become a magistrate in the important Parlement of Bordeaux (as a "lay counsellor", inscribed in October 1557), (Dast Le Vacher de Boisville). Deciding that he preferred tranquillity to engagement, however, he left his judicial office and returned to the family's château. There, he read extensively, reflected deeply, and began to write the famous essays (*Essais*: from "essayer"—to test, to try out) that have influenced all subsequent literature throughout the world. Against his inclinations, Michel de Montaigne was also pulled out of his retreat to serve from 1581 to 1585 as the mayor of Bordeaux, less than ten years after Charles II de Montferrand (of the senior line) had been the city's governor and mayor.

These two connections with the world of law and politics are also reflected in his sister's marriage. For the husband of Jeanne Eyquem de Montaigne was to be Richard de Lestonnac, from 1554 or '57 to 1571, a councillor (*conseiller*) in the Parlement of Bordeaux, where Michel Eyquem had also been a councillor. Like his brother-in-law, Lestonnac associated frequently with the city's literary elite. Since he was a fervent Catholic, his Huguenot wife (Montaigne's sister) sent their eldest of seven children to grow up and be taught in the home of the girl's aunt and uncle (Thomas de Beauregard), both faithful Protestants. Uncle Michel alerted the father as to what was happening, and young Jeanne was brought back to the parental home, where her soul was fought over. Her eventual decision for Catholicism was to earn the lifelong enmity of her mother. Despite this spiritually conflicted childhood, Jeanne grew into what her doting uncle described as "un chef-d'oeuvre" (masterpiece) of nature, "combining such a beautiful soul to such a beautiful body and lodging a princess in a magnificent palace" (*Vies des saints...*, 1950: II, 50; and Coulson, 1964: 224-225).

Later, after founding the first teaching order of nuns in France, Jeanne de Lestonnac said she had learnt much of value from her Protestant period: incorporating religious goals in an educational program, the commitment to educating girls as well as boys, giving a social dimension to instruction, and innovative orientations in teaching (Boisse, 1999: 4-5). Of course, her bordelaise patrons belonged to the Society of Jesus, which modeled most of these same qualities. Jeanne's brother, François

de Lestonnac (1572-1631), had become a Jesuit and died as *recteur* (director) of the College of Poitiers (Féret: III, 405; GeneaNet supplies his dates and names him "Roger").

Obviously an attractive marriage partner, Jeanne de Lestonnac appears to have had twenty-four years of happiness as the *baronne de Landiras*. Five of her seven children with Gaston II de Montferrand-Landiras made it out of infancy, though the eldest son died in late adolescence. The surviving son, after studying with the Jesuits in Rome, was to succeed to the family estates and responsibilities; two daughters were later to enter the religious life and the third daughter married. But between 1592 and 1597, Jeanne de Lestonnac lost, in quick succession, her uncle, her father and, through an accident, her husband. At age 41, she had become a widow.[23]

The fruits of her childhood religious struggles could now move from devoted and pious direction of a family to the service of her faith through prayer, celibacy and female education, though she did not abandon her young children before the eldest attained maturity. Only in 1603, did she enter the Feuillant convent at Toulouse. But the austerities imposed by this order undermined her health within three months and she wisely withdrew. She retired briefly to the château of La Mothe (one of her late husband's *seigneuries*).[24] The end of the year found her living in the Montferrand *hôtel* (substantial private mansion, usually in a city) in Bordeaux, where a severe plague broke out in 1604-1605. Devoting her energies to the sick and suffering, the dowager baroness of Landiras reached the conclusion that God intended her to work among the poor and, especially, to educate their girls. Jeanne de Lestonnac was about to make a significant contribution to what in France is called the Catholic Renaissance.

Jeanne had fallen under the influence of two priests of the Society of Jesus, the famous Counter- or Catholic-Reformation order that had been founded between 1534 and 1540 under the inspiration of St. Ignatius Loyola. Fathers Jean de Bordes and ??? (first name unknown) Raymond were teaching boys at the Collège de Madeleine, in Bordeaux, according to Jesuit principles. They were already dreaming of somehow establishing a comparable school for girls. They put Jeanne de Lestonnac and the two women already following her through the rigours of Loyola's *Spiritual Exercises* (1548), and then helped them establish a school for girls and found a female order. In this enterprise, they were at first supported by Cardinal François d'Escoubleau de Sourdis (1574-1628), archbishop of Bordeaux from 1599. But he began to make difficulties after discovering that he could not persuade Jeanne and her disciples to attach themselves to his preferred Ursulines or otherwise control the new order. Indeed, he later fomented the conspiracy which led to Jeanne's temporary discharge from the leadership of her own order.

Her new order has been variously called *La Compagnie de Marie Notre-Dame*, *Les Soeurs de Notre-Dame de Bordeaux*, and *Les Filles de Notre-Dame* (Communay: lxxiii, also suggests "Jésuites", which underlines that order's initiative in Jeanne's enterprise). The work began and the initial drafts of

---

[23]With a still young eldest son, Jeanne de Lestonnac assumed the direction of the estate's affairs for six years after her widowhood. For example, on 28 July 1597, she received homage from Jean du Fossard when he succeeded to his father's land, called de Cagés (Baurein: III, 126-127), as observed in footnote 19, above.

[24]Recall the Landiras associations with the La Mothe family at the very beginning of history's record of the château.

the rules were written as early as 1606. On 7 April 1607, Pope Paul V (1605-1621) officially approved the new order, and on 8 December 1610, the first five "female companions" (*compagnes*) took their vows. One of these companions had been a Protestant when Jeanne de Lestonnac's personal magnetism first drew them together. Her background and Jeanne's own childhood were reflected in the special attention the new order took to educate and convert Protestant girls.

The rapid popularity of the Company meant that they soon outgrew their original building, which still stands on the rue du Hâ. (Its chapel, in which Jeanne eventually died, started construction in 1616, and has served, ironically, as a Protestant chapel since the French Revolution.) Soon, Jeanne de Lestonnac was travelling to other cities to found new houses. The five original nuns had dedicated themselves to "a life neither uniquely active, nor purely contemplative, but [with] the two together and resembling that of the glorious Virgin Mary" (Boisse: 9). They wanted to penetrate Mary's *mystère* ("spiritual secret") and imitate her attitudes and actions, and they sought to find God in all things.

Jeanne de Lestonnac's qualities of leadership are described by Benedictine historians as follows: "The mother superior was at the same time the friendly and the strong woman, endowed with great powers of persuasion, animated by a supernatural spirit, giving both the maxim and the example, [and] making of obedience the sap of life that invigorates" (*Vies des saints*: 54). Despite the archbishop's later conspiracy against her, she carried herself with humility and tenderness, eventually cleared her name, and returned to her post of leadership. In 1638, two years before her death, she wrote her final amendments of the Company's Rules and Constitutions.

Mère Jeanne received into the order two of her daughters, Marthe and Madeleine de Montferrand-Landiras (both of whom pre-deceased her), and even two granddaughters, Jeanne and Françoise de Chartres-d'Arpaillant. Jeanne de Lestonnac died on 2 February 1640, at the age of eighty-four. She was to be beatified in 1900 by the renowned, reforming Pope Leo XIII (1878-1903), with three healing miracles attributed to her during the 19th century being "authenticated". She was canonized on 15 May 1949 by Pius XII (1939-1958), with two more attributed miracles accepted (Boisse: 25). Let us reiterate that she is the only saint who was born, lived and died in Bordeaux. Numerous statues have been erected in her memory, and so it is a little surprising that the one placed in her memory at the Château de Landiras is in fact a representation of the Virgin.[25]

At the death of Jeanne de Lestonnac, there were thirty daughter houses already established in France and the Spanish Netherlands (now Belgium); today, approximately 2000 *Daughters of Mary Our Lady* work and pray in 120 convents scattered over five continents. Five nuns were to be massacred at the French Cape in South Africa in 1793, another guillotined during the Revolution (in 1794), and more recently (1989) another was murdered in Columbia (Boisse: 11). The nuns of the Company work in schools, parishes, Christian movements, and solidarity organizations, where they combat illiteracy and promote human dignity especially for young females ("Sainte-Jeanne de Lestonnac"). A "Sainte Jeanne de Lestonnac School", for example, may be found on Avenida Lestonnac, in Temecula, California.

Saint Jeanne de Lestonnac's order preceded and may have partly inspired two other remarkable female enterprises in the early 17th century. In a close association with Saint Vincent de Paul (1581-1660), who was simultaneously founding the *Congregation of the Priests of the Mission* in 1633, Saint Louise de Marillac (1591-1660) established the *Filles de la Charité* (Daughters of Charity). Like Jeanne de Lestonnac, Louise de Marillac paid special attention to the poor and outcast. This energetic visionary was beatified in 1919 (after Jeanne de Lestonnac) and canonized in 1934 (before Jeanne). Even earlier, at the other side of France, Saint Vincent's friend and colleague, Saint François de Sâles, the so-called bishop of Geneva, had inspired Jeanne-Françoise Frémiot (1572-1641), since 1601 the widowed baroness de Chantal, to found the *Order of the Visitation Saint-Mary* in 1610. Vincent de Paul, who also knew her directly, called her "one of the holiest people I have ever met on this earth" (Attwater, 1983: 180). She was canonized as early as 1767, almost two centuries before her contemporary saints.

For readers who combine their interest in religion with an interest in fine wines, Jeanne de Lestonnac has one other striking association. On 17 June 1540, Louis de Roustaing, seignior of La Tour, sold a small vineyard, known as Le Domaine de La Mission, to Arnaut de Lestonnac, a burgher and merchant of Bordeaux. The purchaser may have been Jeanne de Lestonnac's grandfather, for the Olive de Lestonnac who leased the land on 30 March 1650 to the Lazarist Fathers[26] was Jeanne's cousin ("Château Haut-Brion"). Arnaut de Lestonnac had foreseen the great potential of the wines of Haut-Brion and had promoted their cultivation. His son, Pierre de Lestonnac, and his granddaughter, Olive de Lestonnac (married to Marc-Antoine de Gourgues, an illustrious *premier président* of the Parlement of Bordeaux), carried on his work. The lease of 1650 became an outright sale in 1664, effected by Olive de Lestonnac's heiress, Catherine de Mullet. Over the next several centuries the Lazarist Fathers nurtured the viniculture of the Domaine of the Mission into one of the great wines of France: "Château La Mission Haut-Brion" ("Château Haut-Brion").

The Montferrand-Landiras Maison at the End of the Ancien Régime

The "Ormée de Bordeaux" (1648-1654) was perhaps the most significant side-event of the Parisian and kingdom-wide rebellion known as the Fronde. The well-known event was a chaos of resistance to the person and policies of Cardinal Mazarin, initiated by the Parlement de Paris and then picked up by the prince de Condé and other nobles. But the Ormée was a popular uprising that gave Bordeaux a distinctively republican municipal government for half a decade. What the Montferrand family thought of it can be easily guessed, but I can't find any of them in the narrative. However, Bernard de Nogaret de la Valette, duke d'Épernon (1592; 1642-1661), the Governor of Guyenne and charged by Mazarin to restore order, installed himself in the château de Montferrand in 1649 (Grasset: 110); when in that year the revolt spread outside the city, the château de Montferrand was ravaged (Sarrazin, 1996: 31).

Through their son, François V, Gaston II and Jeanne de Lestonnac had only one grandchild. This Bernard de Montferrand-Landiras followed his father's military career, but really served his dynasty in two other notable ways. In September

---

[25]The outstretched arms, the serpent entwining the feet, and her standing on a globe (representing the world) all suggest that it is a statue of Mary and not of Jeanne. It is the central focus of pilgrimages to the château.

[26]Members of Saint Vincent de Paul's order are often called "Lazarists" because their initial residence had been the Saint Lazarus Priory in Paris.

1651, he obtained the erection of Landiras from a barony into a marquisate (Communay: lxxiv). And in 1660, he inherited the lands and titles of the senior branch of the house of Montferrand, from which Landiras had been separated since the death of Bertrand III around 1446, more than two centuries earlier. The house now once more combined in one branch both the first and the second baronies of Guyenne. The family's destiny being only two more generations of direct male heirs, however, they would not long enjoy these reunited possessions.

The marriage of Bernard de Montferrand-Landiras to Marie-Delphine ("Delphinette") de Pontac in 1646 or '47 was the second time (the marriage to Jeanne de Lestonnac being the first) that our noble house had married into the Parlement de Bordeaux, where Marie-Delphine's father, Geoffrey de Pontac, had been a *president à mortier* (senior judge).[27] It was in fact common for noble families to marry their sons into judicial or commercial urban families, as the rich dowries accompanying such brides often restored financial liquidity to an aristocratic family's estate. (The practice was rather crudely referred to as "manuring one's fields" and was of course preferred to the selling of portions of the estate that we have noted above and are about to see again below.) The two sons of Bernard and Marie-Delphine were in turn to inherit the lands and titles of the Girondin Montferrand family. During the second's (Léon de Montferrand's) tenure, by a decree of the *Conseil d'État*, on 21 April 1705, the charge of *Grand Sénéchal de Guyenne* was declared hereditary in the Montferrand-Landiras line.

Leon's son, François-Armand de Montferrand-Landiras (1704-1761), sold the "Maison Noble de la Mote [*sic*]" in 1750 to the famous *philosophe* Montesquieu, le Baron de la Brède ("Les Seigneurs de Landiras_2").[28] Then, on 28 June 1751, for 60,000 pounds (*livres*), he sold the *hôtel de Montferrand*, on streets (*rues*) Porte-Dijeaux and Margaux in Bordeaux. The proceeds of this sale allowed him to retire debts on the land of Landiras. He was to be the last male of the house, however, for on 2 October 1751, his only son was murdered on the Amboise Bridge by a *sieur* Ouvrard de Matigny.[29] This unfortunate son was Charles-Hyacinthe, captain of a royal regiment and Count (be it noted) of Montferrand.

The lands and titles of the house, by François-Armand de Montferrand-Landiras's last testament, passed to his two nephews, sons of his sister Marie-Catherine de Montferrand, wife of Étienne François de Brassier, *seigneur* de La Marque, Beychevelle, etc., a *conseiller* in the Parelment de Bordeaux, and immensely prosperous producer of wine (Communay: lxxvi; Figéac, 1996: I, 75 & 122). But both of them died without heirs, and the lands and titles—*le marquisat de Landiras, la baronnie de Montferrand*, etc.—passed to the progeny of Delphine de Brassier, *their* sister. In 1745 she had married Michel-Joseph de

La Roque (or Laroque), baron of Budos (d. 1770, at age 50).[30] This Delphine de Brassier-La Roque, was a local socialite, famous for her gaming parties, especially "le brelan" (a card game involving three of a kind). Her 1787 will indicated her intention of bequeathing to her son her *hôtel* in Bordeaux and the *terre* of Beychevelle (Figeac, 1996: I, 284 & II, 68).[31] To this son, François-Armand de La Roque, and Catherine de Ménoire de Barbe a daughter was born. By her marriage in 1814, Catherine Delphine de La Roque Budos (d. 1860) was to bring what was left of a formerly extensive inheritance to Léon de Brivazac, the son of Jean Baptisite Guillaume Léonard de Brivazac, a lawyer (*avocat*).

The French Revolution and After

In the fall of 1788, however, the crisis in royal finances had forced Louis XVI to summon the Estates-General, and every province in France had to hold local assemblies to elect deputies. In almost every province, the assemblies were divided into three sections, according to their "Ordre" (a term not quite equivalent to the modern idea of "social class"; it distinguished function, rather than ownership), with each Ordre, or Estate, meeting and voting separately. Prior to modern attempts to "rationalize" political institutions, it could be a woman who had the right to political participation and electoral recognition, if she were the person solely possessed of the property so enfranchised (the lady/*dame* where there was no lord/*seigneur*); but a male had to represent her in public assembles. And so, in Guyenne, at the General Assembly of the Three Ordres in the winter of 1788-89, Delphine de Brassier, widow of Michel-Joseph de La Roque, baron de Budos, was represented by her son, François-Armand de La Roque, *chevalier* de Budos. As he was also baron de Montferrand and so first baron of Guyenne, he had his own right to participation. Not to lose the family's second vote, *he* was represented in the assembly by his brother, Charles-François-Armand de La Roque (O'Gilvy, 1856: I, 205).[32] The later meeting of the Estates-General in Versailles,

<hr/>

[27]The son of Geoffroy de Pontac, sgr de Salles (d. 1641), and Delphinette's half-brother, Arnaud de Pontac (1600-1681) had been a magistrate in the Parlement since 1632, and was to be a First President from 1653 to 1673 (Dast Le Vacher de Boisville; GeneaNet). Some sources give the son's superior office to the father!

[28]Alternately, after various litigations and sales, the château de la Motte-Saint-André passed by marriage to the Duhumel family, whose daughter Jeanne Thérèse Duhumel (our geneaology shows "Thérèse-Jeanne du Hamel") married François-Armand de Montferrand. The Société archéologique de Bordeaux says the property was sold and divided up in 1742 ("Jacques Besson").

[29]Montferrand whipped a dog which had run under his horse's legs, and the dog's angry owner shot him. Fleeing justice, the culprit was hanged in effigy (Communay: lxxvii; Grasset: 119-20).

[30]The château de Budos was located only a little south of Landiras. Its family traced itself back to the late 13th century, in fact dating its oldest archival record to the same year that Guilliaume Le Templier had put Landiras on the historical record. Much of the Budos-family information (ca. 1790-1820) in the following paragraphs is obtained or confirmed by Bacque (1908: 27-29). Cf. note 64, in Part One.

Within a few more years, the barons of Brivazac came to enjoy the Montferrand-Landiras succession. It should be noted, though, first, that it was from the La Roque-Budos family that the property was confiscated during the French Revolution and, second, that in 1783 Baurein states "M. de Brassier" was "the present seignior" (III, 208). (The "Privilege du Roi" of the first edition is dated 1783, and this statement was not up-dated for our 1876 edition.)

[31]In 1757, her husband had purchased the *seigneurie* of Beychevelle after the death of the last Duke of Épernon and ordered its château demolished, to be replaced by "un corps de logis bas" that dominated the Gironde (Figeac: I, 144). It might be mentioned that the Montferrands had perhaps two connections to the Épernons: in 1587, Jean-Louis de Nogaret de La Valette, later duc d'Épernon (1554; 1581-1642), had married Marguerite de Foix-Candale; when their son Bernard died in 1661, the title was more or less usurped by *his* grandnephew, Jean-Baptiste-Gaston de Goth (1631-1690), the grandson of Jacques de Goth, marquis de Rouillac, and Hélène de Nogaret, the sister of the just mentioned Jean-Louis de Nogaret de La Valette. Further failures of male heirs saw the *seigneurie* pass through the Zamets to the Pardaillon-Gondrins and its eventual sale in 1751. Chenaye Des Bois (1980), vol. IV, tome VII; and "4. Épernon", *Dictionnaire de Biographie française*, vol. XII (1970).

[32]Interestingly, an O'Gilvy, as a member of a "Régiment irlandais", is found in the Ordre de Saint-Michel, admitted in 1763, as a lieutenant at a captain's rank (Colleville: 327).

very soon moved to Paris, did not develop to the taste of many aristocrats and clergy, and they began to leave the country. La Roque-Budos was to be one of these; in fact, he fled France for England as early as 1789.

Immediately after the events of the summer of 1789 (the fall of the Bastille, the law abolishing feudalism, the Declaration of the Rights of Man and Citizen, e.g.), many aristocrats fled France, usually going to Austria or England. These were the strident opponents of the Revolution, but over the next few years, nobles continued to flee, sometimes because they grew to dislike the unfolding of revolutionary events and sometimes because some little or large thing in their appearance, deportment, speech, actions, dress or friendships drew the attention or aroused the suspicions of neighbours or officials. The Terror from July 1793 to July 1794, in particular, justifiably frightened many. Lest Landiras seem far from Paris, let us remember that the moderately radical leaders of the Revolution's Legislative Assembly (October 1791-September 1792) were called the "Girondins" because of the region many of them represented.[33]

By fleeing in the first year of the Revolution, F.-A. de La Roque-Budos, marquis of Landiras (Marion, Benzacar & Caudrillier, 1911: I, 140, #174),[34] escaped the harrowing experiences of so many of his peers. A *chevalier* of the *Ordre of Saint-Louis*, he had been a captain of a company of dragoons, and so perhaps it was natural that he carried on a military career in exile. He was part of an attempted invasion of France in 1792, passed the years 1795-1797 in the Prince de Condé's army, and was to be found in Russia from 1799 to 1801. The following year, he accepted the general amnesty of Napoleon and returned to France. He was to die in Bordeaux in 1825. For his part, Léon de Brivazac, son-in-law of F.-A. de La Roque-Budos, had emigrated to England in 1792. He participated in the ill-fated "Débarquement de Quiberon", a counter-Revolution invasion of Brittany in June-July 1795, and returned to England with the remnants of his royalist regiment (Figéac: I, 473). Brivazac then remained in London until the general amnesty of the *émigrés* in 1802.[35]

Worth mentioning, though I haven't been able to find the reason, just after the regional Assembly had closed, Charles F.-A. de La Roque-Budos fought a duel at Bechwelle[36] on 11 or 14 March 1789, in which he killed André Joseph de Martin du Tyrac de Marcellus (1745-1789), *comte* de Marc. Marcellus was a *lieutenant du roi en Guienne* and a friend of the *comte* de Fumel (then, the royal garrison commander in Bordeaux and in 1790 the mayor of the newly elected revolutionary council—Auerbach, 5). For this occasion, La Roque-Budos is always identified as "frère de [Marguerite de La Roque-Budos] Mme de Saint-Hérem" (Figéac: I, 236, n. 76; "GeneaNet"; and "Duels"). So, political vehemence or family honour?

The Revolutionary and post-Revolutionary fate of individual estates is rarely easy to ascertain. Usually it was the military member of the family who fled and left the supervision of the estates to others, in this case La Roque-Budos's brother,

Charles-François-Armand de La Roque, *chevalier* de Budos. Even so, it was he and his widowed mother themselves who plundered much of the estate, selling off parts for quick cash in April 1793.[37] In the *commune* of Budos itself, it appears that the La Roque de Budos estate was the only noble land to be sold (Figéac: I, 420). F. A. La Roque received an indemnity of 732,210 francs in 1825 for the family's losses and Dumas de La Roque (how related?), 204,545 francs—both among the few still living, so as to be compensated themselves (Figéac: II, 589, Table XC). By 1831, 39.47% of the bordelaise nobility had recovered their 1789 possessions, but in only 15.45% of the cases was ownership in 1789 and 1831 the same (Figeac: II, 465).

This paucity of compensation was certainly not due to lack of loyalty to the Restoration regime. In 1813, La Roque-Budos was part of a pious, royalist group who met by night, and in 1814, he was among the royal troops who assembled on Louis XVIII's behalf in Bordeaux, in an immediately vain attempt to precipitate Napoleon's fall (Figeac: II, 495, 501-502 & 511). In a similar spirit, Léon de Brivazac preceded the Duke of Angoulême (elder son of the future Charles X) as this prince's entourage entered Bordeaux; thereafter he became part of Angoulême's *garde d'honneur*. We could follow the career of his son Léon II Armand de Brivazac and his 1860 marriage to Anne Louise Caroline de Lur-Saluces, but how far has the Budos story taken us from the *seigneurie* of Landiras? We should not forget that the Baron de Brivazac succeeded to the lands, at least to the titles of Landiras, Budos and so on, but what does this really mean?

One of the famous 18th-century maps by Pierre Belleyme, chief topographer at the Archives Nationales, clearly shows the vineyard and château of Landiras in the 1760s. Because a lord might be identified by only one of the several titles in his possession, not to mention his diverse *terres*, it is hard to get a sense of what portion might be indicated in an estimate of anyone's holdings. But the *Documents relatifs à la vente des Biens nationaux* ("Documents concerning the sale of national properties") shows Charles La Roque-Budos, in reference to a "second" confiscation of lands, as possessing Budos, Landiras, St.-Michel-de-Rieufort, and Illats. On 29 Brumaire Year II (19 November 1793),[38] Landiras itself, "château and surrounding land", is measured at 1200 *journaux* and valued at 213,878 *livres*.[39] This land was divided into numbered parcels and sold over the next several months, from at least 4 Nivôse Year II to 26 Ventôse Year III (i.e., 24 December 1793-16 February 1795). At most auctions, the principal buyer was one Jean Amanieu, *dit* Moine, with various members of the Dutrénit family often

---

[33]Indeed, see Stephen Auerbach, "Politics, Protest, and Violence in Revolutionary Bordeaux, 1789-1794", in *Proceedings of the Western Society for French History* (Vol. 37, 2009), and the works he cites.

[34]Note the presentation of his title. The next entry (#175) refers to "Larroque jeune, dit Larroque-La Tour".

[35]As many as 36.03% of the bordelaise nobility became *émigrés*, including four members of the La Roque-Budos family (Figéac: I, 381). And yet the barons de Brassier, along with the Foix-Candale, were among "le plus brillant parvenu" of the opening of the 19th century (Figéac: II, 611).

[36]Is this actually "Beychevelle", one of the La Roque-Budos family estates?

[37]One source says that Landiras was confiscated and demolished early in the Revolution, its stones being used in essential other buildings ("Les Seigneurs de Landiras_2"). The Château de Budos was similarly torn down and left in ruins. So, balancing the assertion that so much Revolutionary dissipation was due to *sans-culottes* excesses, Figéac makes sure we notice what the great families did themselves (I, 449). Thus, the current château de Landiras dates from the early 19th century.

[38]A completely new calendar was among the more sweeping changes inaugurated by the Revolution (metric measurement perhaps being the most notable and enduring). It chose the retroactive date of the adoption of the republican constitution (22 September 1792) as the start of "Year I" and eliminated the names of months honouring Roman gods and emperors in favour of beautiful names reflecting the seasons of the year; but the calendar was terminated at the end of our 1805.

[39]A *journal* (pl. *-aux*) was the amount of land that could be worked in one day. (One of the inventories of the property was dated 6 Ventose Year III of the French Revolution [i.e., 24 February 1795].)

purchasing several sections, as did Joachim Chalup, among others. A hundred years later the best wine produced in the *commune* of Landiras is called "Château-Darricaut", whose owner was the count R. de Chalup! His produce amounted to 15 *tonneaux* (barrels) of red wine and 30 of white (Cocks & Féret, 7th éd., 1898: 338).[40] Obviously, though at least part of the count's property would include land from the ancient *seigneurie* de Landiras, he possessed neither the château itself nor the right to so name his wines.

Each parcel was numbered and described, as for example the following, bought by Amanieu: #26, "maison et 176 r. vigne"; #37, "maison, parc à brebis et 12 j., 25 r. terres, bois et taillis"; and #68, "maison (écroulée) et 2 j. 7r. pins, taillis". Thus, from these examples alone, we can see that Amanieu acquired three "houses" of which one was dilapidated, a sheepfold, a good bit of land and woods and thickets and pines, and 176 "r." of vineyard.[41] Other parcels listed "two rooms", "granges" (barns), and "chais", this last being cool spaces where wine was fermented in barrels. Almost every parcel was described as having a "maison", so one has to wonder what that term really meant? Were there that many domiciled peasant families on the *seigneurie* of Landiras? From another source, it appears that the actual "ruins of the château", as part of a parcel containing 24 ares, 10 cent. (yielding a revenue of 7 *francs*, 35 *centimes*), along with other parcels, were bought by Édouard Louis Perey.[42]

It is not surprising to find that Jeanne de Lestonnac's "Religieuses de Notre Dame" suffered confiscations too. For February 1792, the *Documents relatifs à la vente des Biens nationaux* indicated that in Bordeaux itself the order owned three houses on rue des Etuves, three houses and a convent on the rue du Hâ, and one house on each of the rue du Pas-St-George and rue Ste-Catherine, for a total worth of 116,601 *livres*.[43]

The scholar A. Communay writes that the barons of Brivazac came to enjoy the Montferrand-Landiras legacy, as, indeed, we have seen. The 1814 marriage of Léon de Brivazac, former *émigré*, to Catherine Delphine de La Roque-Budos, the daughter of *émigré* Charles-F.-A. La Roque, proved more fertile, with four children, than any recent marriage of male descendants (Communay: lxxvii; and O'Gilvy: I, 392). Does this mean that

Michel Figeac's statement that the family's property was not restored even as late as 1831 only shows that he did not take heiresses into account (Figeac: I, 465)? In any case, the uncertainties surrounding many details of medieval Landiras seem to return for its history in modern times.

Terroir and Wines

The remarkable work *Bordeaux ses environs et ses vins classés par ordre de mérite* ["The regions around Bordeaux and their wines classified in order of merit"] (sixteen editions between 1850 and 2001) fills in gaps after the middle of the 19th century, however. For each *commune* in the Bordelaise it lists the best wines in their order of merit and gives names of both wine and proprietor and the production volume. The first two editions do not mention "Château de Landiras", but the editions from 1881 on do, and they estimate its quality of wine relative to its neighbours. Alphonse Bordes was the proprietor from at least 1874, when he possessed 86 hectares,[44] into the early 20th century (Féret: II, 445). By 1929 the owner is François Bordes, which suggests single-family possession for over sixty years. In the same period, the nearby village of Landiras suffered a modest decrease in population, from 1735 to 1605 inhabitants.

We do not know when grapevines were first cultivated on the land adjacent to the château of Landiras, or when its seigniors began to pay particular attention to the potential of the *terroir* for quality wine. Would it be in the 16th century, about the same time that Jeanne de Lestonnac's grandfather began to take special care in the cultivation of *his* estates north of the Garonne—earlier, or later? The freezing winter of 1956 destroyed all the vines in the Bordeaux region, and those of the Château de Landiras were only replanted in the 1980s by the renowned Danish wine connoisseur Peter Vinding-Diers. The property of the Château de Landiras today comprises 75 hectares, of which 26 hectares are under "Appellation d'Origine Contrôlée".[45]

We have very little information on the succession of owners in the mid-20th century. The 14th edition (1991) of *Bordeaux... et ses vins* does not mention the Château de Landiras at all. The 1995 edition, however, names Vinding-Diers as the proprietor, judges the quality of the wine seventh out of twenty-eight, prints a picture of the château, and offers the fullest history of the château of any edition (765).[46] According to the 2001 edition, the wine has regained its second-place ranking and a picture of its label is printed. "S.C.A. Dne La Grave" replaces the name of a private proprietor, and the German Maison Sichel has the exclusive rights to market the wine (Boidron & Lemay, 2001, 16th éd.: 771-772 & 2274). The distinguished wine magazine *Decanter*, sampling the 1998 vintage, described the "excellent balance" of its red, to which it awarded four out of five stars, making it one of the best priced wines in its class (*Decanter*, 2002: 40). In late 2002, a short-lived Canadian-Swiss-French partnership acquired the Château de Landiras and undertook to improve the wine's quality still more. In 2007, Michel Pélissié (co-head, with Jean Nouvel, of an architectural

---

[40]Would this be Marie Antoine "Robert" de Chalup (1861-1926), comte de Chalup (a nobility dating back to 1553 in Périgord)? (GeneaNet: "Marie Antoine 'Robert' de Chalup"; Wikipedia "Familles subsistantes de la noblesse française"). There is a "rue de Joachim Chalup" in the village of Landiras.

In 1874, an A. de Chalup produced a wine called "Aux Arricauds"—four barrels of red wine and twenty of white, from 158 hectares (Féret: II, 445).

[41]"J." = journal/journaux, but I can't explicitly unearth what an "r." was. However, it often preceded the word/term "vigne" and vineyards were often measured in "arpents", which, according to the custom of the region, measured 20 to 50 "ares". An "are" was one hundred square metres, a useful measure where small surfaces of land were especially valuable, as in the case of vineyards; a hundred "ares" made up a hectare. I'm inclined to see the "r" as representing the sound "are".

[42]The *Plan cadastraux de Landiras* [land registry/survey], in the Archives Départementales de La Gironde (Annexe), Bordeaux, is a detailed map showing all the numbered parcels of land. The *Cadastre des Matrices* [registry of standards] (*cote* 3P 3) attaches owners' names to these numbers. Numbers 769-828bis compose the property "Château de Landiras". The ruins of the château are located in #791.

I assume that "10 cent." measures ten hundredths of an "are".

[43]Marion et al., *Documents...Biens nationaux* (108. n. 5) states that twenty-three nuns of the choir and five *converses* claimed gross revenues of 15,792 *livres* in 1790, of which 9160 *l.* were net. (*Soeurs converses* did the menial work in a convent and were not part of the *soeurs de choeur*, who concentrated on more spiritual activities).

---

[44]In that year, four "*tonneaux*" of red wine were produced, and eight of white.

[45]The label for a 2009 vintage has reduced these recent figures to 70 hectares, of which 20 are under cultivation, 15 of red wine and 5 of white. A hectare is a metric measurement of land, equal to 2471 acres or 10,000 square metres. An acre is a traditional measurement of land, equivalent to 4840 sq. yards.

[46]The 14th edition is written-compiled by Édouard Féret, Claude Féret, and Marc-Henry Lemay; and the 15th by Lemay alone.

group), acquired the Château de Landiras. He had earlier, in 1997, purchased "Château Maison Noble", at St-Martin-du-Puy in the Entre-Deux-Mers. With the assistance of François Puerta, Pélissié is continuing to restore the quality of the wine and its reputation.

Conclusion

The château de Landiras, though its wines, can easily echo its previous renown, so long as the property has continuing ownership, sufficient capitalization, and dedicated management. Its glorious history is doubtlessly a thing of the past, but what a legacy! Several archbishops of Bordeaux, *perhaps* a Crusading knight, feudal magnates rubbing shoulders with kings of two countries over several centuries, some marriages into families of magistrates in the Parlement de Bordeaux and at least one mayor of the city, marital associations with both English and French royalty and with the celebrated essayist Michel de Montaigne, and the direct presence for three decades of a devout wife and mother who went on to found a remarkable religious order and eventually to be recognized as a saint. At all these points, the barons of Landiras made a modest contribution to history. Less often noticed, however, is the significance of the impetuous temper of Pierre II de Montferrand-Landiras, whose instigation of the ill-fated English expedition under John Talbot brought a dramatic anticlimax to an already expired Hundred Years' War. Could one describe as "similar" the unfortunate experiences of the barons of Montferrand-Landiras during the French Revolution? In all these ways, the Château de Landiras and its seigniors have played significant roles throughout the High and Later Middle Ages and beyond. To combine all these associations with a quality wine is certainly not unique, but remains nonetheless rare.

Acknowledgements

The author wishes to thank the Discretionary Grant Program, Research and Innovation Committee, of the University of Winnipeg (Winnipeg, Manitoba, Canada), for generously agreeing to fund the publication of these articles. He is also most grateful to Marshall Bailey and Kathleen Sweeney for their making possible the research trip to Bordeaux.

REFERENCES

Anselme, P. [Pierre Guibours] (1967). *Histoire généalogique et chronologique de la maison royale de France, des pairs, grands officiers de la Couronne et de la maison du roi et des anciens barons du royaume*. Paris: Libraires Associez, 1726-1733; New York: Johnson Reprint.

Attwater, D. (1983). Jeanne de Lestonnac. In *The Penguin Dictionary of Saints* (2nd ed.). Penguin.

Auerbach, S. (2009). Politics, protest, and violence in Revolutionary Bordeaux, 1789-1794. *Proceedings of the Western Society for French History, 37*, 149-61.

Bacque, L. (1908). *Histoire de Budos*. Bordeaux: F. Pech.

Bailey, D. A. (2006). Les mystères de la maison des Grailly-Foix-Candale. *Revue de Pau et du Béarn, 33*, 29-41.

Baurein, A. J. (1876). *Variétés bordeloises (1784-86)*. Bordeaux, Féret et Fils.

Boidron, B., & Lemay, M.-H. (2001). *Bordeaux: Ses environs et ses vins classés par ordre de mérite* (16e éd.). Bordeaux: Féret et Fils. Cf. Cocks, Charles.

Boisse, S. C. de. et al. (1999). *Jeanne de Lestonnac 1556-1640 (Dossier historiques et présentation de l'Ordre)*. Christ Source de Vie, No 364 (Avril).

Cadastre des Matrices (cote 3P 3). Archives Départementaux de La Gironde (Annexe), Bordeaux.

Château de Landiras. An Alan Website. Accessed 9 April 2003. http://www.chateaulandiras.com

Château Haut-Brion. http://haut-brion.com/mission/histoires/vincent-fr.htm

Chenaye des Bois, François Aubert de La (1980). *Dictionnaire de la Noblesse* (3rd ed., 1864). Vol. IV. Paris: Berger-Levrault.

Cocks, C., et al. (1984). *Bordeaux ses environs et ses vins classés par ordre de mérite*. Bordeaux: Féret et Fils.

Colleville, [Ludovic], le comte de, et SAINT-CHRISTO, François (n.d.). *Les Ordres du Roi...Ordres royaux militaires et chevaleresques...de 1099 à 1830*. Paris: chez Jouve & Cie.

Communay, A. (1889). *Essai généalogique sur les Montferrand de Guyenne, suivi de pièces justificatives*. Bordeaux: Vve Moquet.

Coulson, J. (1964). *Dictionnaire historique des saints*, trans. Bernard Noël. Paris: Société d'édition de dictionnaires et encyclopédies.

Dast le Vacher de Boisville, J. N. (1896). *Liste générale et alphabétique des membres du Parlement de Bordeaux depuis... 1462 jusqu'à... 1790*. Bordeaux: G. Gounouilhou.

Decanter. October 2002.

D.N.B. = Dictionary of National Biography (1885-1900). Vol. IV.

Dictionnaire de Biographie française, XII (1970). Paris: Letouzey.

Duels. Accessed 13 March 2013. www.tournemire.net/Duels.htm

Féret, É. (1874). *Statistique générale...du département de la Gironde*. Vol. II. Paris: G. Masson; Bordeaux: Féret et Fils.

Féret, É. (1889). *Statistique générale...du département de la Gironde*. Vol. III. *Première partie, Biographie*. Paris: G. Masson; Bordeaux: Féret et Fils.

Figeac, M. (1996). *Destins de la noblesse bordelaise (1770-1830)*. Bordeaux: Fédération historique du Sud-Ouest. 2 Vols.

Garric, A. (n.d.). Léon Armand de Brivazac. *Essai de Généalogie*.

GeneaNet. Marie Antoine "Robert" de Chalup. Accessed 8 March 2013. http://gw4.geneanet.org/charleseric?lang=fr;p=marie+antoine+robert;n=de+chalup

Grasset, J. P., Jean, Ph., & Pastureau, J. L. (n.d.; 1981?). *Le Pays de Montferrand des origines à la Révolution; ou Essai d'histoire locale...* Bordeaux: G.G.E.L.E.P.

Informations Généalogiques. Accessed 2 January 2013. http://www.genealogie33.org/pduc/dat79.htm#19

Jacques Besson. Accessed 7 March 2013. http://www.societe-archeologique-bordeaux.fr/publications/46-jacques-besson.html

La Maison d'Albret. Ascendance d'Henri IV. www.de-bric-et-de-broc.com/France/albret.html

Lemay (1995). *Bordeaux...et ses vins*. See Boidron.

Marion, M[arcel]. Benzacar, J., & Caudrillier, [Gustaaf], eds. (1911-1912). *Documents relatifs à la vente des Biens nationaux. Département de la Gironde*, Vol. I. Bordeaux: Y. Cadoret.

Montferrand. Accessed 3 December 2002. http://perso.club-internet.fr/driout/MONTFERRAND.htm

O'Gilvy, M. (1856-). *Nobiliaire de Guyenne et de Gascogne; Revue des familles d'ancienne chevalerie ou anoblies de ces provinces, antérieures à 1789, avec leur généalogies et armes*. Bordeaux: G. Gounouilhou.

Petit-Dutaillis, Ch[arles]. (1902). Charles VII, Louis XI et les premières années de Charles VIII (1422-1492). Tome 4e, Partie II. In *Histoire de France depuis les origines jusqu'à la Révolution*. (Ernest Lavisse, éd. gén.). Paris: Librairie Hachette.

Plan Cadastraux de Landiras. Archives départementaux de la Gironde (Annexe), Bordeaux.

Ribadieu, H. (1990). *Histoire de la conquête de la Guyenne par les Français*. Pessac (Gironde): Princi Negre.

Sainte-Jeanne de Lestonnac. Innumerable web sites hit by these words.

Sainte-Jeanne de Lestonnac. An Alan Website. Accessed at 9 April 2003. For other information, the websites end in <.../JeanneEnfance>,

<.../JeanneMarriage>, <.../JeanneMort>.
    http://www.chateaulandiras.com/JeanneCompagnie.html
Sarrazin, H. (1996). *La Fronde en Gironde; L'Ormée: Un mouvement
    révolutionnaire, 1648-1654*. Bordeaux: Les Dossiers d'Aquitaine.
Les Seigneurs de Landiras_1, Comité historique de Landiras. Internet
    source. Accessed 2 January 2013 and since.

Les Seigneurs de Landiras_2, Comité historique de Landiras. Internet
    source. Accessed 5 January 2013 and since.
Vies des saints et des bienheureux selon l'ordre du calendrier... (1950).
    Par les RR. PP. Bénédictins de Paris. Paris: Letouzey et Ané. Vol. II.

12

Book Review on *Pakistan and the New Nuclear Taboo*: *Regional Deterrence and the International Arms Control Regime*[*]

Zafar Khan

Department of Politics & International Studies, University of Hull, Kingston upon Hull, UK

Pakistan has always been the focus of international community, strategists, analysts, and academic scholars on various issues more especially on the nuclear issue since Pakistan has embarked its journey from covert to overt nuclearisation of South Asia. Any work in relation to Pakistan's nuclear weapons program ranging from its nuclear policy to its nuclear security has gained a great significance in the realm of politics and international studies. Rizwana Abbasi's maiden volume entitled, *Pakistan and the New Nuclear Taboo*: *Regional Deterrence and the International Arms Control Regime* is a welcome contribution that would certainly be embraced by the Pakistani security planners and strategic community in general and the wider international audience in particular.

Many volumes have already been written on Pakistan's nuclear weapons program, which largely focus on how and why Pakistan went nuclear deliberating mainly on a realist paradigm. The previous volumes, if not substantially, speak little how Pakistan's nuclear behaviour is influenced by the global non-proliferation regime; why the international community failed to prevent Pakistan's nuclear behaviour in terms of its acquisition of nuclear weapons for military purposes; and how the behaviour of nuclear states can better be regulated in the future through international institutions and cooperation. This volume does all of these three essentials in the light of regime theory bolstered with a three-model theoretical approach, that is, looking substantially and observing closely Pakistan's covert and overt nuclear behaviour through the lens of realism, neo-liberalism, and constructivism.

The key aim of this book is that norms, values, and regime still matter despite the presence and influence of hard core realism and neo-realism. Rizwana says, "The aim is to enhance the role of international institutions in changing states' behaviour in order to reduce the risk of nuclear proliferation to as close to zero as possible (p. 36)." That said, she elaborates Pakistan's nuclear behaviour on the basis of a three-model theoretical bases and claims that it is the amalgamation of all these acknowledged theoretical explanations, Pakistan's nuclear behaviour can best be elaborated and understood. However, she emphasises more on the neo-liberal and constructivist argument of cooperation locating Pakistan's position, its commitment, and concerns to the formation, expansion, and sustenance of the non-proliferation regime despite a non-member nuclear weapon state.

[*]Rizwana Abbasi, *Pakistan and the New Nuclear Taboo*: *Regional Deterrence and the International Arms Control Regime*. Oxford, New York, and Bern, Switzerland: Peter Lang, 2012, p. 355, ISBN 978-3-0343-0272-2.

Chapter 1 (pp. 37-79) mainly focuses on the regime theory elaborating mainly the three school of thoughts each with its own significance. Deriving largely the works of Nina Tannenwald and T.V Paul on "nuclear taboo", Rizwana acknowledges and gives equal credence to "nuclear taboo", thereby, introduces "new nuclear taboo" emphasising the rule of both state and international institutions to hamper nuclear proliferation both at its horizontal and vertical levels. Due to nuclear taboo, a normative posture, nuclear weapons have not been used since 1946 to present (p. 58) and norms and cooperation have helped develop and strengthen institutions over the period of time (p. 79).

Under the banner of a three-model theoretical explanation, Chapters 2 and 3 (pp. 81-176) fundamentally observe Pakistan's nuclear behaviour of its pre and post acquisition of nuclear weapons capability. It is interesting to see, as substantially elaborated, that Pakistan's supported the international norms, values and cooperated with the international community in the formation of the non-proliferation regime. However, its normative posture towards the NPT regime reverses to a strategic position when Pakistan's security interest was threatened and the international community failed to prevent Pakistan's adversary to go nuclear. Norms, values and taboo are generally ignored when it comes to national security interest (p. 113). Pakistan's acquisition of nuclear weapons, in a realist paradigm, is read and understood to be security-oriented and adversarial-centric (p. 177). However, these weapons are not used post-acquisition and covert-nuclearisation of South Asia indicating the role of norms, values, and taboo of nuclear weapon in which the rule of international community particularly of the US intervention mattered (p. 153).

Chapters 4 and 5 (pp. 179-248) are basically the exposure of loopholes and weakness in the export and import of nuclear related technology both at the state level (Pakistan) and international level (the NPT regime). Even though Pakistani government denies its involvement on the A. Q. Khan's illegitimate nuclear activities to Iran, Libya, and North Korea, the volume contends, based on reliable sources, that "... Khan's behaviour was ultimately the responsibility of the state due to lack of stringent instituted export controls... (p. 208)." Khan's illegal transfer of nuclear technology remained a wake-up call for Pakistan in general institutionalising its nuclear weapon program and for the global community (committed to non-proliferation) in particular towards developing and strengthening export controls and the nuclear taboo related norms. Rizwana names this Pakistani effort a "new nuclear taboo" (p. 228) which she further calls the "first step in strengthening the counter- proliferation regime (p. 250)."

There has recently been an arms race in South Asia. Given the strength of the book, one could still expect author to provide a substantial and philosophical account on the creation of Arms Control Regime (ACR) in South Asia between the two nuclear rivals to suffice the book title. Amidst the absence of ACR, how Rizwana's stance of new nuclear taboo could help build this regime to prevent the danger of unwanted escalations. The book is silent on this. Nevertheless, it is certainly a value-added to the literature of nuclear studies and can highly be recommended.

13

Russell's Bismarck: Acquaintance Theory and Historical Distance

Thomas Aiello

Department of History, Valdosta State University, Valdosta, USA

The role of acquaintance in Bertrand Russell's theory of descriptions is antithetical and, indeed, antagonistic toward the practice and assumptions of history. In his 1910 paper "Knowledge by Acquaintance and Knowledge by Description," Russell attempts to reconcile direct acquaintance (or its inability to determine the personal self of others) with a descriptive knowledge that is both logical and personal. Russell tries to reconcile the internal and external worlds, attempting to explain access to impersonal knowledge inside a framework that doesn't allow acquaintance with physical objects—he distorts the historical space between researcher and subject. In so doing, he argues for the superiority of acquaintance as an arbiter of knowledge, narrowly avoiding solipsism and wrongly devaluing the most basic of historiograhpical assumptions. His conception creates false historical goals and distorts the space of historical distance, illustrated in this paper through the American slavery studies of Herbert Aptheker, Stanley Elkins, and Kenneth Stampp.

Keywords: Bismarck; Russell; Acquaintance; Description; Aptheker; Elkins; Stampp

Introduction

None can know Bismarck like Bismarck can know Bismarck. In his 1910 paper "Knowledge by Acquaintance and Knowledge by Description," Russell attempts to reconcile direct acquaintance (or its inability to determine the personal self of others) with a descriptive knowledge that is both logical and personal. Russell tries to reconcile the internal and external worlds, attempting to explain access to impersonal knowledge inside a framework that doesn't allow acquaintance with physical objects—he distorts the historical space between researcher and subject. In so doing, he argues for the superiority of acquaintance as an arbiter of knowledge, narrowly avoiding solipsism and wrongly devaluing the most basic of historiographical assumptions. The role of acquaintance in Bertrand Russell's theory of descriptions is antithetical and, indeed, antagonistic toward the practice and assumptions of history, leaving the descriptive knowledge of historians ancillary, sitting quietly in some kind of cosmic second place. His conception creates false historical goals and distorts the space of historical distance, illustrated in this paper through the American slavery studies of Herbert Aptheker, Stanley Elkins, and Kenneth Stampp.

Russell was a public intellectual and political activist for much of his long life, but when he presented his 1910 paper before London's Aristotelian Society, his principal project remained the application of logical analysis to philosophy. Russell's *Principia mathematica* was at Cambridge University Press, awaiting publication[1]. His speeches and published papers defended an atomistic worldview against the assaults of British Idealism. The reference to Bismarck in "Knowledge by Acquaintance and Knowledge by Description" extends only through a few brief pages, but the illustration grounds the article and encapsulates its argument[2].

Descriptions and Acquaintance

Russell's reference to Bismarck illustrates his contention that proper names are descriptions. "The thought in the mind of a person using a proper name correctly can generally only be expressed explicitly if we replace the proper name by a description." (Russell, 1911). He assumes for the sake of the illustration that direct acquaintance with the personal self is possible, but an outside observer attempting to know that self can only access it through description. "If a person who knew Bismarck made a judgment about him," writes Russell, "what this person was acquainted with were certain sense-data which he connected… with Bismarck's body." (Russell, 1911). References to Bismarck rest on descriptions, and those descriptions rest on a direct acquaintance to some aspect of historical knowledge. Descriptions allow functional evaluations of Bismarck, getting the evaluator as close to Bismarck's direct acquaintance with himself as is possible. But "in this we are necessarily defeated, since the actual Bismarck is unknown to us." (Russell, 1911). While each description is subjective and different, the fact of Bismarck's acquaintance with himself grounds each attempt and allows communication about him. "What enables us to communicate in spite of the varying descriptions we employ is

---

[1] Russell's long life lasted from 1872-1970. *Principia mathematica* appeared in three volumes from 1911-1913.

[2] The essay first appeared in print in January 1918 in the book *Mysticism and Logic*, an unorthodox collection of popular philosophical and more technically analytic. "Knowledge by Acquaintance and Knowledge by Description" is among the latter. Ray Monk, *Bertrand Russell: The Spirit of Solitude*, 1872-1921 (New York: The Free Press, 1996), 519-520. Monk's account provides a strong biographical account of Russell's early life. For more biographical information on Russell, see Ray Monk, *Bertrand Russell The Ghost of Madness*, 1921-1970 (New York: The Free Press, 2000); and Ronald W. Clark, *The Life of Bertrand Russell* (New York: Alfred A. Knopf, 1976).

that we know there is a true proposition concerning the actual Bismarck, and that, however we may vary the description (so long as the description is correct), the proposition described is still the same." (Russell, 1911). Acquaintances facilitate descriptions, and descriptions facilitate communication.

Acquaintance, for Russell, is "a direct cognitive relation" of a subject to an object—"the converse of the relation of object and subject which constitutes presentation." (Russell, 1911). Particular sense-data and universal concepts are objects of acquaintance, physical objects and other people's minds are known by description. When a proper name is described, the description is direct. But even in this description acquaintance is necessary. Russell's logical description of a proposition such as "Bismarck is mortal" is $(\exists x)(Bx \& (y)(By \cdot y = x) \& Mx)$[3]. The value any one evaluator places on B (here standing in for "Bismarck"), however, still rests on his or her acquaintance with certain facts about B. So, while description serves to supplement acquaintance with, say, Bismarck's mind, it depends on personally selected historical knowledge about Bismarck—individual acquaintance with some set of facts.

This is indirect access to Bismarck's personal entities. As described by Cora Diamond, "Bismarck, using words that he alone can understand, can reach by the straight road of acquaintance what we can get to only by side-roads, by descriptions." (Diamond, 2000). Russell, however, clearly states that the destination we reach through "side-roads" is not equivalent to Bismarck's direct acquaintance. Though "we often *intend* to make our statement, not in the form involving the description, but about the actual thing described... we are necessarily defeated." (Russell, 1911). If direct acquaintance with Bismarck's self—the relation that is the goal of description—belongs only to Bismarck, and statements about Bismarck reached by description are different than their goal (and can never get there anyway), then either the value of description is compromised or the original direct acquaintance with the self must not be the goal of that description. For Russell, getting close counts, but he never explains what that closeness gives in relation to the original goal. The proposition "which is described and is known to be true, is what interests us," he writes, "but we are not acquainted with the proposition itself, and do not know *it*, though we know it is true." (Russell, 1911).

Russell's potential descriptors attempt to arrive at the knowledge Bismarck has—a perfect knowledge of the self, or something approximate to it—because he has an acquaintance with himself that others do not have. "It is," Russell argues, "very much a matter of chance which characteristics of a man's appearance will come into a friend's mind when he thinks of him; thus the description actually in the friend's mind is accidental. The essential point is that he knows that the various descriptions all apply to the same entity, in spite of not being acquainted with the entity in question." (Russell, 1911). In 1910, there were plenty of people who could have known the living Bismarck and based their knowledge of him on direct acquaintances with the leader. Bismarck for everyone else—those in 1910 without contact and those in 2013 learning through the words of books and professors—can only be known through acquaintance with propositions, which appears farther from Bismarck's knowledge than the friend making "accidental" descriptions. But Russell notes, "We may know that the

so-and-so exists when we are not acquainted with any object which we know to be the so-and-so, and even when we are not acquainted with any object which in fact is the so-and-so." (Russell, 1911). He also describes the distance from Bismarck himself, the "various stages" of removal: "There is Bismarck to people who knew him, Bismarck to those who only know of him through history, the man in the iron mask, the longest-lived of men." (Russell, 1911). The farther we are from the self of Bismarck, the less access we have to the world of Bismarck.

Acquaintance and History

By subordinating distanced knowledge to a direct acquaintance, and by making every description dependent upon some form of personal acquaintance, Russell devalues historical knowledge. If we constantly talk past each other due to various acquaintances with proper names such as "Bismarck," how are we to reconcile statements such as this one made by historian Lothar Gall? "The Reich as created by Bismarck had not only narrowed the historical possibilities for the German nation; it had deformed the nation itself and in so doing had as it were perpetuated itself in its negative consequences." (Gall, 1986). And how far is this statement from Bismarck himself? Does Gall's career of research on the Chancellor still fall short of the personal contact of, say, Baron von Stumm-Halberg or Wilhelm von Kardorff? Could either of them have drawn this conclusion? It bears repeating that Russell posits knowledge by description, a series of those removed acquaintances, as the only method by which one could know Bismarck. But by making that knowledge subservient to a quest for the mind of Bismarck, he sells short the independent value of that description. "Knowledge concerning what is known by description is ultimately reducible to knowledge concerning what is known by acquaintance." (Russell, 1911). This is not the verificationism of Rudolph Carnap, but it sounds like it. Russell makes all understanding dependent on acquaintance with particular sense-data, but the use of the original acquaintance in direct descriptions to represent an entity that can never be known the way the descriptor intends to know it gives Russell's acquaintance theory less surety than logical positivism. He tells us *that* we can know, and *how* to know, but he never tells us *what* we can know—the value of a knowledge filtered through acquaintances and descriptions in relation to the self-acquaintance of our actual subject. Portraying that knowledge as "good enough" does not seem to be good enough.

Referring to Bismarck's reference to himself, Russell notes, "Here the proper name has the direct use which it always wishes to have, as simply standing for a certain object, and not for a description of the object. But if a person who knew Bismarck made a judgment about him, the case is different." (Russell, 1911). Herein lies another inconsistency. Any proposition posited by a distanced evaluator contains only a proper name, and the proper name is a representative of a collection of facts with which the evaluator is directly acquainted. Bismarck the historical actor is not in the impersonal proposition. "Historical actor" itself is simply a possible element to be directly described by the proper name "Bismarck." In other words, each reference to Bismarck in the proposition is an opportunity for potential acquaintances. How can Bismarck's acquaintance with the self be held as the goal of descriptive propositions if such an entity as a self-acquainting Bismarck no longer exists and cannot even be found in language? Russell might respond that

---

[3]Generally translated: There exists an x. x is Bismarck. [If y is Bismarck, then y equals x. (All instances of Bismarck are instances of x.)] x is mortal.

since the bases of every description are direct acquaintances, which lend access to knowledge of the world, and since (in this example) people can have direct acquaintance with the self, then both Bismarck and his self-acquaintance are justly assumed. After all, the theory of descriptions was intended as a method of giving individuals access to knowledge of the world not based on direct experience. But Russell's response would be insufficient, as any direct acquaintance that acts as an element of the direct description "Bismarck"—such as, to use one of Russell's examples, "Bismarck was the first Chancellor of the German Empire"—finds the proper name embedded in the proposition. (Russell, 1911). We are left farther and farther from the knowledge of the intended target with each new proposition attempting to posit that knowledge. No history book, for example, could possibly render a presentation of the first Chancellor of the German Empire without including a proper name. "We can only be assured," he argues, "of the truth of our judgment in virtue of something with which we are acquainted—usually a testimony heard or read." (Russell, 1911). Even if it is taken for granted that the history book's Bismarck is equivalent to the dinner conversation's Bismarck (which perhaps is allowing too much, anyway), it remains a proper name, a stand in for another conglomeration of direct acquaintances, all of which will hinge on the inclusion of the referent's proper name.

Solipsism and Knowledge

For Russell, the theory of descriptions circumvented possible charges of solipsism in acquaintance theory by granting access to knowledge of the outside world. As Cora Diamond paraphrases Russell's arguments in "Knowledge by Acquaintance and Knowledge by Description" and other works of the early 1910s, "the limits of *the* world, about which I can have knowledge, and the objects in which I can denote (whether directly or in some cases only indirectly), lie outside the limits of the realm of my own experience." (Diamond, 2000). But Russell ties everything that can be known to a series of acquaintances, wholly within "the realm of my own experience." Prior to his Bismarck illustration, but in the same paper, Russell notes that physical objects and other people's minds are not "among the objects with which we are acquainted." (Russell, 1911). If our knowledge is dependent on acquaintance with sense data (only cognized at the point in which it comes into contact with our senses, within the realm of personal experience), and that sense data is in aid of grasping truths (such as Bismarck's self awareness) that we can never know, how valid is the knowledge that lies between these two poles? It seems that Russell is masking solipsism, rather than arguing against it. If that knowledge is "indirect," can it be considered whole? Or, perhaps, can it be considered equivalent to *direct* knowledge that we cannot have? Russell does not answer these questions. Nor does he give a firm account of how these two forms of knowledge are cognitively related. The primacy of acquaintance makes even direct descriptions suspect, because in evaluating the logical description of, say, "Bismarck," any evaluator must have direct acquaintances for evidence of B (and those acquaintances will be unique to the evaluator, anyway). "We know that there is an object B called Bismarck," writes Russell, "and that B was an astute diplomatist. We can thus *describe* the proposition we should like to affirm, namely, 'B was an astute diplomatist,' where B is the object which was Bismarck." (Russell, 1911).

Any evaluator of that description will again come to B through a unique set of acquaintances.

That uniqueness—that personalness that characterizes individual acquaintance—does not, for Russell, preclude agreed upon knowledge. "Let us assume that we think of [Bismarck] as 'the first Chancellor of the German Empire.' Here all the words are abstract except 'German.' The word 'German' will again have different meanings for different people. To some it will recall travels in Germany, to some the look of Germany on the map, and so on. But if we are to obtain a description which we know to be applicable, we shall be compelled, at some point, to bring in a reference to a particular with which we are acquainted." (Russell, 1911). Clearly, however, Germany's shape—its border—is a valid particular, and when one participant in communication understands "German" as, "a human within the designated border of Germany," and another assumes, "descendant of the various former Saxon kingdoms," then that communication is not direct. We are constantly talking past each other. But, for Russell, the fact of Bismarck's own self-acquaintance, his existence, makes indirect knowledge—these close approximations to specific agreement—valid. Even if this state of affairs was acceptable, it does not coincide with Russell's theory of descriptions, the goal of which was clarity and specificity. Furthermore, any statement about Bismarck indirectly references Bismarck's personal knowledge, what Diamond calls his "private object." "The quantified proposition," as Diamond notes, "*follows from* Bismarck's private proposition." (Diamond, 2000). This relation between a distanced description (the "quantified proposition") and Bismarck's personal knowledge demonstrates, for Russell, the benefit in the attempt. But even the interpretation of the logic of direct description rests on personal judgments about what sort of knowledge we have about an object we can never truly know (to use the aforementioned example, B), so the relation between the distanced and the personal is constantly changing.

At first glance, this emphasis on the personal can sound like psychologism, and some psycho-historical compromise between acquaintance theory and, say, traditional history or sociology, which claim to know individuals better than they know themselves, would seem appropriate. But Russell was just as disdainful of psychologism in logical formulation as was his predecessor Gottlob Frege. Frege not only sought to corral psychologism, but, like Russell, tried to define away subjectivity in knowledge. His 1892 "On *Sinn* and *Bedeutung*" describes a "common store of thoughts," which humans share "from one generation to another."[4] (Frege, 1892). He would, twenty-six years later, develop his notion of thought further—its objectivity and residence in "a third realm"—explaining that it is independent of subjectivity, "timelessly true, true independently of whether anyone takes it to be true." (Frege, 1918). Thoughts, for Frege, are the mental entities the whole has acknowledged as true, independent of what individuals think about them. What individuals think about them—ideas—act as agents of access from the mind to the outside thought. Thus, thought is objective, and ideas only serve as mediating devices *to* thought, never *from* it. Sense, too, is objective, certainly a more difficult argument to validate considering that it initially seems to stem

---

[4]*Sinn* translates as "sense." *Bedeutung* generally translates as "reference," because "reference" is the closest functional match, but *bedeutung* carries a linguistic weight unequalled by "reference," and so here is retained in the original German. It is also retained in editor Michael Beany's *The Frege Reader*, whose translation was used in this study.

from the interpretation of individual minds—the places from which ideas connect to thought. "The same sense is not always connected," Frege notes, "even in the same man, with the same idea. The idea is subjective." (Frege, 1892). This, however, only hints at what Frege expressed more clearly other places. "The sense of the name," he noted in a 1914 letter to Philip Jourdain, "is part of the thought." (Frege, 1914). If thoughts are found entities—if they are independent of mental creation, simply discovered and agreed upon by those who acknowledge axioms and laws—then the functional display of thought (perhaps not its third realm existence, but surely its useful existence in mind and discourse) is predicated on combinations of senses, which facilitate specificity in meaning. "Without a *Bedeutung*," Frege noted in his 1914 letter, "we could indeed have a thought, but… not a thought that could further scientific knowledge. Without a sense, we would have no thought, and hence also nothing that we could recognize as true." (Frege, 1914).

Acquaintance Theory and Its Role in Slave Histories

Sense and *Bedeutung* helped Frege remove any lurking psychologism, an attempt most historians choose not to make. But psycho-historical models are fraught with difficulties of their own. Historian Kenneth Stampp elaborated an effective critique of historical psychologism and verificationism in the description of American slavery in his 1971 "Rebels and Sambos: The Search for the Negro's Personality in Slavery." (Stampp, 1971). Like Russell and Frege, he tries to carve a middle ground that accounts for knowledge, description, and acquaintance. He criticizes the analysis of historian Herbert Aptheker, who described slaves as active participants in the culture of revolution perpetuated by slave life, as flawed for its childlike faith in the limited source material available. Aptheker's *American Negro Slave Revolts* claimed to have found almost two hundred fifty slave revolts and conspiracies for freedom, each including at least ten slaves. Stampp notes that while white fear and supposition of revolt mean something about slave culture, they do not necessarily mean revolt. By only countenancing written records as absolute proof (and subsequently ignoring bias, literacy rates, etc.), Aptheker skewed historical reality to create of the American slave a perpetually rebelling agent. (Stampp, 1971; Aptheker, 1943) Stampp also critiques historian Stanley Elkins's use of role theory psychoanalysis in evaluations of slave life. Elkins argued that the closed society of North American slavery and the single significance of the master/slave relationship conspired to create a childlike subservience in slaves that kept them docile and impotent, a personality he labeled "Sambo." The mistakes of his argument lie at the polar extreme from those of Aptheker. Elkins applied psychoanalytic models to an assumed group, without first evaluating the historical record to see if his various theoretical models effectively mapped on to the condition of the American slave. Stampp responds by warning of both the danger of applying psychoanalytic categories to historical groups and the contingency of comparative history without primary document research. (Stampp, 1971; Elkins, 1959). Where Aptheker practiced a tunnel-vision empiricism without a rigorous critical examination, Elkins applied critical theory to a subject he had yet to empirically evaluate. It should be acknowledged, however, that Stampp was no Russellian, and did acknowledge the validity of psychology, speech pathology, and other alternative interpretive methods in historical research[5].

(Feinberg & Kasrils, 1983) More importantly, in delineating this middle ground, Stampp never abandoned the general historical contention that proper analysis of documents and source material could lead to an understanding of slavery more complete than any slave or slavemaster could have held. Distanced knowledge was not subordinate. Propositions could render agreed upon knowledge without direct acquaintance.

For Russell, "*Every proposition which we can understand must be composed wholly of constituents with which we are acquainted.*" (Russell, 1911). Those acquaintances create logical propositions that stand in logical relation to other logical propositions. For Diamond, "*If I can take a sentence to stand in logical relations to other sentences, then I can understand that sentence.*" (Diamond, 2000). So interpreters can understand sentences about Bismarck, but that understanding will still contain an element of the personal. "Considered psychologically, apart from the information we convey to others, apart from the fact about the actual Bismarck, which gives importance to our judgment," writes Russell, "the thought we really have contains the one or more particulars involved, and otherwise consists wholly of concepts." (Russell, 1911). Those particulars, it should be remembered, are not physical objects. They are sense data, conveyed by logical propositions. In logic, however, "where we are concerned not merely with what does exist, but with whatever might or could exist or be, no reference to actual particulars is involved." (Russell, 1911). Why is a method unconcerned with particulars used to convey particulars in aid of knowledge of the external world? If an evaluator has logic and Bismarck has self-acquaintance, why is that self-acquaintance held as the goal of inquiry? How can these be considered functionally equal? Perhaps the best counter to the problems of Russell's Bismarck was offered by Frege in 1918:

> Not everything that can be the object of my acquaintance is an idea. I, as owner of ideas, am not myself an idea. Nothing now stops me from acknowledging other men to be the owners of ideas, just as I am myself. And, once given the possibility, the probability is very great, so great that it is in my opinion no longer distinguishable from certainty. Would there be a science of history otherwise? Would not all moral theory, all law, otherwise collapse? What would be left of religion? The natural sciences too could only be assessed as fables like astrology and alchemy. Thus the reflections I have set forth on the assumption that there are other men besides myself, who can make the same thing the object of their consideration, their thinking, remain in force without any essential weakening (Frege, 1918).

Russell's illustration, however, weakens. It leaves many questions unanswered as it attempts to reconcile the internal and external worlds—as he tries to have it both ways in attempting to explain access to impersonal knowledge inside a framework that doesn't allow acquaintance with physical objects. But he cannot have it both ways.

---

[5]Russell, in turn, was no Stamppian. He did, however, later in his life, provide his own evaluation on slavery, though far less nuanced than that of his historian counterparts. Speaking at the Civil Rights Freedom March, 28 August 1963, in Washington DC, Russell declared, "The treatment of the American Negro is an atrocity which has a history of three hundred years in what is now the Untied States of America… He has suffered an experience of systematic terror in which he could, and indeed can today in many parts of the Untied States, be shot down at will." (Feinberg & Kasrils, 1983).

REFERENCES

Aptheker, H. (1943). *American negro slave revolts*. New York: Columbia University Press.

Diamond, C. (2000). Does Bismarck have a beetle in his box? The private language argument in the *Tractatus*. In A. Crary, & R. Read (Eds.), *The new wittgenstein* (pp. 262-292). London: Routledge.

Elkins, S. (1959). *Slavery: A problem in American institutional and intellectual life*. Chicago: University of Chicago Press.

Feinberg, B., & Kasrils, R. (1983). *Bertrand Russell's America: 1945-1970* (Vol. 2). Boston: South End Press.

Frege, G. (1914). Letter to Jourdain. In M. Beany (Ed.), *The frege reader* (pp. 319-321). Oxford: Blackwell Publishing.

Frege, G. (1892). On *Sinn* and *Bedeutung* (originally published 1892). In M. Beany (Ed.), *The frege reader* (pp. 151-171). Oxford: Blackwell Publishing.

Frege, G. (1918). Thought. In M. Beany (Ed.), *The frege reader* (pp. 325-345). Oxford: Blackwell Publishing.

Gall, L. (1986). *Bismarck: The white revolutionary: 1871-1898* (Vol. 2). London: Allen and Unwin.

Monk, R. (1996). *Bertrand Russell: The spirit of solitude, 1872-1921*. New York: The Free Press.

Russell, B. (2004). Knowledge by acquaintance and knowledge by description (Originally published 1911). In *Mysticism and logic*. Mineola, NY: Dover Publications.

Stampp, K. (1971). Rebels and sambos: The search for the negro's personality in slavery. *Journal of Southern History, 37,* 367-392.

14

Hydrological Science and Its Connection to Religion in Ancient Egypt under the Pharaohs

Jonas Eliasson[1,2]
[1]University of Iceland, Reykjavik, Iceland
[2]Kyoto University (visiting), Kyoto, Japan

The history of water management in the Fertile Crescent is closely related to the religion. This is most clear in ancient Egypt in pharaonic time. The class of priests serving under the pharaoh had also many other administrative duties, they had good skill in science, collected hydrological and astronomical data and used it to levy taxes and predict the floods that irrigated the arable land. The special hydrological features of the river Nile make it rather predictable in behavior compared to other major rivers of the region. In this social position the priests had great influence and could use it to stop the pharaoh Ikhnaton in his attempt to establish a monotheistic religion by ousting Amon-Ra and replacing him with Aton. Social life was very colorful at pharaohs' court and the various arts and festivals flourished. The most remarkable of these was the Opet festival where pharaoh himself was the leading figure together with the statues of the gods. The festival was to last 10 days and during that time the river Nile was to change color from grayish to reddish and thereby mark the beginning of the life-giving flood and bear witness to the good relations between the king and the divine powers. This kind of event, an annual prayer by the king to the gods for good harvest was well known in many societies, but it shows the remarkable skills of the Amon-Ra priest that they were ready to predict the onset of the Nile flood within ten days and get away with it.

Keywords: Egypt; Religion; Hydrology; Pharaoh; River Nile

Introduction

When discussing religion in the ancient world, it is necessary to realize that religion, administration and technology could be integrated into a single unit. This article attempts to show how the various natural forces and related technologies were in ancient times believed to be of divine origin. It is important in this respect, to consider that the attitude of ancient peoples, such as Egyptians to divinity, were significantly different from modern perspectives and are often misunderstood by scholars (Hornung, 1982; Hornung, 1999). Egyptian religion was close to shamanism (Morenz, 1992); as the images of the gods from this period show and taboos were common (Assman, 1992). Natural phenomena were controlled by different deities and survival depended on the Nile floods that occurred around the same time every year, irrigated the land and made it fertile as long as the soil remained moist (White, 2003).

During the flood periods nomadic tribes with their herds migrated into Egypt (White, 2003). Such nomads may still be seen on the move south of Sudan in the vast Sudd swamps that the Nile floods once a year and so the land is covered with vegetation. Thus has the Nile valley been, and here (Biswas, 1970), the human race learned the art of increasing harvest by plowing away the natural vegetation, plant grain, harvest it and live off agriculture. Later they learned also to build irrigation systems and keep flood water for later use (Biswas, 1970; Werner, 1983); but now the Aswan dam has taken over this role. The water management led to the agricultural revolution and it provides the basis for the magnificent civilization of ancient Egypt. Science flourished, the main branch being astronomy and calendar computation, which was theological in character (McClellan & Dorn 1983). Connections between astronomy, calendar calculus and religion were actually very common until the present day.

Several hazards were threatening the Egyptian nation, enemy invasions; too small floods that led to drought, too big floods on the other hand could be disastrous for people and livestock alike. When everything was well, the population increased to numbers that the arable land could not sustain with famine as the result. Such events were God's punishment, and the only possible remedy was to have a warrior king who could communicate with god and persuade him to protect the nation. From the perspective of the ancient Egyptians the king Pharaoh was needed to ensure fertility, Nile and all life in the country through his capability to communicate directly with god (Shaw, 2000).

Under the pharaoh was the nobility, such as various officers, priests, generals, constructors and regional commanders (Brugsch-Bey, 1996). The purpose of this article is to show how the administration, technology and religion are interwoven in the realm of ancient Egypt; these were all branches on the same trunk, the survival of the nation by the grace of the gods. Scholars of Egyptology are largely interested in Egyptian antiquities and their relationship to the ancient kingdom of the

Pharaohs. In this article archeology and specific dating are avoided, but when they are mentioned they follow the http:// touregypt.net originally developed in 1994 by the Ministry of Tourism of Egypt, under the direction of Mamdouh al-Beltagi. There are also considerable contributions to Egyptology material on the internet and elsewhere that originates from Zahi Hawass, an Egyptologist, and former Minister of State for Antiquities Affairs in Egypt. Interested readers can find additional information on the: Tour Egypt: http://touregypt.net/ehistory. htm.

Correct dating is difficult in Egyptology, experts agree upon when Alexander the Great was pharaoh, then upon when the Assyrians sacked Thebes about 300 years before, but the rest is a little shaky. Manetho's (Manetho's List, 2012): original list of Egyptian kings and dynasties was never completely accepted and revisions are still being made. As an example (Brugsch-Bey, 1996), means Ikhnaton ascended to the throne 1473 BC but this has now been revised to 1352 BC. Furthermore there is (Newgrosh, Rohl, & van der Veen, 1993), that in the Journal of Ancient Chronology Forum publish theories that there is communication between the first king of Israel, Saul and Ramses II and possibly Ikhnaton in the Amarna letters, described by (Moran, 1992).

Agriculture Creates Superpowers

During the first millennia in written history, the northern hemisphere was sparsely populated with nomadic peoples but the populations increased rapidly when their herds grew (Cunliffe, 1997). They migrated from the steppes to the South. Here, conditions for raising livestock were worse, but agricultural conditions better. In the agricultural revolution large societies and culture are created in the floodplains of the large valleys (Brugsch-Bey, 1996; Hurst, 1951), starting around 5000 BC. These were farming communities; the best known sites are along the Indus in India, Yellow River in China, Euphrates and Tigris in Mesopotamia and the Nile in Egypt. All these rivers, flood, irrigate the land and provide opportunities for farming even though rainfall is in very short supply in the farmland itself.

The art of taming the rivers and cultivating the otherwise arid land turned many an ancient nomadic tripe into a superpower. The largest and most influential area was the Fertile Crescent. Apart from the technical and organizational skills that brought us the wonderful pyramids (Hawass & Lehner, 1997), the Egyptians rose to incredible heights in hydraulic engineering (Kaplan, 2004). The priests operated water level stations, the Nilometers, and built irrigation works (Biswas, 1970), which lead to that the clergy became a very important part of the administration. Divine origin of nature manifested itself in the Pharaonic figure and the River Nile, which brings the water, food and fertility to the nation.

The best conditions for agriculture in the Fertile Crescent were the floodplain around the Nile in Egypt and the floodplain between Euphrates and Tigris in Mesopotamia. All fields are very dry and hot, but the rivers flooded once a year. You can make irrigation, sometimes with little effort, and keep adequate flood water in the irrigation systems after the flood to get one harvest. In this way, the land yields far more food than by cattle herding only. When things are going well the population grows rapidly and powerful kingdoms emerge. Pharaoh's grain stock is growing, pyramids, roads, new dams, canals and locks are built. The best example is the Bahr Yussef canal built around 4300 years ago. It diverts water from the Nile floods into the Fayum (Al Fayyum) oasis near Cairo, doubling the farmland in the oasis and serving as irrigation reservoir.

But floods are not just a blessing. Too large floods damage irrigation works and drown people and livestock. The ancient legend of Noah preserves the story of the flood risk that constantly threatened the civilizations in the Fertile Crescent. The legend is preserved in the Gilgamesh epic from Mesopotamia (Heidel, 1946). It tells the tale of Utnapishtim; he alone survives the great flood. Devastating floods can occur in Mesopotamia if extreme floods hit the big rivers Euphrates and Tigris at the same time. Then the whole valley is flooded, including Ur, the capital of Sumer and the city of Abraham (Werner, 1983). The largest of these floods has left thick sediments of clay in the entire Mesopotamian valley with the exception of the highest hills (Werner, 1983).

When the rain fails the floods can also be too small for the water level to lift itself above the river channel banks and irrigate the land, the canyon in the wall holding the entrance to the Luxor temple (Luxor Temple, 2012) symbolizes this. Then the crop fails with famine as the result, the cause may be many things. Local climatic variations can be everything from unusually small precipitation, to extreme events e.g. global temporary climate change due to volcanic eruption in Iceland (Oman, Robock, Stenchikov, & Thordarson, 2006). Apart from the disasters coming from the Nile, wars were common; the lower part of Egypt was harassed by constant invasions of the peoples to the north, the Egyptians called them Hyksos. They ruled for some time from their capital city Avaris.

The Rise of Hydrologic Technology and Water Management

Considerable documentation exists about water management in the Fertile Crescent. It shows a high level of technical and managerial skills. In the city of Mari in Mesopotamia libraries of clay tablets were found that show a map of the fields and irrigation ditches that provide water to them (Biswas, 1970). A similar map of the irrigation systems along the Yellow River in China exist (Biswas, 1970). It took about 500 years to complete the Chinese system, but according to legends it is the work of Emperor Wu of the Western Han dynasty who reigned 206 BC-9 AD. Then are the famous qanat systems in Persia Iran, they are complex system of tunnels that are dug into the mountains to collect groundwater (Biswas, 1970). Such systems could be diverted into cities without any flood risk, for example to the famous Paradiso gardens in ancient Persia. Today the Taj Mahal Palace in India is the best known place with this type of garden architecture.

But the art of water management rose to its highest levels in ancient Egypt. The largest part of it is desert; the country is almost just a green belt around the river Nile. Living conditions are much better than in Mesopotamia, the floods more regular and droughts not so common. The river flows from south to north, the wind blowing from north to south and it almost never rains. The Nile is navigable up to the first cataract at Aswan and ancient Egypt is from here to the sea. South of Egypt was Nubia, where the Egyptian army frequently battled and took slaves. Originally there were two Egyptian states, but they are united in times of the old kingdom (Dunn, 2012).

Basic Hydrology of the River Nile and the Use of Hydrologic Data in Administration

The White Nile, flows from the Lake Victoria. This is the largest lake in the world with enormous storage effect so in its beginning the White Nile flows very evenly throughout the year. At Khartoum in Sudan the Blue Nile River, which comes from Lake Tana in Ethiopia joins the White Nile. The Blue Nile is a very small river, except in the monsoon rain season in May and June. Then it rains very heavily on the mountains in Ethiopia and the water flows then from all sides into the Lake Tana, so the Lake Tana River crashes with enormous power down the Nile Waterfalls and further along its channel down to Khartoum. The power of the Blue Nile is so great that it stems the White Nile seriously and helps to fill up the Sudd swamps. But four rapids between Khartoum and Aswan slow the flood down, it takes a few weeks for it to fill the river channel, so the flood did not come to Egypt until July, but then usually lasted for two months. Blue Nile has a reddish color but the White Nile grayish, so the color change of the Nile marks the beginning of the flood. This color change was duly noted in the capital Thebes now Luxor, directly opposite the famous royal graves in the Valley of the Kings.

A part of the flood water was stored up inside the irrigation system. The moist soil was plowed as soon as possible and the irrigation system used for the plants and in March the crops were harvested. The land was mostly owned by nobles and priests, which in turn paid taxes to the king. There was considerable persistence in the floods, "good floods" and "bad floods" respectively, had a tendency to group, like in the biblical legend of the seven fat and seven lean years Genesis 41: 17 - 36. Today persistence and autocorrelation of the floods of the Nile are known from the hydrology research on the two thousand years' time series for the water levels of the Nile gathered by the priests (Biswas, 1970; Hurst, 1951).

There were the priests in the temple Karnack and other temples along the river banks who operated the water level measurements of the Nile. They built water level gauges, called Nilometers (Biswas, 1970). These were deep wells of piled stones with a high column in the center of the well with a scale on it where the water level could be read and recorded. This measurement method is still in used **Figure 1**.

With the results of the water level recordings and experience over the years it was relatively easy for priests to calculate the harvest and those accounts were used in levying taxes. This is the only known example of priests playing the role of the internal revenue department using water levels as their evidence. But the priests of ancient Egypt had many official functions so this has been as natural a role for them as doing service in the temple. Their role as priests was to serve the gods inside the Holy of Holiest in the temple, e.g. bring them food once a day.

But temple service was only 3 - 4 months a year for the average priest in other times of the year, he was in administration, e.g. the tax collector who visited the farmers with a record of what each had to pay and charged them accordingly. If they did not pay, there was a police force to take care of that matter (Protecting Civilians, 2012).

The Divine Power and the Royal Power

In ancient Egypt, spiritual and secular authority is one and the same. All natural phenomenon's, the water, the land and the animals were of divine origin and man was too. Top rank was

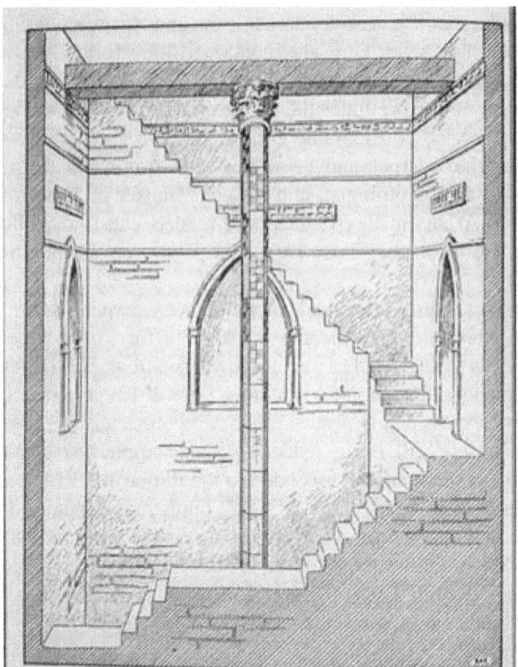

Figure 1.
Nilometer.

the king, the Pharaoh, he descended from the gods but he himself was not a god, even though some past kings did make it to the divine ranks. The most famous of these is Osiris (Morenz, 1992) and his son Horus, whose symbol is the falcon, most sacred of all birds. Egyptian gods were numerous but only 115 are known (Hornung 1982). Many animals like hawks, lions, cats and crocodiles (Dunn 2012) were worshipped. There were gods and goddesses, each could be portrayed with a single icon in the hieroglyphic texts. Sometimes a god appears with the head of an animal, especially the male gods. This animal worship was more practiced in the Fertile Crescent than in the Mediterranean religious systems of the Greeks and the Romans. This suggests that the Egyptian religious system was originally worship of deities in the nature and spirits like in Shamanism, but this does not have to be more than partially correct.

Deities could merge together and change roles, e.g. the sun god Ra sometimes merged with Horus and became Horus-Ra with a human body and a falcon head crowned with a sun-disc. Ra also merged with Amon to become Amon-Ra, who was a god with a ram head and a sun-disc while Amon himself had a human head.

In Manetho's list (Manetho's List, 2012): are 30 Dynasties of Egyptian pharaohs. The rank of the gods varied through the times and there is a possibility that when one king dethroned another and replaced that dynasty with his own, similar revolutions followed in the realm of the gods. As an example, during the eighteenth dynasty 1539-1295 BC Amon-Ra was the supreme god and his power great, but not in the times before and after.

The ancient Egyptians had a great respect for the afterlife and great preparation was needed so the soul of the deceased would receive worthy reception in the realm of the dead. For example, the rite that took place when the heart of the dead were weighed and evaluated before it was accepted. A famous picture from the Book of Dead (Book of Dead, 2013) shows this in **Figure 2**.

Figure 2.
The heart of a scribe being weighed against the feather of Maat from Book of the Dead.

Anubis comes with the deceased by his hand to the ceremony. This is no coincidence, Anubis was the god of mummification, and his role was to assist the deceased on his journey that was both complex and dangerous. Toth with Ibis head comes with the heart of the deceased and a feather from the hair dress of Maat, the goddess of truth, on a tray. Anubis places the heart and the feather on either side of a scale. But the monsters Ammi, representative of the underworld, watches closely, he gets the soul if the heart does not meet the test. If all goes well Horus son of Osiris, former pharaoh and now god, takes the deceased by the hand and follows him into the Holy of Holies where his father and Isis, his mother, wait. Next to Isis waits Maat, presumably to get her feather back.

The Mystery of Ikhnaton

Deities could move up and down the ranks with the help of the king, though it probably has happened more frequently, that the Pharaoh came to power with assistance from the gods. A good example of the former is when Amenhotep IV dethroned Amon-Ra, replaced him with the sun-disc god Aton and took the name Ikhnaton for himself. For this he was nicknamed the heretic king, (Brugsch-Bey, 1996). What is striking here is that the new faith was monotheism, the people was to worship only the god Aton, who had a low rank before Ikhnaton's time.

Researchers do not totally agree how Amenhotep IV got this strange idea. According to the Bible, the Hebrew descendants of Joseph and his brothers, which according to biblical legends came to Egypt in the times of the 15 dynasty or about 1650 BC, (Manetho's List, 2012), lived in the country in Ikhnaton's time. Some believe that Joseph was at the court of Ikhnaton's father, even his viceroy (Minister) see Genesis 41: 37 - 41. This has created wild speculations about that Ikhnaton was in his monotheisms under religious influence from the Hebrews. But many modern scholars believe now that the Old Testament's legend of the Hebrews in Egypt is a myth although this is not explicitly stated (Bimson, 1988). The legend may be true never the less. In Egypt, the Hebrews would have been counted in all writing as Hyksos anyway.

Others still take a more practical approach in the Ikhnaton mystery. The Amon priests were very powerful, owned about 1/3 of the land and did not always do pharaohs' bidding. It may be suggested that the king was simply trying a kind of Cultural Revolution to keep them down in the same way as Mao revolted against his regional commanders in our times. This Ikhnaton did by building in a short time a totally new capital, Akhenaten, which he filled with wonderful works of art in a totally new style. But his administration was not as successful. After his reign 1353-1336 BC (Hornung, 1999); the economy was in total ruin (Akhenaten, 2012). This is understandable as the former administrators, the Amon priests, were totally opposed to Ikhnaton and had every possibility to work against him. Furthermore, a bad infectious disease harassed the country in his time.

Speculations about that Ikhnaton's and Moses' gods were one and the same are very interesting but hardly realistic, (Bimson, 1988). A closer study of these deities shows them very different. That Aton was the lawmaker and supreme judge like Jahve was out of the question, supreme judge was pharaoh. That Jahve should allow brother and sister to wed, as was the custom of Egyptian royalty, no way. Many other arguments can be made.

Arts and Culture at the Court

Further research may uncover new evidence, but until then there is the Egyptian art and craftsmanship to admire, it rose to incredible heights in technology and design under Ikhnaton's rule so all the world is in great depth to this heretic king. There are also speculations that Ikhnaton's art was influenced by the Hebrews. But Ikhnaton's chief art designer and architect were named Bek and there is no evidence that he was not Egyptian. Among the works created in his time is the fabulous statue of Nefertiti, an exquisite work of art, both in form and classical beauty. The death mask of Tutankhamen (ca. 1333-1322 BC) is also a wonder, it was found in his tomb, along with a number of other artworks. He was probably Ikhnaton's son and in his 10 year's reign as King, began the conversion to the old faith. So the new religion was short-lived and the Amon-Ra priests regained all the former powers that Ikhnaton took from them, which is a remarkable testimony to their cunning.

The Opet Festival

The Egyptian gentry loved to pass the time in hunting and parties, just like nobility of all times. But everybody had to stick to his place. The common farmers spent their life more or less in serfdom and we know little of their lives (Hawass, 1997). But the graves of the nobility are full of paintings with stories of how pharaoh was hunting lions while lesser noblemen were hunting pigs or fishing. On these pictures the rank of persons can be judged, the higher the rank, the bigger is the person's body in the picture.

But sometimes the crowd was allowed to participate in the celebrations, especially when they were designed to show the good relations of the administrators, king and priests, to the gods who ruled over the welfare of the people. The best example is the annual Opet festival held on the Nile. It was very popular during the eighteenth dynasty, so popular was that it could lead to hostilities if it was cancelled (Kruchten, 1991).

The purpose of the festival was a meeting between God and pharaoh, to ensure a good flood, the necessary condition for a good harvest. The king should, in other words ensure fertility of the earth by communicating with the gods, a well-known theme in ancient societies, and more may be remaining of this custom than what is commonly accepted. Statues of Amon-Ra were ferried on the Nile from Thebes to the landing site in front of the big temple Karnack (Leprohon, 1999), and carried from there in a great parade by a road lined with statues into the temple. Detailed description of this parade and associated festivities does not exist, and it may also have changed over the hundreds of years the Opet was held. But there were, however, fixed points. Sailing on the Nile with the statues of the gods was one of them.

Another fixed point was the parade into the temple and the mysterious service in the temple. The service was a most secret event, a meeting between the king and god. We can let **Figure 3** represent what happened, even though the picture is from another occasion. There is a man between two gods. His head dress, particularly the Cobra snake figure on the forehead, tells us this is pharaoh himself. On either side of him are Horus and Anubis, guardians of the king and helpers in life and death. They are waiting for the boat at the top right of the image. A closer examination shows that there is Amon-Ra coming, with its ram head symbolizing Amon and crowned with a sun-disc symbolizing Ra. The figure does not leave us in doubt that Pharaoh is a bit nervous, much is at stake that the meeting goes well.

Here we have a ceremony where the king asks the gods to bring the nation her necessities by virtue of their power over the elements (Morenz, 1992). Similar ceremonies were in other communities, the best known the ceremony in the temple of heaven in Beijing where the Emperor prayed for good harvests.

We must admire the Amon priests for daring such an act. Besides computational skills and fairly detailed calendar, which they certainly had (Kline, 1972; Morenz, 1992); they had to have a comprehensive knowledge of the behavior of the Nile flood to be able to predict it within 10 days. To this day, such a prediction is still a problem. This festival is perhaps the best example of how religion, government and technical skills were interwoven in this greatest culture of the world during its time.

Today, the same nation is living in Egypt and then. But the floods of the Nile now stop at the Aswan dam and the Nile crocodile downstream of it is dead. He was one of the main animal gods of ancient Egypt, with him went the last living icon of the old time. But the legacy of Egyptian religion and technical skills still survives to this day, the world is in debt to ancient Egypt, it will never be paid in full (Hornung, 1982).

REFERENCES

Akhenaten (2012). http://en.wikipedia.org/wiki/AkhenatenWikipedia

Assman, J. (1992). When justice fails—Jurisdiction and imprecation in Ancient-Egypt and the Near-East. *Journal of Egyptian Archaeology, 78,* 149-162.

Bimson, J. J. (1988). Exodus and conquest—Myth or reality. *Journal of Ancient Chronology Forum, 2,* 27-40.
http://www.hope-of-israel.org/conquest.html

Biswas, A. K. (1970). *History of hydrology* (pp. xii + 336). New York: American Elsevier Publishing Co.

Book of the Dead (2013).
http://en.wikipedia.org/wiki/Book_of_the_Dead

Brugsch-Bey, H. (1996). Egypt under the Pharaos. London: Bracken Books.

Cunliffe, B. (1997). *The Oxford illustrated history of prehistoric Europe.* Oxford: Oxford University Press.

Dunn, J. (2012).
http://www.touregypt.net/featurestories/animalcults.htm

Hawass, Z. (1997). Tombs of the pyramid builders. *Archaeology, 501,* 39-43. http://archive.archaeology.org/9701

Hawass, Z., & Lehner, M. (1997). Builders of the pyramids. *Archaeology, 501,* 30-46.
http://archive.archaeology.org/9701/abstracts/pyramids.html

Heidel, A. (1946). *The Gilgamesh epic and old testament parallels.* Chicago: University of Chicago.

Hornung, E. (1982). *Conceptions of God in Ancient Egypt: The one and the many* (p. 296).

Hornung, E. (1999). *History of Ancient Egypt. (Translation of Grundzüge der Ägyptischen Geschichte by David Lorton, Trans. Ithaca).* New York: Cornell University Press.

Hurst, H. E. (1951). Long-term storage capacity of reservoirs. *Transactions of the American Society of Civil Engineers, 116,* 770-799.

Kaplan, L. C. (2004). *Technology of Ancient Egypt.* New York, NY: Power Kids Press.

Kline, M. (1972). Mathematical thought from ancient to modern times (pp. xvii+1238). New York: Oxford University Press.

Kruchten, J. M. (1991). The year when the opet festival was not held in Paophi. *Journal of Egyptian Archaeology, 77,* 182-184.

Leprohon, R. J. (1999). Reliefs and inscriptions at Luxor Temple, vol. 1, the festival procession of Opet in the Colonnade Hall, with translation of texts. *Journal of Near Eastern Studies, 584,* 301-303.

Luxor Temple (2012).
http://en.wikipedia.org/wiki/File:Egypt.LuxorTemple.06.jpg

Manetho's List (2012).
http://en.wikipedia.org/wiki/List_of_pharaohs#Existing_primary_old_lists_of_pharaohs

McClellan, J. E., & Dorn, H. (1999). *Science and technology in world history, an introduction.* Baltimore: The Johns Hopkins University Press.

Figure 3.
Pharaoh in the center flanked by Horus left and Anubis right.

Moran, W. (1992). *The Amarna letters.* Maryland: The Johns Hopkins University Press.

Morenz, S. (1992). Egyptian religion. Cornell paperbacks. Ithaca: Cornell University Press.

Newgrosh, B., Rohl, D. M., & van der Veen, P. G. (1993). The el-Amarna letters and Israelite history. *Journal of Ancient Chronology Forum, 6,* 33-64.
http://www.newchronology.org/cgi-bin/somsid.cgi?type=pdf&page=06a033&code=rbhcf1a6&session=1376973446&record=78&subpage=0&hl=The+el-Amarna+letters+

Oman, L., Robock, A., Stenchikov, G. L., & Thordarson, T. (2006). High-latitude eruptions cast shadow over the African monsoon and the flow of the Nile. *Geophysical Research Letters, 33,* L18711.

Protecting Civilians (2012).
http://www.reshafim.org.il/ad/egypt/law_and_order/police.htm

Shaw, I. (2000). *The Oxford history of Ancient Egypt Oxford illustrated histories.* Oxford: Oxford University Press.

Werner, K. (1983). Doubleday books. New York, NY

White, B. L. (2003). Religious foundations of egyptian engineering & science, Ancient Egypt provides an early example of how a society's worldview drives engineering and the development of science. The Egyptian mind, graduate seminar—Under the direction of Dr. Joseph Manning. Stanford: Stanford University.
http://www.strategic-tech.org/images/Egyptian_Engineering_and_Culture.pdf

15

On the Conceptual and Civilization Frames in René Descartes' *Physical Works*

Paolo Bussotti[1], Raffaele Pisano[2]

[1]Research Centre for the Theory and History of Science, University of West Bohemia, Pilsen, Czech Republic
[2]Sciences, Sociétés, Cultures Dans Leurs Évolutions, University of Lille 1, Lille, France

The paper try to provide a contribution to the scientific—historiographic debate concerning the relations between experiments, metaphysics and mathematics in Descartes' physics. The three works on which the analysis is focused are the *Principia philosophiae* and the two physical essays: *La Dioptrique* and *Les Météores*. The authors will highlight the profound methodological and epistemological differences characterizing, from one side, the *Principia* and, from the other side, the physical essays. Three significant examples will be dealt with: 1) the collision rules in the *Principia philosophiae*; 2) the refraction law in *La Dioptrique*; 3) the rainbow in *Les Météores*. In the final remarks these differences will be interpreted as depending upon the different role Descartes ascribed to the three books inside his whole work. The concepts of *intensity* and *gradation* of the physical quantities used by Descartes will provide an important interpretative means. In this paper, we compare the aprioristic approach to physics typical for Descartes' *Principia* with the experimental and mathematical one characterizing Descartes' *Essays*.

Keywords: Descartes; Newton; Collision Rules; Refraction Law; Rainbow; Intensity and Gradation of the Physical Quantities; Science and Society in the XVII Century

An Outline

On Science & Society. The social and civilization environment in which a scientist lives has profound influences on the way how his scientific results and methods are framed (e.g. see Schuhl). This is specifically true for the 17th century, the epoch of the scientific revolution and a century of deep social and political transformations. Nevertheless, we think influence of the social-political situation on the work of a scientist has to be deduced directly from the analysis of his scientific works. In other terms: an analysis of the society in a certain period can be useful to understand the general direction taken by the science in that period, but, in itself, it is not enough to understand the specific work and results of a certain scientist. This kind of general analysis risks to become a sort of an *a priori passe-partout* through which the scientific work is analysed and risks[1] to induce serious misunderstandings on the way in which a certain scientist presented the results of his researches. It is always necessary to begin a historical research—also a research concerning the relations between science and society in a determined period—from the alive, both theoretical and technical work of the scientists. If, in the analysis of the whole work of a scientist, the historian of science reveals some unclearness or internal inconsistencies or a lack of coherence between the methods used by this scientist in different works of his and if all these questions cannot be explained either with technical problems (for example the lack or the misunderstanding of

certain mathematical methods) or with the general methodological and epistemological convictions of the scientist himself, then it is necessary to think of the general structure of the society in that period. Therefore technical analysis of the results and methods used by the scientist is a priori considered and then evaluated within civilization.

On Science. The case of René Descartes (1596-1650) is emblematic in this sense: in his essays *La Dioptrique* and *Les Méthéores* Descartes proposes—among other results—his theory of refraction and of rainbow. Every passage of these two works can be explained taking into account: 1) the level of the science in the 17th century; 2) Descartes' experiments and methods; 3) Descartes' use of mathematics; 4) Descartes philosophical convictions (Hattab, 2009). These books could be understood without taking into account the social non-scientific context in which Descartes lived. The situation as to the *Principia philosophiae* is different at all: we will see in the final remarks of this paper that many results and argumentative structures exposed by Descartes in his *Principia* can be explained taking into account Descartes' epistemological and philosophical convictions, but other parts of the book and some reasoning that appear tormented and unclear can be clarified only considering the particular social situation in which Descartes lived and operated. The sociological analysis becomes hence interesting and can represent a great means to understand the evolution of the scientific ideas only if it is based on the examination of the theoretical-technical results obtained by the scientists and explained in their works. The case Newton and his *civilization science* (Buchwald & Feingold, 2011) is as interesting as the

---

[1]On that see a good essay by Buchwald and Feingold (Buchwald & Feingold, 2011).

one of Descartes: the different social context in which Newton lived allowed him a major freedom than Descartes' (see final remarks of our paper). But in this case, too, the examination becomes interesting basing on Newton's physical and mathematical works. Only in this manner the sociological analysis of science becomes perspicuous and useful for history of science and scientific concepts.

Isaac Newton (1642-1727) explicitly claimed that a model of the solar system had to show the positions held by a planet (Jupiter in the specific case mentioned in the forthcoming quotation) in the course of time, and that this condition cannot be fulfilled following Descartesian physics. Consequently the physical system described by René Descartes (1596-1650) in his *Principia Philosophiae* (1644; see **Figures 1** and **2**) is not a good model of the universe. In his unpublished work *De Gravitatione et aequipondio fluidorum* (Ruffner), Newton criticized the model of the solar system proposed by Descartes in his *Pincipia philosophiae* as follows:

And hence, about the place of Jupiter, which it kept the year before, and with equal reason, about the prior place of a moving body anywhere, according to the doctrine of Descartes [illeg] it is manifest that not even God himself (standing newly established with things) could accurately and in a geometrical sense describe [it], especially when, on account of the changed positions of bodies, it would no longer exist in the nature of things[2].

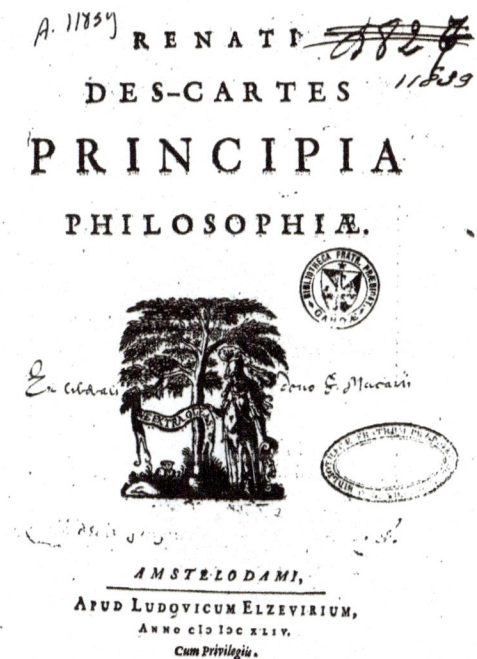

Figure 1.
The frontispiece of the first edition of Descartes' *Principia* (1644)[3].

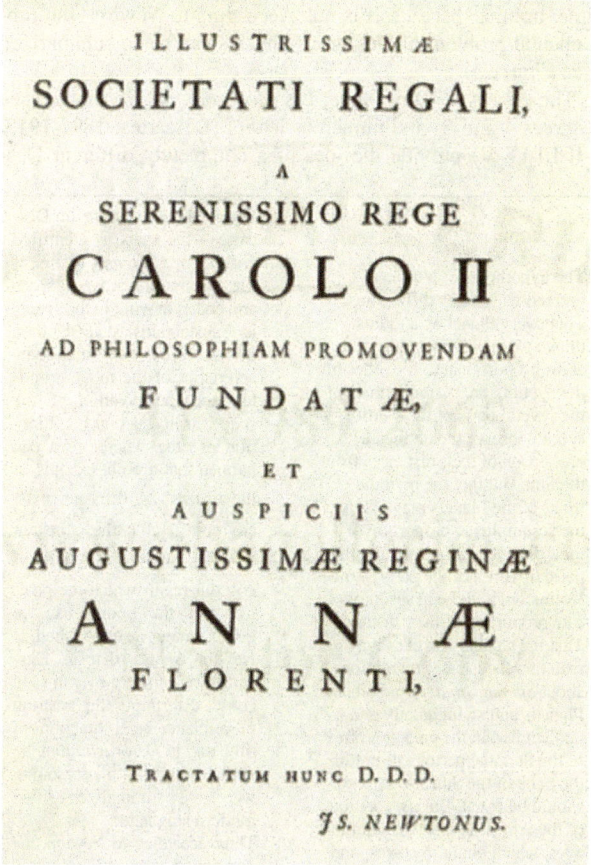

Figure 2.
The frontispiece of the second edition with *General Scholium* by Newton's *Principia* (1713)[4].

Albeit, from an epistemological point of view, it is difficult to exactly identify all characteristics a descriptive-explicative model of physical phenomena should keep, some of them cannot be ignored. Two of these characteristics are:

1) The coherence of the principles that are at the basis of the system, that is the principles must not be mutually contradictory.

2) The possibility to determine quantitative relations between the sizes of the system.

We note that in the classical physical studies, the possibility to express the position of a body as a function of the time, is necessarily a law of motion fundamental for quantitative relations. Generally speaking in order to express such law, it is necessary to determine a physical system in which the space-variable can be decomposed into three (dimensional) mutually perpendicular directions[5]. Then, for every motion, the position of the moving body can be expressed in function of the time i.e. $x = f(t)$, $y = g(t)$, $z = h(t)$. Thus, a law of motion can well interpret a classical physical phenomenon if a Descartesian system (time and each of the three directions) is provided. Hence, time and space have to be uniform quantities as far as they are the bases of the reference systems. A position of a body is a function of

---

[2]"Et proinde de loco Iovis quem ante annum habuit, parique ratione de præterito loco cujuslibet mobilis manifestum est juxta Cartesij [illeg] doctrinam, quòd ne quidem Deus ipse (stante rerum novato statu) possit accuratè et in sensu Geometrico describere, quippe cùm propter mutatas corporum positiones, non ampliùs in rerum naturâ existit" (Newton folios 9, Ms Add. 4003, Cambridge University Library, Cambridge, UK [retrieved via: http://www.newtonproject.sussex.ac.uk/view/texts/normalized/THEM00093]).
[3]Descartes 1897-1913, X-2.

[4]The English translation (1729) was by Andrew Motte (1696-1734) found in the second Latin edition (1713).
[5]That is in modern terms as *rectangular coordinate system* also called *Descartesian* or *Cartesian coordinate system* by three functions for coordinates.

time, but the space itself is not. According to Newton[6] the fundamental problem of Descartes' physics can be so summarized (see **Figure 3**):

The essays *La Dioptrique*, *Les Météores*, *La Géométrie* (see **Figures 4** and **5**) and numerous letters (Descartes, 1897-1913, I-II-III-IV-V) provide the idea of a completely different Des-

The hypotheses of Vortices is pressed with many difficulties. That every Planet by a radius drawn to the Sun may describe areas proportional to the times of description, the periodic times of the several parts of the Vortices should observe the duplicate proportion of their distances from the Sun. But that the periodic times of the Planets may obtain the sesquiplicate proportion of their distances from the Sun, the periodic times of the parts of the Vortex ought to be in sesquiplicate proportion of their distances. That the smaller Vortices may maintain their lesser revolutions about *Saturn*, *Jupiter*, and other Planets, and swim quietly and undisturbed in the greater Vortex of the Sun, the periodic times of the parts of the Sun's Vortex should be equal. But the rotation of the Sun and Planets about their axes, which ought to correspond with the motions of their Vortices, recede far from all these proportions. The motions of the Comets are exceedingly regular, are govern'd by the same laws with the motions of the Planets, and can by no means be accounted for by the hypotheses of Vortices. For Comets are carry'd with very eccentric motions through all parts of the heavens indifferently, with a freedom that is incompatible with the notion of a Vortex. [...]

a) If—as it is the case in Descartes—the space is identified with the *res extensa*, that is, if the separation between space and bodies moving in the space, is substantially denied, then the space has the same characteristics of the moving bodies and the position of the space itself becomes a function of time. Therefore it can happen that a point existing at the instant t_0, does not exist anymore at the instant $t_0 + \Delta t$, so that a system of coordinates in which the positions of the bodies can be given, cannot be established.

b) Newton writes that in Descartes' system not even a God could determine the position of a planet as a function of time and in *De gravitatione* he explains in detail the reasoning we have summarized in a modern language.

c) Thus, according to Newton, the description of the physical world ideated by Descartes in his *Principia Philosophiae* (hereafter *Principia*) does not satisfy the two characteristics needed for a model.

d) Besides these, there are further problems as the consequences of some laws expressed in the *Principia* and contradicted by the experience (as it is the case of the collision rules between two bodies) or the unscrupulous resort to analogy and the lack of clearness as to the relations between experience-experiment and theory.

Figure 3.
Newton's first paragraph on (implicitly) Descartes at the beginning of the *General Scholium*[7].

---

[6]It is well known that Newton spoke of absolute time and absolute space in the general *General Scholium* (Newton, [1713] 1729) where it does not begin with the introduction of the concepts of absolute space and absolute time, but with the prove that the vortices-theory of Descartes is untenable. Likely Newton introduced explicitly his concepts of absolute space and time as an epistemological answer to Descartes' theory. In this manner the initial part of the *General Scholium* can be interpreted as the physical refutation of Descartes' theory and the second part as the epistemological refutation. On historical-philosophical conceptualization around Newtonian colour theory and the new analytical theories one can see Panza (Panza, 2005, 2007), Blay (Blay, 1983, 1992, 2002), Rashed (Rashed) and on Newtonian Optik Hall (Hall, 1993; see also Halley, 1693). On Fresnel's optic one can also see Rosmorduc, Rosmorduc and Dutour (Rosmorduc J, Rosmorduc V, Dutour) interesting for our aims.
[7]Newton, [1713] 1729: p. 387. Recently on Newton a critic French edition is remarkable (Panza, 2004).

cartes. He supplied substantially correct modelling of phenomena, as the refraction (*Ivi*, *La Dioptrique*, discours II, VI) with the consequent genial explanation of the rainbow and of other optical effects (*Ivi*, *Les Météores*, discours VIII, VI). Sometimes analogy brought him to incorrect explanations, as it is the case for the origin of the colours (*Les Météores*, discours VIII, VI). However, in these cases, too, a profound attempt to make the theory coherent with the facts is present. The idea to measure and to quantify the sizes constitute the conceptual and methodological basis of *La Dioptrique* and of *Les Météores* even if the transcription into mathematical terms is not always explicit. Particularly *La Géométrie* (*Ivi*, VI) deserves a separate series of considerations: despite mathematical problems are dealt with (hence not directly connected with the knowledge of the external world), the new modelling proposed by Descartes—the analytical geometry—will be fundamental for science, too, because of the idea to transcribe geometrical data into an analytical form. The Essays and some letters arouse hence a different impression from that given by the *Principia*.

In the *La Dioptrique* (and *Les Météores*) he was able to provide—plausible, even if non always exact—early models of the phenomena as refraction, rainbow and origin of the colours considering empirical data and framing them into a theoretical structure, as it will be clarified in the third section of our paper. Differently from this approach, in the *Principia*, as well known,

DISCOURS
DE LA METHODE
Pour bien conduire sa raison, & chercher
la verité dans les sciences.
PLUS
LA DIOPTRIQVE.
LES METEORES.
ET
LA GEOMETRIE.
Qui sont des essais de cete METHODE.

A LEYDE
De l'Imprimerie de IAN MAIRE.
cI Ic c xxxvII.
Avec Privilege.

Figure 4.
The frontispiece of *Discours de la méthode* (1637)[8].

---

[8]Descartes 1897-1913, VI. *Discours de la Méthode* (*Ivi*: pp. 1-79). It includes *La Dioptrique* (*Ivi*: pp. 80-228), (*Ivi*, *Les Météores*: pp. 231-366), *La Géométrie* (*Ivi*: pp. 367-485). *Le Monde* (*Ivi*, XI-1: pp. 3-118). For the Latin edition (1644) of the *Principia* see *Ivi*, VIII-1; for the French translation (1647) see: *Ivi*, IX-2.

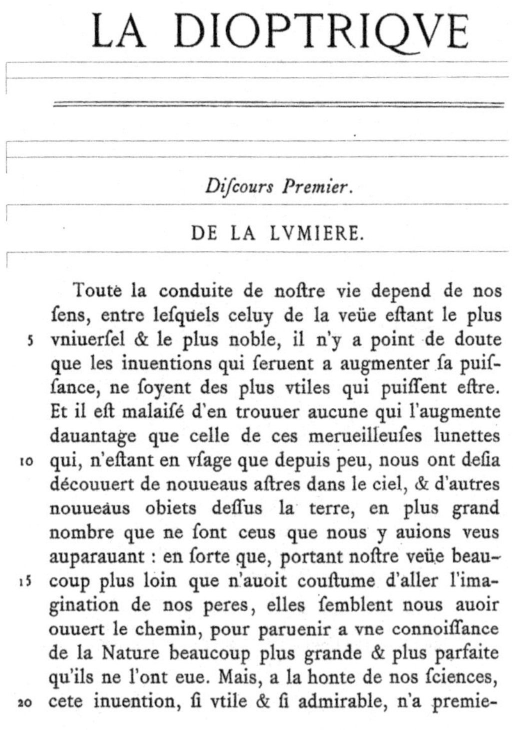

LA DIOPTRIQVE

Difcours Premier.

DE LA LVMIERE.

Toutè la conduite de noftre vie depend de nos
fens, entre lefquels celuy de la veüe eftant le plus
5 vniuerfel & le plus noble, il n'y a point de doute
que les inuentions qui feruent a augmenter fa puif-
fance, ne foyent des plus vtiles qui puiffent eftre.
Et il eft malaifé d'en trouuer aucune qui l'augmente
dauantage que celle de ces merueilleufes lunettes
10 qui, n'eftant en vfage que depuis peu, nous ont defia
découuert de nouueaux aftres dans le ciel, & d'autres
nouueaus obiets deffus la terre, en plus grand
nombre que ne font ceus que nous y auions veus
auparauant : en forte que, portant noftre veüe beau-
15 coup plus loin que n'auoit couftume d'aller l'imagination de nos peres, elles femblent nous auoir
ouuert le chemin, pour paruenir a vne connoiffance
de la Nature beaucoup plus grande & plus parfaite
qu'ils ne l'ont eue. Mais, a la honte de nos fciences,
20 cete inuention, fi vtile & fi admirable, n'a premie-

Figure 5.
The first page of the *La dioptrique* (1694)[9].

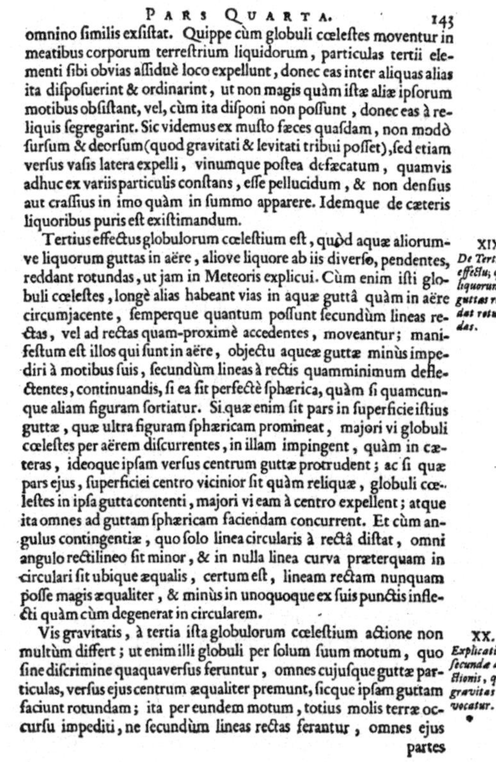

Descartes tried to supply a global physical theory looking for
its foundation in few basic notions without resorting to any
quantification. He limited his speeches with qualitative and
analogical arguments. Descartes does not seem to fully catch
the difficulty and complexity of some problems as the nature of
gravity and of magnetism (*Le Monde ou Traité de la lumière*
(hereafter *Le Monde*), Descartes, 1897-1913, XI; *Id.*, *Principia*,
IX-2, Part IV, § 20-27: pp. 133-183). The example of gravity is
particularly significant: Descartes' mechanisitic conception
brought him to think that the origin of gravity (to consider as a
phenomenon taking place on the earth) depends on the effects
of the quick movement of the particles ("particulae") of the
second element around the earth (*Principia*, 1644, VIII, Part IV,
§ 20-21)[10] (see **Figures 6** and **7**).

The earth itself and the bodies on the earth are mostly composed of particles belonging to the third element. They are
heavier than those of the second element surrounding the earth.
The movement of the particles of the second element exerts a
pressure on the bodies composed by particles of the third element so that they tend to the centre of the earth. In synthesis
this is the mechanistic conception of gravity exposed by Descartes. A consequence of this conception is the theoretical impossibility to determine a relation between *mass* as physical
measurable quantity and *quantity of matter* as (classical Descartesian) conception of internal part of an object (see **Figure 8**).

A consequence is that the explanation between what is the
mass (physical measure) and what is the quantity of matter
(mathematical interpretation) was not easily identifiable due

---

[9]Descartes, 1897-1913, VI.
[10]As to the theory of the particles composing the three elements (Descartes,
1897-1913 [*Principia*, 1644, III, § 48-53] VIII-1: pp. 102-107) and in particular the chapter 52 (Descartes 1897-1913, VIII-1: p. 105, line 11-30)
titled *Tria esse huius mundi aspedabilis elementa*.

---

omnino fimilis exfiftat. Quippe cùm globuli cœleftes moventur in
meatibus corporum terreftrium liquidorum, particulas tertii elementi fibi obvias affiduè loco expellunt, donec eas inter aliquas alias
ita difpofuerint & ordinarint, ut non magis quàm iftæ aliæ ipforum
motibus obfiftant, vel, cùm ita difponi non poffunt, donec eas à re-
liquis fegregarint. Sic videmus ex mufto fæces quafdam, non modò
furfum & deorfum (quod gravitati & levitati tribui poffet), fed etiam
verfus vafis latera expelli, vinumque poftea defæcatum, quamvis
adhuc ex variis particulis conftans, effe pellucidum, & non denfius
aut craffius in imo quàm in fummo apparere. Idemque de cæteris
liquoribus puris eft exiftimandum.

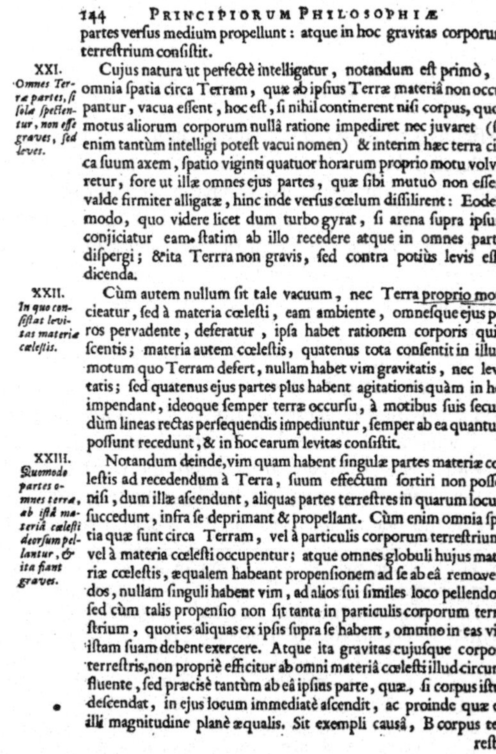

Tertius effectus globulorum cœleftium eft, quòd aquæ aliorum-
ve liquorum guttas in aëre, aliove liquore ab iis diverfo, pendentes,
reddant rotundas, ut jam in Meteoris explicui. Cùm enim ifti globuli cœleftes, longè alias habeant vias in aquæ guttà quàm in aëre
circumjacente, femperque quantum poffunt fecundùm lineas rectas, vel ad rectas quam-proximè accedentes, moveantur; mani-
feftum eft illos qui funt in aëre, objectu aquecæ guttæ minùs impe-
diri à motibus fuis, fecundùm lineas à rectis quamminimum defle-
ctentes, continuandis, fi ea fit perfectè fphærica, quàm fi quamcun-
que aliam figuram fortiatur. Si quæ enim fit pars in fuperficie iftius
guttæ, quæ ultra figuram fphæricam promineat, majori vi globuli
cœleftes per aërem difcurrentes, in illam impingent, quàm in cæ-
teras, ideoque ipfam verfus centrum guttæ protrudent; ac fi quæ
pars ejus, fuperficiei centro vicinior fit quàm reliquæ, globuli cœleftes in ipfa gutta contenti, majori vi eam à centro expellent; atque
ita omnes ad guttam fphæricam faciendam concurrent. Et cùm an-
gulus contingentiæ, quo folo linea circularis à rectà diftat, omni
angulo rectilineo fit minor, & in nulla linea curva præterquam in
circulari fit ubique æqualis, certum eft, lineam rectam nunquam
poffe magis æqualiter, & minùs in unoquoque ex fuis punctis infle-
cti quàm cùm degenerat in circularem.

Vis gravitatis, à tertia ifta globulorum cœleftium actione non
multùm differt; ut enim illi globuli per folum fuum motum, quo
fine difcrimine quaquaverfus feruntur, omnes cujufque guttæ particulas, verfus ejus centrum æqualiter premunt, ficque ipfam guttam
faciunt rotundam; ita per eundem motum, totius molis terræ occurfu impediti, ne fecundùm lineas rectas ferantur, omnes ejus
partes

*XIX.
De Tertio
effectu, quòd
liquorum
guttas red-
dat rotun-
das.*

*XX.
Explicatio
fecunda a-
ctionis, quæ
gravitas
vocatur.*

Figure 6.
Descartesian gravity and magnetism.

---

partes verfus medium propellunt: atque in hoc gravitas corporum
terreftrium confiftit.

*XXI.
Omnes Ter-
ræ partes, fi
fola fpecten-
tur, non effe
graves, fed
leves.*

Cujus natura ut perfectè intelligatur, notandum eft primò, fi
omnia fpatia circa Terram, quæ ab ipfius Terræ materià non occu-
pantur, vacua effent, hoc eft, fi nihil continerent nifi corpus, quod
motus aliorum corporum nullà ratione impediret nec juvaret (fic
enim tantùm intelligi poteft vacui nomen) & interim hæc terra circa fuum axem, fpatio viginti quatuor horarum proprio motu volve-
retur, fore ut illæ omnes ejus partes, quæ fibi mutuò non effent
valde firmiter alligatæ, hinc inde verfus cœlum diffilirent: Eodem
modo, quo videre licet dum turbo gyrat, fi arena fupra ipfum
conjiciatur eam ftatim ab illo recedere atque in omnes partes
difpergi; &ita Terra non gravis, fed contra potiùs levis effet
dicenda.

*XXII.
In quo con-
fiftat levi-
tas materiæ
cœleftis.*

Cùm autem nullum fit tale vacuum, nec Terra proprio motu
cieatur, fed à materia cœlefti, eam ambiente, omnefque ejus po-
ros pervadente, deferatur, ipfa habet rationem corporis quie-
fcentis; materia autem cœleftis, quatenus tota confentit in illum
motum quo Terram defert, nullam habet vim gravitatis, nec levi-
tatis; fed quatenus ejus partes plus habent agitationis quàm in hoc
impendant, ideoque femper terræ occurfu, à motibus fuis fecundùm lineas rectas perfequendis impediuntur, femper ab ea quantum
poffunt recedunt, & in hoc earum levitas confiftit.

*XXIII.
Quomodo
partes o-
mnes terræ,
ab iftà ma-
teriâ cœlefti
deorfum pel-
lantur, &
ita fiant
graves.*

Notandum deinde, vim quam habent fingulæ partes materiæ cœleftis ad recedendum à Terra, fuum effectum fortiri non poffe,
nifi, dum illæ afcendunt, aliquas partes terreftres in quarum locum
fuccedant, infra fe deprimant & propellant. Cùm enim omnia fpatia quæ funt circa Terram, vel à particulis corporum terreftrium,
vel à materia cœlefti occupentur; atque omnes globuli hujus materiæ cœleftis, æqualem habeant propenfionem ad fe ab eà removen-
dos, nullam finguli habent vim, ad alios fui fimiles loco pellendos;
fed cùm talis propenfio non fit tanta in particulis corporum terreftrium, quoties aliquas ex ipfis fupra fe habent, omnino in eas vim
iftam fuam debent exercere. Atque ita gravitas cujufque corporis
terreftris, non propriè efficitur ab omni materià cœlefti illud circum-
fluente, fed præcisè tantùm ab eà ipfius parte, quæ, fi corpus iftud
defcendat, in ejus locum immediatè afcendit, ac proinde quæ eft
illi magnitudine planè æqualis. Sit exempli causâ, B corpus ter-
reftre

Figure 7.
Descartesian gravity and magnetism[11].

---

[11]**Figure 6**: Descartes 1897-1913 [*Principia*, 1644, VIII-1, Part IV, § 20-21]
IX-2: pp. 210-211 [Full Latin version: *Ivi*, VIII-1: pp. 1-348].

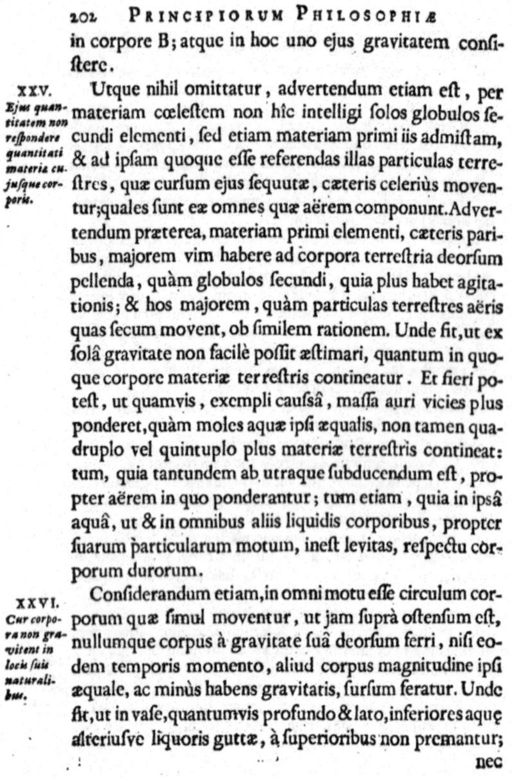

202 PRINCIPIORUM PHILOSOPHIÆ

in corpore B; atque in hoc uno ejus gravitatem confistere.

XXV.
Ejus quantitatem non respondere quantitati materiæ cujusque corporis.

Utque nihil omittatur, advertendum etiam est, per materiam cœlestem non hîc intelligi solos globulos secundi elementi, sed etiam materiam primi iis admistam, & ad ipsam quoque esse referendas illas particulas terrestres, quæ cursum ejus sequutæ, cæteris celeriùs moventur; quales sunt eæ omnes quæ aërem component. Advertendum præterea, materiam primi elementi, cæteris paribus, majorem vim habere ad corpora terrestria deorsum pellenda, quàm globulos secundi, quia plus habet agitationis; & hos majorem, quàm particulas terrestres aëris quas secum movent, ob similem rationem. Unde fit, ut ex solâ gravitate non facilè possit æstimari, quantum in quoque corpore materiæ terrestris contineatur. Et fieri potest, ut quamvis, exempli causâ, massa auri vicies plus ponderet, quàm moles aquæ ipsi æqualis, non tamen quadruplo vel quintuplo plus materiæ terrestris contineat: tum, quia tantundem ab utraque subducendum est, propter aërem in quo ponderantur; tum etiam, quia in ipsâ aquâ, ut & in omnibus aliis liquidis corporibus, propter suarum particularum motum, inest levitas, respectu corporum durorum.

XXVI.
Cur corpora non gravitent in locis suis naturalibus.

Considerandum etiam, in omni motu esse circulum corporum quæ simul moventur, ut jam suprà ostensum est, nullumque corpus à gravitate suâ deorsum ferri, nisi eodem temporis momento, aliud corpus magnitudine ipsi æquale, ac minùs habens gravitatis, sursum feratur. Unde fit, ut in vase, quantumvis profundo & lato, inferiores aquę alteriusve liquoris guttæ, à superioribus non premantur;

nec

It can happen i.e. that, albeit a mass of gold is twenty times heavier than a quantity of water of the same size, it does not contain twenty times the quantity of matter contained in that mass of water, but only four or five times [...][12]

Figure 8.
Some Descartes' arguments on matter concept[13].

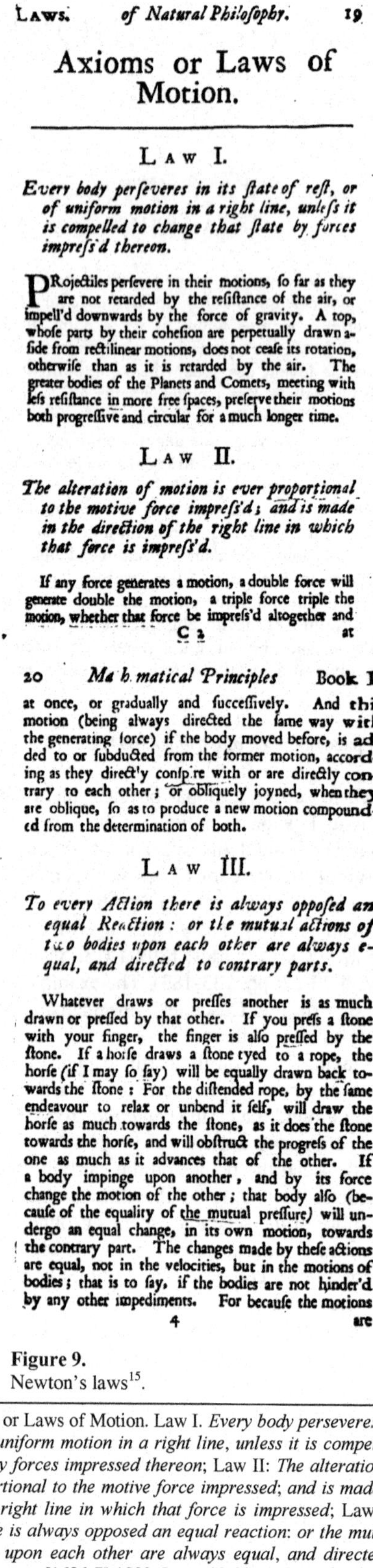

LAWS. *of Natural Philosophy.* 19

Axioms or Laws of Motion.

LAW I.

Every body perseveres in its state of rest, or of uniform motion in a right line, unless it is compelled to change that state by forces impress'd thereon.

PRojectiles persevere in their motions, so far as they are not retarded by the resistance of the air, or impell'd downwards by the force of gravity. A top, whose parts by their cohesion are perpetually drawn aside from rectilinear motions, does not cease its rotation, otherwise than as it is retarded by the air. The greater bodies of the Planets and Comets, meeting with less resistance in more free spaces, preserve their motions both progressive and circular for a much longer time.

LAW II.

The alteration of motion is ever proportional to the motive force impress'd; and is made in the direction of the right line in which that force is impress'd.

If any force generates a motion, a double force will generate double the motion, a triple force triple the motion, whether that force be impress'd altogether and

C 2   at

20   *Mathematical Principles*   Book I.

at once, or gradually and successively. And this motion (being always directed the same way with the generating force) if the body moved before, is added to or subducted from the former motion, according as they directly conspire with or are directly contrary to each other; or obliquely joyned, when they are oblique, so as to produce a new motion compounded from the determination of both.

LAW III.

To every Action there is always opposed an equal Reaction: or the mutual actions of two bodies upon each other are always equal, and directed to contrary parts.

Whatever draws or presses another is as much drawn or pressed by that other. If you press a stone with your finger, the finger is also pressed by the stone. If a horse draws a stone tyed to a rope, the horse (if I may so say) will be equally drawn back towards the stone: For the distended rope, by the same endeavour to relax or unbend it self, will draw the horse as much towards the stone, as it does the stone towards the horse, and will obstruct the progress of the one as much as it advances that of the other. If a body impinge upon another, and by its force change the motion of the other; that body also (because of the equality of the mutual pressure) will undergo an equal change, in its own motion, towards the contrary part. The changes made by these actions are equal, not in the velocities, but in the motions of bodies; that is to say, if the bodies are not hinder'd by any other impediments. For because the motions

4   are

Figure 9.
Newton's laws[15].

their difficulties of transcription into quantitative physical terms. The mechanistic and *a priori* conviction of Descartes brought hence him to the impossibility to have a well defined conception of space and of mass[14]. This is a substantial, not only formal difference. In fact, the scientific framework of the treatises can deceive. For example, in *Principia*, Newton wrote eight definitions and the three *laws* (or *axioms*) at the beginning (see **Figure 9**).

Therefore one can get the impression he started from these to explain the phenomena analysed in the three books of *Principia*. Actually, the two introductory sections (*definitions* and *axioms*) give an Euclidean order to the text that is different from the way in which Newton reached to determine the nature of the phenomena. The definitions and the laws were enucleated on the basis of the phenomena, not before a detailed examination

---

[12]"Et fieri potest, ut quamvis, exempli caussa, massa auri vicies plus ponderet, quam moles aquae ipsi aequalis, non tamen quadruple vel quintuplo plus materiae terrestris contineat [...]" (Descartes [*Principia*, 1644, Part IV: p. 202] VIII-1: p. 213, line 16). The translation is ours.
[13]*Ibidem.*
[14]The concept of mass from physical and mathematical standpoint was a hard concept until 19th century for new theories i.e. like chemistry and thermodynamics, machines theory (Pisano, 2010, 2011). For example Lazare Carnot (1753-1823) explicitly was ambiguous (Gillispie & Pisano 2013: p. 377) on the concept of force (Carnot, 1803: p. xj, p. 47) and mass assuming both of Descartesian and Newtonian assumptions (Carnot, 1803: p. 6). Ernst Mach (1838-1916) wrote interesting speeches on that (Mach, ([1896] 1986): pp. 368-369) tried to formulate an operative interpretation of mass using the third principle of mechanics (Mach, 1888, [1896] 1986)).

[15]"Axioms; or Laws of Motion. Law I. *Every body perseveres in its state of rest, or of uniform motion in a right line, unless it is compelled to change that state by forces impressed thereon*; Law II: *The alteration of motion is ever proportional to the motive force impressed; and is made in the direction of the right line in which that force is impressed*; Law III: *To every action there is always opposed an equal reaction: or the mutual actions of two bodies upon each other are always equal, and directed to contrary parts.*" (Newton, [1686-7] 1803, I: pp. 19-20; *Italic style* and capital letters belong to the author). (Newton, [1686-7] 1803, I: p 2; author's *italic* style and Capital letters). On forces and their geometrical interpretation one can see De Gandt (De Gandt, 1995).

and comprehension of the phenomena themselves. Instead in Descartes' *Principia* the laws, and above all the ideas concerning the constitution of matter, were thought almost independently from phenomena and, afterwards, applied to them.

On the *Principia Philosophiae*

In this section, we will deal with the cases in which the physical laws established by Descartes in his *Principia* are self-contradictory and contradicted by the experience itself, particularly on the collision rules theory.

Some Historiography on Descartes' Collision Rules

The historiography concerning Descartes' collision rules is conspicuous. Here we analyze only those studies directly connected with the logic of our reasoning[16].

Ernst Cassirer (1874-1945) stresses that the collision rules are self-contradictory, even if he does not enter into details. Consequently such rules do not provide a unified picture and, hence, a model of the phenomenon. Cassirer ascribes this situation to the fact that Descartes

[...] leaves the continuous and patient development of his deductive-mathematical premises and passes directly to explain concrete particular phenomena that are very complex[17].

Nevertheless, it is necessary to point out that in other cases of complex phenomena, as the refraction and the rainbow, Descartes is faithful to the mathematical approach of his own work.

Pierre Boutroux (1880-1922) after having eulogized Descartes for the introduction of the inertia principle and the conservation of the quantity of motion principle, writes as to the collision: "Unfortunately, Descartes makes a very serious mistake, that is surprising from his part"[18]. The mistake consists in the fact that Descartes did not catch the vectorial nature of the quantity of motion. The mistakes in the collision rules are due, according to Boutroux, to this misconception.

René Dugas (1897-1957) claims there is more than one reason why Descartes did not succeed in the explanation of the collision: a) lack of distinction between elastic and inelastic collisions (Dugas, [1954] 1987: pp 150-151); see also 1954; b) existence of dissymetries with regard to the reasons that can produce, increase or diminish the quantity of motion of a body; c) lack of comprehension of the vectorial nature of velocity (*Ivi*). Dugas adds that the experience is anyway necessary for a correct formulation of the collision rule (*Ivi*). Furthermore he underlines that from Descartes' correspondence, it is possible to deduce he had carried out some experiments, but that, between experimental results and principles, he had chosen the principles. Therefore Dugas ascribes the failure of Descartes' collision rules to an unclear comprehension of the basic principles connoting the motion quantity (theoretical reason) and to the lack of serious experiments on this subject (empirical reason).

Pierre Costabel (1912-1989), after having analysed the collision rules in Descartes claims:

It has been said and repeated the Descartesian collision rules are only an outline. Nevertheless, it has been stressed that the principles, of which such rules would be an outline, were already acquired in Descartes' thought. Actually we believe that things work in the opposite manner. These rules are only an outline because they are the expression of a thought that is still researching[19].

By the way, still Costabel's opinion that Descartes proposed only some outlined rules in the work he considered the result of his most mature thought in physics appears disputable.

Recently, Stephen Gaukroger discusses that Descartes' physics is based upon modelling drawn from statics and tries to explain the genesis itself of the collision rules on this basis. He proposes an interesting examination of the fourth rule (Gaukroger, 2000: pp. 60-80).

Peter McLaughlin, analyses the Descartesian concept of *determination* of a motion. He also frames the Descartesian rules inside a context deriving from statics and, in this way, he tries to provide an explanation of such rules (McLaughlin, 2000: pp. 81-112).

Beyond the principles explicitly formulated in his works, likely Descartes also resorted to some principles of minimum exposed in some of his letters. Gary C. Hatfield mentions a letter on 17 February 1645 to Clerselier[20] (1614-1684) in which Descartes wrote:

[...] when two bodies in incompatible modes collide, some change in these modes must truly occur, so as to render them compatible, but that this change is always the least possible [...][21].

McLaughlin also points out that Descartes resorts to a "principle of minimal modal change" (McLaughlin, 2000: p. 99). He also tries to interpret the meaning of *mode*. In particular, he remarks that *determination* and *velocity* of a motion are two different *modes*. It is then maybe possible to think that the collision rules are conceived so that the modal change is the less possible. In this manner, for example, in the rule 4, the change of the *determination* of the body B represents a *modal change* less than the one existing if the body C, too, would move, because, in this case, two *modes* would change: *determination* and *velocity*.

The existence of *principles of minimum* in Descartes' corpus is reasonable by what he wrote in the fifth *discours* of the *Les Météores* concerning with form of the clouds under the action of irregular winds:

[...] figure which can least [assume the form and] prevent

---

[16]With regard to the various factors on which historiography of science depends, see: Kragh, 1987; Pisano & Gaudiello, 2009a, 2009b; Kokowski, 2012; Poincaré, [1923] 1970, [1935] 1968; Rossi; Taton, 1965, 1966; Westfall, 1971.

[17]"[...] er den stetigen Gang und den geduldigen Ausbau seiner deduktivmathematischen Voraussetzungen verläßt, um unvermittelt zu der Erklärung verwickelter konkreter Sonderphänomene". (Cassirer, [1906] 1922: p. 479). The translation is ours.

[18]"Malheureusement, Descartes commet une erreur très grave et qui est bien surprenante da sa part". (Boutroux, 1921: p. 677). The translation is ours.

[19]"On a dit et redit que les règles cartésiennes du choc ne sont qu'une esquisse, mais on l'a fait en sous-entendant que les principes dont elles seraient l'esquisse étaient déjà fermes dans la pensée de Descartes. La réalité nous parait différente. Ces règles ne sont qu'une esquisse parce qu'elles sont l'expression d'une pensée en état de recherche". (Costabel, [1967] 1982: pp. 141-[152]158). The translation is ours. See also Costabel, 1960.

[20]Clerselier is an important figure in the scientific frameworks of Descartes. He edited and translated many Descartes' works i.e. *Correspondences* (1657, 1659, 1667), *Le Monde* (1667) and *Principes* (1681).

[21]"[...] *lors que deux cors se rencontrent, qui ont en eux des modes incompatibles, il se doit véritablement faire quelque changement en ces modes, pour les rendre compatibles, mais (que) ce changement est tousiours le moindre qui puisse être [...]*." (Descartes, 1897-1913, IV: p. 185, line 13). Author's *italic*. See also Hatfield, 1979, p. 133.

[opposes less resistance to] their movement [...][22]

The plurality of approaches through which many distinguished scholars and historians tried to explain the reasons that led Descartes to formulate collision laws that are self-contradictory and not confirmed by experience, proves that this question is not clear at all. Therefore, every explanation has, at least partially, a conjectural and hypothetical character.

Collision Dynamics and Physics-Mathematics Arguments

The study of the collision rules between two bodies is a subject on which the literature was relatively abundant in Descartes' age (McLaughlin, 2000: pp. 81-112). Descartes established seven rules (Descartes, 1897-1913, *Principia*, VIII-1: pp. 69-69; see **Figure 10**).

Descartes did not make distinction between elastic and inelastic collision. However, considering the structure of his reasoning above exposed, he was referring to elastic collisions on a surface without friction. It is known that only the first one of these previous rules is correct. A part from this, *do these rules have an inner coherence—for inner coherence we mean the property according to which no contradictory conclusions can be draw from the principles*? Let us see an example in order to consider two bodies B and C, the first one of mass 5, the second one 7.

Let C be at rest and let B move with velocity v. After the collision, C remains at rest, while B inverts the direction of its motion (by using rule 4).

Let us now imagine that B increases its mass with continuity and that C decreases it with continuity, in a way that the sum of the sizes remain invariable. When B has size 7 and C size 5,

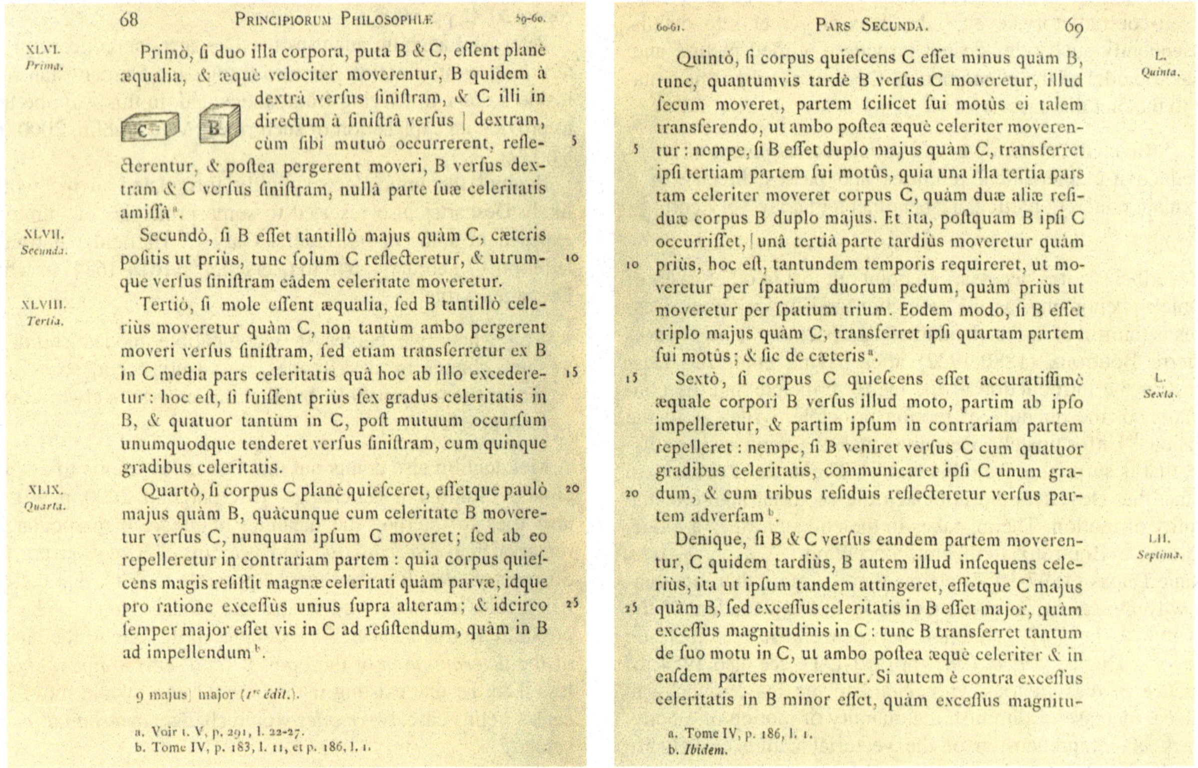

68 PRINCIPIORUM PHILOSOPHIÆ. 59-60.

XLVI. *Prima.* Primò, ſi duo illa corpora, puta B & C, eſſent planè æqualia, & æquè velociter moverentur, B quidem à dextrâ verſus ſiniſtram, & C illi in directum à ſiniſtrâ verſus | dextram, cùm ſibi mutuò occurrerent, reflecterentur, & poſtea pergerent moveri, B verſus dextram & C verſus ſiniſtram, nullâ parte ſuæ celeritatis amiſſâ [a].

XLVII. *Secunda.* Secundò, ſi B eſſet tantillò majus quàm C, cæteris poſitis ut priùs, tunc ſolum C reflecteretur, & utrumque verſus ſiniſtram eâdem celeritate moveretur.

XLVIII. *Tertia.* Tertiò, ſi mole eſſent æqualia, ſed B tantillò celeriùs moveretur quàm C, non tantùm ambo pergerent moveri verſus ſiniſtram, ſed etiam transferretur ex B in C media pars celeritatis quâ hoc ab illo excederetur: hoc eſt, ſi fuiſſent priùs ſex gradus celeritatis in B, & quatuor tantùm in C, poſt mutuum occurſum unumquodque tenderet verſus ſiniſtram, cum quinque gradibus celeritatis.

XLIX. *Quarta.* Quartò, ſi corpus C planè quieſceret, eſſetque paulò majus quàm B, quâcunque cum celeritate B moveretur verſus C, nunquam ipſum C moveret; ſed ab eo repelleretur in contrariam partem : quia corpus quieſcens magis reſiſtit magnæ celeritati quàm parvæ, idque pro ratione exceſſûs unius ſupra alteram; & idcirco ſemper major eſſet vis in C ad reſiſtendum, quàm in B ad impellendum [b].

9 majus] major (*1re édit.*).

a. Voir t. V, p. 291, l. 22-27.
b. Tome IV, p. 183, l. 11, et p. 186, l. 1.

60-61. PARS SECUNDA. 69

L. *Quinta.* Quintò, ſi corpus quieſcens C eſſet minus quàm B, tunc, quantumvis tardè B verſus C moveretur, illud ſecum moveret, partem ſcilicet ſui motûs ei talem transferendo, ut ambo poſtea æquè celeriter moverentur: nempe, ſi B eſſet duplo majus quàm C, transferret ipſi tertiam partem ſui motûs, quia una illa tertia pars tam celeriter moveret corpus C, quàm duæ aliæ reſiduæ corpus B duplo majus. Et ita, poſtquam B ipſi C occurriſſet, | unâ tertiâ parte tardiùs moveretur quàm priùs, hoc eſt, tantundem temporis requireret, ut moveretur per ſpatium duorum pedum, quàm priùs ut moveretur per ſpatium trium. Eodem modo, ſi B eſſet triplo majus quàm C, transferret ipſi quartam partem ſui motûs; & ſic de cæteris [a].

LI. *Sexta.* Sextò, ſi corpus C quieſcens eſſet accuratiſſimè æquale corpori B verſus illud moto, partim ab ipſo impelleretur, & partim ipſum in contrariam partem repelleret: nempe, ſi B veniret verſus C cum quatuor gradibus celeritatis, communicaret ipſi C unum gradum, & cum tribus reſiduis reflecteretur verſus partem adverſam [b].

LII. *Septima.* Denique, ſi B & C verſus eandem partem moverentur, C quidem tardiùs, B autem illud inſequens celeriùs, ita ut ipſum tandem attingeret, eſſetque C majus quàm B, ſed exceſſus celeritatis in B eſſet major, quàm exceſſus magnitudinis in C : tunc B transferret tantum de ſuo motu in C, ut ambo poſtea æquè celeriter & in eaſdem partes moverentur. Si autem è contra exceſſus celeritatis in B minor eſſet, quàm exceſſus magnitu-

a. Tome IV, p. 186, l. 1.
b. *Ibidem.*

1) If two bodies B and C, whose mass[23] is equal, go one against the other with the same speed, then, after the collision, they bounce back in the starting direction with unmodified speed; 2) In the same situation, but with B greater than C, the body C, after the collision, bounces back in the original direction and the two bodies proceed unified in that direction; 3) If B and C have the same size, but B is quicker than C, then, after the collision, C bounces back and, *mutatis mutandis*, the situation is the same as in the rule 2; 4) If C is bigger than B and C is at rest, whatever the speed of B is after the collision, C remains at rest and B bounces back in the direction from which it was coming; 5) If C is smaller than B and C is at rest, when B collides with C, the two bodies proceed unified, according to the principle of conservation of the quantity of movement; 6) If C is at rest and B and C have the same size, and if B hits C, after the collision, C will move in the same direction and verse as B, while B itself bounces back; 7) If B and C move in the same verse and C is bigger and slower than B and the excess of the velocity of B is greater than the excess of the size of C, then B transfers part of its movement to C, so that the two bodies move with the same velocity in the same verse. The rule also considers the symmetric case in which the excess of speed of B is less than the excess of size of C.

Figure 10.
Collision rules arguments[24].

[22]"[...] la figure qui peut le moins empêcher leur mouvement […]". (Descartes, 1897-1913, VI: p. 286, lines 28-29). The translation is ours.

[23]The word used by Descartes for *mass* is—in general—"mole" (Descartes, 1897-1913, VIII: p. 68, line 9) when he speaks of the third rule of the collision and other occurrences. In the *Principia* Descartes uses the word "corpus" plus an adjective ("major" or "minor"). For example, at the beginning of the fifth collision rule, we read: "Quinto, si corpus quiescens C esset minus quam B […]" (Descartes, 1897-1913 Principia VIII: p. 69, line 1). We have translated these words with *mass* because other translations would be even worse and without refereeing to modern concept of the mass. On the history of the concept of mass, at first glance one cans see Jammer (Jammer, 1961).

[24]Descartes, 1897-1913, VIII: pp. 68-69.

after the collision, B pushes C and the two bodies prosecute their motion unified (rule 5).

Thus, because of the continuity principle, a physical state necessarily exists in which, after the collision, B remains at rest and this must happen when B is as great as C.

The conclusion of this reasoning, deduced by applying the rules 4 and 5, is that when a body B of size m and speed v strokes a body C—that is at rest—of the same size, B remains at rest and C prosecutes in the same direction and verse as B and with speed v.

However, this results contradicts the rule 6.

Beyond the lack of inner coherence, there is also the problem that the Descartesian rules of the collision contradict the daily experience concerning the collisions themselves in an evident manner. In the Principia, *Descartes*—who was aware of this—underlined (Descartes, 1897-1913, IX-2, §53) that his rules are referred to ideal situations that can be hardly experimented, after having concluded the paragraph 52 claiming that "these rules [of collision] are so evident that no empirical confirmation is necessary"[25]. In this part of his scientific framework the relation between experience and modelling-theory would provide that i.e. single events of a phenomenon are determined by circumstances that are contingent in respect to an *a priori* theoretical model. Thus this kind of approach is typically deductive and aiming to test a final theoretical reasoning. As a matter of fact, the eventual inconsistency between theory and experience depends either on such circumstances or on the inadequacy of the model to represent the phenomenon to which it was applied[26].

The lack of an agreement between experiences-data and modelling-theory is typical of a scientific theory, especially physics and chemistry. For example, a unit of measurement is effectively a standardised quantity of a physical (and chemical) property, used as a factor to express occurring quantities of that property. Therefore, any value of a physical quantity is expressed as a comparison to a unit of that quantity. In the physics mathematics[27] domain one generally precedes by means of calculations, therefore the units of measurement are not a prior-

ity in terms of a solution to an analytical problem (Pisano, 2013; Lindsay, Margenau, & Margenau). In this sense, the physical (and chemical) nature of the quantities is not a priority[28]. One may discuss the role played by a certain science in history (e.g., physics), focusing solely on the historical period, the kind of mathematics adopted and the relations between experiments and theory in the analysed historical period (Pisano, 2011). For our aim, the most important aspect is the role played by the relationship between physics and mathematics adopted in a scientific theory in order to describe mathematical laws—e.g., the second Newtonian mathematical law of motion or, in the case of Descartes's *Principia*, the lack of such mathematical structure and its conesquences (Nagel, 1961, 1997). On the other hands, the *time* is a crucial physical magnitude in mechanics (Truesdell, 1968) but in the aforementioned, the *time* (and *space*) is also a mathematical magnitude since it is a mathematical variable in variations (later derivatives) operations aimed to interpret a certain phenomenon. Most importantly, if we lose the mathematical significances of time and space magnitudes, we would lose the entire mechanical paradigm. Nevertheless, the approaches to conceive and define foundational *mechanical-physical quantities* and their *mathematical quantities* and interpretations change both within a physics mathematics domain and a physical one (Duhem). One could think of mathematical solutions to Lagrange's energy equations (Lagrange, 1778, 1973; Panza, 2003) rather than the crucial role played by collisions and geometric motion in Lazare Carnot's algebraic mechanics or Faraday's experimental science (Faraday, 1839-1855; Heilbron; Pisano, 2013) with respect to André-Marie Ampère (1775-1836) mechanical approach in the electric current domain and finally the physic mathematics choices in James Clerk Maxwell (1831-1879) electromagnetic theory (Maxwell, 1873; Pisano, 2013). Physical science makes use of experimental apparatuses to observe and measure physical magnitudes. During and after an experiment, this apparatus may be illustrated and/or and designed. Generally, this procedure is not employed in pure mathematical studies. Thus, one can claim that experiments and their illustrations can be strictly characterized by physical principles and magnitudes to be measured. A modelling of results of the experimental apparatus allows for the broadening of the hypotheses and the establishment of certain theses. If one avoids study-modelling experimental results, one may generate an analytical scientific theory since there is no interest in the nature of physical magnitudes and their measurements.

In the Descartesian rules on the collisions this eventual lack mostly concerns: a) Descartes, in physics, guessed the importance of conservation principles, but, in the collision rules, he was not able to exploit this fundamental and correct idea in a suitable manner; b) a lack of an adequate mathematical interpretation which could be helpful for the fully comprehension of a phenomenon; and c) the impossibility to operate adequate measure since the lack of fully knowledge of the concept of physical quantities for some substances (i.e., one can think of the concept of velocity, rather mass, or temperature, heat etc.)

[25]"Nec ista egent probatione, quia per se manifesta". (Descartes, 1897-1913, [*Principia*, VIII]: p. 70, line 12). The translation is ours.
[26]On that Thomas Samuel Kuhn (1922-1996) proposed (Kuhn, [1962] 1970) that some contradictions between facts and theory are simply ignored by the scientists until a *dominant paradigm* provides exhaustive explanations of the majority of phenomena in which, in a certain period, the scientific community is interested. In particular see *Anomaly and the Emergence of Scientific Discoveries* (Kuhn, [1962] 1970, Chap. VI: pp. 52-65) and the *The Response to Crisis* (Kuhn, [1962] 1970, Chap. VIII: pp. 77-91, in particular pp. 80-82; see also Osler, 2000). Besides that, Paul Feyerabend (1924-1994) has shown—basically through an analysis of Galileo's work—that some experiences are often neglected and that the *critics of experience* is constituted by *ad hoc* argumentations ideated by the scientists to achieve his/her theoretical purposes (Feyerabend, 1975, chaps. 5-8; see also 1991). On Galileo, recently one can see: Festa, 1995, Pisano, 2009a, 2009b,
[27]One of us stressed the relationship between physics and mathematics in the history of science by means of many studies. Among physicists, mathematicians, historians and philosophers who are credited with study of mathematical physical quantities by means of experiments, modelling, properties, existences, structures etc. one can strictly focus on how physics and mathematics work in a unique discipline physics mathematics (or, if one prefers, mathematics physics). Thus, it is not a mathematical application in physics and vice-versa but rather a new (for example in the 19th century) way to consider this science: a new discipline physics mathematics and not mathematical physics, where the change in the kind of infinity in mathematics produces a change in both significant physical processes and interpretations of *physical quantiti*es (Pisano, 2013: pp. 39-58; see also 2011: pp. 457-472).

[28]For instance, one can see an analogous situation concerning heat and temperature concepts in the analytical theory of heat (Fourier, 1807, 1822) with respect to Sadi Carnot's thermodynamic theory (Pisano, 2010, 2011; Gillispie & Pisano, 2013; Pisano, 2010). I briefly note that physics considers the indispensable agreement between theoretical data and observations—experimental data (including the properties of magnitudes) to establish a physical theory. Generally, such arguments are not considered rigorous by physics mathematics.

and the lack of experiments on collision; even considering the whole described picture, it is hard to conceive how it is possible. Thus, a conclusion would be that, in many cases, the lack of a mathematical quantitative treatment prevented Descartes to realize his procedures were not always correct.

Quantification of Physical Reasonings

In his physical works Descartes frequently takes position against the *essentialism* typical of the *Scholastic* because he thinks that such an approach cannot help in anyway to understand the physical phenomena. Particularly he points out the necessity to give a clear and quantitative form to the principles and to the problems themselves of physics. However, Descartes' physical conception is not free from essentialist aspects. For example

> [...] a consequence of his first law of motion, Descartes insists that the quantity conserved in collisions equals the combined sum of the products of size and speed of each impacting body. Although a difficult concept, the "size" of a body roughly corresponds to its volume, with surface area playing an indirect role as well. This conserved quantity, which Descartes refers to indiscriminately as "motion" or "quantity of motion", is historically significant in that it marks one of the first attempts to locate an invariant or unchanging feature of bodily interactions[29].

Descartes seemed to have understood—in the second *discours* of the *La Dioptrique* on the decomposition of the motion and of the *determination* of a motion—that velocity has a direction[30] besides a modulus (Descartes, 1897-1913, VI: pp. 93-105). While, in the *Principia* no quantitative specifications with regard to the role that the modulus and the direction[31] of velocity should get in the physical phenomena is provided.

In the end, concerning his quantitative physical reasonings we can mainly claim:

1) Important concepts and rules—as quantity of motion, and significant rules, the seven collision laws—are introduced by Descartes (*Principia*) in a manner that they could not be expressed in an adequate mathematical terms.

2) The three physical parts of the *Principia* (the second, the third and the fourth ones) are inscribed into a physical conception that, in many regards, is still linked to the *Scholastic* ontologism.

Relying upon his researches on the fluid dynamics exposed in the second book of his *Principia*, Newton argued that the vortices, of which Descartes imagined the universe was composed, cannot be stable (Newton, [1713] 1729, II, *General Scholium*: pp. 387-388). This means the physics of Descartes' *Principia* does not satisfy to the minimal requests for it to be translated into quantitative terms in a quantitative model. If Descartes had tried this operation, likely, he would have noticed the physical and factual inconsistencies to which his principles brought. For example, he could have seen that his collision rules were self-contradictory. Coherently with what he himself had claimed in various passages of *Regulae ad directionem ingenii* (Descartes, 1897-1913, X: pp. 351-488; see **Figure 11**) and of *Discours de la méthode* (Descartes, 1897-1913, VI: pp. 1-78). As a matter of fact, in the 13th *regula* Descartes claims (Descartes, 1897-1913, X: pp. 430-438) that every problem has to be divided and analysed into a series of enumerated parts whose knowledge is absolutely certain.

According Descartes, for a phenomenon[33], one should carry out a large series of experiments and after a profound analysis, to consider only those who are really suitable to comprehend such a phenomenon and to exclude the others. Moreover, this reasoning is also valid as to single parts of an experiment. Thus Descartes should have specified the experiments on which his collision rules were based. This would have been important to interpret into mathematical terms their results and in order to make sure the concepts which he used were perspicuous. Nevertheless, as above seen, he acted in a completely different way as to the collision rules (this was also the case for concepts as *force, pressure, power*). Thus, he would have realized how difficult a satisfactory introduction of a conceptual structure suitable to explain the physical phenomena is. In other words,

> [Descartes] expresses so well the basic idea of a mathematical physics, but he fails to specify how he want to make sure physics susceptible to mathematical treatment. For sure, he completely underestimated the difficulty of this task: it is clear when with a candor typically of scholastic he propose as example to represent by means of a

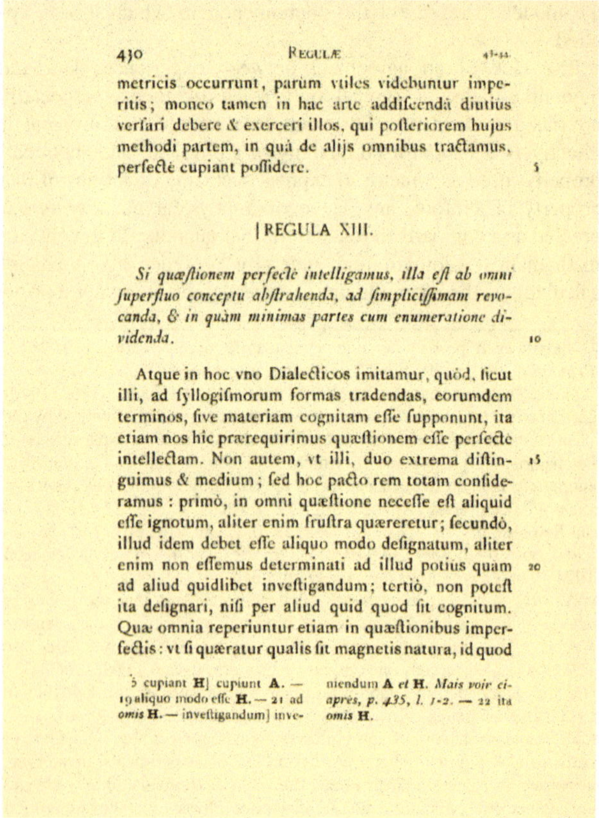
430 REGULÆ 43-44.

metricis occurrunt, parùm vtiles videbuntur imperitis; moneo tamen in hac arte addiſcendâ diutiùs verſari debere & exerceri illos, qui poſteriorem hujus methodi partem, in quâ de alijs omnibus tractamus, perfectè cupiant poſſidere.

| REGULA XIII.

Si quæſtionem perfectè intelligamus, illa eſt ab omni ſuperfluo conceptu abſtrahenda, ad ſimpliciſſimam revocanda, & in quàm minimas partes cum enumeratione dividenda.

Atque in hoc vno Dialecticos imitamur, quòd, ſicut illi, ad ſyllogiſmorum formas tradendas, eorumdem terminos, ſive materiam cognitam eſſe ſupponunt, ita etiam nos hic prærequirimus quæſtionem eſſe perfectè intellectam. Non autem, vt illi, duo extrema diſtinguimus & medium; ſed hoc pacto rem totam conſideramus : primò, in omni quæſtione neceſſe eſt aliquid eſſe ignotum, aliter enim fruſtra quæreretur; ſecundò, illud idem debet eſſe aliquo modo deſignatum, aliter enim non eſſemus determinati ad illud potiùs quàm ad aliud quidlibet inveſtigandum; tertiò, non poteſt ita deſignari, niſi per aliud quid quod ſit cognitum. Quæ omnia reperiuntur etiam in quæſtionibus imperfectis : vt ſi quæratur qualis ſit magnetis natura, id quod

5 cupiant **H**] cupiunt **A**. — 19 aliquo modo eſſe **H**. — 21 ad *omis* **H**. — inveſtigandum] inveniendum **A** *et* **H**. *Mais voir ci-après, p. 435, l. 1-2.* — 22 ita *omis* **H**.

Figure 11.
Regulae ad directionem ingenii[32].

[29]Slowik, § 4. Author's quotations.

[30]This does not mean that he had completely caught the concept of vector. Nevertheless his conception might be indented as *orientation* (*direction* and *versus*).

[31]This happens i.e. more than once, at the beginning of the second *discours* of the *La Dioptrique*. The word recurs by Descartes to indicate a direction is "costé" (i.e. see: Descartes 1897-1913, [*La Dioptrique*], VI: pp. 94-95).

[32]Descartes, 1897-1913, X: p. 430 [pp. 351-488]).

[33]Descartes, particularly quotes Gilbert's experiments with the magnets (Descartes, 1897-1913, X: pp. 430-438).

line the degree of whiteness, without making allusion to the difficulties inherent in the measurement of a qualitative intensity[34].

In the *Principia,* an eloquent mechanistic conception (Dijksterhuis 1961) is provided: "[...] every modification of the matter as well as the diversity of all its forms depends on motion [...]"[35]. The interplay between *gradation* and *intensity* of the considered quantities plays an essential role especially when he enumerates some of the fundamental properties of the particles composing the three elements (Descartes, 1897-1913, X, III part, § 52 and § 53: pp. 105-107). The intensity of the velocity of these particles decreases with a continuous *gradation* from the first to the third element: the first one is composed of very small fluted particles whose motion is extremely quick; the second one by small circular particles, that anyway are a little bit bigger and less quick of those composing the first element; finally, the third element is constituted by the biggest and slowest particles. The form of the particles and the different intensity of their speed is the cause of being the first element the luminous, the second the transparent and the third the opaque. Given these presuppositions, one could expect a transcription of all these physical relations into quantitative terms, also considering that many scientists (Galileo is the most famous example) had already given a mathematical form to their physics. Actually, in the *Principia* there is no mathematization of the physical relations (Panza, 2006).

On the Two *Essays, La Dioptrique* and *Les Météores*

The two *Essays* were written as appendices to the *Discours de la méthode* to illustrate concrete applications of the theoretical precepts previously exposed. However, *La Dioptrique* and the *Les Météores,* do not give the impression to follow pre-established methodological precepts (Braunstein), rather they show the lively work of the scientist and because of this they are so interesting. The language used by Descartes is the French because these texts also had a practical scope (construction of lenses and telescopes) and therefore they had to be understood by the artisans who, in general, were not confident with the Latin. The purposes of the *La Dioptrique* and of the *Les Météores* are clear. It is possible to identify four conceptual centres, whose treatment is based on rather diversified methodological approaches (see **Figure 12**):

Since the second conceptual centre is the most significant from a historical-scientific point of view and it is the one in which Descartes follows explicitly a quantitative approach, we will address two themes treated there: 1) the law of refraction; 2) the rainbow. We will see that the approach is completely different from that connoting the *Principia.*

Reflexions on the Law of Refraction

In the second *discours* of the *La Dioptrique* Descartes (see **Figures 13(a)** and **(b)**) determines the law of refraction.

The main purpose of the *Dioptrique* was the improvement of optical instruments. To this end, Descartes derived the sine law of refraction by analogy with the inflection of the motion of a tennis ball upon entering water[40].

Let us imagine (**Figures 13(a)** and **(b)**) that a ball K is thrown from A to B and that it meets the surface of the cloth CBE in B. If one supposes that K has a sufficient power to break the cloth, then the ball will continue its movement beyond the cloth, losing a certain fraction of its velocity—let us suppose half of the initial velocity—Descartes claims that, if the *determination* (Descartes, 1897-1913, VI: p. 97, line 14 and following pages) of the movement is decomposed into two components, the one parallel and the other perpendicular to the cloth, only the perpendicular component will be modified by the encounter with the cloth, while the parallel will not be. If now the three perpendiculars AC, HB, FE to CBE are drawn, so that $HF = 2AH$, the ball will reach the point I of the circumference of radius AB in a time which is the double to the one needing to cover the part AB. A questions arises: *how is it possible to determine the point I?* The ball maintains its *determination* to proceed in the horizontal direction, therefore it will cover a double space in a double time in the direction parallel to the cloth. Thus, the point I is the one whose projection BE on the cloth CBE is the double of CB. Descartes argues that if a means is posed at the place of the cloth, that, as the water, opposes a major resistance to the motion of the ball than the air (supposed to be over the water), then the law determining the change of the ball motion in the passage from one mean to the other one, is the same as the law determining the passage of the ball between two portions of the same means separated by the cloth.

Let us now suppose (**Figure 13(b)**) that the ball, once reached B (let t be the time needed for the passage from A to B) does not miss its velocity[41], but rather receives a push so that the velocity increases by 1/3. In this case, if we carry out a construction analogous to the previous one, the ball will reach the point I in a time equal to $2/3t$, so that the projection BE on the separating surface is equal to $2/3CB$. This depends on being the velocity along the horizontal *determination* unmodified. Descartes claims that the action of light has the same behaviour as the motion of the ball (Buchwald). Hence, if a light ray starts from a less refracting means and reaches a more refracting means (according to Descartes, this happens, for example, in the passage from the air to the water) the component of motion *determination* parallel to the separating surface will remain unmodified, whereas, according to the nature of the two means, the perpendicular component will be modified. Therefore as in the following **Figure 14**:

The ratio between segments as KM and NL is invariant, namely

$$\frac{KM}{NL} = \frac{AH}{gI} = ...$$

---

[34]Dijksterhuis, [1950] 1977: p. 71, see also pp. 60-82. The translation is ours. Still interesting is Dijksterhuis, 1961.
[35]Descartes, 1897-1913, VIII: pp. 52-53. The translation is ours.

[40]Darrigol 2012, Chap. 2. (Author's italic). For our aim, in this highlightly book an interesting account concerning Newton's optic is presented (*Ivi,* Chap. 3).
[41]In this context Descartes often speaks of *force de son mouvement* (a kind of motion force: Descartes, 1897-1913 VI: p. 100, lines 1-2) and also uses the word *vitesse* (velocity). In our specific case, the translation of *force de movement* with velocity does not look to betray Descartes' thought. *Force de movement* looks a concept similar to quantity of motion, but since the mass is an invariant in the interaction described by Descartes, the translation velocity looks appropriate. In this case, too, the lack of scientific concepts and of a language universally codified makes these notions similar to various post-Newtonian concepts in the history, but not perfectly identifiable with them.

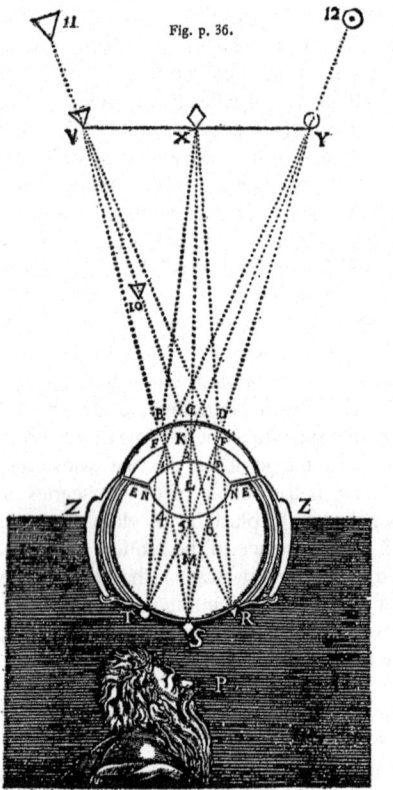

116   OEuvres de Descartes.   37:

VXY, au moins fi vous faites en forte que cet œil

Fig. p. 36.

retiene fa figure naturelle, proportionnée a la diftance

Figure 12.
The mechanism of the vision according to Descartes[37].

1) The first *discours* of the *La Dioptrique* poses, in substance, the bases for the prosecution of the treatment. Descartes carries out some considerations on the nature of the light (in part they are used and developed in the successive *discours*), but specifies that in the Essays he will deal with the problems how the light is spread rather than what is its nature[36]. Given these aims, Descartes explains he will limit to illustrate the easiest manner to conceive the light in relation to the phenomena he has to clarify. He will rely upon experiences and hypotheses, as the astronomers do in order to describe the motions in the skies. Therefore the first *discours* of the *La Dioptrique* represents the true methodological introduction to the two "physical" Essays rather than the *Discours de la méthode*; 2) The second conceptual core, which is the broadest and the most important, includes the *discours* II-IX of the *La Dioptrique* and the *discours* VIII-X of the *Les Météores*. Here Descartes faces, in the *La Dioptrique*, the theme of the refraction, of the form of the eye and of the vision-mechanism, of the properties of the lenses and of the most suitable form the lenses must have to reach their purpose (correction of sigh-defects, magnification of the objects, and so on). In the *discours* VIII, IX and X of the *Les Météores* Descartes exposes the theory of the rainbow and of the parhelions. The treatise is developed in a quantitative form. The author resorts to the experiments and reaches to explanations of phenomena that, even if not correct or based upon correct presuppositions, provide anyway a substantially perspicuous picture of the phenomena; 3) The third conceptual core includes the 10th *discours* of the *La Dioptrique*. This core could be defined the *practical* one because Descartes proposes projects of machineries to construct optical instruments with as most perfect as possible lenses. This is an interesting document of history of scientific technology (even if almost no one of the projected machines was built); 4) Finally, the initial seven *discours* of the *Les Météores*, that concern subjects as the nature of the winds, the clouds formation, the causes of the precipitations, etc., have—in comparison to the other parts of the Essays—a style which is nearer to the one used by Descartes in his *Principia*. Actually, subjects dealt with in an original manner are not missing, as it is the case in the sixth *discours* with regard to the form assumed by the snow-flakes.

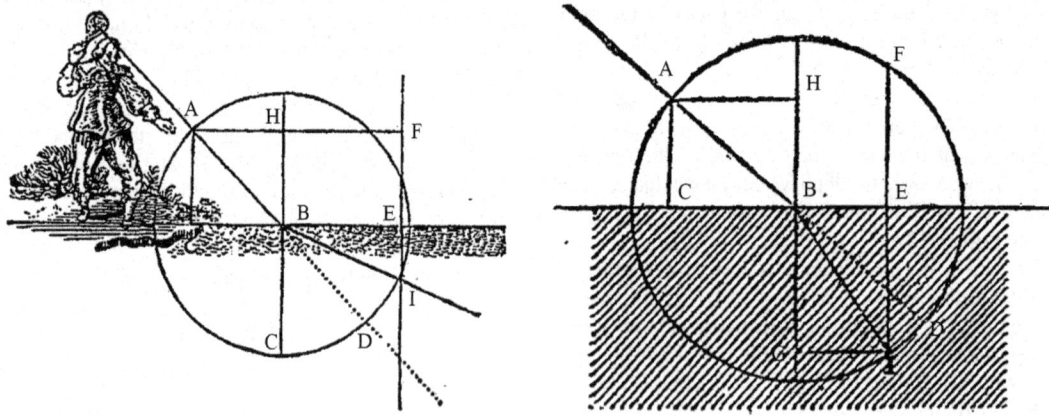

Figure 13.
(a) Analogy between the movement of a ball and a light ray[38]; (b) The ball in B receives a push. Analysis of the consequences[39].

---

[36]The reference text as to Descartesian ideas on light is *Le Monde ou le Traité de la Lumière*, published posthumous in 1664. The chapters 13 and 14 are those specifically dedicated to light. Numerous paragraphs of the third part of *Principia* concern the nature of light inside the context of Descartes' theory of matter (Descartes, 1897-1913, VIII) Descartes tries to explain what light is, what its effects are, how the stars irradiate. The literature on Descartesian theory of light is huge and it is impossible to provide even general indications. Recently for a very good and definitive history of optic see Olivier Darrigol (Darrigol, 2012, and all references cited). The Essays constitute the second volume of the Italian translation of Descartes' scientific works (Descartes, 1983). The editor Lojacono added an adequate list of references and suggesting (Descartes, 1983: pp. 95-110; see also: Sabra, 1967; Tiemersma, 1988; Malet, 1990; Armogathe, 2000; Schuster, 2000; Shapiro, 1974; Schuster, 2013).

[37]Descartes, 1897-1913 [*La Dioptrique*, V *discours*], VI; p. 116.

[38]Descartes, 1897-1913 [*La Dioptrique*, I *discours*] VI; p. 91.

[39]Descartes, 1897-1913 [*La Dioptrique*, II *discours*] VI; p. 100.

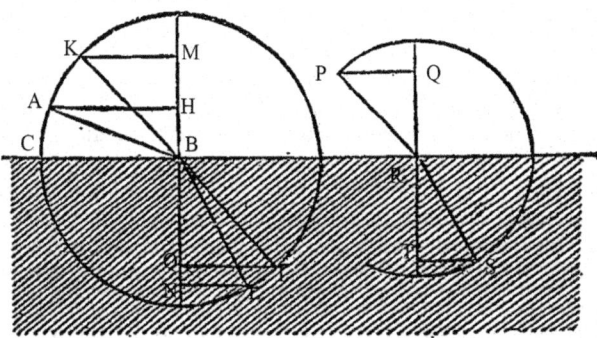

Figure 14.
Determination of the motion and its components[42].

These previous segments are the *sinus* of the incidence and of the refraction angles respectively. The law of refraction is, thus, formulated like this: *the ratio between the sinus of the two angles is a constant and depends on the refraction index of the two means* (Descartes, 1897-1913, VI: pp. 101-102).

The argumentation proposed by Descartes does not claim to be a demonstration of the refraction law, rather an explanation that makes it deductively plausible. Nevertheless, there are many questions concerning the picture proposed by Descartes:

1) What is exactly the *determination* of a motion?

2) Can the analogy of the ball that perforates the cloth (see **Figure 13**) be legitimately extended to the light rays?

3) Does the nature of light have an influence on the refraction law?

These questions are, as a matter of fact, doubts on the legitimacy of Descartesian argumentation. On the other hand, Newton represents a conceptual and linguistic line of separation for physics because the concepts used in pre-Newtonian physics were—in general—not defined. One holds on the common use of the words, or one oscillates between the common use and forms of specification that were not always univocal or even mutually coherent[43]. Therefore no surprise if Descartes did not define the concept of *determination*. In any case, the *determination* does not look *tout court* identifiable with the direction of a movement because Descartes uses the word *direction*, too, when he speaks of movement. The concept of *determination* has been studied for a long time by Descartes' scholars (many in: Mclaughlin, 2000) because undoubtedly it is difficult to enucleate. It is maybe possible to think that Descartes intended by *determination* the tendency of a body to reach the points of its actual direction. These point are really reached or would be reached if no impediment subsists. In the example of the second *discours* of the *La Dioptrique*, the ball has a *determination* towards *D*, however this point is not reached because of the impediment of the cloth. The *determination* would hence be a tendencies inherent to the motion of the body, while the direction is a geometrical line. This is an interpretation because the concept of *determination* remains, in any way, problematic.

As to the analogy between motion of the ball and action of

light, Descartes assumes it without any further discussion and justification. He underlines anyway that this analogy is not complete because the ball is deviated far from the normal to the surface of the cloth by the cloth itself, while if a light ray passes from a less dense to a more dens means, the ray approaches the normal, as well known. This brought Descartes to the wrong conclusion that, given two means with different density, light, in its movement, encounters less resistance in the more dense means. However, according to Descartes the light propagates instantaneously in every means. Therefore one cannot claim that, according to Descartes, the light speed is major in a dense means rather than in a less dense means. Rather Descartes explains that since light is "[…] an action by a very subtle matter that fulfils the pores of the other bodies"[44]. Such action is hindered by more "soft" bodies, as air, rather than by less "soft" bodies, as water. Hence, as light encounters less resistance to spread in the water rather than in the air, this is the reason why in the passage air/water light approaches the normal.

The conceptual equipment used by Descartes to determine the refraction law is hence tied to notions that are not always well defined (as the one of *determination* of a motion), to analogies and to wrong ideas; despite this the formulation of the law is correct[45]. This induces us to think that the whole equipment exposed to the reader in the second *discours* of the *Dioptrique* is not directly connected to the way in which Descartes discovered the refraction law. Rather it looks to have the aim to convince the reader and to frame optics inside the mechanistic project Descartes had already in his mind when he wrote the Essays. In a brilliant and profound paper Schuster underlines that:

> Descartes was willing to try to ride out likely accusations that the premises are empirically implausible, dynamically ad hoc, and in some interpretations, logically inconsistent, because the premises provided elegant and more or less convincing rationalisations for the geometrical moves in his demonstration[46].

The premises were confused and wrong, but the model was elegant and worked. Schuster produces convincing evidences in favour of the thesis that the refraction law was ideated by Descartes through an itinerary based upon his studies of geometrical optics. If this is true, the law was deduced independently of dynamic considerations added by Descartes in a second time.

Conceptual Streams behind Descartes' Law of Refraction

The physical-geometrical core of Descartesian argumentation can hence be connected to the idea of decomposing a

---

[42]Descartes, 1897-1913 [*La Dioptrique*, II *discours*], VI: p. 101.

[43]In this sense, a classical example is the concept of force. Many scholars used it in the 16th and 17th centuries. There is an abundant and interesting literature on this subject, that allowed—in great part—to clarify how different authors used this term. In this case, too, before Newton had given his definition of force, this word did not have a univocal meaning.

[44]"[…] une action reçue en une matière très subtile, qui remplit les pores des autres corps […]" (Descartes, 1897-1913,VI: p. 103, lines 13-14). The translation is ours.

[45]We do not enter here into either the problem concerning the relations between Descartes and the other authors who, substantially, had understood refraction law, as Willebrord Snel van Royen called Snellius (1580-1626), Claude Mydorge (1585-1647) and Thomas Harriot (1560-1621) or the fundamental role Johannes Kepler (1571-1630) had in this studies on refraction (Pisano and Bussotti 2012; see also Malet 1990). The notes to the first and second *discours* of the *Dioptrique* (Descartes 1983) are thorough in this regard. See also Schuster 2000.

[46]Schuster, 2000: p. 271. Particularly Schuster has recently published an important contribution to the mechanistic Descartes' conception (Schuster 2013).

movement in two mutually perpendicular components. Descartes could hence imagine to decompose the motion of a light ray into these two components, without introducing the mechanical analogy of the ball or the concept of *determination*. His convictions on the nature of light induced him to introduce these notions. There was no necessity connected to the physical-geometrical argumentation to do that because the argumentation itself would have lost nothing of its validity without the mechanical analogy of the ball.

The further element to take into account is that Descartes led many experiments concerning the refraction and optics in general. In order to prove this, three examples are indicative: a) at the beginning of the third *discours* of the *La Dioptrique*, the experiment on the way in which eye forms the imagines (Descartes, 1897-1913, VI: pp. 105-106. The problem of the vision is further specified in the fifth and sixth *discours*, of the same work, pp. 114-147); b) in the tenth *discours* of the same text the affirmation that, in order to establish the most suitable form for a hyperbolic lens and the best position for its focus "[...] experience will teach better than my reasoning"[47]. Thus Descartes realized that the "[...] exact proportions are not so necessary that they cannot be changed a little bit"[48]. Hence, in this case, geometry is a guide for the form of the lens, but it does not determine such form in an absolute and univocal manner; c) the experiments with an ampoule full of water (VIII *discours* of the *Les Météores*) to comprehend the rainbow phenomenon. The experiments in optics are hence a fundamental aspect of Descartes' works. The genesis of the discovery of refraction law can perhaps summarized this way:

1) Descartes knew the tradition of geometrical optics studies;

2) He had realized—and this is a great, even if not exclusive, merit of his—that the physical phenomena can be understood only if quantities that remain invariable are determined;

3) He had carried out a plurality of experiments. All these facts brought him to intuit and to formulate the refraction law in a correct way. The other argumentations we have seen, were introduced because of philosophical convictions and to make the law plausible, but they do not play a role in the discovery of the law and—it is necessary to add—they are extraneous to the nature of the phenomenon.

The situation for the case here analysed is far different from that of the *Principia*: the refraction law is a paradigmatic example of a reasoning in which the mathematical apparatus is poor, but an easy formalization of Descartes' reasoning shows its consistency and correctness. In fact, it is enough:

1) To decompose the motion of light in a vectorial form[49], according to the parallel and perpendicular components to the incidence surface.

2) To use a symbolic notation to indicate the angles.

3) To introduce the concept of incidence and refraction angle. All this is clear in Descartes' treatise, even if the reasoning is not completely symbolized. Therefore a coherent quantification is possible, while it was not the case with the collision rules introduced in the *Principia*.

The *La Dioptrique* shows that a mathematical structure exists at the basis of Descartesian reasoning: let us consider the VIII *discours*, where Descartes exposes the focal properties of the parabolic and hyperbolic lenses. Furthermore, in the last part of the second book of his *Geometry*, Descartes extends the study of reflection and refraction to the oval lenses (Descartes, 1897-1913, VI: pp. 424-441). The treatment is, in this case, highly formalized and completely expressed in mathematical terms. Descartes carried out experiences and experiments. He mathematized the results and proposed explicative models based on the quantification of the phenomena. Because of this, the role of Descartes in the scientific turning point of the 17th century is relevant. The concepts of *gradation* and intensity represent an interesting instrument through which Descartes' ideas on refraction can be interpreted. First of all, *gradation* is the basis of refraction itself: if the different transparent materials had not different refraction indices, the phenomenon itself would not exist. Therefore gradation of the refraction indices represents the basis of this optical phenomenon. Since every material has its own index, it is possible to construct a graduated scale: the refraction indices represent the intensity with which every material refracts light. Descartes, by discovering the exact form of refraction law, made the intuitive idea that the materials have different refraction powers perspicuous. In this manner he ideally established a scale of *gradation*, even thought Descartes ideas that most dense materials also are the most refracting is wrong.

The Rainbow

The eight and most important *discours* of the *Les Météores* is dedicated to the rainbow (Maitte, 1981, 2006; Ronchi & Armogathe, 2000).

The way in which Descartes faces the rainbow problem presents an excellent epistemological model for the genesis of the scientific discovery. It is also indicative of the non univocal manner in which Descartes addressed the problems of physical arguments. The most significant aspects are three:

1) The use of experience to catch the properties of the phenomena;

2) Scientific quantification of the reasoning to obtain perspicuous results;

3) Elements of Descartes' mechanistic conceptions that influenced his rainbow theory.

From the beginning, Descartes resorts to experience in an appropriate manner (Descartes, 1897-1913, [VIII *discours*], VI: pp. 325-327). In an initial phase of his work, his purpose is to realize, in a qualitative manner, what the invariants characterizing the rainbow phenomenon are: since rainbow is visible not only in the sky, but also, for example, in the fountains in which the water is illuminated by sun rays under particular conditions depending on the way in which the sun rays hit the drops of water in respect to the observer, Descartes reasoned this way (see **Figure 15**, on the right our paraphrase).

This means the rainbow is not necessarily connected to atmospheric events as the rains. Furthermore Descartes observes that the size of the water drops does not have any influence on the phenomenon. He remarks that if the ampoule is raised and suspended by a machinery, which is not described in the text, but that can be easily imagined, the conclusion is the following: a sun ray hits the ampoule (that is the drop of water) in *B*, it is refracted by the water in *C*. From here it is reflected in *D*, from

---

[47]"[...] l'experience enseignera mieux que mes raisons" (Descartes, 1897-1913, VI: p. 202, lines 9-10). The translation is ours.

[48]"[...] proportions ne sont pas absolument nécessaires, qu'elles ne puissent beaucoup être changées". (Descartes, 1897-1913, VI: pp. 201-202). The translation is ours.

[49]Even if, probably, Descartes did not catch the concept of vector in its generality, he himself proposed to decompose the *determination* of a motion into two mutually perpendicular components, as we have seen.

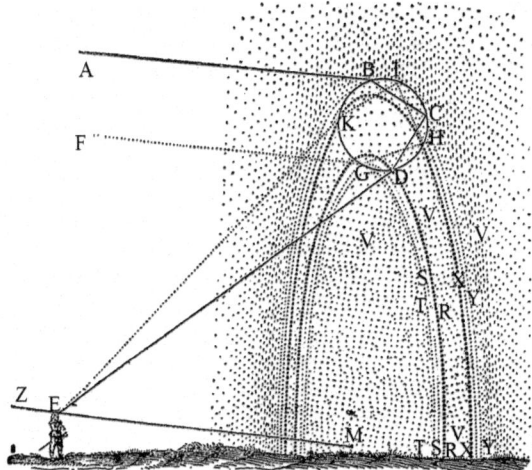

[...] this arc [the rainbow] can appear not only in the sky, but also in the air near us, every time there are many drops of water illuminated by the sun, as the experience shows in some fountains. Therefore I established easily that the rainbow depends only on the way in which the light rays act on the drops and on the inclination with which the rays reach our eyes from the drops[50]. If *AB* or *ZM* indicate the direction Sun-eye, when the angle *DEM* is about 42 degrees, then a brilliant red appears in the part *D*. Such colour continues to be present whatever is the movement of the ampoule, as long as the angle *DEM* remains 42 degrees. As soon as this angle is increased, even of a very small quantity, the red disappears. While, if the size of the angle is reduced, the red pencil of light is divided into less brilliant pencils in which the other colours of the rainbow appear. If the size is further diminished, every colour disappears. However, when the angle *KEM* is 52 degrees, the zone *K* is illuminated by a red, that is less brilliant than the one present in *D* when

DÊM is 42 degrees. If the angle *KEM* is made broader, the other colours appear in zones as *Y*. These colours have a minor intensity than the red in *K*. If the size of the angle is either slightly diminished or made it much bigger, every colour disappear. It is likely that at this stage, Descartes had already understood the role of reflection and refraction in rainbow genesis. However, to have a confirmation he carries out the following experiment: he poses an obscure and opaque body in one of the points of the lines *AB*, *BC*, *CD* e *DE*. He remarks that the red colour disappears. While, if the whole ampoule is covered, excluded the points *A*, *B* e *D*, and no obstacle disturbs the action of the rays *ABCDE*, the red continues to be present.

Figure 15.
Explanation of the rainbow in the *Les Météores*[51].

where it is refracted to the observer in *E*. Consequently the red appearing in *D* is given by two refractions and one reflection. The red in *K* of the second rainbow is given by one refraction of the ray in *G*, followed by one reflection in *H*, a further reflection in *I* and a refraction in *K* until the ray reaches *E*. Since there are two reflections and two refractions, the red is less intense. In this way, the general nature of the phenomenon is explained. Two questions are still to be answered:

1) Why does the rainbow appear when the angles DEM and KEM are respectively 42 and 52 degrees?

---

[50]"[...] cet arc ne peut pas seulement paroistre dans le ciel, mais aussy en l'air proche de nous, toutes fois & quantes qu'il s'y trouve plusieurs gouttes d'eau esclairées par le soleil, ainsi que l'expérience fait voir en quelques fontaines, il m'a esté aysé de iuger qu'il ne procède que de la façon que les rayons de la lumière agissent contre ces gouttes, & de là tendent vers nos yeux". (Descartes, 1897-1913 [VIII *discours*], VI: p. 325, line 10). The translation is ours.
[51]Descartes, 1897-1913 [VIII *discours*], VI: p. 326.

2) What is the cause of the rainbow colours?

Descartes answers the first question through the following very acute reasoning: let the drop of water be represented by the circumference (see **Figure 16**).

In the picture traced by Descartes there are many elements that characterize a great part of the scientific discoveries:

1) The use of the experience to achieve a global qualitative vision of the studied phenomenon.

2) The resort to the experiment having in mind not only the questions, but also a series of possible answers.

3) The quantification of the data and resort to the demonstration to explain the phenomena in a perspicuous way.

The concepts of *gradation* and *intensity* represent once again

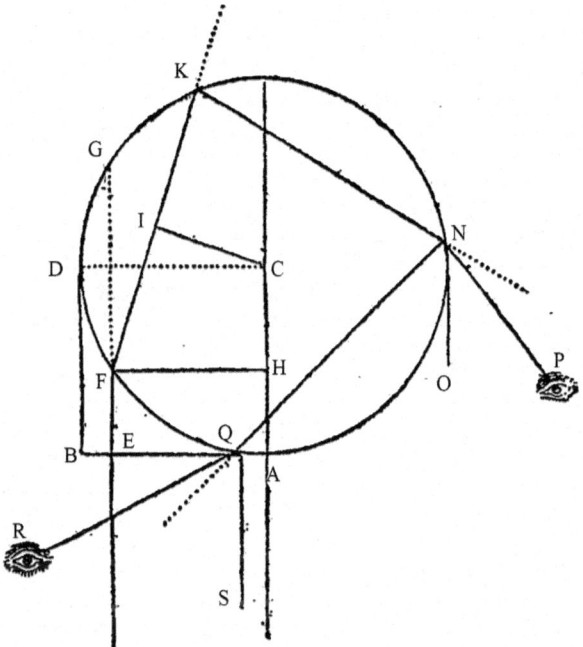

Let *F* be the point of the drop in which the solar ray strikes. Let this ray be refracted in *K*, from *K* reflected to *N* and from here refracted towards the eye in *P* or reflected to *Q* and from *Q* refracted towards the eye in *R*. This figure is hence a model of the first and of the second rainbow. Traced the perpendicular *CI* to *FK* from the centre *C* of the circumference, it results that $\frac{HF}{CI}$ is the ratio between the refraction indices of the air and of the water. In fact, let us trace the radius *CF* and the tangent at the circumference in *F*, in the triangle *FCC'*, the sine of the angle *C'FC* is *CC'* = *FH*, but *C'FC* is equal at the incidence angle and *CFI* is the angle of refraction. Since the refraction index water-air is known, the ratio of *FH* to the radius *CD* is known. It is therefore possible to determine the ratio of *IC* with these two quantities. Thus, it is possible to establish the size of the arcs *FG* and *FK* hence to calculate the angle *ONP*. If the position of the point *F* in which the solar ray strikes the drop varies, the angle *ONP* will vary in a way that can be calculated. The calculation shows that, when *F* varies—it is enough to limit the analysis at the quarter of circumference *AD*—the rays that come out with an angle *ONP* of about 40 degrees are more numerous than the rays that come out with other angles. This explains why the first rainbow is visible when the angle *DEM* in figure 9 is about 42 degrees. In an analogous way, it is possible to prove that most part of the angles *SQR* are about 52 degrees. This explains the second rainbow.

Figure 16.
Geometrical model of the rainbow in the *Les Météores*[52].

---

[52]Descartes, 1897-1913 [VIII *discours*], VI: p. 337.

a lens through which the physical phenomenon can be observed and the work by Descartes interpreted: *gradation* and *intensity* are inherent (**Figure 15**) to the angles between the lines *EM*, *ED* and *EM*, *EK*. When the degrees of these two angles vary, the two arcs of the rainbow either subsist with the different colours or disappear at all. The intensity of the colours is a function of these angles, too. The **Figure 16** can be interpreted as a model that provides a geometrical representation of the *gradation* of the angles. The reasoning and the calculation demonstrate why those particular sizes (42 and 52 degrees) are the *critical* ones for the rainbow. Inside a context that, for many aspects can be defined of a *modern physical context*, the angular *gradation* justifies the existence of the rainbow. This *gradation* is connected to the intensity of chromatic *gradation* by an elegant functional link.

For sure Descartes aims to explain the nature of the colours. Thus, he provides an interesting answer, in part based on experiments carried out with an optical prism and in part on his mechanistic convictions. Namely, in his theory of the colours, he takes into account the empirical data, but tries to explain them by means of presuppositions tied to the way in which he conceives the nature of light. If, as to refraction law, the analogy of the balls was not the central core of the argumentation, here the idea that the action of light is transmitted by the particles of the subtle matter is essential for the explanation.

Descartes constructs a mechanic model in which he imagines that a subtle matter composed of little spheres having a determined velocity of translation is present. The reciprocal collisions among these particles and/or the collisions with some other body can modify this velocity and also induce a rotational motion in each single particle. He claims the colours depend on the motions of the particles that constitute the subtle matter and that transmit the action of light. At different velocities of rotation correspond different colours. This idea is brilliant, but (differently from what had happened in the rest of the *discours* on the rainbow) no relation between modelling and physical phenomenon is shown; such relation is only supposed. Furthermore a direct connection between the experiment with prism and the supposed explanation of this experimental result is missing. There is no demonstration. Thus Descartes replaced the facts of the chromatic world with a set of other facts relative to the motion of the supposed particles, but these motions are as difficult to be explained as the colours themselves. The modelling proposed is not easier than the phenomenon because it contains the same number of elements: simply Descartes replaces the facts of a certain *world* with the facts of another world. There is no precise assumption that explains why the world of the particles is, from an epistemological and physical point of view, easier than the chromatic world and justifies hence why the world of the particles should provide an explanation for the chromatic world. Because of this, the model is not explicative. In a sense, the reasoning could be inverted until reaching a supposed explanation of the motion of the particles by means of the colours and not vice versa. The way of reasoning proposed by Descartes in this case is more similar to that of the *Principia* than to the one connoting the rest of the *discours* on the rainbow, even if the form in which the subject is exposed and the fascination of Descartesian speculations give an appearance of plausibility to Descartes' theory of colours. Again, in this case, *gradation* and intensity are also cardinal concepts. When the *gradation* of the velocities and of the motions of the spheres of the subtle matter vary, a corresponding variation of

the chromatic scale exists. Therefore the two concepts of *gradation* and *intensity* can provide a good perspective description through which to analyse Descartes' *physical works*.

Conclusion

Notes on Science & Society Civilization

Usually a discussion concerning history of science and technique/technology is presented such as a discipline within the history of science for understanding eventual relationship between science and the development of art crafts produced by non–recognized scientists in a certain historical time. The relationship between science and science and society and consequent civilizing by science is centred on the possibility that the society effetely developed a fundamental organization in capacity to *absorb* science and produce technologies (i.e., water and electrical supply, transportation systems etc.). Thus, *a development civilization was necessary parallel to development of the science within society? Is effetely happened that? Did Descartesian and Newtonian physical works develop as a response to the needs of society?* Alexandre Koyré (1892-1964) strongly remarked the history of science and the role played by mathematics between Newton and Descartes (Koyré, 1965, Chapter III) in the history of scientific thought. Through the intuition that the fundamentals of scientific theories contain two basic choices, Koyré' intellectual matrix (Pisano & Gaudiello, 2009, 200b) has been cleared up.

> The new science, we are told sometimes, is the science of craftsman and engineer, of the working, enterprising and calculating tradesman, in fact, the science of rising bourgeois classes of modern society. There is certainly some truth in this descriptions and explanations [...]. I do not see what the *scientia activa* has ever had to do with the development of the calculus, nor the rise of the bourgeoisie with that of the Copernican, or Keplerian, astronomy theories. [...] I am convinced that the rise and the growth of experimental science is not the source but, on the contrary, the result of the new *theoretical*, that is, the new *metaphysical* approach to nature that forms the content of the scientific revolution of the seventeenth century, a content which we have to understand before we can attempt an explanation (whatever this may be) of its historical occurrence[53].

> [...] I shall therefore characterize this revolution [the birth of the modern science] by two closely connected and even complementary features: (a) the destruction of the cosmos and therefore the disappearance from science—at least in principle, if not always in fact—of all considerations based on this concept, and (b) the geometrization of space, that is, the substitution of the homogeneous and abstract—however now considered as real—dimension space of the Euclidean geometry for the concrete and differentiated place-continuum of pre-Galilean Physics and Astronomy[54].

According to the Russian historian[55] we can consider that: 1) the history of scientific thought has never been entirely separated by philosophical thought. 2) the most important scientific revolutions have always been determined by a replacement of

[53]Koyré, 1965: pp. 5-6.

philosophical speculations. Thus i.e., the history of scientific thought (i.e. for physical Descartesian and Newtonian sciences) has not developed by *vacuum*, but it moves in a set of ideas, foundational principles, or axiomatic evidences.

Final Remarks on Descartes' *Physical Works*

Particularly in this paper we have highlighted the two different ways in which 3) Descartes developed his physical research-frames in his *Physical Works*: a) typical of an essentialist and aprioristic way of thinking, b) based on experiments and mathematization. The differences between, the physical *Essays Dioptrique* and *Météores*, and the *Principia*, concern both the content and the methodological aspect. These differences regard the way in which the scientific work is addressed. The approach of the *Essays* can be epistemologically interpreted:

1) Descartes presents his experimental and theoretical work as a scientist.

2) He realizes that science and technique have deep connections. Therefore he had the idea to address the essays basically to the artisans.

3) Descartes had close relations with export artisans as Ferrier. He fully understood the role that science could play in the construction of machines.

4) Descartes thought machines were fundamental for the future of mankind.

5) The mechanistic convictions of Descartes are apparent from many passages of the two *Essays*, even if these conceptions do not play a fundamental role for the discoveries exposed in the *La Dioptrique* and in the *Les Météores*.

The *Essays* present hence Descartes as a producer of the scientific work. On the basis of his whole scientific work, likely Descartes was one of the first scientists to have the idea that, in a physical theory every phenomenon must be explained on the basis of a precise law. However, the perspectives of the scientific work were not completely rosy:

1) In Descartes' epoch it was already clear that experiments were the basis of physics and they would have been still more in the future;

2) The costs for the research were increasing more and more. From here the necessity of financial supports;

3) In Descartes' time, ecclesiastical censorship continued to represent a problem;

4) Descartes was profoundly surprised by Galileo's conviction. He wrote in a letter to Mersenne in November 1633:

> In fact, I cannot imagine that he, who is Italian and well-liked to the Pope himself—as far as I know—was considered a criminal for no other reason but he wanted to establish the earth movement. I am aware that this conception was censured by some cardinals. However—as far as I remember—I had heard that it had continued to be taught in Rome itself[56].

Therefore in the first half of the XVII century the social and political situation was difficult for the scientists. In fact, new discoveries were emerging with a rhythm far more rapid than in the previous centuries, but, at the same time, the financial supports to develop research depended on the power holders and not on the scientists themselves. The aim of the power holders was of course to use the science for their scopes. Furthermore the ecclesiastic censorship was strong. If we take into account this picture, it is perhaps possible to understand the approach of the *Principia*. This book is the expression of personal Descartes' physical and metaphysical ideas (as the mechanistic conception) and of his desire to become—despite his declaration in a contrary sense—a sort of new scientific authority. From here the encyclopaedic character of the book arises, whose intention is to face all problems of physics. However, at the same time, the *Principia* can be interpreted as a book profoundly influenced by the social situation we have rapidly outlined. This situation is also connected to the most convenient way to present science. Descartes wanted to make science acceptable to the Church and to the power people with whom he would have had contacts. In this manner, for example, the paragraphs III, 16-19 of the *Principia* can be explained, where the validity of the systems of Ptolemy (II century AD), Nicolaus Copernicus (1473-1543) and Tycho Brahe (1546-1601) is denied. Descartes shows that, in his own system, the earth has to be considered, as a matter of fact, at rest. This assertion can be interpreted as an insurance for Catholic Church. The insistence on the fact that, in determining physical laws, deduction is far more important than experiments, is one of the most evident ideas expressed in the *Principia*. This idea is in part coherent with what Descartes really thought, but in part it has the aim to show that experiment—namely a *fine* enquire on the world that can modify the world itself—with its potentially *subversive* value, has a secondary importance. In other terms: science is not dangerous from a social point of view and can hence be accepted by the power holders. As a matter of fact, we have seen that, when Descartes produces science, he cannot renounce to experiment. The *Principia* can hence been interpreted as the text that concludes a phase of the scientific revolution, namely the phase in which the social role of the scientists was not yet clear. The scientists were not yet, in every aspect, institutional figures, as they became in the second half of the 17th century[57]. Because of all these reasons, the *Principia* are a text that presents a relevant historiographic interest. It is not always easy to distinguish what Descartes wrote to justify the scientific work and to make it acceptable to whom could valuate this work potentially dangerous from a social point of view from what he wrote for a real conviction. Finally, main comparisons between Descartes's and Newton's conceptions we carried out summarized by the following table as relevant dissimilarities between these two scientists, with regard to the subjects deal with in our paper (see **Table 1**).

---

[54]Koyré, 1965: pp 6-7. In the following explaining of Alexandre Koyré' choice for the history of science: "*The destruction of the cosmos*" that is a replacement of the finite world, as it had been hierarchically classified by Aristotle, with the infinite universe. "*The geometrization of space*": that is a replacement of Aristotle' physical (concrete) space with the abstract space of the Euclidean geometry. (Pisano & Gaudiello, 2009a, 2009b).

[55]A conference (1954, Boston) of *American Association for the Advancement of Science.* Cfr.: *The scientific Monthly*, 1955; Koyré, 1971.

[56]"Car ie ne me suis pû imaginer, que luy qui est Italien, & mesme bien voulu du Pape, ainsi que l'entens, ait pû estre criminalizé pour autre chose, sinon qu'il aura fans doute voulu establir le mouvement de la Terre, lequel ie sçay bien auoir elle autresfois censuré par quelques Cardinaux; |mais ie pensois auoir oüy dire, que depuis on ne laissoit pas de l'einseigner publiquement, mesme dans Rome" (Descartes, 1897-1913, I: p. 271, lines 2-9). The translation is ours. Moreover, we remark that a possible problem with ecclesiastical censorship induced him to avoid the publication of *Le Monde*, as he wrote in the same letter (Descartes, 1897-1913, I).

[57]By concerning the social and political situation in 17th century and the relations with science, one can see the following works: Heilibron, 1979; Dear, 1995, 1987; Kokowski, 2004; Gorokhov, 2011.

Table 1.
Descartes and Newton's main arguing.

Descartes	Newton

General Conceptions

A) In the *Principia Philosophiae* Descartes exposed his mechanistic conception. An attempting to unify the whole physical world on the bases of few principles and rule is present; the treatment was not mathematized and accurate definitions are missing. The geometric model proposed provided weak indications about the positions of the bodies in function of the time. Important laws are introduced as the inertia law and the law of the conservation of movement. The main reference are the *Principia Philosophiae* (Descartes, 1897-1913, Inertia law, VIII-1, II part, § XXXVII: pp. 62-63; the conservation of movement: *Ivi*, § XXXIX and § XL: pp. 63-65). Nevertheless, since a mathematical and definitional apparatus is missing, it is difficult—and probably in part wrong—to interpret Descartesian conception of *inertia* and *quantity of motion* as in the Newtonian and post-Newtonian physics.

B) In the Essays, *La Dioptrique* and *Les Methéores* Descartes deals with specific problems connected to reflection and refraction. Here the proposed models are mathematical or, at least, can be easily acceptably mathematized; demonstrations are presented. The refraction-law is expressed (Descartes, II Discours of the *La Dioptrique* in: Descartes, 1897-1913, VI: pp. 93-105).

A) According to Newton, a mechanical model has to foresee the positions of the bodies through mathematical relations between the space variable and the time variable. In general, a physical model must supply precise laws and deductions expressible in a mathematical form (for example in the Author's Preface, Newton writes: [...] and then from these forces, by other propositions, which are also mathematical, we deduce the motions of the Planets, the Comets, the Moon and the Sea" (Newton, [1713] 1729, I, Preface: p. A2; see also *Ivi*, II, *General Scholium*: p. 392) Definitions (8), *axioms* or *laws* (3) are exposed in the initial section of the *Principia* (Newton, [1713] 1729, I, Definitions: pp 1-18). *Axioms* or *laws* plus their corollaries: pp 19-40). For the first time a physicist feels the need to provide definitions of the quantity he is dealing with.

B) Generally speaking the structure of *Principia* looks Euclidean, but, Newton introduced his apparently abstract formulations in order to explain, from a unitary point of view, physical phenomena.

Connection theory-experience

A) In the *Principia Philosophiae* there is an insufficient connection between theory and experience. In some cases—as in the one of the movements of the planets—there are intrinsic difficulties to connect theory and experience because no provisional model is supplied, but only a descriptive one. In other cases, as the collision rules, experience is not coherent with theoretical rules (Descartes, 1897-1913, VIII-1, second part, §§ XLVI-LII: pp. 68-70). Descartes ignore the experience, claiming that many conditions can influence the experiments and the experience (*Ivi*, § LIII: p 70). But a *critics of experience* is lacking.

B) In the *Essays* the experience and the experiments play a fundamental role. Descartes analyzed many empirical details and explains them through the theory. The experience and the experiments guided him to develop his theory (See i.e., how Descartes focused on the experience of the rainbow colours to explain this phenomenon in *Les Météores* (Descartes, 1897-1913, VI: pp. 325-344).

A) The experience and the experiments are the bases of Newton's physics. He is explicit in the *Optiks*, where a plurality of experiments is presented and the theory is clearly constructed to provide a model to the phenomena deriving from experiments (Newton, [1704] 1730: p. 1). A profound *critics of experience* is *implicitly* presented because Newton specifies the experimental conditions and the effects that could perturb the results of the experiments (Newton, [1713] 1729, II: pp. 202-205).

B) The *Philosophiae Naturalis Principia Mathematica* (Newton, [1713] 1729, et editions) too, have their source of inspirations in the phenomena (no really experimental) and in the attempt to explain and foresee the phenomena; i.e, the second section of the third book of the *Philosophiae Naturalis Principia Mathematica* is titled *The Phaenomena or Appearances* (Newton, [1713] 1729, III: pp. 206-212)

Fundamental concepts: space, time, mass

A) In the *Principia Philosophiae*, the space cannot be distinguished from *res extensa*. It is always relative (Descartes, 1897-1913, VIII-I, II part, Question X: p. 45).The time is relative (Descartes, 1897-1913, VIII-I, I part, questions LVI-LVII: pp. 26-27).

B) It is known that a scientific (i.e., by magnitudes) distinction between mass and weight was problematic at that time.

A) The absolute time exists (before than in the famous general *General Scholium*, Newton spoke of absolute space and time in the *General Scholium* posed as a conclusion to his Definitions. (Newton, [1713] 1729, I: pp. 9-18). Both were introduced also as an answer to the problems present in Descartes' physics explained by Newton himself (Newton, [1713] 1729, II, *General Scholium*: pp. 387-393).

B) The mass is clearly distinguished by the weight (*Ivi*, definition I: p. 1). Even if Newton's concept of mass can be criticized for well known reasons, the concept of mass was (within his physical mathematical system) reasonable at that time.

Problems connected to the cultural environment

A) Descartes had to face a series of problems that in Newton's land and time wee far less serious: 1) Catholic censure of Copernican theory; 2) role of the scientist still not well defined. Power holders could think that scientists were dangerous for the social order; 3) scarce financial support. Since the *Principia* are Descartes' world-system and the most conspicuous manifest of his way of thinking, he tried and intermediation between his ideas and possible dangerous consequences.

B) This is one of the reasons why the *Principia* are such a tormented text. In the Essay (*La Dioptrique*, *Les Météores*, *La Géométrie*) dealing with more specific arguments, he did not have these problems and the treatment was clearer and more coherent.

A) Newton did not deal with the problems addressed by Descartes because of: 1) Different period: end of the 17th begin of the 18th century. 2) Different land: England where the Catholic censure was not effective. 3) Newton represents a scientist who is perfectly integrated in the system; rapidly the scientists were becoming persons with public roles and well defined social positions.

B) Newton was completely free to publish his works without the problems faced by Descartes.

C) Comment: Newton's theoretical conceptions are not *directly* influenced by the social and political environment. He was free, as to the subjects he dealt with, and he had non problems with censure. The influence of the social and political environment was *indirect* as far as it allowed Newton to develop freely his researches.

When a thought does not have clear and delineated scopes, it likely results tormented, often self-contradictory and difficult to frame into an organic picture. Under this point of view, *Le* is different from the *Principia*: in this original and pleasant brief treatise Descartes exposes his mechanistic conceptions and his theory of light, based upon them. But in this case, the scope is clear—independently of the correctness of the basic ideas expressed in *Le Monde*—and the argumentation is linear. Finally, even if, as Scott and Koyré claimed

> Thus Descartes' hypothesis at least has the merit of explaining the nature of weight without recourse to any occult force acting across space. More than that, it is easy to detect in it a groping after a universal law; the mechanism by which a body falls to the earth is in the last resort the same as that which keeps the planets in the solar vortex [...][58]

> [...] thought of course unsuccessful, attempt at a rational cosmology, an identification of celestial and terrestrial physics, and therefore the first appearance in skies of centrifugal forces [...][59]

Descartes had in physics the merit to have tried a unique explanation for the gravity on the Earth and for the orbital movements of the planets (unification of terrestrial and celestial physics), this has happened with a form more coherent with a mentality typical of an aprioristic conception of the physics rather than the one connoting an observative-experiment-quantitative approach.

Acknowledgements

We want to express our gratitude to anonymous referees for precious comments and helpful suggestions.

REFERENCES

Armogathe, J. R. (2000). The rainbow: A privileged epistemological model. In: S. Gaukroger, J. Schuster, & J. Sutton (Eds.) (2000) *Descartes' natural philosophy* (pp. 249-257).

Barbin, E., & Pisano, R. (2013). *The dialectic relation between physics and mathematics in the xixth century*. Dordrecht: Springer.

Blay, M. (1983). *La conceptualisation newtonienne des phénomènes de la couleur*. Paris: Vrin.

Blay, M. (1992). *La naissance de la mécanique analytique la science du mouvement au tournant des XVIIe et XVIIIe siècles*. Paris: Presses Universitaires de France.

Blay, M. (2002). *La science du mouvement de Galilée à lagrange*. Paris: Belin.

Boutroux, P. (1921). L'histoire des principes de la dynamique avant Newton. *Revue de Métaphysique et de Morale, 28*, 657-688.

Buchwald, J. Z., & Feingold, M. (2011). *Newton and the origin of civilization*. Princeton, NJ: The Princeton University Press.

Braunstein, J. F. (2008). *L'histoire des sciences: Méthodes, styles et controverses*. Paris: Vrin.

Buchwald, J. Z. (1989). *The rise of the wave theory of light: Optical theory and experiment in the early nineteenth century*. Chicago: The University of Chicago Press.

Carnot, L. (1803). *Principes fondamentaux de l'équilibre et du mouvement*. Paris: Deterville.

Cassirer, E. ([1906] 1922). *Das erkenntnisproblem in der philosophie und wissenschaft der neuern zeit*. Berlin: Bruno Cassirer.

Costabel, P. ([1967] 1982). *Demarches originales de descartes savant*. Paris: Vrin.

Costabel, P. (1960). *Leibniz et la dynamique: Les textes de 1692. Histoire de la pensée*. Paris: Hermann.

Darrigol, O. (2012). *A history of optics: From Greek antiquity to the nineteenth century*. Oxford: The Oxford University Press.

Dear, P. (1987). Jesuit mathematical science and the reconstitution of experience in the early seventeenth century. *Studies in the History and Philosophy of Science, 18*, 133-175.

Dear, P. (1995). *Discipline & experience. The mathematical way in the scientific revolution*. Chicago, London: The University of Chicago Press.

De Gandt, F. (1995). *Force and geometry in Newton's principia*. Princeton, NJ: The University of Princeton Press.

Descartes, R. (1897-1913) Œuvres de Descartes. 12 vols. Adams C, Tannery P (eds). Paris; Discours de la méthode et Essais, Specimina philosophiae. vol VI Principia philosophiae, Latin version vol VIII, Principia philosophiae French translation vol IX; Physico-mathematica vol X, Le Monde ou Traité de la lumière, vol XI (Id, 1964-1974 par Rochot B, Costabel P, Beaude J et Gabbery A, Paris).

Descartes, R. (1964-1974). *Oeuvres. Adam J et Tannery A. Nouvelle présentation par Rochet E, et Costabel P, 11 vols*. Paris: Vrin.

Descartes, R. (1983). *Opere scientifiche. Vol 2. Lojacono E (ed). Discorso sul metodo, la diottrica, le meteore, la geometria*. Torino: UTET.

Dijksterhuis, E. J. (1961). *The mechanization of the world picture*. London: The Oxford University Press.

Dijksterhuis, E. J., Serrurier, C., & Dibon, P. ([1950] 1977). *Descartes et le cartesianisme hollandais*. Paris: Presses Universitaire de France.

Dugas, R. ([1950] 1955). *Histoire de la mécanique*. Neuchâtel: Editions du Griffon.

Dugas, R. ([1954] 1987). La pensée mécanique de Descartes. In: G. Rodis Lewis (Ed.), *La science chez descartes* (pp. 145-162). New York and London: Garland Publishing.

Duhem, P. M. (1977). Aim and structure of physical theory. Princeton, NJ: Princeton University Press.

Faraday, M. (1839-1855). *Experimental researches in electricity, 3 vols*. London: Taylor.

Festa, E. (1995). *L'erreur de Galilée*. Paris: Austral.

Feyerabend, P. (1991). *Dialogues sur la connaissance*. Paris: Seuil.

Feyerabend, P. K. (1975). *Againts the method*. London: New Left Books.

Gaukroger, Schuster, J., & Sutton, J. (2000). (pp. 60-80).

Gaukroger, S., Schuster, J., & Sutton, J. (2000). *Descartes' natural philosophy*. London and New York: Routledge.

Gillispie, C. C., & Pisano, R. (2013). *Lazare and sadi carnot. A scientific and filial relationship*. Dordrecht: Springer.

Gorokhov, V. (2011). Scientific and technological progress by Galileo. In H. Busche (Ed.), *Departure for modern Europe. A Handbook of early modern philosophy (1400-1700)* (pp. 135-147). Hamburg: Felix Meiner.

Hall, A. R. (1993). *All was light. An introduction to Newton's optick*. Oxford: The Clarendon Press.

Halley, E. (1693). An instance of the excellence of the modern algebra in the resolution of the problem of the foci of Optik Glasses Universally. *Philosophical Transaction, 17*, 960-969.

Hatfield, G. C. (1979). Force (God) in Descartes' physics. *Studies in History and Philosophy of Science, 10*, 113-140.

Hattab, H. (2009). *Descartes on forms and mechanisms*. Cambridge: The Cambridge University Press.

Heilbron, J. L. (1979). *Electricity in the 17th and 18th centuries: A study of early modern physics*. Berkeley, CA: The University of California Press.

Jammer, M. (1961). *Concepts of mass in classical and modern physics*. Cambridge, MA: The Harvard University Press.

Kokowski, M. (2004). Copernicus's originality: Towards integration of

---

[58]Scott, [1952] 1987, p. 184.
[59]Koyré, 1965, p. 65. See also *Id.*, 1934, 1957, 1961, 1966.

contemporary copernican studies. Warsaw-Cracow: Instytut Historii Nauki. Polish Academy of Science. Wydawnictwa IHN PAN.

Kokowski, M. (2012). The different strategies in the historiography of science. Tensions between professional research and postmodern ignorance. In A. Roca-Rosell (Ed.), *The circulation of science and technology. Proceedings of the 4th international conference of the European society for the history of science* (pp. 27-33). Barcelona: Societat Catalana d'Història de la Ciència i de la Tècnica (SCHCT). http://taller.iec.cat/4iceshs/documentacio/P4ESHS.pdf

Koyré, A. (1934). *Nicolas copernic, des révolutions des orbes celeste.* Paris: Alcand.

Koyré, A. (1957). *From the closed world to the infinite universe.* Baltimore: The Johns Hopkins University Press.

Koyré, A. (1961). *Du monde de "à-peu-près" à l'univers de là précision.* Paris: M Leclerc et Cie-Armand Colin Librairie. (*Id*, Les philosophes et la machine. Du monde de l' "à-peu-près" à l'univers de la précision. Études d'histoire de la pensée philosophique)

Koyré, A. (1971). *Études d'Histoire de la pensée philosophique.* Paris: Gallimard.

Koyré, A. (1965). *Newtonian studies.* Cambridge, MA: The Harvard University Press.

Koyré, A. (1966). *Études galiléennes.* Paris: Hermann.

Kragh, H. (1987). *An introduction to the historiography of science.* Cambridge: The Cambridge University Press.

Kuhn, T. S. ([1962] 1970). *The structure of scientific revolutions.* Chicago, IL: The Chicago University Press.

Lagrange, J. L. (1788). *Mécanique analytique.* Paris: Desaint.

Lagrange, J. L. (1973). *Œuvres de Lagrange.* Seconde édition. Courcier, I-XIV vols. (in X). Paris: Gauthier-Villars.

Lindsay, R., Margenau, B., & Margenau, H. (1946). *Foundations of physics.* New York: John Wiley & Sons.

Mach, E. (1883 [1996]). *The science of mechanics—A critical and historical account of its development.* 4th edition. La Salle: Open Court-Merchant Books.

Mach, E. (1986). Principles of the theory of heat, historically and critically elucidated. B. McGuinness (ed.), (vol. 17). Boston, MA: Reidel D Publishing Co.

Maitte, B. (1981). *La lumière.* Paris: Seuil.

Maitte, B. (2006). *Histoire de l'arc–en–ciel.* Paris: Suil.

Malet, A. (1990). Gregoire, Descartes, Kepler and the law of refraction. *Archives Internationales d'Histoire des Sciences, 40,* 278-304.

Maxwell, J. C. (1873). *A treatise on electricity and magnetism.* Oxford: The Clarendon Press.

McLaughlin, P. (2000). Force, determination and impact. In Gaukroger S., Schuster, J., & J. Sutton (Eds.) (2000) (pp. 81-112).

Nagel, E. (1961). *The structure of science: Problems in the logic of scientific explanation.* New York: Harcourt-Brace & World Inc.

Nagel, T. (1997). *The last word.* Oxford: The Oxford University Press.

Newton, I. ([1713] 1729). *Philosophiae naturalis principia mathematica.* London: Motte.

Newton, I. ([1686-7] 1803). The mathematical principles of natural philosophy. London: Symonds.

Newton, I. (1666). *De gravitatione et aequipondio fluidorum.* Ms Add. 4003. Cambridge: The Cambridge University Library. http://www.newtonproject.sussex.ac.uk/view/texts/normalized/THEM00093

Newton, I. (1803) *The mathematical principles of natural philosophy.* London: Symonds.

Newton, I. ([1704] 1730). *Opticks: Or, a treatise of the reflections, refractions, inflections and colours of light.* 4th edition. London: William Innys.

Osler, M. J. (2000). *Rethinking the scientific revolution.* Cambridge: The Cambridge University Press.

Panza, M. (2003). The origins of analytic mechanics in the 18th century. In H. N. Jahnke (Ed.), *A history of analysis. Proceedings of the American Mathematical Society and The London Mathematical Society* (pp. 137-153). London.

Panza, M. (2004). *Newton.* Paris: Belles Lettres.

Panza, M. (2005). Revision of Italian translation of Descartes' correspondence on mathematical matters with addition of some critical notes: René Descartes, *Tutte le lettere, 1619-1950.* In G. Belgioioso (Ed.), *Critical notes* (pp. 103-105, 254, 482-491, 556-557, 663-669). Milano: Bompiani.

Panza, M. (2007). Euler's introductio in analysin infinitorum and the program of algebraic analysis: Quantities, functions and numerical partitions. In R. Backer (Ed.), *Euler reconsidered. Tercentenary essays* (pp. 119-166). Heber City, UT: The Kendrick Press.

Panza, M., & Malet, A. (2006). *The origins of Algebra: From Al-Khwarizmi to Descartes.* Special issue of *Historia Mathematica* 33/1.

Pisano, R. (2013). Historical reflections on physics mathematics relationship in Electromagnetic theory. In E. Barbin, & R. Pisano (Eds.), *The dialectic relation between physics and mathematics in the 19th century* (pp. 31-58). Dordrecht: Springer.

Pisano, R. (2009a). On method in Galileo Galilei' mechanics. In H. Hunger (Ed.), *Proceedings of ESHS 3rd conférence* (pp. 147-186). Vienna: Austrian Academy of Science.

Pisano, R. (2009b). Continuity and discontinuity. On method in Leonardo da Vinci' mechanics. *Organon, 41,* 165-182.

Pisano, R. (2010). On principles in Sadi Carnot's thermodynamics (1824). Epistemological reflections. *Almagest, 2,* 128-179.

Pisano, R. (2011). Physics-mathematics relationship. Historical and epistemological notes. In E. Barbin, M. Kronfellner, & C. Tzanakis, (Eds.), *European Summer University History And Epistemology In Mathematics* (pp. 457-472). Vienna: Verlag Holzhausen GmbH-Holzhausen Publishing Ltd.

Pisano, R., & Bussotti, P. (2012). Galileo and Kepler. On theoremata circa centrum gravitates solidorum and mysterium cosmographicum. *History Research, 2,* 110-145.

Pisano, R., & Gaudiello, I. (2009a). Continuity and discontinuity. An epistemological inquiry based on the use of categories in history of science. *Organon, 41,* 245-265.

Pisano, R., & Gaudiello, I. (2009b). On categories and scientific approach in historical discourse. In H. Hunger (Ed.), *Proceedings of ESHS 3rd Conference* (pp. 187-197). Vienna: Austrian Academy of Science.

Poincaré, H. ([1923]1970). *La valeur de la science.* Paris: Flammarion.

Poincaré, H. ([1935]1968). *La science et l'hypothèse.* Paris: Flammarion.

Rashed, R. (1992). *Optique et mathématiques. Recherches sur l'histoire de la pensée scientifique en arabe.* Aldershot: Variorum.

Ronchi, V. (1956). *Histoire de la lumière.* Paris: Colin.

Rosmorduc, J., Rosmorduc, V., & Dutour, F. (2004). *Les révolutions de l'optique et l'œuvre de Fresnel.* Location: Adapt-Vuiber.

Rossi, P. (1999). *Aux origines de la science moderne.* Paris: Seuil-Points/Sciences.

Ruffner, J. A. (2012). Newton's de gravitatione: A review and reassessment. *Archive for History of exact Sciences, 66,* 241-264.

Sabra, A. I. (1967). *Theories of light from Descartes to Newton.* London: Oldbourne,

Schuhl, P. M. (1947). *Machinisme et philosophie.* Paris: Vrin.

Schuster, J. A. (2000). Descartes opticien: The construction of the law of refraction and the manufacture of its physical rationales, 1618-1629. In Gaukroger, J. Schuster, & J. Sutton (2000) (pp. 258-312).

Schuster, J. A. (2013). *Descartes-Agonistes. Physico-mathematics, Method and Corpuscular-Mechanism 1618-1633.* Dordrecht: Springer.

Scott, J. F. [1952] 1987). *The scientific work of René Descartes.* New York: Garland Publishing.

Shapiro, A. E. (1974). Light, pressure, and rectilinear propagation: Descartes' celestial optics and Newton's hydrostatics. *Studies in History and Philosophy of science, 5,* 239-296.

Slowik, E. (2009). Descartes' physics. E. N. Zalta (Ed.), *The Stan-ford Encyclopedia of Philosophy.* Stanford, CA: The Stanford University Press.

Taton, R. (1965). Alexandre Koyré, historien de la « révolution astronomique. *Revue d'histoire des sciences et de leurs applications, 18,* 147-154.

Taton, R. (1966). *Histoire générale des sciences*. 5 vols. Paris: PUF, Quadrige.

Tiemersma, D. (1988). Methodological and theoretical aspects of Descartes' treatise on the rainbow. *Studies in History and Philosophy of science, 19*, 347-364.

Truesdell, C. (1968). *Essay in the history of mechanics*. New York: Springer.

Westfall, R. S. (1971). *The construction of modern science. Mechanism and mechanic*. New York: Wiley & Sons Inc.

16

Italy and Mozambique: Science, Economy & Society within a History of an Anomalous Cooperation

Luca Bussotti[1], Antonella De Muti[2]
[1]Centro de Estudos Internacionais ISCTE-IUL, Lisbon, Portugal
[2]Federal University of Minas Gerais, Belo Horizonte, Brazil

In this article the authors aim at showing how an "anomalous" international and very intense cooperation between Italy and Mozambique was born. In fact, Italy has not a strong colonial tradition, especially in Mozambique, so it seems interesting to try to understand the reason why this former Portuguese colony has become the Italian most important partner in its cooperation activity. This analysis is based on the main hypothesis related to the birth of international bilateral cooperation: they have been seriously considered in order to explain the origin of this strange relationship, but they cannot completely clarify this particular case. According to the Italian social and political recent history, the privileged relationship with Mozambique is due more to a "bottom up" process than to geo-strategic or economic reasons. The fact that Mozambique had belonged to a weak Western power such as Portugal certainly gave Italy the opportunity to penetrate more easily in this country than in the ones which had been under the strong dominion of France or England. One of the most important results of this "anomalous" cooperation has to be found in the scientific fields (such as geology, architecture, biotechnologies) and in its impact on the development of Mozambique.

Keywords: Italy; Mozambique; Bilateral Cooperation; Origins; Comparative History; Institutions; Science; Economy & Society

Introduction

This study aims at understanding why and through which modalities the cooperative relationship between Mozambique and Italy has taken its exceptional character and lasting commitment.

Even though its first cooperation Act was only passed in 1979, Italy got involved in cooperation activity with Mozambique since the years of the liberation struggle and the period immediately after the independence of this former Portuguese colony (1975).

Indeed, it seems difficult to explain how such an intense relationship was born, since even the brief Italian colonial experience was far from being in Mozambique, having concentrated, at the level of sub-Saharan Africa, especially in Ethiopia and Somalia. However, Mozambique is, up to now, the favorite destination of the official development assistance (ODA) from Italy, the eighth world power.

The answer to such a question, in fact, appears to be substantially different from the one that can be given for the European countries with strong colonial traditions. Actually they established, in Africa as elsewhere, "natural" cooperation relations with the newly independent countries because of the previous ties to their former political domains. This has resulted, in the majority of cases, in extensive partnerships. Let's consider, for example, France, whose former colonies have been influenced in financial, monetary, cultural, economic and even military terms, as recently demonstrated by the case of Mali. As Gabas pointed out, the priority of France cooperation has always been to establish a "Francophony-Africa-Mediterrean trio"; its image continues to be that of a country strictly linked to its colonial past (Gabas, 2005: 249). The relationships between the UK and its former african colonies were based, for a long time, on the "imperial" Britannic vision; even after decolonization, during the 1950s and 1960s, "the prevailing economic models emphasized investments" (Paquement, 2010). Much more problematic have been the relationships between Portugal and PALOP (Moita, 1985; Ferreira, 1994), Spain and Equatorial Guinea (Velloso, 2007), Belgium and Congo (Gerard-Libois, 1970; Vanthemsche, 2012).

Nothing similar can be said as regards Italy, substantially free of a colonial past, and whose foreign politics have always been characterized by a sort of "international equilibrium" between its Atlantic position (NATO membership and close relations with the USA), the European and Mediterranean vocation and the search for a dialogue between Israel and Palestine (Puri Purini). These options changed in 2001, when Berlusconi and his Government made stronger relations with Bush's Unites States and Putin's Russia, reducing his commitment in Europe. The African perspective has never been a priority for Italian Government.

In recent years Berlusconi has developed a favoured relation with Ghaddafi and, in the Middle East, with Israel, instead of encouraging the dialogue with the Palestinians.

For this reason, the answer to the basic question about why Mozambique is the main objective of Italian ODA, will also allow us to reject models that are, perhaps, too often taken for granted, but that cannot apply to the case here analyzed. The reference is to that model of the international Western cooperation with the developing countries, first of all the American one, whose key features are rooted in the European Recovery Program (ERP) or Marshall Plan. The ERP was launched immediately after the Second World War in order "to help" those European Countries (such as Italy) whose industrial apparatus had been dramatically destroyed and which had to enter the forum of "democratic" nations (Truman doctrine). The same principles—economic growth and democratization, according with a "top-down" approach and an accentuated bilateralism instead of multilateralism—oriented the birth and the goals of USAID (created in 1961), a powerful "Cold War" instrument against the Soviet Union in the area of developing countries. Despite clear differences, the politics of international cooperation carried out by the European Countries most engaged in this activity (the Netherlands, Sweden, Norway, etc.) have to be embedded in the same globalized context, in which the principles of Western democracy and free market had to constitute the new pillars of the former European colonies in Asia and Africa. For these reasons this kind of cooperation has been the target of several criticisms over the years, almost all of them from the point of view opposite to the liberal conception, or even of Marxist tendency, from the Dependency Theory to the current positions of an economist like Jeffrey Sachs (Frank, 1966; Cardoso & Faletto, 1979; Amin, 1977; Grieco, 1988; Sacks, 2005).

Through this research we get to the conclusion that other channels have been used to develop the special relationship between Italy and Mozambique. This is due to three key factors: first, the permanent pressure from the Italian "civil society" on its politicians; second—paradoxically—the lack of a clear Italian strategy in its international and African politics which allowed the acceptance—from a political perspective—of Mozambique as the priority country for international Italian cooperation. Finally, a geo-political reason, since Mozambique had been colonized by a weak European power such as Portugal, which, on its leaving, left a vacuum in which the Italian ambitions were able to fit. So, it is possible to say that, the building of bilateral relations between Italy and Mozambique was initially rooted in "informal" mechanisms, and only subsequently was institutionalized at a formal level.

This article consists of three parts: in the first, a summary of the main lines of the development of the Italian cooperation both in general and with Mozambique will be presented, accompanied by essential statistical data; in the second, we will try to formulate hypothesis in order to understand why Italy chose Mozambique as its main cooperation partner; finally, we will show the conclusion of our research.

In terms of methodology, the research has been based on a number of sources: the official ones, published by the Italian Foreign Ministry, the archives of the Ministry itself in Rome, testimonies on the birth of the cooperation relationships between the two countries (on the Italian side as well as the Mozambican), the available bibliography, though not too wide.

Mozambique in the Italian Cooperation

The Birth of Italian International Cooperation

After the end of the Second World War, Italy was in quite difficult conditions. The Country had to be almost completely rebuilt, especially in the North, where the largest part of its industrial apparatus was concentrated. So, from 1945 to 1960, the efforts of the Italian politics were focused on internal targets more than on foreign policy. Moreover we have to remember that Italy was a "losing power", and had a low international credibility. In addition to this, according to the reasons above mentioned, Italy entered NATO in 1949 notwhistanding the hard political battles led by the Communist and the Socialist Parties inside and outside the Parliament, and only in 1955 joined the United Nations. It is now easier to understand the reason why, differently from what happened for the other European powerful States, Italy began to deal with cooperation with developing countries very late.

The first steps of the Italian Government in the international cooperation were 1) to manage the relations with Somalia, a former colony, of which Rome had had the fiduciary administration until 1960; 2) The approval of two laws (the No. 1033/1966 and the No. 75/1970) regarding the international volunteer service, with the aim to give technical assistance to developing Countries; 3) The approval of the Law 1222/1971, the first specifically directed to the international cooperation, with a budget of 50 billion liras in 5 years. Once more, it was not a law dealing with all the aspects of international cooperation, but an act which aimed at regulating the activity and the legal status of public servants working in the technical cooperation with the developing countries, giving special provisions to Somalia. According to Gallizioli, because of the lack of a clear strategy of its international (and African) politics, 80% of the budget went to fatten the bureaucracy of the international organizations. Between 1971 and 1979 the private fluxes for International cooperation overcame the public ones (Gallizioli, 2009).

This first phase of the Italian international cooperation was characterized by a total confusion in terms of institutional competence: the funds for Somalia administration were managed by four ministries and the Italian Central Bank. The total budget for Somalia was of 90 billion liras (about 50 million euro) in the 1950s and of 60 billion liras in the following decade. The confusion can be explained by the fact that Italy hadn't decided yet whether to include this activity inside the structure of the Ministry of Foreign Affairs or to create an external agency.

A new phase began with the approval of the law 38/1979, following to which a Department for the Cooperation to Development was created within the Ministry of Foreign Affairs. It is possible to affirm that the 1980s were the "Golden Age" of international Italian cooperation.

The last phase began with the approval of the law 49/1987, which stated that the cooperation for development was part of Italian foreign policy (art. 1). In this period (1989), Italy reached its maximum in terms of ODA (0.41% of the GNP), differently from what was happening in the other European countries. The increase of ODA, in percentage, was relevant, passing from 0.08% to 0.19% of GNP over the two first years of the 1980s, reaching 0.35% in 1984. In 2003 not even 0.20% of the GNP was invested in international cooperation, leaving Italy at the last place in Europe and the second lowest position inside OSCE.

This downward trend continued in the 2000s, when the budget for the ODA passed from 732 million euro in 2008 to 86 in 2012.

As the Minister for Cooperation and Integration, Andrea Riccardi, said in December 2011:

The Italian aid for development is stagnant. We are far from the European objective of 0.5 per cent and 0.7 per cent of the UN. Last year we reached a historic minimum (0.15 percent of GDP) ending in second last place in the ranking of donors, only followed by Korea. For 2012, the forecast is for a further decrease[1].

Italy started from these "institutional" bases and didn't have a clear strategy, but even though Mozambique has constantly represented the priority country for the Italian international cooperation. In order to explain the reason and the way in which this "anomalous" cooperation has been improved along the years, it is necessary to investigate outside the institutional level. The hypothesis which can be formulated is connected with the ability of the Italian "civil society" to influence the Italian government at making the cooperation with Mozambique a priority in its African politics.

The Position of Mozambique in the Italian ODA

After many years in which its resources were distributed to a large number of countries, the Italian Cooperation accepted the recommendations of the OSCE/DAC Peer Review 2004, *Note for programming guidelines* 2007-2009[2], deciding to focus its aid on the Sub-Saharan African countries and on those in post-conflict situations (DAC, 2009). In addition, the various geographical areas were assigned two different levels of priority, and the aid was addressed to the areas of health, education, environment, alternative and renewable resources, public and global good and gender equality (DAC, 2009).

Mozambique, which has been assigned priority level 1, has, so far, firmly maintained the privileged position it has enjoyed since its independence (Development CO, 2012).

From 1982 to 2009, this country received € 764 million in grants and loans of which 105.9 million euro in aid credit; to these figures it must be added the resources arising by debt cancellation in 2002, amounting to 557.3 million euro (IDEM). Mozambique has also been selected, the only one among all the countries supported by the Italian Cooperation, for the implementation of a project for direct support to the state budget, the Budget Support, and chosen, along with Vietnam, as the target country for twinning business.

In the reports published by the Italian Cooperation, we read:

Over the past five years, the aid from the Italian Cooperation in sub-Saharan Africa was more than 1000 million Euros, targeted to interventions involving a total of 34 out of the 46 countries in the region. The main beneficiaries of the aid have been Mozambique, Ethiopia and Sudan.

In 2010, about 54 million were released as gift (spread over 34 countries and recipients) while 10 million euros were granted in aid credit.

Mozambique was the largest recipient of Italian aid, with 21 million provided in 2010, followed by Somalia (10 million), Ethiopia (8 million), Sudan (7,000,000). Other beneficiary countries were Kenya, Uganda and Senegal[3].

The action of the Italian Cooperation in Mozambique started immediately after its independence and continued, without interruption, until the present day, despite relevant reductions.

Due to the development of its political-economic situation, supported by its institutional stability, Mozambique seems to represent a virtuous case in the much criticized system of international cooperation (Carrino, 2005), that was able, in this case, to transform the emergency humanitarian aid (during the bloody civil war that swept the country until 1992) in real development cooperation (World Bank, 2008).

Mozambique always appears at the forefront of Italian ODA. **Tables 1** and **2** indicate the main Italian bilateral aid recipient countries from the years 1987-1988 until the years 2008-2009, from which it is evident its privileged position, similar, but often even more favored than that of Ethiopia, a former Italian colony.

In recent years, following the evolution of the international geopolitical frame in which the Italian interests are located, new priorities have arisen as for the allocation of the resources. The new situation has led to the displacement of urgent interventions in conflict and crisis areas, especially after the changing of the balance on the world stage, such as the dissolution of the Soviet Union, the Balkan war (1991-1995) the Afghan conflict (2001) and the Iraqi (2003-2011), the lasting instability on the Middle East chessboard, the explosion of migration flows.

The "Strange" Birth of a Cooperative Relationship: Hypothesis

The reason for such a large commitment in men and resources of the Italian cooperation in that distant country in Sub-Saharan Africa rises interesting questions, which we will try to answer through the analysis of what the general motivation of the ODA allocation are considered to be, trying to assess the extent to which Mozambique meets the criteria that are placed at the basis of the interventions, categorized as follows (Isernia, 1995; Raimondi/Antonelli, 2001):

1) geo-economic reasons: they presuppose economic implications resulting from the geographic proximity, as was the case with the support of Italy in countries such as Albania, the former Yugoslavia or the African Mediterranean countries;

2) political-economic reasons: they appear when an industrialized state does not intend to have relationships with a developing one for political-ideological reasons (US cooperation with some "rogue states" through Japan);

3) international political motivation: they arise from the relevance of geo-political unstable areas or places of conflict that represent a threat to world peace (see Iraq and Afghanistan);

4) post-colonial motivation: industrialized countries concentrate their aid in their former colonies, to help their growth;

5) economic motivation: it is a form of cooperation from de-

---

[1]Conference in the occasion of the 40th anniversary of IPALMO, 1971-2001: "*Ieri, oggi domani, quattro decenni di trasformazioni geo-economiche-politich*", speech by the Minister for International Cooperation and Integration Andrea Riccardi, Rome December 12th, 2011.
http://www.integrazione.gov.it/ministro/discorsi/2011/12/conferenza-ipalmo-anniversary.aspx, accessed January, 2012.

[2]DIPCO 14/2007 it is the weekly bulletin of the DGCS (General Direction for Development Cooperation) in which all the resolutions of the general manager and the executive committee, as well as notices, documents and international reports are recorded.

[3]For information about the financial commitment of the Italian cooperation for development, see: A. Raimondi, G. Antonelli, *op. cit.* See also the annual reports on the implementation of the policy of development cooperation on the site.
http://www.cooperazioneallosviluppo.esteri.it/pdgcs/italiano/Pubblicazioni/intro.html

Table 1.
Italian ODA (1987-1998) values expressed in millions of US dollars.

Countries	Tot	Countries	Tot	Countries	Tot
1987/88	usd	1992/93	usd	1997/98	usd
Mozambique	266	Mozambique	195	Madagascar	67
Somalia	268	Tanzania	199	Mozambique	65
Ethiopia	233	China	166	Haiti	44
Tanzania	174	Egypt	141	Uganda	40
China	136	Argentina	144	Ethiopia	39
Tunisia	104	Tunisia	103	Malta	24
Sudan	97	Morocco	89	Albania	22
Egypt	94	Sierra Leone	100	Argentina	20
India	63	Ex Yugoslavia	91	Ecuador	20
Senegal	59	Albania	81	China	20

Source: Raimondi/Antonelli, 2001.

Table 2.
Italian ODA (2002-2009) values expressed in millions of US dollars.

Countries	Tot	Countries	Tot	Countries	Tot	Countries	Tot
2002/03	usd	2006	usd	2007	usd	2008/09	usd
Mozambique	231	Nigeria	755	Iraq	480	Iraq	429
Rep Congo	225	Iraq	485	Morocco	83	Afghanistan	92
Tanzania	67	Serbia	129	Ethiopia	105	Ethiopia	60
Ethiopia	48	Ethiopia	105	Lebanon	65	Palestine	55
Tunisia	35	Cameroun	63	Afghanistan	62	Lebanon	48
Guinea Bissau	35	Zambia	51	Sierra Leone	44	Albania	43
Afghanistan	33	Lebanon	44	Mozambique	43	Liberia	38
China	31	Afghanistan	32	China	42	Ivory Coast.	34
A.N.P	26	Mozambique	30	St. Vincent & Grenadine	41	Mozambique	30
Albania		Albania	30	Serbia	23	Sudan	27

Source: OSCE/DAC, *Peer Review*, Italy, various years.

veloped countries, aimed to achieve specific economic dividends, especially favoring their own business in the underdeveloped countries, and exploiting its natural resources.

In the case of the relationship Italy-Mozambique, the first three points are evidently to be rejected *a priori*. We will focus, therefore, on the last two, particularly on point 4.

Post-colonial reasons: In our opinion, a first, possible answer for the massive Italian commitment in Mozambique can be sought in the establishment of "political" non-governmental relations among some leaders of political parties and organizations in Italy and Mozambique.

In this first case, Italy, after trying to implement its foreign policy and cooperation in its former colonies, with which, however, didn't succeed in maintaining strong ties, turned to the territories "belonging to weak colonial powers because the relationships with the other countries belonging to former strong colonial powers were essentially precluded" (Calchi Novati, 1997).

This opinion was substantially shared by Ennio Di Nolfo,

according to whom:

As a matter of fact, Mozambique, like other Portuguese colonies, was one of the privileged sectors of the Italian penetration, being Portugal a weak power, so having Italy the possibility or hope to get more benefits than those which could be obtained from other colonies belonging to France or Britain) (*Di Nolfo*, 1997).

Therefore, Italy probably intended to create its own area of political and economic influence in a country of ancient Portuguese colonization that, even from a geographical point of view, was closer to its former colonies and had reached independence in the period in which Italy had just begun to structure its cooperation policy.

Another important element to be taken into account was the conditioning resulting from the commitments arising from its participation in the Atlantic Pact. How it makes us keenly note Calchi Novati:

NATO, and in general East-West policy, gave Italy the opportunity to intervene much more on the world stage. Among other things, being accepted among the great liberal democracies of the West was considered itself a foreign policy objective, indeed the only true big goal attained by our foreign policy (Calchi Novati, 1997).

Even after the ending of the "bloc politics", the influence of the Atlantic Alliance has remained strong. Italy has therefore tried to take advantage of the conflicts within the NATO (Romano, 2002) to recover those positions that were closer to his original interest, and had partly to set aside due to its dependence from the ally (Calchi Novati, 1997). The Italian support to Mozambique in the period when the country was a Socialist Republic, can be placed in this perspective.

The one above described, however, represents the already "institutionalized" phase of the cooperation between Italy and Mozambique. The question that now arises is how these results were reached. "Political non-governmental relations" played in this case a decisive role. They came before the strategic options in the "official" Italian foreign policy were taken, but then they facilitated its implementation and consolidation. Here is what the first Italian ambassador in Maputo, Claudio Moreno (in office from 1976 to 1980), protagonist of the events of those years, says: *The friendship with Mozambique was born through the thin network of diplomatic contacts woven by Italy, which led to the opening of the first embassy of a Western country in Maputo.*

The Role of Italian Political Organizations and Civil Society in the Birth of Bilateral Cooperation Italy-Mozambique

Moreover, Italy was one of the first Western countries to promote a joint committee and a cooperation agreement with Mozambique. Moreno also emphasizes the important role that the pressures and initiatives on the government by the PCI and the PSI had in order to encourage the birth of the Italian development cooperation with Mozambique.

The above presented situation suggests that, in the decade 1970-1980, at least three social actors were able to influence the institutional choices in favor of Mozambique. They are the mirror of the Italian political peculiarity in the context of the Cold War. Actually, Italy was a country in which the socialist and the catholic traditions worked together for the building of popular democracy and international stability. These two tendencies were not only of political nature: they were of cultural, ethical, philosophic nature too. Their different ideas of solidarity made a convergence of interests towards Mozambique that was possible, thanks to other, important international reasons, too, that we will present later.

The most significant forces that contributed to the choice Mozambique as the privileged Italian international partner are the following:

The left wing parties, both in their direct relations with the Central Government and in those with the local governments, especially in the so called "Red Towns" (towns with a left wing local government); which represented the first example of decentralized cooperation.

The Catholic Church, especially through some of its organizations, which were able to influence the Christian Democrat Party (DC) in power, in order to develop good relations with Mozambique, in addition to NGOs of different inspiration;

Italian academic world, widely present from the beginning of the Italian cooperation with Mozambique, and even more after the failure of the Somali experience in the 1980s.

1) If in the "First Republic" the left wing parties never had direct responsibility in central government, the same cannot be said with regard to local governments that gave a decisive contribution to cooperation with Mozambique[4]. Although there isn't a wide literature on the subject, with the exception of very few studies (Lanzafame/Podaliri, 2004), we can find a large numbers of contributions of journalistic or propagandistic nature, as well as the testimonies of those who lived in the first person that extraordinary season that can help us to rebuild the development of this unique relationship. The first contacts between members of the political and intellectual Italian and Mozambican worlds took place in the early sixties. At that time, a strong anti-colonial attitude and a feeling of solidarity with developing countries had developed in the Italian public opinion, involving more and more sectors of the society: from intellectuals, to the Church, from organizations of various kind to students as well as ordinary people. This attitude spread to the institutions, giving impulse to a series of initiatives of solidarity from cultural, religious and political forces even before an interest by the government was born (Calchi Novati, 1997). Dina Forti, for many years responsible for the contacts with the liberation movements in developing countries on behalf of PCI, tells that in 1962, two years before the declaration of armed struggle, was contacted by Marcelino dos Santos, one of the main leaders of FRELIMO, of whom she had never heard about. Dos Santos asked her to arrange a meeting with one of the PCI leaders to talk about Mozambique and the rising of its independence movement. Giancarlo Pajetta, head of the International Department, agreed with great interest to meet him[5]. At the time, many Italian municipalities as Piacenza, Grosseto and Trento gave their support to the anti-colonial struggle In October 1964, the Reggio Emilia communist ruled city council, following the FRELIMO decision to start the armed insurrection, sent to the guerrilla leaders a message of support to the liberation struggle of the people of Mozambique. A few years later, in 1966, José Luís Cabaço, a young FRELIMO activist, who later held important government positions, arrived in Italy with two objectives: to study sociology

at Trento University and create a network of relationships that might have helped in the fight against the Portuguese colonialism: the objective was actually met. Although he never directly took part in the commissions dealing with cooperation, the Mozambican statesman became an adviser to the Foreign Minister Joaquim Chissano and President Samora Machel for issues concerning Italy, because of his deep knowledge of the country[6]. So Luis Cabaço recalls the climate of fervor and renewal that Italy experienced in the Sixties and Seventies:

It is not possible to understand the cooperation between Italy and Mozambique if we do not remember the peculiarity of the Italian democracy in the post war period, its partisan tradition and, in particular, the dream of a historic compromise between the Catholic and socialist positions as regards social justice. With the advent of anti-colonial struggle, the means of communication between our two peoples expanded the missionary experience, incorporating components of political identity which took off from the hands of the Portuguese colonial government its control on this relationship. This spaces opened the way to the first interventions of a Catholic Church committed in favor of the destiny and the aspirations of colonized people... Also the role played by the political left winged forces on the issue of the Third World grew (Cabaço, 2003: 9).

It was in this atmosphere that the idea of organizing a conference of solidarity with the peoples still under the Portuguese colonial rule arose. It was held in Rome from 24 to 26 June 1970 and was attended by representatives of Angola, Guinea Bissau and Mozambique. Personalities belonging to the world of culture and politics from all the parties gave their support to the event. On this occasion, an official meeting between representatives of the Portuguese colonies and Pope Paul VI was arranged. It had a great importance since it represented the legitimacy, from a political and moral point of view, of the national liberation movements in those countries. The meeting with the Pope was organized by Marcella Glisenti, founder of the bookstore Paesi Nuovi in Rome, who had always been interested in issues linked to the Third World. Paesi Nuovi was connected to the DC, but, at the same time, Marcella Glisenti was part of IPALMO, whose President was Gian Paolo Calchi Novati, an academic professor of left tendency. This meeting represented the most effective initiative arising from the alliance between the democratic Catholicism and the Marxist tradition in favor of the liberation struggle of the African Portuguese colonies. In an indirect form, the European enemy was represented by Portugal, a State member of the NATO, but that did not collect any political sympathy in the main Italian parties. The political leaders who took part in the event were the leaders of the movements fighting for independence: Agostinho Neto from Angola, Amilcar Cabral from Guinea Bissau and Marcelino dos Santos from Mozambique:

...They were received as representatives of Angola, Mozambique and Guinea Bissau, so indirectly recognized as independent countries and not as Portuguese colonies. That caused, of course, the official protests of Portugal... (GLISENTI, 1993: 14).

Another important consequence of the Rome Conference was the birth of the "policy of twinning", chiefly supported by the eminent parasitologist Silvio Pampiglione, a doctor known for

---

[4]Interview with Ambassador Claudio Moreno, 28th January 2011.

[5]Some information are taken from our meeting with Dina Forti, that took place in her house in Rome on 26th January 2011; She recalled some events very clearly, others she had forgotten because of the old age or she preferred not to talk about. We have only used information that could be confirmed.

[6]Interview with L. Cabaço, former State Work Secretary and acting Minister of Information in the transitional government, Minister of Transport and Communications (1 Government), Minister of Information 1981-1986, and Member of Parliament (Maputo November 29th 2010).

his humanitarian commitment in countries emerging from colonialism. It is so possible to say that the academic cooperation with Mozambique has its origin in this meeting: as a matter of fact, Pampiglione will be one of the first doctors to go to Mozambique, developing the first Italian cooperation programs.

So, in the same year 1970, the PCI entrusted three Italian cities councils with the task of managing relations with the three African countries: Angola was assigned to Prato, Guinea Bissau and Cape Verde to Arezzo and Mozambique to Reggio Emilia.

While the twinning projects with the other two cities did not produce lasting fruits, the one between Reggio Emilia and Mozambique remains one of the most meaningful and successful model of what was called "diplomacy from below" (Lanzafame/Podaliri, 2004: 15) the first example of decentralized cooperation. Even today there are cases of cooperation carried out at the level of local government: it is worth remembering the Cooperation Agreement between the Autonomous Province of Trento and the Province of Sofala in 2001.

About the twinning with Reggio Emilia, Giuseppe Soncini, then president of the Hospital Santa Maria Nuova in the city, said that he was contacted by the direction of the Communist Party who entrusted him with the task of creating a link with Mozambique. He confesses that, fascinated by the personality of Amilcar Cabral, would have preferred to deal with Guinea Bissau, but he accepted the Party guidelines, succeeding in giving birth to an unique and very successful experiment, one of the most striking examples of the involvement of local authorities: a partnership between the Reggio Emilia hospital and the guerrilla hospital, only a few huts in the Mozambique forest.

In 1972, Soncini organized an expedition across the border of Tanzania, to the northern areas of Mozambique freed by the guerrilla, to bring solidarity and concrete help. Besides him, other people took part in the expedition: Lanfranco Turci head of the Department of Health of the Emilia Romagna region, Angelo Pisi, vice mayor of Reggio Emilia, journalist Marisa Musu and Franco Cigarini, a photographer and documentary film maker on behalf of Reggio Emilia city council. The film *Ten days with the guerrillas in freed Mozambique*, shot by Franco Cigarini, remains as an evidence of the expedition. It is the first documentary movie on the liberation struggle in Mozambique that arrived in Europe[7].

From 24 to 25 March 1973 the "National Conference of Solidarity with the struggle of Independence of Angola, Guinea and Mozambique" to which Samora Machel took part, was held in Reggio Emilia. Also this conference was supported by a large number of Italian politicians and intellectuals belonging to various political groups, such as PCI, PSIUP, PSI, DC.

During these meetings, the foundation of the friendship between the Italians and the representatives of the guerrillas, later rulers of Mozambique, was laid; a friendship that remained unchanged over the years. Among other measures in favor of Mozambique, the municipality of Reggio Emilia organized, from 1979 onwards, the sending of three cargo ships carrying humanitarian aids.

After independence, President Samora Machel personally invited Dina Forti in Mozambique with the delicate task of holding an institutional position on behalf of the government, thanks to the relations of friendship and respect that he and the leaders of FRELIMO had for her.

The Catholic Church has always considered Mozambique as an important target of its mission. It is quite impressive the number of articles, reports, interviews that the newspaper of the Italian Catholic bishops, "L'Osservatore Romano", published since Mozambique independence. Although the majority of the articles are concentrated in two years, (1988: the visit in Mozambique of the Pope; 1992: the General Peace Agreement in Rome, thanks to the mediation of the Sant'Egidio Community), the activity of the Church in Mozambique is constantly reported with a very special attention by the newspaper (BUSSOTTI, 2011). When Samora Machel died, in 1986, although his clear anti-religious tendencies, "L'Osservatore Romano" commented the event in a very worried tone, because of the strategic transformation that Machel had been operating in the economic politics of Mozambique (Chillà, 1986). Many of the DC politicians, who took part in various Italian Governments, were strictly linked to the Church, especially to the missionary wing, particularly sensitive to the Mozambican reality. Among the politicians already mentioned, Piero Bassetti, Luigi Granelli (who occupied the charge of Minister), Carlo Fracanzani (who was Vice-Minister), were the exponent of this "missionary wing" in the Italian Government. Of course, they directly influenced the option for Mozambique, especially in the 1970s, when, in Italy, for the first and last time in its history, DC and PCI formed a government of national unity (1976), in order to fight the common struggle against terrorism. Coincidentally, these are the years in which Mozambique reached its independence, so it was quite easy, for the DC politicians, to comply with the requests coming from the PCI and the Catholic Church. Even if the Italian government never recognized the FRELIMO during the national liberation struggle, Mozambique was officially recognized immediately after its independence. Hence, the Italian central authorities began the building of an aid program. What had happened in the two meetings in Rome and Reggio Emilia helped in this sense: Minister Fanfani agreed, for example, to meet President Samora Machel and this represented a great political event. The Italian Government itself directly became active in Mozambique, with the massive program of development cooperation, which we have mentioned above. Andreotti, for a long time Minister of Foreign Affairs and one of the most prominent members of DC, gave a great attention to the relations with East and Africa, focusing on Mozambique, as demonstrated by the many visits to the country he made, and by the support given to peace process. His purpose was to fit into the spaces that the great powers had left free in the international arena, as Cabaço remarked[8]. Going to Mozambique, to take office, the first italian Ambassador Claudio Moreno was accompanied by a small delegation of doctors, including Professor Pampiglione, Professor Cresta and Dr. Monasta that immediately were engaged in a support program in Maputo Central Hospital as well as in the Medicine Faculty of the University Eduardo Mondlane. The Italian position appeared to be completely different from that of other countries. Ambassador Claudio Moreno says that Italy was very well seen at governmental level. As a demonstration of it, he tells that, while at that time all the Mozambicans that held institutional positions, were not allowed to have relationships with Western embassies, they were not forbidden to

---

[7] A testimony about the expedition from Reggio Emilia to the guerrilla camps has been given by William Turci, Lanfranco Turci's brother, in a conversation in Maputo, where he moved in the period immediately following the independence, working for the Italian cooperation at first and then becoming an entrepreneur (November 2010).

[8] L. Cabaço, quoted interview.

have contacts with the Italian[9]. Later the "Tangentopoli" storm wiped out some of the protagonists of the first phase of cooperation with Mozambique, but it did not interrupt the relationship of solidarity between the two countries. The most relevant event showing the good relations existing between these two countries was registered in 1981, when President Samora Machel went to Rome on an official visit and was received at the Quirinale by President Sandro Pertini (Fondazione Sandro Pertini, 1981); Machel returned in Rome in 1985, and, on that occasion, was received by Pope John Paul II. The words of Mario Lanzafame, sum up the birth, institutionalization and strengthen of the Italy-Mozambique cooperation:

... as solidarity... turns into cooperation, as activists in the labor movement, executives, professionals in the health field and administrators transformed the theory and practice of proletarian internationalism, as it was called, in solidarity at first and then in cooperation; as individual believers, militant in social Christian organizations, important Christian Democrat leaders made use of their government positioning to offer the opportunity of creating at first supportive relationships and then relationships linked to a more general framework of development models, as anti-colonialist and emancipation movements... build relations and connections, that leave deep traces to the present time: what they kept from the experience gained during the season of the struggle and what they left behind when they became leaders of their countries; as professionals or volunteers, individually at first and then in partnerships, built and put into practice solidarity, international cooperation and humanitarian intervention (Lanzafame, 2005).

Strong relationships were also created with many NGOs, among which the most active were Molisv and CUAMM, but also with IPALMO, that so much would have done in the birth and development of university cooperation in Mozambique. One of the highest points in the relationships between Italy and Mozambique is represented by the signing of the Rome Peace Agreement, in 1992, which, thanks to the mediation of the Catholic Church and Sant'Egidio Community, put an end to a civil war that had lasted 16 years. After the signing of the peace agreement, the UN sent international troops to Mozambique (Onumoz), to manage the peace transition (Couto, 2000), in which also Italian soldiers took part.

2) Italian universities did not have a strong tradition in the activity of international cooperation, especially with Africa. However, the cooperation with Somalia had obtained, as one of its best results, the opening of the Somali University. The political situation in Mozambique and its friendly relationship with the Italian Government made possible to develop some initiatives in this field. Mozambique needed technical assistance: socialist countries could not guarantee all these necessities, so Italy entered a space quite empty. Personal relations too had an important role. In 1976, together with the first Italian Ambassador, Moreno, some academic professors leaved to Mozambique, beginning to cooperate with this country, initially in the field of health and, from 1977, through programs of technical assistance with the Faculty of Geology. In 1978 the commitment of Italian academic cooperation involved other faculties, such as Agriculture, Economics, Medicine and Architecture. The Italian universities most involved in these first programs were Rome, Viterbo, Udine and Venice. In 1983, the first bilateral agreement of academic cooperation Italy-Mo-

zambique was signed. These programs continue till today even if with some difficulties, due to the financial situation of Italy.

3) In the Seventies IPALMO played a relevant role in the building university cooperation. This institute has been defined as "... (a) kind of pressure group, a real aid lobby", led by Piero Bassetti and Giampaolo Calchi Novati (Calchi Novati, 1997). The successes achieved in this specific field of cooperation, certainly persuaded the two parts to go on with the academic relationships. As a direct impact of this commitment on the country's development, it is possible to mention, the following areas in which the scientific international cooperation between Italy and Mozambique was carried out:

a) *Geology*: 10 *square degrees of the provinces of Nampula, Zambézia and Cabo Delgado were cartographated, and a great quantity of petrographic, geological and geophysical data gathered. New areas of mining interest, the ones that only began to be exploited in the Nineties, were identified in the Seventies thanks to the Italian scientific cooperation. Hydro-geological maps of Maputo and Gaza provinces were produced.*

b) *Architecture: between 1996 and 2009, many studies were performed, among which: a survey on the Maputo corridor, the main road connection between Mozambique and South Africa; the analysis of the growth of urban centres and their suburbs; the classification of the architectural heritage of the country and, finally, the elaboration of town planning schemes referred to various cities, among which Matola. Rules for the civil constructions were defined. It is important to point out that the Architecture faculty of the Mondlane University eas established thanks to a direct partnership with the University of Rome, La Sapienza.*

c) *Agriculture: Both the "Sunflower Project" in South Mozambique, creating a new variety of sunflower, more suitable for the local climatic features and the experimentation on the njiemba bean, helped Mozambique to diminish its structural food deficit.*

d) *Medicine: an important research was published, at the end of a program aimed to study and identify the main characteristics of infectious diseases, such as enteritis, sexually transmitted diseases, otitis and parasitosis.*

e) *An international Centre of Biotechnology was set up, that has established itself as one of the most prominent centers of excellence in the area of applied sciences in Mozambique.*

Also cases of failure were registered, such as the cooperation between the Faculty of Economics of the Eduardo Mondlane University and the Faculty of Economics of the "Tor Vergata" University in Rome, but they did not interrupt the scientific cooperation between the two countries.

4) The external factors. Besides inner factors, external reasons too contributed to the development of the relationship between Italy and Mozambique. At a geo-political level, in fact, Italy had tried, without success, to play a political and economic role in its former colonies. Its following step was, therefore, to "enter" the territories "belonging to weak colonial powers, as the relationships with the rest of the former colonial world was interdicted to us" as Gian Paolo Calchi Novati points out at the conference "L'Italia nell'era della colonizzazione e del neocolonialismo" (Calchi Novati, 1997).

According to this interpretation, Italy opportunistically "entered" the former Portuguese colony, due to the weakness of Portugal, as Ennio Di Nolfo stated in the above mentioned conference:

Mozambique, as the other Portuguese colonies, has been one

---

[9]C. Moreno, quoted interview.

of the privileged sectors for Italy, being naturally Portugal a weak power, and leaving to Italy the possibility or the hope to obtain here more vantages than in the other colonies belonging to France or Great Britain (Di Nolfo, 1997).

So, a very plausible reason for the italian commitment in the cooperation with Mozambique might be its attempt to create a zone of political and economic influence, considering the proximity of Mozambique to the former Italian colonies. Another external reason could be its position as a member of NATO. As Calchi Novati stresses:

Nato, and generally the East-West politics, gave Italy interesting chances for intervening in the international scenario. The simple fact to be part of the great Western democracies was considered a goal, or better, the only, real goal of our foreign politics effectively achieved (Calchi Novati, 1997).

This ability, from the Italian side, to insert its foreign strategy inside the framework of the Cold War and of the NATO too, permitted it to act according to a high level of originality and freedom. Adding the fact that Samora Machel, in spite of the marxist choice of the government, was never willing to close international relations with the Western countries, it is then possible to explain the reason why these external factors approximated the two countries. Without former colonies towards which to direct its political strategy, Italy switched its attention to the areas of tensions rather than to those of stability (Romano, 2002).

The Importance of Economic Factors

Looking for the reasons that are at the basis of the Italian cooperation in Mozambique we cannot forget the economic aspects, which are many and long-standing, although for the most part, so far unknown.

To understand the importance of Mozambique for the Italian economy and the commitment of the Italian Cooperation in this country, we must go back to the period immediately after independence, in which many Italian companies were engaged in the building of important infrastructures.

The Corumana dam is the most important contract signed between Italy and Mozambique after independence. In 1982 the Banco de Moçambique made a financial agreement with Mediocredito bank for a 13 billion dollars loan for the building of the dam. The works were entrusted to the consortium Co.bo.co (Condotte d'Acqua, Bonifica-IRI, Lega delle Cooperative).

To the same period dates the construction of the Pequenos Libombos dam, whose building was entrusted to the Consorzio Strade-Italstrade and to the Calzoni Company. The total value of the works was of 110 million dollars for which Mozambique signed an agreement with Mediocredito bank (Repubblica, 10/7/1984:10).

Other Italian companies took charge, over the years, of the rebuilding of power lines (SAE/Sadelmi in the Centre-North, ENEL between Cahora Bassa and South Africa), aqueducts (CMB in Beira, CMC in Pemba), the railway line Maputo—Swaziland (Consorzio IRSA—Ansaldo/Astaldi), roads (CMC and Astaldi), the completion of the first optic fiber telephone connection (Italtel). In recent years, Italy has had a role in Mozambican economy through ENI oil exploration and the cultivation of oil palm and jatropha for the production of fuels.

The great Italian works in Mozambique continued, even if on a smaller scale, during the nineties and the new millennium, until the inauguration, of the bridge over the Zambezi River, in 2009.

Although the works were carried out by a Portuguese consortium, the Italian company Trevi played an important role in its construction, having built the foundations of the pillars. Through their contributions the European Commission (€35 million), Italy (20 million) and Sweden (18 million), allowed making true the old Mozambican dream of joining the north and the south of the country, separated by the Zambezi River.

Italian cooperation in the infrastructure sector has never stopped: a project for the construction of the Nhacangara dam (in the province of Manica) for an amount of more than 60 million euro and the one for the drainage of a part of the city of Maputo are in progress. (Ministero Degli Esteri-Coopera-Zione Allo Sviluppo, 2012).

Currently the CMC OF Ravenna is in charge of the rehabilitation of the sewer system of Beira, Mozambique's second largest city, the building of highways and other civil works[10].

In recent years, thanks to the continuation of the aid on the one hand and the investment growth on the others, the Italian presence in Mozambique has definitely strengthened and has been supported by the "Africa Plan" of the Ministry of Foreign Affairs and the Ministry of Economic Development (MISE).

From 2008, the will to create economic ties between the two countries, which also can take advantage of the thirtyfive-year friendship between Italy and Mozambique, has become pressing. There's the Italian intention to benefit from the position of the African country which has one of most promising economies in the SADC thanks to its vast natural resources not fully exploited yet (lo Cascio, 2010).

As a result of this renewed commitment, exports increased (compared to 2008) to more than 63% (from 24 to 39 million euro, the highest value in the last ten years), placing Italy in the ninth position among Mozambique supplying countries (data 2009).

Simultaneously to the growth of exports, there has been a reduction in imports by 38%, the Italian trade deficit thus passing from about 236 million to about 121 million (data 2010).

Cooperation has thus been an effective lever for raising and expanding the partnership between Rome and Maputo and to support the renewed interest of Italian companies in the Mozambican market.

Recently, moreover, the ENI research for oil and natural gas in northern Mozambique that began a few years ago, have borne fruit. At the end of 2011, the Italian oil company announced the discovery of a huge natural gas field off the coast of Cabo Delgado, estimated at 30 billion cubic meters, which could radically change Mozambican economy, creating at the same time, a major source of income for the Italian company (Daly, 2011; Smith, 2012; Garzilli, 2012): "... (the) greatest discovery of hydrocarbons that Eni has ever done... the increase 20% at one swoop of the world reserves of the six-legged dog, "as stated by the Eni CEO Paolo Scaroni (Il Sole 24 Ore, 21/10/2011).

The opening of a new phase of economic relations between the two countries as a result of the exploitation of natural gas fields discovered by ENI, not separated by the continuation of co-operation relationships, still required by the Mozambican government, was also outlined by the Italian Minister of Foreign Affairs Terzi, during his official visit to Mozambique on May

---

[10]CMC has been in Mozambique since 1982, when the Pequenos Libombos dam was built and (under the name of CMC Africa Australe Lda.) is the greatest building company in the country employing 3.000 workers and with 100 million euro turnover. Source: "Il Sole 24 Ore" Speciale, numero 41, 17th October 2008, p. 27.

4th, 2012 (Ministry of Foreign Affairs, 2012).

Conclusion

The here presented study intended to check the initial hypothesis, according to which the cooperation between Italy and Mozambique had an "atypical origin" denying, to some extent, the established paradigms in this respect. Actually, from the available data, it can be concluded that the reasons that usually lead European countries to engage in cooperative relationships with developing countries, do not apply to the Italian case, at least as regards the relationship with Mozambique.

The almost complete absence of a colonial history made so that Italy had to "create" areas of influence in the African context, which didn't take place neither through a planned project, nor, much less, through an "institutionalized" modality. The main way to enter Mozambique in a such massive manner has been through a "bottom up" strategy, thanks to the political relations of leftist Italian forces with FRELIMO in a first time, and then through the Catholic movements too. From the moment in which Mozambique gained independence from Portugal, its government established good diplomatic and bilateral official relations with Italy, taking advantage of all the political relationships developed throughout the years thanks to the activism of local institutions.

This led to a long period of cooperation, even if with limited economic benefits in comparison with the amount of the investments, as clearly indicated in the above study. However, the impacts on the scientific field have been relevant, since great progresses have been made in the knowledge of geology, agriculture, medicine, architecture and urban planning.

It is possible that the current situation will change this framework, as the ENI investment in Cabo Delgado gas seems to show. It would be quite interesting to understand if and how the strong bilateral relations between Italy and Mozambique have been able to open the doors to ENI, or if it has been the result of an independent activity of this great company. But this is another issue, which would need a new and different research.

Acknowledgements

A special thank to prof. Maurizio Vernassa, director of the PhD School in geopolitics at the University of Pisa, for the support given to this research, presented today in the journal AHS.

REFERENCES

Amin, S. (1977). *Capitalism in the age of globalization*. London: Zed Books.

Bertulli, C. (1974). *Croce e spada in Mozambico*. Roma: Coines.

Bussotti, L. (2011). Il Mozambico nella stampa italiana. Il caso de "L'Osservatore Romano"e de "La Repubblica". In Bussotti/Ngoenha (Eds.), *Le grandi figure dell'Africa Lusofona* (pp. 127-160). Udine: Aviani.

Cabaço, L. (2003). *La polvere e la pioggia*. Maputo: Ambasciata d'Italia-Ufficio per la Cooperazione allo Sviluppo.

Calchi Novati, G. P. (1997). *L'Italia nell'era della decolonizzazione e del neocolonialismo*. Paper presented at the First Workshop CONICS, "La Cooperazione allo sviluppo nella politica estera italiana". Sala Morosini, Roma: Ministero Affari Esteri.

http://www.uniurb.it/scipol/dmg.htm#convegni

Cardoso, F. H., & Faletto, E. (1979). *Dependency and development in Latin America*. University of California Press

Carrino, L. (2005). *Perle e Pirati, Critica della cooperazione allo sviluppo e nuovo multi-lateralismo*. Trento: Erickson.

ChillÀ, A. (1986). *Mozambico al bivio fra miseria e convivenza pacifica* (p. 3). L'Osservatore Romano.

Daly, J. C. K. (2011). *Is Mozambique the Next African Energy Superpower?* OILPRICE.COM.

http://oilprice.com/popup9.html

Di Nolfo, E. (1997). *Cooperazione e politica estera: opzioni strategiche, opzioni geografiche*. Paper presented at the First workshop CONICS, "La Cooperazione allo sviluppo nella politica estera italiana". Sala Morosini, Roma: Ministero Affari Esteri.

http://www.conics.it/word/atticonics.pdf

Frank, G. (1966). *The Development of Underdevelopment*. Monthly Review Press.

Gabas, J.-J. (2005). French Development Co-operation Policy. In P. Hoebink, & O. Stokke (Eds.), *Perspectives on European Development Co-operation*. Oxon/New York: Routledge.

Garzilli, E. (2012). *L'Italia in Mozambico: organizzazioni umanitarie e affari sui giacimenti di gas*. Il Fatto Quotidiano.

Glisenti, M. (2003). *La polvere e la pioggia*. Maputo: Ambasciata d'Italia-Ufficio per la Cooperazione allo Sviluppo.

Grieco, J. M. (1988). Anarchy and the limits of cooperation: A realist critique of the newest liberal institutionalism. *International Organization, 42*, 485-507.

Il Sole 24 Ore, (2008). Numero Speciale, 41.

Lanzafame/Poliadri (2004). *La stagione della solidarietà sanitaria a Reggio Emilia: Mozambico 1963-1977—Un esempio ante litteram di cooperazione decentrata*. Torino: L'Harmattan Italia, Logiche Sociali.

Lanzafame, M. (2005). La stagione della solidarietà a Reggio Emilia: Mozambico e Africa Australe.

http://www.boorea.it/Sezione.jsp?idSezione=32

Lo Cascio, C. (2010). Intervista per Newsletter Consorzio Italy.

Ministero Degli Affari Esteri (2013). Cooperazione Allo Sviluppo, Linee guida della cooperazione allo sviluppo per gli anni 20011.

http://www.cooperazioneallosviluppo.esteri.it/pdgcs/documentazione/PubblicazioniTrattati/2011-01-01_LineeGuida20112013agg.pdf

Osce/Dac (2012). *Dac Peer Review, Italy various years*. Paris.

http://www.oecd.org/

Pertini, S. (1981). *Bibliografia degli scritti e discorsi di Sandro Pertini (1924-2007)*. voce n. 929: Discorso pronunciato il 14 ottobre 1981 nel palazzo del Quirinale a Roma, in occasione della visita ufficiale in Italia del presidente della Repubblica popolare del Mozambico Samora Machel, in SD II, 279-281. www.fondazionepertini.it

Raimondi/Antonelli (2001). *Manuale di Cooperazione allo sviluppo*. Torino: SEI.

Relazioni annuali sull'attuazione della politica di cooperazione allo sviluppo sul sito.

http://www.cooperazioneallosviluppo.esteri.it/pdgcs/italiano/pubblicazioni/intro.html

Romano, S. (2002). *Guida alla Politica Estera italiana da Badoglio a Berlusconi*. Milano: RCS Libri S.P.A.

Smith, D. (2012) *Africa's resource curse throws shadow over Mozambique's energy bonanza*. "The Guardian", guardian.co.uk

Terzi, G. (2012). Intervento nella sua visita in Mozambico del 4 maggio.

http://www.esteri.it/MAE/IT/Sala_Stampa/ArchivioNotizie/Approfondimenti/2012/05/20120504_Mozambico.htm

(2013). *The End of Poverty: An Interview with Jeffrey Sachs*.

http://www.motherjones.com/politics/2005/05/end-poverty-interview-jeffrey-sachs

World Bank (2008). *Beating the Odds: Sustaining Inclusion in Mozambique's Growing Economy*. Washington.

http://econ.worldbank.org/external/default/main?pagePK=64165259&theSitePK=469372&piPK=64165421&menuPK=64166093&entityID=000334955_20080822070929

17

On the New Boson Higgs's Studies at the CERN-ATLAS Experiment. The Emergency of a Historical Discovery[*]

Raffaele Pisano[1,2]

[1]Sciences, Sociétés, Cultures dans leurs Evolutions, University of Lille 1, Lille, France
[2]Research Center for Theory and History of Science, University of West Bohemia, Plzen, Czech Republic

This paper is a summary of the interview-workshop to Aleandro Nisati (12 December 2012, SEMM-*Service Enseignement et Multimédi*a) co-organized by UFR Physique, University of Lille 1, France (Raffaele Pisano, Remi Franckowiak, Bernard Maitte and Lisa Rougetet), ATLAS Experiment Team (CERN, Genève, Switzerland), in persons of the cited Italian scientist—already *Physics coordinator* at ATLAS—and his colleague, Steven Goldfarb (CERN-University of Michigan, USA). The latter kindly answered to the questions on the ATLAS detector, LHC machine and CERN-ATLAS laboratories proposed by the participants. Distinguished lectures by historians of science at University of Lille 1 (Bernard Maitte, Bernard Pourprix and Robert Locqueneux) specialist on history of physics opened the workshop session.

Keywords: History of Physics; Science and Society; Standard Model Higgs Boson

A Short Introduction on the Discovery

On July, 4th 2012, the ATLAS experiment presented a preview of its updated results on the search for the Higgs Boson. (**Figure 1**). The results were shown at a seminar held jointly at CERN and via video link at ICHEP, the International Conference for High Energy Physics in Melbourne, Australia (Atlas Collaboration, 2012; CMS Collaboration, 2012). At CERN, preliminary results were presented to scientists on site and via webcast to colleagues located in hundreds of institutions around the world. Aleandro Nisati was *ATLAS Physics coordinator*.

The Higgs boson is the only missing elementary particle of the *Standard Model* (SM) of particles and fields. In the SM, the non-zero vacuum expectation value of the Higgs field breaks the electroweak gauge symmetry. It is the simplest process capable of giving mass to the gauge bosons and elementary fermions. Its quantum would be a scalar boson, the only one in this theory. A brief overview of the searches for this particle with the *A Toroidal LHC ApparatuS* (ATLAS) detector at the *Large Hadron Collider* (LHC) is given. In particular, the latest results of the search for this particle at the LHC are summarized and discussed, focusing on the recent observation of a new boson by the experiments ATLAS and *Compact Muon Solenoid* (CMS, the main experiments) at the LHC, with a mass around 126 GeV. Preliminary available data show that this particle is consistent with the boson predicted by the SM. More data are needed to perform precision measurements of the physics properties of this new boson, and verify whether this is the Higgs boson predicted by Standard Model.

Interview to Aleandro Nisati

The latest results concerning the discovery of a new boson (m ~126 GeV) were experimented by *A Toroidal LHC Appa-*

[*]Short review.

Figure 1.
Higgs decay to four electrons recorded by ATLAS in 2012 (Bottom). Higgs decay to four muons recorded by ATLAS in 2012. Images credit: URL (last checked 14 January 2013). http://www.atlas.ch/news/2012/latest-results-from-higgs-search.html. Nisati Workshop Brochure organized at University of Lille 1, France.

ratuS (ATLAS) and *Compact Muon Solenoid* (CMS) at the Large Hadron Collider (LHC) and recently exposed at SISFA 2012 Congress where I interviewed Aleandro Nisati (*I.N.F.N. Sezione di Roma-CERN*, Italy/Switzerland), *ATLAS Physics co-*

ordinator who had a major role in the discovery and key-note at the Congress. This new particle is effetely consistent, within the current available experimental accuracy, with the *Standard Model Higgs boson* (SMHB).

But, what is the importance of the Higgs boson?

Nisati: the Higgs boson is the only missing elementary particle of the *Standard Model* (SM) of particles and fields. Here the non-zero vacuum expectation value of the Higgs field breaks the electroweak gauge symmetry. It is the simplest process capable of giving mass to the gauge bosons and fermions.

What about preliminary available experimental data?

Nisati: the quantum associated to this field is a spin-0 particle, the Higgs boson. An indirect constraint on the Higgs boson mass of $m_H < 185$ GeV at 95% confidence level (CL) has been set using global fits to electroweak precision data. Direct searches (up to 2011) excluded at 95% CL a SMHB with mass $m_H < 114.4$ GeV and $147 < m_H < 179$ respectively. The search for this particle was pursued at the LCH looking in particular to high mass resolution channels: the diphoton and the 4-lepton final states. The data sample used in the analysis was based on about 5 fb^{-1} of proton-proton collisions data taken at $\sqrt{s} = 7$ TeV (2011) and 5.5 fb^{-1} taken at $\sqrt{s} = 8$ TeV data (early 2012). In the diphoton final state, both ATLAS and CMS observed an excess of events around the $\gamma\gamma$ invariant mass of 125 - 126 GeV, on top of a smooth background produced mainly by SM $\gamma\gamma$ process. Jet-jet and γ-jet processes, a potentially dangerous background with jets misidentified as photons, are suppressed thanks the robust photon identification and reconstruction provided by the high-performance electromagnetic calorimeters of these two experiments. An excess of events is observed also in the H→ZZ*→4-lepton channel (where for leptons only electrons and muons are considered). In this case, the dominant background is represented by the SM diboson production ZZ*→4-leptons (irreducible background) and by Z + jets processes, where jets can be mis-reconstructed as electrons or muons. Also in this case, the robust electron and muon identification in both experiments allows a strong reduction of Z + jets events below the irreducible background. Finally, this excess is observed also in the low mass resolution channel H→WW*→lvlv, in a mass interval fully consistent with the 125 - 126 GeV mass, where the excess is observed in $\gamma\gamma$ and 4-leptons. The statistical combination of these results for ATLAS, and independently for CMS, leads to the observation of an excess of events at around 125 GeV mass with at least 5-sigma significance (corresponding to a probability ~4×10^{-7}) per experiment.

Are these results well-matched with historical theoretical theory hypothesed by Higgs last century?

Nisati: at this stage the results are compatible with the hypothesis that the new particle is the *Higgs boson* predicted by the SM. We have to wait to claim that the boson discovered is exactly *Higgs Boson*; particularly, observing this new particle also in final states with fermions, such as H→ττ and H→b-bbar.

What is the main consequence if Higgs boson is confirmed?

Nisati: in case, SM will receive one of the strongest support from experimental results. On the contrary, deviations of this particle from the *Standard Model Higgs boson* will inevitably indicate new physics at the energy scale of the LHC. In both cases, a new extraordinary and exciting era in particle physics just opened up.

Conclusion

Thus, is seems that, more data are needed to perform precision measurements of the physics properties of this new boson, and verify whether this is the Higgs boson predicted by *Standard Model*.

Pisano: *Maybe new reflections on the history of the World and its live components might be near to have a crucial founded hypothesis?*

Acknowledgements

I would like to express my sincere gratitude to Aleandro Nisati for his friendly and precious collaboration. I also thank Bernard Maitte, Remi Franckowiak, Bernard Pourprix, Robert Locqueneux, and Lisa Rougetet for co-authoring in the workshop-interview and further process during workshop organizing terms.

REFERENCES

ATLAS Collaboration (2012). Observation of a new particle in the search for the standard model higgs boson with ATLAS detector at the LHC. *Physics Letter B 716, 1,* 1-29. URL (last checked 14 January 2013).
http://www.sciencedirect.com/science/article/pii/S037026931200857X

CMS Collaboration (2012). Observation of a new boson at a mass of 125 GeV with the CMS experiment at the LHC. *Physics Letter B, 716,* 30-61. URL (last checked 14 January 2013).
http://www.sciencedirect.com/science/article/pii/S037026931200858

Higgs, P. W. (1964). Broken symmetries and the masses of Gauge Bosons. *Physics Review Letter, 13,* 508-509.

Higgs, P. W. (1966). Spontaneous symmetry breakdown without Massless Bosons. *Physics Review Letter, 145,* 1156-1163.

READINGS

Lévy-Leblond, J. M. (1996). *Aux contraires, l'exercice de la pensée et la pratique de la science.* NRF Essais, Paris: Gallimard.

Lévy-Leblond, J. M. (2006). *De la matière: Relativiste, quantique, interactive.* Paris: Seuil, Traces Écrites.

Locqueneux, R. (2009). *Une histoire des idées en physique.* SFHST, Paris: Vuibert.

Kibble, T. W. (1967). Symmetry breaking in non-abelian gauge theories. *Physics Review Letter, 145,* 1554-1561.

Pisano, R., & Casolaro, F. (2012). A historical inquiry on geometry in relativity. Reflections on late relationship geometry-physics (Part Two). *History Research, 2,* 56-64.

Pourprix, B. (2009). *D'où vient la physique quantique?* Paris: Vuibert et Adapt.

Pourprix, B. (2010). La naissance de la physique quantique: Rupture et continuité. *Bulletin de l'union des professeurs de physique et de chimie, 104,* 1037-1050.

Pourprix, B. (2013). La genèse de l'atome de Bohr (forthcoming). *Images de la physique 2012.* Paris: CNRS.

The ALEPH, DELPHI, L3, OPAL, SLD, CDF and D0 Collaborations (2010). Precision electroweak measurements and constraints on the standard model. CERN-PH-EP-2010-095.

Appendix

Notes on Aleandro Nisati

Aleandro Nisati is I.N.F.N. (*The Italian Institute of Nuclear Physics*) physicist researcher and scientific associate at CERN on LHC (*Large Hadron Collider*), Geneva. His research regards with new and strange particles producing a large publishing-and-spreading-job within the ECFA (*The European Committee for Future Accelerators*) particularly on Higgs searches, as well as studies of muon production, in proton-proton collisions at the LHC. He is one of the main founding physicists of one of the two main experiments at LHC, *A Toroidal LHC ApparatuS* (ATLAS) where he has been recently Physics Experimental Coordinator: scientific program and the project on muon detection and spectrometer, trigger system. Nisati also designed the first-level muon trigger algorithm, as well as the one of the second-level and for that he was elected chair of the Trigger/DAQ Institutes Board until 2007, and Higgs group co-convener for next two years. Recently (2012) he is also coordinator of the "ATLAS Input to the European Strategy Preparatory Group". ATLAS (and CMS, the main experiments at LHC) has found in summer 2012 a strong evidence of the production at the LHC of a new boson with mass near 126 GeV. This new particle is consistent, within the current available experimental accuracy, with the *Standard Model Higgs boson.*

18

The Roots of the Theoretical Models of the Nanotechnoscience in the Electric Circuit Theory

Vitaly Gorokhov[1,2]
[1]Institute of Philosophy, Russian Academy of Sciences, Moscow, Russia
[2]Institute of Technology Assessment and System Analysis, Karlsruhe Institute of Technology,
Karlsruhe, Germany

In the contemporary nanotechnoscience makes natural-scientific experimentation constitutive for design, while research results are oriented equally on interpreting and predicting the course of natural processes, and on designing devices. Nanoystems can be seen as nanoelectrical switches in a nanocircuit. In nanocircuit structure, we find traditional electronic components at different levels, realized on the basis of nanotechnology. In nanotechnoscience explanatory models of natural phenomena are proposed, and predictions of the course of certain natural events on the basis of mathematics and experimental data are formulated, on the one hand, as in classical natural science; as in the engineering sciences, on the other hand, not only experimental setups, but also structural plans for new nanosystems previously unknown in nature and technology are devised. In nanotechnoscience different models (equivalent circuits with standard electronic components) of electric circuit theory are used for the analysis and synthesis of nanocircuits, and a special nanocircuit theory is elaborated. So nanotechnology is, at the same time, a field of scientific knowledge and a sphere of engineering activity—in other words, NanoTechnoScience, similar to Systems Engineering as the analysis and design of complex micro- and nanosystems.

Keywords: History of Science; History of Engineering Science; Nanotechnoscience; Electric Circuits Theory; Electronic Nanocircuit; Circuits Models of Nanosystems; Natural Science; Engineering Science; Science and Engineering

Introduction

Contemporary technoscience makes natural scientific experimentation inseparable from design, while research results are equally oriented to interpret and predict the course of natural processes and to design structures.

Engineering theory is oriented not toward interpreting and predicting the course of natural processes but toward designing engineering schemes. Natural scientific knowledge and laws must be considerably specified and modified in engineering theory to be applicable to practical engineering problems. To adapt theoretical knowledge to the level of practical engineering recommendations, technical theory develops special rules that establish a correspondence between the abstract objects of engineering theory and the structural components of real engineering systems and operations that transfer theoretical results into engineering practice. Engineering sciences are specific because their engineering practice replaces experiments, as a rule. It is engineering activity that checks the adequacy of theoretical engineering conclusions and serves as a source of new empirical knowledge.

In the nanotechnoscience is equal important the explanation and prognostication of the course natural processes (like in natural science) and multiplying of structural schemes of nanosystems (like in engineering science). Electron beam lithography system is at the same time experimental investigation system and is used for the nanofabrication as so-called "nanowriter".

It is well-known that, in nanotechnoscience, constructs from various scientific theories—classical and quantum physics, classical and quantum chemistry, structural biology, etc.—are used, whereas, in nanosystems, different physical, chemical and biological processes take place. However one can also construct the circuit on the basis of definite nanosructures, such as, e.g., a super-heterodyne radio receiver on the nanolevel (see: Bhushan 2004: p. 240).

In the nanotechnoscience for analysis and synthesis of the nanocircuits also are used the different models (equivalent circuits with standard electronics components) of the electric circuit theory and is elaborated a special nanocircuit theory. In the structure of the nanocircuits we can find many different traditional electronic components ("molecular-scale electronics") realized on the nanolevel with the help of nanotechnology: first, there are electronic elements, second, electronics blocks, and third, large-scale nanosystems.

The Structure of NanoTechnoScience

In nanotechnoscience, on the one hand, explanatory models of natural phenomena are drawn up and predictions of the course of certain natural events on the basis of mathematics and experimental data are formulated as in classical natural science, and, as in the engineering sciences on the other hand, not only experimental arrangements are constructed, but also structural plans of new nanosystems previously unknown in nature and technology (**Figure 1**).

Three main levels in the theoretical (ontological) schemes of a nano scientific theory can be discerned, namely mathematically oriented functional schemes, "flow" schemes reflecting natural processes going in the investigated or constructed system, and structural schemes representing its structural parameters and engineering analysis, i.e. systems structure.

The *functional scheme* is oriented on the mathematical description and fixes the general idea about the system (for example, nanosystem), irrespective of the method of its realization. The units of this scheme reflect only the functional properties of the elements of the system for the sake of which they are included in it to attain the general objective and reflect certain mathematical relations. The blocks of this scheme reflect only those functional properties of the systems elements, for which they are incorporated and which contribute to achieving the common purpose. The blocks express generalized mathematical operations and their relations are particular mathematical dependences. But they can be expressed as a simple decomposition of interrelated functions aimed at achieving the customer-prescribed common purpose of system under investigation and/or design. Such a functional scheme is used to construct a system algorithm and determine a system configuration.

Flow schemes (for example, flow block diagram) describe natural, for instance, physical processes taking place in the technical system and connecting its elements into a single whole. The units of such schemes reflect various operations performed in the natural process by the elements of the technical system while it is functioning. These are based on natural-scientific concepts first of all physical processes.

In the nanotechnology they present not only physical (electrical, mechanical, hydraulic, etc.) processes, but also chemical and biological ones, that is to say any natural processes in general. The blocks of these schemes reflect various operations performed by the elements of the nanotechnological system during its function. In the extreme general terms, "flow" schemes represent not only natural processes, but also any flow of "substance" (matter, energy or information).

Structural schemes reflect the structural arrangement of elements and linkages in the given system and presuppose its possible realization. They are the theoretical drafts of the systems structure to elaborate a project of the experimental situation together with the experimental equipment. Hertz for example developed structural schemes and a conceptual apparatus corresponding to them—such concepts as the dipole and vibrator. The scrupulous description of test equipment designs (e.g., of mirror material, shape and dimensions, etc.) was combined with the general description of experimental measurement situations, the latter being a prototype of future electric circuits of the radio receiver and radio transmitter. In the nanotechnology can be another realization as in the traditional electronics but the structural scheme is similar. For example, the one of the main elements of electric circuits—capacitor can receive in nanotechnology another construction as conventional Faraday capacitor but has the similar representation as two-terminal network-capacitive resistance.

The structural scheme gives nodal points of "flows" (operating processes) which can be equipment items, parts of or even entire complicated systems. The elements of the latter are regarded in them as having not only functional properties, but also properties of the second order, i.e. those undesirable properties which are added by a definitely realized element, for instance, non-linear distortions of the amplified signal in the

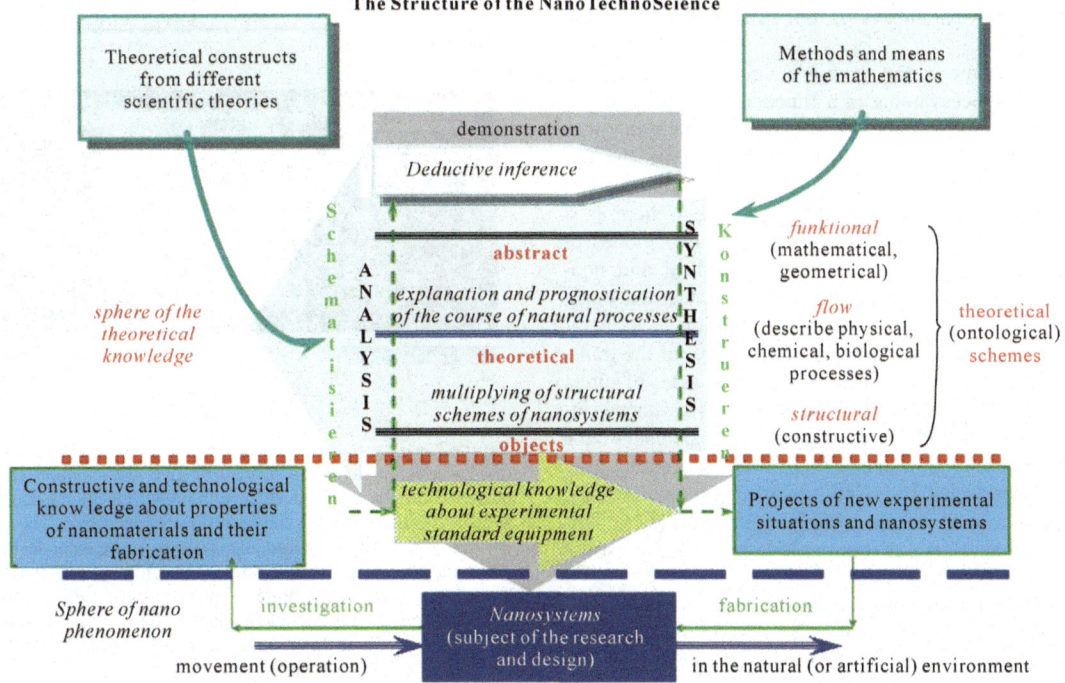

Figure 1.
The structure of NanoTecnoScience.

amplifier. These schemes represent constructive-technical and technological parameters, i.e. they reflect specific problems cropping up in engineering practice. In modern man-machine and nanobio hybrid systems, such a realization can be of diverse types and even be a non-engineering and non-physical one. Therefore, the terms "technical parameters", "construction" are not apt here. The case in point is the configuration of systems, their general structure.

From the radio electronics point of view it makes no difference what kind of the realization has the circuit (also as nanostructure). His blocs and elements can be represented in all cases as the correspondent equivalent circuits with standard electronics components.

Let us consider the specific features of the above-mentioned theoretical schemes of engineering science, referring to the electric circuit theory.

Even structural schemes of electric engineering are idealizations of real electric circuits. They omit many of particular characteristics of an electrical device, such as its overall dimensions, weight, assembly techniques, etc. (they are specified during design work and manufacture, i.e. during engineering itself). Such schemes give general structural and technical, and manufacturing parameters of standardized structural elements (resistors, inductance coils, batteries, etc.), which will be used in further analysis, namely, their types and dimensions taken from catalogues, operating voltage, the best arrangements and connection types, screening. In the electric circuit theory, such schemes are initial ones. They are taken in the ready-to-use form from other, more special electric engineering disciplines are subjected to theoretical analysis.

One should differentiate between the structural theoretical scheme and various types of real engineering schemes (e.g., wiring diagrams). Principal elements of the structural scheme are a power source, load (electric power receiver) and idealized structural elements, connecting them and represented by special symbols. Numerous parameters of real structural elements are omitted.

The "flow" scheme of the electric circuit theory reflects an electromagnetic process going in a functioning electric device and the circuit itself is a set of elements and their relations (connections), forming a current path. The latter has the following parameters: voltage, strength, power, amplitude, phase and frequency (for sinusoidal current). In addition, there exist various kinds of this process (and their respective modes of circuit function): direct and alternating, periodical and non-periodic, steady-state and transient currents, etc. Current transformation is either the quantitative transformation of its parameters (for example, current strength and voltage) or the transformation of the pattern of its variation in time (say, of direct current into alternating current or vice versa). Resistance, inductance, capacitance, which are further idealizations of the corresponding structural elements of the electric circuit (the resistor, inductor, capacitor), and ideal current and voltage sources can be considered as "flow" scheme elements. This "semiotic constructor" makes it possible to represent any structural element of the structural scheme.

To each element of the "flow" scheme there corresponds a specific physical process whose detailed description is beyond the scope of the electric circuit theory which takes it into account, however. (For example, resistance represents irrecoverable losses of electric energy in the circuit, resulting from its transformation into other forms of energy-thermal, chemical,

etc.) In the electric circuit theory, this process is expressed by a definite relationship of physical parameters of an element, say, voltage versus current strength or electric charge versus voltage, and the number of appropriate units of measurement (ohm, farad, hertz, etc.) Electric circuit elements form branches which are joined by means of ideal electric connections (i.e. connections free of resistance, inductance, capacitance) to form nodes and loops.

Similar in nanotechnology nanoinsulators and nanoconnectors for optical nanocircuits may be considered to be complex circuit elements, C_1, C_2 and L (see **Figure 2**): "it is possible to characterize complex arrangements of (plasmonic and non-plasmonic) optical nanocircuit elements using the circuit theory" (Silveirinha, Alù, Li, & Engheta, 2007: p. 64).

Distributed-parameter circuits ("A distributed parameter is a

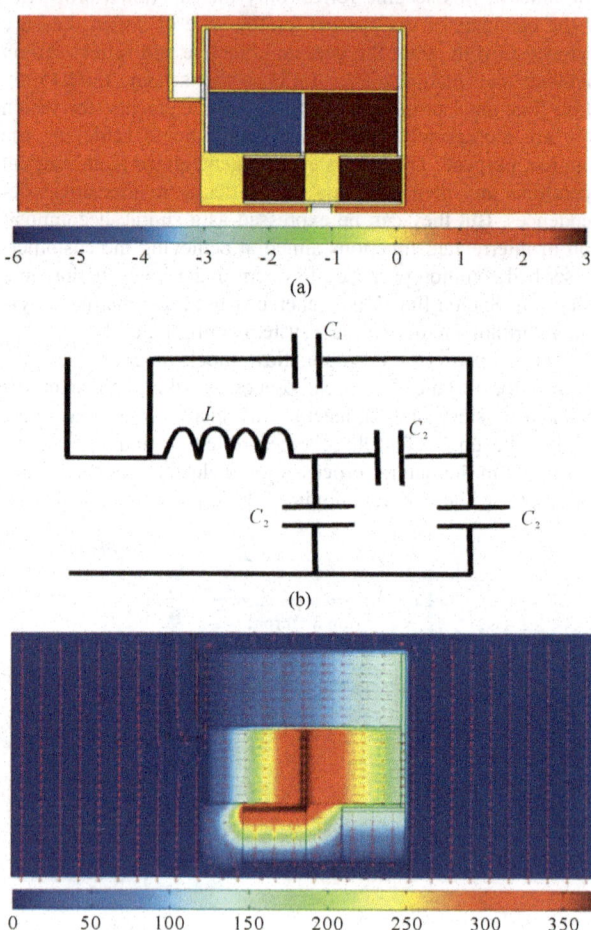

Figure 2.
(a) An optical nanocircuit formed by five nanomodules (four nanocapacitors and one nanoinductor), mimicking the function of the circuit shown in (b). Here a 2D configuration is considered. The value of the permittivity for each nanomodule is shown in the color scale in (a). The white region represents a material with a high permittivity (EVL). (c) Two-dimensional (2D) finite element method (FEM) "quasi-static" simulation of optical nanocircuit in (a). Here the color scheme shows the optical potential distributions, and the arrows shows the direction (not the amplitude) of displacement current in each nanomodule. We note how high the value of optical potential reaches in some of the nodes of this nanocircuit, due to the LC resonance (Silveirinha, Alù, Li, & Engheta, 2007: p. 63).

parameter which is spread throughout a structure and is not confined to a lumped element such as a coil of wire" (Wilson, 2007), e.g., homogeneous lines, are theoretically presented for engineering analysis as distributed-parameter circuits equivalent to them under given operating conditions (e.g., in a particular frequency band). The distributed-parameter circuit can be analyzed within the framework of the electric circuit theory and with the use of the electromagnetic field theory. Moreover, the flow scheme of substitution, derived within the framework of the electric circuit theory can be represented by different functional schemes (e.g., the potential diagram or two-ports). Similar in the nanotechnoscience can be described the geometry of two-nanotube transmission line and his RF circuit model (Burke, 2004: p. 3).

Functional schemes of the electric circuit theory are diagrams, graphical forms of the mathematical description of the electric circuit state, To each functional element of this diagram there corresponds a particular mathematical relationship, say, current strength versus voltage in some circuit section, or a particular mathematical operation (say, differentiation or integration). The arrangement and characteristics of functional elements correspond to the flow circuit scheme. Thus, in the circuit analysis, say, with the aid of the graph theory, circuit flow scheme elements (inductances, capacitances, resistances, etc.) are substituted, in accordance with definite rules, by a special ideal functional element—unistor, letting current to flow only in one direction. The resultant homogeneous theoretical scheme can be handled with the use of topological methods of circuit analysis (Starzyk & Sliwa, 1984). Thus, the functional schematic circuit diagram corresponds to a particular equation set and, at the same time, it is equivalent to some flow scheme.

Nanosystem as Electronic Nanocircuit-Models from the History of Science

The nanomachines can be regarded as nanoelectrical switches in the nanocircuit. In nanotechnology define a nanomachne also as the nanocircuit. "Nanotechnological constructions are to reproduce traditional electronic components (switches, diodes, transistors, etc.) on a nanoscale. One main goal of this effort is to open up new dimensions of data processing, namely through the storage of large amounts of data in the smallest possible space... Because of the intermediary position of the nanoscale, it is also called 'mesoworld'" (Schiemann, 2005).

In the nanocircuit structure we can find traditional electronic components ("molecular-scale electronic components") of the different levels realized on the base of the nanotechnology:

1) First of all, such electronic elements as an electronic switch (e.g. transistor), wires, inductors and *capacitor* or *battery cell*;

2) Second, electronic units (blocs) as antenna ("radiates transmitted power in narrow beam for maximum 'gain' and receives backscattered signal from targets") or modulator ("to 'trigger' the transmitter operation at precise and regularly recurring instants of time") (Barrett, 2000-2002: p. 23);

3) Third, complex nanosystems as a hole (e.g. nanocomputer).

Nanoinductors, Nano-Capacitors, and Nano-Resistors

In the **Figure 3** you can see three basic circuit elements at optical frequencies—nanoinductors, nano-capacitors, and nano-resistors. "There is not that much difference between a battery

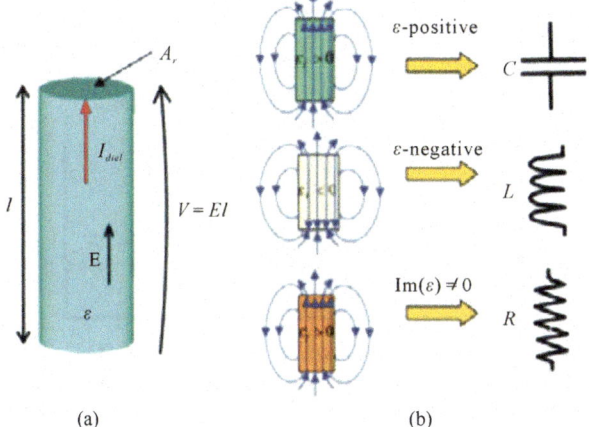

(a)   (b)

Figure 3.
(a) Geometry of a generic subwavelength nanocircuit element in the form of a nanowire with length l and cross-section T A; (b) Equivalent circuit model for the nanowire depending on the electrical properties of the material (Silveirinha, 2007).

and a *capacitor*... Conventional Faraday capacitors store electric charge between parallel charged plates that are separated by an insulating dielectric material. Instead of flat parallel plates, capacitors that come in tubes use two metallic foils separated by an electrolyte-impregnated paper in a "sandwich" that is rolled up into the tube. For these devices, nanotube thin films can increase the surface area of the conducting foil due to the nanotubes' very small size, orderly alignment and high conductivity. "Nanotubes provide a huge surface area on which to store and release energy-that is what makes the difference..." (Johnson, 2005).

Atomic-Scale Transistor and "Electronic Tube"

In nanoscience, such wave processes are investigated at the level of the single electron, atom, or molecule, as well as of the cluster of atoms and molecules. And at the basis of this research, for example, of the the wave function, a new nanosystem can be constructed, which is in principle similar to radio equipment or to those of its elements, such as the atomic-scale transistor (see **Figure 4**), which "can be reversibly switched between a quantized conducting on-state and an insulating off-state by applying a control potential relative to a third, independent gate electrode" (Xie, 2007), or "electronic tube" as two-dimensional nanostructure. Electron transport in nanostructures on helium films (Leider & Klier, 2008: p. 182). This is in principal similar with the three-electrode radio tube in the traditional electronic device. In engineering, schematic diagrams are more important than in science, since the peculiarity of engineering thought is operating with schemata and models. And these models adopt today from the history of science.

The atomic-scale transistor "can be reversibly switched between a quantized conducting on-state and an insulating off-state by applying a control potential relative to a third, independent gate electrode. For this purpose, an atomic-scale point contact is formed by electrochemical deposition of silver within a nanoscale gap between two gold electrodes, which subsequently can be dissolved and re-deposited, thus allowing open and close the gap". Here is the effect of this electrochemical cycling process and is discussed "the mechanisms of formation

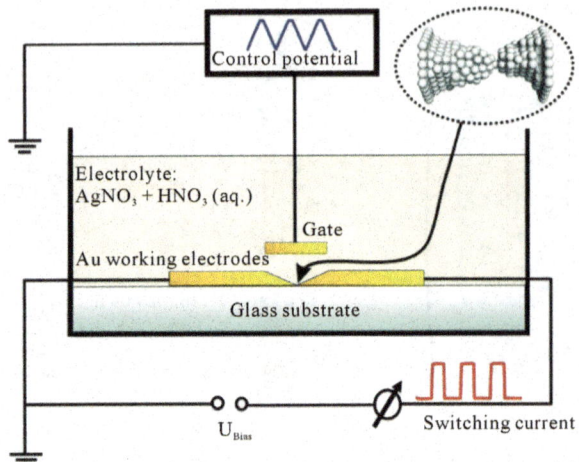

Figure 4.
Illustration of the experimental setup. "Silver quantum point contacts are electrochemically grown within a nanoscale gap between two electrodes deposited on a substrate. After repeated electrochemical deposition/dissolution processes, a bistable contact configuration is formed, and the reproducible switching of the contact between the two Au working electrodes is achieved by means of an independent gate electrode" (Xie, 2007: p. 115).

and operation of the atomic-scale quantum transistor" (Xie, 2007: p. 115).

In recent study of the nanotechnoscience is constructed "a molecular logic gate in a microfluidic system based on fluorescent chemosensors by detecting the changes in intensity as a response to various inputs (pH, metal ions)" (Berger, 2007) (see **Figure 5**). In principle mode of functioning of this electronic switch not differ from the coherer—an electrical component formerly used to detect radio waves, consisting of a tube containing loosely packed metal particles (filing in coherer of Branly (see **Figure 6**) by Popov's receiver or nickel powder (by Marconi). The waves caused the particles to cohere, thereby changing the current through the circuit (see Gorokhov, 2006: pp. 21-22).

Miniaturized Antenna on the Micro- and Nanometer Scale

We can speak about for instance nanoantenna sensors in the visible and infrared regime: "In order to detect electromagnetic radiation, one needs two basic elements: 1) a physical structure that efficiently couples to the radiation—the antenna; and 2) a rectifying element that converts the high-frequency AC signal to a low-frequency signal that can be detected by electronic means. Antenna structures and rectifying diodes have long been studied and applied for radio waves, television signals, cell phones, and so on. Recent work has shown that miniaturized antennas on the micro- and nanometer scale can be tuned to infrared and visible radiation, and that these nanoantenna structures can be integrated with metal-oxide-metal (MOM) rectifying diodes. The sensor consists of a MOM diode integrated together with a dipole antenna" (Bernstein, 2006: pp. 133-138).

Analogy between an early Hertzian antenna to operate at microwave frequencies and the nanodimer antenna see in **Figure 7**. "The pioneering work of Hertz at the end of the nineteenth century is at the foundation of the modern antenna science and engineering, and therefore of an important part of current wire-

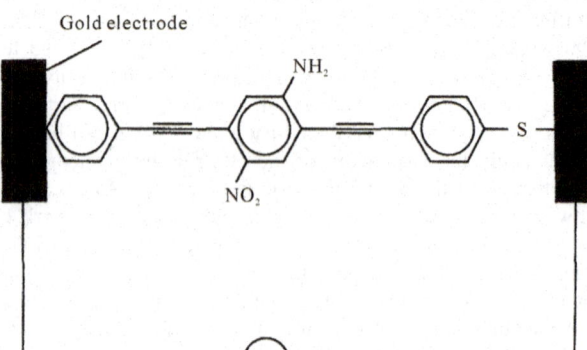

Figure 5.
"Illustration of *an electronic switch* made of a conducting molecule bonded at each end to gold electrodes. Initially it is nonconducting; however, when the voltage is sufficient to add an electron from the gold electrode to the molecule, it becomes conducting. A further increase makes it nonconducting again with addition of a second electron" (Pool & Owens, 2003: p. 351).

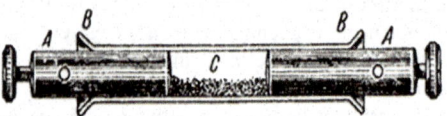

Figure 6.
Coherer of branly (Gorokhov, 2006: p. 48).

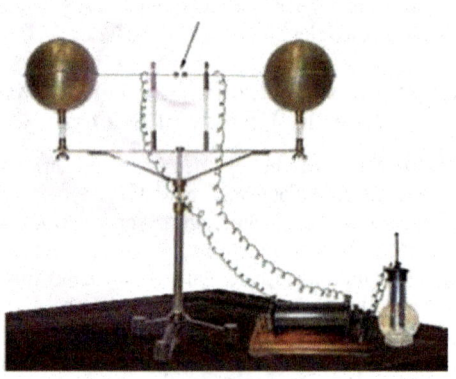

(a)

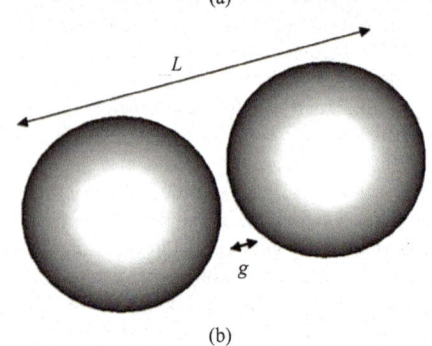

(b)

Figure 7.
Analogy between two dimer antennas: (a) An early Hertzian antenna to operate at microwave frequencies; (b) The plasmonic nanodimer antenna in the form of two closely spaced spherical nanoparticles (Alù, 2008: 195111-1).

less technology. His intuition of driving oscillating charges distributed over two closely spaced spherical capacitors... has proven successful for generating the first class of working radiators, and it has paved the way to myriads of wireless applications in the current technology... Currently, the theory and practice of RF antenna design is well established, and the old geometry of Hertz's first antennas... would definitely look outdated, compared with the myriad of different antenna designs currently available for numerous different purposes and applications... However, for different reasons *the optical nanoantenna science is still in its early stage*, and the recent experiments on optical nanoantennas may be well compared with the first attempts performed by Hertz... In this context, we have recently proposed a general theory that may bring and utilize the concepts of input impedance, radiation resistance, antenna loading, and matching of optical nanoantennas in order to translate the well-known and established concepts of RF antenna design into the visible regime" (Alù, 2008: 195111-1). This is right for nanocircuits at all.

Micrometer-Scale Silicon Electro-Optic Modulator

In radio electronics and radiolocation, modulation is the process of varying one or more properties of a high frequency periodic waveform to receive a modulating signal with help of modulator. "Because of the high rate of switching (many hundreds of pulses per second) and the very short time intervals being used (a few microseconds at the most for the pulse duration) the transmitter operation cannot be controlled by normal switches or relays. The circuit which does this switching, and also supplies the input power required by the oscillator, is the modulator. It is an electronic circuit which is 'triggered' by the output from the master timing unit and which produces a d.c. pulse whose duration is determined by the circuitry of the modulator. This d.c. pulse of controlled pulse duration, recurring at the precise instants of time determined by the master timing unit, is used to switch the oscillator on and off (Barrett, 2000-2002: p. 16). The same nanoblock as modulator we can see in the nanotechnology. "Much of our electronics could soon be replaced by photonics, in which beams of light flitting through microscopic channels on a silicon chip replace electrons in wires. Photonic chips would carry more data, use less power and work smoothly with fiber-optic communications systems. The trick is to get electronics and photonics to talk to each other... Now Cornell University researchers have taken a major step forward in bridging this communication gap by developing a silicon device that allows an electrical signal to modulate a beam of light on a micrometer scale... Their modulator uses a ring resonator—a circular waveguide coupled to a straight waveguide carrying the beam of light to be modulated. Light traveling along the straight waveguide loops many times around the circle before proceeding... The ring is surrounded by an outer ring of negatively doped silicon, and the region inside the ring is positively doped, making the waveguide itself the intrinsic region of a positive-intrinsic-negative (PIN) diode. When a voltage is applied across the junction, electrons and holes are injected into the waveguide, changing its refractive index and its resonant frequency so that it no longer passes light at the same wavelength. As a result, turning the voltage on switches the light beam off... The PIN structure has been used previously to modulate light in silicon using straight waveguides. But because the change in refractive index that can be caused in

silicon is quite small, a very long straight waveguide is needed. Since light travels many times around the ring resonator, the small change has a large effect, making it possible to build a very small device. Tests using a pulse-modulated electrical signal produced an output with a very similar waveform to the input at up to 1.5 gigabits per second" (Steele, 2005).

Nanotechnology-Complex Electronic Circuitry with Multiple Junctions and Interconnects

An important area for development within molecular manufacturing is *systems design* of the extremely complex molecular systems. "Although the design issues are likely to be largely separable at a subsystems level, the amount of computation required for design and validation is likely to be quite substantial. Performing checks on engineering constraints, such as defect tolerance, physical integrity, and chemical stability, will be required as well" (Arnall, 2003: p. 37). "Because the switches are so tiny, they operate in the realm of quantum physics, which opens the possibility of using the switch to make a multi-bit memory device... The researchers also used the switches to form the basic binary logic gates required to make computer processor chips. They made an AND gate using two switches formed from a single silver sulfide wire and two platinum wires combined with a resistor that restricts electric currents to specific voltages. An AND gate produces a 1 only if both inputs are 1. They made an OR gate using two switches formed from two silver sulfide wires and a single platinum wire combined with a resistor. An OR gate produces a 0 only if both inputs are 0. They made a NOT gate using one switch combined with two resistors and a capacitor, which briefly stores electric charge. A NOT gate turns an input of 1 into 0 and vice versa" (Smalley, 2005).

Analysis and Synthesis of the Nanocircuits from the Point of View of the Electrical Circuits—Historical Transfer of the Methodology for the Research of the New Types of the Technical Systems

Following the paradigm of the electric circuit theory nanocircuits may be considered in different frequency regimes as complex circuits consists of the three basic elements of any linear circuit, R, L, and C. For example, pass-band optical nanofilter can be described as parallel RLC resonance (see **Figure 8**) and stop-band optical nanofilter als series LC resonance. fabricating nanofilters in optical lumped nanocircuit devices... The importance of transplanting the classical circuit concepts into optical frequencies is based on the possibility of squeezing circuit functionalities (e.g., filtering, waveguiding, multiplexing...) in subwave length regions of space, and on correspondingly increasing the operating frequency with several orders of magnitude. Moreover, nowadays the interest in combining optical guiding devices, as optical interconnects, with micro- and nanoelectronic circuits is high..., since it is "Following the nanocircuit theory, we show how it is possible to design such complex frequency responses by simple rules, similar to RF circuit design, and we compare the frequency response of these optical nanofilters with classic filters in RF circuits. These results may provide a theoretical foundation for not still possible to perform all the classic circuit operations in the optical domain. Introducing new paradigms and feasible methods to bring more circuit functionalities into the optical domain would rep-

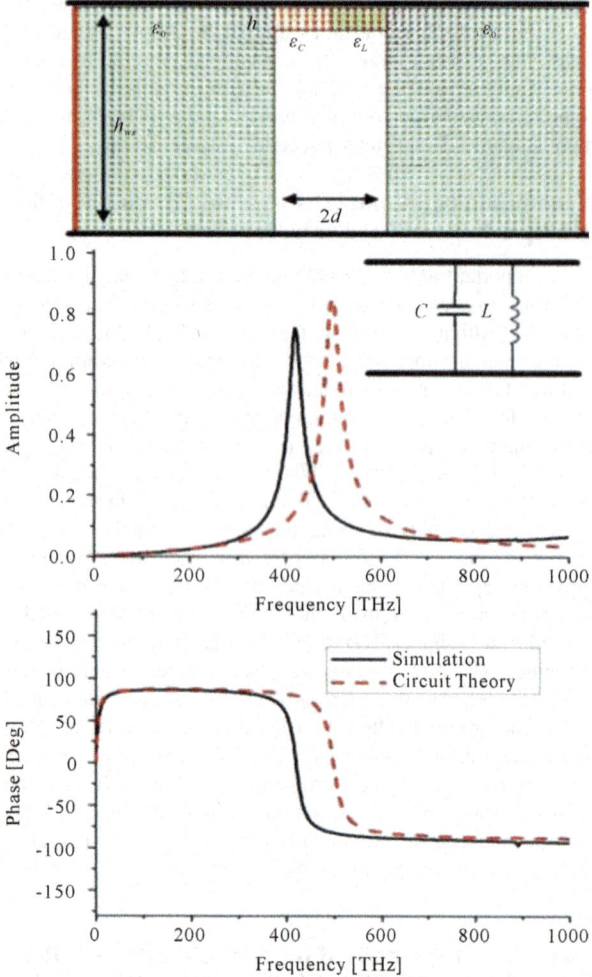

Figure 8.
Transfer function (amplitude and phase) and electric field distribution at the resonance for an optical pass-band nanofilter formed by two nanorods juxtaposed in parallel in a waveguide, one made of silicon and the other made of silver (Alù, Youngy, & Engheta, 2008: 144107-4).

resent an important advance in nanoelectronics technology... we have introduced and discussed the fundamental concepts for developing a novel paradigm for optical nanocircuits, with the aim to extend classic circuit concepts, commonly available at RF and lower frequencies, to higher frequencies and in particular to the optical domain. Specifically, we have discussed... how a proper combination of plasmonic and non-plasmonic nanoparticles may constitute a complex nanocircuit at infrared and optical frequencies, for which the conventional lumped circuit elements are not available in a conventional way. After introducing the nanocircuit concepts for isolated nanocircuit elements..., and after having applied them to model infinite stacks of nanoelements to design nanotransmission lines and nanomaterials..., we have been interested in analyzing in details how the connections and interactions among the individual nanoelements may be modeled and designed in a complex optical *nanocircuit board* with functionalities corresponding to those of a classic microwave circuit" (Alù, Youngy, & Engheta, 2008: 144107-1).

In principle, the both procedures analysis and synthesis are similar since the synthesis of a new technical system involves

the analysis of the existing similar devices.

The engineering theory function is by "shuttle" iteration. First, an engineering problem consisting in construction of some technical system is formulated. Then it is represented as an ideal structural scheme which is then transformed into a natural process scheme showing technical system function. To analyze and mathematically model this process, a functional scheme representing particular mathematical relationships is constructed. The engineering problem is thereby reformulated into a scientific problem, and then into deductively solved mathematical problems. This upward way is termed the *analysis of schemes*.

The reverse way—the *synthesis of schemes*—makes it possible to use the available structural elements, more specifically the corresponding abstract objects, to synthesize a new technical systems (more specifically, its ideal model, theoretical scheme) in accordance with definite rules of deductive transformation, calculate basic parameters of the object and simulate its function. The solution obtained at the ideal model level is gradually transformed to the engineering level where such engineering parameters as overall dimensions and weight of parts, types of connections, connection and part screenings from side electromagnetic effects, the best structural arrangements, etc., considered to be secondary parameters from the ideal model viewpoint, are taken into account and additional theory-correcting computations are performed. Thus, the lower level of engineering-theory abstract objects (structural schemes) directly involves empirical (structural & technical and manufacturing) knowledge, and is intended for utilization in engineering. It is this last fact that largely determines the specific feature of design-oriented engineering theory: to its abstract objects there must correspond a class of hypothetical technical systems which have not been created yet. Therefore, both analysis and synthesis of theoretical schemes of technical systems are important in engineering theory (see **Figure 1**).

In the analysis of an electric circuit in the electric circuit theory, the initial scheme is a structural diagram of an electric device. In conformity with the problem being solved, it is substituted by an equivalent flow scheme valid for the functional mode of the device, the substitution being done in accordance with special rules. Further transformations of the latter scheme are aimed at obtaining simpler schemes which will be more suitable for computations. With this aim in view, special theorems are proved, definite scheme transformation rules formulated and standard design methods described. The synthesis of schemes consists in finding electric circuit elements which can ensure the required functional mode meeting the conditions specified in the form of a certain mathematical relationship. To simplify synthesis, use is made of standard schemes, tables of standard circuits and corresponding mathematical relationships. In engineering practice, pure synthesis is extremely rare; certain parameters of a technical system and its elements are generally specified as early as in the problem statement and synthesis is often reduced to mere updating of an earlier device. Moreover, engineering practice always uses traditional empirical structural schemes, usually ready-to-use ones. Therefore, synthesis is reduced to analysis and what is to be determined is a few parameters of the newly designed circuit. At this stage the engineer often resorts to iteration methods, based on successive approximation; he approaches to the solution step by step, returning to the initial problem more than once. In mature engineering practice associated with mass and series production, technical systems are constructed of standard elements. There-fore, in theory, synthesis also involves the combination of standard idealized elements in accordance with standard rules of theoretical scheme transformation. Analysis is also reduced to the same procedure.

It is possible to extend the classic circuit concepts, commonly available at microwave and lower frequencies, to higher frequencies and in particular to the optical domain (**Figure 9**). "We have developed accurate circuit models at optical wavelengths to characterize the equivalent impedance of the envisioned nanocapacitors and nanoinductors. It has also been shown that the induced displacement current may leak out of the subwavelength nanocircuit elements, causing strong coupling between the nanoelements and the neighboring region. To circumvent this problem, we have introduced the concept of optical nanoinsulators for the displacement current... We have confirmed, both analytically and numerically, that *nanocircuit elements... may be accurately characterized using standard circuit theory concepts* at optical frequencies, and in particular they may indeed be characterized by an equivalent impedance for nanocircuit elements. We have further explained how to apply the proposed circuit concepts in a scenario with realistic optical voltage sources. We have also studied how to ensure a good connection between the envisioned lumped nanoelements... This has led us to consider unit nanomodules for lumped nanocircuit elements, which may be regarded as *building blocks* for more complex nanocircuits at optical wavelengths" (Silveirinha, Alù, Li, & Engheta, 2007: p. 64).

Analytical quasi-static *circuit models* ("modeled theoretically") for the coupling among small nanoparticles excited by an optical electric field in the framework of the optical lumped nanocircuit theory in **Figure 10** are of importance in the *understanding* of complex optical nanocircuits at infrared and optical frequencies.

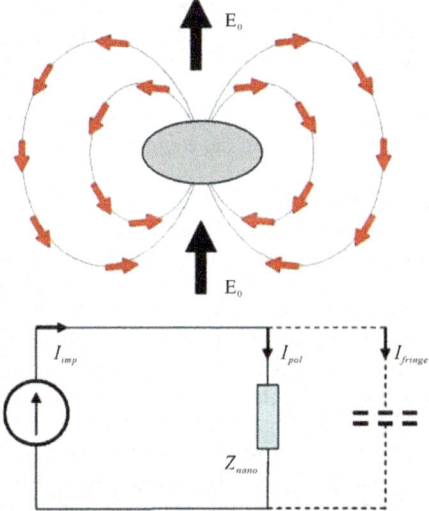

Figure 9.
(Color online) A nanoparticle illuminated by a uniform optical electric field E_0 (black arrows) may be viewed in terms of the circuit analogy presented... as a lumped impedance *nano Z* excited by the impressed current generator *imp I* and loaded with the fringe capacitance associated with its fringe dipolar fields (red arrows) (Alù, Salandrino, & Engheta, 2007).

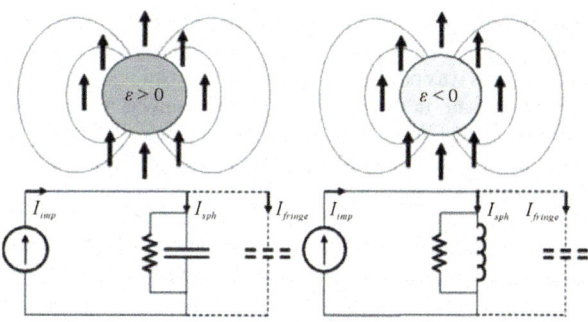

Figure 10.
A basic nanocircuit in the optical regime, using the interaction of an optical wave with an individual nanosphere. (left column) A non-plasmonic sphere with $\varepsilon > 0$, which provides a nano-capacitor and a nano-resistor; (right column) A plasmonic sphere with $\varepsilon < 0$, which gives a nano-inductor and a nanoresistor. Solid arrows show the incident electric field, and the thinner field lines represent the fringe dipolar field from the nanosphere (Engheta, Salandrino, & Aiu, 2004: p. 12).

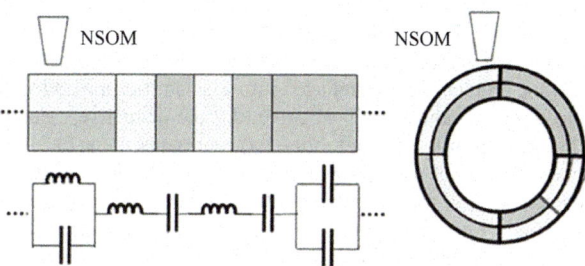

Figure 11.
Nanocircuit synthesis. (Top left) Conceptual nanocircuit formed by rectangular blocks of plasmonic and non-plasmonic segments; (bottom left) Its *equivalent circuit*; (right) A closed "nano-loop" (Engheta, Salandrino, & Aiu, 2004: p. 13).

Synthesizing nanocircuit elements in the optical domain using plasmonic and non-plasmonic nanoparticles from three basic circuit elements, i.e., nanoinductors, nano-capacitors, and nano-resistors see for example in **Figure 11**.

"All these concepts are important steps towards the possibility of synthesizing a complex optical *nanocircuit board* with the functionalities analogous to a classic microwave circuit (e.g., filtering, waveguiding, multiplexing...)". Such approach "would allow one to *quantitatively* design and *synthesize* desired nanocircuits (such as nanofilters, nanotransmission line, parallel and series combination of nanoelements, etc.) at optical frequencies using properly designed collections of nanoparticles acting as "lumped" nanocircuit elements. This concept may open doors to design of more complex nanocircuits and nanosystems in the optical domains" (Alù, Youngy, & Engheta, 2008).

This methodology is typical for the engineering sciences at all and was developed already in the theory of mechanisms in the end of the 19th century. For example Fr. Reuleaux defines in his "Kinematics of Machinery. Outlines of a Theory of Machines" (Reuleaux, 1875) kinematic analysis and synthesis as follows: Kinematic analysis consisted in decomposing the existing machines into their component mechanisms, chains, links and pairs of elements, i.e., in determining the kinematic composition of the machine involved. The final result of that analysis was the choice of kinematic pairs, links, chains and mechanisms to be used to assemble a machine for carrying out the required motions. Reuleaux differentiated between direct and indirect synthesis. The former concerned the compositions of mechanisms which could effect particular changes of the body worked. This was possible when the mechanism was reduced to a kinematic pair. In that situation, the solution was the choice of a proper design for the elements of that pair. According to Reuleaux, the main method of theoretical synthesis of new mechanisms was indirect synthesis, i.e., the preliminary solution of all problems of a particular type, among which the method sought could be found. Such synthesis was possible because the number of realizable mechanisms was limited. First, all possible simple chains were investigated, which could be used to obtain a number of mechanisms by changing the ratio of various links to that chain, transforming some links of that chain into a fixed member, replacing some mechanism pair by another one, etc.

The operation of nanotheory is realized also as in the engineering theory by the iteration method. At first a special engineering problem is formulated. Then it is represented in the form of the structural scheme of the nanosystem which is transformed into the idea about the natural process reflecting its performance. To calculate and mathematically model this process a functional scheme is constructed. Consequently, the engineering problem is reformulated into a scientific one and then into a mathematical problem solved by the deductive method. This path from the bottom to the top represents the analysis of schemes (the *bottom up* approach). For instance, this can be the investigation of "the possibility of connecting nanoparticles in series and in parallel configurations, acting as nanocircuit elements" (Salandrino, 2007). The way in the opposite direction— the synthesis of schemes (the *top down* approach)—makes it possible to synthesize the ideal model of a new nanosystem from idealized structural elements according to the appropriate rules of deductive transformation, to calculate basic parameters of the nanosystem and simulate its function. Nanocircuit synthesis can be, for example, a synthesizing nanocircuit elements in the optical domain using plasmonic and non-plasmonic nanoparticles (Engheta, Salandrino, & Aiu, 2004).

Conclusion

Thus, the engineering theory function consists in solving particular engineering problems with the aid of theory-evolved procedures, type analyses which are suitable in various, more special (scientific and engineering) studies and engineering practice. The creation of new procedures of this kind, the elaboration of rules and proofs of theorems concerning the adequacy of equivalent transformations and allowable approximations, the construction of new standard theoretical schemes pertains to the engineering theory advance on the frontiers of the theoretical research in engineering sciences, and its findings, are stated in primary publications (first of all, in articles) whereas textbooks and monographs provide examples of the engineering theory function, theoretically classify and systematize proven methods of engineering problem solution, demonstrate their compatibility with the general system of theoretical knowledge of the engineering discipline involved. In the natural scientific theory primary importance are flow schemes, but not structural schemes. Both the mathematical apparatus and experiments are for natural scientist just a means of prediction and explanation of the natural processes. For example, Hertz in principle worked as an engineer, when designing new experimental equipment. But he did not mean to find some technical

application for his experimental devices. One of the major problems of the well-developed engineering theory function in "copying" of type structural schemes for various engineering requirements and conditions. Then the solution of any engineering problems, the construction of any new systems will be theoretical supported. This is the essence of the constructive function of engineering theory (theory in engineering science), its lead of engineering praxis. His solution result is cast into practical-methodical recommendations (for designer, inventor, production engineer, etc.). To its abstract objects there must correspond a class of hypothetical technical systems which have not been crated yet. Therefore, in the engineering theory is important not only analysis, but first of all synthesis of theoretical schemes of technical systems. So nanotechnology is at the same time a field of scientific knowledge and a sphere of engineering activity, in other words—NanoTechnoScience— similar with Systems Engineering as the analysis and design of complex man/machine systems but now as large-scale micro- and nanosystems. That is why is very important to investigate the historical sources of the nanotechnological methods in the history of science and technology.

The engineering theory function is aimed at approximation of the theoretical image of an technical system, its equivalent transformation into some new, simpler scheme which will be more suitable for computations, at the reduction of complex cases to simpler and standard ones for which a ready-to-use solution exists, Therefore, the major attention of the engineering theorist is directed at evolving standard solutions of engineering problems, standard design-simplifying methods. It also largely determines the nature of engineering theory supporting the validity of such equivalent transformations and approximations. No matter whether the analysis, synthesis of schemes or mere engineering computations are done, the following general "algorithm" of engineering theory function can be formulated (see **Figure 12**).

1) In the starting point of the process of the theoretical solution of a new engineering problem, the initial conditions of this problem, engineering requirements and limitations and possible analogies with previously solved problems are formulated in terms of structural & technical and manufacturing knowledge. This procedure can be termed the engineering problem conceptualization.

2) The empirical description shall be theoretically formulated in concepts and notions which are standard for the engineering theory involved. This procedure can be termed the identification of the engineering problem with a scientific problem, i.e. the setting-up of a correspondence between the technical system under design and investigation and a particular theoretical scheme of the engineering theory involved. The result is a structural scheme constructed of idealized elements taken from a standard elements catalogue.

3) The so constructed structural scheme is transformed into a simpler type scheme by the first-order approximation. The transformation is accompanied by singling out technical system parameters which are the most important in the problem involved. Equivalent transformations (the formation of substitution schemes) are used to form flow schemes for various modes of technical system function, specified in the problem statement. If a complex flow scheme cannot be approximated, in one or several steps, to the simplest type diagram for which there exists a standard theory—evolved solution (if even these manipulations are not required, the solution is found directly from table

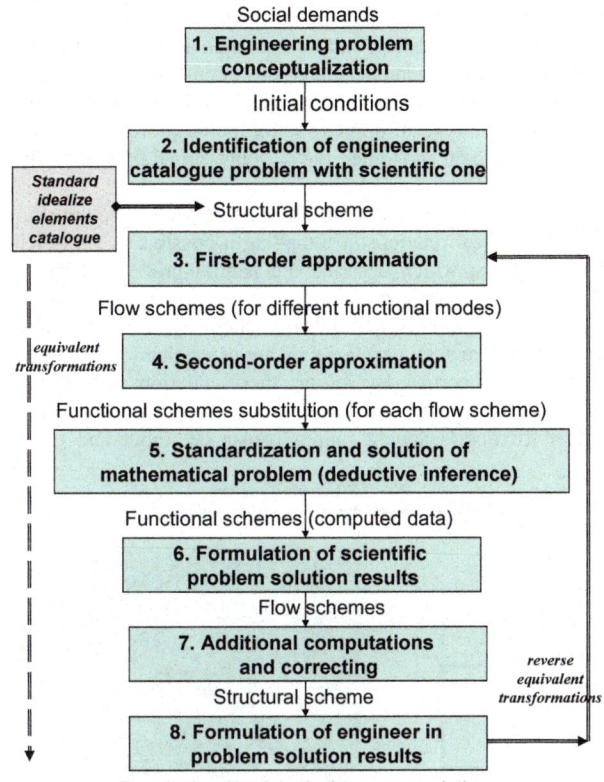

Social demands

Figure 12.
General algorithm of engineering theory function.

formulas), it is substituted by an equivalent functional scheme in accordance with definite rules of correspondence.

4) A functional scheme constructed with the aid of the second—order approximation is used to formulate an equation set to be solved by special mathematical methods (e.g., by matrix ones). These equations are obtained on the basis of physical (Ohm's, Kirchhoff's and other) laws setting up, for example, a relationship between circuit current parameters and circuit element parameters. Their concrete numerical values known from the problem statement make it possible to determine unknown current and circuit element parameters through solving the equations.

5) The functional scheme is used to solve the mathematical problem using a standard computational procedure and standard problem solution methods based on previously proved theorems. To this end, the functional scheme is reduced to a standard one in accordance with definite rules of substitution. Thus, in the electric circuit theory, mixed connections are transformed into simpler, series and parallel ones, multiloop circuits are turned into single—loop ones, etc. In the electric circuit theory, such simplifying transformations are based on specially proved equivalence of some type schemes (e.g., of a "delta" and "star" and vice versa) and relevant theorems (say, the equivalent current and voltage source theorem) which give more computationally suitable schemes. This makes it possible to substitute certain circuit sections by other, equivalent and scheme—simplifying ones. The problem solution result obtained, by mathematical methods is translated to the flow scheme level by reverse equivalent transformation. Scientific problem solution results are formulated. Several flow schemes (for various functional modes)

are then synthesized into an engineer object structural model.

7) Then the solution is adapted to a specific case and partly modified, i.e. additional computations are done and structural and engineering amendments introduced. It is necessitated by the fact that both the analysis and synthesis of schemes are invariably based on a compromise, trade—off between the complexity and accuracy of computations, on approximate methods and standard artificial techniques. The findings of theoretical computations must be corrected to take account of various engineering, social, economical, ecological and other requirements. It may call for the incorporation of new elements satisfying these requirements into theoretical schemes; these elements may be considered as connotations (additional, accompanying attributes) of these schemes. Framing a system of connotations which are incorporated into engineering-theory theoretical schemes as special elements may make it necessary to multiply return to previous stages (the iteration procedure) in order to construct new flow and structural schemes (corrected for these connotations), perform new approximations, equivalent transformations and computations. One of the major problems of well-developed engineering theory function is "copying" of type structural schemes for various engineering requirements and conditions. Then the solution of any engineering problems, the construction of any new engineering systems of a given type will be theoretically supported. This is the essence of the constructive function of engineering theory, its lead of engineering practice. Otherwise its function will amount only to solving routine engineering problems.

8) The final procedure of engineering theory function is that the solution result is cast into practical methodological recommendations (for the designer, inventor, etc.).

The constructive application of nanoscience as technoscience is expressed in its guidance of development in engineering practice. In nanotechnoscience, therefore, a prediction of the flow of natural processes on the nanolevel is just as important as the replication of the structural diagram of a new nanosystem (for example, a spintronic component, such as the "spin valve"). The superconductivity re-entrant phenomenon opens genuine prospects for building a very rapidly operating device, the "superconducting spin valve" for superconducting spintronics. Graphene electronics could even manipulate electrons as quantum-mechanical waves (similar to light waves made up of photons) rather than as particles.

It is very important to differentiate real fabricated "large scale MEMS" or "large-scale carbon nanotube devices" as three dimensional nanostructures from equivalent circuit modelled their components. **Figures 13(a)** and **(b)** show "scanning ion microscope (SIM) image of inductor (L), resistor (R) and capacitor (C) in a parallel circuit structures with free space nanowiring" (Bhushan, 2004: p. 187).

The "electrical engineering" schematic diagrams reflect physical processes which take place within the elements and units of radio engineering devices. Such diagrams deal with the calculation of parameters and the mapping of electric currents in standard electrical elements such as resistors, capacitors, and inductors. Of course, these devices can be called electrical circuit only with reservations. Use is made of electronics theory to describe the physical processes in the new radio engineering elements such as, for example, electron tubes or semiconductor devices. But to calculate of the parameters of these devices in which they are included use is, as a rule, made of traditional equivalent circuit (resistors, capacitors and inductors). As the physical processes in elements of radiolocation devices (klystrons, magnetrons, cathode ray tubes, antennas, etc.) operating in new radio engineering regimes are different, it was necessary to modify the former methods of their calculation and representation or to develop new ones, as well as to develop new mathematical resources. The process was also stimulated by the need to investigate and develop methods of internal noise suppression in elements of radiolocation equipment (for example, the schrot effect in electron tubes). Similar is in the nanotechnology.

It is well-known that, in nanotechnoscience, constructs from various scientific theories—classical and quantum physics, classical and quantum chemistry, structural biology, etc.—are used, whereas, in nanosystems, different physical, chemical and biological processes take place. One can, however, also construct a circuit on the basis of definite nanosructures, such as, e.g., a super-heterodyne radio receiver on the nanolevel (**Figure 14**).

One of the important methods in the engineering sciences and also nanotechnscience is an approximation. The implementation of engineering theory involves a sequence of so-called approximations. For example, in electronics, the two-port theory is used to analyze complex circuits, the parameters of which are difficult to determine, owing to the awkwardness of the computations. Approximation is the substitution of some mathematical functions or designs by other, very similar, simpler functions or designs, which are equivalent in the desired aspect and for which known solutions exist, or can easily be obtained. In engineering sciences, this is a method for solving engineering problems on the basis of theoretical models and with the aid of a series of equivalent substitutions and transformations. The method of approximation is essentially a compromise between the accuracy and the complexity of designs. Accurate approximation usually involves complex mathematical relationships and computations. An oversimplified equivalent scheme of a technical system affects the accuracy of computations. The approximating expression or scheme must ex-

press the nature of the function or scheme under approximation as accurately as possible, and be as simple as possible, in order to simplify the mathematical solutions of engineering problems. Any approximation calls for a special substantiation of solution adequacy, one type of approximation being preferable for one functional mode and other types being preferable for other-modes).

The two-port concept is introduced to facilitate the transition to mathematical relationships, making it possible to apply Kirchhoff's laws, which describe the natural process of current flow in the two-port circuit, and the corresponding equations in the matrix form. The coefficients of these equations are called two-port parameters, because they are determined solely by the two-port's properties. By solving these equations with the aid of the matrix theory, one can determine the structural parameters of two-ports sought—input resistance, input and output

L, C, R Circuit Structure

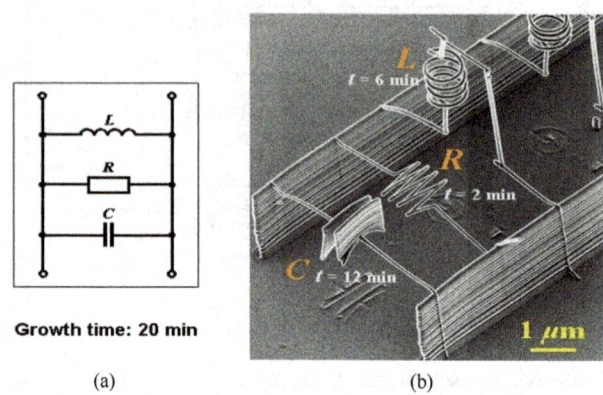

Growth time: 20 min

(a)   (b)

Figure 13.
Scanning ion microscope (SIM) micrograph of inductor (L), resistor (R) and capacitor (C) structures: (a) equivalent circuit modelled (b) three dimensional nanostructure (Bhushan, 2004: p. 186).

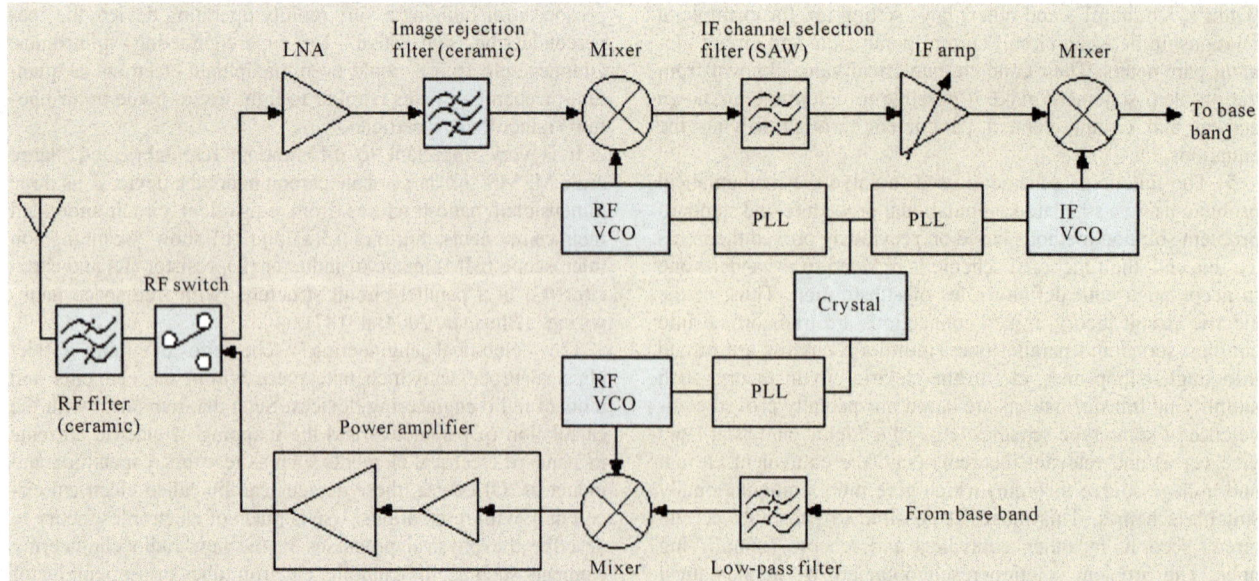

Figure 14.
Schematic of a super-heterodyne radio architecture (VCO = voltage-controlled oscillators, radio frequency (RF) and intermediate frequency (IF), SAM = self-assembled monolayer, PLL = phase-locked loop, LNA = low-noise amplifier) (Bhushan, 2004: p. 240).

power, insertion loss, etc. A number of theorems (the reversibility theorem, equivalent oscillator theorem, etc.) are proved in two-port theory. Its use makes it possible not only to simplify the computations, but also to synthesize new models by deductive equivalent transformation of two-ports. Such a transformation gives the most economical and effective engineering solutions. It indicates natural restrictions on these transformations, the main types of two-ports and the types of their connections. It should be noted that, in analyzing complex circuits, these are preliminarily transformed into a combination of simpler two-ports, the parameters of which are taken from special tables. Matrices for each of them are then used to carry out mathematical operations (addition, multiplication, etc.), depending on their connection type.

Several types of mathematical methods correspond to the same engineering theory. This is due to the fact that ideal objects are investigated at different levels. We have just considered the two-port theory and its mathematical apparatus. However, electric circuit analysis also involves the concept of a one-port making up larger structural "building-blocks", or units. (The one-port is a two-pole circuit section to which a difference of potentials is applied and which carries current.) Any amplifier, oscillator, filter, etc. can be considered to be a sum of capacitors, inductors, resistors, current and voltage sources. The latter are also idealizations, i.e., circuit theory deals with a comparatively small number of ideal elements and their combinations, representing these ideal elements at the theoretical level, and not with a great variety of radio-device structural elements differing in their characteristics, principles of operation, designs, etc. To apply the mathematical apparatus, further idealization is required; each of the above elements can be considered to be an active or passive one-port.

The methodological investigation of the history of science is very important to understand a methodology of the new scientific fields.

REFERENCES

Ahmed, H. (1991). Nanostructure fabrication. *Proceedings of the IEEE, 79,* 8.

Alù, A., & Engheta, N. (2008). A Hertzian plasmonic nanodimer as an efficient optical nanoantenna. *Physical Review B, 78,* 19. http://repository.upenn.edu/cgi/viewcontent.cgi?article=1500&context=ese_papers

Alù, A., Salandrino, A. & Engheta, N. (2007). Coupling of optical lumped nanocircuit elements and effects. *Optics Express, 15,* 21. http://repository.upenn.edu/cgi/viewcontent.cgi?article=1477&context=ese_papers

Alù, A., Youngy, M. E., & Engheta, N. (2008). Design of nanofilters for optical nanocircuits. *Physical Review Letters B, 77,* 144107. http://repository.upenn.edu/cgi/viewcontent.cgi?article=1436&context=ese_papers

Arnall, A. H. (2003). *Future technologies, today's choices nanotechnology, artificial intelligence and robotics; a technical, political and institutional map of emerging technologies.* A Report for the Greenpeace Environmental Trust, London: Department of Environmental Science and Technology Environmental Policy and Management Group, Faculty of Life Sciences, Imperial College London, University of London. http://www.greenpeace.org.uk/MultimediaFiles/Live/FullReport/5886.pdf

Barrett, D. (2000-2002). Radar theory. http://www.radarpages.co.uk/theory/ap3302/sec1/sec1contents.htm

Berger, M. (2007). Towards wet computing. *Nanowerk L.* http://www.nanowerk.com/spotlight/spotid=3559.php

Bernstein, G. H., Chua, L. O., Csurgay, A. I. et al. (2006). Biologically-inspired cellural machine architectures. In W. S. Bainbrige, & M. C. Roco (Eds.), *Managing nano-bio-infocogno innovations: Technologies in society. National Science and Technology Council's Subcommittee on Nanoscale Science, Engineering, and Technology.* Dordrecht: Springer.

Bhushan, B. (Ed.) (2004). *Springer handbook of nanotechnology.* Berlin, Heidelberg, New York: Springer-Verlag.

Burke, P. J., Li, S., & Yu, Z. (2004). Quantitative theory of nanowire and nanotube antenna performance. http://arxiv.org/PS_cache/cond-mat/pdf/0408/0408418v1.pdf

Cox, D. M. (1999). High surface area materials. In R. W. Siegel, E. Hu, & M. C. Roco (Eds.), *Nanostructure science and technology. A worldwide study. R & D status and trends in nanoparticles, nanostructured materials, and nanodevices.* Final Report Prepared under the Guidance of the Interagency Working Group on NanoScience, Engineering and Technology (IWGN), National Science and Technology Council (NSTC). Maryland: WTEC, Loyola College. http://www.wtec.org/loyola/nano/final/ch4.pdf

Engheta, N., Salandrino, A., & Aiu, A. (2004). Circuit elements at optical frequencies: nano-inductors, nano-capacitors and nano-resistors. http://arxiv.org/ftp/cond-mat/papers/0411/0411463.pdf

Gorokhov, V. (2006). Die karlsruher experimente von heinrich hertz und die rolle ferdinand brauns für die entstehung der radiotechnik als theorie und praxis in Deutschland und in Russland. In *Jahrbuch des Deutsch-Russischen kollegs 2004/2005.* Aachen: Shaker Verlag GmbH.

Johnson, R. C. (2005). Nanotubes enable dense supercapacitors. http://www.automotivedesignline.com/showArticle.jhtml?printableArticle=true&articleId=60405658)

Józsa, C., Tombros, N., Popinciuc, M., Jonkman, H. T., & van Wees, B. J. (2008). Graphene spintronics—Injection and transport. In *NIM workshop "interactions in hybrid nanosystems",* Frauenwörth.

Leider, P., & Klier, J. (2008). Electron transport in nanostructures on helium films. In Th. Schimmel et al. (Eds.), *Nanotechnology—Physics, chemistry, and biology of functional nanostructures: Results of the first research programme Kompetenznetz "Funktionelle Nanostrukturen" (Competence Network on Functional Nanostructures).* Stuttgart: Landesstiftung Baden-Württemberg.

Pool Jr., Ch. P., & Owens, F. J. (2003). *Introduction to nanotechnology.* Hoboken, NJ: John Wiley & Sons.

Ray, D. L. (2008). The end of the silicon era? Carbon nanotubes, the next great leap. http://www.nanowerk.com/spotlight/spotid=5706.php

Reuleaux, F. (1875). *Kinematics of machinery outlines of a theory of machines.* London: Macmillan and Co.

Roth, S., & Kern, D. (2008). Self-assambly of carbon nanotube transistors. In Th. Schimmel et al. (Eds.), *Nanotechnology—Physics, chemistry, and biology of functional nanostructures: Results of the first research programme Kompetenznetz "Funktionelle Nanostrukturen" (Competence Network on Functional Nanostructures).* Stuttgart: Landesstiftung Baden-Württemberg.

Salandrino, A., Alù, A., & Engheta, N. (2007). *Parallel, series, and intermediate interconnections of optical nanocircuit elements part 1: Analytical solution.* http://arxiv.org/ftp/arxiv/papers/0707/0707.1002.pdf

Schiemann, G. (2005). Nanotechnology and nature. On two criteria for understanding their relationship. *HYLE—International Journal for Philosophy of Chemistry, 11,* 1. http://www.hyle.org

Schmid, G. et al. (2006). *Nanotechnology. Assessment and perspectives.* Berlin, Heidelberg: Springer

Sherrity, S., Wiedericky, H. D., Mukherjeey, B. K., & Sayerz, M. (1997). An accurate equivalent circuit for the unloaded piezoelectric vibrator in the thickness mode. *Journal of Physics D: Applied Physics, 30.* http://ext1.rmc.ca/academic/physics/ferroelectrics/Scanneddocuments/ferro6.pdf

Silveirinha, M. G., Alù, A., Li, J., & Engheta, N. (2007). Nanoinsulators and nanoconnectors for optical nanocircuits.
http://arxiv.org/ftp/cond-mat/papers/0703/0703600.pdf

Smalley, E. (2005). *Nano bridge builds logic*. The Latest Technology Research News.
http://www.trnmag.com/Stories/2005/012605/Nano_bridge_builds_l ogic_012605.html

Song, L., Zhao, Y., Sun, L., & Xie, S. (2008). Water filled in single-walled carbon nanotubes. *NIM Workshop "Interactions in Hybrid Nanosystems"*, Frauenwörth.
http://www.nano-initiative-munich.de/fileadmin/media/events/Book_ of_Abstracts_28_4_08_final_klein.pdf

Steele B. (2005). Making the big step from electronics to photonics by modulating a beam of light with electricity.
http://www.news.cornell.edu/stories/May05/LipsonElectroOptical.ws .html

Starzyk, J. A., & Sliwa, E. (1984). Upward topological analysis of large circuits using directed graph representation. *IEEE Transactions on Circuits and Systems, CAS-31*, 4.

Wilson, B. (2007). Distributed parameters.
http://cnx.org/content/m1043/latest/

Xie, F.-Q., Obermair, Ch., & Schimmel, Th. (2007). Configuring a bistable atomic switch by repeated electrochemical cycling. *V International Conference on Microelectronics and Computer Science. Nanoscale Phenomena—Fundamentals and Applications, "NANO-2007"*, Kishinev.

Evaluating National Socialism as a "True" Fascist Movement

Angelo Nicolaides

HOD Department of Hospitality, Tourism and PR Management, Vaal University of Technology,
Vanderbijlpark, South Africa

The terms "Fascism" and "Nazism" are often linked, and at times they are regarded as one and the same ideology. The question raised is what is the distinction between Fascism and National Socialism or Nazism? A closer look at the ideas of fascism and National Socialism reveals certain affinities and overlaps with other ideologies, like Socialism, Liberalism and Conservatism. Fascism had many contradictory strands and despite deep unresolved tensions between ideas of race, nation and state in both National Socialism and fascism, the former is regarded as a "true" fascist movement. This article strives to ascertain the main differences and similarities between National Socialism and fascism and to ascertain if National Socialism could be considered to be a "true" fascist movement.

Keywords: Fascism; National Socialism; Totalitarianism

Introduction

The popular view taken concerning the issue of National Socialism and Fascism is a paradox one, concerning the mixtures of populations which on the one hand, looks to a new fascist individual, and ultra-elitism and contempt for the masses on the other hand, and this in no way makes National Socialism any less fascist than say Italian Fascism. Even though there some intellectual confusions and a lack of coherence between National Socialism and Fascism they undoubtedly belong to the same ideological family (Rocco, 1982: pp. 42-44). In both National Socialism and Fascism, ideas are combined with highly emotive xenophobic and vicious forms of Nationalism. The "roots of fascism are traceable to the antagonisms between growing industrial monopolization and the democratic system" (Marcuse, 1973: p. 410). In order to allow monopoly capitalism to survive the working class opposition had to be neutralized. This meant that the existing democratic institutions could no longer serve as effective vessels for capitalism. For production to continue and profits to be kept up, totalitarian terror was required. This was the case in both National Socialism and Fascism. They were both used to repress the working class in the interests of big business, banks and various other major financial concerns. Both National Socialism and Fascism were mass movements of middle class reaction against Socialism and Liberalism in a period of serious political and social upheaval and crisis in Europe (Morgan, 2003: pp. 17-25).

Origins

The origins of the Third Reich were to be found in the eco The origins of the Third Reich were to be found in the economic destabilization of the 1920s. The twenties modernization wave broke up the "old" politics and created political space for new right-wing movements, except among industrial workers and the unemployed who were the "most immediately dependent on modernization" (Betz, 1994: p. 25), and failed to rally to the Italian Fascists and German Nazis in nay great numbers.

The Nazi and Fascist states were "propelled towards ever more radical measures by their own inherent instability" (Mason, 1990: p. 49). As F. L. Carsten remarked: "There was no 'Fascism' anywhere in Europe before the end of the First World War" (Carsten, 1980: p. 63). Ernst Nolte in his *Three Faces of Fascism*, more or less concurs with Carsten's view. Hugh Trevor-Roper commented that: "The public appearance of Fascism as a dominant force in Europe is the phenomenon of a few years only. It can be precisely dated. It began in 1922-1923 with the emergence of the Italian Fascist Party... it came of age in the 1930s in Germany... it ended in 1945 with the defeat of two dictators" (Trevor-Roper as quoted in Woolf, 1968: p. 18).

Fascist and National Socialistic thought also originated in terms of the Communist view, as "the openly terroristic dictatorship of the most reactionary, most chauvinistic and most imperialist elements of finance capital" (Turner, 1975: p. 119). The psychological character of certain classes, especially the lower middle class and socially deprived adolescents after the First World War in Italy and Germany also favored the growth of Fascism and National Socialism. Richard Koenigsberg in Hitler's Ideology: a Study in Psychoanalytic Sociology, also noted that "Hitler's ideology offered 'a means whereby his fantasies might be expressed and discharged at the level of social reality'" (Koenigsberg, 1975: p. 85). The lower middle classes in Germany and Italy after the First World War, suffered alienation, self-hatred and loss of security, which allowed them to develop sadistic traits of character which moulded the authoritarian personality (Laquer, 1979: pp. 465-467). However, neither Fascism nor National Socialism (Nazism), was class-based. In fact, Fascism always maintained that it was a national ideology. It rejected class struggles and class antagonisms and was "leftist" in orientation in terms of propaganda that was portrayed about it. This is why it was able to achieve what it did and it appealed to all social classes. It was mainly the working classes though that joined its ranks. In order to review the degree to which Italian Fascism characterizes a combination of aspects of nationalism and socialism, it is critical to differentiate between the political ideologies and how they were interpreted in different settings.

In Italy

When the Italian Fascist movement was created at the meeting of the *Fasci di Combattimento* in Milan on March 21st 1919, Mussolini and his then handful of supporters regarded the new movement as a left wing challenger for the working class votes which were at that time being handed to the Italian Socialist Party (PSI). This primary Italian Fascist movement included a combination of socialists who supported Mussolini, nationalists, forward thinkers, national syndicalists and war veterans from the First World War. Ideologically viewed then, Fascism developed out of the convergence of these groups and predominantly around the belief that Italy could and should be regenerated to its classical glory. The combination of different systems of ideological belief or practice namely, nationalism and socialism into what Mussolini described as "National Socialism" or Fascism was what resulted in Italy. The Marxists view of Italian Fascism was that it was the final drive of a rapidly collapsing middle class in its frantic effort to hold onto its strong socio-economic position in a scenario where the working class was rapidly gaining ground. The Fascists undoubtedly included many from the middle class in their ranks but they also incorporated the working classes and wealthy aristocrats.

Michael Mann, who is a Marxist historian, stated in his book *Fascists*, that the rise of right-wing authoritarian movements between the two world wars is to be understood as "nation-statism building not a cage but a concentration camp". This interpretation is essentially at odds with the Marxist interpretations of Fascism. Marxism *per se*, regards Fascism as a brutal endeavor to preserve capitalism from the challenges of left-wing mobilizations directly after World War I. Mann is also averse to regarding Fascism as a totalitarian "political religion" which emerged as a reaction against modernization and democracy. By the late 1930s, the basic thought was that Fascism and National Socialism was an aspect of a moral and religious crisis in Western civilization and while most of Europe passed through challenging economic times in the period between the wars, Fascists did not try to seize power in countries where the state had well-established democratic institutions and a strong foundation for infrastructural control. Benedetto Croce and R. Collingwood saw Fascism and National Socialism as a denial of human liberty. Croce argued that Fascism was a corruption of Italian liberty and stated that: "authoritarian governments endure only among decadent peoples" (De Ruggiero, 1927: p. 343).

Support by industrialists and Capitalists for Fascism was wide-ranging especially between different countries. A point of congruence amongst Fascist minded citizenry in countries where Fascism emerged was to be found in the powerful vested interests in the growth of the nation-state. The majority of the military and civil service personnel and especially the public-sector and manual laborers opted to become Fascists. Fascists recruited from both the ranks of the proletariat as well as the bourgeoisie. In this regard, G. L. Mosse regarded Fascism and especially National Socialism as a: "deeply rooted cultural malaise" (Mosse, 1966: pp. 15-34). De Felice, (1977: p. 176) expresses the opinion that Mussolini established a support base and also encountered many adversaries in every social class. If taken in a sociological context, Fascism was the result of a

rapid development and modernization, or even the particular manner of industrialization in both Italy and Germany (Barrington, 1967: p. 88). Fascism was seen as a possible route to modernization, but when compared to Germany, industrialization and modernization came late to Italy. The problem is that Germany was highly industrialized by the late 1920s, but Italy lagged relatively far behind. Then in terms of socio-economic criteria, Italian Fascism and Nazism should not be in the same category (Turner, 1975: p. 132). If rapid modernization is thus linked to Fascism then, in this respect, it does not adequately explain what happened in Italy and Germany.

Fascists were not in the least afraid of the revolutionary working-classes and in fact recruited vigorously from their ranks. In fact, in June 1914, Benito Mussolini personally took part in the violent and confrontational "Red Week" in which Fascists displayed there power. The advocates of Fascist ideology intended to display it as an amalgamation of nationalism and socialism. As early as the late 19th Century, nationalists including Corradini lambasted liberal Italian politicians on the basis that they had failed miserably in their feeble attempts to modernize the Italian economy. They had also not promoted Italian interests abroad in terms of colonial adventures and above all else, they had not protected the interests of the working classes.

Corradini maintained that Italy was a "proletarian nation" which had become embroiled in the international social Darwinist struggle for survival with far more dominant European states. Italy could only regenerate itself if class conflicts acme to an end and diverse classes in society began to work together to build national unity which was essential for economic growth and meaningful colonial expansion. The latter was especially needed as it would provide Italy with the much desired status of a great power. In 1938, Mussolini replaced the Chamber of Deputies with the Chamber of the Fasces and Corporations (*Camera dei Fasci e delle Corporazioni*). This Chamber was constituted of a number of delegates who were appointed by each of the corporations, plus a number of delegates appointed by the National Fascist Party.

Mussolini described the institutional transformations as follows:

"*We have constituted a Corporative and Fascist State, the State of national society, a State which concentrates, controls, harmonizes, and tempers the interests of all social classes, which are thereby protected in equal measure. Whereas, during the years of demo-liberal regime, labor looked with diffidence upon the State, and was, in fact, outside the State and against the State, and considered the State an enemy of every day and every hour, there is not one working Italian today who does not seek a place in his Corporation or syndical federation, who does not wish to be a living atom of that great, immense living organization which is the national Corporate State of Fascism*". (Lowell Field, 1968: p. 16)

The initial programmes of the *Fasci di Combattimento* were in a sense left-wing and the growth of Italian Fascism from 1920 and 1922 was essentially due to the expansion of the rural and provincial squads which often opted to use violence against socialist organizations and members as a means of defending especially upper and middle class interests. By 1922 the Fascists claimed that they would address the restraints of laissez faire capitalism and this would be by means of a Corporatist Third Way which was a middle-path between communism and capitalism. Industries were to be managed in terms of corporatist principles in which every industry would have corporatist organizations. The members of these bodies would represent employers and workers who were mentored by fascist officials. These would collectively make economic decisions to support the fascist cause by also improving the wages of workers. In practice however, the corporatist experiment was relatively unsuccessful and although there were some minor reforms the corporatist experiment by and large failed since Mussolini was under the control of wealthy financiers and industrial elites who continued to exploit the workers.

Venetian financiers, essentially controlled Mussolini, but in the eyes of the world he was perceived as Duce of the Fascists and Head of Government. For Mussolini, the fascist Italian was to be created on a par with the Renaissance Italian (Smith, 1975: p. 174). The Grand Council of Fascism (*Gran Consiglio del Fascismo*) was a very important organ and ostensibly idiomatic of the Fascist Party, the government ministers including the Presidents of the Senate and the Chamber and the commander of the *Squadristi* militias. A number of Fascist candidates were to be voted for and voters had to either accept or reject the notion of a unitary state. It was the Grand Council which was also tasked with submitting to the King the names of suitable candidates who could be elected as Head of Government. There were wide-ranging parliamentary limitations in Italy and the power of the fascist dictatorship grew as the independence of the judiciary became severely compromised. All political parties in Italy, other than the Italian Fascist Party were gradually abolished and the independent trade unions were replaced by fascist syndicates. Any other political groups were allowed to exist only if they remained uncritical of fascism and Mussolini. The media were very strictly monitored and censured and used predominantly as a puppet of fascist propaganda which promoted the idea that true identity could be found in the community of the nation and the nation preceded the individual. All class struggles could be counterbalanced by nationalism which was vehemently opposed to the liberal bourgeois conception of life, and both Germany and Italy as nations transcended division. It was nationalism that would prepare the nation for self-sacrifice, heroism and conflict. The bourgeois by comparison, tended to undermine these ambitions and wasted time and effort on the pursuit of materialistic desires and petty parliamentary politics. In Nazi Germany, the nation was imbued with a quasi-religious aura, but this was not the case in Italian fascism. Ironically, it was the Grand Council which initially supported Mussolini that decided to oust him in July 1943. Mussolini tried to justify his ruthless regime through the requirement for efficiency and getting things done effectively in a weakening Italian state, but the Second World War soon exposed the vast military and logistical limitations of the fascist corporate state.

Fascism was thus a "conjunctural phenomenon" which combined heterogenous social class and generational support. Juan Linz expressed it as a "novel response to the crisis... of the pre-war structure and party systems" in both Italy and Germany (Laquer, 1979: p. 18). Nolte suggested that: "Fascism is anti-Marxism which seeks to destroy the enemy by the evolvement of a radically opposed and yet related ideology" (Nolte, 1969: pp. 20-21). In his typology *Three Faces of Fascism*, originally published in German in 1963, Nolte subdivided it into four distinct stages of development. Pilsudski's Poland was regarded as a pre-Fascist state, while the *Action Francaise* was seen as a being in the early fascist phase of development. Mussolini's Italy was a "normal" Fascist state, while Germany's National

Socialists were regarded as extreme, hyper-nationalistic and almost radical Fascists (Nolte, 1969: p. 21). Nolte saw both Fascism and Nazism as having originated as "anti-Marxism", which set out to destroy the opposition by the use of virtually identical methods. Both were resistance to practical transcendence and "anti-Christian Catholicism", but this ignores the fact that many were Catholics, especially in Italy. Both were driven by fear or "angst" of transcendence which in both Italy and Germany was directed against groups who symbolized transcendence. This was anticipated by Friedrich Nietzsche (Nolte, 1969: p. 440).

In Italian fascism, nationalism was more traditional and was in essence a form of patriotism and xenophobic imperialism. Fascism represented the seeking out of a "third way" between communism and capitalism which was intended to free society from the alienation of an industrial society and so liberal democracy and parliamentary government were rejected. The fascist movement was more characterized by what it stood against than what it stood for.

How Were Fascism and Nazism Totalitarian in Nature?

A totalitarian state is one in which the leadership has total authority and control over every aspect of the lives of citizenry. There is neither public nor private life and a dictator or ruling elite who use terror to subdue the masses. In a totalitarian state, propaganda is used extensively to control the hearts and minds of people. This was the case in both Fascist Italy and Nazi Germany. In both states all the individual liberties that liberals' tended to value, were heavily reduced. Only total obedience to the totalitarian state would serve the national interests. The fascist totalitarian state was dominated by the political elite and especially by Mussolini. Fascists based much of their theories on the work of the German philosopher Nietzsche and political scientists including Pareto, Mosca and Michels. Mussolini, Gentile and Primo de Rivera admitted that their vision of the state was totalitarian. Hitler shared this vision but linked it to the notion of control by force. Freedom was not individualistic but rather coincided with the purpose of the state.

The Nazi state was internally chaotic with no real top-down control and the Nazis worked with an existing state bureaucracy, many of whom only joined the ranks of the Nazis in 1939. The S.S. and other militarized elements worked in tandem with the state police and the army. Hitler had total control in this "organizational jungle" (Broszat, 1981: p. 358). Hitler and Mussolini thus had vital roles in their respective totalitarian states. A stated by Gentile: "It is always the few who represent the self-consciousness and will of an epoch" (Gentile, 1928: p. 291). Despite the authoritarian nature of each state, both had traditionally entrenched interests and constantly changing alliances which forced Hitler and Mussolini to make concessions (Laquer, 1979: p. 411). Although Corporations were part of the ancient Volk in Germany, Italy had more complex relationships with the ideas of "syndicalism" and "corporation". Mussolini's state would to a large extent direct and control syndicates for the ends of the nation but there was nothing comparable in Italy.

It was believed that both Mussolini and Hitler possessed the requisite political insights to effectively lead their respective countries and their political powers should thus be virtually unrestricted. National Socialism was undoubtedly a type of fascism but it was a lot more racially focused than Mussolini's

Fascism. In both states, there were bureaucracies created to organize and maintain reigns of terror. The citizens of Fascist Italy and Nazi Germany would live untouched as long as they were loyal to Mussolini and Hitler respectively. Mass psychology was the methodology employed to control the citizenry. In Germany, the state could not be primary once the *Fuhrerprinzep* was created. It was Hitler as the Fuhrer who came to embody the sovereign authority of the state. Consequently all state authority was Fuhrer authority. In Italy, parties were considered to be compromising and they were merely stifling the national interest. Only propaganda would win them over (Schmitt, 1985: p. 50).

Differences and Similarities between Fascism and Nazism

The most profound difference between Fascism and Nazism was the centrality of the race issue. In the case of Nazi Germany there was a strong *Volk* tradition whereas in Italian fascism this is absent. The Germanic *Volk* factor alienated French Fascists like Drieu de Rochelle or Spanish Fascists like Primo de Rivera and even Mussolini. The latter referred to Germany in the 1930s as a "racialist lunatic asylum" (Mosse, 1966: p. 314). Italian Fascists never reached the intense levels of anti-Semitism that prevailed in Germany. Another distinguishing mark is the intensity of terror and controlled violence which was markedly less in Italy (Turner, 1975: p. 17). The Italian Fascists vindicated their desire for colonialist expansion into parts of Africa, for example, in terms of their perceived racial superiority relative to the Africans and also gradually adopted a greater anti-Semitic mentality as their alliance with Hitler developed. Human nature assumed an interesting character in both Fascism and Nazism. Many young fascists were encouraged to think of violence in almost romantic terms. Violence is what linked the individual with the unconscious and it encouraged the "hero" idea of the *Übermensch*. Ultimately the idea of the *Übermensch* provided a strong theoretical basis for Fascism in Italy. Proponents of Fascism used Nietzsche's "*Übermensch*" or "superman" notion to validate their behaviour. Friedrich Nietzsche had reasoned that some members of humanity were endowed with a superior will and imagination, and as a consequence of this would as a matter of course, tend to dominate society and ruler the weaker masses. Unconditional inequality was biologically determined and irremovable and all Nazis accepted an inequality of races. The Aryan who was at one with the landscape and fellow Aryans, was considered superior in all respects to Jews, Slavs and Negroes. Hitler described Aryans as the "genius" race, but some Aryans were born to be superior to others. The genius or hero-figure could allow great things to be accomplished by peoples through his efforts. As Hitler put is: "The progress and culture of humanity are not a product of the majority, but rest exclusively on the genius and energy of the personality" (Hitler, 1939: pp. 310-313).

A related point about genius or leader figures was made in Italian fascism but it was not premised in accounts of either racial or biological genius, but rather on the interpretation of the sociological writings on elitism of *inter-alia*, Gaetano Mosca, Robert Michels and Vilfredo Pareto. It was these writers who assisted the generation of suspicions concerning parliamentary democracy which were rife amongst fascists. The element of self-deluding pomposity and neurosis was also a strong feature of both Hitler's and Mussolini's visions of their own roles (Smith, 1975: p. 127). Mussolini regarded himself as a man excluded from communing with others as if it was a divine law. He even introduced the Roman salute instead of the handshake as he reviled any physical contacts (Smith, 1975: pp. 128-139). Since fascists believed that human nature was corrupted by liberal democratic ideals, change was necessary. In the case of National Socialism, this campaign was duty-bound to produce a "Volk-bound German man" (Pois, 1986: p. 70). Mussolini desired that the fascist Italian had to be unburdened of wrong ideas and be recreated to be on a par with the Renaissance Italian (Smith, 1975: p. 174). For Germans such as Rosenberg the Nazis, the Aryan already existed but had to be protected against racial mixing however for Himmler and the Waffen SS, the new German man had to be selectively bred for the future and inferior races had to be eliminated. This was a popular ideology and as Heiden (1939: p. 98) stated: "The great masses of the people did not merely put up with National Socialism. They welcomed it".

This notion was developed into the idea of the "superman" by later Fascists and Nazis. The Fascists and Nazis also accepted that totalitarian dictatorships were justified, as only a superior leader could fully exemplify the collective will of the masses. Both Italian and German fascist writers referred to Fascism as a state of mind or way of being. Nazis often proclaimed that one should "think with the blood". The masses were for the most part viewed as being instinctual or herd-like and they could thus easily be manipulated by the superior few. Thus crude forms of social Darwinism combined with the doctrine of the *Herrenvolk* or "master-race". Mussolini believed that all people were untrustworthy and selfish while Hitler was distrustful of all and hateful to all (Bullock, 1962: pp. 30-38).

The Nazis believed, as Hitler had stated in *Mein Kampf* (My Struggle), that the Aryan Germans were the master race and where thus superior to all others and were especially far more advanced than the Jews. Fascists also asserted also that individuals are all fundamentally competitive by nature rather than collaborative, and both an individual and a nation are caught up in a social Darwinist fight for the survival of the fittest where the "end justifies the means" in a Macchiavelian type approach. A number of fascists argued that it was only possible for individuals to arrive at their full potential through there physical participation in an often brutal struggle against both domestic and international opponents. Consequently using violence to crush any domestic political opponents is acceptable, as is resorting to war in order to achieve desired foreign policy objectives. Little attention was given outside Germany to the issue of living space or *Lebensraum*. This lay behind Hitler's foreign policy for the eastward expansion of Germany into Russia and the ultimate decimation of the Slavonic races. By contrast, Italian expansion was usually perceived in terms of European imperialism. In Germany it was linked almost obsessively to the issue of race since National Socialism was irrationalist and everything was judged from the perspective of race (Nolte, 1969: pp. 570-575). The German state was subservient to the Volk and to the racial issue, but in Italy, the Fascist movement strove towards rational modernization. In both Fascism and Nazism there were marked subdivisions. Alexander de Grand, in his study on Italian Fascism, speaks of conservative, technocratic, national, syndicalist and *Squadrismi* typologies of fascism. Nolte speaks of pre, early, normal and radical fascisms. This gradual evolving of National Socialism and Fascism is another link between them (Roberts, 1979: p. 318).

Both National Socialism and Italian Fascism sought to bring about national and social unity in single-party systems which were highly totalitarian in nature. In fascism, politics took priority over economics and the focus was on the nation. Economics was thus determined by national objectives. In both National Socialism and Italian fascism, economic practices were a combination of socialist and liberal policies. The corporate state would integrate employers and employees in Italy and politics as expressed in the nation state. This was considered to be spiritually as well as morally superior to economics. In the case of National Socialism, race and Volk occupied the key position in thinking. In both Germany and Italy, the idea was for self-sufficient economy gathering its economic resources for the national ends. In the case of both states it was linked to the war footing in the 1030s. In Germany from 1936 onwards, the aim was for economic self-sufficiency in preparation for international conflict (Bullock, 1962: pp. 358-359).

The main ambiguity of both the German and Italian fascist regimes was that they used "a battery of economic controls to which left-wing governments, outside the Soviet Union, could still only aspire to". Yet the beneficiaries of these proposals were groups which supported more right-wing parties (Milward in Laquer, 1979: p. 411). Sternhell explains the development of fascist ideology in both Italy and Germany as a logical and reasonable response to the pervading practical political circumstances. The hatred for the bourgeois order and hatred of their values is a visible theme in both Italian fascism and Nazism (Sternhell, 1994: pp. 93-99).Certainly both Hitler and Mussolini appeared to have very little interest in economic theories, as long as their nationalist and imperialist ambitions could be underpinned. As Mosse noted on National Socialism: "It nationalized when it wanted to nationalize... It allied itself with big business when it wanted such an alliance", overall it seemed to lack any specific economic commitment (Sternhell, 1994: pp. 93-99). Fischer (1996) stated: "*In the past fifteen years, the long-entrenched thesis that National Socialism represented the revolt of the Mittelstand (the middle-class, bourgeoisie) has undergone decisive revision. Although few historians would deny the Nazi party's success among the German middle classes in recruiting party members and drawing voters, sophisticated statistical work, much of it drawn from newly-explored regional archives, has shown that the Nazi constituency was much more diverse than once imagined. Recent scholarship now argues that support for the Hitler movement extended to all social classes. Moreover, although the Nazi party performed especially well in Protestant regions, it did not fail to attract Catholics. In short, National Socialism evolved into a genuine Volkspartei (party of the nation) that transcended the class and milieu-based politics of the Weimar period...*".

In the area of Fascist attacks on intellectualism, it is difficult to isolate Fascist themes or ideologists although the Italians had Giovanni Gentile who "built" up much of the doctrine of fascism for Mussolini. The National Socialists did not have anyone as distinguished in their ranks. The National Socialist interpretation of the term "social" was distinct from that of the Italian fascists as the former focused on the racial *Volkisch* dimension rather than on the state. An individual was constituted through the community which was constituted in terms of racial soul (*Volkseele*). Nature was regarded as a life force which gave both meaning and purpose to humans and their Volk (Mosse, 1978: p. 15). It was the emotive, instinctive life

of people that linked them to their Volk and also to their inner life-force of nature. People could be glorified, therefore, according to their oneness with nature, and not through their dominance over it. Unlike the Italian fascists, the Nazis celebrated in a bogus, and almost mystical sense, peasant life, country landscapes and nature. It was the landscape which imbued people with their inner life force. Hitler's love of animals and the fact that he was a vegetarian are related to this standpoint. As in the case of leaders in Nazism, the leadership membership of the Fascist movement was derived from amongst war veterans and in particular, former commissioned and non-commissioned officers. Members were also recruited from the ranks of the white collar workers and the educated middle class.

Madden (1987) has shown that National Socialists emanated from all social classes in large volumes. Fischer (1978) also assessed the class orientation of the members of the *Sturm Abteilung* (S.A., Stormtroopers or Brownshirts) and uncovered that "the workers are over-represented in the S.A." (p. 140). From 1933-1934, some 69.9% of the S.A. emanated from the working class compared to 53.2% from the German population in general. Italian Fascists as well as Nazis criticized liberal democracy on the grounds that political parties and various pressure groups appealed to the selfish egoism of certain people and increased social conflicts at a time when national unity was desirable. Both Hugh Trevor-Roper and Ernst Nolte view fascism as a result of tyranny and megalomania on the parts of Mussolini and Hitler respectively. Alan Bullock states that fascism "was to Hitler the instrument of his ambition" (Bullock, 1962: p. 237).

Conclusion

Both Fascism and Nazism were highly totalitarian in nature. Both had one powerful leader, who came to epitomize the general will of the nation. The leaders felt at ease in invading all areas of both public and private life and this was justifiable as it supposedly served the "greater good". Each state sought to bring about national and social unity in single-party systems which were totalitarian in nature and although there were some differences between fascism and National Socialism, there were enough similarities between them for them to be treated as part of the same movement in which the masses could be won over by extensive propaganda (Mosse, 1978: p. 128). Sternhell is of the opinion that Nazism was not "truly fascist" on account of its form of racism (Sternhell, 1994: pp. 93-97) whereas R. de Felice viewed Italian fascism as being fundamentally different from Nazism on account of Nazism's atavistic tendencies (De Felice, 1977: pp. 20-26). Philip Moran sees Italian fascism and German National Socialism as belonging to the same "family" as both were mass movements of the "middle-class reaction against liberalism and socialism in an era of severe political and social crises" (Morgan, 2003: p. 8). This is somewhat distinct from the view of Reinhard Kuhnl who asserts that "National Socialism was 'fascist' but was also its own movement with its own criteria which are not directly connected to capitalism or to capitalist desires" (Mosse, 1996: p. 48) and had an "unquestionable revolutionary nature" (De Felice, 1977: p. 191). Vajda, in Fascism as a mass movement, sees Italian fascism and National Socialism as original European phenomena which expressed the traditions and tendencies of Europe and should thus be understood as part of the development of the ideological and political structure of the West. Both are bourgeois and both are equally opposed to liberalism each had a bourgeois form of power with aggressive expansionist aims against people with in similar economic and cultural levels as well almost identical social systems (Vajda, 1976: p. 26). In both, fascism appealed to individuals and portions of the mainstream elite whom it promised to serve more efficiently and effectively than the ruling existing parties. There were without doubt great linkages between fascism and National Socialism (Turner, 1975: pp. 84-86). While they have similarities and differences, the differences do not preclude National Socialism from being viewed as a truly Fascist movement. Essentially the congruence between them far outweighs any dissimilarities. Critically, in both, violence was a preferred tool to use in harnessing support and in obtaining desired objectives.

Even though National Socialism was unique in that it had the Aryan myth and racism and extreme anti-Semitism based on supposed biological superiority. Some Germans saw Jewishness as a cultural or spiritual problem, but to others it was regarded as a racial problem. It was often associated with the bourgeois life and even Bolshevism. The Jews soon became the central focus point of nationalistic hatred in Germany. The frustration with their lives drove many Italians and Germans to seek new strengthening of their nations in what became hypernationalistic drives to monopolize politics, social organization and even education and cultural affairs (Turner, 1975: pp. 44-52). It is evident that both Italian Fascist and German Nazi leaders were able to rise to power as the existing leaders were unable to halt the threat, perceived or real, from the radical left. They were essentially unable to forge any consensus top diffuse the threat from the radical left and attract support to win a majority in the parliaments, and so fascist movements tended to develop in nations with strong left-wing movements (Carsten, 1980: p. 233). The use of terror and violence in fascist Italy and Nazi Germany against enemies of the state and the removal of pluralism in both states further emphasized that they were very similar in orientation. Both states used mass psychology and extensive propaganda campaigns to great effect. Both states idolized their leaders manipulated the masses. There is no doubt that National Socialism was a variation of Italian fascism and a true fascist movement.

Both National Socialism and Italian fascism were revolutionary in nature and were mass movements that mobilized the populace and both vilified the west as a plutocracy and aimed at destroying the existing order so that a Volk or nation could finally triumph and both hated traditional elites. Renzo de Felice sees Italian fascism as emanating from a radical left-wing enlightenment (De Felice, 1977: pp. 14-33). Both were inhuman as they negated the freedom and dignity of the people and each was linked to the notion of adaptability and was ascribed to certain socio-economic conditions in countries transforming into industrial societies. The researcher believes that there are thus enough similarities between National Socialism and fascism per se for us to categorize them as being in the same "family' of ideology and National Socialism was thus a truly fascist movement". "To the historian fascism is Janus-faced. One face looks forward, in the spirit of the Enlightenment, to the rational control and direction of human life; the other face looks backwards to a much simpler more primitive life, when men struggled to live", National Socialism fits the bill (Skidelsky, 1975: p. 288).

REFERENCES

Betz, H. G. (1994). *Radical right-wing populism.* New York: St. Martins.

Broszat, M. (1981). *The hitler state.* London: Longman.

Bullock, A. (1962). *Hitler: A study in tyranny.* London: Konecky & Konecky.

Carsten, F. L. (1980). *The rise of fascism.* London: Batsford.

De Felice, R. (1977). *Interpretations of fascism.* Cambridge: Harvard U.P.

De Ruggiero, G. (1927). *The history of European liberalism.* Oxford: Clarendon Press.

Fischer, C. J. (1978). The occupational background of the S.A.'s rank and file membership during the depression years, 1929 to mid-1934. In P. Stachura (Ed.), *The shaping of the Nazi state.* London: Croom Helm.

Fischer, C. J. (1996). *The rise of national socialism and the working classes in weimar Germany.* Oxford: Berghahn Books.

Gentile, G. (1928). *Philosophic basis of fascism.* Milan: Foreign Affairs 6.

Heiden, K. (1939). *One man against Europe.* Penguin: Harmondsworth, Middlesex.

Hitler, A. (1969). *1939 Mein Kampf.* London: University of Chicago Press.

Koenigsberg, R. (1975). *Hitler's ideology: A study in psychoanalytic psychology.* New York: Library of Social Sciences.

Laquer, W. (1979). *Fascism: A readers guide.* London: Routledge.

Lowell Field, G. (1968). *The syndical and corporative institutions of italian fascism.* New York: AMS Press.

Madden, P. (1987). The social class origins of Nazi party members as determined by occupations, 1919-1933. *Social Science Quarterly, 68,* 263-280.

Mann, M. (2004). *Fascists.* Cambridge: Cambridge University Press.

Marcuse, H. (1973). *Reason and revolution.* New York: Oxford University Press.

Morgan, P. (2003). *Italian fascism 1919-1945.* New York: Taylor & Francis.

Mosse, G. L. (1966). *The crisis of German ideology.* London: Weidenfeld & Nicolson.

Mosse, G. L. (1978). *Nazism: A historical and comparative analysis.* Oxford: Basil Blackwell.

Nolte, E. (1969). *Three faces of fascism.* New York: Mentor.

Pois, R. (1986). *National socialism and the religion of nature.* London: Croom Helm.

Roberts, D. (1979). *Syndicalist tradition and Italian fascism.* Manchester: Manchester University Press.

Rocco, A. (1982). *The political doctrine of fascism.* Denver: Alan Swallow.

Skidelsky, R. (1975). *Oswald Mosley.* London: Macmillan.

Smith, M. (1975). *Mussolini.* New York: Weidenfeld and Nicolson.

Sternhell, Z. (1994). *The birth of fascist ideology.* Princeton: Princeton University Press.

Turner, H. A. (1975). *Reappraisals of fascism.* New York: New Viewpoints.

Vajda, M. (1976). *Fascism as a mass movement.* New York: Palgrave Macmillan.

Woolf, S. (1968). *European fascism.* London: Weidenfeld and Nicolson.

20

Megalithism and Tribal Ritualism: A Passage through the Kurumbas of Attappadi

Manjula Poyil

Department of History, Nirmlagiri College, Kannur University, Kerala, India

The study of mortuary practices of Megalithic communities and its use as the basis for reconstructing the past society is unique in archaeology as it represents the direct and purposeful culmination of conscious behavior of the followers of this cultural trait. There are voluminous studies on the Megalithic builders of South India, including Kerala, written by prominent archaeologists and anthropologists from the early decades of the nineteenth century. Most of them ignored the continuity of Megalithic tradition, except a scant reference to the erection of funeral edifices among tribes like the Kurumbas and Mudugas of Attappadi and Mala-arayans of the Thiruvananthapuram district of Kerala. A study of the living Megalithic practices provides clues to ethnographic parallels, existing belief systems and habitation sites of the present communities. The present study discusses the cultural aspects of the rituals related to living Megalithic tradition among the Attappadi tribes, of the Palakkad district of Kerala. The study of the mortuary practices of the Kurumbas raises two important questions-firstly, how far this tribe can be seen as the actual successor of Megalithic builders of Kerala and, secondly, how does the social differentiation within the Kurumba community got reflected in its mortuary practices, just like the Megalithic builders of the past.

Keywords: Megalith; Kurumbas; Secondary Burial; Cheeru; Living Tradition

Introduction

The present study deals with the existence of Megalithic[1] traits as a living tradition among the Kurumba tribe of Attappadi. The study of mortuary practices of Megalithic community and its use as a basis for reconstructing the past society is unique in archaeology because it represents the direct and purposeful culmination of conscious behavior of the followers of this cultural trait. There are several studies on the Megalithic traits of tribal communities in India (Hutton, 1992: pp. 242-249; Mawlong, 1990: pp. 9-14; Grigson, 1932; Bondo, 1950) but barring a few, most of the studies on the tribes of Kerala ignored the continuity of Megalithic tradition among tribes like the Kurumbas and Mudugas of Attappadi and Mala-Arayans of the Thiruvananthapuram district. A study of such living Megalithic practices provides clues to ethnographic parallels, existing belief systems and habitation sites of the present communities. The present study discusses the cultural aspects of the rituals related to living Megalithic tradition in Attappadi, the Palghat district of Kerala. A study of the mortuary practices of the Kurumbas raises two important questions-firstly, how far this tribe can be seen as the actual successor of Megalithic builders of Kerala and, secondly, how does the social differentiation within the Kurumba community got reflected in its mortuary practices,

just like among the Megalithic builders?

Kerala, situated on the South-Western Coast of India, preserves the heritage of a rich Megalithic culture in the form of a wide variety of burial monuments and of a survival of megalithic cult among the various tribal communities who inhabit on the slopes of the western ghats, which still provides a pristine habitat for more than 36 varieties of tribal communities. Among these, Kurumbas have a close affinity with Megalithic communities because they erected funeral memorials only after the performance of an elaborate secondary burial. The Kurumbas, the most archaic among the 3 tribes of Attappadi (the other two being Irulas and Mudugas), lives in the dense forest adjoining the Silent Valley of Palghat district of Kerala, which is a part of the Nilgiri biosphere. There are two divisions among the Kurumbas-Palu-Kurumbas and Alu-Kurumbas. Alu-Kurumbas are concentrated in South-Western, Southern, South-Eastern and Eastern slopes of the Western ghats, and in the upper elevations of the Nilgiris. The Kurumbas of Attappadi are Palu-Kurumbas and they are concentrated in the lower elevations of the ghats. Both these groups are shifting cultivators and they used to live in separate hamlets. Each hamlet is a closely knit kin group with nuclear families. These tribal communities have an unfailing faith in animism and ancestor-spirits (Tylor, 1871: p. 424) which determined the nature of their mortuary practices, though slight changes existed between the two due a difference in the physical environment. There are 14 Palu-Kurumba hamlets scattered in different parts of south-western Attappadi. Among these Thodikki hamlet is the most prominent and has a com-

---

[1]The word *Megalith* is derived from two words, *Mega* means big and *Lith* means stone. It is a custom of erecting huge funeral edifices over the relics of the dead. Along with the corpse all the belongings of the deceased are also deposited.

manding position regarding funeral ritual related to all the hamlets. From the archaeological point of view Todikki acquires a predominant position because it is from here that reports about the Kurumba tradition of erecting dolmen-like Megaliths came first.

Historiography

Historical writings on the living tradition of Megalithic practice in Kerala are very few. Most of the studies are concentrated on the typology of monuments, their individual and common features, comparison with those of other parts of India and the world, and the belief systems associated with Megalithism. The first notable effort in this direction was made by L. A. Krishna Iyer, who studied extensively the Megalithic culture of the whole region of Kerala. He noticed, for the first time, the similarity between the ancestor worship of the Megalithic people and the tribal practices. In his two important works, *The Prehistoric Archaeology of Kerala* (Iyer, 1948) and *Kerala Megaliths and their Builders* (Iyer, 1967) as well as in his article *The Disposal of the Dead among the Primitive Tribes of Travancore* (Iyer, 1939: pp. 61-62)", he pointed out that certain Travancore tribes like the Mala-Arayans erected dolmens over their graves like the Megalithic people. In his famous work, *Travancore Tribes and Castes* in 3 Volumes, he studied the burial customs of various tribes of Travancore and found that burial was the common mode of disposal of the dead and they deposited grave goods along with the corpse.

In his *Early Man in Wynad* (John, 1975: pp. 125-131) and *The Megalithic Culture of Kerala*, (John, 1978: pp. 485-489) K. J. John studied the survival of Megalithic culture among the lower caste Hindus and tribal communities of Malabar. He pointed out that majority of the tribes who live on the Western Ghats practice a burial custom which is very close to Megalithism of the ancient days. He argued that the cult of Muthappan and *teyyam* ritual dance is a cultural relic of the tribal tradition of ancestor worship.

Dieter B. Kapp in his remarkable article, "The Kurumbas' Relationship to the 'Megalithic' Cult of Nilgiri Hills (South India)" (Kapp, 1985: pp. 493-534) examined the past and present relationship of the Nilgiri Kurumbas towards megalithism. The most significant features of this article is that it presented the erection of dolmens, stone circles and various other lithic remains as a pointer to the cult of megalithism as a living tradition among them even today.

Megalithic Traits in Kurumba Burial Practices

Disposal of the Dead

"The onset of death is universally the subject of ritual, and there is not a single human society that simply throws the body out as a mass of decaying protoplasm" (Murphy, 1989: p. 211). And, for the Kurumbas, rituals are very elaborate, complex and weird. Their mortuary practices had three phases-pre-burial, burial and post-burial or secondary burial. According to Alekshin, the most important component of burial practice is ritual-the activities sanctioned by tradition that occur before, during, and after the burial and are considered essential to the transfer to the other world of deceased members of the community, both those forming its nucleus and others related by blood (Alekshin, 1987: pp. 137-138). Most important pre-burial ceremonies are

announcement of death, purification ceremonies, funeral dance etc. Interment and mourning are the most common ceremonies of the second phase. Through interment the corpse is put inside the pit dug in the ground and the grave is filled, after inhuming the body inside it, with earth. Their graveyard, which is located away from the settlement in the forest, is known as *Chodalai* and graves are dug by expert gravediggers from the tribe. The grave is 6-feet deep and has a side cavity called *Allekkuzhi*, where the body of the deceased is placed and well protected with bamboo mats.

Grave-Goods

The corpse will be interred with a variety of goods including the personal possessions of two varieties-one domestic possessions of the deceased person like different kinds of food materials and water, clothes, ornaments, pottery, money, a cane basket known as *tekku* which contains different varieties of grains and second varieties are implements like knife, hoe, axe, spade, sickle, digging stick etc. Grains such as rice, millet, ragi, kora, thuvara, etc. also are mainly interred. Money is the token for the ferry charge to cross the river in the land of the dead for the spirit. After interment Kurumbas used to fix a stone as a burial mark at the head. All these grave goods gives us important historical clues like the type of their economy, type of metals used by them, their dietary pattern, anthropological data, belief in life after death etc.

Social Differentiation

It has been suggested that the social position of the departed is one of the important elements of the burial practices. It consists of the collection of material elements—the burial structure, the assemblage of grave goods, and the position of the deceased-required for a person of a particular age and sex to be transported to the other world (Alekshin, 1987: pp. 137-138). This social differentiation is reflected in mortuary ceremonies and clearly in the deposition of grave goods. The burials of infants are devoid of grave goods. On the basis of productive activities grave goods of men and women vary. Being an agricultural and hunting community, the Kurumba men are engaged in hunting and fishing and in various agricultural activities like ploughing while the women are involved in reaping, making baskets for keeping grains and digging tubers. Hence the most prominent grave goods deposited in men's graves are hoe, fish hooks, arrows, axe etc. whereas those in the graves of women are sickle, digging stick, needle and cane basket. Besides, a Kurumba woman is buried along with her precious and semi-precious ornaments. Thus their burial deposits appear to be richer than those of men.

Secondary Funeral and Erection of Memorial

The secondary burial ceremony of the Kurumbas is popularly known as *Cheeru*, (Poyil, 2009: pp. 31-38) which is protracted and very elaborate. Through this ceremony Kurumbas make necessary arrangements for the spirit's journey to the land of the dead. The Kurumbas called their spirit *Nikal* or shadow. The ceremonies connected with *cheeru* are spread over four days. This post-burial ceremony is conducted after the death of 101 members in a settlement; hence it took 10 to 20 years or more between two *cheerus*. This long interval between two *cheerus* is also caused by the huge expenditure incurred in celebrating this event. The prime ceremony is the collection of specific bones, i.e., clavicle, of the dead from the graveyard. The clavicle of the person who had died first after the last *cheeru* is collected first. A decorated funeral car known as *gudikettu* is constructed with a sacred chamber called *gubbe* at the bottom. The collected bones are kept inside the *gubbe* till the end of *cheeru*. The funeral rites are accompanied by funeral song, dance and music, feast and blood sacrifice.

At the end of the *cheeru* bones are taken to a sacred place known as *nikalumalai* or shadow-land, situated in the forest away from each Kurumba settlement, where the remains of the forefathers are kept. Then the bones are put inside a dolmen-like structure known among Kurumbas as *malikai* or *matinati*. A fitting farewell to the spirits is indispensable because the soul or *nikal* remains alive after death and it hovers around the hamlet to cause harm to the members of the entire hamlet. Hence it is essential to provide a permanent abode for the spirits.

Conclusion

Burial practices are significant archaeological sources for the analysis of past and present human societies. Thus knowledge of the living Megalithic tradition is helpful in unfolding the past history of early Iron Age communities. It would also enable us to trace out the antiquity of those communities who follow megalithism presently. In order to extract this information, tribal burials have to be excavated carefully and all the grave-goods accurately recorded so that a comparative investigation with tribal funerary ceremonies would be possible.

REFERENCES

Alekshin, V. A. (1983). Burial customs as an archaeological source. *Current Anthropology, 24,* 137-138.

Bondo, E. W. (1932). *Highlander*. London: Oxford University Press.

Grigson, W. (1950). *Maria gonds of bustar*. Oxford: Oxford University Press.

Hutton, J. H. (1992). The meaning and methods of erection of monoliths of Naga tribes. *Journal of Royal Anthropological Institute, 52,* 242-249.

John, K. J. (1975). Early man in Wynad. *Journal of Kerala Studies, II,* 125-131.

John, K. J. (1978). The megalithic culture of Kerala. In V. N. Misra, & P. Bellwood (Eds), *Recent advances in Indo-Pacific pre-history* (pp. 485-489). New Delhi: Oxford and IBH Publishing Co.

Kapp, D. B. (1985). The Kurumbas' relationship to the "megalithic" cult of Nilgiri hills (South India). *Anthropos, 80,* 493-534.

Krishna Iyer, L. A. (1939). The disposal of the dead among the primitive tribes of Travancore. *Man in India, XIX,* 61-62.

Krishna Iyer, L. A. (1948). *The pre-historic archaeology of Kerala.* Trivandrum: L.K. Balaratnam.

Krishna Iyer, L. A. (1967). *Kerala megaliths and their builders.* Madras: University of Madras.

Mawlong, C. (1990). Classification of Khasi megaliths: A critic. *Proceedings of Northeast India History Association,* Imphal, 9-14.

Murphy, R. F. (1989) *Cultural and social anthropology: An overture* (3rd ed.). Eagle Wood Cliffs, NJ: Prentice Hall.

Poyil, M. (2009). Farewell ritual and transmigrating souls: Secondary funeral of the Kurumbas of Attappadi. *The Anthropologist, 11,* 31-38.

Tylor, E. B. (1871). *Primitive culture, I.* London: John Murray.

21

Borderland Theory as a Conceptual Framework for Comparative Local US and Canadian History

Claire Parham

Siena College, Loudonville, New York, USA

My book *From Great Wilderness to Seaway Towns: A Comparative History of Cornwall, Ontario and Massena, New York, 1784-2001* compared the two towns at different historical moments from 1784 to 2001 by utilizing Oscar Martinez's borderland theory and argued that the shared experiences of Cornwall and Massena's residents based on their borderland locations lead them to follow comparable patterns of social and economic development. As former American colonists, both area residents wanted to develop towns identical to their former communities. The founders of Cornwall and Massena and their descendants, therefore, challenged national values and beliefs and developed a distinctive society and culture of their own. In contrast to Seymour Lipset who argued that the organizing principles made the two countries different, my research suggests that Louis Hartz was closer to the mark when he stated "the differences between the two countries are less significant than the traits common to both." To determine the how the lives of Massena and Cornwall residents' lives were affected by their border locations, I highlighted key events and experiences that caused these men and women to develop common values and beliefs and adhered to the methodology of local historians.

Keywords: Canada; US Local

When I began researching the history of Massena, New York and Cornwall, Ontario in 1996 as a possible dissertation topic, I searched not only for historical documents, but also a methodology and theoretical framework to analyze the economic, political, and social values of these two border towns. The only literature that existed at that time either concerned the lives of residents on the US/Mexican border or the contrasting national values of the United States and Canada. I, therefore, like many local historians, came up with my own model and approach to evaluate the history of Massena and Cornwall. In "A Manifesto: The Defense and Illustration of Local History," Paul Leuilliot stated, "Sometimes for lack of a model, the local historian must invent a method of approach… For local history this method may differ from the method appropriate for general history—for the simple reason that a history of a sector must develop its own original hypothesis for discovery and inquiry" (Leuillot, 1977: p. 14). By using Oscar Martinez's borderlands milieu theory and local history techniques as a methodological and research framework, I compiled my own interpretation of the relationship and differences between the residents of these two border towns.

Canadian and American scholars' research comparing and contrasting the values, experiences, and beliefs of residents of these two nations has tended to reflect two broad schools of thought. Seymour Lipset laid the groundwork for the first hypothesis, known as the value-orientation theory in his 1963 paper, "The Value Patterns of Democracy: A Case Study in Comparative View." Recently, in *Continental Divide: The Values and Institutions of the United States and Canada*, he surmised his 30-year sociological analysis of the cultural and institutional differences between Canada and the United States. Lipset made specific assertions about how the establishment of businesses, personal relationships, governments, and churches by Canadians and Americans reflected their opposing economic, social, and religious values. Since the American Revolution, all sectors of Canadian and American society have diverged because of the countries' contrasting organizing principles. Canadians are more class aware, law-abiding, elitist, and collectively oriented, while Americans pride themselves on living in an egalitarian, classless society, and thrive on individualism and personal achievement. Even with the increasing melding of the economies and popular culture of Canada and the United States since World War II, fundamental developmental differences guarantee that the two nations will never be economically, socially, or politically identical (Lipset, 1990: pp. 120-122).

Many scholars questioned the relevance of Lipset's value-orientation approach in explaining cultural changes in the United States and Canada after World War II. In 1973 Irving Horowitz challenged the contemporary merits of Lipset's theory based on the growing economic and cultural similarities between the United States and Canada. In his essay, "The Hemispheric Connection: A Critique and Corrective to the Entrepreneurial Thesis of Development with Special Emphasis on the Canadian Case," he argued that the behavioral and value differences between the United States and Canada were not historically linked to the nations' conflicting revolutionary ideologies, as Lipset suggested, but were instead based on a lag between the two countries' social development. Once Canada completed its social and economic evolution, Horowitz stated, the country would become more like the United States and less like Great Britain. This transformation began following World War II, as the increasing level of crime, education, and religious participation in Canada narrowed the cultural gap between the United States and Canada. Horowitz, therefore, concluded that "Lipset's thinking is premised on a continuation of pre-World War II tendencies rather than post World War II trends" (Horowitz, 1973: p. 346).

In the last fifteen years, numerous books have surfaced in which scholars compare the United States and Canada on a national level. Firstly, *Fire and Ice: The United States, Canada, and the Myth of Converging Values'* author Michael Adams pointed out how Canadians and Americans are not getting more like each other, but instead are diverging in many important ways. Jason Kaufman who penned *The Origins of Canadian and American Political Differences* critiqued the public and political policy of the United States and Canada from colonialism to the present day by framing his argument around five specific differences between American and Canadian development: economic; collectivism, social services, and voter alignment; comparative federalism; individual and civil rights; and identity politics. Finally, David M. Thomas and Barbara Boyle Torrey's five-section edited collection *Canada and The United States: Differences that Count* allowed various authors to comment on the values, politics, beliefs, and social policies of each nations' leaders and citizens.

A second group of scholars offered a glimpse into the lives of border residents in the American and Canadian Pacific region. Led by Wallace Stegner's *Wolf Willow*, a poignant reflection of growing up on the Montana/Saskatchewan border at the turn of the twentieth century, researchers in this new vein analyzed various aspects of life in borderland regions. Sterling Evans divided his contributors' essays, *The Borderlands of the American and Canadian Wests: Essays on Regional History of the Forty-Ninth Parallel*, into five sections addressing regional definition, colonization of borderlands, agricultural economies and labor markets, and environmental issues. While both groups of comparative historians studied local and regional experiences, a void still exists in terms of the lives of residents in the North American Atlantic border region over an extended period of time.

In *Border People: Life and Society in the US-Mexico Borderlands*, Oscar Martinez outlined a set of criteria to evaluate the uniqueness of border town life and used oral interviews to prove his theory. His most useful tool for US and Canadian historians was his argument that inhabitants of border towns function in an environment called the "borderlands milieu". These circumstances are defined as "unique forces, processes, and characteristics that set borderlands apart from interior zones" (Martinez, 1994: p. 10). According to Martinez, residents of border towns face the constant threat of foreign invasion, deal with heterogeneous populations, interact with foreigners, and feel separated or isolated from their countrymen.

Martinez also offered three models of borderland's interaction: alienated, coexistent, interdependent, and integrated. He ascertained that the settlers of interdependent borderlands experience circumstances making their lives stand out from the national norm. Borderlanders witness a flow of money and people that created opportunity to establish social relationships across the border. This fluid relationship also fostered fear among men and women of outsiders because of their continued exposure to people of varying ethnic background. Due to their remote location, farmers, shopkeepers, and religious leaders acquired a sense of otherness and thought of themselves as different from people in interior regions. In the case of US/Canadian border, according to Martinez, several Hollywood films portrayed the border as a place that offered escape, a second chance, an opportunity to forget, and safety and comfort for those in need. Politically, town leaders have often seen laws as being made by distant, insensitive, and excessively nationalistic politicians. The sparse number of residents and voters and remoteness from centers of power limit their political clout often resulted in the proposals of their leaders for social and economic improvements being frequently ignored by decision makers. Finally, borderlanders differed from residents of their national heartland because of their exposure to foreign economies, increased employment opportunities, and consumer choices unavailable to those in heartland (Martinez, 1994: pp. 23 & 25).

My book *From Great Wilderness to Seaway Towns: A Comparative History of Cornwall, Ontario and Massena, New York, 1784-2001* compared the two towns at different historical moments from 1784 to 2001 by utilizing Oscar Martinez's borderland theory and argued that the shared experiences of Cornwall and Massena's residents based on their borderland locations lead them to follow comparable patterns of social and economic development. As former American colonists, both area residents wanted to develop towns identical to their former communities. The founders of Cornwall and Massena and their descendants, therefore, challenged national values and beliefs and developed a distinctive society and culture of their own. In contrast to Seymour Lipset who argued that the organizing principles made the two countries different, my research suggested that Louis Hartz was closer to the mark when he stated "the differences between the two countries are less significant than the traits common to both" (Hartz, 1964: pp. 1-48).

To determine how their border locations affected the lives of Massena and Cornwall residents' lives, I highlighted key events and experiences that caused these men and women to develop common values and beliefs and adhered to the methodology of local historians. In "A Manifesto: The Defense and Illustration of Local History" by Paul Leuilliot, he described the different techniques and elements of doing local history and chronicling the lives of common people. Firstly all of the research methods utilized by local historians are more flexible, more qualitative then quantitative, and many times experimental. Also, the researchers in this realm concern themselves with the invisible aspects of daily life impacting peoples' values and beliefs including age-old traditions and folklore. Local history overflows into the history of mentalities, of attitudes toward life, death, money, and innovation. Unlike most historians, whose work centers on colossal events and actions of leaders on a national scale, I specifically exposed the differences in terms of values, development, and social and economic experiences of borderland residents in juxtaposition with their countrymen in other regions. As Leuilliot concluded, my concerns and methodology differed from academic and national historians and included both primary and secondary sources. I exposed the differences between national and local values and experiences and showed why the heartland of the United States and Canada is different from the borderland (Leuillot, 1977: pp. 6-26).

In 2009, my book entitled *The St. Lawrence Seaway and Power Project: An Oral History of the Greatest Construction Show on Earth* expanded my analysis of the interplay between Cornwall and Massena residents with outsiders, the regional interdependence in terms of trade and social relationships, and the limited political clout of local leaders in terms of lobbying state and local officials for funding for social and infrastructure programs. As Martinez asserted, certain border regions experience a greater flow of economic and human resources across the border, greater trade and consumerism, and a sense of otherness from those in the interior sections that triggers fear of outsiders and a political inferiority complex. However, the lack of long-term social and economic impact of the St. Lawrence Seaway project on the area contradicted Martinez's argument that borderland areas thrived after World War II both socially and economically. Instead my research supported Paul Leuilliot's assertion that local areas serve as indicators of future national trends. Both Cornwall and Massena residents witnessed deindustrialization and a loss of population due to the movement of manufacturers south in search of cheaper labor and operating costs.

The Settlement of Cornwall and Massena

Cornwall, Ontario and Massena, New York are two towns separated by a narrow expanse of the St. Lawrence River on the northern New York/Canadian border. Besides being close geographical neighbors, settlers arrived in each locale in the closing decades of the eighteenth century. In 1784 no longer welcome in the former colonies United Empire Loyalists and their families relocated to Royal Township #2, later renamed Cornwall. Northeastern farmers migrated to Massena leaving family homesteads in New England and New York in search of cheap and abundant land on the newly opened frontier. As Martinez suggested, both area's founding families saw their new homes as places that offered a second chance and an opportunity to forget. Initially, both groups of settlers struggled to become economically self-sufficient and foster cultural and political institutions among a widespread and often transient population. Settlers' shared spiritual beliefs gave them the strength to endure the harsh frontier conditions and enhanced their relationships with their neighbors.

Cornwall and Massena's isolated borderland location encouraged these men and women to adopt contrasting religious values and beliefs to those in other regions of the United States and Canada. During the frontier days, in the absence of ministers, Cornwall and Massena inhabitants took charge of their spiritual lives by organizing congregations and recruiting new worshipers as a way to create social bonds between members of scattered and often transient populations. Many worshippers saw their faith as a way to deal with the harsh conditions and isolation of frontier living. Like the pioneers who settled the American West, the loyalists experienced starvation, financial uncertainty, and loneliness.

While many of the loyalists and their families practiced the more structured faiths of Presbyterianism, Anglicanism, and Roman Catholicism, recruiting full-time ministers and priests, proved difficult as many members of the British clergy viewed Canada as an unsettled frontier and its parishes as an undesirable assignment. Therefore, settlers started their own congregations and conducted their own services without the guidance of a minister. Lay readers not only presided over sporadic services,

but also performed weddings and funerals. The Presbyterians, the most prominent faith in the area from the early days of settlement and traditionally one of the most nationally organized religions, altered the deference of local worshippers to the authority of church leaders as it had in the former American colonies. While Cornwall Presbyterians still accepted the Book of Common Prayer and stressed ceremony and Christian discipline, parishioners retained their ability to excommunicate members and to ordain their own minister. In 1839, 961 residents attended services at St. John's Presbyterian Church (Upper Canada Return of Population and Assessment, Volume 1: p. 574).

Methodism appealed to many Cornwall residents based on its simple doctrines and organization and its evangelical traveling preachers. John Wesley, the faith's creator, stressed the role of the individual in seeking salvation and preached that perfection was available to those who desired it with the aid of the Holy Spirit. While a superintendent oversaw and defined the circuits that traveling preachers serviced, it was the weekly class meetings that were the foundation of Methodism. Occasional camp meetings, held by two or more ministers, also served as a source of group consciousness based on shared spiritual values. These planned gatherings made settlers feel less isolated and part of a community. Ministers preached about the central values and motivation of settlers' including self-sufficiency, social equality, and individualism. The conversion experience itself provided worshippers with a release from the anxiety and frustration associated with frontier life. By 1839, the number of Cornwall Methodists had risen to 160 (Upper Canada Return of Population and Assessment, Volume 1: p. 574).

The religious experience of Massena residents mirrored that of their Cornwall neighbors as they too organized congregational and voluntary associations. Between 1800 and 1840 Massena Congregationalists and Methodists met weekly for prayer services as traveling preachers only periodically visited. These loosely organized congregations served as the town's central social and cultural organizations. Congregationalists also periodically reaffirmed and strengthened their spirituality by observing days of fasting and humiliation and attending weekly prayer meetings. This faith offered Massena settlers some regularity in their lives, while still appealing to their desires to have a personal relationship with God. During early settlement, the Methodists were the only challengers for the souls of the Massena faithful. Beginning in 1805, circuit riders charged with preaching to worshippers in Malone, Ogdensburg, Potsdam, and Massena infrequently conducted services in private homes and schoolhouses (Prince, 1961: p. 1). Most riders successfully gained new followers because, unlike their Protestant counterparts, they ventured into the backwoods areas and preached to members of the rural community.

Political Organization

Politically, the founding fathers of Cornwall saw the laws and structures that distant leaders requested they implement as insensitive and nationally oriented. Regardless of the fact that the loyalists and Massena residents now lived on opposite sides of the border, both still harbored comparable political goals and values. These former soldiers and prominent farmers did not desire a strong paternalistic government and did not defer to authority. Cornwall residents, unlike their counterparts in the neighboring towns of Alexandria and Kingston, never developed hierarchical political structures. Instead, Cornwall settlers, similar to Massena residents, demanded a democratic, popularly elected government. Loyalists attempted to establish the same participatory government structure they had in their former home towns. Residents wanted town meetings and local courts administered by officials who concerned themselves solely with the financial and legal administration of the towns, and who did not interfere with individuals' rights. While Cornwall loyalists initially failed in their efforts to gain a democratic local government, their protests exhibited their desire for the same political system that their American neighbors implemented after the Revolution. Like other frontiersmen, they insisted on a degree of political autonomy which set them apart from other Canadians and angered provincial government officials.

The attempt to establish an organized governing structure in Cornwall exposed the differing political beliefs of the former military commanders and common citizens. National government officials first attempted to formalize the structure of town government by ordering settlers of the royal townships to hold town meetings in 1787. In Cornwall a conflict arose between former military leaders, and local activists, over who should conduct the meetings and be eligible for election as town delegates. When the gathering was held on July 12, 1787, local activists led by Patrick McNiff forced Samuel Anderson, the current town magistrate and a group of fellow officers to leave the proceedings by threatening their lives. The citizens who remained at the meeting elected 10 representatives, including McNiff. However, Anderson and the other regiment commanders challenged the election. In response to the controversy, dominion officials set aside the idea of locally appointed officials administering town affairs, and instead created a regional and national political structure that controlled town affairs from above (Senior, 1983: p. 62, Report of Ten Inhabitants..., and Ensign Francis McCarty Deposition).

Massena residents established a democratic government from the town's inception. In 1802 the New York State Legislature passed the original county charter empowering the residents of Massena to establish locally based legal and political structures. Judges of the court of common pleas and circuit court decided criminal and civil complaints, while town meetings administered by elected officials authorized the construction of roads, allotted funds for the poor, and dealt with other miscellaneous town matters. Early town officials included a supervisor, town clerk, assessor, overseer of the poor, commissioner of highways, and superintendent of schools. The first town meeting took place in Massena in 1803 at the home of Peter Tarbell. The locally elected Massena government concentrated on completing road projects and developing a social welfare system (Podgurski, Prince, & Peers, 1959: p. 5).

The Canal Era

For much of the nineteenth century, Massena and Cornwall politicians found their demands ignored by state and national officials concerning the development of waterpower along the St. Lawrence River, and therefore, took matters into their own hands. A debate raged over the practicality of constructing a canal for the purpose of converting the energy produced by the current of the St. Lawrence River into electricity for public and private use. Local citizens and politicians realized the economic opportunity offered by channeling this natural resource, but could not convince state officials of the validity of their proposal or garner the necessary private monies to bankroll the construction.

The members of the Upper Canada Parliament initially discussed the Cornwall canal project in 1816 because of the difficulties military commanders encountered transporting their troops and supplies up and down the St. Lawrence River during the War of 1812. In 1818 members of a provincially appointed commission studied the specific geographic and economic aspects of such an undertaking. Following lengthy parliamentary debates about the waterway's merit and substantial price tag, national officials authorized the Cornwall Canal project on February 13, 1833. A decade later, contractors completed the original 11 1/2-mile-long canal. Constructed between 1834 and 1843, the Cornwall Canal, the third in a series of nationally funded projects built along the St. Lawrence River between Montreal and Cornwall, improved inland water transport and expanded the country's hydro-generated power. However, soon after the conclusion of the project, the Canadian government's transportation minister realized that the water depth and width of the locks could not adequately accommodate the ships of the age and improvements continued for several decades (Pringle, 1934: p. 3; The Chronological History..., 1934: p. 1).

The first political defeat in the US came in 1833 when local Massena officials presented a petition to the New York State Legislature that described the power canal and its potential financial attributes. While the proposition peaked the interest of enough of the members to warrant a feasibility survey, the enormous expense of the undertaking, including the purchase of large amounts of privately owned land, the employment of large numbers of workers, costly machinery and materials, compounded with the lack of industries to purchase the power, caused the proposal to be tabled until 1897. Learning from past mistakes, Henry Warren, a local real estate magnate, garnered an impressive list of five foreign investors committed to funding the multi-million dollar construction and acquired the property rights to the necessary land, prior to making a presentation to the legislature. Among the original investors was Albon Man, a long-time annual visitor to Massena Springs, who wished to give something back to the community that had furnished him with so many memorable vacations over the years. With Man's help, Warren enlisted the financial backing of three of his friends, M. H. Flaherty, C. A. Kellogg and Charles Higgins—a situation that left the men in Albany with little choice but to approve the measure (Podgurski, Prince, & Peers, 1959: p. 7). Upon the project's completion, it had silenced its critics by convincing the Pittsburgh Reduction Company to build a plant in Massena and lease power from the newly formed St. Lawrence River Power Company.

The Arrival of Foreigners

Cornwall and Massena's locations near the canals forced residents to deal with foreigners sooner than their immediate neighbors. The Board of Works and private contractors employed more than 1000 Irish laborers on the Cornwall Canal between 1834 and 1842. Most laborers lived in shanty huts near the canal site and shopped at the company store. Poor living conditions and high unemployment rates led to violence. Historian J. F. Pringle notes, "Hundreds of men were employed on the various contracts and it was only natural that there should be a rough element that were constantly making trouble" (Pringle, 1934: p. 3; The Cornwall Canal, 1887: p. 1). Local inhabitants distrusted the Irish canal workers and expected them to abide by the law and adopt Canadian religious and social values. As Oscar Martinez indicates, "In the case of isolated villages, discord with other groups may arise out of fear and resentment triggered by encroachment from outsiders" (Martinez, 1994: p. 17).

When canal workers murdered deputy sheriff Ewen Stuart in 1834 and former lieutenant governor Albert French two years later, animosity arose between the Irish laborers and long-time Cornwall inhabitants, and exposed the latter's fear and lack of tolerance for immigrants. After canal workers repeatedly committed violent crimes, many residents considered the roads bordering the canal unsafe for travel and took alternate routes. In September 1835, Cornwall magistrates applied to Lieutenant Governor John Colbourne for military assistance in maintaining order and public safety until the project's completion. According to a *Cornwall Observer* editor, "After this sacrifice of one of our most respected townsmen, Sir John Colbourne cannot refuse two companies at least to guard our jail and maintain our laws" (Editorial, 1834: p. 1). In 1836, the troops arrived and remained stationed in Cornwall until 1843.

Lehigh Construction managers promised Massena town officials at the inception of construction in 1897 that the canal workers and their families brought to Massena to work on the waterway project would not negatively affect the surrounding community. As company officials strove to be self-sufficient in terms of housing and supplies, they constructed Camp Bogart on the north side of town consisting of a dining hall, kitchen, and several 20 by 50 feet buildings, each housing up to three workers and their families. As the project progressed, there was not enough room at Camp Bogart for the increasing number of workers, and many were forced to live in shacks or sand dugouts made of old boxes and lumber near the canal site. The cluster of primitive buildings, referred to as White City, was located on North Main Street, and extended from the town border to the canal site. According to local journalist, Anthony Romeo, "Life during the canal days was appalling. The Italian and Hungarian workers and their families spent subzero winter nights in tarpaper shacks with no running water" (Romeo, 1961: p. 2).

Town residents became increasingly worried about the surge in crimes committed by canal workers, much of which was reported in the local newspaper. Canal workers not only got into frequent skirmishes with each other, but also with the St. Regis Indians. This behavior reinforced Massena residents' aversion to foreigners. The Massena police chief did not hire additional constables as most job foremen preferred to personally deal with the indiscretions of their workers. However, several incidents described in the *Massena Observer* required the assistance of law enforcement personnel. Even though these violent acts were not directed at members of the general public as they had been in Cornwall, they aroused a great deal of fear and concern for public safety.

From Agriculture to Industry

Contrary to Martinez's argument that the isolation of border towns resulted in their economic underdevelopment and neglect prior to World War II, following the construction of power canals on the St. Lawrence and Grasse Rivers, Cornwall and Massena became major regional manufacturing centers. Wealthy Montreal entrepreneurs financed Cornwall's initial factories. More than a dozen manufacturing operations, including a paper mill and a men's clothing factory, joined these enterprises by the early twentieth century. Massena's first major manufacturing firm was an aluminum processing plant constructed by the Pittsburgh Reduction Company in 1903, later known as the Aluminum Company of America (Alcoa). The workers recruited by the owners of these large enterprises altered the population of Cornwall and Massena and increased the number of local residents employed in manufacturing.

In the second half of the nineteenth century, Cornwall's economy shifted away from agriculture to manufacturing as Canadian entrepreneurs gravitated toward favorable locations for factories near canals and dams. Manufacturers recognized the St. Lawrence canals as accessible transport routes for their raw materials and the accompanying dams as sources to power their waterwheels and produce electricity. Municipal bonussing program implemented by town officials additionally provided mill owners with start-up cash, tax incentives, and emergency loans. Andrew Hodge, a former mill operator and current town councilor, stated, "This municipal council duly recognizing the importance of manufacturing in this country… pledges to aid and assist all cotton, woolen and other similar factories which may be established within the municipality" (Senior, 1983: p. 227).

George Stephen became the first to set up a factory incorporated as the Cornwall Manufacturing Corporation along the Cornwall Canal in 1867. His primary investor, Sir Hugh Allan, served as a silent partner and Stephen served as vice president. The factory's looms driven by waterwheels allowed workers to produce Canadian tweed blankets and flannels for a national and international market. The facility included a dye house, storehouse, and tenant cottages for workers in addition to the main mill building. By 1887 Stephen employed 750 workers with an average monthly payroll of $18,000 (Parham, 2004: p. 35).

Following the success of Stephen's mill, Andrew and Robert Gault, Bennett Rosamond, a partner of Stephen's in Mississippi, Montreal businessmen Edward MacKay and Donald Smith, and Cornwall mill owner John Harvey, financed two other cotton plants. Similar to Stephen, the workers in each facility produced woolen goods for Montreal merchants to sell wholesale and retail. Each of the manufacturers solicited incentives and long-term tax exemptions from local officials. In 1903 the three mills' owners jointly employed 1463 workers, produced goods valued at $1,647,347, and paid $446,588 in wages (Senior, 1983: p. 233; Pringle, 1980: p. 294; Parham, 2004: p. 37).

John Barber and a group of Toronto investors also located a major paper mill in Cornwall because of the area's ample water-borne power. The Cornwall canal provided Barber with waterpower for his machinery and paper processing. The waterway also offered him a direct transportation route for his raw materials from northern Ontario and for his finished product to various ports, including Montreal. In 1882 Barber completed construction of a $141,674, 33-acre facility on the north end of the Cornwall canal. He also purchased $126,397 of the latest water-powered machinery and hired 100 employees. Surprisingly, Barber received no bonuses or incentives from the town. The operation of his paper machines around the clock on every day but Sunday reflected the success of his new operation (Pringle, 1980: p. 295; Harkness, 1946: p. 236; Senior, 1983: p. 234).

The most important social effect of industrialization on Cornwall was an increase and diversification of the population.

From 1870 to 1891 many French Canadians from surrounding towns and impoverished British subjects from overseas came to Montreal in search of employment. Unlike many areas of Canada during these decades where town officials battled a recession, Cornwall leaders welcomed three new mills, whose employment needs exceeded the local supply. With the poor conditions in the surrounding rural areas, French Canadians moved into town to fill these new factory jobs. By the turn of the century, 1105 individuals had immigrated to Cornwall, with 466 new residents arriving between 1881 and 1890. The town's total population increased from 5081 in 1871 to 6790 in 1891 (Census of Canada, 1871: Table 4, p. 274; Census of Canada, 1901: Table 17, p. 459; Census of Canada, 1941: Table 10, p. 113). As French Canadians spoke a different language from existing residents, they relied on each other for financial and spiritual support and security. In Cornwall the Quebecois became active members in the Catholic Church as a means of dealing with their new unfamiliar surroundings.

The abundance of inexpensive power created by the Massena canal caught the attention of the nation's largest aluminum processing company—Pittsburgh Reduction Company—later known as the Aluminum Company of America (Alcoa). Founded in Pittsburgh, Pennsylvania in 1888 under the watchful eye of Charles Martin Hall, the inventor of a low cost way of producing aluminum, and with the financial backing of a group of young entrepreneurs headed by Alfred Hunt, the company monopolized the national market within a few short years. For almost a decade, the Pittsburgh Reduction Company resisted expansion and concentrated on improving its Pittsburgh operation. But, the constant protesting of workers and the astronomical price of electricity encouraged the company to seek alternate manufacturing sites with more favorable conditions, first in Niagara Falls in 1895 and seven years later in Massena near the new power canal. The locale presented the company with two long sought luxuries—affordable electricity and a docile labor supply (Carr, 1952: p. 2).

Following a May 15, 1902 visit to Massena by company executives Arthur Davis, Charles Hall, and E. S. Fickes, Pittsburgh Reduction purchased 100 acres of land east of the canal. Two months later contractors began construction of a $1 million facility that included five 550-feet long production buildings, a storage yard, and company-owned railroad tracks. Alcoa officials also purchased the entire annual output of the newly finished powerhouse from the owners of the St. Lawrence Power Company. Davis, Hall, and Fickes expected their new Massena factory to eventually become Pittsburgh Reduction's main processing plant. At the inception of production on August 24, 1903, Pittsburgh Reduction's Massena managers hired 67 men to manufacture aluminum wire, cable, and cooking utensils (Massena Alcoan..., 1952: p. 7).

Within three years, company executives approved the construction of a new reduction facility and enlarged the original wire department, thereby doubling the factory's production capacity and increasing the number of workers to 581. Alcoa employees also deepened the Massena Canal, updated the generators and turbines in the powerhouse, and constructed another pot room, rolling mill, and a larger wire mill. By 1910, company managers employed 171 men and boys in the reduction division, 59 in the carbon plant, 140 in the fabricating plant, and 269 in the power division (Internal Alcoa Document).

The success of Alcoa encouraged the establishment of other manufacturing companies including a silk mill, insulating company, a macaroni factory, and a lingerie factory. These businesses provided jobs for the wives and daughters of aluminum workers and local female residents who wanted to supplement their family's income. Also the construction of Diamond Creamery in 1907, a cooperative producer of condensed milk financed by farmers and local investors, served as another source of employment outside of farming and aluminum production.

Massena's population and social life changed with the influx of foreigners to work at Alcoa. The town's population quadrupled and diversified with the arrival of European immigrants. These immigrants initially consisted of Italians and Jews from New York City, and later of recent arrivals from Eastern Europe, Central America, and Scandinavia who adhered to different cultures and religious traditions that taxed the patience of local residents and stressed the available housing market. The transformation that took place in the first half of the twentieth century pressured this small town to come to terms with its new identity as an industrial center and with the difficulties of dealing with a diverse population.

To combat local residents' uneasiness, Pittsburgh Reduction officials constructed separate housing for workers and managers in previously undeveloped areas of town. Throughout the next several decades, Alcoa officials also enrolled their immigrant workers in company-sponsored Americanization programs, in which instructors taught new families the English language and the basic elements of American history. On a municipal level town councilors approved funding for a larger police force and the construction of more schools to accommodate the increasing number of school-age children. However, the implementation of these initiatives did not erase the intolerance community members held for outsiders and their unfamiliar customs.

In addition to dictating where its workers' resided, Alcoa controlled other aspects of their lives as a preventative measure to guard against complaints about unruly behavior outside the factory walls. Doctors treated injured workers and the ailments of their immediate family in an on-site hospital in order to dispel the idea that immigrants had poor hygiene, lacked respect for medical care, and therefore, contributed to the ill health of the community and burdened local health care facilities. Company officials also organized bowling leagues and created a local baseball team that played matches against neighboring towns. Both measures gave members of the community and Alcoa workers a common social experience with the hopes of improving the tenuous personal relations. However, company executives underestimated the power of the long history of local biases and dislike for outsiders that dated back to the early encounters with the St. Regis Indians. It would take more than fancy housing and sports teams to overcome these heartfelt feelings.

A local reporter provided the first documented example of the misconceptions Massena residents harbored about immigrants in his account of a visit to 600 illegal Chinese immigrants detained at the county jail in 1901. Under the title, "Hundreds of Chinese: Yellow Tide Still Streams," the writer told of the deplorable conditions in the jail where the Chinese men were housed and described it as the "black hole of Calcutta", an obvious reference to the perception of the poor living conditions in India. He continued by expressing amazement at the jovial attitudes of the inmates and assumed that this behavior was based on the conditions at the jail being more favorable then those left behind in their homeland. In the remainder of his commentary, the writer repeatedly exhibited his ignorance of foreign cultures and his support of the popular opinion that Asians were naturally weak and childlike. The most memorable portion of the article detailed the attempts by local boys to teach the Chinese how to play American football. Throughout this example, the author compared the awkwardness of the physical movement of the Chinese in comparison to the skillfulness of the young Americans highlighting his narrowmindedness and intolerance for foreign cultures (Hundreds of Chinese..., 1901: p. 6).

The Seaway Politicians

Politically both towns' leaders continued to be ignored in the twentieth century by state lawmakers in their quest to improve their regional economies and future prospects with the construction of the St. Lawrence Seaway and Power project. Based on the remoteness of the area and the sparse number of voters, in order for their voices to be heard, their campaigns lasted decades and finally achieved their goals when national security matters added a global component to their demands. Without the effort of these individuals, the Seaway would have slipped off the national radar without being constructed. Most Cornwall and Massena politicians believed the future economic survival of the region hinged on the completion of the St. Lawrence Seaway project. Aaron Horovitz, Lionel Chevrier, Thomas Bushnell, and Dr. Rollin Newton all recognized the potential of the cheap water power and transportation for attracting new businesses. They spent their lives pressing for the passage of Seaway legislation by Canadian and US national officials. Without the perseverance of these men, the project never would have come to fruition.

Aaron Horovitz was the most influential and longest serving twentieth century Cornwall politician. Horovitz, a native of Romania, established the Prince Clothing Company along with his brother Louis in 1911. In 1930 Horovitz became the mayor of Cornwall and the first Jewish leader of a Canadian town. Between 1930 and 1956 Horovitz occupied the mayor's office for 18 years, the longest tenure in Cornwall history. His expertise as a business owner helped him settle the labor disputes and worker housing problems of the 1930s, handle the earthquake devastation of 1944, and convinced him of the importance of the Seaway project for the survival of current manufacturers and the future economic development of Cornwall (Horovitz to Seek Reelection, 1956: p. 2).

Horovitz spent his final years as an elected official promoting the economic benefits of the St. Lawrence Seaway project to local business leaders and politicians. In a speech to the Cornwall Board of Trade in May 1954, he described how the completion of the power and transport elements of the Seaway would boost the local economy and job market. Horovitz emphasized the reluctance of many business owners to locate plants in Cornwall without the passage of national legislation to fund the Seaway. He indicated that many company executives had decided to construct operations in other towns due to cheaper electricity and transportation. A positive outcome for ongoing negotiations depended upon the Seaway project approval. The completion of the waterway would cause manufacturers to flock to Cornwall and provide long-term employment for area residents. Horovitz ended his speech by stating "we are close to a transition period in Cornwall, and planning for the future is essential" (Horovitz, 1954).

Lionel Chevrier earned the title as one of the most well-known national leaders from Cornwall in the twentieth century. He was hailed by the press and the people of Cornwall in the 1950s as "Mr. Seaway" due to his efforts from 1930 to 1953 to convince Canadian and American officials to pass the St. Lawrence Seaway legislation. Chevrier was born in Cornwall in 1903, the son of Joseph Chevrier and the former Melvina DeRepentigny, both French Canadian Catholics. His parents came to Cornwall on their honeymoon and moved to the area in 1890 because of the promising business opportunities. By the time Lionel was born, his father, Joseph, owned a thriving grocery business and later became a Centre Ward councilor and Cornwall's first French Canadian mayor (Good, 1987: p. 15).

Chevrier followed in his father's footsteps in terms of politics and inherited his father's dream of constructing the Seaway. Lionel attended the Centre Ward Separate School and the Cornwall Collegiate Institute before enrolling at the University of Ottawa in 1917. Following graduation he attended a seminary for a year and then went to law school at Osgoode Hall. Lionel was admitted to the bar in 1928 and set up a practice with George Stiles, a well-known Cornwall lawyer, and Howard Hessell, a former classmate. Upon his return to his native town, he became a member of the Board of Trade and was appointed secretary of that organization from 1931 to 1934. In that position he prepared and presented an in-depth study regarding all the ramifications and possible local effects of the proposed St. Lawrence Seaway project. A summary of the information Chevrier uncovered was released to the public and he made numerous speeches to civic organizations. His report put the Seaway back on the national political agenda in the US and Canada. According to biographer Mabel Tinkiss Good, this research project on the Seaway and his connection with the board brought Chevrier into the national spotlight and led him into an unplanned political career. When the liberal party leadership sought a spirited and well-spoken political candidate for one of Ontario's parliamentary seats in 1935, Chevrier fit the bill (Good, 1987: p. 51).

In 1935 Chevrier won a seat in Parliament for the Liberal party. He began a three-decade-long undefeated political career highlighted by his constant efforts to promote the Seaway. In May 1943 Chevrier was appointed assistant to the Minister of Munitions and Supply, C. D. Howe, in the MacKenzie King government. Two years later, King appointed him Minister of Transport offering him the perfect opportunity to promote the Seaway project at home and abroad. By January 1953, Chevrier and other leaders, including Prime Minister Laurent recognized that American interest in the waterway and power project had dwindled and determined that Canadian contractors should complete the project exclusively on the Canadian side. Months later, President Harry S. Truman and the US Congress passed the Wiley-Dondero bill and the project was undertaken jointly. In 1954 Chevrier assumed the post of president of the St. Lawrence Seaway Authority, a position he held for three years (Good, 1987: pp. 53-56).

During the Great Depression and times of global conflict, the leaders of Massena also kept the vision of the Seaway alive as state and national leaders paid more attention to social programs and the war effort. All of the leaders of Massena prior to the construction of the St. Lawrence Seaway spoke of the project as the key to the area's future economic success. Their lifelong commitment, public campaigning, lettering writing, and speech making led national leaders to approve the St. Lawrence

Seaway bill.

Thomas Bushnell had a long local political career, but his dedication to the Seaway project caught the eye of state officials almost garnering him a coveted trustee position in the newly formed New York State Power Authority in 1943. He was born in 1889 in Palmyra, New York, a town between Rochester and Syracuse, the son of a Civil War veteran.

Bushnell lost his first mayoral race to W. Gilbert Hawes by three votes in 1929. Bushnell defeated Hawes two years later by a margin of 1312 to 1037. In 1933 Bushnell was challenged by Ira Dishaw, but won the contest 1364 to 1062. Two years earlier he was considered by local Democrats and Republicans as a strong contender for one of the trustee positions with the New York State Power Authority. Although he was not appointed to the board by Governor William Harriman, Bushnell remained a strong proponent of the Seaway and for a time became the project's unofficial spokesmen. As mayor he had traveled with other area politicians and business leaders to the Hotel Franklin in Malone to encourage Warren Thayer, a state senator from Chateaugay, to cast his vote in favor of the Power Authority bill. Bushnell also presented a speech at a meeting of the Great Lakes Association in Toronto in 1934 in which he expressed support for the Seaway project and its benefits for Massena. The following year he lost the mayoral race to Dr. Rollin Newton (Prince, 1967: p. 5).

Dr. Rollin Newton was the most important leader in Massena in first half of twentieth century. He was a major supporter of the Seaway project, a champion of infrastructure improvements, including better roads and sewers, and the benefactor of the town's first hospital. Newton was born in Stockholm, New York in 1872. He attended Brasher and Stockholm High School and graduated from Potsdam Normal School in 1896. Prior to entering the University of Buffalo Dentistry College, Newton studied law under Judge Preston in Parishville and taught at his alma mater. Upon completion of dental school, he operated practices in Troy and Parishville, New York before assuming the patients of Dr. C. S. Ober in Massena in 1900. While Newton arrived in Massena by train, his father brought his dental equipment by sleigh. He opened his first office in the Russell business block, but moved his practice several times over the next five decades (Prince, 1967: p. 5).

Like Bushnell, Newton became convinced of the imminent federal approval of the Seaway and power project and made it his life's mission to keep the project in the national spotlight as well as garner support from other local residents. His most rudimentary method of spreading the gospel of the Seaway was to explain the social and economic promise for the area during and after the construction of the various facilities to any captive audience including many of his dental patients undergoing lengthy procedures. In an article in the *Massena Observer*, publisher Leonard Prince described his first teeth cleaning experience in 1928 and being apprised of the many reasons why the Seaway needed to be built and assured that the United States Congress would pass the project bill during its next session. Prince admits that while his hope waned as the years passed and no construction began, Massena natives led by Newton remained confident the Seaway would eventually be completed (Prince, 1967: p. 6).

After Newton conceded defeat to O. T. McGuiggan in 1945, he turned his attention full-time to convincing state and federal lawmakers of the urgency of passing the St. Lawrence Seaway legislation. As President of the Northern Federation Chamber of Commerce, he wrote to Senator George Aiken of Vermont, a long-time supporter of the Seaway, and attached a press statement sent to the *Rochester Times Union*, *Syracuse Post Standard*, and *Buffalo Evening News*. The opinion piece outlined the importance of developing the hydro-electric potential of the St. Lawrence River and challenged Seaway opponents to a public debate (Newton, 1945).

Contrary to most borderland residents, Horovitz, Chevrier, Bushnell, and Newton demanded the attention of state and federal policymakers and gained redemption for their efforts when the Seaway project commenced in 1954. The persistence of local leaders kept the Seaway in the spotlight. This group recognized the reluctance of state and national officials to provide funding for any economic or social programs that did not appeal to a national constituency and took it upon themselves to become the promoters of the economic future of the region. As Martinez indicated national politicians foster laws and policies that impact the masses and often neglecting isolated border areas. However, even with little political clout, Chevrier rose to a national leadership position and was able to gain passage of the Seaway and power dam project that for several decades fostered the economic prosperity of Cornwall, his hometown. Rather then sit back idly and criticize distant federal officials, each learned to work the system and the media to his advantage and gained prominence through hard work and perseverance.

The St. Lawrence Seaway and Power Project

The St. Lawrence Seaway and Power Project is often referred to as the "eighth wonder of the world." Covering 265 miles from Montreal, Quebec to the Great Lakes, the undertaking remains the largest jointly-built power production and waterway in the twentieth century. Twenty-two thousand workers labored on the simultaneously built, five sections of the project erecting dams and locks and dredging channels. On the Canadian side, engineers, property agents, and carpenters acquired and flooded 22,000 acres and seven villages, and moved 531 houses and 18 cemeteries. Operating engineers manned $75 million in equipment, while laborers poured six million cubic yards of concrete in all weather conditions (Parham, 2009). Dedicated contractors and their employees made financial and personal sacrifices to finish the job on time and on budget.

From 1954 to 1958, Massena and Cornwall residents witnessed an invasion of transient workers with different accents, religious beliefs, and social lives due to their towns' roles as the headquarters of the Seaway and Power Project. Prior to 1954, local politicians, church leaders, and school principals had dealt with issues related to the arrival of new residents with differing values and traditions during canal construction in the nineteenth century and the successive period of industrialization. Cornwall and Massena residents mutually disliked their towns being invaded by outsiders and even though Seaway and power dam workers and their families temporarily altered Cornwall and Massena's populations and social institutions, residents' clung to their regional identity. Historically, the residents of these two border towns had been exposed to outsiders from various regions of the country with different social and religious values sooner than their more homogeneous rural neighbors. But as in the past, residents would resist the cultural and social change and try to cling to their traditional values.

In August 1957 during the peak of construction on the US side PASNY contractors employed 6672, while Ontario Hydro contractors employed 6007 in June 1956. The maximum combined employment of 11,924 skilled and unskilled workers was recorded by Seaway officials in August 1957 (Parham, 2009). According to David Manley, a fifteen year old laborer on the project, "Some of the workers were local including some Indians from the reservation. Others came from Georgia, Alabama, Florida, and Virginia, particularly the engineers. Many worked in the spring and summer and returned home in the winter because of the cold" (D. Manley, personal communication, July 24, 2004).

On the Canadian side Bob Goodrich, the head of the employment office for Ontario Hydro, indicated that many of men constructing the Canadian side of the power dam had worked on the Niagara Falls project that had just been completed by Hydro. At that time, the agency had a core group of workers who moved from one power project to another. Other workers were from Cornwall or recruited through the Employment Service Office as demand warranted (B. Goodrich, personal communication, March 6, 2004).

John Dumas, the son of a *Watertown Daily Times* reporter, described the diversity of workers who came to live and work in his home town. "I am not sure there was any mold to build the construction workers that came here. They were all kind of different. We had one that stayed at our house as a matter of fact. We had a large four bedroom house in downtown Massena and used only three, so my grandmother rented a room to a construction worker. Our renter was a nice old southern man named, Seth. He told some great stories about going out in the woods of Kentucky or Louisiana and picking up a bear cub and trying to outrun Mama bear" (J. Dumas, personal communication, August 3, 2004).

College students comprised a large portion of the seasonal worker population in the US and Canada. During the summer months, they often filled laborers or machine operators' jobs. David Flewelling asserted, "In 1957 I was nineteen and I flunked of college. As part of a northeastern cooperative program I had spent previous summers making a dollar an hour as a labor foreman and chief laborer. In March of 1957 I hitchhiked from Pine River Junction to Massena, New York. The St. Lawrence Seaway was a big draw in those days because workers were in short supply and contractors were paying men high wages. I was hired the first week I was there by Perini as a draftsman on the Grasse River Lock doing rebar lift drawing. I was there from March until mid-July" (D. Flewelling, personal communication, November 30, 2004).

Besides diversifying the population of Massena and Cornwall, the Seaway workers and their wives established social relationships on both sides of the border allowing for a cultural transfer to take place through extensive border crossings and increased trade and consumer consumption. As Ambrose Andre, a concrete inspector for the Corps of Engineers explained, "I met my wife one Friday night at Picky's bar. She was a school teacher and was there with a friend. We chatted a little and to make a long story short, my friend and I picked them both up. The fellow I was with knew them both, so that helped. I took her home and made plans for a date a few nights later and we were married six months later" (A. Andre, personal communication, July 17, 2004).

Ray Singleton who worked on the American side as an operating engineer married a women from Cornwall exemplifying the cross border interaction highlighted by Martinez. "We went on strike in Massena and I spent a lot of time at the bars. That is when I met, Melba, the gal I married" (R. Singleton, personal communication, June 22, 2005). His wife Melba elaborated, "I would go over to Massena with four or five of my friends including my best friend Bessie, who had a little black car. We would drive over to dance and have a good time and go home. We were all in our late twenties and worked for Bell Telephone. A lot of people from Cornwall traveled to Massena and spent an evening over there. Cornwall didn't have places like that where you could go and dance and have a drink" (M. Singleton, personal communication, June 4, 2005). John Dumas explained, "At that point in time Cornwall's drinking age was 21 and ours was 18. Because of the lower drinking age, the Canadians were attracted over here by the droves" (J. Dumas, personal communication, August 3, 2004).

Seaway workers and their wives also enjoyed Massena's borderland location as it allowed greater access to shopping and personal services. Joyce Eastin, the wife of an Uhl, Hall and Rich engineer, reminisced, "I remember one time several of us went shopping in Cornwall. We would go and shop and stop and have lunch and come home particularly when the kids were in school" (J. Easton, personal communication, February 26, 2005). Her friend Ann Marmo added, "One of my favorite places to shop and get my hair done was across the river in Cornwall. I don't think I thought there were any good beauticians at the time in Massena. In those days the prices were much better in Canada than in the US especially on woolens goods, and clothing, so some of us would go over for the whole day and have some fun. We were different than the local women" (A. Marmo, personal communication, June 15, 2005).

Even the workers enjoyed the ability to cross the border to buy consumer goods. Jim Cotter explained, "We could go over to tailor shops in Canada and get tailor made clothing because subsequent to World War II Canadians encouraged skilled craftsmen from Europe to migrate to Canada and so there were things available over there that weren't available on the American side. They had some great hardware stores where you could find horseshoes that you couldn't find west of the Mississippi" (J. Cotter, personal communication, September 11, 2004).

The construction of the St. Lawrence Seaway was portrayed as an economic bonanza for Massena and the surrounding St. Lawrence County communities that bordered the St. Lawrence River. Numerous reports were published that marketed the area as a perfect location for manufacturing firms due to the availability of cheap electricity and the easy access to the Great Lakes and the Atlantic for transportation of finished goods. Plans were drawn up for the reconstruction of the town's roads and five schools were erected to accommodate the current and anticipated long-term increase in school aged children. However, once the bulldozers left town, the project had only enticed one new manufacturing operation, and the talk of economic grandeur fell by the wayside. The neighboring Canadian town of Cornwall, however, managed to take advantage of the opportunity and until recently was referred to as the southern capital of Ontario. The reason for Massena's lack of progress and failure to live up to the expectations of the Seaway planners has long been debated by local economic development officials. A main component of this stagnation can be credited to the area's historically ethnocentric mentality and its desire not to revisit its past social problems.

Conclusion

From the early days of settlement, the men and women of Cornwall and Massena created organizations that benefited and complemented their lifestyles in terms of government structures and houses of worship. Due to their isolated locations on their nation's periphery, these residents thought of themselves as different from people in the interior sections, causing a sense of otherness reflected in their development of similar economic, social, and political values and practices. They often saw laws as rules made by distant, insensitive and excessively nationalist politicians and often dealt with unruly residents and immigrant workers as they saw fit. The sparse number of voters and their distance from the center of power should have limited their political clout resulting in their demands for social and economic assistance and improvements being frequently ignored by decision makers. However, both area business men and politicians raised the money and garnered national approval for the construction of canals and eventually rallied for the construction of the St. Lawrence Seaway and power project. When national and state officials ignored these areas based on their isolated location, local leaders who had garnered political office based on their visions of the future forged ahead with their demands and kept them in the national spotlight even when their terms in office ended.

According to Martinez, towns like Massena and Cornwall should not have prospered or attracted manufacturing prior to the end of World War II. This however, is one of the main areas where the border towns in northeastern New York and southern Canada differed from those on the Mexican/US border. Their economic success in the nineteenth and early twentieth century occurred solely based on their geographical location that up until that point had been a disadvantage. The accessibility for manufacturers to cheap water power, navigable waterways, and non-union workers coupled with financial incentives from local government officials resulted in the industrialization of these two towns earlier than in other areas. Increasingly, the workers who manned the machines at these factories spoke different languages and harbored spiritual and cultural values and continued to diversify the population of Cornwall and Massena sooner than other regions. Crimes committed by these new arrivals often led to ethnic tension and social uneasiness that was played out on the front pages of the newspapers and in the criminal courts.

While the St. Lawrence Seaway and Power Project had been portrayed by economists and politicians as an economic bonanza, for the residents of Cornwall and Massena, it was another bout with an invasion of outsiders who threatened their quiet small town lives. At the beginning of the Seaway project in 1954, Cornwall and Massena residents still harbored a mutual dislike for men and women who held different spiritual beliefs or spoke a foreign language. Area inhabitants found the untamed lifestyle of Seaway workers to be unacceptable, and tried to curb their behavior with an increase in law enforcement and crime prevention initiatives. Local parish leaders also added extra Sunday services to accommodate workers' schedules. While Massena natives on the surface appeared more accepting of newcomers, they were happy to see them leave after the project's completion. With these workers came new cultures and religious traditions that taxed the patience of local residents.

The borderland location of Massena and Cornwall offered opportunities for greater consumer choices and transborder human relations for workers, their wives, and many single women during the St. Lawrence Seaway and Power Project. Many crossed the border to shop, dine, or meet a prospective mate. The geographical location of these two towns offered a unique experience for workers and their families, most of whom had labored on and lived near projects being constructed in the middle of nowhere. In this case, these temporary borderlanders established social and economic relationships across the border as had early settlers. These shared experiences fostered the development of similar beliefs and values that stood out from the national norm. As Jim Cotter, an engineer on the Seaway project concluded, "I've always felt that Massena residents due to their closeness to the Canadian border felt a greater attachment to Canada then they did to the United States" (J. Cotter, personal communication, September 11, 2004).

My research, therefore, offers a new interpretation of the life of residents on the US/Canadian border since the American Revolution. Like other borderlanders around the globe, Cornwall and Massena residents lived in a unique human environment and developed a set of values and beliefs that contrasted that of their compatriots in the heartland based on shared social and economic experiences. By exploring the lives of common people and being flexible with my analysis and source material, I uncovered a different perspective to existing US/Canada history that has an ideological, national or northwestern focus. Combining the techniques of local historians and the theory of Mexican/US border scholars, I have provided a framework for other scholars to expose the differences in values, economic progress, and social ethnocentrism of local border residents in the US and Canada from those in the heartland.

REFERENCES

Carr, C. C. (1952). *Alcoa: An american enterprise*. New York: Rinehart and Company.

Census of Canada (1871). Table 4. 274.

Census of Canada (1901). Table 17. 459.

Census of Canada (1941). Table 10. 113.

The Cornwall Canal (1887). *The Cornwall standard-freeholder*. 1.

Chevrier, L. (1954). Speech to Cornwall board of trade.

Chronological History of the Past Half Century (1934). *The Cornwall Standard-freeholder*. 1-10.

Editorial (1834). *Cornwall observer*. 1.

Ensign Francis McCarty Deposition, 12 January 1787.

Gates, C. (Ed.) (1894). *Our county and its people: A memorial of St. Lawrence County, New York*. Syracuse, NY: D. Mason and Company.

Guillet, E. (1933). *Pioneer days in upper Canada*. Toronto: University of Toronto Press.

Good, M. T. (1987). *Chevrier: Politician, statesmen, diplomat, and entrepreneur of the St. Lawrence seaway*. Stanke.

Harkness, J. G. (1946). *Stormont, dundas and glengarry: A history 1784-1945*. Oshawa: Mundy-Goodfellow Printing Company, Limited.

Hartz, L. (1964). *The founding of new societies*. Harcourt: Brace and World Inc.

Horovitz to Seek Reelection (1956). *Cornwall standard-freeholder*. 2.

Horowitz, I. (1973). The hemispheric connection: A critique and corrective to the entrepreneurial thesis of development with special emphasis on the Canadian case. *Queen's Quarterly*, 80.

Hundreds of Chinese: Yellow Tide Still Streams. (1901). *Massena Observer*, 6.

Leuillot, P. (1977). A manifesto: The defense and illustration of local history. In R. Forster and O. Ranum (Eds.), *Rural society in France* (pp. 14-26). John Hopkins University Press.

Lipset, S. (1990). *Continental divide: The values and institutions of the United States and Canada.* New York: Routledge, Chapman, and Hall.

Martinez, O. (1994). *Border people: Life and society in the US-Mexico borderland.* Tucson: University of Arizona Press.

Massena Alcoan 50th Anniversary Issue, June 1952.

Massena Manuscript Census, 1905-1925.

McInnis, E. (1982). *Canada: A political and social history.* Toronto: Holt, Rinehart, and Winston of Canada, Limited.

Naylor, R. T. (1975). *The history of Canadian business, 1867-1914, volume two, industrial development.* Toronto: James Lorimer and Company Publishers.

Newton, R. A. (1945). Correspondence to Senator George Aiken.

New York State Census, 1845, 1855 and 1875.

Parham, C. P. (2004). *From great wilderness to seaway towns: A comparative history of Cornwall, Ontario, and Massena, New York, 1784-2001.* Albany: SUNY Press.

Parham, C. P. (2009). *The St. Lawrence seaway and power project: An oral history of the greatest construction show on earth.* Syracuse: Syracuse University Press.

Park, J. H. (1990). *Internal Alcoa document from April 4, 1990.* Workforce History.

Podgurski, N., Prince, L., & Peers, R. (Eds.) (1894). *The Massena story.*

Prince, L. (1961). Circuit riders brought Methodism to Massena; meetings held in homes. *Massena Observer,* 1.

Pringle, J. F. (1980). *Lunenburgh or the old eastern district.* Belleville: Mika Publishing.

Report of Ten Inhabitants of Township #2 on Meeting of 12 January 1787.

Romeo, A. (1951). Our town. *Massena Observer,* 2.

Senior, E. K. (1983). *From royal township to industrial city: Cornwall 1784-1984.* Belleville: Mika Publishing.

The Cornwall Canal (1887). *Cornwall Observer,* 1.

Town Council Minutes (1878) 412-413.

Upper Canada Returns of Population and Assessment, Volume 1, 574.

22

Considerations on Mechanism Designs as Suitable for Cultural Heritage Evaluation

Marco Ceccarelli

LARM: laboratory of Robotics and Mechatronics, University of Cassino and South Latium, Cassino, Italy

Technological developments can be considered part of Cultural Heritage that deserves to be preserved for historical records and memories to a large public. Such a preservation can be also useful from technical viewpoints both to track past evolutions and to understand future trends. In this paper both designs and approaches for mechanism design are illustrated as worthy of being considered elements of Cultural Heritage with both above mentioned values mainly but not only for engineers. Examples of mechanism inventions and design algorithms both for whole machines and mechanism components are reported to show how technical achievements are and can be considered for Cultural Heritage in a broad sense and application, not only for technical use.

Keywords: History of MMS; History of Machines; Cultural Heritage; Past Mechanism Designs

Introduction

It is well understood that a memory of the past helps for a sure identity of subjects, communities, and persons. Such a good memory is today identified as Cultural Heritage mainly but not only for preservation of past developments and achievements in the broad sense of humanity experience (UNESCO, 2010).

In technical fields such an attention to memory of the past is addressed as History of Science and Technology, including History of Engineering in its specific expertise. History of MMS (in the past TMM) is the historiographical area dealing with history and evolution of MMS (Mechanism and Machine Science), and it is related to technical insights on Mechanism Science thanks to the activity of a community mainly referring to the IFToMM PC (Permanent Commission) for History of MMS (Koetsier, 2000).

Works on History of MMS with engineering viewpoints have been published in Proceedings of HMM Symposium series in the years 2000-2012, (Ceccarelli, 2000, 2004, Ceccarelli & Yang 2008, Koetsier & Ceccarelli, 2012) and in books of a series that has been recently started by Springer on History of MMS (available at http://www.springer.com/series/7481).

Even in the past, and since the beginning of a well-recognized discipline on TMM (Theory of Machines and Mechanisms) (now MMS) attention has been devoted to History of TMM to track and record technical past of MMS developments, like for example in (Chasles, 1837; Reuleaux, 1875; De Jonge, 1943; Dimarogonas, 1993; Ferguson, 1962; Hartenberg & Jacques Denavit, 1956; Nolle, 1974; Roth, 2000), just to cite few significant literature sources.

Only recently History of MMS is recognized with technical contents not only for memory purposes (to give credits to inventors and scientists, and to track evolution of engineering procedures and theories), but even for orienting future developments along well-identified directions of MMS development. But this approach cannot be yet recognized as a technical Cultural Heritage of MMS achievement, since this historical awareness is still restricted to a small well identified technical community and is not available to a wide public of the society for a general understanding and appreciation.

Tangible MMS products can be recognized in machines that have been built and operated successfully, but even unsuccessfully, in the past as a contribution to the evolution of Technology and Society at local and worldwide levels. Even plans, drawings, and patents are recognized as MMS products with value of Cultural Heritage and in fact, they are often stored and used in museums and exhibitions of History of Science and Technology. Intangible MMS products can be also considered as referring to acquired knowledge that has been expressed in theories, algorithms, and reasoning for design and operation of machines. In general, those intangible MMS products are difficult to be identified and stored when they have been not reported in specific reports or books on corresponding tangible MMS products. In addition, even when reported in written documents or books those intangible MMS products are not considered worth full of consideration for Cultural Heritage since their technical contents make very often difficult the understanding and fruition from non-expert public. Thus, the true contribution remains hidden or even forgotten in old books or manuscripts in libraries and personal archives.

---

*Corresponding author.

This paper is an attempt to address attention both to tangible and intangible products of MMS activities, but with a novel attention referring to a technical content that can be understandable even to a large public and can be useful to current professionals. Indeed, the paper is aimed at illustrating the values of tangible and intangible MMS products with few significant examples. The analysis of tangible MMS products as whole masterpieces or mechanism components is extrapolated in a similar approach to evaluate intangible MMS products such as conceptual designs, theories, and algorithms. Summarizing, this paper is an attempt in the direction of illustrating how History of MMS in its many different aspects but with technical contents can be interpreted and made available as part of Cultural Heritage for Humanity, both for memory preservation and future use of acquired knowledge in MMS expertise.

Cultural Heritage

The concept of Cultural Heritage has been developed starting for preservation of archaeological/monumental goods of great significance for history of humanity. In the last two decades interest on problems and aspects of Cultural Heritage has been broadened to a large variety of areas, but still as concerning with memories of Human Society evolution referring to Archaeological and Architectural Goods. The goals for Cultural Heritage are recognized today both in goods as material objects, like an artistic masterpiece, an architectonic building, or a monument, and in developments of immaterial achievements, like a language or dialect, a folkloristic celebration, or human attitudes. The main aim of Cultural Heritage is the preservation of those goods and developments for the future generation both for their memory and use, in the general area of History of Humanity.

In general, Cultural Heritage is defined as the legacy of products of human ingenuity in the form of physical artifacts and intangible attributes of a group or community that are inherited from past generations, maintained in the present and bestowed for the benefit of future generations, as indicated in (UNESCO, 2010).

Physical or tangible Cultural Heritage products are understood as buildings and historic places, monuments, artifacts, etc., that are considered worthy of preservation for the future. These include objects significant to the Archaeology, Architecture, Science or Technology of a specific culture. Nature aspects are also important parts of a culture, encompassing the territory and natural environment, including what is scientifically known as biodiversity. The significance of physical artifacts can be interpreted against the backdrop of socioeconomic, political, ethnic, religious and philosophical values of a particular group of people. Of course, intangible Cultural Heritage is more difficult to preserve than physical objects.

The heritage that survives from the past is often unique and irreplaceable, which places the responsibility of preservation on the current generation. In general small objects such as artworks and other cultural masterpieces are collected in museums and art galleries for fruition to a large public.

Rules and laws have been developed in a recent past in order to clarify the values of Heritage items and to establish criteria and procedures for identifying and assigning credits of cultural products. Significant is the Convention Concerning the Protection of World Cultural and Natural Heritage that was adopted by the General Conference of UNESCO in 1972 (UNESCO,

2010). Then, many other standards and agreements have been elaborated at national and international levels, but mainly within the frames of architectonic goods.

In extending the above concepts to technical areas and particularly to engineering fields of MMS, we may consider as tangible goods the machinery and their components together with their mechanical designs still functioning or not, and we may consider as intangible goods procedures and algorithms for designing and operating those machines.

But how to identify a machine or a development in MMS as a piece of Cultural Heritage? This is usually done for traditional heritage goods by using historical studies, but considerations are also used in the frames of aesthetics, anthropology, nature preservation, and other Humanity disciplines, even by looking at economic aspects and legal constraints. Thus, from historical viewpoint it is not difficult to identify a piece worth full of memory preservation, mainly from a far past. Activities for Cultural Heritage identification can be carried out with a very complex and multidisciplinary tasks. Motivations and evaluations always come from viewpoints dealing with historical considerations such as from History of Humanity, History of Art, History of Architecture, and so on. Similarly, machines and their theoretical backgrounds can be identified as piece of Cultural Heritage by using historical studies, technical interpretations, evaluations of their impacts on the Society developments and influences on Technology, by looking yet at economic aspects and social behavior that the affected.

Preservation and fruition of goods are important aspects for Cultural Heritage value but they are also challenging activities since usually they contrast to each other. In general, goods of Cultural Heritage are stored, shown, and used in museum frames with constraints of permitting visit to a large public with just a visual inspection. In addition, more and more is requested an interaction of a visitor/user with a piece of Cultural Heritage in order to let get direct experience of significance of a piece of Cultural Heritage at large. Machine designs and their theoretical backgrounds can be stored similarly in museums and exhibitions with their tangible product counterparts but requiring specific explanations for those technical characteristics of non fairly easy understanding.

MMS developments, both as tangible and intangible products, can be studied and evaluated to create frames that can be considered for Cultural Heritage as per the significance and contribution of Technology in evolving the Humanity. This paper is aimed at proposing how History of MMS can contribute to an expansion of Cultural Heritage to technical contents by considering machines together with the corresponding engineering knowledge.

Mechanism and Machine Science

The paper is focused on potential contributions of the specific area of Mechanism Design (MD) in Cultural Heritage of technical developments. MD is a part of Mechanical Engineering (ME), since MD can include several aspects of ME as indicated in the definitions of MMS and MD as reported in IFToMM terminology. MD is linked to the broader MMS area that includes all those aspects dealing with mechanisms. In fact, MD is a specific focus on structure and functionality of mechanisms as part of machines when they are designed and operated through the outputs from all those other engineering aspects. MMS is the wide area of disciplines in mechanical engineering that address attention to technological developments and engineering problems that are related to mechanical systems both in their theories and applications. A clear definition of MMS is given by IFToMM, the International Federation for the Promotion of MMS (www.IFToMM.org) as (Ionescu, 2003): "Branch of science, which deals with the theory and practice of the geometry, motion, dynamics and control of: machines, mechanisms and mechanism elements and systems thereof, together with their application in industry and other contexts, in biomechanics and the environment. Related processes, such as the conversion and transfer of energy and information, also pertain to this field".

Scholars and professionals working in MMS are devoted at several levels to the many aspects that are aimed at the innovation and application of machinery in all the fields of Technology and Science. In general, machines and mechanisms are identified with their scope of transmitting or elaborating energy into motion application for the purpose of a task. Thus, interest on historical evolution of MMS can be recognized for modern developments and trends in the mechanical aspects of functioning of any system. But today for an optimized functioning other aspects than mechanical ones are also considered fundamental for machine components, such as from electric, electronic, and software fields by leading to the modern concept of Mechatronics. Thus, even disciplines from other engineering areas are now involved in MMS activities with a vision of integration of systems of different nature. Therefore, the character of science for MMS is recognized as an evolution from TMM (Theory of Machines and Mechanisms) not only for the theoretical wide backgrounds that involve even other sciences like for example Physics and Mathematics, but even for the purpose of understanding those multi-disciplinary mechatronic systems that are the today machines. Within this science view of MMS it is considered fundamental also the knowledge and understanding in historical evolutions of machines and their theoretical backgrounds.

The communities working on MMS are aggregated in societies at local, national, and international levels even with different focuses both within academic and professional frames. In particular, the MMS community can be well characterized by indicating the main international bodies that are also linked to those national and local entities. They are IFToMM and ASME, American Society of Mechanical Engineering. Within their activities, through many divisions and committees on specific technical fields, they carry out activities for advanced formation, coordination of international research activities, editorial plans, and conference organizations to facilitate the circulation of achievements and discussion of novel problems. Other forum of discussion and achievement presentation for MMS areas are the several journals that are published at national and international frames as linked to those engineering societies or international publishers.

The History of MMS is addressed with a wide activity within the above-mentioned technical frames, but with the peculiar character of being attached to engineers' interest with engineering approaches mainly for understanding and future developments of past achievements. It is worth to mention the IFToMM Permanent Commission for History of MMS and ASME Committee for History and Heritage in Mechanical Engineering. With their activity they promote a consideration of the past in MMS mainly for technical scholars and professionals. Nevertheless, efforts are attempted to direct those ac-

tivities also to a large public, like for example with a IFToMM book series on history of MMS see http://www.springer.com/series/7481) and an ASME inventory of Landmarks (ASME, 1996).

History of MMS for Cultural Heritage

In **Figure 1** summary of main aspects that can contribute to an evaluation of a product in History of MMS as Cultural Heritage good is represented by stressing the multidisciplinary of such an evaluation with the above-mentioned considerations. The scheme has not the aim to be exhaustive and indeed a complementary view is needed as contributed by historians of Cultural Heritage. The concept and corresponding list of necessary steps in **Figure 1** are indicated to stress that the achievements in MMS can be treated as any other products of Cultural Heritage in Technology. Thus, this overview is thought convenient to show the feasibility of such a consideration and not to propose new procedures.

Evaluation and identification of a mechanism design for Cultural Heritage with characters in **Figure 1** can be outlined similarly to traditional Cultural Heritage procedures with the following steps:
- get general information, as a first screening activity of matter of interest in multidisciplinary contexts
- search for original documents and source of information, as regarding an investigation of historical sources with multidisciplinary views
- validate the documents and sources by means of a historiographical work, even with help of historians
- analyze the document for technical soundness as related to its time
- understand the technical influence and effects on technical developments of the time and subsequent periods
- consider the social impact in society developments
- evaluate other aspects for quoting the document as valuable as product of Cultural Heritage with fruition for a large public
- submit the document interpretation to the community for validating the value as product of Cultural Heritage.

The above procedure summarizes a complex activity that will require a multidisciplinary approach with cooperation of experts also in areas other than in Cultural Heritage. An existing approach can be considered that one that has brought and brings pieces of technical achievements in terms of built machines and textbooks in Science museums. But most of the time those exhibitions are aimed only at surprising visitors with past solutions, which have some modern appearance or content. Signifi-

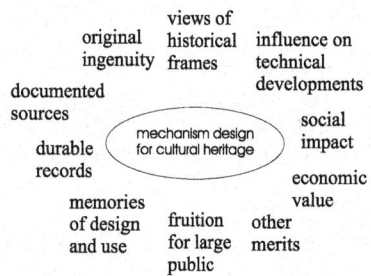

Figure 1.
Main aspects for evaluating mechanism designs as products for cultural heritage.

cant examples with aspects for large public fruition can be indicated in the Smithsonian Museum in Washington, British Museum in London, and Science Museum in Milan. The fails of MMS exhibits in the cited museums can be understood in the fact that those exhibits show just some products but they do not give the possibility to have an overview of their MMS characters with even the corresponding theoretical backgrounds. A complete fruition of a mechanism design as product for Cultural Heritage will require a more wide understanding and explanation both in a mechanical design and theoretical aspects. Since a preliminary stage of such awareness it would be convenient to convince technical experts and historians that even mechanism designs both in constructions and procedures, are worth full to be considered as product for Cultural Heritage in a broad sense and not only as a show of the past expertise.

Attempts in direction of building collections of mechanism designs are experienced in a recent past, but mainly in the form of products (models, books, machine scaled reconstructions) for museum exhibitions or just in archives but with a limited access to a large public. Significant examples can be indicated in the mechanism collections in Bauman Technical University in Moscow (Russia), Cornell University in Cornell (USA), Dresden Technical University (Germany), and Turin Technical University (Italy), just to cite few significant ones. The cited University collections are not available to a general public and they are mainly focused on technical issues. A very recent focused plan towards Cultural Heritage of mechanism designs can be considered in the European project "Thinkmotion" (7FP EU project: CIP-ICT-PSP.2009.2.3 for years 2010-2013), whose aim is to make the History of MMS available to a large public by means of a digital library through the Europeana webpage of the European Community.

A Short Outline of MMS Developments

Over the time changes of needs and task requirements in Society and Technology have required continuous evolution of mechanisms (the term is used as mechanical system) and their uses, with or without a rational technical consciousness. In past evolution, technical knowledge has made possible to propose more and more solutions enhancing mechanisms and their uses in order to satisfy demands with updated aspects for Technology and Society.

Mechanisms and machines have addressed attention since the beginning of Engineering Technology and they have been studied and designed with successful activity and specific results. But TMM (Theory of Machines and Mechanisms) has reached a maturity as independent discipline only in the 19-th century. Today we refer to TMM as MMS because of a more wide engineering area of interest and application of mechanism concept.

The historical developments of mechanisms and machines can be divided into periods with specific technical developments that, according to author's personal opinion, can be identified and characterized by referring to significant starting events such as:
- Utensils in Prehistory;
- Antiquity: 5-th cent. B.C. (Mechanos in Greek theatre plays);
- Middle Ages: 275 (sack of the School of Alexandria and destroy of Library and Academy);
- Early design of machines: 1420 (the book Zibaldone with designs by Filippo Brunelleschi);
- Early discipline of mechanisms: 1577 (the book Mechanicorum Liber by Guidobaldo Del Monte);
- Early Kinematics of mechanisms: 1706 (the book Traitè des Roulettes by Philippe De La Hire);
- Beginning of TMM: 1794 (Foundation of Ecole Polytechnique);
- Golden Age of TMM: 1841 (the book Principles of Mechanism by Robert Willis);
- World War Period: 1917 (the book Getriebelehre by Martin Gruebler);
- Modern TMM: 1959 (the journal paper Synthesis of Mechanisms by means of a Programmable Digital Computer by Ferdinand Freudenstein and Gabor N. Sandor);
- MMS Age: 2000 (re-denomination of TMM by IFToMM);

The historical evolution to the current MMS can be shortly outlined by looking at developments that occurred since the Renaissance. Mechanisms and machines were used and designed as means to achieve and improve solutions in other fields. Specific fields of mechanisms grew in results and awareness so that first personalities were recognized as brilliant experts, like for example Francesco Di Giorgio Martini and Leonardo Da Vinci among many others, as emphasized in (Ceccarelli, 2008). At the end of Renaissance Mechanics of Machinery addressed a great attention also in Academic world, starting from the first classes given by Galileo Galilei in 1593-98 (Ceccarelli, 2006). The designer figure evolved to a professional status with strong theoretical bases finalizing a long process only in 18-th century. In Renaissance prominent was the activity of closed small communities of pupils/co-workers after "maestros" and "maestros" (Ceccarelli, 2001, 2008). Academic activity increased basic knowledge for rational design and operation of mechanisms. First mathematizations were attempted and fundamentals on mechanism kinematics were proposed by first investigators, who were specifically dedicated to mechanism issues, like for example Philippe De la Hire among many others. The successful practice of mechanisms was fundamental for relevant developments in Industrial Revolution during which many practitioners and researchers implemented the evolving theoretical knowledge in practical applications and new powered machines. The 19-th century can be considered the Golden Age of TMM since relevant novelties were proposed both in theoretical and practical fields. Mechanisms were the core of any machinery and any technological advance. A community of professionals was identified and specific academic formation was established worldwide. TMM gained an important role in the development of Technology and Society. Several personalities expressed the fecundity of the field with their activity, like for example Franz Reuleaux among many others. The first half of 20-th century saw the prominence of TMM in mechanical (industrial) engineering but with more and more integration with other technologies. A great evolution was experienced when with the advent of Electronics, it was possible to handle contemporaneously several motors in multi-d.o.f. applications of mechanisms and to operate 3D tasks with spatial mechanisms. The increase of performance (not only in terms of speed and accuracy) required more sophisticated and accurate calculations that have been possible with the advent of Informatics means (computers and programming strategies). Technically, MMS can be seen as an evolution of TMM as having a broad content and view of a Science, including new disciplines, even with multidiscipline contents.

Systems, inventions, theories, algorithms, applications and general technical events are part of this evolution that can be considered forming Cultural Heritage of MMS developments. Those achievements have been developed by a community and in particular by individuals, whose efforts and activities are also interesting and indeed worth full of consideration for Cultural Heritage value, as pointed out with technical emphasis in the book series, and particularly in its Volumes 1 and 7, in which biographical notes are combined with memories and modern interpretation of those achievements.

Examples of Theories and Algorithms

Intangible goods for a Cultural Heritage of MMS can be considered intellectual activities and results such as for example theories, algorithms for analysis and synthesis, formulation of design criteria and performance indices, machine operation strategies, modeling of structures, kinematic concepts.

Although the above intangible products can be stored in publications that can be themselves tangible goods, those products of MMS achievements in terms of acquired knowledge require specific attention for preservation both in understanding and interpreting original value for the future, also for a suitable fruition by a large public.

In the following, few examples of those MMS heritage products are reported with a short discussion both to show samples from different historical periods and to illustrate peculiarities of their evaluations as well as their values for Cultural Heritage with the above-mentioned aspects.

In **Figure 2** a page of handwritten treatise by Francesco di Giorgio in (Galluzzi, 1991) is shown as a record of an early classification of machines referring to pumping systems. Likewise the case of disk records of songs, the product itself is a piece of Cultural Heritage (as in fact it is considered as a very valuable document in a science museum). But its great value for Cultural Heritage can be better recognized in the conceptual achievement of considering different mechanical designs of machines as referring to a unique topology, even with a very early concept of kinematic inversion (as in the middle right figure) in which an inverted crank-slider mechanism can be identified. This is an example of early theoretical works that can be appreciated without formulation but with relevant MMS achievements that deserve preservation and consideration in future generations.

Figure 3 shows schemes by Guidobaldo Del Monte in his book (Del Monte, 1577) as very early kinematic models to study the motion capability of basic machines. They can be considered fundamental in tracking the historical evolution of abstraction of machine structures and operation that has a fundamental role in computational engineering both for design and operation of systems.

Another example is the notation proposed by Charles Babbage in 1826 for mechanism catalogue (Babbage, 1826). This notation was not considered efficient in his time and it was very quickly forgotten. But the attempt is well recorded and even mentioned in other proposals for a language of mechanism catalogue (Ceccarelli, 2000). This can motivate the need of preservation of its formulation and logics as an intermediary step of the evolution to a successful modelling that is used today. There are many of those classifications that are based on logics and rules that can be understood as intangible products that deserve to be preserved in their original state, although

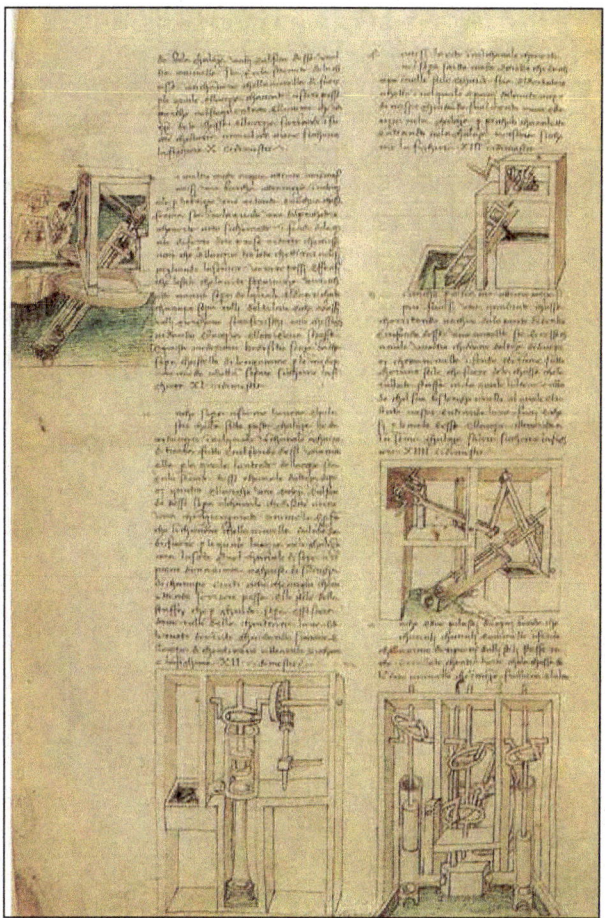

Figure 2.
Hand written manual for pumping systems by Francesco Di Giorgio (1439-1501).

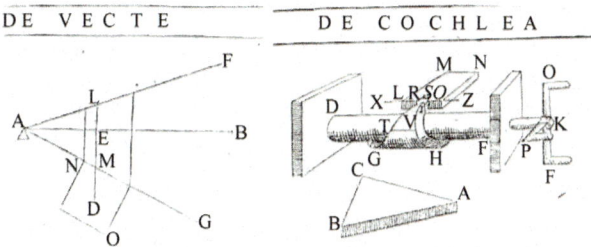

Figure 3.
Schemes of basic elementary machines/mechanisms as studied by Guidobaldo Del Monte in 1577.

nowadays they are not anymore used. This is a specific chapter of the history of MMS and its consideration will require specific attention and new evaluation as concerning a value for Cultural Heritage.

An example is illustrated in **Figure 4**, (Allievi, 1895), in which planar mechanisms are classified by using theoretical properties in tracing special loci in coupler curves as defined and understood by using kinematic properties and formulation. In such an evaluation significant are not only kinematic concepts but even aspects of mathematics and mechanical engineering at the same time. It is a heritage product since it is even representative of a reasoning that was under development at the

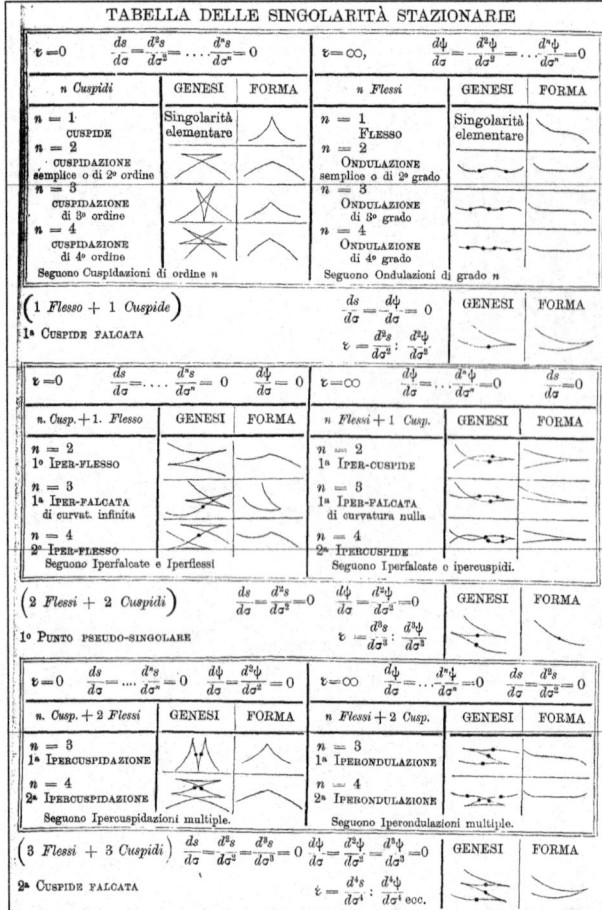

Figure 4.
A classification of coupler curves by Lorenzo Allievi published in (1895).

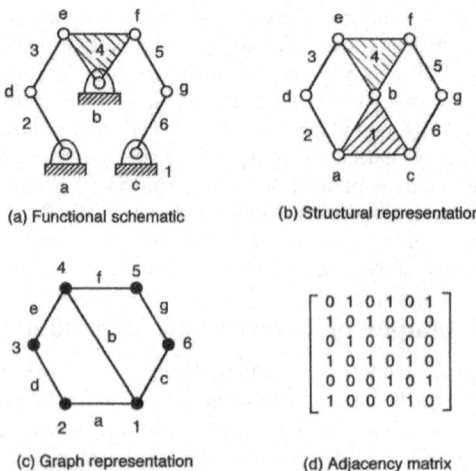

Figure 5.
A mathematization of mechanism models by using graphs by Tsai L.W. in 2001.

end of 19-th century.

Similarly, in modern time it is significant the encyclopaedic classification by Artobolevski (1975-1980), also for the social implication and general influence in more large area than only research and mechanical engineering. In this case the work can be understood as a tool for facilitating the understanding of machines and mechanisms even to a public with only basic knowledge on mechanisms since the classification is worked out with an illustration-based approach. The rich approach and the exhaustive collection can be considered itself a masterpiece for preservation of mechanisms in current practice, but in the history of mechanism design.

Figure 5 is an example that even very modern achievements of theories and algorithms can be considered suitable for preservation. This is the case of the modeling and formulation in terms of a mathematics-oriented output for development of expert systems as applied to mechanism design in (Tsai, 2001).

Other examples of theories and algorithms that deserve consideration as products for Cultural Heritage can be considered the graphical techniques that the advent of Informatics and computer calculations have made obsolete, although they are still of great interest from conceptual viewpoints. Those techniques are outlined and indeed stored in several publications during the 19-th century but a unique frame is not yet available and indeed sometimes differences are given from one author to

another.

Other theories can be considered as those that brought to modern mathematizations and computer-oriented algorithms, whose background is often underestimated, like for example first developments of Screw Theory or algebraic approaches for mechanism analysis and synthesis. Emblematic is the case of the deduction of the sixth order formula for the coupler curve of a four-bar linkage that in modern texts is not even mentioned. Another past algorithm with modern yet interest is the analysis procedure through vector polygons, that was developed in 19-th century.

The above examples can give both samples of what could be considered intangible products of Cultural Heritage from MMS achievements but also they show the problems and peculiarities for identifying them and indeed what and how preserving their heritage values. The abstraction and even formulation behind and after acquired knowledge are what can be considered valuable aspects for Cultural Heritage. But they are complex and difficult to store with those contents of Cultural Heritage that are so far considered for the traditional heritage from mankind developments, mainly with aspects for fruition by large public that makes significant a preservation.

Main difficulty with preservation of theories and algorithms can be understood in providing suitable fruition frames for a large public so that they can fully understand and appreciate such heritage products. Up to now only expert historians with a significant technical background can fully appreciate and indeed use those past algorithms and procedures so that easily they are lost.

Examples of Inventions and Mechanisms

Similarly but with somehow more easy understanding it is possible to indicate and identify examples of tangible products of MMS that can be considered for Cultural Heritage. They are systems with their designs and operations whose remains can have a direct interpretation of historical value and significance in society developments with a fairly easy understanding.

Thus, prototypes of successful past machines, even from a recent past like those in **Figure 6** can be successfully identified as goods that indicate developments of the MMS both in terms

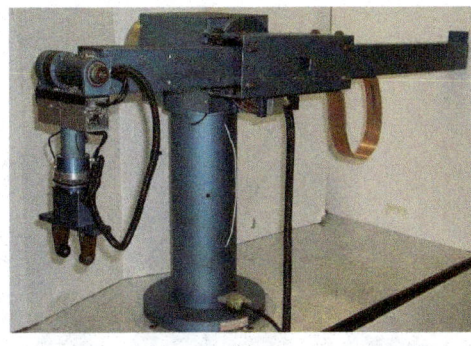

(a)

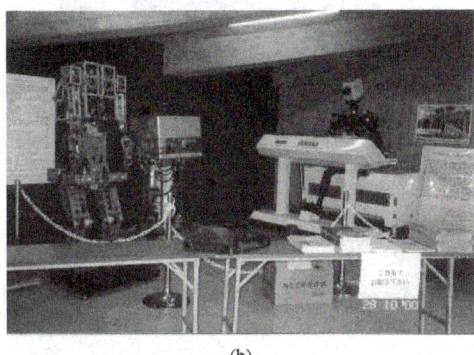

(b)

Figure 6.
Examples of system prototypes valuable as products of Cultural Heritage from robotics: (a) An early prototype of Stanford arm as stored for archiving purposes at the all of Compute Science School in Stanford University (USA); (b) Early robots from 1970' to 1980' at a show corner in Waseda University in Tokyo (Japan).

of knowledge and enhancement of quality of life. For example, the History of Robotics with a wide understanding, as indicated for example in (Ceccarelli, 2001), is full of products that have been naturally preserved by users and appreciated in general by a large public so that they are still sources of considerations for history, preservation, but also for further developments and thinking in mankind enhancements. The prototypes in **Figure 6** are fundamental achievements in mechanism designs for robots and they have been preserved since the beginning of Robotics as a memory of the efforts in developing them but also to show those achievements to a large public (indeed engineering students) with a first approach of Cultural Heritage in engineering fields. Those examples are indicative that mainly in technological and engineering achievements the past is not strongly related to the time and valuable past achievements can be recognized in their historical value when they have stimulated changes and improvements in mankind developments, as today we experience with accelerated rapidity. However, the examples in **Figure 6** are much more than only pieces of products, since they are the results of knowledge achievements with conceptual contents as well.

But not only big achievements with impressive shows are worth full of preservation in Cultural Heritage of MMS. In fact, even those achievements that have contributed, even considerably, but with a slow but incisive influence on the progress are worth full to be considered. Emblematic examples are the machines and mechanisms that have been developed during the Renaissance to give new impulse to society development. They

are already recognized of historical value but not in a full sense of Cultural Heritage since most of the time they are preserved for showing just the past skills in engineering and technology. In **Figures 7** to **11** examples of different machines from different periods are illustrated as from such exhibitions with no other goals. In **Figure 7(a)** the machine significance is even reproduced in an architectonic decoration of an important building of the time. In **Figure 7(b)** a wheelchair mechanism is shown as a complementary furniture of a aristocratic palace. This is a case in which a mechanism design has been fundamental for the quality of life but somehow not recognized as a technical achievements, likewise only in the last decades new medical devices are considered of priority interest since the growth of elder population.

In **Figure 8** examples are shown in terms of vehicles that are stored as decoration both in technical environments of Univer-

(a)

(b)

Figure 7.
Exhibitions in palace museums: (a) A 16-th cent. basso-relief as decoration of Urbino Palace celebrating machine design with gears; (b) A 19-th cent. Wheelchair with suspension mechanisms and steering back wheel at Chigi Palace in Ariccia (Rome).

(a)

(b)

Figure 8.
Exhibition of machines of the past: (a) A steam machine for road construction in the campus of school of engineering in Las Palmas (Spain); (b) Steam powered locomotive from late 19-the century in a garden square in Brescia (Italy) with details of the force transmitting Stephenson mechanism.

(a)   (b)

Figure 9.
A iron production plant preserved as Science Museums in Mexico: (a) overall view of the structures; (b) a show of a mechanism for a large gripper.

Figure 10.
A power plant of 1910's as art museum in Rome.

Figure 11.
An exhibition of a collection of ancient Chinese lock mechanisms at Tainan University (Taiwan).

sities and also in city frames. Sometimes, like the case in **Figure 8(b)** some emphasis, even through colored repainting, is

given to the past complex mechanisms that were used in those vehicles. It is also remarkable that the size of machinery is not today a limitation in such a preservation, as it is the case in **Figure 9** where a successful attempt of a Cultural Heritage preservation is achieved by using a large industrial plant as a museum that is dedicated to the corresponding technology in order to illustrate also the social life during its working times. The potentiality of industrial plants for Cultural Heritage sites can be also demonstrated by the cases in which they are used as museum frames not only for the specific technical areas they represent, but even as stimulating space for museum exhibition of arts, like for example the case in Rome where a plant of the 1910's with diesel engines for energy production is used to host exhibition of Roman sculptures, **Figure 10**.

In **Figure 11** a museum room is shown as specifically dedicated to preservation of lock mechanisms within a frame illustrating historical evolution and variety of solutions. This show room is a very peculiar case since it has been established thanks to the interest and efforts of Prof. Hong-Sen Yan, but mainly as due to his curiosity and passion in those specific mechanisms of the past. Several other collections of mechanism designs exist with a similar motivation and they are indeed hidden either in University frames with reduced availability for a public fruition or in museum frames with limited estimation and explanation of influence in the cultural development of the society. An example of such university collections is illustrated in **Figure 12** in which wood models of mechanisms that were used for teaching purposes, are now just stored with no possibility of understanding and fruition.

Significance of past mechanism designs is also appreciated when reconstructions are proposed in order to fully study the design and operation of the achievements. In some cases reconstructions are even shown with the aim to make understandable the functioning of the past mechanism designs to a wide public, as in the examples of **Figure 13**. Those reconstructions can be still considered products of Cultural Heritage since they preserve and make available past machinery that had influence in the society evolution. However, for a full heritage evaluation, preservation should include also a procedure on how they have been originally designed and even the technology and process that made possible their operation at the time of their success.

Conclusion

Cultural Heritage has the aim to identify and preserve significant achievements of humanity developments in durable

Figure 12.
Wood mechanism models from early 1950' at the school of Engineering of La Sapienza University of Rome (Italy).

(a)

(b)

Figure 13.
A modern reconstruction of past mechanisms: (a) a module of Babbage mechanical calculator at Science museum Elder in Las Palmas (Spain); (b) a functioning reconstruction of ancient Chinese wind mill at a Taiwan University in 2008.

records and memories that can be useful to future generations, not depending on the fashion of the time. This paper is an attempt to present achievements from Mechanism and Machine Science, both in physical products and intangible knowledge, as worth fully being considered elements of Cultural Heritage for a wide public that can recognize ultimately the significance and contribution of MMS in humanity developments. The proposed examples are chosen to show both the wide range of time and place, and the variety of achievements in MMS as products of Cultural Heritage value. Each of these examples will need indeed a specific study and consequent evaluation as relevant product of Cultural Heritage. The purposes of those examples are also to show a continuity of those MMS achievements both in time and contents during the MMS history.

REFERENCES

Allievi, L. (1895). *Cinematica della biella piana.* Napoli: Regia Tipografia Francesco Giannini & Figli.

Artobolevsky, I. I. (1075). *Mechanisms in Modern Engineering* (Vol. 5). Moscow: Mir Publisher.

ASME Int. History and Heritage (1997) *Landmarks in Mechanical Engineering.* West Lafayette: Purdue University Press.

Babbage, C. (1826). On a method of expressing by signs the action of machinery. *Philosophical Transactions of the Royal Society, 116,*

250-265.

Ceccarelli, M. (1998). Mechanism Schemes in Teaching: A Historical Overview. *ASME Journal of Mechanical Design, 120,* 533-541.

Ceccarelli, M. (2000). Classifications of mechanisms over time. *International Symposium on History of Machines and Mechanisms—Proceedings of HMM.* Dordrecht: Kluwer Academic Publishers, 2000): 285-302.

Ceccarelli, M. (Ed.) (2000). *International Symposium on History of Machines and Mechanisms—Proceedings of HMM.* Dordrecht: Kluwer Academic Publishers.

Ceccarelli, M. (2001). A Historical Perspective of Robotics toward the Future. *Fuji International Journal of Robotics and Mechatronics, 13,* 299-313.

Ceccarelli, M. (Ed.) (2004). *International Symposium on History of Machines and Mechanisms—Proceedings of HMM.* Dordrecht: Kluwer Academic Publishers.

Ceccarelli, M. (2006). Early TMM in Le Mecaniche by Galileo Galilei in 1593. *IFToMM Journal Mechanism and Machine Theory, 41,* 1401-1406.

Ceccarelli, M. (2008). Renaissance of Machines in Italy: From Brunelleschi to Galilei through Francesco di Giorgio and Leonardo. *IFToMM Journal Mechanism and Machine Theory, 43,* 1530-1452.

Ceccarelli, M., & Yan, H.-S. (Eds.) (2008). *International Symposium on History of Machines and Mechanisms—Proceedings of HMM.* Dordrecht: Springer.

Del Monte, G. (1577). *Mechanicorum liber.* Pesaro.

Chasles, M. (1837). Apercu historique sur l'origin et le développement des méthodes en géométrie..., Mémoires couronnés par l'Académie de Bruxelles (Vol. 11, 2nd ed.). Paris.

De Jonge, A. E. R. (1943). A brief account of modern kinematics. *Transactions of the American Society of Mechanical Engineer, 65,* 663-683.

Dimarogonas, A. D. (1993). *The origins of the theory of machines and mechanisms, modern kinematics—Developments in the last forty years.* New York: Wiley, 3-18.

Ferguson, E. S. (1962). *Kinematics of mechanisms from the time of Watt.* Contributions from the Museum of History and Technology paper 27, Washington, 186-230.

Galluzzi, P. (Ed.) (1991). *Prima di Leonardo—Cultura delle macchine a Siena nel Rinascimento.* Milan: Electa.

Hartenberg, R. S., & Denavit, J. (1956). Men and Machines... an informal history. *Machine Design,* 75-82,101-109,84-93.

Koetsier, T. (2000). Mechanism and machine science: Its history and its identity. *International Symposium on History of Machines and Mechanisms—Proceedings of HMM.* Dordrecht: Kluwer Academic Publishers, 5-24.

Koetsier, T., & Ceccarelli, M. (Eds.) (2012). *Explorations in the History of Machiens and Mechanisms—Proceedings of HMM,* Dordrecht: Springer.

Ionescu, T. (Ed.) (2003). Standardization of Terminology. *IFToMM Journal Mechanism and Machine Theory, 38,* 7-10.

Nolle, H. (1974). Linkage coupler curve synthesis: A historical review —I and II. *IFToMM Journal Mechanism and Machine Theory, 9,* 147-168,325-348;

Reuleaux, F. (1875). *Theoretische Kinematic—Chapter 1.* Braunschweig.

Roth, B. (2000). The search for the fundamental principles of mechanism design. *International Symposium on History of Machines and Mechanisms—Proceedings of HMM.* Dordrecht: Kluwer Academic Publishers, 187-195.

Tsai, L.-W. (2001). *Mechanism design: Enumeration of Kinematic Structures according to Function.* Boca Raton: CRC Press.

UNESCO (2010). Cultural heritage. http://portal.unesco.org/culture/

23

Immigrants in the United States of America

Stacy Ragsdale

Department of Filology and Languages, UNED University, Madrid, Spain

Immigrant population has formed over many hundreds of years. Newcomers have arrived in large waves when jobs were plentiful and resources were unlimited; and immigration slowed during times of economic recession. Early immigrants were predominantly White Europeans that farmed the land and tried hard to find enough food to eat and a warm place to live. The Industrial Revolution brought new types of jobs which required communication and skills. Today there are 38.5 million immigrants living in the United States the majority of which are Latino. The job market has become very competitive for these new immigrants, so competitive in fact, that American residents are pressuring politicians to pass anti-immigration legislation thus making the immigration integration process very difficult. This article investigates the immigration movement in the United States and events that have molded the United States in which we live today.

Keywords: Immigration; Legislation; Education; History; Integration; Obstacles

A Nation of Immigrants Is Born

The Statue of Liberty has long symbolized the beginning of a new life for millions of immigrants fleeing poverty and hardship hoping to pursue happiness in the United States of America. It is the subject for Emma Lazarus' poem "The New Colossus".

"Not like the brazen giant of Greek fame, with conquering limbs astride from land to land; here at our sea-washed, sunset gates shall stand a mighty woman with a torch, whose flame is the imprisoned lightning, and her name Mother of Exiles. From her beacon-hand glows worldwide welcome; her mild eyes command the air-bridged harbor that twin cities frame. "Keep ancient lands, your storied pomp!" cries she with silent lips. "Give me your tired, your poor, Your huddled masses yearning to breathe free, the wretched refuse of your teeming shore. Send these, the homeless, tempest-tossed to me, I lift my lamp beside the golden door!" (Lazarus, 1968)

Lazarus' famous poem is engraved on a tablet cemented to the pedestal on which the Statue of Liberty stands. The Statue of Liberty was the first monument most immigrants saw upon their arrival and it seemed to welcome them to the United States.

Immigration to the United States can be detected as early as 15,000 BC and it still continues today. Throughout history there have been periods of massive immigration mixed with other periods in which immigration was strictly regulated and so the numbers dropped dramaticallyImmigration arrival to the US has generally come in what historians call "waves". The first major wave of immigration begins in the early 1800s and ends around 1890. After a lull in arrivals, the second important immigration wave comes in 1890 and lasts until the early 1920s.

The third massive immigration wave begins in the 1930s near the end of the Great Depression and continues until present day.

Newcomers have arrived in large waves when jobs were plentiful and resources were unlimited; and immigration has slowed during times of economic recession. Early immigrants were predominantly White Europeans that farmed the land and tried hard to find enough food to eat and a warm place to live. The Industrial Revolution brought new types of jobs that required communication and skills. In 2011, the Pew Hispanic Research Center estimated that there were 40.4 million immigrants living in the United States (Pew Hispanic Research Center, 2013) the majority of which were Latinos. The job market has become very competitive for these new immigrants. So competitive, in fact, that Americans are pressuring politicians to pass anti-immigration legislation thus making the immigration integration process very difficult.

Early Immigrants Put down Roots in Ethnic-Like Settlements

The first US settlers that arrived to the United States endured many hardships to make their dreams of a home in a new land a reality. The voyage to the US posed other obstacles to immigration. Passage was expensive and the journey could take from six weeks to six months. "Immigrants were packed into steerage. The usual height of the steerage deck was from 4 to 6 feet and the lower deck was hardly more than a black hole... No provisions were made for ventilation, the only fresh air came in through the hatches and these had to be closed during storms" (Wittke, 1993). Passengers were required to bring and cook their own food which could not stay fresh and immediately became mouldy and rotten. Diseases such as typhus, cholera, and smallpox were common on such a crowded and dirty journey. In his book, *A People's History of the United States*,

Howard Zinn publishes a contemporary account of one of these voyages:

> "On the 18th of May 1847, the "Urania", from Cork, with several hundred immigrants on board, a large proportion of them sick and dying of the ship fever, was put onto quarantine at Grosse Isle. This was the first of the plague-smitten ships from Ireland which that year sailed up the St. Lawrence. But were driven in by an easterly wind, and of that enormous number of vessels there was not a one free from the taint of malignant typhus, the offspring of famine and of the foul ship-hold... a tolerably quick passage occupied from 6 to 8 weeks... Who can imagine the horrors of even the shortest passage in an emigrant ship crowded beyond its utmost capacity of stowage with unhappy beings of all ages, with fever raging in their midst... the crew sullen or brutal from very desperation, or paralysed with the terror of the plague-the miserable passengers unable to help themselves or afford the last relief to each other, one-fourth, or one-third, or one-half of the entire number indifferent stages of the disease; many dying, some dead; the fatal poison intensified by the indescribable foulness of the air breathed and rebreathed by the gasping sufferers-the wails of children, the ravings of the delirious, the cries and groans of those in moral agony! ... there was no accommodation of any kind on the island... Hundreds were literally flung on the beach, left amid the mud and stones to crawl on the dry land how they could... May of these... Gasped out their last breath on that fatal shore, not able to drag themselves from the slime in which they lay..." (Zinn, 1995)

The hardships of immigration did not end with the journey over the sea. Once newcomers arrived they faced the challenging chore of setting up new homes in a foreign land. Jamestown established by the English in 1607, was located along the James River and has been reported as being "soggy and mosquito-plagued". Settlers at Jamestown had to build new homes, hunt or grow their own food. Many were not used to hard work and immediately became ill. Colonial immigrants felt homesick, as they would probably never see their families or country again. Many settlers packed up their belongings and tried to return home by ship. Lord Delaware who was a governor from London forced them to return to Jamestown and continue attending the mandatory church services. The Jamestown settlers endured many hardships, such as starvation, harsh winters, and hostility from the Powhatan Indians. In 1610, Jamestown settlers faced a very harsh winter that was later to be known as "the starving time". This period, characterized as a time with no food or water, drove settlers to eats rodents, cats, snakes, and even walking boots. "One settler later claimed that some residents had turned to cannibalism, and that one neighbour had killed, 'salted' and eaten his pregnant wife... By the end of that terrible season, more than half of Jamestown's settlers had perished" (Beschloss, 2009).

Immigrants that came before the 1800s established their own ethnic colonies in different parts of the US. The earliest settlers came mostly from Spain and France and founded the first U.S. cities: Pensacola (1559) and San Augustine (1565) by the Spaniards and Fort Caroline (1564) by the French. In the Rio Grande valley, Spaniards later founded Santa Fe in 1607-1608 and Albuquerque in 1706. Spaniards settled in New Mexico and Florida, and the French all along both sides of the Missis-

sippi river all the way North to Canada. Later, the English came and settled along the east coast in Virginia and Pennsylvania. The Dutch followed and settled in along the Hudson River in New York, while the Irish-Scots settled in western Pennsylvania and in the southern US Ethnic-like settlements in which inhabitants maintained their own cultural traditions and languages began to form throughout the New World (Wittke, 1939).

Some nationalities held tightly to their own ways and were reluctant to embrace a new culture and language; as a result, many Englishmen began to resent these new neighbors. In 1753, Benjamin Franklin wrote the following about the German Americans: "Few of their children in the country try to learn English. The signs in our streets have inscriptions in both languages... Unless the stream of their importation could be turned...they will soon outnumber us so that we will not preserve our language and even our government will become precarious" (Bush & Putnam, 2010). The large German population was beginning to make Franklin and other citizens fear that the US would become overwhelmingly German.

Germans were not the only immigrants that were feared and disliked, the Irish also faced discrimination when they began to immigrate in large numbers. In *A Power Governments Cannot Suppress*, author Howard Zinn describes "there was virulent anti-Irish sentiment in the 1840s and 1850s, especially after the failure of the potato crop in Ireland killed one million people and drove millions more abroad, most of them to the United States". "No Irish Need Apply", a phrase that often appeared in employment ads, symbolized the prejudice that existed against the Irish immigrants. Benjamin Franklin disliked the Irish, whom he called "a low and squalid class of people" (Zinn, 2007).

Even before the US was established as a country, coexistence between ethnic groups was not trouble-free. Germans were generally criticised for the way they clung to their native language. Irish and were numerous and some considered them lazy. The Dutch also felt the sting of criticism. Dr. Drew Hamilton found the Dutch "both old and young... and remarkably ugly... in their persons slovenly and dirty" (Hoobler, 2003). Early colonist had never encountered such ethnic diversity in their homeland and this adjustment was proving to be challenging.

The United States won its independence from the British in 1776 and elected George Washington as its first president. Washington welcomed immigration however he encouraged them not to come as "clannish groups but as individuals, prepared for intermixture with our people, then they would be assimilated to our customs, measures and laws: in a word, soon become one people". John Quincy Adams held similar views and called for new immigrants to "cast off the European skin, never to resume it" (Schlesinger, 1998). He encouraged looking forward to posterity instead of backwards toward ancestry. With the birth of a new country, government needed a way to govern and communicate with their new colonies and states; so they became motivated to educate colonists.

English Becomes the US Common Language

Although all of the US government business is conducted in English and many states have named English as their official language; the United States as a country has no declared official language. The United States were born on land discovered by the Spanish, inhabited by Native Americans, and later settled by English, Dutch, Germans; but the English language finally prevailed. Perhaps the reason lies in the fact that the early English settlers came here to stay and build a home, while other nationalities came for other purposes.

When Christopher Columbus discovered the New World, he and his men came looking for riches that would impress the King and Queen of Spain and would secure funding for future expeditions. The Columbus expedition came and returned but did not settle. Later, the French and Dutch came to the New World to make fortunes in trade before returning to their home country. Why was it that none of these languages installed itself in the New World? The first English colony in which the Pilgrims settled in 1619 was Jamestown. Settlers had not been able to worship freely in England so they came to the New World to practice religious freedom and create a community in which they could advance Christianity. The Puritan's bible was written in English; therefore in order to learn about religion, people needed to know English to understand about God. Learning English became a top priority for future generations so children could read the bible and worship. The first year in the New World, many Pilgrims died from lack of food, cold, and illness. Those who survived did so thanks to the Native Americans that helped the Pilgrims; one in particular named Squanto saved the Pilgrims and communicated with them in English. Squanto had been kidnapped years earlier by English sailors and taken to England. Due to the success of English colonies, the arrival of English immigrants increased. "By the end of the seventeenth century, English was being heard and taught along more than a thousand miles of the eastern coast" (Bragg, 2003).

Shortly after, in 1620, 102 passengers set sail on the Mayflower toward the new world. Forty one of them were Pilgrims that had left England in order to pursue a religious freedom. The rest of the passengers were indentured servants, craftsmen, women, and children that had obtained the right to settle on land claimed by the Virginia Company near the Hudson River. However, their voyage left them near Cape Cod, far north of their destination. Although they tried to sail south, sand bars made navigation difficult so the pilgrims decided to settle in Plymouth. Some passengers were unhappy with the new settlement and threatened to live as they pleased without reguard to their neighbors. As a result, colony leaders drafted the Mayflower Compact, a document pledging allegiance to England yet simultaneously establishing a form of self government that would ensure the general good of the colony. Thus another group of Englishmen settled on the east coast (Constitutional Rights Foundation, 2002).

By 1776, the use of English was spreading but other nationalities held on tightly to their native language. German was the principle language used around eastern Pennsylvania, as a matter of fact, "the first US Census reported 8.7 percent of American spoke it as their first language" (Gonzalez, 2000). There were over 30 newspapers published in German and early German bilingual education was established.

Some accounts tell a story that the colonist were prepared to adopt German as a common language and abandon English as a protest toward English colonial policy. On his Language Policy Web Site Emporium Archives (1997-2008), James Crawford, writer, lecturer, and formerly the Washington editor of *Education Week*, blogs about the legend of Frederick Muhlenburg. The Muhlenberg legend relates a story that the German language failed to become the official language of the United States because of Muhlenberg's one vote. Crawford believes that this legend derives from a similar vote related to publishing some of the federal laws in German while Muhlenberg was the Speaker of the US House of Representatives. "In 1795, the House defeated this proposal on a 42-41 vote, in which Muhlenberg may have stepped down from the Speaker's chair to break a tie. Existing records, however, make it impossible to ascertain what role, if any, the Speaker played. It is known that he was never fluent in German." (Crawford, 2013)

According to English journalist Bill Bryson, any allegation that there was a vote to install German as the official language is absolutely false. "The only known occasion on which German was ever an issue was in 1795 when the House of Representatives briefly considered a proposal to publish federal laws in German as well as in English as a convenience to recent immigrants, and that proposal was defeated. Indeed, as early as 1778, the Continental Congress decreed that messages to foreign emissaries be issued "in the language of the United States" (Bryson, 1994). In 1900, Germans continued to be one of the largest minorities living in the US until the post World War I era when the US began an Americanization policy.

In their investigation "Good Old Immigrants of Yesteryear Who Didn't Learn English: Germans in Wisconsin," Miranda E. Wilkerson and Joseph Salmons suggest that early immigrants did NOT immediately learn English upon their arrival as many believe. "The full range of evidence shows that into the twentieth century, many immigrants, their children, and sometimes their grandchildren remained functionally monolingual many decades after immigration into their communities had ceased. Qualitative data from the 1910 US Census, augmented by qualitative evidence from newspapers, court records, literary texts, and other sources, suggest that Germans of various socioeconomic backgrounds often lacked English language skills. German continued to be the primary language in numerous Wisconsin communities, and some second- and third-generation descendants of immigrants were still monolingual as adults" (Salmons & Wilkerson, 2008).

Furthermore Germans were not barred from certain types of jobs due to their monolingual status; "In Hustisford, Germantown, and Kiel, monolinguals worked in a variety of settings, not only as farmers and laborers, but as stonemasons, blacksmiths, cheese makers, tailors, and butchers, not to mention preachers, teachers, and foremen. In an urban setting such as Sheboygan, monolinguals were similarly widely distributed across occupations." (Salmons & Wilkerson, 2008)

Another way in which English was spread was by conquering or purchasing territories. Louisiana was a colony of France that became United States property through the Louisiana Purchase in 1803. This land acquisition more than doubled the size of the country. When Louisiana became a state in 1812, most of the residents spoke French so their public documents were written in French and their courts and schools operated in both French and English. The governor at that time, Jacques Villere did not speak a word of English. By 1840, Englishmen had settled in all parts of Louisiana and French had become a second language. English began to prevail as more English speakers settled there (Gonzalez, 2000). "It would be the French who would give the opening English needed to flood over North America (Bragg, 2003)." President Jefferson immediately had Captain Meriwether Lewis and William Clark to find a river that would facilitate trade to the west coast. The Gold Rush of

1849 would draw English-speaking colonists west.

When miners discovered gold in 1848 in California, millions crossed the United States in attempt to settle in California and find their fortune. This significant event redistributed the US population, and became known as the Gold Rush. "As news spread of the discovery, thousands of prospective gold miners traveled by sea or over land to San Francisco and the surrounding area; by the end of 1849, the non-native population of the California territory was some 100,000 (compared with the pre-1848 figure of less than 1,000). A total of $2 billion worth of precious metal was extracted from the area during the Gold Rush, which peaked in 1852" (History.com, 2013). The English language travelled west with many gold seekers

The transition from Spanish to English for Mexicans living on territories annexed by the US in the Treaty of Guadalupe Hidalgo took a much longer time. Most residents eventually learned English but kept Spanish and became bilingual. Similarly in 1898, the US occupied Puerto Rico and tried to impose English as one of the official languages. When Anglo administrators tried to impose English as the language of instruction, many students dropped out of school and the entire education system almost collapsed.

Negro slaves coming in were also forced to adopt English as their new language. They were processed through a receiving station called Sullivan's Island in Charleston, South Carolina. Half of the slaves that were taken from the West Indies were unloaded here. These immigrants came from West Africa where there were hundreds of local languages being spoken at that time. On the voyage to the New World, speakers of the same language were broken up in order to avoid mutinies and to keep slaves powerless. Many of these slaves began to use a form of "pidgin" English, a simplified form of speech with a limited vocabulary used for communication between people with different languages. This form of English would develop further as it came ashore; so many slaves arrived speaking a form of English. Slaves were not allowed to learn the written form of English so that their masters would have more control over them (Bragg, 2003).

Thus the English language came and spread throughout the United States as a common language. "In 1789, 90 percent of America's four million white inhabitants were of English descent" (Bryson, 1994). Before the American Revolution, colonist considered themselves Englishmen and did not want to break away from the motherland. It took long consideration and hot debate to convince all of the colonies to declare independence.

As we have seen, US immigrants from different parts of the world adopted the English as their language, but immigrants also left their mark on the English language. By the end of the sixteenth century, there were words from fifty different languages being used as "English" (Bragg, 1994). English was able to grow by incorporating such words as "rendezvous" (French), "pyjamas" (Hindustani), "alcohol" (Arabic), "cafeteria" (Spanish), "taekwondo" (Korean), and "breeze" (Portuguese). Newcomers brought their foods and spices such as goulash (Hungarian), ravioli (Italian), chilli (Mexican), and bratwurst (German); thus transforming British English into US English, the language of a melting pot.

Industrial Revolution Brings Changes

The colonial period ended and immigration continued its course through the Industrial Revolution. The invention of Fulton's steam engine made transatlantic travel speedier, however new obstacles awaited immigrants upon their arrival to the US. Newcomers now needed to pass inspections and exams in order to remain in the US. Early immigrants were received at the dock in New York. Their muscles and teeth were inspected to see if the immigrant could withstand hard work, later the inspection took place at Ellis Island. Once newcomers had passed inspection and were free to stay, they would likely encounter a "runner". New York was infested with runners, who were hired to take advantage of immigrants by leading them into hotels, boarding houses, or train stations. These establishments would in turn overcharge the immigrant for everything and take advantage of them.

In 1903, a new immigration record was set when 857,046 foreigners arrived in the United States. Ellis Island, an immigration station in New York Bay was built and many of these new immigrants passed through its doors. In the years before World War I, a new group of immigrants began to arrive from Asia. These newcomers settled primarily on the west coast. These immigrants were not processed at Ellis Island; they went through Angel Island immigration station in San Francisco. Based on the 1890 US Census, it is stated that 20% of the country's Chinese immigrants had settled in San Francisco, the main port of entry on the west coast at that time. San Francisco was the first US city to have a Chinatown, founded in 1850s (Yans-McLaughlin & Lightman, 1997). The graph (**Figure 1**) (Scholastic, 2010) details US immigration growth by decade.

Chinese settlers were not the only oriental immigrants arriving in the 1850s; the Japanese outnumbered the Chinese. More than 100,000 Japanese immigrated to the United States between 1900 and 1925. Unlike the Chinese, Japanese immigrants did not tend to settle in San Francisco or other West Coast cities during the late 19th and early 20th centuries. The majority of Japanese migrated to Hawaii, a US territory that had not yet become a state. As more immigrants arrived, the Japanese eventually replaced native Hawaiians as the most numerous group on the island chain.

Benjamin Franklin's concerns reappeared in the late 1800s because many native-born Americans, once again, feared that the great influx of immigrants might cause a loss of control over their country. In the 1860s, the Chinese were welcomed as cheap labour that would build our railroads. Later there was a job shortage and then Chinese were seen as a threat. In the early 1900s, both the Japanese and the Chinese encountered prejudice and even violent attacks. Angry native-born Americans began to demand legislation that restricted Chinese and Japanese immigration. *The Naturalization Act of* 1870 and *The Chinese Exclusion Act of* 1882 were passed in response to public opinion and aimed to curb immigration from China. A "gentlemen's agreement" was made in 1908 to end immigration from Japan. These laws radically cut Chinese immigration for the next 10 years and prohibited Chinese residents from becoming citizens (Hernández, 2007).

Congress passed *The Naturalization Act of* 1906. This Act required all immigrants to speak English in order to become nationalized citizens and languages other than English were to be discouraged. Up until this time, immigrants didn't really need to learn English beyond the conversational level because prior to the 1800s, they lived same ethnic communities and spoke their native tongue. Most immigrants were farmers or craftsmen and had little need for a new language. During the

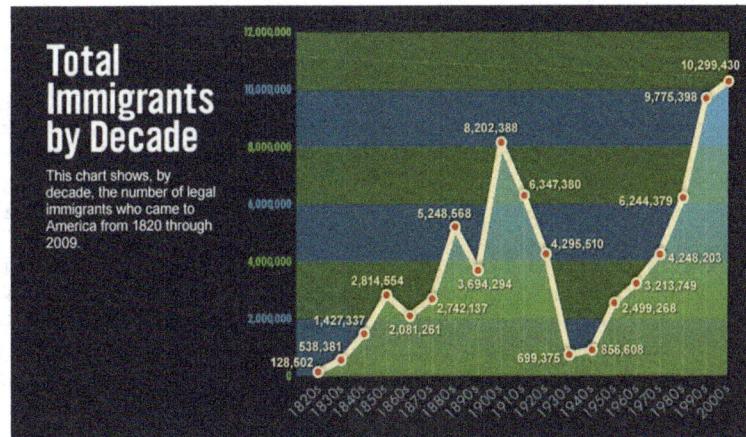

Figure 1.
Total Immigrants by Decade Source: teacher.scholastic.com.

industrial revolution, most immigrants worked in factories and were able to do their jobs with little or no English.

The Naturalization Act of 1906 was a clear message from the US government: learn the predominate language and adopt the white majority culture or go back home. Before passage of this law, newcomers had continued to settle in ethnic-like neighborhoods making it simple for them to interact in their own language and keep their culture alive. More importantly, the lack of English knowledge had never been a barrier to entering the job market. Most immigrants easily found jobs in factories even though they knew that these jobs were often underpaid and offered hazardous conditions. *The Naturalization Act of* 1906 was one of the factors that encouraged English language learning but it was not the only cause.

The Industrial Revolution slowly caused US industries to require workers that could learn new skills and communicate in English. In the 1800s many Chinese immigrants had jobs that required little English. They worked as miners, railroad construction workers, cooks, and laundrymen. By the 1900s English became an obstacle as they became entrepreneurs. Lack of English skills made merchants vulnerable to "unscrupulous suppliers, complaining customers and thieves" (Chang, 2003). Shop workers had to find non-verbal ways of communicating such as saving the last piece of merchandise and showing it to the supplier as a way of re-ordering more supplies. In public school, classes had been given in English since the 1800s. Chinese children also learned English by reading English-language newspapers, listening to the radio, watching movies and reading comic books.

In the early twentieth century Henry Ford revealed his concern about non native workers when he stated, "These men of many nations must be taught the American ways, the English language, and the right way to live" (Meyer, 1980). Ford had discovered that most of his employees did not speak English and communication problems forced Ford to spend a large amount of money on company interpreters. These issues resulted in the opening of The Ford School in 1914.

Ford Motor Company started an "Americanization" program to help new immigrants adapt to the mass production system. In order for employees to collect their full salary of 5 dollars a day, they had to live in a single family home and not in an apartment. As a result, many immigrants moved outside their ethnic neighbourhoods. Ford offered English classes to employees that

participated fully in this program. By the mid-1920s, most states had instituted English-only instructional policies in both private and public schools, which was essentially a form of submersion education for immigrant children.

Ford was not the only company to look for its own solutions for teaching immigrant workers English. In 1918, over one thousand immigrant US steel workers in Gary, Indiana were enrolled in "opportunity classes". The curriculum designed by Peter Roberts of the Young Men's Christian Association, YMCA, dealt with citizenship education. Robert's classes taught immigrants everyday words and phrases related to home and work, buying, selling, and travelling. Reading and Geography also formed part of the curriculum followed by "patriotic texts". "The final phase of the YMCS program prepared the worker for the naturalization exam." (Betten, 1976)

In the 1920s, anti-immigration sentiment became even more widespread. Nativists, those who favoured the interests of certain established inhabitants of an area or nation as compared to claims of newcomers or immigrants, lobbied vigorously for even more restrictions. Congressman Albert Johnson of Washington worried that because the county was letting in newcomers from countries that "did not embrace or even know democracy, our capacity to maintain our cherished institutions stood diluted by a stream of alien blood" (Hernandez, 2007). So Johnson proposed *The Emergency Quota Act of* 1921 and *The Immigration Act of* 1924, (Johnson-Reed Act) that set up a new quota system and restricted Italian, Jewish, Polish, and Asian immigration. As a result, only half a million immigrants were admitted into the United States during the 1930s, compared with the 4 million who had come during the 1920s.

Embracing Ethnic Diversity?

Because few jobs were available during the Great Depression, non-English speakers had no alternative but to take positions with unsafe working conditions, long hours, and 7-day-work weeks. Sometimes immigrants received low pay or none at all, but they were unable to defend themselves because they didn't speak English. Resentment toward immigrants in the workplace was common, especially when work was scarce and job competition was fierce. The Second World War would revive the US economy and bring more positions to the ailing US job market.

A surge in US nationalism overtook the country due to the war victory and people began to believe that nationalism was the glue that would bind the country together. Franklin D. Roosevelt said in 1943, "The principle on which this country was founded and by which it has always been governed is that Americanism is a matter of the mind and heart: Americanism is not and never was, a matter of race and ancestry. A good American is one who is loyal to our creed of liberty and democracy." (Schlesinger, 1998)

Another consequence of World War II was that "the United States began to recognize once again the importance of foreign languages, foreign language education, and cooperation with (as opposed to fear of) speakers of other languages which naturally led to a greater interest in ESL education. The US army was in need of bilingual soldiers for posts in Germany; however, few Americans spoke German. This was one of the factors that caused many linguists and educators in the 1950s to put a lot of effort into English as a Second Language, ESL, research and producing a variety of ESL teaching methods that are still used, at least in part, today" (Your Dictionary The History of ESL). The 1940s marked the beginning of an expansion for ESL programs.

If it seemed that the US was beginning to embrace the idea of ethnic diversity in the US during these post WWII years, President Johnson removed all doubts in 1965. On Sunday October 3, 1965, President Lyndon B. Johnson signed the Immigration and Nationality Act at the foot of the Statue of Liberty in New York Harbour. "Our beautiful America was built by a nation of strangers... from a hundred different places or more that have poured forth into an empty land, joining and blending in one mighty and irresistible tide" (Meacham, 2009). The bill that Lyndon signed on that day would transform the United States into a society of diverse cultures, religions, and ethnic groups. Immigration Nationality Act, INA, eliminated the quota by nationality system and gave preference to skilled workers and family of US residents.

The 1965 law marked the beginning of a massive wave of immigration to the US. Even though the Nationality Act of 1965 did not cause an immediate increase in population, most historians believe that the Immigration and Nationality Act of 1965 opened the doors to the third wave of immigration that is still in progress today. This wave began slowly and Latin American and Asian arrivals were twice as high as that of the Europeans marking a shift from a predominately European immigrant population to a Latino one.

Throughout the 80s, immigration continued to rise and more than 8 million new immigrants came that figure increased between 1991 and 2000 to 9.1 million. European immigration decreased to 705,000 in the eighties and then as a result of the fall of communism in the 1990s, 1.3 million Europeans came. Uncounted illegal immigrants add significantly to that total according to McLaughlin and Lightman. Later in an attempt to curb illegal immigration, the Immigration Reform and Control Act was passed in 1986. This act established sanctions against employers who hired illegal immigrants and offered amnesty for illegal immigrants requesting legal status. An agricultural guest program was set up for alien laborers.

By the 1990s, immigrants were coming mostly from Asia, South and Central America, according to Mei Ling Rein author of *Immigration and Illegal aliens: Burden or Blessing.* These immigrants were more likely to be women, around the age of 29, with a technical occupation such as a labourer, machine

operator or service occupation. Mexico was the county with the most immigrants (131,575) in 1998. Mexico was followed by China (36,884), India (36,482), Philippines (34,466) and the Dominican Republic (20,387). These immigrants wanted to live in a community where they felt comfortable, one that had lots of jobs, and hopefully had friends and family already living in that same community. Unfortunately 40% of new immigrants that came in 1998 only wanted to live in two states: California (25.8%) and New York (14.6%). Florida, Texas, New Jersey and Illinois were other popular destinations. The chart below (**Figure 2**) (US Census Bureau, 2004) illustrates data found in the U.S. Census Bureau Current Population survey of 2004.

Immigrants during these years were more likely to be poor. According to Rein, "in 1999 more than one third (36.3%) of foreign born full time, year round workers earned less than $20,000 compared to one fifth (21.3) of their native counter parts." In 2003, the majority of Latino immigrants earned between $25,000 and $39,999 each year while the majority of whites earned over $80,000. The wage gap between immigrants and whites was extremely wide (Rein, 2002).

In their book, *The Color of Wealth: The Story Behind the US Racial Wealth Divide*, Meizhu Lui and Barbara use home ownership data from 2003 to point out that all immigrant groups were not faring equally as well. Among white residents 75.4% owned a home while only 48.1% of African Americans and 46.7% of Latinos did so. Fifty six percent of Asian/Pacific Islanders owned homes and fifty four percent of Native Americans did as well. There was also a large variation in the values of the homes owned. According to data compiled by Barbara J. Robles, analysis or federal Bank survey of consumer finances, the mean White primary residence value was $141,769 in 2003, the Negro primary residence value was $45,476, and the Latino primary residence value was the lowest at $53,548 (Meizhu, Robles, Leondar-Wright, Brewer, & Adamson, 2006).

US Immigrants Today

Today's immigrants are different from early immigrants for several seasons. The early immigrant population was predominantly European; modern day immigrants come mostly from Latin America and Asia. Early immigrants were rural farmers; today the immigrants that arrive are urban workers. Early immigrants came to the United States to stay and had little possibility of returning home and there was little contact with their country of origin. Today's immigration allows for more back and forth movement between the country of origin and the US

White and Hispanic Income		
Yearly Earnings in 2003	Percentage of Whites	Percentage of Latinos
0 - $14,999	6.5%	16.48%
$15,000 - 24,999	9.35%	18.26%
$25,000 - 39,999	15.50%	22.60%
$40,000 - 59,999	18.71%	17.90%
$60,000 - 79,999	15.81%	11.07%
$80,000	34.13%	13.67%

Figure 2.
White and Hispanic income in 2003; Source: US Census Bureau Current Population survey 2004, Table FINC-03, p. 13.

Also advanced technology allows immigrants to stay in touch with their homeland.

Perhaps the most important transformation has occurred within the US itself; the US has shifted from an agricultural based economy then to an industrial economy and finally to an information-based economy, therefore, today's immigrant is experiencing a lack of low-skilled jobs. The following table (**Figure 3**), based on Passel and Cohn's Pew Hispanic Research Center report (Passel & Cohn, 2012), illustrates the make-up of the US immigrant population in 2009 and 2010.

Many of the factory and farm jobs that were available to early immigrants, have moved to other countries and the US job market is now a difficult place for unskilled workers. The US economy has shifted from agriculture, to industry, then services, and finally information. As Steve Denning at Forbes magazine explains, "In 1900, it took a large portion of the US population to produce enough food for the country as a whole. With better farming practices, fewer people were needed. At the beginning of the 1930s, more than a fifth of all Americans still worked on farms. A much smaller percentage was actually needed. Today, 2 percent of Americans produce more food than we can consume. The Great Depression, was about finding jobs for all those who were no longer needed on farms." (Denning, 2012).

As a result of these economic changes, the number of unskilled jobs available has decreased. A college degree, excellent English skills and job training are now necessary to succeed. According to authors Katharine Davies Samway and Denise McKeon:

"whereas our immigrant grandparents generally needed no more than oral, interpersonal communication skills in English, at most, in order to succeed in the United States, today's immigrants must reach high levels of literacy in order to participate beyond the poverty level. Consequently, simply placing newcomers in an English-speaking environment will not adequately prepare them to participate fully in the life of the nation" (Samway & McKeon, 1999).

Immigrants now need to be well educated to succeed in the United States, and educational institutions are the key to help-

	2009	2010
Total (thousands)	39,929	39,313
Mexico	11,747	11,707
Central America	2989	3015
Carribean	3749	3529
South America	2740	2675
South/East Asia	9985	9743
Middle East	1384	1353
Europe and Canada	5798	5847
Africa and Oceania	1501	1414
Other	37	30

Figure 3.
Revised immigrant population living in the US 2009-2010; Source: Pew Hispanic Research Center.

ing immigrants obtain better jobs. Unfortunately immigrant children are not performing as well in US public schools school as native-born White children are. The Department of Education measures national reading and math proficiency through the NAEP, National Assessment of Educational Process. In 2011, of the 8th graders in the "all" category, 24% of them were reading below proficient level while 36% of Latinos scored below proficient on the NAEP reading evaluation. Also 27% of all children scored below level in Math, but the figure was 39% for Latinos. This gap between White and Hispanic academic performances is known as the Hispanic Achievement Gap. Addressing this gap would ensure a prosperous future for US Hispanics.

In 2010, the foreign-born population was 38.5 million residents, 12.5% of the total US population. Over half of them (53.1%) came from Latin America, over a quarter of them (27.7%) came from Asia, 12.7% came from Europe, 3.9% came from Africa, and 2.7% came from "other" regions (Grieco & Treveyan, 2010). Of the 20.5 million immigrants from Latin America, 56% of them came from Mexico and China sent the most immigrants from Asia. Of those immigrants 79% entered the US before the year 2000. Eighty per cent of the population speak only English at home.

Today's immigration population is much more geographically diverse. Only fifty six percent of the total foreign-born population lives in the traditional immigration states: California (9.9 million), New York (4.2 million), Texas (4.0 million), and Florida (3.5 million). The other 46% settled in non-traditional Midwestern or southern states. Many states that have not typically had large Latino populations are experiencing growth in their Hispanic population. In Georgia, the Latino population has grown by 96.1% from 2000 to 2010; Alabama increased by 144.8%, Mississippi by 105.9%, Tennessee by 134.2%. Latino population is still increasing in traditionally Latino states but at a slower rate; California increased by 27.8%, Arizona by 46.3, Texas by 41.8%, and Florida by 57.4%; but there are now large increases in other states (US Census, 2010).

The modern immigrant work force is made up of diverse backgrounds. The poorest and least skilled workers are immigrating to the United States along with the most educated and wealthy workers. The immigrant work force has increased from 14.6 million in 1994 to 29.7 million in 2010; however an important shift has taken place. For the first time in the year 2007, the number of skilled workers outnumbered the lower-skilled workers. According to a report published by the Brookings Institution and based on census data, "30% of the county's working-age immigrants, regardless of legal status, have at least a bachelor's degree, while 28% lack a high school diploma" (Bahrampour, 2011). The report also found that more highly skilled immigrants came from India, China, and the Philippines; while Mexico and Central America tended to send lower skilled labour. These skilled immigrants tended to work in coastal cities or metropolitan areas. Lower skilled workers were more common in the areas near the US Mexican border. Even though an immigrant has a higher education, their foreign credentials are often not recognized in the US therefore, half of the US immigrants are working at a job for which they are over quailfied.

Immigration expert Joseph Chamie claims that without immigration, the US population growth would decrease by as much as 80%. The United States relies on immigration to keep growing as a nation. Furthermore the US must look to immigration in order to complete its aging work force. Finally, tax dollars from foreign workers are needed to finance our government. The US cannot ignore the integration of these newcomers (Chamie, 2005).

According to Professor Jimenez at Stanford University, "the recent inflow of immigrants is integrating reasonably well" (Jimenez, 2011). However, the current economic downturn, a shift in the types of jobs that are now available, and unauthorized status of many immigrants are some of the causes that are impeding today's immigrants from integrating more easily. Furthermore, competition for the few available jobs on the market is causing anti-immigrant sentiments, which in turn, generates unfavorable immigration legislation.

Anti-immigrant legislation leads to an increase in illegal immigration. The most alarming characteristic of today's immigrants is that of the 38.5 million immigrants living in the United States, one third of them are illegal. "Seven out of ten unauthorized immigrants are in the labour force" (Jimenez, 2011). Legal status is one of the most influential factors of integration. Immigrants that do not have permission to live and work in the United States are likely to earn lower salaries, live below the poverty line, and be excluded from health care. Federal law allows the children of illegal immigrants to attend public schools but only ten states offer in-state tuition to these students. Many immigrants, particularly Hispanics, come to the US because they need jobs in order to survive. Mexicans, Central Americans, and others will continue to come because work is a necessity. No amount of restrictive legislation will stop them.

REFERENCES

Associated Press Staff (2010). Multicultural approach has failed. *The Washington Post*, October 18, A12.

Bahrampour, T. (2011). Foreign labor's skill level on rise. *The Washington Post*, June 9, A1.

Beschloss, M. (2009). March to freedom, the Jamestown paradox. *Newsweek*, November 30, 56.

Betten, N. (1976). *Polish American steelworkers: Americanization through industry and labor* (pp. 31-42). Champaign: University of Illinois Press.

Bragg, M. (2003). *The adventure of English, the biography of a language* (pp. 152-268). New York: Arcade Publishing.

Brewton, S., & Brewton, J. (1968). *America forever now, a book of poems* (p. 247). New York: Thomas Y. Crowell Company.

Bryson, B. (1994). *Made in America, an informal history of the English language in the United States* (p. 59). New York: William Morrow and Company Inc.

Bush, J., & Putnam, R. (2010). A better welcome for our immigrants. *The Washington Post*, July 3, A19.

Chamie, J. (2005). *Education, immigrant integration and demography. Education and immigrant integration in the United States and Canada.* (pp. 7-12). Washington DC: The Woodrow Wilson International Center for Scholars and The Migration Policy Institute.

Chang, I. (2003). *The Chinese in America: A narrative history* (p. 166). New York: Penguin Group.

Constitutional Rights Foundation (2002). The mayflower compact. http://www.crf-usa.org/foundations-of-our-constitution/mayflower-compact.html

Crawford, J. (2013) The Muhlenburg legend, language policy web site

emporium archives (1997-2008). http://www.languagepolicy.net/archives/can-muhl.htm

Samway, K., & McKeon, D. (1999). *Myths and realities, best practices for language minority students* (p. 28). Portsmouth: Heinemann.

Denning, S. (2012) Is the US in a phase change to the creative economy? *Forbes*, January 31. http://www.forbes.com/sites/stevedenning/2012/01/31/is-the-us-in-a-phase-change-to-the-creative-economy

Faiola, A. (2010). Official's views on Muslim immigration divide Germany. *The Washington Post*, September 10, A14.

Gonzalez, J. (2000). *A history of Latinos in America harvest of the empire* (p. 209). London: Viking Penguin Group.

Grieco, E., & Trevelyan, E. (2010). Place of birth of the foreign born population 2009. *American Survey Briefs*, October, 1-5. http://www.census.gov/prod/2010pubs/acsbr09-15.pdf

Hernández, R. E. (2007). *Immigration* (p. 41). Broomall: Mason Crest Publishers.

Staff Writer (2013). The history of ESL. http://esl.yourdictionary.com/about-esl/the-history-of-esl.html

History.com (2013). The Gold Rush of 1849. http://www.history.com/topics/gold-rush-of-1849

Hoobler, D., & Hoobler, T. (2003). *We are American, voices of the immigrant experience* (p. 33). New York: Scholastic Inc.

Jimenez, T. (2011). *Immigrants in the United States: How well are they integrating into society* (pp. 1-4)? Washington DC: Migration Policy Institute.

Lui, M. Z. et al. (2006). *The color of wealth: The story behind the US racial wealth divide* (p. 133). New York: The New Press.

Meacham, J. (2009). Who we are now? *Newsweek*, January 20, 39.

Meyer, S. (1980). Adapting the immigration line: Americanization in the Ford Factory 1914-1921. *Journal of Social History, 14,* 70.

Passel, J., & Cohn, D. (2012) *US foreign-born population: How much change from 2009 to 2010* (p. 1)? Washington DC: Pew Hispanic Research Center.

Pew Hispanic Research Center (2013). A portrait of the 40 million, including 11 million unauthorized a nation of immigrants. http://www.pewhispanic.org/2013/01/29/a-nation-of-immigrants

Rein, M. (2002). *Immigration and illegal aliens blessing or burden* (p. 93)? Farmington Hills: Gale Group Inc.

Salmons, J., & Wilkerson, M. E. (2008). Good old immigrants of yesteryear who didn't learn English: Germans in Wisconsin. *American Speech, 83,* 259.

Scholastic (2010) Immigration: Stories of yesterday and today, immigration data and table based on data from the US department of homeland security and elaborated by teacher.scholastic.com. http://teacher.scholastic.com/activities/immigration/immigration_data/index.htm

Schlesinger, A. M. (1998). *The disuniting of America: Reflections on a multicultural society* (pp. 30-31). New York: W. W. Norton & Company.

US Census Bureau (2010). US census data.

US Census Bureau (2010). US census data.

US Census Bureau (2004). Current population survey, Table FINC-03, p. 135.

Wittke, C. (1993). *We who built America, the saga of the immigrant* (p. 15). Cleveland: Case Western Reserve University.

Yans-McLaughlin, V., & Lightman, M. (1997). *Ellis Island and the peopling of America, the official guide* (pp. 1-20). New York: The New Press.

Zinn, H. (1995). *A people's history of the United States, 1492-Present* (p. 221). New York: Harper Perennial Publishers.

Zinn, H. (2007). *A power governments cannot suppress* (p. 250). San Francisco: City Lights Book.

Permissions

The contributors of this book come from diverse backgrounds, making this book a truly international effort. This book will bring forth new frontiers with its revolutionizing research information and detailed analysis of the nascent developments around the world.

We would like to thank all the contributing authors for lending their expertise to make the book truly unique. They have played a crucial role in the development of this book. Without their invaluable contributions this book wouldn't have been possible. They have made vital efforts to compile up to date information on the varied aspects of this subject to make this book a valuable addition to the collection of many professionals and students.

This book was conceptualized with the vision of imparting up-to-date information and advanced data in this field. To ensure the same, a matchless editorial board was set up. Every individual on the board went through rigorous rounds of assessment to prove their worth. After which they invested a large part of their time researching and compiling the most relevant data for our readers. Conferences and sessions were held from time to time between the editorial board and the contributing authors to present the data in the most comprehensible form. The editorial team has worked tirelessly to provide valuable and valid information to help people across the globe.

Every chapter published in this book has been scrutinized by our experts. Their significance has been extensively debated. The topics covered herein carry significant findings which will fuel the growth of the discipline. They may even be implemented as practical applications or may be referred to as a beginning point for another development. Chapters in this book were first published by Scientific Research Publishing Inc.; hereby published with permission under the Creative Commons Attribution License or equivalent.

The editorial board has been involved in producing this book since its inception. They have spent rigorous hours researching and exploring the diverse topics which have resulted in the successful publishing of this book. They have passed on their knowledge of decades through this book. To expedite this challenging task, the publisher supported the team at every step. A small team of assistant editors was also appointed to further simplify the editing procedure and attain best results for the readers.

Our editorial team has been hand-picked from every corner of the world. Their multi-ethnicity adds dynamic inputs to the discussions which result in innovative outcomes. These outcomes are then further discussed with the researchers and contributors who give their valuable feedback and opinion regarding the same. The feedback is then collaborated with the researches and they are edited in a comprehensive manner to aid the understanding of the subject.

Apart from the editorial board, the designing team has also invested a significant amount of their time in understanding the subject and creating the most relevant covers. They scrutinized every image to scout for the most suitable representation of the subject and create an appropriate cover for the book.

The publishing team has been involved in this book since its early stages. They were actively engaged in every process, be it collecting the data, connecting with the contributors or procuring relevant information. The team has been an ardent support to the editorial, designing and production team. Their endless efforts to recruit the best for this project, has resulted in the accomplishment of this book. They are a veteran in the field of academics and their pool of knowledge is as vast as their experience in printing. Their expertise and guidance has proved useful at every step. Their uncompromising quality standards have made this book an exceptional effort. Their encouragement from time to time has been an inspiration for everyone.

The publisher and the editorial board hope that this book will prove to be a valuable piece of knowledge for researchers, students, practitioners and scholars across the globe.

List of Contributors

Danilo Capecchi
Dipartimento di Ingegneria Strutturale e Geotecnica, Università La Sapienza, Rome, Italy

Donald A. Bailey
Department of History, University of Winnipeg Winnipeg, Manitoba, Canada

M. R. Manmathan
Department of History, Farook College, Calicut University, Kerala, India

Theodore John Rivers
Independent, Forest Hills, USA

Peter N. Kirstein
History Department, St. Xavier University, Chicago, USA

Thomas J. Straka
School of Agricultural, Forest, and Environmental Sciences, Clemson University, Clemson, USA

Wei Hu
Department of Computer Science, Houghton College, New York, USA

Raffaele Pisano
Sciences, Sociétés, Cultures dans leurs Evolutions, University of Lille 1, Lille, France
Research Center for Theory and History of Science, University of West Bohemia, Plzen, Czech Republic

Agamenon R. E. Oliveira
Polytechnic School of Rio de Janeiro, Federal University of Rio de Janeiro, Rio de Janeiro, Brazil

Donald A. Bailey
Department of History, University of Winnipeg Winnipeg, Manitoba, Canada

Zafar Khan
Department of Politics & International Studies, University of Hull, Kingston upon Hull, UK

Thomas Aiello
Department of History, Valdosta State University, Valdosta, USA

Jonas Eliasson
University of Iceland, Reykjavik, Iceland
Kyoto University (visiting), Kyoto, Japan

Paolo Bussotti
Research Centre for the Theory and History of Science, University of West Bohemia, Pilsen, Czech Republic

Luca Bussotti
Centro de Estudos Internacionais ISCTE-IUL, Lisbon, Portugal

Antonella De Muti
Federal University of Minas Gerais, Belo Horizonte, Brazil

Vitaly Gorokhov
Institute of Philosophy, Russian Academy of Sciences, Moscow, Russia
Institute of Technology Assessment and System Analysis, Karlsruhe Institute of Technology, Karlsruhe, Germany

Angelo Nicolaides
HOD Department of Hospitality, Tourism and PR Management, Vaal University of Technology, Vanderbijlpark, South Africa

Manjula Poyil
Department of History, Nirmlagiri College, Kannur University, Kerala, India

Claire Parham
Siena College, Loudonville, New York, USA

Marco Ceccarelli
LARM: laboratory of Robotics and Mechatronics, University of Cassino and South Latium, Cassino, Italy

Stacy Ragsdale
Department of Filology and Languages, UNED University, Madrid, Spain

CPSIA information can be obtained
at www.ICGtesting.com
Printed in the USA
LVOW06*1443111017

552032LV00004B/39/P

9 781632 404909